Sustainable Economics

Context, Challenges and Opportunities
for the 21st-Century Practitioner

SUSTAINABLE ECONOMICS

CONTEXT, CHALLENGES AND OPPORTUNITIES FOR THE 21ST-CENTURY PRACTITIONER

KEITH SKENE and ALAN MURRAY

Routledge
Taylor & Francis Group
LONDON AND NEW YORK

First published 2015 by Greenleaf Publishing Limited

Published 2017 by Routledge
4 Park Square, Milton Park, Abingdon, Oxon OX14 4RN
605 Third Avenue, New York, NY 10017

Routledge is an imprint of the Taylor & Francis Group, an informa business

Cover by Sadie Gornall-Jones

British Library Cataloguing in Publication Data:
A catalogue record for this book is available from the British Library.

ISBN-13: 978-1-78353-154-7 [hbk]
ISBN-13: 978-1-78353-151-6 [pbk]

Contents

Figures

Tables

Preface

Wealth, power, health, food, water, peace and happiness: imagine something that threatened these central foci of aspiration, such deeply ingrained descriptors of the human condition. For this reason, global sustainability is the most contentious issue facing all of us today, whether you are the president of a nation, the CEO of a major company or the parent of a young family.

Sustainability, whose very definition itself remains contentious, elicits hugely polarized opinions at every hurdle, because it has the potential to threaten the bastions of power, wealth and control so cherished by many. Yet the threats of ignoring the subject target much more basic necessities, such as food, water, clean air, soil and security, posing challenges that reach into every home on the planet. The perturbation of planetary balance, as a consequence of our insatiable exploitation of its resources, brings with it such apocryphal warnings as floods, famine, disease, war and indiscriminate mayhem. Economic, social and environmental issues all demand resolution, yet these three theatres of human activity appear immiscible.

The debate over the future of our planet and, in particular, that fate of the human race, in terms of how we should conduct ourselves economically, has two significant factions. The actively or passively optimistic schools of thought, sometimes referred to as **cornucopians** (after the ancient Greek horn of plenty, that overflowed with fruit), hold to the belief that the Earth will continue to provide the resources we need for continued economic growth and that a business-as-usual approach will suffice. The pessimistic school of thought, sometimes referred to as the **Malthusian** movement (after Thomas Malthus, the 18th-century curate who wrote of the dangers of an expanding human population), proclaims the end of the world as we know it unless drastic action is taken.

The stakes are incredibly high, yet much of the argument on either side stands on ankles made of clay, fundamentally weakened by outdated theory, inappropriate metaphor and baseless extrapolation, devoid of meaningful data and appropriate context. This book aims to present a clear picture of current thinking on sustainability, examining the history of the issues and suggested solutions. We explore the strengths and weaknesses of the many and diverse schools of thought. The book is targeted at enabling the modern business student and practitioner to disentangle the complex, often convoluted debate relating to sustainability. It provides the tools necessary to lead their organizations through the murky waters of current times and prepare for the challenges of the future. Innovation and leadership are central to this journey, and it is hoped that this book will contribute to the preparation of the next generation of business professionals.

Note for tutors and students

An extensive pack of electronic supporting materials is available online for free download. This includes a series of 10 lectures totalling around 500 slides with outlines and templates, and a web-linked reference search engine, allowing you to instantly search and access the cited references in this textbook.

1
Human economic activity: an environmental impact assessment

This chapter provides an historical context for the current economic, societal and environmental climate, examining the concepts of progress, economic growth, and development. The onset of agriculture, urbanization and economics are traced back to the agrarian revolution, some 10,000 years earlier. We explore the implications of change throughout human history in terms of impact on the environment and provide a detailed analysis of the impact of business activity on the environment. The importance of ecosystem services for environmental, societal and economic security are evaluated. Human, social, manufactured and natural capital are compared and contrasted. Cornucopian, cautious optimist and Malthusian positions are examined, Bearing in mind that many MBA and EMBA students may lack a scientific background, we set out the key basic principles underpinning the science of sustainability, allowing the reader to more fully interact with this topic and make clearer judgements when faced with contrasting viewpoints.

Learning aims and objectives

- To chart the economic–social–environmental relationship through human history
- To examine how risks to our existence have changed through time
- To evaluate how current business practice has emerged
- To evaluate the impact of current business practice
- To understand how source and sink issues impact on our planet
- To appreciate how environmental damage impacts on economics and society
- To examine how feedback effects environmental perturbation

Learning outcomes and experiences

- Understanding the link between business, society and the environment
- Understanding the origins and nature of the modern world
- Appreciating the consequences of a destabilized environment
- Appreciating how positive feedback acts to heighten environmental damage
- Defining sustainability in a meaningful way
- Understanding how very different opinions can exist relating to the issues of environmental sustainability

1.1 Progress and the Golden Age

> Nature has fixed no limits on our hopes
>
> Marie Jean Antoine Nicolas de Caritat, Marquis of Condorcet (Condorcet, 1955 [originally 1779], p. 173)

Kungliga Djurgården is an island in central Stockholm and was, formerly, a hunting estate of the Swedish royal family. The name literally means "royal game park". In many ways, the esoteric collection of buildings and structures on this island highlights the journey of the human race.

A large part of the island houses the Skansen Museum, where scores of old buildings from across Sweden have been relocated to the island, allowing you to visualize what life was like hundreds of years ago. Quaint and simple, the impression is one of how far we have progressed. The smell of ruminant manure and the sight of predatory bears and wolves, interspersed among Sami huts of mud and logs, combine to present a disturbing glimpse of where we have come from, the Agrarian Age. Living shoulder to shoulder with such apparent squalor and danger seems far removed from the sophisticated surroundings of Stockholm itself.

Leisure opportunities are embraced throughout the island, from the myriad yachts and motor launches moored along the shore, to the innocently named Green Grove (Gröna Lund), a terrifying amusement park where people pay to be twisted, dropped, spun and contorted beyond the point of screaming. Progress brings increased leisure time, no longer having to work endless hours among the moose manure and the wolves of Skansen.

The cultural past is further celebrated nearer the shore in the Nordic Museum, housed in a magnificent Danish Renaissance building which is more cathedralesque than the Storkyrkan itself. Again the impression is of how far we have travelled and how we have progressed in so many aspects of life, from interior decoration to fashion.

Finally, hugging the shoreline, in a building that resembles a Shinto temple from one aspect and a huge modern barn conversion from another, sits one of the great lessons of our imperfect past: the *Vasa*. On first entering this vast museum, the impression is not one of failure, but of extraordinary achievement. In front of you, there sits a massive wooden ship from a different age. At 69 m long, 11 m wide and some 52 m in height, the *Vasa* was state-of-the-art naval architecture when it set sail on its maiden voyage in 1628. At this time, the Swedish Empire stretched across the Baltic, and was expanding. The *Vasa* was to represent the sophistication and power of Sweden, resplendently embellished with ornate carvings designed to set the King in a suitable context. These included the emperors of Rome, ancient Greek gods and rampant lions. This wasn't just a warship. It was an all singing, all dancing, all sailing advertising machine for King and country.

However, the ship *was* a warship, and King Gustav II Adolf was determined that it would be the most powerful warship on the planet. Very late in the design process, he insisted that the ship should have a second layer of gun ports on its port and starboard sides, housing a total of 64 bronze cannon. The ship's designers bowed to his wish. You didn't argue with the King.

Unfortunately, this was a major design flaw. These huge cannon made the boat top-heavy, with insufficient room for ballast below the water line, and, shortly after setting sail on her maiden voyage on 10 August 1628, in amenable weather conditions, the boat keeled over and sank. And so this magnificent vessel, proclaiming the power and majesty of the Swedish war machine, ultimately represented failure. Ornate and beautiful as it was, it possessed the hydrostatic qualities of the *Venus de Milo*. The huge museum houses a boat that couldn't stay afloat, and represents the interference of a king who knew nothing of design.

On emerging from this massive time capsule into the modern, sophisticated capital city with its smoothly running trams, trains and ferries, all is again well with the world. While the past may have had some highlights, the impression left is that we have progressed so far from the agrarian lifestyle of Skansen and the errors and flaws of the *Vasa*. Interference by the state and a lack of technological skill sank the ship. The path of progress, as encapsulated in the Enlightenment, would have no time for church or state, and would proclaim technology and reason as the engines of change.

It is a widely held view that the history of humankind traces a journey of progress. Each generation improves on the last one, and we are steadily moving forward towards a much more wonderful life. New breakthroughs in engineering, medicine and agriculture continually hit the headlines. We are travelling into a bigger, brighter and better future. The vertical line of improvement also lies at the heart of much of our understanding of biological evolution. The tree of life branches out and reaches further towards the sky, with humankind at the top. The process of scientific thinking itself is also seen as continually testing ideas, weeding out the less good and replacing them with improved versions.

It was the Enlightenment that set out the principles of this journey, and state and church were not its only targets. The Marquis of Condorcet, one of the leading French Enlightenment thinkers, stated that "Nature has fixed no limits on our hopes" (Condorcet, 1955 [originally 1779]; p. 173). Nature, which had dictated to the human race and shaped our sojourn, was no longer to be worshipped, feared and tolerated. Just as the theologians before them, who took aim at the pantheistic worship of nature seen to be present in Celtic Christianity, so the modern humanist tradition levied the same attack at any consideration of nature as a player in the calculations underpinning progress. In the same way as the grip of kings and papal powers would be loosened, nature would no longer limit the Enlightenment dream. Progress highway would not circumnavigate the ancient woodland; it would bore straight through it.

And economics lay at the heart of the Enlightenment. Adam Smith (1723–90), perhaps the most influential of all of the Enlightenment thinkers in terms of shaping the world we know today, set out the economics of the

Enlightenment. Smith emphasized a move away from protectionism to free trade (laissez-faire economics), governed by an invisible hand rather than the ruling classes. He saw economics as delivering social cohesion and paving the way to a productive, prosperous and happy existence for all. Virtuous self-interest could lead to invisible co-operation.

Two central pillars of modern economics, **growth** and **development**, follow the Enlightenment mantra, that we are on a journey to bigger and better things. In fact, in terms of development, the world is often divided into **developing** and **developed** nations, the former still on a journey to the utopia already enjoyed by the latter. **Economic growth** is defined as the sustained increase in wealth over time measured in the real **per capita** production of goods and services.

Progress has a unit of measurement: the **gross domestic product.** Gross domestic product (GDP) is defined as the monetary value of all the finished goods and services produced within a country's borders in a specific time-period. GDP is usually calculated on an annual basis. It includes all of private and public consumption, government outlays, investments and exports less imports that occur within a defined territory. The concept was framed in its current form by Simon Kuznets (1901–85).

Since GDP is the unit of progress, it has taken centre stage and has re-characterized our perception of success. Based on GDP, economic growth "has become a national virility symbol" (Hywel Jones, 1975; p. 1). Negative economic growth is looked on as a very bad thing. Two successive quarters of negative growth can be termed a **recession**, while two years of negative growth can qualify as a **depression** (note that many definitions exist for recession and depression, but all involve sustained periods of negative economic growth as measured by GDP). Economic growth is also seen as delivering sociological wellbeing. Samuelson and Nordhaus (1995; p. 402) wrote: "The GDP and related data are like beacons that help policy-makers steer the economy towards the key economic objectives".

Economic growth is viewed as not merely as a good thing, but as essential evidence of progress. "To continue to progress, humanity needs more economic growth, not less" (Atlantic Institute for Market Studies, 2003). Indeed, economic growth is also implicated as a central pillar to global security: "Domestically and internationally, the tolerance of the poor and middle classes for the existence of wealthier classes and countries depends on a belief in economic growth" (Delaney, 2005). Warnings are made relating to any suggestion of reducing growth in order to protect the environment. Lord Stern has commented that:

> It is neither economically necessary nor ethically responsible to stop or drastically slow economic growth to manage climate change. Not only would it be analytically unsound, it would also pose severe ethical difficulties and be so politically destructive as to fail as policy (Stern, 2009; p. 3).

He had earlier stated that "stabilisation of greenhouse-gas concentrations in the atmosphere is feasible and consistent with continued growth" (Stern, 2006; p. xi)

1.1.1 Human development

Human development is the second important aspect of progress, viewing humans as not merely a means of production but as an end-point (Streeten, 1994). Incorporating the societal face of the Enlightenment, it describes the ongoing journey towards a better world, where humans, through knowledge, industry, reasoning and technology, maximize their potential, their comfort, their longevity and their contentment.

The United Nations has even developed a unit of measurement for development, the GDP of society, called the **Human Development Index** (HDI). This index combines measurement of education, earnings (measured by gross national income per capita) and health, and each year the nations of the Earth are assessed. In 2013, Norway ranked as the most developed nation on Earth, while Niger finished in 187th and last place.

A recent phenomenon has been to tie development to sustainability, in the term **sustainable development**. Sustainable development is development that meets the needs of the present without compromising the ability of future generations to meet their own needs (Brundtland, 1987).

This very much echoes a much earlier definition of income by Sir John Hicks (1946) who defined **income** as the amount (natural or financial) one could consume during a period and still be as well off at the end of the period. Thus sustainability is fundamentally framed within human development, which is itself grafted to economic growth. This locates the solution space for our concerns related to our planet within the current growth-based economic model. Thomas Friedman states: "I start from the bedrock principle that we as a global society need more and more growth, because without growth there is no human development and those in poverty will never escape it" (Friedman, 2008; p. 186).

American President Ronald Reagan aligned himself with Enlightenment thinking, rejecting any limitation to growth, and claiming that: "There are no great limits to growth because there are no limits of human intelligence, imagination, and wonder" (Reagan, 1983).

1.1.2 Issues with the growth dogma

The idea that economic growth can continue, unrelenting, bringing with it human development and leading to some form of utopia, unhindered by nature, is not the only cockerel in the hen-house. Many economists and politicians express serious concerns that continued economic growth will not deliver a perfect world. Indeed, many of the benefits of economic growth have been questioned. As early as 1961, Robert Theobald observed: "An economy of abundance is under present rules also an economy of waste and repetition—indeed without this waste the economy would slump. Nobody, however, can be optimistic about the survival of a society with such values" (Theobald, 1961; p. 2). Professor Tim Jackson has noted:

> The myth of growth has failed us. It has failed the two billion people who still live on less than $2 a day. It has failed the fragile ecological systems on which we depend for survival. It has failed, spectacularly, in its own terms, to provide economic stability and secure people's livelihoods (Jackson, 2009a; p. 5).

Jim Yong Kim, appointed President of the World Bank in 2012, has written that: "the quest for growth in GDP and corporate profits has in fact worsened the lives of millions of women and men" (Millen *et al.*, 2000; p. 7). Hannah Arendt (quoted in Beiner, 1999; p. 124) observed that "Economic growth may one day turn out to be a curse rather than a good, and under no conditions can it either lead into freedom or constitute a proof for its existence."

UN Secretary General Ban Ki-moon has attacked GDP, saying "We need to move beyond gross domestic product as our main measure of progress, and fashion a sustainable development index that puts people first" (Ban Ki-moon, 2012). On the subject of how to measure progress, Simon Kuznets, the father of GDP, stated:

> Distinctions must be kept in mind between quantity and quality of growth, between its costs and return, and between the short and the long term. Goals for more growth should specify more growth of what and for what. The welfare of a nation can scarcely be inferred from a measurement of national income (Kuznets, 1962; p. 29).

Professor William Rees suggests that economic growth cannot solve poverty. The lifestyles currently enjoyed by the high-income North cannot be extended to the low-income South using prevailing technologies without the depletion of existing stocks of natural capital and the deterioration of vital life-support functions. Contemporary political rhetoric represented by the prevailing growth-based economic "development" paradigm is fundamentally incompatible with ecological and social sustainability (Rees, 2001, 2002).

Given that GDP does not take account of degradation of natural resources, the depletion of energy resources, and the effects of pollution on health and the environment, it has been suggested that a better index that included environmental damage should be implemented. This approach is called **green accounting.** In the USA, efforts were made to develop such an index, which was called the **integrated economic and environmental satellite accounts** (IEESA). However, this approach was abandoned in 2005 (Abraham and Mackie, 2005).

1.1.3 Economic growth and a sustainable future: having your cake and eating it

If GDP is not to be reassessed to include environmental damage, some have asked what would be required to "decouple" the economy from its material basis so that GDP growth could continue while increases in certain material throughputs (e.g. CO_2 emissions) gradually declined to sustainable levels. Tim Jackson has pointed to the importance of distinguishing between "**relative**" and "**absolute**" decoupling of economic output and environmental pressure. Relative decoupling implies a reduction in the environmental pressure per unit of economic output. Certainly energy intensity (energy used per unit GDP) has dropped over the last 40 years in "developed" nations (Goldemberg and Siqueira Prado, 2013). However, in many countries moving into the industrial and information ages, environmental damage continues to increase. Indeed, the reduction in energy intensity in the developed world is often due to externalization of energy expenditure to other countries.

Absolute decoupling means an absolute reduction in environmental pressure. Thus, since economic growth damages the environment, then if economic growth is assumed to continue, economic damage will also continue. Jackson (2009b) argues that absolute decoupling is an essential condition for economic activity to remain within ecological limits.

A second approach is to regard intellectual growth as a means to deliver sustainable economic growth (Hepburn and Bowen, 2012). Economic growth can therefore be sustained with zero material growth and increasing intellectual growth, allowing for a drag exerted by pollution. This fundamentally represents an Enlightenment approach, emphasizing human reasoning and technology as the solution space. Dematerializing the economy through reasoning and technology would appear to deliver improved economic output as well as improved environmental health. Improved energy and material intensity would also greatly decrease current subsidies related to material and energy consumption.

1.1.4 Sources and sinks

While debate continues as to the benefits and costs of growth on human wellbeing, and the suitability of GDP as a measure of such wellbeing, the society–economy axis is not the only area of disagreement. The environment–economy axis has attracted much attention of late. WWF Chief Emeka Anyaoku has noted:

> What we currently measure as development is a long way away from the EU and the world's stated aim of sustainable development. This is because economic decisions routinely ignore natural capital expenditure. Economic indicators are essential, but without natural resource accounting, ecological deficits will go unnoticed and ignored. It is as if we spent our money without realizing that we are liquidating the planet's capital (Anyaoku, 2007).

The debate has focused on two questions. First, does economic growth negatively impact on the environment? Second, will the environment negatively impact on economic growth? These questions revolve around two areas: **source-related issues** and **sink-related issues**.

Source-related issues make reference to the use of our planet as a resource. Economic growth requires raw material and there are concerns that we may run out of such material (e.g. oil, soil, phosphate, lithium, fish and fresh water). Such shortages could mean that economic growth slows, or stops.

Sink-related issues appertain to industrial and domestic waste, such as carbon dioxide, nitrogen and phosphate fertilizers, ozone, methane and dioxins. As the by-products of economic growth increase in concentration, they significantly impact on the environment. Environmental perturbation in turn has the potential to impact on economic growth.

There are three positions in the environment–economy debate:

1. **The Cornucopian position**: this position stresses that concerns over resource shortage are unproven, and in fact there are basically

limitless resources available. Many economists have an optimistic attitude towards the problem since they believe that resource scarcity, signalled by price increases, will stimulate both technological progress and substitution of natural resources with capital (Dunn, 1992; Weidenbaum, 1992). As Nordhaus and Tobin stated (1973; p. 523), "If the past is any guide for the future, there seems to be little reason to worry about the exhaustion of resources which the market already treats as economic good". Economic growth and progress more generally are neither limited nor constrained by the environment, and technology will always keep us ahead of the game, easily replacing any failings in ecosystem function. The American economist, Henry George (quoted in Simon, 1993) famously quipped "Both the jayhawk and the man eat chickens; but the more jayhawks, the fewer chickens, while the more men, the more chickens!" Increasing prosperity will lead to a positive feedback on environmental care, and a negative feedback on population growth, thus righting the wrongs under the guidance of Adam Smith's invisible hand. This is the most optimistic school and is Enlightenment-based, where humanity will overcome all adversity. It views the concept of limitation as weak-minded and lacking in faith in our abilities. Described by Manes (1990; p. 104) as "myopic utilitarianism", it is criticized for excluding the environment and society from its considerations.

2. **The cautious optimist position**: this position proposes that environmental limitations will create some drag on economic growth, caused by negative feedback from a perturbed environment. Stationary growth is possible, provided that loss in natural capital is balanced by technology. This is represented by **Hartwick-Solow sustainability**, in which the total sum of all changes in capital stocks must be zero. The Hartwick-Solow sustainability rule states that it is sustainable to consume at constant or increasing levels, even while nonrenewable resources decline, provided the total capital stock (natural and human-made) is maintained, by investing rents from natural stock into human-made stock.

3. **The Malthusian position**: environmental limitations are significant enough to prevent sustained growth in consumption and production. Often referred to as "deep ecology" (Naess, 1990), this school of thought posits that increasing pressure from geometric

population growth, combined with increasingly scarce resources and environmental perturbation, will bring the economic growth to a halt, or worse, collapse. Notable exponents of this viewpoint in the 20th century include John Maynard Keynes, Nicholas Georgescu-Roegen and Sir John Hicks. Bill McKibben, in his book, *Eaarth, Making a Life in a Tough New Planet* (McKibben, 2010), has stated that the planet is irrevocably broken while James Lovelock, in his most recent book, *The Vanishing Face of Gaia, a Final Warning: Enjoy it While You Can* (Lovelock, 2009), concludes that there is only a small chance that we can reverse climate change.

So what impact has economic growth had on the environment, and can nature truly limit our hopes? What does the future hold? Will progress road lead to a New Jerusalem, or is the final destination Sodom and Gomorrah? What is the cost of progress?

1.2 A brief history of planetary exploitation

> History is a relentless master. It has no present, only the past rushing into the future. To try to hold fast is to be swept aside.
>
> John F. Kennedy (2005).

On a sunny day, walking along a mountain path high in the Grampian Mountains in Eastern Scotland, you can gain the impression of a world unsullied by human activity and unperturbed by the huge wheel of economic growth that churns and rotates inexorably onward. All seems well with the world. The flowers grow, the bees buzz and the birds sing like they always have done. Yet scientific research paints a very different picture of the health of our planet. Indeed over 20 years ago, a group of leading scientists released the following statement:

> We the under-signed senior members of the world's scientific community hereby warn all humanity of what lies ahead. A great change in our stewardship of the earth and the life on it is required if vast human misery is to be avoided and our global home on this planet is not to be irretrievably mutilated (UCS, 1992).

Indeed, in the intervening years since this statement, all indicators have pointed to a worsening situation. Huge increases in biodiversity loss and habitat fragmentation, two-thirds of the most important fisheries over-exploited, a 30% increase in atmospheric carbon dioxide levels in the past 200 years, ozone depletion, widespread pollution of fresh water, and increasingly unpredictable weather events. According to WWF's *Living Planet Report*, 35% of the world's natural wealth has been lost over the past 30 years alone.

Yet there are very different views as to where these events will lead us. The Gaian hypothesis, as developed by James Lovelock and others in the 1970s, presents the Earth as a self-regulating system, with stable atmospheric and oceanic processes. Anything that perturbs this system, such as humans, will be expelled, and equilibrium will be restored. However, the history of the Earth tells a very different story, and we need to go back to the first and most notable pollution event on our planet to see why this is the case.

This first pollution episode was not of human making, but ultimately would lead to the making of humans. In fact the masters of this dramatic incident were invisible to the naked eye, each one just one millionth of a metre across. This event was the Great Oxygenation Event and occurred some 2.4 billion years ago, changing the planet completely and leading to mass extinction (Price *et al.*, 2012). Yes, oxygen was the first significant pollutant made by a living organism on Earth. Oxygen is a waste product in the conversion of sunlight to sugar, in much the same way that carbon dioxide is a waste product when sugar (or its fossilized form, fossil fuel) is burned. Oxygen is produced when water molecules are split into hydrogen and oxygen in the process called photosynthesis. Today, most of life relies on oxygen, but before photosynthesis, on early Earth, there was no oxygen in the atmosphere, and life forms didn't use it. In fact these early life forms were poisoned by it. Today, we find the distant relatives of these ancient, oxygen-hating bacteria hidden away in low oxygen environments such as bogs and lake-bottom mud.

What is interesting is that the Great Oxygenation Event did not lead to the creatures responsible being expelled from the living planet. Rather, the entire planet changed irrevocably. In fact the original inhabitants of the planet were banished from most of their former habitats. In the atmosphere, oxygen levels increased, and some of the oxygen was converted into ozone, which formed a layer high above the planet. Ozone reduced the ultraviolet radiation hitting the Earth, allowing life to emerge from the oceans on to land without having its DNA fried. We see its benefit when we observe the effects of damage to the ozone layer today. Two-thirds of Australians will have experienced skin cancer by the time they are 70 years old. From 1982 to 2010, melanoma diagnoses increased by around 60%, according to Cancer Council Australia (2014).

The use of the water-splitting reaction also led the way to the sun becoming the source of life-giving energy, rather than the Earth. The path was open for a huge increase in complexity, diversity and opportunity within the biosphere. Indeed the first mass pollution event would have a greater effect than anything that has happened since. Mass extinctions have come and gone, wiping out 98% of life on the planet at times, but never has the impact been so fundamental.

Yet today, another species, multicellular, oxygen-dependent and land based, a product of all the changes set in place by the first great pollution event, is challenging this record. Huge planetary perturbation at many levels, caused by the waste products of our activities, is occurring, threatening all aspects of life on our planet. Humans couldn't be more different from the tiny cyanobacteria that created such havoc so long ago, yet we have the potential to reset the planet in a similar way. And the changes being made by our activities are so profound, that they are being picked up in the geological record of the planet, leading to the development of the concept of the **Anthropocene**. The Anthropocene is the geological epoch shaped by humans (Crutzen, 2002). A contentious term, representing a geological epoch covering the period during which human activity has had a significant global impact, as evidenced by changes to atmospheric and geospheric records. Human activity now alters physico-chemical processes such as biogeochemical cycles, ocean–atmosphere transfers, and the flux of sediments (Steffen *et al.*, 2011). Stratigraphic records will reflect accelerated mass transfer of sediments through erosion and sedimentation.

The Anthropocene represents the period of time over which human activity initiated the transformation of Earth system behaviour and altered environmental processes. There is some blurring between its use within a scientific, geological context, when referring to a geological epoch, and in casual reference. This is much like the Gaian hypothesis, which became embraced by the New Age movement as an outworking of Mother Earth.

Although claimed as a recent, transcendent term, the Anthropocene as a concept has existed for over 100 years. Terms such as the **Anthropozoic** (Stoppani, 1873), **Psychozoic** (Le Conte, 1879), and **Noosphere** (Le Roy, 1927) were conceived to denote the idea of humans as new global forcing agents. In the 1990s, the term **Anthroposphere** found widespread use in Chinese literature.

The Anthropocene was formally introduced in 2000 by Nobel laureate and former IGBP vice-chair Paul Crutzen (b.1933) and colleague Eugene Stoermer (1934–2012) in IGBP's Global Change newsletter (Crutzen and

Stoermer, 2000). The term and concept quickly became popular. In 2003, the term yielded 416 web hits; by 2012 that number had increased to over 500,000. Over 200 scientific papers referred to the Anthropocene in 2012.

So when did the Anthropocene begin? Some say it started with the industrial revolution, around 250 years ago, as fossil fuel use increased to perturb CO_2 and methane levels in the atmosphere. However, others argue it began some 12,000 years ago, with sediment loading of rivers and oceans accompanying early agriculture. It has been demonstrated that carbon dioxide levels began to rise beyond expected levels some 8,000 years ago, associated with forest clearance, while methane broke expected levels some 5,000 years ago, linked to rice paddy-field development (Ruddiman, 2003).

Indeed such was the CO_2 enrichment of the atmosphere that temperatures rose by an estimated 2°C, preventing an expected glaciations event in Canada. Around 1,000 years ago, a series of bubonic plague events led to the abandonment of many farming areas. These farms were replaced by forest which led to a drop in CO_2 levels, thought to have contributed to the little ice age between AD1300 and AD1900 (van Hoof *et al.*, 2006). Thus it is argued that these examples clearly show that human forcing of the atmosphere and of sedimentation led to measurable climatic and geological changes long before the industrial revolution.

1.2.1 The four ages of planetary exploitation

To understand the relationship between economics, society and the environment, we need to understand the history of this relationship. To do this we will examine the four stages of the human story: the Hunter-Gatherer Age, the Agrarian Age, the Industrial Age and the Information Age (Fig. 1.1).

1.2.1.1 The Hunter-Gatherer Age

Stretching back to the origin of *Homo sapiens*, and other members of the genus *Homo*, our earliest period was spent, like many other animals, foraging and hunting for food within the natural environment. Indeed it is estimated that some 95% of our time on Earth was spent in this age (given that modern humans are first noted some 200,000 years ago, and the Hunter-Gatherer Age was replaced as the main lifestyle descriptor around 10,000 years ago). Pre-dating human existence, *Homo habilis* (2.33 Mya) possessed tools while *Homo erectus* (1.8 Mya) used both tools and fire.

Hunter-gatherer communities still exist on the planet, but are very rare and threatened. The Hunter-Gatherer Age is often reflected on as primitive,

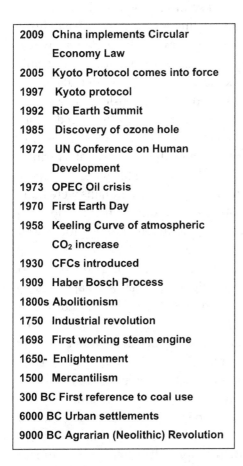

2009	China implements Circular Economy Law
2005	Kyoto Protocol comes into force
1997	Kyoto protocol
1992	Rio Earth Summit
1985	Discovery of ozone hole
1972	UN Conference on Human Development
1973	OPEC Oil crisis
1970	First Earth Day
1958	Keeling Curve of atmospheric CO_2 increase
1930	CFCs introduced
1909	Haber Bosch Process
1800s	Abolitionism
1750	Industrial revolution
1698	First working steam engine
1650-	Enlightenment
1500	Mercantilism
300 BC	First reference to coal use
6000 BC	Urban settlements
9000 BC	Agrarian (Neolithic) Revolution

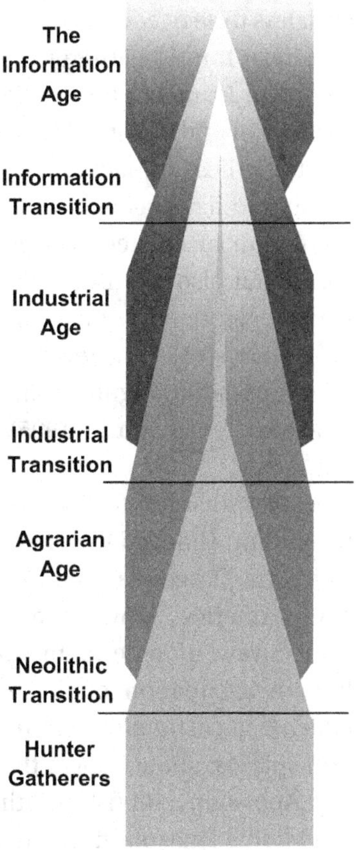

FIGURE 1.1 The key ages of humankind and key events along the way. Note the overlap within the ages.

stressed, uncomfortable and deprived, in terms of insufficient resources and low aspiration. Certainly the remnants of this age today appear to reinforce such thinking. This reflects a significant change in values. Today, self-sufficiency is equated with subsistence or poverty. Prosperity is equated with producing a narrower range of products while purchasing a wider range of products.

Fundamentally, there are many misconceptions of this period. First, even the hunter-gatherers of today only forage for 3–5 hours per day, and spend a lot of the rest of the time resting or participating in leisure activities (Hayden, 1981 p. 407). It should be remembered that today's habitat is much poorer than previous times due to the vast devastation that humans have unleashed on such landscapes, and so originally there was probably even less time needed to forage and hunt. Ethnographic studies have shown that most hunter-gatherer communities remaining on the planet, such as Yolngu in Arnhem Land or the!Kung people in the Kalahari, are, arguably, egalitarian and devoid of leadership (Knauft 1994; Winterhalder 2001).

The earliest impact on the environment by human-like ancestors is thought to have been around 500,000 years ago, with the advanced implementation of fire technology. This allowed survival in colder, temperate zones, but also required either food storage or the use of meat in winter, when vegetation was not available. This niche shift would have implications at an ecosystem-wide level. By the middle Palaeolithic, humans were hunting prime-adult ungulates, and this indicates that they were now top of the food chain (Gaudzinski, 1995). This also implies that their populations were low.

While transition to the Agrarian Age (often referred to as the Neolithic revolution) changed the environment, earlier (40–45,000 years ago) change to hunting large mammals occurred, leading to extinctions in Europe. In North America, South America, and Australia, about 72%, 80%, and 86%, respectively, of large mammal genera ultimately became extinct with the human occupation of those continents (Diamond, 1992). Pimm *et al.* (1995) have estimated that the Polynesians exterminated more than 2,000 bird species, about 15% of the world total, using only Palaeolithic technology. Appearance of fish hunting in the Upper Palaeolithic, while absent in the Middle Palaeolithic, is thought to indicate a food crisis on land due to population pressure (Klein, 1999). By the Upper Palaeolithic, the appearance of decorative objects may indicate a switch to tribal identification, moving away from the egalitarian HGC and towards the onset of "nationality" (White, 1993). Such tribal developments also point towards division of labour and social stratification.

The Hunter-Gatherer Age is marked by humans having little energetic impact on their environment, and generally working within the environmental context. Environmental disasters would have had significant impacts on humans, as they did on all of the other species. Indeed, because humans existed at or near the top of the food chain, perturbation of primary productivity, through meteor impacts or volcanic eruptions reducing incoming radiation, would have potentially destructive effects. If the environment could no longer sustain a given human population, then that population would decrease. For example, the explosion of the super-volcano Toba on Sumatra 70,000 years ago was thought to have almost wiped out the

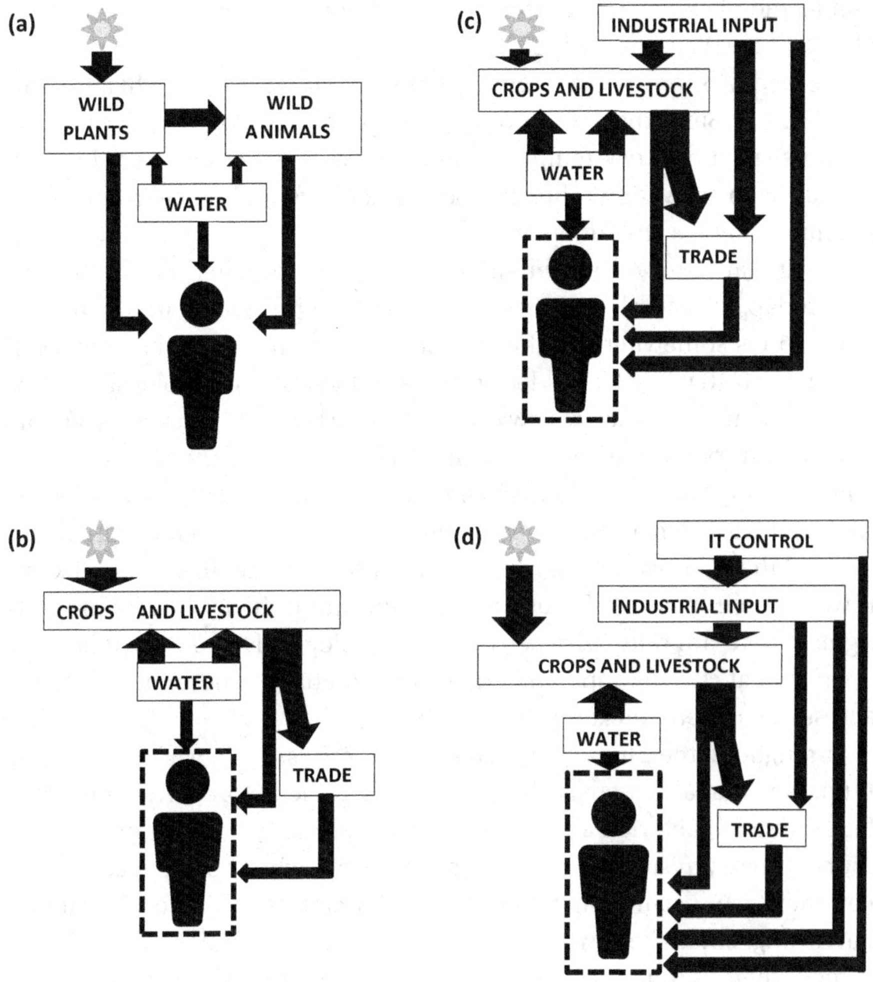

FIGURE 1.2 Feedback loops through human history. (a) Hunter-Gatherer Age; (b) Agrarian Age; (c) Industrial Age; (d) Technology Age. Dashed box: urbanization. Each arrow represents an existentialist risk, where a break would threaten our survival.

human race, leading to a genetic bottleneck, due to the sun's radiation being blocked out (Williams *et al.*, 2009).

The feedback loop between environment and humans was tight and short (see Fig. 1.2). Since there was little capacity for food storage or preservation, a poor season of ecosystem function in terms of growth and productivity would mean starvation. Thus the population size and its behaviour were attenuated by the environment.

Looking at the **ages of humanity** (Fig. 1.1), we see that there is historical overlap. Indeed all four ages are currently represented among human populations somewhere on this planet. However, it was the emergence of land reform that finally has led to the annihilation of the oldest of these ages, the Hunter-Gatherer. Now there is no free land to roam across, and no easy migratory route to escape environmental change. The oldest, longest and, arguably, the most successful period of human existence has not failed itself, but has fallen foul of property rights. Of course even if the human race decided that they wanted to return to a hunter-gatherer lifestyle (unlikely), it would be impossible for us to do so, and not only because of property rights. There are only 2 ha per capita of ecologically productive land on the planet at current population densities, and this is unevenly distributed across the planet (Wackernagel *et al.*, 1999).

Throughout the Hunter-Gatherer Age, there is evidence of increasing human capital and increasing hunting of large herbivores. The only problem with an egalitarian and uncoordinated population is that of the **common property resource model of economics**—where the tragedy of the commons can occur with neither motive for conservation nor sustainable harvesting, since there was no ownership. In other words, if nothing was owned, then nothing needed to be externalized, including responsibility. Tragedy of the commons and the common property resource model refer to the observation that if a resource of limited quantity is accessed by a population, then there is likelihood that the resource will be over-exploited, to the detriment of the population, because individuals will continue to use the resource with no concern for the greater population.

Although discussed for many centuries, it was ecologist Garrett Hardin who published the seminal paper on this topic in 1968 (Hardin, 1968). He emphasized the danger if individuals becoming alienated from wider society, in that self-interest would threaten the greater whole. His paper focused on population growth, but included the implications of such growth on nonrenewable resources. Hardin's position was that legislation was needed to curb individualism. Others have argued that communities have the capacity to alter their behaviour, without the need for government intervention. Indeed, this latter school would argue that the further away from local control a system is, the greater risk to the resource base (Ostrom *et al.*, 1999).

However, the tight and short feedback loop already referred to (Fig. 1.2) would ensure that environmental accountability did weigh on each individual and each family unit. If you cut down the fruit tree to burn as wood, there will be no more fruit. In an island such as Australia, for the first 60,000 years there was only really an internal market, whereas for the last 200 years this has changed to an increasingly external market. The introduction of external trade shifts the accountability, as revenue provides escape from the consequences of environmental feedback. However, both the buyer and the seller can avoid the responsibility, as it becomes externalized to both.

Another advantage of the hunter-gatherer relates to the source and diversity of their diet. Wild populations of food-bearing plant species have much greater diversity than agricultural plants, providing a broader range of strategies against environmental distress and disease. Furthermore, foraging in a seasonal context would mean they would have been rather well buffered against interannual environmental variability because of their dietary breadth, particularly given the ecological intelligence required (Helle and Helama, 2007). Furthermore, an irony exists in terms of perceived scarcity of resources for these early people. In reality, scarcity is central to modern capitalist economics, enforced where necessary (via cartels), in order to maintain profit margins.

So the shift from hunter-gathering to a trade-based age led to the exclusion of the environment, not only from feedback, but from value. The changes that occurred through the Agrarian Age and the Industrial Age, along with the philosophical position taken by the Enlightenment, where nature and its feedback were viewed as no longer limiting progress, all led to the dissociation and divorce of our marriage to the environment. Yet it has been observed that human enterprise is bound by the dimensions of the biosphere (Dilworth, 2010). And so the separation is only imagined, rather than true, for the marriage cannot be annulled in real terms, no matter how abusive we are to the bride. Only our deaths can bring an end to this special relationship, and by annoying the bride, ultimately, we face her wrath. Separation has brought with it increased vulnerability from many sources (Fig. 1.2). Even Adam Smith, the founding father of modern economics, noted: "Labourers, and those who do not labour at all, are all equally maintained by the annual produce of the land and labour of the country. This produce, how great soever, can never be infinite, but must have certain limit" (Smith, 1863; p. 136).

Adam Smith recognized three components of price: rent, profit and wages. A fourth component (replenishment of natural capital) was included in rent. In other words, the maintenance of environmental wellbeing was considered a necessary cost. He commented:

> These three parts [rent, profit and wages] seem either immediately or ultimately to make up the whole price of corn. A fourth part, it may perhaps be thought, is necessary for replacing the stock of the farmer, or for compensating the wear and tear of his labouring cattle, and other instruments of husbandry. But it must be considered that the price of any instrument of husbandry, such as a labouring horse, is itself made up of the same three parts (Smith, 1863; p. 21).

1.2.1.2 The Agrarian Age and the urban revolution

Around 12,000 years ago, just as the last ice age was ending, a period of dramatic change occurred in human behaviour. While the industrial revolution has often been observed as the most significant transition in human history, in fact the transition from the Hunter-Gatherer Age to the Agrarian Age was much more elemental, laying the foundations for all that was to come. To this extent it was the human race's Great Oxygenation Episode.

Three developments in particular would pave the way to the modern world.

1. The onset of agriculture
2. The onset of urbanization
3. The onset of economics

These events would dramatically shift the relationship between economics, society and the environment (Fig. 1.2; Fig. 1.3).

One of the ongoing debates is related to the following question: what came first, the city or the farm? The city-first argument posits that urbanization led to cross breeding of gathered seeds, in turn producing the more useful crops that would form the basis of the Agrarian Age (Jacobs, 1970). The farm-first argument claims that without extensive agriculture, the populations of cities could never have been sustained (Bairoch, 1988). What we do know is that these two defining aspects of human history, urbanization and agriculture, both arrived around the same time.

The archaeological and ethnographic records throughout the world show that the transition from hunting and gathering to farming eventually

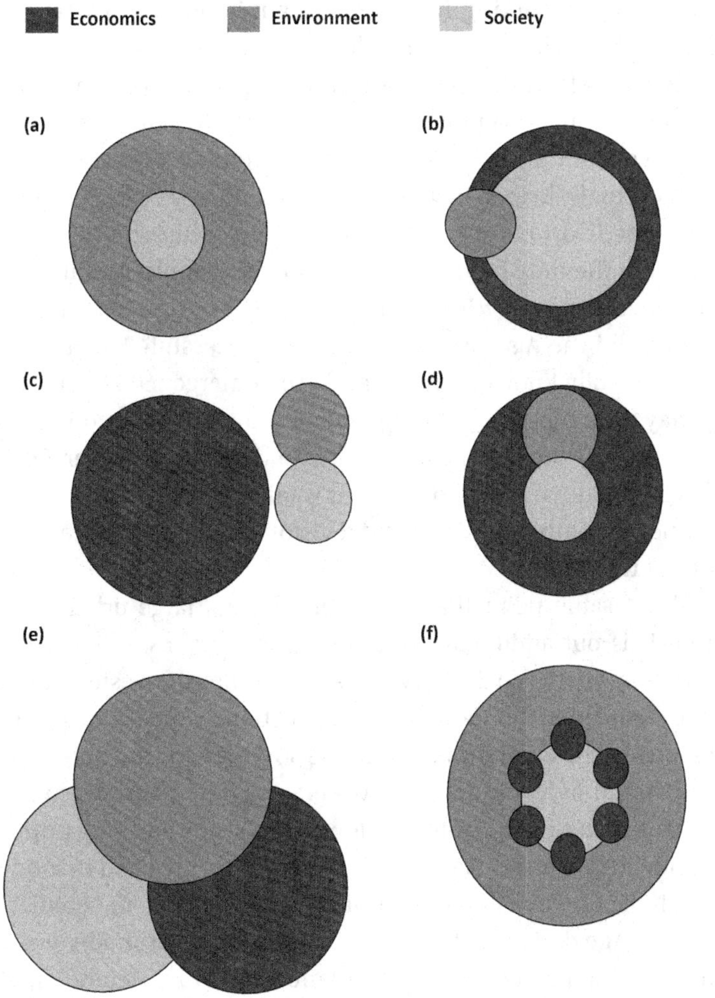

FIGURE 1.3 Different world-views on the relationship between economics, the environment and society. (a) The Ancient Biocentric Model or hunter-gatherer relationship, where society was entirely shaped by and dependent on the environment; (b) The Enlightenment Model, where the environment was viewed as one of the constraints from which progress would free humankind, with the economy dominating; (c) The Technocentric Model, with economics being the only player; (d) The Post-Slavery Model, acknowledging the existence of society and environment; (e) The Triple Bottom Line Model, where sustainability emerges from the overlap of all three sectors; (f) The Pluriverse Model of co-existent non-globalism, a pluralist movement (see text for references).

resulted in longer working hours, lower adult stature, worse nutritional condition and heavier disease burdens, usually acquired from the herds of animals with which the humans now co-habited (Diamond, 1998). Only certain species could be cultivated, and this lead to a decline in diversity of diet, and a concentration on a very limited number of easily grown crops. This would actually lead to increased vulnerability, as evidenced by the Irish Potato Famine (Gorta Mór) of the 19th century which hit an island where potatoes were the only food for some 3 million people, 1 million of whom starved to death. *Homo vulnerabilis* was created by our own making.

Why then did the Agrarian Age prove so successful? The answer to this may never be fully known, but certainly the emergence of a less equitable society may have played a role, aligned with the birth of economics, where trade of surplus production could generate wealth and power. On one side of the social divide of rich and poor sat wealth, comfort and laziness, while on the other sat ambition, drive and a vision of a better future. Politics was also born at this time.

Around the same point that agriculture began, large urban centres also appeared. This put additional strain on agriculture, as a division of labour began to emerge between the harvesters and the non-harvesters, and this division has continued to this day. The intensification of harvesting led to increasing pressure on the environment, and the soil. Soil erosion and water supply became an issue, as less suitable areas were converted into agricultural fields.

The generation of surplus food allowed a peasant farming population to also provide for a warrior class, who would not be involved in food production, much like the division of labour between worker and soldier ants. As the Agrarian Age demanded sedentary lifestyles, territoriality was a necessity and a consequence, and so the land had to be defended. However, division of labour alone was not sufficient to create social stratification based on unequal distribution of wealth. Sedentary lifestyles also allowed for possessions, unlike nomadic lifestyles, and thus this wealth could be converted into material possessions. It would have been difficult to carry a Badmington cabinet or a Pinner Qing Dynasty vase around with you while foraging for fruit or pursuing a squirrel.

This is where the third development came into place: economics, or, more fundamentally, trade. Now, resource exploitation could increase even more, as material could be traded. This required food to be stored. As the soon-to-be-cursed trader in a biblical passage in Luke 12:18 proclaimed: "I will tear down my barns and build bigger ones and there I will store all my grain ... take life easy: eat, drink and be merry."

This is summed up as **the surplus theory of social stratification**, which states that surplus of food supply allows populations to increase while allowing greater leisure time, particularly for those no longer involved directly in food production. This surplus can support a new urban population of specialized craftsmen, merchants, priests, officials, and clerks (Childe 1946; p. 18). Increase in leisure provides an opportunity for occupations that are not absolutely necessary for the needs of everyday life. Food surplus can be implicated in determining the complexity of the social organization, the division of labour and degree of specialization, the form of ownership, exchange, and inheritance of property in addition to the development of ceremonies, crafts and arts (Jacobs and Stern, 1947; pp. 125-6).

And so economics was born. The nomad had no ability to store and trade, and thus only when he stopped, farmed and built a house could he start trading at any meaningful level. Urbanization created centres for trade. Only then could exploitation of fellow humans become viable, and social stratification begin. Interestingly, the ruling classes that emerged had to ensure that their population did not outnumber the peasants (thus challenging any concept of Darwinian fitness reflecting reproductive output); otherwise there would be insufficient food to feed them. This was solved by having the eldest son as the inheritor of the estate, with other disinherited offspring force to leave and seek another set of peasants needing a leader (a common event in animals, with the added advantage of avoiding inbreeding). In medieval times, disinherited noblemen riding on horseback with a small group of servants searching for available fiefdoms became a common sight across Europe, and the knights of the crusades were often recruited from this nomadic outcome of the Agrarian Age.

The Agrarian Age became more methodologically intensive and sophisticated with time. One interesting biogeographical outcome was that the centres of origin for most of the crops that became the main staples of humans were not the most productive current locations. This is because the greatest hotbeds of plant diversity tend to be located on relatively poor soils as a rule (for example the Fynbos in South Africa, or the laterite soils of south-west Australia). The same applies to the oceans, where resplendently diverse coral reefs are found in low-nutrient waters and are destroyed by high nutrient levels.

However, with trade of seeds, people living in the more fertile but less diverse areas would actually have greater success than the diverse but nutrient-poor locations, giving them an economic advantage. This advantage would have a profound impact on the geopolitical landscape. Around

88% of all humans alive today speak some language belonging to one or another of a mere seven language families, all originating in the early Holocene from two small areas of Eurasia that happened to become the earliest centres of agricultural domestication—the Fertile Crescent and China. Fertile soils laid the foundations for economic power, control, linguistics and empire.

Early slash and burn approaches gave way to post-forest agrarian systems such as hoe-based, hydraulic (river), wet rice, fallowing, pasturing and rain-fed cereals. During the Medieval period, animal-drawn agriculture was developed further. Increasing exploration of the planet, particularly by Europeans, brought movement of species such as potato and corn while cultivation of tropical species such as sugar cane, tea and coffee increased dramatically.

The metabolism of the Agrarian Age was essentially based on solar energy and carbon, and as agriculture spread and intensified, this involved the loss of forested land. It is estimated that 30–50% of the CO_2 enrichment of the atmosphere is accounted for by changes in vegetation.

Up until the 20th century, we lived within a "controlled solar energy system" (Sieferle, 2001), where labour was invested in transforming ecosystems and increasing yield of utilizable biomass. It has been estimated that before the beginning of industrialization, Central Europe had an energy return on investment (EROI) of ten to one (Krausmann, 2004). In other words, there was ten times more food energy harvested as consumed by each farm hand. That would mean that for every farm worker, nine nonfarm workers could be fed.

And the Agrarian Age seamlessly became industrialized in the 20th century with mechanized, chemical-dependent and highly specialized systems of cultivation and breeding now to be found in advanced countries and, to a lesser extent, in some developing countries. In many of these latter countries, the use of high-yield seeds, mineral fertilizers and pesticides is high.

Humans now manipulated the land rather than being reliant on the environment. Control had been wrested, somewhat, from nature, and taken into our hands. Our ecological intelligence was not that useful to us any longer, and became diminished. Alongside this, impacts included increased soil erosion, habitat destruction and increasing population pressure in addition to increased urbanization, requiring further intensification of agriculture. This placed increasing strain on the environment. But things were about to get much worse.

1.2.1.3 The Industrial Age

The industrial Age, accompanied by the Enlightenment, represents a fascinating marriage between philosophy, technology, empire and wealth. At a time of revolution and rebirth, Europe and, later, the USA led the way in a transformative movement that would alter all of the aspects of our lives. This unstoppable wave that continues to sweep across the world, took food production with it, transforming it into industrial agriculture.

In 1906, this industry began to produce nitrogen fertilizers, using vast amounts of energy to do so and contributing significantly to greenhouse gas emissions. Now soils could be supplemented with chemical fertilizer, hugely increasing productivity and meaning that crop rotation was not needed. Today, 40% of the world's human population is dependent on crops grown using artificial fertilizers. This figure represents 2.8 billion people. The use of huge mechanized approaches has led to larger and larger fields, with the destruction of natural field boundaries, greatly impacting on wildlife and on natural pest control. This machinery also leads to compacted soil. Pesticides, herbicides and huge amounts of fresh water are required, as natural controls of pests, disease and water cycling are destroyed. In fact more energy is invested into agriculture than is obtained from the food. On top of this, we waste around 40% of the food that we produce. We are not a leaky colander, but a huge sinkhole.

Sociologically, the Industrial Revolution also brought an increased polarization between the rich and the poor, while liberating population growth and increasing generational overlap thanks to people living longer. It also was to deliver environmental damage of unprecedented savagery. Today we are faced with the challenges created by the Industrial Revolution: a damaged ozone layer; highly perturbed atmospheric gas content; threats to ocean and atmospheric circulation patterns; soil erosion; rising sea levels; species extinction; water, land and air pollution; salinization; a distended population; a resource and energy crisis.

As we have noted already, mass deforestation, and changes in CO_2 and methane levels in the atmosphere had begun at the outset of the Agrarian Era, some 10,000 years ago. Lead pollution from Ancient Greek and Roman periods was about one tenth of that of the 19th century (Hong *et al.*, 1994), while copper pollution (mostly from production of coinage and military ware) would not be exceeded until 1750. A further peak in Cu pollution was noted 1,000 years ago due to industrial activity in the Sung dynasty in China (Hong *et al.*, 1996). A peat core from a Swiss bog revealed significant enrichments of arsenic, antimony and lead extending back to Roman times, indicating that the anthropogenic fluxes of these metals have exceeded the natural fluxes for more than 2,000 years (Shotyk *et al.*, 1996).

Urbanization and economics, both originating in the Agrarian Age, would now form the foundations of the Industrial Age. During the late 15th century through to the late 16th century, there was a significant increase in trade and colonial activity, allowing the accumulation of much greater surpluses. It was during this period when, according to Wallerstein (1974), the capitalist world economy was formed. The latter part of the 18th century saw machine-based industries and steam energy developing in England. This in turn led to a significant demographic transformation, with people flocking to cities for work. The steam energy, combined with iron, transformed transport as the age of steam emerged. Steam stood as the bridge between coal and available power, transforming what had been possible previously.

During the Industrial Age, energy transition was characterized by a shift from the use of energy flows with low power density, in the form of biomass that is regrown annually, to the exploitation of large-scale energy deposits that had accumulated over geological eras and which existed in concentrated forms such as coal, oil and gas, with a high power density (Smil, 2003).

Energy now came from the **subterranean forest**, as Sieferle (2001) put it. By 1800, 900 kg of coal per capita per year was already being used in the UK, while 90% of total global coal extraction occurred in the UK. In 1900, over 70% of coal extracted globally was used by only four countries: UK, USA, Germany and France. By 1850, the annual coal combusted in the United Kingdom had reached the equivalent of the fuelwood that could be produced from a virtual forest area the size of the entire country (Krausmann and Kowalski, 2013). Steam engines enable the conversion of coal into mechanical power. This led to a dramatic increase in the available power compared with the previous regime. Resource use also increased dramatically. In the United Kingdom, materials used increased from 60 to 400 million tonnes per year between 1750 and 1900.

Chemical industry began to develop in the 19th century, and the 20th century saw steel production escalate, along with the replacement of coal by oil and electricity. Electrical and petrol engines became dominant, the latter liberating transport. The petrochemical industry became a rampant business, leading to huge production of trains, planes, ships and vehicles, with vast use of nonrenewable resources in terms of structure, aside from the damaging emissions. Some 30 tonnes of material are used in the production of a car, while motorways use vast resources for construction, using

Box 1.1: Consumption of resources over the last century

During the last 100 years, global population quadrupled to 6.4 billion and global economic output as measured by GDP grew more than 20-fold (Maddison, 2001). Total material extraction increased 8-fold, with building material 34-fold, ores/industrial minerals 27-fold, and biomass 3.6-fold. From 1948 to 1973, *per capita* use of materials increased by more than 50% while the use of nonrenewable minerals increased by 340%. Humanity currently uses almost 60 billion tonnes of materials per year. As a consequence, material intensity (i.e. the amount of materials required per unit of GDP) declined, while materials use *per capita* doubled from 4.6 to 10.3 tonnes per capita per year (Krausmann *et al.*, 2009).

around 40,000 tonnes of materials per km (see Box 1.1 for increasing consumption information).

Electricity generation is hugely inefficient. It requires vast amounts of energy, with up to 60% of the primary energy lost in conversion and transmission. The new green fuel, ethanol, is estimated to consume six times as much energy in its manufacturing as it provides as a fuel.

Thus, provided with the rich resources of a planet ripe for the picking, we have set about our industrial journey in a most inefficient and destructive way, making it difficult to see how this represents an Enlightenment. Rather, to many, this recent period of human existence resembles more an age of environmental **endarkenment**, with our species now so distant from its environmental context that it fails to see the significance of the damage done.

1.2.1.4 The Information Age

Much as the Industrial Age emerged from within the Agrarian Age, so the Information Age has arisen almost seamlessly from within the Industrial Age. Of course across the planet, all four of the ages of humanity still exist in some form of tense co-existence. But undoubtedly, the Information Age is reaching into almost every aspect of life for many of us. This age has brought new opportunities, but also new vulnerabilities.

While ancient analogue computers have existed from as early as 4,500 years ago (for example, the Sumerian abacus), the ability to share information as well as to carry out manipulation of data was not fully realized until the development of the Internet and the World Wide Web, along with the availability of cheap personal computers. The silicon chip, fundamental to the birth of the modern personal computer era, was initially designed by

Robert Noyce in 1959, improving on a germanium chip developed by Jack Kilby six months earlier. The Internet has existed in a basic form since the 1960s. However, the first functioning Internet available to the man in the street did not become available until the early 1990s, perhaps ushering in the Information Age in its true form.

The Internet has revolutionized so many aspects of life. From education to business, from communication to crowd-sourcing and from politics to philanthropy, humans have felt empowered and enriched by being able to communicate with a potential audience of 2.4 billion users. Mobile phones, used by 6 billion humans worldwide, are now integrated with World Wide Web access, increasing further the connectivity. However, while the Internet is very resilient to random failures, it is highly susceptible to hacking and viral attack. This increases the vulnerability of the human race, as we become reliant on computing for such essential aspects as transport, medical implants, power distribution and banking (Fig. 1.2).

The second development of the Information Age was the establishment of economic globalization. The seeds for this were planted during the formation of global bodies such as the International Monetary Fund (1944), World Bank (1944), and the United Nations (1945). Economic globalization had been accompanied by cultural globalization, accelerated through population movement and the Internet. Globalization can again be seen as driven by Enlightenment philosophy, where the bringing together of our global technology and reasoning can best fit us for a better future and pave the way to a utopia. However, the loss in diversity and the impact of free trade on resource exploitation in developing countries are areas of concern. Chris Whynacht observes (Whynacht, 2011; p. 8) that "Smith would never have supported the globalization of international capital markets or the drawing down of global stocks of natural capital without replenishing them through rental expenses before paying profits."

A third important development of the Information Age is the use of orbiting satellites in communication, meteorology, television, navigation (Navstar and GPS), remote sensing, military purposes, and search-and-rescue, not to mention detecting potentially threatening space rocks (if only the dinosaurs has mastered space technology). So reliant have we become on satellites that the repercussions of them losing functionality has opened up a new level of vulnerability for us, one not on the planet, but in space.

The Information Age has been predicted long before it occurred. The Marquis of Condorcet, Enlightenment philosopher and revolutionary, wrote that a significant technical advance would be made:

> uniting a great number of objects in an arranged and systematic order, by which we may be able to perceive at a glance their bearings and connections, seize in an instant their combinations, and form from them the more readily new combinations (Condorcet, 1955, p. 173).

The concept of the **noosphere** (the sphere of human thought) is seen by its key protagonists (Vladimir Vernadsky and Pierre Teilhard de Chardin), as the next phase of planetary development, following on from the geosphere and then the biosphere. Teilhard de Chardin (1971; p. 110) conceived of computational power and connectivity, the Information Age, delivering this noosphere:

> Here I am thinking of those astonishing electronic machines (the starting-point and hope of the young science of cybernetics), by which our mental capacity to calculate and combine is reinforced and multiplied by a process and to a degree that herald as astonishing advances in this direction as those that optical science has already produced for our power of vision.

Teilhard de Chardin saw increasingly complex social networks as contributing to the noosphere, leading eventually to the Omega point, which he felt was the goal of history, akin to the destination of the path of progress of the Enlightenment. The noosphere is represented by integration and unification. As a result of Teilhard de Chardin's predictions, he has become known as the patron saint of the World Wide Web.

As Michael Benedikt describes it in his Collected Abstracts from the First Conference on Cyberspace:

> Cyberspace is a globally networked, computer-sustained, computer-accessed, and computer-generated, multi-dimensional, artificial, or virtual reality. In this world, onto which every computer screen is a window, actual, geographical distance is irrelevant. Objects seen or heard are neither physical nor, necessarily, presentations of physical objects, but are rather, in form, character, and action, made up of data, of pure information. This information is derived in part from the operation of the natural, physical world, but is derived primarily from the immense traffic of symbolic information, images, sounds, and people that constitute human enterprise in science, art, business, and culture (Benedikt, 1990; p. 1).

Although defined as a different age, the Information Age has not reduced the huge resource exploitation and economic growth of the Industrial Age, but rather, in many ways, has exacerbated it. Up to 60 different metals are incorporated into electronic equipment and in such tiny amounts that they are almost impossible to recycle efficiently. Energy requirements are also high, and include consumption related to production, data centre consumption, PC consumption, and consumption related to peripheral devices. Huge amounts of energy are needed for heating, cooling and ventilation of equipment. The Internet consumes around 860 TWh annually according to estimates (Gelenbe, 2009), the same as the entire nation of Japan. At least 2% of global carbon emissions are directly due to IT systems and further increases are expected since new IT applications are developed every day (Anderson *et al.*, 2008). By 2020 the global carbon footprint is expected to double. Cloud computing is a field where new green opportunities are coupled with new environmental risks (Sissa, 2011).

While the Information Age is often touted as delivering sustainability by reducing the carbon footprint, by up to 20% according to The Climate Group (Webb, 2008), Hilty *et al.* (2006) demonstrated, through the use of simulations, that the future impact of ICT on the global carbon footprint could be marginal because positive and negative effects would cancel each other out. The shift to mobile units has led to a decreased energy use of software, but static units are still designed under an infinite energy principle, while the supportive infrastructure for both static and mobile units is similar.

Measures to reduce the energy footprint include increasing the life-span of units, replacing DSL with optical units, locating servers close to green energy sources, reducing power usage, switching servers between different time zones or wind speed areas, developing more energy-efficient hardware such as solid state discs compared with hard disc drives, clock gating (reducing CPU clock speeds), power gating (closing down parts of the chips) and reduced redundancy.

Computing now controls most industrial activity, just as industry took control of agricultural processes at the onset of the Industrial Age. Hence vulnerabilities related to the Information Age threaten not only industry, but agriculture. The whole tower could come toppling down. Threats from satellite damage due to solar flares or geomagnetic reversal, from hackers and from power outages pose issues from above (sun), below (geomagnetism) and all around (hackers) (Fig. 1.2).

On the positive side, information technology can be used for greater efficiency at design, manufacture, use and recycling phases of the product life-cycle. Computing can also find optimal solutions to complex problems, allowing visualization of large data sets. However, such models are reliant on the parameters and purity of the data supplied. There are three kinds of lie: lies, damned lies and computer modelling, to misquote Mark Twain (and, allegedly, Benjamin Disraeli). While models can be deliberately designed for a specific outcome, favourable to the paymaster, more often they fail because of a lack of knowledge, the famous "unknown unknowns" of Donald Rumsfeld.

Information technology offers the potential for reinforcing otherwise nebulous concepts, such as energy efficiency, by reporting real-time energy use to the consumer, for example. This allows individuals to monitor and adjust their own energy behaviour, hence encouraging energy efficiency in home, work and travel (Webb, 2008).

Time, in terms of labour, costs more than energy. Information technology has been focused on time efficiency as opposed to energy efficiency (Spreng, 1993). Thus while promoting economic growth, it neither contributes to society (since it generates unemployment by saving on working hours) nor to the environment (since it uses energy and creates huge waste). Furthermore, since its goal is time efficiency, its success is not measured in environmental and societal currency. While new technology continues to deliver the Enlightenment dream, if the dream itself is flawed, then technology will never deliver sustainability. Ultimately, very few cars of themselves have killed anyone, but many have died at the hands of drivers.

Recent work on existential risk (risk to the survival of intelligent life on the planet) points to technology as the greatest threat to human kind (Bostrom, 2013). While we have developed strategies to survive natural existential risks of many kinds (super-volcanoes, disease pandemics, tsunamis, earthquakes, etc.) over many thousands of years, it is the power that future technologies are likely to provide us with in terms of manipulating the natural world for our own ends that poses the greatest risk. Ironically, the very cornerstone of the Enlightenment, technology, is considered our greatest threat today (Fig. 1.2).

1.2.1.5 Summary of the ages of humankind

The history of humankind has been a journey of change, as all journeys are, but the drivers of change have altered. The Hunter-Gatherer Age, in which we have spent 95% of our time on Earth, was shaped by the environment, and our existence relied on our relationship with nature. The feedback loops were simple, rapid and direct, stemming from the sun and the rain. The rest was the outcome of the particular food web of which we were a part. Carbohydrates were the dominant chemicals while our energy was mostly dedicated to acquiring the food and water needed to sustain us. We existed in an egalitarian relationship socially and with the environment. Human capital represented the only limit to human economic development (e.g.

the number of fishermen limited the number of fish caught), if economics even existed.

The Agrarian Age still relied on the sun and water, but we began taking control of the food webs, altering them to suit our needs. Soon these outcomes formed the basis of profits, allowing trade, and settlements facilitated the development of trade routes and export/import. Carbohydrate was still the dominant chemical. Our energy was spent creating agricultural surplus, or trading this surplus, as an economic system developed. Inequality entered not only human society, but the human–environment relationship. In the Agrarian Age, the environment was now a source and a sink. Man-made capital limited economic development (e.g. the number of fishing boats limited the number of fish harvested).

The population underwent division of labour (food producers and those not involved in agriculture), and with a sedentary, trading race, social stratification emerged. With the basics more than taken care of, wealth, power and tokenism prevailed. This lead to wider uses of renewable and non-renewable resources, and with an increasingly large trading floor, industrialization of production emerged, ushering in the Industrial Age. Our energy was spent creating wealth either for ourselves or our employers, and inequality increased at both the social and environmental levels.

The Industrial Age superseded the Agrarian Age by industrializing agriculture, while colonialism all but wiped out the remnants of the Hunter-Gatherer Age, except in areas where the colonial powers could see no exploitative advantage. In the early Industrial Age, man-made capital limited the potential for economic development (e.g. the ability of an automobile factory to make lots of cars), but in the later stages, it is the natural capital that limits that development (e.g. insufficient lithium to make enough batteries for the new generation of electric cars). It is fossil fuel deposits, not the number of refineries, that limit oil production; it is the area of forest, not the number of saw mills, which limits forestry. We attempt to solve the fishing and forestry issues by introducing plantation forests and fish farms—cultivated natural capital—a hybrid, but still reliant on natural capital (topsoil, water, sunlight).

The Information Age now controls the financial, industrial, agricultural and cultural domains of our existence, and we live in a largely controlled world. While improving our social interactions and enhancing industrial efficiency, the Information Age has so far not altered our relationship with the environment in any meaningful way. Its replacement of humans in the workplace may also erode social structure while enhancing economic growth. It is yet to be seen if this will change, but at present it merely contributes to the source and sink exploitation of our existence, while introducing new risks due to our increasing dependence on technology. While the Information Age excludes environmental considerations within its solution space, then its solutions will continue to fail nature, and further erode the natural capital of our planet.

Each age has brought a population explosion, as technology has raised the carrying capacity by allowing access to greater energy resources for humans. Through the ages of humankind there has been a shift from using portable utilitarian, easily acquired, replaceable, easily recycled artefacts to using heavy, elaborate, multi-resource artefacts requiring prolonged manufacture, maintenance, and increased waste. From the Agrarian Age onward, with the advent of economics came the age of possession, inequality, envy, greed and individualism: **the age of the plastic crown.**

1.3 What is perturbed, why and the consequences

This section examines the feedback between business activity, society and the environment, demonstrating how these three areas have significant implications for each other. Three environmental impacts are identified: climate destabilization, non-greenhouse gas pollution and habitat destruction and exhaustion.

1.3.1 The three arenas

Human activities currently take place in three arenas: economics, society and the environment (see Fig. 1.3). Whatever we do in any one arena tends to impact on any other arena. Each arena also has completely unique requirements and sustainability issues, and these often come into conflict with the requirements and sustainability issues of the others. Economics has growth, equity and efficiency as its objectives. Society has empowerment, participation, social mobility, institutional development, cultural identity and social cohesion as its objectives. The environment has thermodynamics as its driver and succession, population dynamics, ecosystem function, resilience and recovery as its responses as we shall explore in Chapter 4 (see Goodland and Daly, 1996).

In our present position, humans will wish to continue actively participating in these three arenas, and so we would hope for sustainability in all three. Sustainability depends on the maintenance of capital. There are four types of capital associated with these three arenas: human capital, social capital, natural capital and human-made capital.

Human capital consists of education, health and nutrition of individuals, integration within society, dignity, human rights, representation and achieving potential. The concept of human capital is often examined in terms of the work potential of a given human, i.e. what contribution he or she can make to the economy. A measure of human capital, the **Human Development Index**, uses health (life expectancy), wealth (income) and education as its criteria. GDP has been viewed as too narrow an index with which to measure development, focusing only on income. In an attempt to "humanize" the assessment of development, economists Mahbub ul Haq and Amartya Sen focus on three criteria: **income** (measured by Gross National Income per capita), **health** (measured by life expectancy at birth) and **education** (measured by adult literacy and primary, secondary and tertiary education participation).

Each criterion is calculated by dividing the observed figure for a particular nation by the highest value globally. These proportions are then multiplied together and the third root is taken, giving a geometric mean. Criticisms centre around the material focus of the index. Furthermore, while marrying economic and social measures, the index does not include any environmental impact assessment. Thus the index cannot be used in any consideration of sustainable development. Businesses that cultivate human capital tend to outperform those that do not do this (Crook *et al.*, 2011). Some others replace human capital with cultural capital (e.g. Bourdieu, 1986). At this point it is worth recalling the different types of capital.

- **Social capital**: this includes cultural identity, diversity and context, community, institutions, sovereignty, representation, equality, networking, group sourcing and diversification potential. The Social Capital Foundation (www.socialcapital-foundation.is/) discusses the concept as follows: "Social capital is about revitalizing the community link, and can be defined as a set of mental dispositions and attitudes favouring cooperative behaviours within society". The concept of social capital recognizes an emergent value in groups of individuals, as opposed to individual, human capital. Thus the sum of human capital does not equal social capital. Rather, social capital forms the context for human enrichment.

- **Human-made or manufactured capital**: "capital generated via economic activity through human ingenuity and technological change; the produced means of production" (Berkes and Folke, 1993; p. 1). Much debate surrounds the idea that human capital gains could offset natural capital losses. One position claims that this is possible, and therefore insists that natural capital loss need not be problematic. Another position claims that this is not possible, and that natural capital should be maintained at all costs. Both sides of this debate will be examined in Chapter 5.
- **Natural capital**: the flow of goods and services from ecosystems. For example a forest offers wood, shelter, water cycling, soil stability and nutrient cycling. Recently efforts have been made to value natural capital. The Boreal forests in Canada have been valued at US$3.7 trillion, while global natural capital has been valued at US$33 trillion per year (Costanza *et al.*, 1998). These figures represent the cost of replacing the services provided by the natural world. Natural capital is the only form of capital that we cannot make. Therefore consumption of natural capital is liquidation. Its production is driven by its own self-organizing character. It had been viewed as a free and infinite good, but now it is becoming limiting.

Economic sustainability requires that total capital is kept constant. It does not require any particular type of capital to remain constant. For example, natural capital could decline, provided there was an increase in one or more of the other types of capital. Social sustainability focuses on social and human capital, ignoring human-made and environmental capital, while environmental sustainability requires natural capital to be sustained.

The issue is that business practice currently undermines sustainability in all three arenas, and thus poses a significant threat to our ongoing activities in each. Figure 1.4 shows how these impacts are manifest. Economic growth relies on resource acquisition, use and waste. This waste is generated in the acquiring, manufacturing, use and breakdown of materials. All of these activities use the environment either as a sink (for dumping waste) or as a source (for mining/harvesting resources). Examples of sink issues include nutrient run-off (eutrophication), toxic mining till, ozone destruction, greenhouse gases, sulphur dioxide, pesticides and herbicides. Examples of source issues include deforestation, wetland drainage, fishery collapses, excessive hunting of wild animals such as elephants, whales and Siberian tigers, soil erosion and declining phosphate reserves.

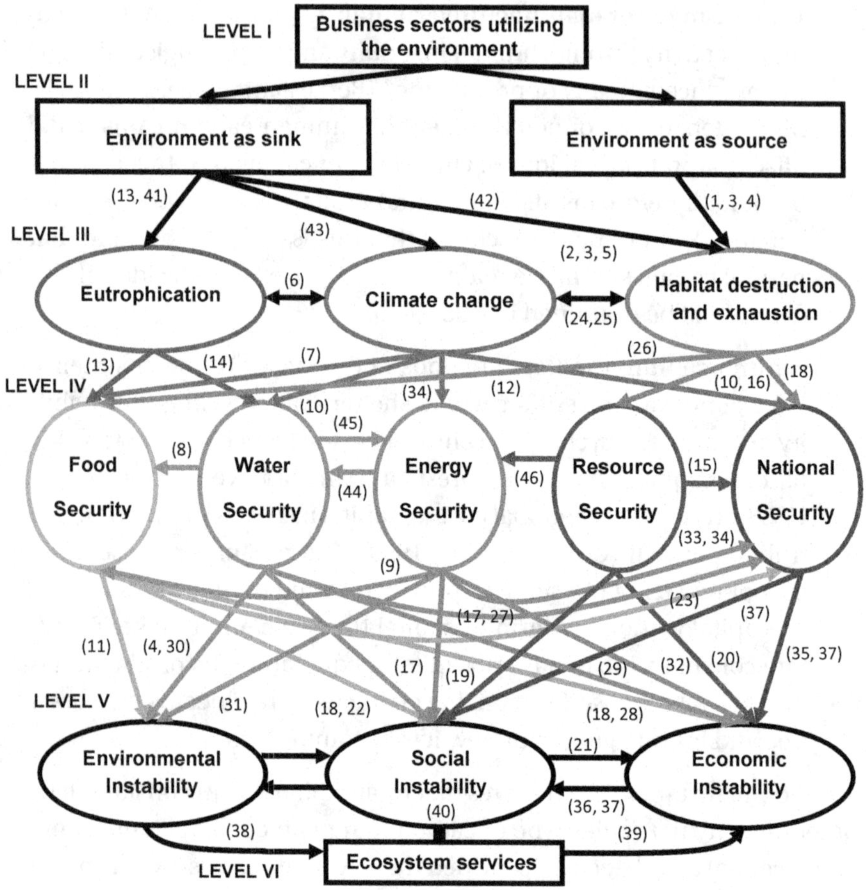

FIGURE 1.4 The relationship between economic activity, ecosystem services and security. Significant literature on the Economy–Environment–Society–Economy (EESE) cycle is provided as a starting point for further work.

(1) Sprohge and Sirisom, 2011; (2) Cochard, 2011; (3) Koh *et al.*, 2011; (4) Dobrovolski *et al.*, 2011; (4) Newburn *et al.*, 2011; (5) Mantyka-Pringle *et al.*, 2012; (6) Moss *et al.*, 2011; (7) Beddington *et al.*, 2011; (8) Fereres *et al.*, 2011; (9) Karp and Richter, 2011; (10) Howard *et al.*, 2011; (11) Chappell and LaValle 2011; (12) Farah and Rossi, 2011; (13) Lal, 2007; (14) Falkenmark, 2001; (15) Webersik, 2010; (16) Scheffran and Battaglini, 2011; (17) Arnold, 2009; (18) Gunasekera *et al.*, 2011; (19) Barrett 2013; (20) Keay and Metcalf, 2011; (21) Okpala and Jonsson, 2002; (22) Schanbacer, 2010; (23) Messer, 2009; (24) Ehrlich *et al.*, 1993; (25) Oldeman, 1998; (26) Zhang and Liu, 2006; (27) Ozturk *et al.*, 2013; (28) Timmer, 2000; (29) Gallopin and Rijsberman, 2000; (30) Pfister *et al.*, 2009; (31) Omer, 2008; (32) Ikein, 2009; (33) Kalicki and Goldwyn, 2005; (34) Scheffran and Battaglini, 2010; (35) Lewis, 2009; (36) Perreault and Valdivia, 2010; (37) Burns and Price, 2009; (38) Lant *et al.*, 2008; (39) Fisher *et al.*, 2008; (40) Shackleton *et al.*, 2010; (41) Egertson *et al.*, 2004; (42) Zhang *et al.*, 2007; (43) Küstermann *et al.*, 2008; (44) Dominguez-Faus *et al.*, 2013; (45) Bizikova *et al.*, 2013; (46) Bustamante and Gaustad, 2014

The input/output rules (waste emissions should be within natural assimilative capacity and harvesting rates should be within regenerative capacity of nature in the case of renewable resources, or in the case of nonrenewable resources, depleted at a rate at which human technology can find renewable replacements for them) have clearly been broken (Goodland and Daly, 1996). Sink issues lead to non-greenhouse gas pollution, climate destabilization and habitat destruction and loss, while source issues impact on habitat destruction and exhaustion (Level III in Fig. 1.4). Climate destabilization impacts on habitats due to desertification and sea level rise. As a consequence of these three problems, five key areas are threatened (Level IV, Fig. 1.4): food security, water security, energy security, resource security and national security. Many of these also impact on each other. Energy insecurity threatens food security and water security. Food, water, energy and resource insecurity threaten national security, while water security threatens food security.

With these five central areas of human life destabilized, it follows that the environment, the economy and society will become unstable (Level V, Fig. 1.4). Environmental instability means that ecosystem services (such as water cycling, nutrient cycling and crop pollination) collapse, thus further threatening economic and social security. Ecosystem services consist of the important functions that the natural world undertakes which have significant implications for human survival and wellbeing. They come under four categories:

1. Supporting services such as nutrient cycling, oxygen production and soil formation. These underpin the provision of the other "service" categories.
2. Provisioning services such as food, fibre, fuel and water.
3. Regulating services such as climate regulation, water purification and flood protection.
4. Cultural services such as education, recreation, and aesthetic value.

Damage to ecosystems through anthropogenic impacts greatly affects the ability of these ecosystems to maintain these services. References for all of these interactions are detailed in Fig. 1.4.

The three impacts of pollution, climate destabilization and habitat destruction have been termed "the three modern horsemen of the apocalypse" (Skene, 2011; p. 140), which, ironically, have emerged as a result of our attempts to avoid the three original apocalyptic horsemen of Malthus: disease, famine and war. The road to progress, taking us from the impoverishment of our ancestors to the prosperous future we strive for, has created challenges which are so great as to undermine our very existence. And these new horsemen are likely to revive the three Malthusian horsemen, as food, water and national security become undermined, leading to greater susceptibility to disease.

In the next chapter we will return to Level III of Fig. 1.4 and examine each of these three horsemen that have emerged from the abuse of the input/output rules. But first some time for reflection.

1.4 Debate, discussion and further thought

1. Can technology save the planet?
2. Should technology represent a separate pillar of sustainability?
3. Is economic growth sustainable?
4. How exactly does business impact on the environment and what are the consequences does this have on the social and economic arenas?
5. What are the greatest threats to sustaining our existence on Earth?
6. What are ecosystem services and how are they threatened?
7. Can we really replace ecosystem services with technology?
8. Carbon is overemphasized in terms of sustainability. Discuss.
9. How do human, social, manufactured and natural capital (i) complement (ii) antagonize one another, and how should we visualize a balance between them if we hope to plan towards a sustainable future?

References

Abraham, K. and Mackie, C. (2005). *Beyond the Market: Designing Nonmarket Accounts for the United States*. National Academies Press, Washington DC.

Anderson, D. and 17 other authors. (2008). A Framework for Data Center Energy Productivity. White Paper #13: Metrics & Measurements. The Green Grid, Beaverton, OR. pp. 1-14.

Anyaoku, E. (2007). In connection with the Beyond GDP Conference on 19–20 November 2007.

Arnold, C.A. (2009) Water privatisation trends in the United States: human rights, national security and public stewardship. William & Mary Environmental Law and Policy Review 33: 785-850.

Atlantic Institute for Market Studies (2003). Speech to Nova Scotia Forest Products Association, 17 January 2003.

Bairoch, P. (1988). *Cities and Economic Development: from the Dawn of History to the Present.* University of Chicago Press, Chicago.

Ban Ki-moon (2012) Remarks to the high-level delegation of mayors and regional authorities. New York, USA, 23 April 2012.

Barrett, C.B. (2013). *Food Security and Sociopolitical Stability.* Oxford University Press, Oxford.

Beddington, J., Asaduzzaman, M., Fernandez, A., Clark, M., Guillou, M., Jahn, M., Erda, L., Mamo, T., Bo, N. Van, Nobre, C.A., Scholes, R., Sharma, R. and Wakhungu, J. (2011) Achieving food security in the face of climate change: Summary for policy makers from the Commission on Sustainable Agriculture and Climate Change. Copenhagen, Denmark: CCAFS.

Beiner, R. (1999). The civic argument for socialism. In. Avnon, D. And De-Shalit, A. (eds.) *Liberalism and its Practice.* Routledge, London.

Benedikt, M. (1990) *Collected Abstracts from the First Conference on Cybernetics.* School of Architecture, University of Texas, Austin.

Berkes, D. and Folke, C. (1993). A systems perspective on the interrelationships between natural, human-made and cultural capital. Ecological Economics 5: 1-8.

Bizikova, L., Roy, D., Swanson, D., Venema, H.D. and McCandless, M. (2013). *The Water–energy–food Security Nexus: Towards a Practical Planning and Decision-support Framework for Landscape Investment and Risk Management.* International Institute for Sustainable Development.

Bostrom, N. (2013). Existential risk prevention as global priority. Global Policy, 4(1), 15-31.

Bourdieu, P. (1986). The forms of capital. In: Richardson, J. (Ed.) *Handbook of Theory and Research for the Sociology of Education.* Greenwood, New York. pp. 241-58.

Brundtland, G. (1987). *Our common future: Report of the 1987 World Commission on Environment and Development.* Oxford University Press, Oxford.

Burns, R.N. and Price, J. (2009). *The Global Economic Crisis and Potential Implications for Foreign Policy and National Security.* The Aspen Institute, Washington D.C.

Bustamante, M.L. and Gaustad, G. (2014). Challenges in assessment of clean energy supply-chains based on byproduct minerals: A case study of tellurium use in thin film photovoltaics. Applied Energy. In press.

Cancer Council Australia (2014). www.cancer.org.au/about-cancer/types-of-cancer/skin-cancer.html

Chappell, M.J. and LaValle, L.A. (2011). Food security and biodiversity: can we have both? An agroecological analysis. Agriculture and Human Values 28: 3-26.

Childe, V.G. (1946). *What Happened in History.* Penguin, New York.

Cochard, R. (2011). Consequences of deforestation and climate change on diversity. In: Trisurat' Y., Shrestha, R.P. and Alkemafe, R. (eds.). *Land Use, Climate Change and Biodiversity Modelling: Perspectives and Applications.* IGI Global, Hershey, PA. pp. 24-51.

Condorcet M.J.A. de (1955, originally 1779). *Sketch for a Historical Picture of the Progress of the Human Mind.* Translated by June Barraclough. Weidenfeld & Nicolson, London.

Costanza, R., d'Arge, R., De Groot, R., Farber, S., Grasso, M., Hannon, B., Limburg, K., Naeem, S., O'Neill, R.V., Paruelo, J., Raskin, R.G., Sutton, P. and van den Belt, M. (1998). The value of the world's ecosystem services and natural capital. Ecological Economics: 25(1): 3-15.

Costanza, R., Graumlich, L.J. and Steffen, W.L. (2007). *Sustainability or Collapse? An Integrated History and Future of People on Earth.* MIT Press, Cambridge, MA.

Crook, T.R., Todd, S.Y., Combs, J.G., Woehr, D.J. and Ketchen Jr, D.J. (2011). Does human capital matter? A meta-analysis of the relationship between human capital and firm performance. Journal of Applied Psychology, 96(3), 443.

Crutzen, P.J. (2002). Geology of mankind. Nature 415 (6867): 23-32.

Crutzen, P.J. and Stoermer, E.F. (2000). The Anthropocene. Global Change Newsletter, v. 41, pp. 17-18.

Delaney, D.M. (2005). What to do in a failing civilization. Proceeding of CACOR 3(6): 16-21.

Diamond, J. (1992). *The Third Chimpanzee.* Harper Collins Publishers, New York.

Diamond, J. (1998) *Guns Germs and Steel: a Short History of Everybody for the Last 13000 Years.* Vintage, London.

Dilworth, C. (2010). *Too Smart for our Own Good: The Ecological Predicament of Humankind.* Cambridge University Press, Cambridge.

Dobrovolski, R., Diniz-Filho, J.A.F., Loyola, R.D. and de Marco Junior, P. (2011) Agricultural expansion and the fate of global conservation policies. Biodiversity and Conservation 20: 2445-59.

Dominguez-Faus, R., Folberth, C., Liu, J., Jaffe, A.M. and Alvarez, P.J. (2013). Climate change would increase the water intensity of irrigated corn ethanol. Environmental Science and Technology 47(11): 6030-7.

Dunn, J.R. (1992). America the beautiful: accomplishments of environmental protection in the US. National Review (6 July 1992): p. 34.

Egertson, C.J., Kopaska, J.A. and Downing, J.A. (2004) A century of change in macrophyte abundance and composition in response to agricultural eutrophication. Hydrobiologia 524: 145-56.

Ehrlich, P.R., Ehrlich, A.H. and Daily, G.C. (1993). Food security, population and environment. Population and Development Review 19: 1-32.

Falkenmark, M. (2001). The greatest problem: the inability to link environmental security, water security and food security. International Journal of Water Resources Development 17: 539-54.

Farah, P. and Rossi, P. (2011) National energy policies and energy security in the context of climate change and global environmental risks: a theoretical framework for reconciling domestic and international law through a multi-scalar and multilevel approach. European Energy and Environmental Law Review (EEELR). Kluwer Law International 20: 232-44.

Fereres, E, Orgaz, F. and Gonzalez-Dugo, V. (2011). Reflections on food security under water scarcity. Journal of Experimental Botany 62: 4079-86.

Fisher, B., Turner, K., Zylstra, M., Brouwer, R., de Groot, R., Farber, S., Ferraro, P., Green, R., Hadley, D., Harlow, J., Jefferiss, P., Kirkby, C., Morling, P., Mowatt, S., Naidoo, R., Paavola, J., Strassburg, B., Yu, D. and Balmford, A. (2008) Ecosystem services and economic theory: integration for policy-relevant research. Ecological Applications 18: 2050-67.

Friedman, B. (2005). *The Moral Consequences of Economic Growth.* Alfred A. Knopf, New York.

Friedman, T.L. (2008). *Hot, Flat, and Crowded: Why We Need a Green Revolution--and How It Can Renew America.* Farrar, Straus and Giroux, New York.

Gallopin, G.C. and Rijsberman, F. (2000) Three global water scenarios. International Journal of Water 1: 16-40.

Gaudzinski, S. (1995). Wallertheim revisited: a re-analysis of the fauna from the Middle Palaeolithic site of Wallertheim (Rheinhessen/Germany). Journal of Archaeological Science 22: 51-66.

Gelenbe, E. (2009). Steps towards self-aware networks. Commun. ACM 52: 66-75.

Goldemberg, J. and Siqueira Prado, L.T. (2013). The decline of sectorial components of the world's energy intensity. Energy Policy 54: 62-5.

Goodland, R. and Daly, H. (1996). Environmental sustainability: universal and non-negotiable. Ecological Applications 6(4): 1002-17.

Gunasekera, D., Newth, D. and Finnigan, J. (2011). Reconciling the competing demands in the human–earth system. Ensuring food security. Economic Papers 30: 296-306.

Hardin, G. (1968). The tragedy of the commons. Science 162: 1243-8.

Hayden, B. (1981) Subsistence and ecological adaptations of modern hunter/gatherers. In: Harding, R.S.O. and Teleki, G. (eds.), *Omnivorous Primates: Gathering and Hunting in Human Evolution.* New Columbia University Press, New York. pp. 344-421.

Helle, S. and Helama, S. (2007) Climatic variability and the population dynam¬ics of historical hunter-gatherers: The case of Sami of northern Finland. American Journal of Human Biology 19: 844-53.

Hepburn, C. and Bowen, A. (2012) Prosperity with growth: economic growth, climate change and environmental limits. Grantham Research Institute on Climate Change and the Environment, Working Paper No. 93.

Hicks, J.R. (1946). Income. Chapter 14 of *Value and Capital* (2nd Edition: Clarendon Press, 1946), reprinted in Parker, R.H., Harcourt, G.C. and Whittington, G., Readings in the Concept and Measurement of Income (2nd Edition: Philip Allan, 1986).

Hilty, L.M., Arnfalk, P., Erdmann, L., Goodman, J., Lehmann, M. and Wäger, P.A. (2006). The relevance of information and communication technologies for environmental sustainability: A prospective simulation study. Environmental Modelling & Software 21(11): 1618-29.

Hong, S., Candelone, J.P., Patterson, C.C. and Boutron, C.F. (1994). Greenland ice evidence of hemispheric lead pollution two millennia ago by Greek and Roman civilizations. Science 265: 1841-3.

Hong, S., Candelone, J.P., Patterson, C. and Boutron, C. (1996). History of ancient copper smelting pollution during roman and medieval times. Science 272: 246-9.

Howard, W., Welch, L.D., Gold, T., Goodman, S., Kern, P., Youngblut, C., Owens, M., Hughes, B., Warner, M. and Butts, K. (2011) Report of the Defense Science Board Task Force on trends and implications of climate change on national and international security. Office of the Under Secretary of Defense for Acquisition, Technology and logistics, Washington D.C. 20301-3140.

Hywel Jones, G. (1975). *An Introduction to Modern Theories of Economic Growth.* Thomas Nelson and Sons, London.

Ikein, A. (2009). The potential power of West African oil to the economies and energy security interest of Euro-America in the 21st century. Journal of Sustainable Development in Africa 10: 540-56.

Jackson, T. (2009a). *The Prosperity Without Growth: the Transition to a Sustainable Economy.* The Sustainable Development Commission, London.

Jackson, T. (2009b). *Prosperity Without Growth: Economics for a Finite Planet.* Earthscan, London.

Jacobs, J. (1970) *The Economy of Cities.* Vintage, London.

Jacobs, M. and Stern, B. (1947) *Outline of Anthropology.* Barnes and Noble, New York.

Kalicki, J.H. and Goldwyn, D.L. (eds.) (2005). *Energy and Security: Towards a New Foreign Policy Strategy.* Johns Hopkins University Press.

Karp, A. and Richter, G.M. (2011). Meeting the challenge of food and energy security. Journal of Experimental Botany 62(10): 3263-71.

Keay, I. and Metcalf, C. (2011) Property rights, resource exploitation and long-run growth. Journal of Empirical Legal Studies 8: 792-829.

Kennedy, J.F. (2005). *Designing a new range of topical products: The ALLERMYL® story*. VIRBAC Laboratories, Medical Department, Carros, France.

Klein, R.G. (1999). *The Human Career: Human Biological and Cultural Origins*. University of Chicago Press, Chicago, IL.

Knauft, B. (1994). Culture and cooperation in human evolution. In: Sponsel, L.E. and Gregor, T. (ds.) *The Anthropology of Peace and Nonviolence*. Boulder: Lynne Rienner, Boulder, CO. pp. 37-67.

Koh, L.P., Miettinen, J., Liew, S.C. and Ghazoul, J. (2011) Remotely sensed evidence of tropical peatland conversion to oil palm. Proceedings of the National Academy of Sciences 108: 5127-32.

Krausmann, F. (2004). Milk, manure and muscular power. Livestock and the industrialization of agriculture. Human Ecology 32 (6): 735-73.

Krausmann, K. and Kowalski, M.F. (2013) Global socio-metabolic transitions. In: Singh, S., Haberl, H., Chertow, M., Mirtl, M., Schmid, M. (eds.) *Long Term Socio-Ecological Research: Studies in Society–Nature Interactions Across Spatial and Temporal Scales*. Springer, New York. pp. 339-68.

Krausmann, F., Gingrich, S., Eisenmenger, N., Erb, K.-H., Haberl, H. and Fischer-Kowalski, M. (2009). Growth in global materials use, GDP and population during the 20th century. Ecological Economics 68(10): 2696-705.

Küstermann, B., Kainz, M. and Hülsbergen K-J. (2008) Modeling carbon cycles and estimation of greenhouse gas emissions from organic and conventional farming systems. Renewable Agriculture and Food Systems 23: 38-52.

Kuznets, S. (1962). How to judge quality. The New Republic, 20 October 1962.

Lal, R. (2007). Anthropogenic influences on world soils and implications to global Food Security. Advances in Agronomy 93: 69-93.

Lant, C., Ruhl, J.B. and Kraft, S. (2008). The tragedy of ecosystem services. BioScience 58: 969-74.

Le Conte, J. (1979). *Elements of Geology*. D. Appleton & Co., New York.

Le Roy, E. (1927). *L'Exigence Idéaliste et Le Fait de L'Évolution. (Idealistic Exigency and the feat of Evolution)*. Boivin: Paris.

Lewis, J.I. (2009). Climate change and security: examining China's challenges in a warming world. International Affairs 85: 1195-213.

Lovelock, J. (2009). *The Vanishing Face of Gaia: A Final Warning: Enjoy It While You Can*. Allen Lane, Santa Barbara, CA.

Maddison, A. (2001). *The World Economy. A Millennial Perspective*. OECD, Paris.

Manes, C. (1990). *Green Rage: Radical Environmentalism and the Unmaking of Civilization*. Back Bay Books, New York.

Mantyka-Pringle, C.S., Martin, T.G. and Rhodes, J.R. (2012). Interactions between climate and habitat loss effects on biodiversity: a systematic review and meta-analysis. Global Change Biology 18(4): 1239-52.

McKibben, B. (2010). *Eaarth: Making a Life on a Tough New Planet*. Henry Holt and Company, New York.

Messer, E. (2009). Rising food prices, social mobilizations, and violence: conceptual issues in understanding and responding to the connections linking hunger and conflict. NAPA Bulletin 32: 12-22.

Millen J.V., Irwin, A. and Kim J.Y. (2000) Introduction: What is growing? Who is dying? In: Kim, J.Y., Millen, J.V., Irwin, A. and Gershman, J. (eds.) *Dying for Growth: Global Inequality and the Health of the Poor.* Common Courage Press, Monroe, ME. pp. 3-10.

Moss, B., Kosten, S., Meerhoff, M., Battarbee, R.W., Jeppesen, E., Mazzaro, N., Havens, K., Lacerot, G., Liu, Z., De Meester, L., Paerl, H. and Scheffer, M. (2011) Allied attack: climate change and eutrophication. Inland Waters: Journal of the International Society of Limnology 1: 101-105.

Naess, A.D.E. (1990). *Ecology, Community and Lifestyle.* Cambridge University Press, Cambridge.

Newburn, D.A., Brozovic, N. and Mezzatesta, M. (2011). Agricultural water security and instream flows for endangered species. American Journal of Agricultural Economics, Agricultural and Applied Economics Association 93: 1212-28.

Nordhaus, W.D. and Tobin, J. (1973). Is growth obsolete? In: Moss, M. (ed.), The Measurement of Economic and Social Performance, Studies in Income and Wealth. Vol. 38, National Bureau of Economic Research, pp. 509-32.

Okpala, A.O. and Jonsson, P.O. (2002). Social attributes and economic instability in Africa. Journal of Applied Business Research 18: 87-93.

Oldeman, L.R. (1998). *Soil Degradation: A Threat to Food Security?* Report 98/01, International Soil Reference and Information Centre, Wageningen.

Omer, A.M. (2008). Energy, environment and sustainable development. Renewable and Sustainable Energy Reviews 12: 2265-300.

Ostrom, E., Burger, J., Field, C.B., Norgaard, R.B. and Policansky, D. (1999). Revisiting the commons: local lessons, global challenges. Science 284: 278-82.

Ozturk, S., Sozdemir, A. and Ulger, O. (2013). The real crisis waiting for the world: oil problem and energy security. International Journal of Energy Economics and Policy 3(S): 74-9.

Perreault, T. and Valdivia, G. (2010). Hydrocarbons, popular protest and national imaginaries: Ecuador and Bolivia in comparative context. Geoforum 41: 689-99.

Pfister, S., Koehler, A. and Hellweg, S. (2009). Assessing the Environmental impact of freshwater consumption in LCA. Environmental and Science and Technology 43: 4098-104.

Pimm, S.L., Russell, G.J., Gittleman, J.L. and Brooks, T.M. (1995). The future of biodiversity. Science 296: 347-50.

Price, D.C. and 29 others (2012). *Cyanophora paradoxa* genome elucidates origin of photosynthesis in algae and plants. Science 335: 843-7.

Reagan, R. (1983). Address to the University of South Carolina, Columbia, Sept. 20, 1983 www.reagan.utexas.edu/archives/speeches/1983/92083c.htm

Rees, W.E. (2001). Concept of Ecological Footprint. In: Levin, S (ed.), *Encyclopedia of Biodiversity Vol. 2.* Academic Press, San Diego, pp. 229-44.

Rees, W.E. (2002). Globalization and sustainability: Conflict or convergence? Bull. Sci. Technol. Soc. 22(4): 249-68.

Ruddiman, W.F. (2003). The anthropogenic Greenhouse Era began thousands of years ago. Climate Change 61: 261-93.

Samuelson, P.A. and Nordhaus, W.D. (1995). *Economics.* 15th edition. McGraw Hill, New York.

Schanbacer, W.D. (2010). *The Politics of Food: The Global Conflict Between Food Security and Food Sovereignty.* Praeger, Santa Barbara, CA.

Scheffran, J. and Battaglini, A. (2010). Climate and conflicts: the security risks of global warming. Regional Environmental Change 11 S1: 27-39.

Scheffran, J. and Battaglini, A. (2011). Climate and conflicts: the security risks of global warming. Regional Environmental Change 11(1): 27-39.

Shackleton, C., Shackleton, S.E., Gambiza, J., Nel, E., Rowntree, K., Urquhart, P. and Ainslie, A. (2010). Livelihoods and vulnerability in the arid and semi-arid lands of southern Africa: exploring the links between ecosystem services and poverty alleviation. Nova Publishers.

Shotyk, W., Cheburkin, A.K., Appleby, P.G., Fankhauser, A. and Kramers, J.D. (1996). Two thousand years of atmospheric arsenic, antimony, and lead deposition recorded in an ombrotrophic peat bog profile, Jura Mountains, Switzerland. Earth and Planetary Science Letters 145(1): supplement E1-E7.

Sieferle, R.P. (2001). *The Subterranean Forest: Energy Systems and the Industrial Revolution.* Translated from the German original by Michael P. Osman. The White Horse Press, Cambridge.

Simon, J. (1993). Economic thought about population consequences: Some reflections. Population Economics 6: 137-52.

Sissa, G. (2011). Utility computing: green opportunities and risks. CEPIS UPGRADE 4: 16-21

Smil, V. (2003). *Energy at the Crossroads. Global Perspectives and Uncertainties.* The MIT Press, Cambridge, MA.

Skene, K.R. (2011). *Escape from Bubbleworld: Seven Curves to Save the Earth.* Ard Macha Press, Angus, UK.

Smith, A. (1863). *An Inquiry into the Nature and Causes of the Wealth of Nations.* T. Nelson and Sons, London.

Spreng, D. (1993). Possibilities for substitution between energy, time and information. Energy Policy 21(1): 13-23.

Sprohge, H. and Sirisom, J. (2011). Coal mining: the neglected environmental threat. In: Kreiser, L. Ashiabor, H., Sirisom, J. and Milne, J.E. (eds.). *Environmental Taxation and Climate Change: Achieving Environmental Sustainability through Fiscal Policy. Critical Issues in Environmental Taxation Volume X.* Edward Elgar Publishing Ltd, Cheltenham, Glos., UK. pp. 129-43.

Steffen, W., Grinevald, J., Crutzen, P. and McNeill, J. (2011). The Anthropocene: conceptual and historical perspectives. Philosophical Transactions of the Royal Society A 369: 842-67.

Stern, N. (2006). *Stern Review on the Economics of Climate Change.* Government Economic Service, London.

Stern, N. (2009). *A Blueprint for a Safer Planet: How we can Save the World and Create Prosperity.* The Bodley Head, London.

Stoppani, A. (1873). *Corsa di Geologia.* Bernardoni and Brigola, Milan.

Streeten, P. (1994). Human development: means and ends. The American Economic Review 84(2): 232-7.

Teilhard de Chardin, P. (1971). *Man's Place in Nature.* Fontana Books, London.

Theobald, R. (1961). *The challenge of Abundance.* New York, C.N Potter.

Timmer, C.P. (2000). The macro dimensions of food security: economic growth, equitable distribution and food price stability. Food Policy 25: 283-95.

UCS (1992). World Scientists' Warning to Humanity, Union of Concerned Scientists' statement posted at: www.ucsusa.org/ucs/about/page.cfm?pageID=1009

van Hoof, T.B., Bunnik, F.P., Waucomont, J.G., Kürschner, W.M. and Visscher, H. (2006). Forest re-growth on medieval farmland after the Black Death pandemic—Implications for atmospheric CO_2 levels. Palaeogeography, Palaeoclimatology, Palaeoecology 237(2): 396-409.

Wackernagel, M., Onisto, L., Bello, P., Linares, A.C., Falfán, I.C.L., Garcia, J.M., Guerrero, A.I.S. and Guerrero, M.G.S. (1999). National natural capital accounting with the ecological footprint concept. Ecological Economics 29: 375-90.

Wallerstein, I. (1974). *The Modern World-System, vol. I: Capitalist Agriculture and the Origins of the European World-Economy in the Sixteenth Century.* Academic Press, London.

Webb, M. (2008). Smart 2020: Enabling the low carbon economy in the information age. The Climate Group, Technical Report.

Webersik, C. (2010). *Climate Change and Security.* Praeger Publishers, Santa Barbara, CA.

Weidenbaum, M.L. (1992). Leviathan in Rio: The UN Gearing Up For its Massive "Earth Summit" in June. National Review, Apr. 27, 1992, p. 44.

White, R. (1993). Technological and social dimensions of "Aurignacian-age" body ornaments across Europe. In: Knecht, H., Pike-Tay, A. and White, R. (eds.), *Before Lascaux: The Complex Record of the Early Upper Paleolithic.* CRC, Boca Raton, FL. pp. 277-300.

Whynacht, C. (2011). Rediscovering the steady state of classical economics: discussion on the origin of the economic theory of sustainability. Dalhousie Journal of Interdisciplinary Management 7: 1-14.

Williams, M.A.J., Ambrose, S.H., Kaars, S. van der, Ruelemann, C., Chattopadhyaya, U. and Chauhan, P.R. (2009). Environmental impact of the 73ka Toba super-eruption in South Asia. Palaeogeography, Palaeoclimatology, Palaeoecology 284: 295-314.

Winterhalder, B. (2001). The behavioral ecology of hunter-gatherers. In: Panter-Brick, C., Layton, R. and Rowley-Conwy, P. (eds.) *Hunter-Gatherers: An Inter-disciplinary Perspective.* Cambridge: Cambridge University Press, Cambridge, UK. pp. 12-38.

Zhang, H. and Liu, L. (2006). Main progress and prospects of land resource ecological security research. Progress in Geography 25: 77-85.

Zhang, K., Yu, Z., Li, X., Zhou, D. and Zhang, D. (2007). Land use change and land degradation in China from 1991–2001. Land Degradation and Development 18: 209-19.

2
The three horsemen of the modern apocalypse: climate, pollution and habitat

The chapter examines the causes, consequences and response of both business and government to climate destabilization, non-greenhouse gas pollution and habitat destruction and exhaustion. Complexities of climate destabilization and extreme weather events, including the challenges of measuring and interpreting climate data are examined. Positive feedback and non-linear climatic response are explained. Sceptical positions are outlined and critiqued. Significant global meetings, and their successes and failures are outlined, including the Kyoto Protocol, Rio 1992, COP15, COP18 and Rio +20. Pollution arising from non-greenhouse gas pollutants is at least as serious a threat to the Anthropocene. These sink or output issues pose significant challenges. Of greatest concern are agricultural run-off, manufacturing waste and end-of-use waste. Financial implications of either ignoring or addressing these waste issues are compared, and legislative programmes, with their impact on business, are investigated. As natural habitats are converted to resources for humans, consequential damage to crucial ecosystem services will impact on business. Of further concern is the over-exploitation of these finite resources, leading to instability of supply chains. We examine the concept of peak resources and the Hubbert Curve.

Learning aims and objectives

- Explain what is meant by the terms non-linear climate response and positive climatic feedback
- Define the term "thermocline"
- Outline the changes in climate over the Earth's history
- Outline the key direct and indirect impacts of climate destabilization on industry, the environment and society
- Outline the impacts of agriculture on our planet
- Define the concept of eutrophication and explain why it is such an important issue
- Define what we mean by a waste hierarchy
- What do we mean by habitat destruction and habitat erosion? Why might habitat erosion be the more dangerous of the two?
- Outline the main causes and consequences of: deforestation; coral reef decline; wetland disappearance
- Define what we mean by a **Hubbert Curve**

Learning outcomes and experiences

- What are the central sceptical positions on climate destabilization?
- How is oceanic circulation affected by the climate, and what repercussions do these effects have?
- Explore the interactions between eutrophication and climate destabilization
- What are the causes and consequences of climate migration?
- How does the impact of climate destabilization differ across the planet? What makes particular areas more vulnerable to climate destabilization than others?
- What are the economic consequences for eutrophication?
- How has politics impacted on waste management?
- Discuss resource exhaustion in terms of peak minerals, peak soil, peak timber, peak fish and peak human population
- Explain why the terms **renewable resources** and **nonrenewable resources** are potentially misleading

2.1 Climate destabilization

This section is entitled **climate destabilization**, rather than **climate change** or **global warming**. This is because, in the first place, our climate has been changing since the planet first formed, and second, the effects will not be uniform across the planet and are not solely related to warming.

There has been no greater, more vehement, polarized and public debate than that regarding the science of climate destabilization. Indeed, never before has scientific research come under such a spotlight of interrogation. A particularly controversial incident involving senior members of the research community led to eight separate reviews including a parliamentary select committee report in the UK. Three questions have dominated the agenda: Is it happening at all? Did we cause it? What impact will it have? To answer these questions, we need to understand the history of climate.

Climate *change* has been occurring since the Earth first existed. Over time, levels of atmospheric gases have altered, sometimes dramatically. For example the atmospheric content has changed from 4.5 billion years ago to the present day. The biggest changes have been the huge increase in nitrogen and oxygen, and the massive reduction in carbon dioxide levels, from 90% to around 0.04% in 2013.

The content of the atmosphere is very important. Carbon dioxide, carbon monoxide, methane, water vapour, nitrous oxide, ozone and chlorofluorocarbons all are capable of absorbing radiation reflected from the planet surface and re-radiating some of this energy back to Earth, thus raising the temperature. These gases have become known as **greenhouse gases**. These greenhouse gases have all been increasing over the last 200 years (and longer) due to human activity, and these increases have continued, unabated, over the last 25 years (Fig. 2.1). HCFC-22 (Fig. 2.1) is particularly dangerous as it acts as a powerful greenhouse gas and in ozone depletion. Although not as powerful as banned CFCs used to be, and although it is less used in the western world, eastern and southern countries are increasing its use. As can be seen, it has increased from trace amounts in 1980 to 200ppt in 2010. Used in air-conditioning units, which are undergoing a huge increase in sales in India and China (20% annual increase), this has created a significant threat to both our climate and our skin.

Greenhouse gases all absorb radiation coming from the Earth that would otherwise disappear into space. The gas particles act as tiny radiators, bouncing the radiation back towards the planet as heat. This leads to the planet warming. The facts are well established. We have known for over 100

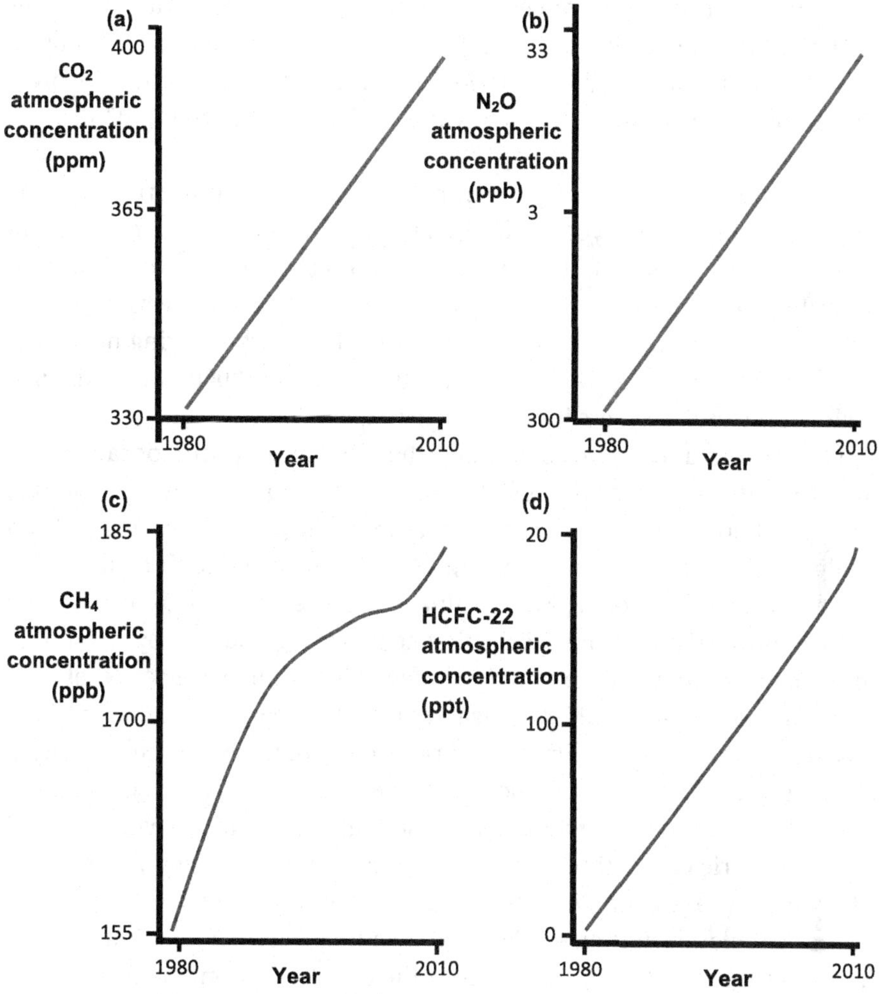

FIGURE 2.1 Greenhouse gas atmospheric concentrations over the last 30 years (data from www.esrl.noaa.gov/gmd/aggi). (a) Carbon dioxide; (b) nitrous oxide; (c) methane; (d) chlorodifluoromethane (HCFC-22), a powerful ozone-depleting and greenhouse gas.

years that these gases act in this way, and for the last 40 years that the levels of these gases are increasing in the atmosphere. We also know that increases in these gas concentrations will lead to increasing temperatures.

Another repercussion of increasing temperatures is a change in ocean circulation. Oceans play a very important role in redistributing heat around the globe. These currents can either be wind-generated, or **thermohaline**. Thermohaline circulation involves the gradual evaporation of surface water, increasing the salt concentration, until the more salty water becomes so dense that it sinks down. A loop forms, driven by the sinking, a bit like a fan belt that is turned by the rotation of a wheel. A second wheel involves the temperature. As the water moves into cooler areas, it cools and becomes denser.

Thus a combination of salt concentration and temperature drive the sinking. The Atlantic Conveyor, for example, brings as much heat to the UK in winter as does the sun. If it didn't do this, our temperatures would be considerably lower in winter. Around 10,000 years ago, the conveyor stopped working due to dilution of the salt from glacial melt water, bringing ice age conditions back to the UK (Broecker, 2000; Marotzke, 2000). Most disturbingly, it only took 70 years for the ice age to take hold.

As ice melts and dilutes sea water, the circulation of the oceans alters and slows down. This is because the sea water is not as dense and doesn't sink. Furthermore, increasing temperatures will prevent the water from cooling as much, therefore reducing density increase due to cooling. The wheel slows, and so does the belt. A final repercussion of the disappearance of the North Atlantic Conveyor is that sea levels would rise by about one metre since there would be no down flow. This, along with sea level rises due to glacier melt, would significantly threaten many coastal areas. This has implications for the climate in various parts of the world. Interestingly, although global temperature increase drives the slowing of the circulation, in Northern Europe, this will lead to a cooling, particularly in winter.

Atmospheric circulation will also be impacted by the greenhouse effect. This has important implications for many parts of the world. The monsoonal circulation patterns will be affected, causing very serious consequences for South-East Asia, including the two most populous countries in the world, China and India. Monsoons are generated due to differences in heating between oceans and land. Heating of the atmosphere will reduce the monsoonal circulation. In India alone, 125 million tonnes (or 18%) of rain-fed cereal production potential could be lost. The jet streams, so pivotal in terms of rainfall and temperature for areas such as mainland Europe, will also be impacted. The Northern polar jet stream is set to move northward, bringing warmer and wetter conditions to European winters.

These impacts have significant repercussions. These are fundamentally related to heat and water. Some areas will become cooler and others warmer, while some areas will become drier, and others wetter. This will impact on agriculture, particularly in terms of droughts, water-logging, soil erosion and salinity. Tropical cyclones and hurricanes are likely to increase in occurrence and intensity as oceans warm (Emanuel, 2013). Sea levels will rise, due to glacial melt and oceanic circulation changes, combined with more extreme rainfall events. As global temperatures rise, greater evaporation from oceans will lead to increasing amounts of water vapour in the atmosphere, leading to this intense rain. Changes in oceanic and atmospheric circulation will also lead to changes in where the rain falls, increasing the risk of drought in other areas.

Drought and floods both increase the risk of soil removal, through wind and water erosion respectively, undermining agricultural productivity further. Although more than 99.7% of the world's food comes from the soil, each year more than 10 million hectares (25 million acres, an area larger than Portugal) of crop land are degraded or lost, as rain and wind sweep away topsoil. In developing nations, soil is being depleted up to approximately 10–40 times faster than it is being built up in nature (Pimentel, 2006).

These problems are exacerbated by deforestation, because trees play a central role in moving water from the soil to the atmosphere, preventing run-off, and their roots also stabilize soil. A third impact is that because trees absorb energy, which then evaporates water from their leaves, this evaporation reduces the atmospheric pressure above forests. Thus, forests set up a pressure difference and moist air moves into the continents from the oceans, bringing water into these otherwise dry areas. Therefore, deforestation greatly increases the risk of drought for continental areas (Makarieva *et al.*, 2006).

Heat related human mortality is expected to rise by 257% by 2050 (Hajat *et al.*, 2014). Mortality due to heart disease will increase (Clearfield *et al.*, 2014). Infectious diseases are also predicted to increase with rising temperatures, as insect vectors of diseases such as malaria and dengue fever increase their potential range. A wide range of other viral diseases impacting on humans will increase under climate change (Singh, 2014). Corals become more susceptible to fungal and bacterial diseases in warmer water. Climate disruption has also been linked to the amphibian disease, chytridiomycosis, which threatens these organisms with extinction, with unpredictable weather events thought to increase the risk (Altizer *et al.*, 2013).

Finally, many of the impacts of climate destabilization have secondary effects, called positive feedback. In other words, the impact leads to another event which further increases the impact. There are two types of secondary effect: those produced as a consequence of the initial perturbation, and those emerging from human actions designed to repair the initial damage. Examples of the first type include the warming of the permafrost and

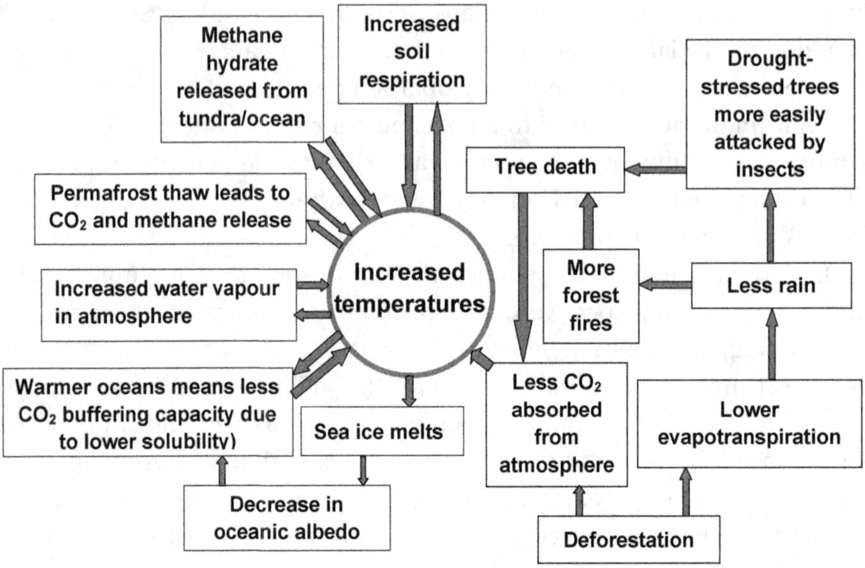

FIGURE 2.2 Positive feedback in climate destabilization. Increasing temperatures lead to a range of effects that result in forcing further changes.

oceans, releasing methane which itself is a significant greenhouse gas. The release of large amounts of this gas from ocean reserves may also promote submarine slope failure and consequent tsunami generation. Examples of the second type include deforestation and agricultural displacement from land now used to grow green fuel crops, exacerbating the water and food security issues. Figure 2.2 sums up potential feedback impacts.

Climate destabilization has been linked to many of the great societal collapses over human history. The Mayan civilization collapsed because of drought (Hodell *et al.*, 2005). Failed monsoons accounted for the demise of the Tang Dynasty, Yuan Dynasty and Ming dynasty in China (Lee and Zhang, 2013). The Akkadian empire of Mesopotamia experienced an abrupt collapse when a shift to more arid conditions occurred 6,180 years ago (Cullen *et al.*, 2000). Parts of low-latitude north-eastern Africa and south-western Asia suffered regime-changing drought, causing major disruption about 4,300 years ago (Drysdale *et al.*, 2006).

The Tiwanaku civilization of the central Andes was devastated when a prolonged period of drought led to the collapse of the agricultural base about 1,000 years ago (Weiss and Bradley, 2001). Environmental problems also contributed to the decline of the Polynesians of Pitcairn Island, Easter

Islanders, Greenland Norse, Anasazi and even the Roman Empire (Flannery, 1994; Diamond, 2005; Costanza *et al.*, 2007). Thus, many scientists and anthropologists fear that such destabilization will have a significant impact on the modern world, exacerbated by the other repercussions of our current economic practice.

2.1.1 Sceptics

How often has been overheard the comment relating to climate destabilization that takes the form of: "This greenhouse effect will be no bad thing—just think ... we'll be growing grapes in Grimsby, and no more cold winters either". Interestingly, this idea goes back to the very first scientist to link atmospheric CO_2 levels and temperature increase. Svante Arrhenius, Nobel laureate and discoverer of the greenhouse effect, saw the rise in temperature from atmospheric CO_2 as having a positive impact:

> We often hear lamentations that the coal stored up in the earth is wasted by the present generation without any thought of the future, and we are terrified by the awful destruction of life and property which has followed the volcanic eruptions of our days. We may find a kind of consolation in the consideration that here, as in every other case, there is good mixed with the evil. By the influence of the increasing percentage of carbonic acid in the atmosphere, we may hope to enjoy ages with more equable and better climates, especially as regards the colder regions of the earth, ages when the earth will bring forth much more abundant crops than at present, for the benefit of rapidly propagating mankind (Arrhenius, 1908; p. 63).

The Royal Society identified eight misleading but common sceptical positions (Royal Society, 2007):

- The Earth's climate is always changing and this is nothing to do with humans
- Carbon dioxide only makes up a small part of the atmosphere and so cannot be responsible for global warming
- Rises in the levels of carbon dioxide in the atmosphere are the result of increased temperatures, not the other way round
- Satellites do not support the theory of global warming
- Computer models which predict the future climate are unreliable and based on a series of assumptions

- It's all to do with the Sun—for example, there is a strong link between increased temperatures on Earth and the number of sunspots on the Sun
- The climate is actually affected by cosmic rays
- The scale of the negative effects of climate destabilization is often overstated and there is no need for urgent action

A milder form of scepticism recognizes that climate destabilization is real, but will be slow and moderate enough to allow us to adapt to it, through measures such as geo-engineering, GM crops and altered architecture. This is a fundamental Enlightenment approach, where reason and technology will come to our rescue. This position also believes that within a few decades, the climate will plateau around a new, manageable stable state. Since oil is likely to run out anyway, then the main driver of global warming will disappear.

Clear rebuttals of all of these points have been made in a number of lucid reports (e.g. Royal Society, 2007; Allison *et al.*, 2009; Anderegg *et al.*, 2010). By far the bulk of scientists are now agreed that there is a significant risk to our planet from climate destabilization. The change will occur more quickly and more extremely than previously thought, and will last for thousands of years (Archer 2009; Solomon *et al.*, 2009). In the most recent report from the Intergovernmental Panel on Climate Change (IPCC), the situation was summarized as follows: "Continued emission of greenhouse gases will cause further warming and long-lasting changes in all components of the climate system, increasing the likelihood of severe, pervasive and irreversible impacts for people and ecosystems" (IPCC, 2014). If significant mitigation strategies are not taken, then there is a very tangible risk to our own survival. Concerns are no longer limited to scientists. Economist Robert Repetto stated that "There are many reasons to doubt whether adaptive measures will be timely and efficient, even in the US where the capabilities exist" (Repetto 2008; p. 5). Economist Lord Stern reflects that "adaptation will be necessary on a major scale, but the stronger and the more timely the mitigation, the less will be the challenge of adaptation" (Stern 2009: 71).

Many of the impacts of climate destabilization, when modelled over time, are strongly right-skewed. This means that there is a significant risk of a sudden escalation in impact after a given time (Tol, 2005). Thus although things seem to be slowly changing at present, at any point there could be a rapid acceleration caused by positive feedback spirals, as mentioned earlier (Fig. 2.2). This is known as **non-linear climate response**.

An example of non-linear climate response is the oceanic circulation system, where although the direct effect may only be a slight, sea level rise, drop in temperature in the north-east Atlantic, additional impacts on sea ice and clouds, the strength of trade winds, ventilation of the North Pacific, the strength of the Asian monsoon, the quantity of atmospheric carbon dioxide and water vapour, all may mean that the final outcome could be amplified. Three further important potential non-linear climate responses are the West Antarctic ice sheet destabilization, ecosystem service degradation, and intense hydrologic variation. A significant pulse of volcanism in Iceland, at the end of the last glaciation, flags a link between ice unloading and volcanism (McGuire, 2010).

Many sceptics claim that the rate of carbon release and temperature rise are either not linked or have already stabilized recently. This is clearly not the case. Furthermore, others have argued that potential impact has been overestimated. Again, the evidence does not support this position. Global carbon dioxide emissions from fossil fuels in 2008 were 40% higher than those in 1990. Over the past 25 years temperatures have increased at a rate of 0.19°C per decade, in very good agreement with predictions based on greenhouse gas increases. A wide array of satellite and ice measurements now demonstrate beyond doubt that both the Greenland and Antarctic ice-sheets are losing mass at an increasing rate (Screen *et al.*, 2013). Melting of glaciers and ice-caps in other parts of the world has also accelerated since 1990. This leads initially to flooding in dependent rivers, but later to drought, as glacial melt is no longer available. Thus a given location will experience extremes of climate as a result. Current sea-level rise has also been under-estimated: satellites show recent global average sea-level rise (3.4 mm per year over the past 15 years) to be ~80% above past IPCC predictions.

2.1.2 Impact on business and security

It is widely accepted that climate destabilization will have major impacts on economics and national security. Depending on the magnitude of 21st-century destabilization, negative impacts are expected on water, food, human health (Adger *et al.*, 2007) and, ultimately, economic growth (Stern, 2006; Nordhaus, 2008). Kellie-Smith and Cox (2011; p. 886) conclude that "navigating the climate–economy system to a soft landing will require massive efforts in both mitigation and adaptation, but may also require lower but more sustainable rates of global economic growth".

Climate destabilization will also lead to huge numbers of human, animal and plant migrants, disturbing ecosystems and cultures alike. Mediterranean biomes are expected to shift 300–500 km northward if a 1.5°C warming were to occur, which could mean that Mediterranean ecosystems would become more desert-like. The threat to national security from migration is clearly evident. The total number of human migrants driven by climate destabilization could rise to 150 million by 2050, up from 25 million in the mid-1990s (Myers, 2002).

Climate destabilization will pose the greatest challenges for weak states. According to the predictions of the IPCC, the Middle East and North Africa will be the most affected regions during global climate destabilization. By the end of this century, this region is projected to experience an increase of 3–5°C in mean temperatures and a 20% decline in precipitation. The Stern Report observed (Stern *et al.*, 2006; p. 16): "Climate-related shocks have sparked violent conflict in the past, and conflict is a serious risk in areas such as West Africa, the Nile Basin and Central Asia". It is worthwhile noting that population growth, soil degradation and unequal land distribution combined to create the conditions for the genocide in Ruanda in the 1990s (Percival and Homer-Dixon, 1995).

Climate destabilization will act as a **threat multiplier** that is likely to exacerbate existing vulnerability of a region to current climatic and non-climate stresses. A threat multiplier is defined as that which exacerbates threats caused by persistent poverty, weak institutions for resource management and conflict resolution, fault lines and a history of mistrust between communities and nations, and inadequate access to information or resources. President Barrack Obama makes direct connections between climate destabilization, security and violent conflicts stating that "urgent dangers to [our] national and economic security are compounded by the long-term threat of climate change, which if left unchecked could result in violent conflict, terrible storms, shrinking coastlines and irreversible catastrophe" (Obama, 2009).

Tol (2010) and Solarz (2012) identify the two biggest threats for the EU as migration and lack of consensus between the 27 states which are clustered in three different climatic zones. One man's meat may well be another man's poison, as each climatic zone, from Mediterranean to boreal, will face very different problems. If the EU were one state the threat of climate destabilization could be more easily addressed but the EU is a federation of 27 independent states and agreement on required responses to emerging challenges is time-consuming and difficult.

Current assessments of the cost of climate destabilization focus on agriculture and forestry, water resources, coastal zones, energy consumption, air quality, and human health (for example Stern *et al.*, 2006). However, these cost assessments are fundamentally underestimates because of omissions of important aspects such as: redesigning urban water management systems (be it for more or less water); costs of saltwater intrusion in groundwater; implementing safeguards against increased uncertainty about future circumstances; increasing costs of cooling power plants; ocean acidification harming remaining shellfish and fisheries; increased extratropical storm damage. However, these pale into insignificance compared with the collapse of the West Antarctic ice sheet, which would raise sea levels by 3.3 m. A rise in sea level of 1.5 m would displace 17 million people from the Bangladesh delta region alone. River deltas are at risk from sea-level rise and salinization. For a 50 cm sea-level rise, salt water would penetrate 9 km into Nile aquifers, affecting agriculture and the whole economy.

The increased rise in sea level will affect developing and developed countries. Risk of damage to low-lying port facilities, airports, roads, rail lines, tunnels, pipelines, power lines, etc. is particularly large. Many of these facilities are concentrated on coastlines of the Atlantic Ocean, Pacific Ocean and Gulf of Mexico. The economies of Central American and Caribbean nations are primarily based on agriculture, hydropower and fisheries. Climate destabilization makes these areas particularly vulnerable (Ramirez and Butts, 2011).

The German Advisory Council anticipates that a global warming of 2–4°C would lead to a drop of agricultural productivity worldwide and that this decrease will be substantially reinforced by desertification, soil salinization and water scarcity (WBGU, 2007). The 2007 Report of the **Intergovernmental Panel on Climate Change** (IPCC, 2007) states that the resilience of many regional ecosystems is likely to be exceeded in this century by an unprecedented combination of climate destabilization associated disturbances, such as flooding, drought, wildfire, insects, and ocean acidification, and the global change drivers of land use change, pollution, fragmentation of natural systems, and the over-exploitation of resources.

2.1.3 Key climate destabilization conferences and outcomes

Over the last 40 years there have been numerous global conferences addressing the issue of climate destabilization. Here is a summary of the outcomes of these meetings.

2.1.3.1 UN Conference on the Human Environment, Stockholm, June 1972

115 nations represented, leading to the setting up of the United Nations Environment Programme (UNEP) and to many governments establishing specialist departments for environmental issues. Viewed as a success and led to tangible outcomes such as a ban on whaling.

2.1.3.2 United Nations Conference on Environment and Development (the Earth Summit) Rio 1992

At its time the largest and most costly diplomatic meeting in history, the Earth Summit at Rio de Janeiro took place in June 1992; 180 nations were represented. The summit set out to cover everything from ozone to oceans, from climate to conservation and from poverty to biotechnology. The agenda has since been recognized as being too wide-ranging (Palmer, 1992; Little, 1995). Bruce Bebbitt summed up the event as "a chaotic process more akin to a street brawl than a diplomatic meeting" (Babbitt, 1992; p. 28). Only two hard legal outputs resulted, the Rio Framework Convention on Climate Change, which had no targets, and the Rio Framework Convention on Biological Diversity, which was not signed by the USA. The overall outcomes were presented in a 40-chapter volume called Agenda 21, which required some US$300 billion to implement in. However, this money was never pledged, leaving Agenda 21 with neither teeth nor legs.

2.1.3.3 Kyoto 1997 (COP3)

The Kyoto Protocol finally addressed the weakness of no targets in the Rio Framework Convention on Climate Change. However, the outcome was that some countries could actually increase their emissions, and much false accounting went on in the background, aimed at easing the burdens on particular countries. The outcomes were many and included the emergence of carbon trading, discussed in Chapter 3. There were many issues with the protocol, including a lack of proper scientific consideration of carbon sequestration and, in particular, the questionable role of forestry in this process (Faure *et al.*, 2003). As in so many of these attempts at global action on environmental issues, the Kyoto Protocol was not binding. While 191 countries ratified the protocol, Andorra and the USA refused to do this, and in 2012, Canada withdrew from it.

Since Kyoto, there has been a COP meeting every year. Here is a brief summary of their achievements.

- **COP4 Buenos Aires, Argentina**: November 1998. Established deadline for finalizing Kyoto Agreement, targeted for the year 2000.

- **COP5 Bonn, Germany**: October 1999. Continued work to resolve issues towards finalizing Kyoto Protocol.
- **COP6 The Hague, Netherlands**: November 2000. The summit collapsed when the USA insisted it should receive special concessions for carbon sinks, an idea refuted by the rest of the members. The EU and US could not reach agreement and the American president, George Bush, stated he was against the Kyoto Protocol.
- **COP7 Marrakech, Morocco**: October 2001. Produced the Marrakech Accord, commonly referred to as the Kyoto rule book.
- **COP8 New Delhi, India**: October 2002. With the Kyoto Protocol in limbo (due to insufficient numbers of countries ratifying it) this summit dealt with surrounding issues.
- **COP9 Milan, Italy**: December 2003. First discussion of an adaptation fund to help developing countries face the challenges of climate destabilization.
- **COP10 Buenos Aires, Argentina**: December 2004. Russian finally ratify Kyoto Protocol, allowing it to pass into force, aiming to reduce carbon emissions to 5.2% of the 1990 levels by 2012.
- **COP11 Montreal, Canada**: November 2005. First post-Kyoto ratification summit, agreed to continue GHG level negotiations beyond 2012, the year when the Kyoto Protocol ends. USA (largest global GHG emitter) and Australia refuse to sign agreement. A second important outcome was the ratification of the Marrakech Accord.
- **COP12 Nairobi, Kenya**: November 2006. Adaptation was a major theme of this summit, held in a region that will suffer significantly from climate destabilization. A review of the Kyoto Protocol would be carried out by 2008.
- **COP13 Bali, Indonesia**: December 2007. Debate was dominated by what should succeed the Kyoto protocol, with no resolution. The EU called for emissions to peak in 10–15 years time, but USA, Russia, Australia, Canada and Japan object. Little progress.
- **COP14 Poznań, Poland**: December 2008. Post-Kyoto talks continued without resolution. An adaptation fund to help developing nations face the consequences of climate destabilization was

agreed, but only based on a 2% levy on carbon trading, instead of a suggested 3%. This led to the collapse of negotiations.

- **COP15 Copenhagen, Denmark**: December 2009. Recognized as a low point, with the USA, Brazil, China, India and South Africa agreeing a deal, the Copenhagen Accord, without consulting or including the remaining 187 nations present. This resulted in the Accord having no legal standing.
- **COP16 Cancun, Mexico**: November 2010. Viewed as a success, the Cancun Accord locked in the nations responsible for 80% of global emissions to reduction targets, including China and USA. The Green Climate Fund, for adaptation among developing countries, was greatly expanded in value.
- **COP17 Durban, South Africa**: November 2011. A divisive meeting with India claiming intimidation and China calling for greater responsibility to be placed on the developed world for past emissions. Green Climate Fund management framework agreed.
- **RIO +20**: held 20 years after the Earth Summit of 1992, Rio +20 occurred in June 2012. This huge events with 45,000 participants and 100 heads of state, saw the President of USA, the prime minister of the UK and the Chancellor of Germany failing to attend. Its aim was to establish a new set of goals to replace the Millennium Development Goals, which would expire in 2015, and to initiate the Green Economy initiative, a strategy to implement sustainability into economics. It also wanted to create a global organization for the environment. On all counts, the summit failed.
- **COP18 Doha, Qatar**: November 2012. USA refuses to increase its 17% reduction of emissions target for 2020, while the EU fail to reach any agreement on emission targets due to opposition from Poland. Work continued towards a new protocol to replace Kyoto, targeted at 2015.
- **COP19 Warsaw, Poland**: November 2013. Deemed unsuccessful by the media, attempts at holding "developed" nations responsible for historic carbon emissions predictably failed. 132 countries walked out of the talks in an all-time low. Hope of a significant agreement by Paris 2015, to replace the Millennium Development Goals, looks unlikely.

- **COP20 Lima, Peru**: December 2014. A modest set of procedural outcomes paving the way towards a new global climate agreement in Paris in December 2015 were arrived at after 30 hours beyond the planned end of the meeting, but otherwise, little progress was made on larger looming issues, such as compensation to developing nations and new market-driven approaches.

2.2 Non-greenhouse gas pollution

Climate destabilization, related to greenhouse gas emissions, has dominated government, research and tabloid agendas in recent times. The focus has been on carbon. However, climate is only one of the three apocalyptic horsemen that threaten business and human survival. Pollution arising from non-greenhouse gas pollutants is at least as serious a threat to the Anthropocene. These sink or output issues pose significant challenges.

Of greatest concern are agricultural run-off, manufacturing waste and end-of-use waste. We examine each of these and investigate modern approaches to counteract these problems. Financial implications of either ignoring or addressing these waste issues are compared, and legislative programmes, with their impact on business, are investigated. Organizations involved in this area include the Joint Group of Experts on the Scientific Aspects of Marine Environmental Pollution (GESAMP), the Food and Agriculture Organization of the United Nations, the Global Environment Facility and the Global Alliance on Health and Pollution (GAHP).

2.2.1 Agricultural fertilizers

While climate destabilization has grabbed all of the headlines, with atmospheric carbon dioxide reduction dominating agendas, another very important set of elements have avoided such notice: phosphorous (P), potassium (K) and nitrogen (N). These three elements together form the largest pollution event facing our planet since the great oxygen revolution some 2.4 billion years ago, and pose potentially a greater threat to the biosphere than does carbon dioxide. For while CO_2 levels have been 300 times higher than current levels in the past, P, K and N levels have never approached current concentrations.

The importance of these elements comes from the fact that they are the most limiting on plant growth. Essential to all species, their concentrations determine how much of the sun's energy enters the biosphere. They act like the security guards of energy flow. So if you are a species with a huge population (say 7 billion) then you need a lot of energy to stay alive, let alone live an active life or become obese. The surface area of the planet suitable for agriculture is limited, and with continual harvesting year after year, the soil gradually loses its nutrients to successive generations of crops that absorb the nutrients. So the only ways currently available to increase yield are to replace the lost nutrients, convert poor land to farmland (e.g. by draining wetlands or clearing forests) and make the good land even more productive. This is done by adding fertilizers to the soil.

P, K and N are the major fertilizers applied to agricultural fields across the world. This is not a recent development. Farmers in the Agrarian Age had to use manure (N, P and K), urine (N), wood ash (P), guano (P), blood (N and K), seaweed (K) and fallow fields (N) in order to enrich the soil and replace the nutrients harvested within the crops of the previous year. As far back as the Neolithic, farmers focused on recycling nutrients (Bogaard *et al.*, 2013).

Today things are very different. We are now in the age of exploitation and waste. Phosphorus is mined from rock phosphate, nitrogen is fixed using the highly energy-expensive Haber-Bosch process and potassium is mined from ancient marine salts. The nutrients are placed in the soil in huge quantities, in soluble forms, and then most of the applied quantity is washed into the rivers, lakes and oceans.

Nitrogen fertilizer is the only nutrient that can be synthetically made from nitrogen gas. The others (P and K) rely on mining of exhaustible sources. These sources are also unevenly spread across the planet, meaning politics may come into play in the future. Canada and the former Soviet Union have 70% of the world's potash, while Morocco has 85% of the world's high grade rock phosphorus. While potassium is unlikely to run out, financially viable mines will become scarce, and countries possessing these sources will be able to hold the world to ransom. Phosphorus extraction has intensified, partly due to the increasing needs of China, and even with currently uneconomic sources included, the global reserves will be depleted within 70 years, according to the US Geological Survey.

And so it is ironic that given their scarcity, the damage done by these fertilizers is because of excessive application and run-off. Deforestation also leads to increasing loss of nutrients from soils because of increased flow-through of groundwater (which is no longer travelling up trees and into the atmosphere). Nitrogen fertilizers in the soil are also broken down into gaseous nitrogen, which then dissolves in rainfall, often falling on natural ecosystems. In 1977, 32 million tons N per year were being applied in the form of fertilizer, while by 2005 this had risen to 88 million tons N per year (Smil, 2003).

So what do these high levels of N, P and K do once they are washed from the fields? They create an effect called eutrophication. Eutrophication is defined as the increased rate of primary production and accumulation of organic matter.

Eutrophication allows for a huge increase in plant growth, which is why it is a consequence of farming practice in the first place. However, in waterways, it leads to small plants and algae growing and reproducing rapidly, and forming a thick layer on the surface. This blocks the light, leading to the death of larger aquatic plants. This upper layer then dies and bacteria begin to decompose it. This bacterial breakdown absorbs vast quantities of oxygen, leading to fish and invertebrate death. In Europe, Asia and North America, 50% of lakes are now eutrophic (ILEC/Lake Biwa Research Institute, 1988–93).

In the seas, algal growth increases rapidly, leading to coral death and greatly impacting on coastal fisheries. Again significant falls in oxygen levels lead to serious problems, particularly around river estuaries. Extreme events lead to toxins from cyanobacteria increasing, killing all fish and mammals. These areas are known as dead zones. These toxins can also enter the human chain, causing liver and brain damage. An example of this is paralytic shellfish poisoning. Coastal winds can blow a toxic aerosol onshore, leading to irritation of eyes and lungs in humans.

Eutrophication leads to a rapid loss of biodiversity, thus undermining the functionality of the ecosystems involved. It massively disrupts the balance of nature, as almost all natural ecosystems function under low-nutrient conditions and are damaged by eutrophication (Fig. 2.3). Increased nitrogen and phosphorus availabilities also enhance the replication rate of aquatic viruses. Lesions in marine coral communities caused by infections of *Aspergillus* fungi grow at faster rates under high nitrate availability.

2.2.2 Economic costs of eutrophication

Eutrophication in England and Wales is estimated to cost US$105–60 million per year (Pretty *et al.*, 2003), while in the US, the costs approach US$2.2 billion (Dodds *et al.*, 2008). Mitigation costs are also high. The reduction of

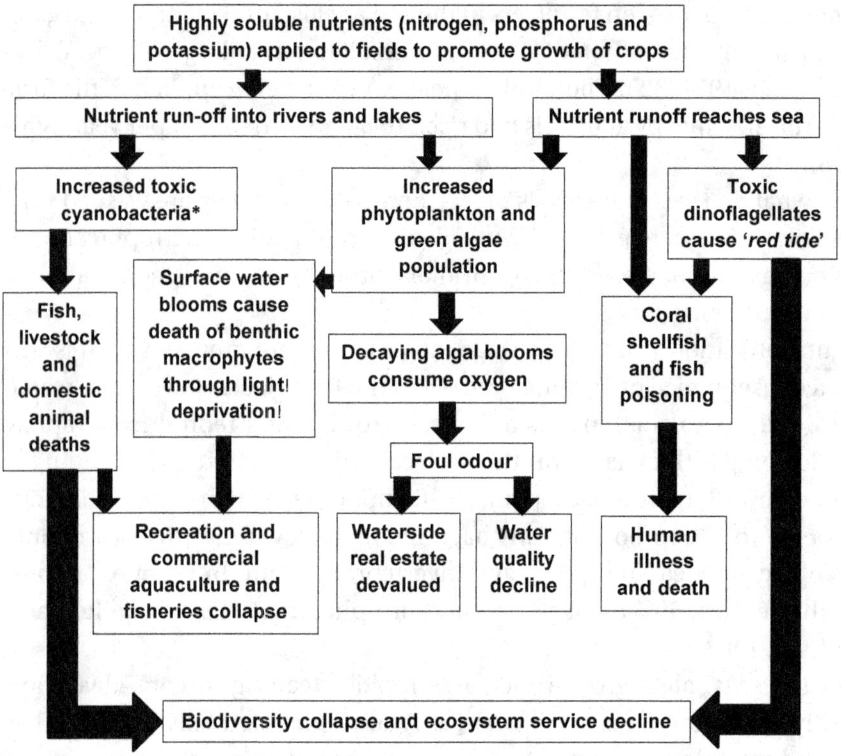

FIGURE 2.3 Eutrophication cascade, demonstrating that the application of fertilizers onto fields of crop and forage quickly move into the natural environment, causing widespread damage ecologically, socially and economically.

phosphorus pollution into Lake Mjøsa in Norway cost US$110 million alone (Løvik, 2009). The loss of coral reefs, in part due to eutrophication, threatens the $375 billion per year in goods and services that these structures offer. At present, 30% of the world's corals are at elevated risk of extinction (Hay and Rasher, 2010).

An additional problem is that once an ecosystem has been poisoned by excess nutrients, it is unlikely to recover easily. Duarte *et al.* (2009) put it this way: "the expectation that ecosystems can be returned to an idealized past reference status by virtue of reducing direct human pressures is as likely as the existence of Neverland."

2.2.3 Positive feedback

Unfortunately, other anthropogenic damage to coastal waters will exacerbate the impact of eutrophication due to positive feedback. Historical overfishing has altered coastal food webs, removing ecological buffers (Duarte, 2009) and rendering coastal ecosystem more prone to eutrophication (e.g. Heck and Valentine, 2007). Chemical contaminants, coastal habitat degradation and invasive species all add to the problems (Paine *et al.*, 1998; Breitburg *et al.*, 1999; Rabalais, 2004).

In the Baltic Sea, climate destabilization is expected to change precipitation patterns in drainage basins. This is expected to lead to an increase in mean annual river flows in the northern drainage basins and a decrease in mean annual river flows in the southern basins. Changes in run-off and river flows explain 71–97% of the variability in land–sea fluxes of nutrients (HELCOM, 2007). Climate destabilization will therefore affect the magnitude of future nutrient loads to the Baltic Sea (Lindkvist *et al.*, 2013). Recent modelling indicates extreme impacts of climate destabilization on agriculture (Rosenzweig *et al.*, 2014). Lakes are also vulnerable to the combined impact of nutrient enrichment and climate change (Jones and Brett, 2014). Figure 2.4 explores how climate destabilization and eutrophication act together. With coastal eutrophication, increased above-ground leaf biomass, decreases in the dense, below-ground biomass of bank-stabilizing

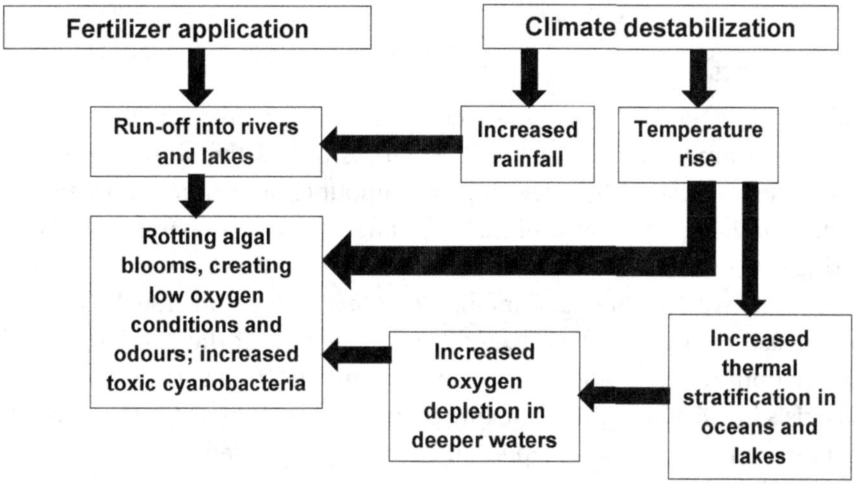

FIGURE 2.4 Interaction between eutrophication and climate destabilization, demonstrating that climate destabilization magnifies the damage done by eutrophication.

roots and increased microbial decomposition of organic matter are expected in estuaries. Alterations in these key ecosystem properties reduced geomorphic stability, resulting in creek-bank collapse with significant areas of creek-bank marsh converted to unvegetated mud (Deegan *et al.*, 2012). Herbicides and pesticides are also routinely sprayed on fields, leading to significant death among wild plants and animals.

In addition to agricultural run-off, it has been estimated that some 40% of agricultural food product is wasted between field and fridge. Thus the excessive application of fertilizers and habitat destruction that is synonymous with modern agriculture is placed in an even more wasteful context.

While agricultural waste contributes 80% of the total waste in Ireland, and 20% of the total waste in the UK, agriculture is by no means the only business sector contributing to non-greenhouse gas pollution. Each year 1.8 billion tonnes of waste is produced in Europe, averaging 3.5 tonnes per person. Of this, mining waste represents 29% of the total, construction waste is 25% of total, municipal waste is 14% of the total, 2% is industrial waste and 1% is hazardous waste. In addition to this, 17 million vehicles are scrapped each year (data from http://scp.eionet.europa.eu/themes/waste).

Waste is formed at every point in a product's life-cycle, from birth (mining and manufacturing), through life (pollution from functioning and repair) to death (disposal and replacement). Every tonne of consumer waste generates five tonnes of manufacturing waste and 20 tonnes of resource extraction waste (Meadows *et al.*, 1992).

2.2.4 Politics

Following the Second World War, economic regeneration took precedence over environmental concerns and countries across the world entered a heightened industrial frenzy, using vast amounts of resources and energy while producing mountains of waste. Changing social pressure in the West during the sixties included greater environmental awareness, perhaps first seen in the work of Rachel Carson, *Silent Spring* (Carson, 1962). Governments also responded, as reflected by the creation of the Department of the Environment (DoE) in the British Government in November 1970. The Oil Crisis in 1973 brought to the fore fears of raw material shortages which accentuated the resource depletion concerns expressed within *Limits to Growth* (Meadows, D.H. Club of Rome, 1972). The British Labour government's green paper *War on Waste*, published in 1974, was a reaction to these fears.

Waste has changed both qualitatively and quantitatively through the ages of humankind. The hunter-gatherer produced organic waste that was part of the cycling of nutrients, easily reassimilated by the myriad of organisms involved in natural recycling. Agrarian waste became more of an issue, both in terms of increasing agricultural waste and urban waste. As industrial processes began, new, non-organic waste emerged and this became the trademark of the Industrial Age.

In the current Information Age, the much more complex possessions, such as cars, machinery, computers and mobile phones pose a new problem: tiny traces of many elements, each too small in volume to recycle. In the United States alone, 140,000 computers and almost half a million mobile units are scrapped each year (EPA, 2011). Each computer manufactured results in 500 kg mining waste (Vereecken *et al.*, 2010).

Certain components create more waste than others. For example, tin, gold and silver all create 2,000 times the weight of useful product as waste, while copper, zinc and platinum create over 100 times the useful product weight as waste. Huge volumes of acidified water waste are also generated. Brominated flame retardants and dioxins from burning plastics (a method frequently used in informal recycling centres) both pose serious health risks (Sepúlveda, 2010). Significant wastes also emerge from the green energy sector, such as carcinogenic cadmium-polluted water from solar panel production. Rare earth metals, central to much green technology including large wind turbines, produce a panoply of toxic, hazardous waste in their extraction, including radioactive uranium and thorium.

Recent emphasis has been placed on the concept of a waste hierarchy (Fig. 2.5). In this scheme, there is a preferred order of actions: prevention, re-use, recycling, energy recovery and disposal.

- **Prevention** charges the product designer with having great responsibility in the process of waste management, wherein waste is designed out of products at the outset, both in terms of manufacture, use and breakdown.

- **Re-use** focuses on the service industry and the designer, in terms of easy maintenance, along with possible secondary use of component parts. Thus, if a product breaks down irreparably, at least part of it can be used in building another product, without the need of manufacturing from scratch. Thus the scrap yard becomes a spare parts unit. This may require greater universality of components, allowing interchangeability between models and even brands. For

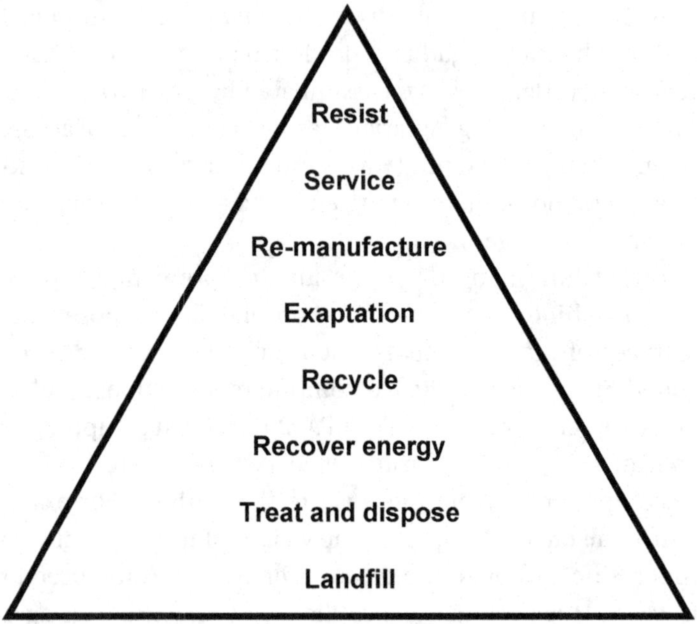

FIGURE 2.5 The waste hierarchy emphasizes the preferred ways to deal with waste. While modern theory emphasizes reduce, re-use and recycle, resisting the acquisition of the product in the first place is the preferred option. Exaptation refers to re-using the object for a completely different purpose without increasing the waste associated with it.

example, charging units for phones and computers are notorious for only fitting one brand.

- **Recycling** comes only third in the hierarchy, as the process consumes energy and contributes to the manufacturing costs, as the recycled material must be re-formed in order to be used again.
- **Energy recovery** systems harvest the output power and use it as input power in the same or another process. At another level, during product formation, energy is often needed to convert material into a particular form, and during recycling it may be possible to utilize this chemical potential to carry out work.
- If all else fails, then **disposal** is the only remaining solution, but its place at the bottom of the hierarchy indicates that this is the last resort, and something to be avoided at all costs where possible. Landfills are environmental hazards, and seldom contribute

anything useful to a sustainable future. Their long-term impacts are also understudied. Landfills in the UK currently contribute 3% of greenhouse gas emissions.

2.3 Habitat destruction and exhaustion

As natural habitats are converted to resources for humans, consequential damage to crucial ecosystem services will impact on business. Of further concern is the over-exploitation of these finite resources, leading to instability of supply chains. We examine the concept of peak resources and the Hubbert Curve. The consequence of resource insecurity on business is examined in a number of case studies. Key organizations involved in habitat issues include the United Nations Forum on Forests, World Conservation Union (IUCN) and the Inter-organization Programme for the Sound Management of Chemicals.

Nordhaus and Tobin (1972; p. 14) wrote:

> The prevailing standard model of growth assumes that there are no limits on the feasibility of expanding the supplies of nonhuman agents of production. It is basically a two-factor model in which production depends only on labour and reproducible capital. Land and resources, the third member of the triad, have generally been dropped.

As we have already noted, ecosystems services lie at the heart of any truly sustainable future. Ecosystems are fundamentally and inextricably linked to their habitats, and thus habitat destruction is not merely the loss of pretty forests where we can take the dog for a romp. Habitat destruction represents total loss of functionality.

Furthermore, what may look like a functioning habitat may not be functioning at all. In Scotland today, driving through the countryside, it appears that there is abundant forest. However, this is not the case. Most of the forest that is visible is industrial forest, with trees packed together excluding light from the ground, preventing the formation of the understorey, and whose sole purpose is wood production. It has no functionality in terms of being a forest. In reality it has as much in common with a forest ecosystem as a brick wall.

Habitat erosion is the reduction in functionality of a habitat. Habitats do not need to be erased to lose functionality. Species extinctions, pollution, high levels of ultraviolet radiation, soil erosion, eutrophication, fragmentation and altered water courses all weaken and alter habitats and damage the crucial interactions between species (Fortuna *et al.*, 2013). Furthermore, introduction of exotic, invasive species, as facilitated by human transport, greatly undermines ecosystem function. As Professor Daniel Janzen (Janzen 1974; p. 48), a Kyoto Prize winner, observed, there is a "much more insidious kind of extinction: the extinction of ecological interactions".

These "**dead man walking**" (a phrase originally referring to death row prisoners in American penitentiaries) ecosystems, once damaged, may be beyond recovery, and, while giving the semblance of functionality, are little more than the fractal morphological vestiges of a thriving ecology. Ecosystems operate at a system level, where functionality is an emergent quality reliant on interaction. Furthermore, since ecosystems emerge from hundreds (or even thousands) of years of ecological succession, they cannot be rebuilt by humans. Thus habitats once destroyed are generally lost for the long term.

2.3.1 Deforestation

The history of deforestation and the history of humankind are inextricably linked. While climatic change over millions of years has altered forest distribution, it is the human impact that has had the most devastating effect. Half of Britain's forests were already gone by the time the Romans invaded. By 1600, more than one third of New Zealand's forests were destroyed, while on Easter Island, all the forest had disappeared by 1700, with catastrophic consequences for the human population. Recent work demonstrates that declines in the provisioning of services will initially be slow but will then accelerate as species from higher trophic levels are lost at faster rates (Dobson *et al.*, 2006).

Humans impact on forests in a number of ways. First they have always used wood for construction of buildings and boats. In fact wood was the most important source of building material for millennia. Wood was also important in the charcoal (essential in World War II in the production of charcoal absorbers in 40 million gas masks), tanning and food smoking industries.

Wood is used as fuel (and again was the most important fuel for millennia). Much of the Irish oak woodlands were consumed in iron smelting, as oak was one of the few woods that could generate sufficient temperatures. Forests had a very different value prior to the industrial revolution. Initially, forests were sources of fruit and animals, as well as shelter.

Fruit shrubs and trees are naturally found in forests, forming understorey layers. They rely on animals to pollinate and disperse their seeds, and so do not require wind for this purpose. Hence they grow well within forests. Animals that eat the fruit (frugivores) are therefore also associated with forests, and so early hunter-gatherers would have found the forest as a bountiful source of food. During the Agrarian Age, diet shifted to crops and domestic meat, and the link between man and forest declined. Indeed, many viewed forests as places where attackers could hide. This was still the case in the 1960s, when **Agent Orange**, a defoliant, was sprayed over the forests of Vietnam by the American military to expose the Viet Cong, with devastating consequences to future generations in terms of birth defects, miscarriage and cancer.

As the Imperial Era arrived, and with it the Industrial Age, forests were viewed as essential for military ship building. In many ways the great empires of Spain, England and France, were built of wood, in the form of warships and transport ships. Another important reason for an empire's leaders to protect forests was for royal hunting grounds. The New Forest in England was planted under the command of William the Conqueror in 1079 for hunting. However, with metal and concrete replacing wood as building material and with coal replacing wood as timber, forests became valued only for industrial production related to furniture, paper and Christmas trees. Ecosystem function was no longer required in the world of industrial forestry.

A major driver of forest destruction is agriculture. From our earliest times, we have cleared woodland to free up land for crop and pasture. As populations have grown, this tendency has increased. Ultimately crops need land, and animals need forage, and so food production has always been linked to deforestation. Today in the Amazon rainforest, 80% of deforestation is for cattle ranching.

Ironically, another major contributor to deforestation is the growth of crops for green fuels. The European Union has deemed that 5.75% of its automotive fuel should come from plants. These plants are grown mostly in Asia, where, between 1985 and 2000, 87% of Malaysian forests have been replaced by oil palm, while each year an area half the size of Belgium is converted from rainforest to oil palm in Indonesia. Since 1980, Cambodia, Laos, Vietnam, Thailand and Burma have lost one third of their forest. The Orangutan Foundation International estimates that some 5,000 apes are dying each year because of oil palm growth. In many ways, the car is replacing the beef industry as the main driver of deforestation.

Cash-rich crops such as coffee, which share climatic optima with rainforest, have further contributed to deforestation. Once removed, the forest ecosystem has little chance of recovery, because the bulk of the nutrients are in the trees, not the soil. Under the heavy rainfall typical of this area, the remaining soil is quickly eroded, leading to eutrophication in adjoining rivers and devastation on what remains of the land. Soon fertilizers must be applied to allow forage crops to grow, exacerbating the problems. Land-use activities, especially deforestation, are also a major source of greenhouse gases, accounting for 8–20% of all global emissions (Houghton, 2005).

Poor soil management is a problem throughout the world. With climate destabilization comes harsh rainfall and drought, leading to crop failures and massive soil loss. Soil is the foundry of life, averaging just 15 cm in depth, and is the foundation for the entire food pyramid, on top of which we are precariously perched. Great civilizations have been destroyed through soil erosion. Deforestation, overgrazing and intensive agriculture, beginning in the Agrarian Age, now means some 10 million hectares of crop land are washed away each year. An area big enough to feed all of Europe has been degraded beyond repair.

In China, 18 kg of soil is lost for every kg of food produced, with soil being depleted 54 times faster than it is being formed and costing US$42 billion per year in lost productivity. Babylon, Antioch and the Mayan civilization are all thought to have fallen because of soil erosion and mismanagement, with silt blocking irrigation channels and deforestation contributing to soil loss. Lester W. Brown, President of the Earth Policy Institute has commented: "Civilization can survive the loss of its oil reserves ... But it cannot survive the loss of its soil reserves" (Brown, 2011).

Desertification resulting from soil erosion is an increasing problem. Nigeria loses 350,000 ha of crop and rangeland per year (about the area of Yosemite National Park), while salinization (high salt levels), caused by excessive irrigation in dry regions, is a severe threat, with one third of all irrigated land in Shanxi province of China salinized. This figure is 50% for Australia.

2.3.2 Coral reefs

Huge habitat destruction caused by a combination of on-land activities (industrial run-off, soil erosion, agricultural spraying) and water-based activities (dragnetting, antifouling agents on ships, ballast water from tankers) has degraded the reefs, leading to significant threats to the biological and physical structure of the oceans. Coral reefs often protect coastal areas from erosion, and so their disappearance will have significant consequences for coastal human communities.

2.3.3 Wetlands

The drainage of wetlands in order to convert them to agricultural land and real estate has been devastating. By 1993, over half the world's wetlands had been destroyed (McLeod *et al.*, 2011). Wetlands not only house huge amounts of wildlife, but they store vast amounts of carbon and water, buffering against flooding. They also filter pollution and protect coastlines against erosion and are important in groundwater replenishment. Their destruction has significant consequences for a region. An important source of greenhouse gases is the release, via land-use conversion, of carbon from tidal marshes, mangroves, and sea-grass beds. These coastal carbon stocks are increasingly referred to as "**blue carbon**". It has been estimated that up to 1 billion tonnes of wetland carbon is being lost each year, leading to economic damages of US$6–42 billion annually (Pendleton *et al.*, 2012).

2.3.4 Resource exhaustion

Sink issues, such as climate destabilization, pollution of soils and rivers and the loss of biodiversity have tended to dominate the agenda recently rather than concerns relating to the depletion of minerals (**source** issues). However, anxiety relating to resource exhaustion has been raised for thousands of years. Early in the 4th century BC, Plato, referring to the disappearance of forests in Attica, wrote: "What now remains compared with what then existed, is like the skeleton of a sick man, all the fat and soft earth having been wasted away, and only the bare framework of the land being left" (Plato, 1961; 389c).

In 1924, geologist Ira Joralemon concluded:

> the age of electricity and of copper will be short. At the intense rate of production that must come, the copper supply of the world will last hardly a score of years. Our civilization based on electrical power will dwindle and die (Joralemon, 1924).

In 1945, Harold Williamson described the role of "**prophesies of scarcity**" in generating a conservation response for both renewable and nonrenewable resources (Williamson, 1945). Harrison Brown, in his provocative book, *The Challenge of Man's Future* (Brown, 1954), argued that the full development of every nation on the planet, to a level already present in the West, would lead to a total collapse of Earth's natural resource base.

These ideas were further developed by Kenneth Boulding. In his landmark essay, "The economics of the coming spaceship Earth", written in 1966 (Boulding, 1966), he set out his now famous analogy of the spaceship. In this paper, some of which was based on his earlier work (Boulding, 1945; Boulding, 1950), he explained how, as humans have increased in numbers and in their intensity of resource exploitation, the planet has changed from an open world, with apparently limitless assets, to a closed world, akin to a spacecraft. On board spacecraft Earth, we now must carefully use and recycle what we have left, otherwise we risk extinction. He suggested that we must turn from a **cowboy economy**, where consumption and production rule, maximizing throughput, to a **spaceman economy**, where maintenance of stock and minimal throughput are key.

More recently, some 14 raw materials have been judged by the European Commission to be "critical": antimony, beryllium, cobalt, fluorspar, gallium, germanium, graphite, indium, magnesium, niobium, platinum group metals, rare earth metals, tantalum, and tungsten (European Commission, 2010). The whole topic of resource exhaustion centres around one particular graph, thanks to the work of the geophysicist M. King Hubbert.

2.3.5 The Hubbert Curve: a history of peak oil

In the 1950s, Hubbert noted that a couple of centuries earlier, production (in tonnes per year) of petroleum was essentially zero. He reasoned that production would rise to one or more maxima after which it would decline back to zero in another century or two. No matter how erratic the production turns out to be, the curve of production of any finite resource over time (years) will fundamentally be described by the Gaussian Error Curve which starts at zero, rises to a maximum and then returns to zero. The area under the curve from zero to infinity represents the total mass of that resource measured in tonnes. This curve became known at the **Hubbert Curve** (Fig. 2.6). The Hubbert Curve traces the increasing exploitation of a resource, from early low levels, where the resource is not particularly central to any human process, followed by increasing supply, reflecting increasing demand as its usefulness becomes realized. However, as readily abundant sources of the resource become exhausted, supply reaches a maximum before curving

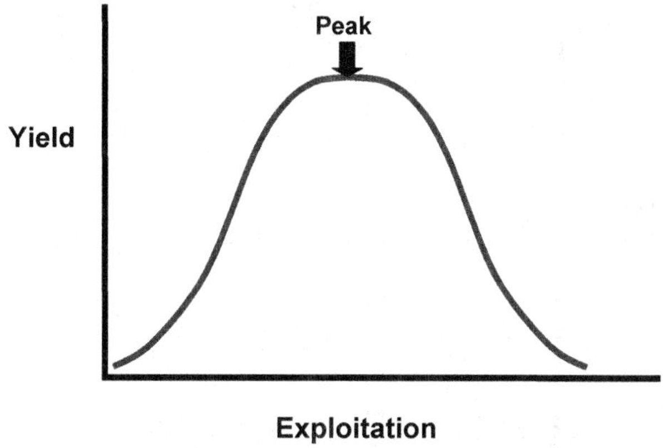

FIGURE 2.6 The peak oil or Hubbert Curve. As exploitation increases, yield increases, but, as the resource is limiting (Boulding's "spaceship Earth") then yield decreases with increasing exploitation (Hubbert, 1956; Brandt, 2007). The tipping point for many of the world's resources may have already occurred, or will occur in the coming years.

downwards. The end of the upward curve usually means that supply is now lagging demand, and thus consumers begin to feel the pain of a shortage. Following the peak, which would be expected to post-date supply crisis, the situation becomes worse, as supply actually starts to decline. At this stage, less abundant, more technically difficult deposits are being exploited, and the supply becomes increasingly poor.

The most important point on this curve is the time, or date, at which maximum production is reached. This point is called the **peak**. In the case of petroleum production in the US, the peak occurred in 1972, just as Hubbert had predicted years earlier. Only the development of Alaskan fields allowed some rebound up until 1985, when a new decline followed. Hubbert also predicted that global conventional oil production would peak around the year 2000, which has proved to be slightly inaccurate given that conventional oil production has only plateaued recently (see Bardi, 2005). This phenomenon is now commonly referred to as **peak oil**.

It should be noted that the predicted volume of oil to be produced at the peak was 37% too low, and that Hubbert's predictions relating to coal and natural gas ran badly amiss. Hubbert predicted that US oil production would peak at 3 billion barrels per year. Production in 1970 was 4.1 billion barrels. Hubbert predicted that global coal production will peak in 2150 at about 6.4 billion metric tonnes. However, actual production reached that

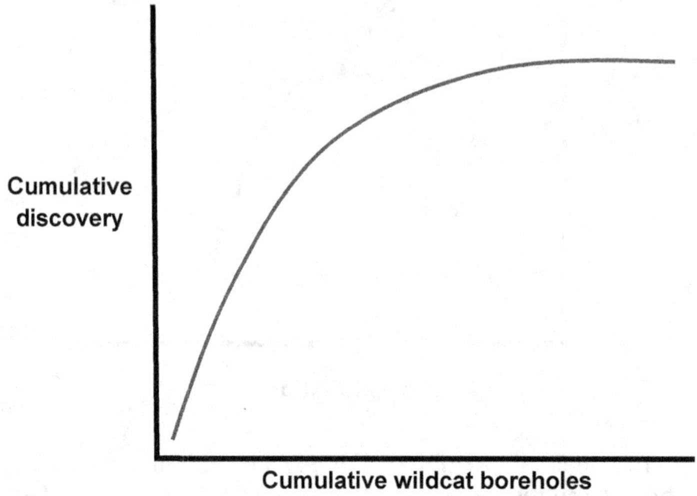

FIGURE 2.7 The creaming curve compares the cumulative number of boreholes drilled in search of new oil (wildcat boreholes) with the cumulative number of successful discoveries of viable mineral sites. The curve initially increases rapidly, with successful wildcats converting to mineral wealth, but then levels off, with less and less mineral wealth generated, due to a reduced volume of undiscovered deposits.

level in 2007 and is still growing rapidly. Hubbert also predicted that US gas production would peak at 14 trillion cubic feet per year in 1973 whereas actual production was 21 trillion cubic feet in 2009 (Smith, 2012).

Many of the discovery process models within the oil industry are based on the use of **creaming curves** (Fig. 2.7). The creaming curve basically describes the decreasing returns between the exploration activity and the total discoveries for one given region. Basically with finite resources, greater effort is needed to maintain production. This means that production cost increases with time. This is the key concept used by the oil industry to characterize the dynamic process of the development of an oil producing region through exploration.

Geologists tend to support the concept of peak oil, while economists tend to be oil optimists, arguing that the real issue lies not in diminishing resources but with the cartel of OPEC, which involves maximizing profits and stopping exploration in the most resource-rich regions of the world. Middle East countries that offer the best perspectives for new discoveries are also less extensively explored.

The oil optimists argue that Hubbert got it wrong in much the same way as they argue that Malthus also got it wrong with regards to demography (e.g. Smith, 2012). According to economists, the main shortcoming of the peak oil theory is its static methodology. It fails to take into account a central plank of the Enlightenment: technology. The driver of this technological progress comes from rising commodity prices, meaning that technological advancement in exploration, production and processing will compensate for falling primary resource stocks. By ignoring the nature of the causal effects in the minerals markets, optimists believe that the Hubbert Curve becomes an invalid tool.

More recent forecasts endeavour to take into account the dynamic relationship between economic variables and the impacts of new resources and technologies. Another criticism is that while the Hubbert peak may work for a single oil well, it is less useful globally, given the heterogeneity of reserves, exploitation and demand. If we open an oil well today, it will be out of step with a neighbouring oil well opened 40 years ago.

A recent analysis by Maggio and Cacciola (2012) estimated peak values for oil (of 30 gigabarrels/year) would be reached in 2015, peak natural gas values (of 132 trillion cubic feet/year) in 2035 and peak coal values (of 4.5 tonnes of oil equivalent/year) would be reached in 2052. As Richard Heinberg (2007) has pointed out, peak petroleum will be quickly followed by *Peak Everything*. So many business sectors are dependent on petroleum, and so the peak of world petroleum will impact on all of these sectors.

2.3.6 Peak minerals

Most of the peak studies so far have focused on the case of oil, and Giurco *et al.* (2010) note that there exist fundamental differences between oil and many minerals. Metals are elements and hence are indestructible. Once they are mined and put into use they do not disappear but can be recycled. This can mean that if recycling increases, then raw resource mining can decrease. For example, steel production in the US has continued on a high level based on scrap even though iron ore production has not grown at the same pace (Ericsson and Söderholm, 2010).

A crucial signature of the peak minerals phenomenon is declining quality and grade. Figure 2.8 shows how ore quality has declined significantly over the last 150 years in Australia. Recently compiled historical data sets (Mudd, 2009) show that long-term trends for copper, nickel, lead, silver and zinc ore grades in Australia are also all declining. The industry's response is to dig

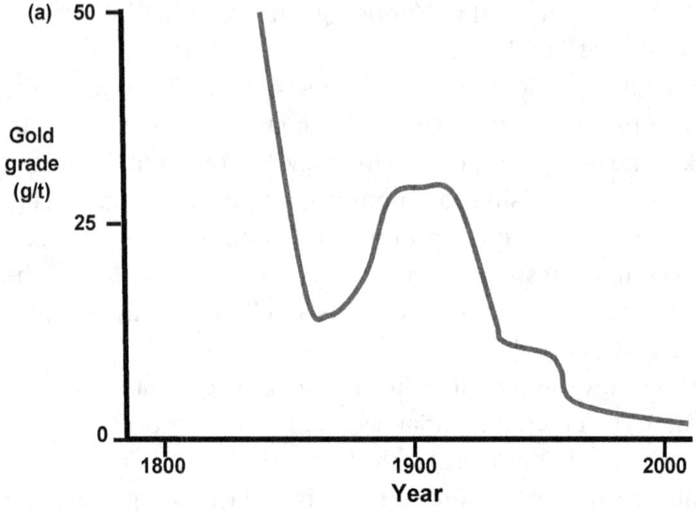

FIGURE 2.8 Gold ore quality (gold grade) in Australian mines measured as grammes per tonne, through time (data from Mudd, 2009; 2010).

deeper, dig wider and use more capital, energy, labour and water to extract a diminishing concentration of material. This leads to greater waste outputs, in terms of dirty water, tailings and waste rock, and to more significant pollution. Also, governments are under greater pressure to release previously protected land for exploration and exploitation.

Figure 2.9 shows the water consumed per kg gold produced with increasing gold grade. The higher the grade, the purer the gold deposits. As can be seen, as gold becomes scarce (towards the left side of the graph), lower grade deposits will be mined, meaning a rapid escalation in water used. Figure 2.10 (cyanide/gold) shows that cyanide consumption, essential in the extraction process of gold, follows a similar trend, increasing exponentially with decreasing gold grade.

Waste generated from uranium, gold and copper mining has greatly increased recently (Mudd, 2007), again indicating that ore quality has declined and peak levels for these metals have been passed. Fundamentally, the discussion about mineral resource depletion is as much about falling resource quality as a reduction in resource quantity. It is clear that the Hubbert Curve not only signifies decreasing yield, but increasing environmental damage.

Damage from mining is long-term and is devastating for the surrounding ecology and water quality. During the 1980s, the Australian government

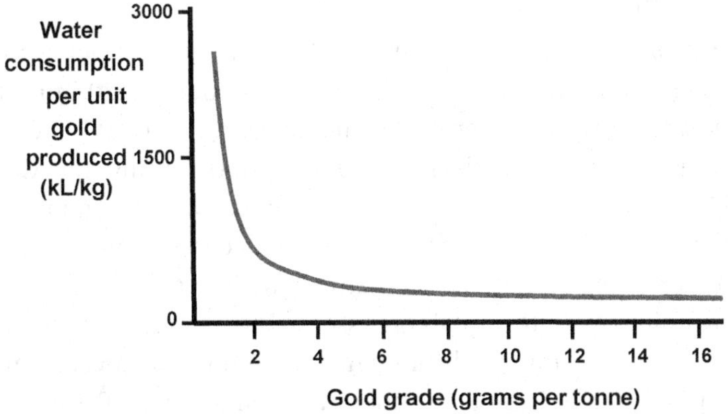

FIGURE 2.9 Water consumed per unit of gold mined, in kl per kg of gold refined with increasing ore quality (data from Mudd, 2009; 2010).

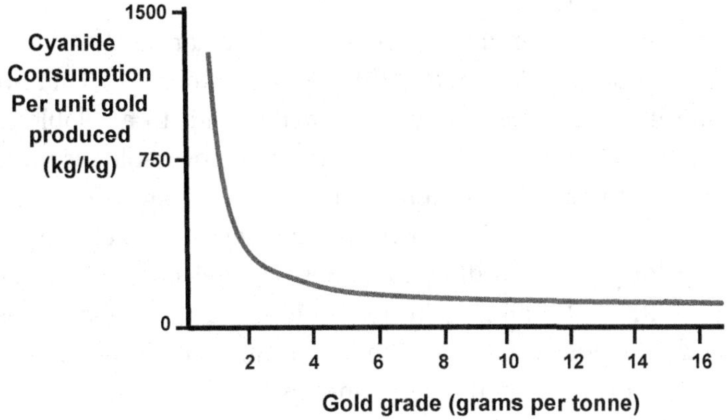

FIGURE 2.10 Cyanide consumption per unit of gold produced with increasing ore quality (gold grade). As gold grade declines, reflecting increasing scarcity, pollution increases.

spent AUS$25 million in rehabilitating the former Rum Jungle mining field in the Northern Territories, a uranium and copper mine. As recently as 2007, the adjacent East Finniss River was still heavily polluted with acid mine drainage leaching from waste rock dumps (Mudd, 2010).

2.3.7 Peak lithium

Lithium has found itself at the centre of recent peak mineral concerns, because of its importance in renewable energy technology. Lithium was originally used as a lubricant in aeroplane engines starting in WWII, but became extremely important in nuclear fusion weaponry during the Cold War. Demand increased further with its use in the glass and aluminium industry. However, the end of the cold war saw demand decline. Then the use of lithium ion batteries increased rapidly, particularly in terms of powering vehicles, while lithium niobate crystals are essential for mobile phone technology.

Around 25 million tonnes of lithium metal is viable to recover from known resources plus another 5 million tonnes in marginal stocks. Extraction so far totals only 0.5 million tonnes, while current production of lithium is roughly 25,000 tonnes per year (Kushnir and Sanden, 2012). The presently known lithium resources excluding the ocean will only be exhausted this century if large-scale use of predominantly BEV sized batteries comes into play, or if batteries are not recycled.

However, if environmental lobbies such as in Salar de Uyuni in Bolivia, the second largest global source of lithium, and other political and social forces come into play, there may be a greater limit to available lithium. Indigenous people in many of the areas where recoverable resources exist also have claims that could interfere with supply. Such are the concerns that significant question marks hang over the concept of the electric car as a replacement for petroleum-driven engines. Each electric car battery contains 4 kg of lithium. If all cars in the world (around 1 billion) were converted, we would require a total of 4 million tonnes of lithium. In reality, the high quality graphite needed for the anodes (25 kg per battery) would be even more limiting. Currently there are no other materials to replace either lithium or graphite for the same energy output.

2.3.8 Peak platinum and uranium

Platinum is an important metal in fuel cells, and it has been calculated that if all 1 billion cars in the world were using these fuel cells, supplies would run out in 15 years (Cohen, 2007). Again, platinum cannot be replaced with an alternative metal without weakening performance. Uranium or more specifically uranium 235, the isotope required for nuclear fission power generation and for nuclear warheads, is viewed as having peaked in the production. Current supply meets only 58% of demand.

Germany, the Czech Republic, France, DR Congo, Gabon, India, Bulgaria, Tajikistan, Hungary, Romania, Spain, Portugal, UK, and Argentina have all already reached uranium production peaks (OECD, 2008). Although there is disagreement over exactly how long uranium supplies will last, given a decline in nuclear reactors following the Japanese tsunami and the hope of fast breeder reactors converting other form of uranium into uranium 235, it is understood that peak uranium has been reached across the planet. This, combined with increasing shortages of other important metals involved in nuclear power generation, poses a significant challenge to a post-oil planet in terms of energy generation, given the shortages of key metals required in other "green" energy generation strategies already noted.

Recent design strategies have involved a rapid increase in the use of minor metals, and in using a broad pallet of these in a given product. As mentioned before, as many as 60 different metals can be found in a computer today. Many medical technologies contain over 70 metals. This poses huge problems in terms of recycling, particularly because often, very small amounts of each metal are found in each component (Reck and Graedel, 2012).

In addition to lithium, many other metals now form the heart of the renewable energy industry, with recent emphasis on rare earth metals. Cadmium (Cd), cobalt (Co), and lanthanum (La), used along with lithium in rechargeable batteries; gallium (Ga), indium (In), selenium (Se), and tellurium (Te) are crucial to thin-film photovoltaics; dysprosium (Dy) and neodymium (Nd) are key in high-strength magnets; hafnium (Hf) is an essential component of nuclear control rods and new generation computer chips (Reller, 2011).

These metals are not rare *per se*, but occur at very low concentrations, and so require huge processing costs, energetically and environmentally, to extract sufficient quantities of them. While supply of the major base metals are not threatened at present, many of the daughter metals are not so secure. Gallium, indium, and neodymium are singled out as elements of particular concern from a long-term supply standpoint. Many additives such as chromium, molybdenum and manganese in steel or in paints, or the new age of high-tech metals such as indium, geranium and tantalum, included in nanotechnology and micro-electronics, are extremely difficult to recycle. Indium is thought to have as little as ten years supplies left at current usage (Cohen, 2007), threatening LED flat-screen technology.

While design has moved towards more complex combinations of metals that are difficult to extract and recycle, a sustainable future requires a move in the opposite direction, minimizing the number of materials, utilizing materials whose extraction has low ecological impact, and designing the products for re-use and recycling.

2.3.9 Peak phosphorus

As we have noted already, phosphate is a limited resource, but is central to our food supply chain. Without phosphate fertilizer, the modern industrial agriculture machine would grind to a halt; 90% of mined phosphorus is used in food production. Phosphorus cannot be synthesized by humans (unlike ammonium fertilizer from nitrogen gas, which represents 78% of the atmosphere), and so the mining of this resource, and the careless waste of it creating the issues of eutrophication mentioned earlier, mean that in many ways, peak P poses the greatest challenge to our own survival.

We may have no petroleum to drive to the food store, but without phosphorus, there would be very little food in the store. Fundamentally, a lack of petrol in our tanks is less likely to kill us than a lack of food in our stomachs. With current global P reserves estimated to be depleted in 50–100 years, peak phosphorus production is predicted to occur by 2030 (Cordell *et al.*, 2009). Western Europe and India are already completely dependent on imports (Jasinski, 2006). Meanwhile, the quality of deposits is deteriorating and production costs are escalating. The demand for phosphorus is predicted to increase by 50–100% by 2050 (Steen, 1998). Rosmarin (2004) estimates that close to 25% of the 1 billion tonnes of phosphorus mined since 1950 has ended up in water bodies, or is buried in landfills.

White and Codwell (2009) observe that while oil and phosphorus are both nonrenewable resources, two differences remain. Oil once consumed cannot be recycled, whereas phosphorus, as a basic element can (as can metals). A second difference is that oil can be replaced by other forms of energy once it runs out, whereas phosphorus cannot be replaced.

2.3.10 Peak soil

Peak soil probably occurred around 10,000 years ago. Given that the Agrarian Age saw practices that increased soil erosion, we have been sitting on an ever-decreasing volume of soil ever since. This is because soil takes so long to form. Only industrialized fertilizer production has rescued us, but the phosphorus peak will reveal the damaged underbelly of agriculture. As mentioned earlier, soil loss is increasing and climate destabilization, combined with greater industrialization, have exacerbated an already serious problem. Reduced soil resource will have devastating consequences in many ecosystem services, and on food supply.

2.3.11 Peak timber

Over the past few decades, tropical timber production in many Asia–Pacific countries has displayed a rapid increase followed by a peak and then decline: a Hubbert curve. Because trees often take 30–40 years to regrow, and because cutting results in deforestation and the extraction of most of the nutrients within the ecosystem, continued forestry is unsustainable. Furthermore, the soil left will be quickly washed away, given the heavy tropical rains in these areas. Thus diminishing nutrient resources mean that large-scale timber extraction leads to the trees resembling a nonrenewable resource. Shearman *et al.* (2012) suggest that we have now passed peak timber in tropical regions.

2.3.12 Peak fish

The oceans are under increasing pressure as habitats. These pressures stem from a combination of over-harvesting and pollution, leading to extreme pressure on fish populations. The Newfoundland fisheries have suffered catastrophic failures as far back as 1980 and have never recovered. The North Sea is in crisis at present. Table 2.1 shows the major fisheries of the world and clearly demonstrates that **peak fish** has been reached in all of them with significant decline now under way across the planet. This will have very significant impact on the human race, particularly in island communities who rely on fish protein as an essential part of their diet.

Fishery	Harvest potential	Year potential	Decline from peak
East central Atlantic	4	1984	−22%
South-east Atlantic	3	1978	−53%
West central Atlantic	2	1987	−28%
East central Pacific	3	1988	−13%
North-east Pacific	4	1990	−12%
South-west Pacific	1	1991	−13%
Antarctic	0.2	1980	unavailable
World	82	1999	unavailable

TABLE 2.1 Declining major fisheries/peak fish levels in each fishery, year peak fish levels were reached and decline from peak

Source: FAO, 1999; McGinn and Peterson, 1999

2.3.13 Peak people

Population growth, according to Enlightenment philosophers, is positive. A larger population allows for greater division of labour, leading to greater prosperity. Originally population growth was viewed as militarily important (enough young men to fight) but later it was seen as a strength economically. However, with so much of our support network fundamentally in decline, we must face the fact that the human population may soon peak.

David Pimentel, an agricultural scientist at Cornell University, has estimated that a sustainable world population, living at the dietary level of the average American, is about 2 billion people. The world population in late 2011 is estimated to have reached 7 billion people and was growing at the rate of approximately 1% per year. Furthermore, many of the poorest countries in the world are now increasing their ecological footprints as they gain wealth and spending power.

Thus our population and our resources are on a collision course. As the population continues to grow and increase in its per capita expectations, placing greater demands on ecosystem services and consuming more and more of the planet's resources, there can surely only be two outcomes:—a decline in our resources or a decline in our population. Scarcity of renewable resources causes additional burdens for a nation's budget and increases demands from poorer populations. Weak governments may find it difficult to resolve a problem with economic tools and the use of power against demands of population may escalate leading to social unrest.

Resource optimists claim that resource shortages are remediable through market flexibility and substitution, posing no threat to long-term exponential economic growth. With falling rates of fertility and population growth, world population will stabilize, according to this view, at manageable levels. While population growth rates are indeed falling, they are still positive, meaning the growth in total population continues. Indeed, the average annual increase has barely changed since reaching a maximum in the 1990s. 2% of 100 is still more than 15% of 10.

This implies a net addition of 2–3 billion people above the current global population of 7 billion before stabilization. Further, the fastest addition to population is occurring in those areas that can least support it: sub-Saharan Africa and poorer parts of Asia and the Middle East. The very real issue of carrying capacity (peak people), as global population reaches levels that strain food and other essential life-support systems (see Fig. 1.2), continues. Another pressing issue is the social problem of supporting a growing cohort of elderly people, an unavoidable result of population stabilization.

Finally, although many of the metals that furnish our luxury western lifestyles are threatened, it is peak phosphorus, peak soil and peak food that pose a much more serious challenge. However, peak oil, and associated peaks in the energy metals, will also impact greatly on food production, as agriculture is heavily dependent on energy to produce nitrogen fertilizers and run machinery.

2.3.14 Nonrenewable renewables and renewable nonrenewables

While resources are classically divided into nonrenewable (such as metal ores, oil and coal) and renewable (such as timber, topsoil, biodiversity and fresh water, produced by ecosystem services), in reality, recycling offers the chance to "renew" the metal stocks of the world more readily than we can replenish the produce of ecosystem services, given the damage we have done to the natural engine of renewal. Fishery collapses, deforestation, salinization and soil erosion and desertification, in addition to eutrophication, climate destabilization, ocean acidification and decreasing planetary albedo all make it less likely that any form of natural renewal can keep pace with our use of these crucial resources.

It has been estimated that changes in renewable resources will contribute more to social turmoil in coming decades than climate destabilization or ozone depletion. Scarcity of renewable resources is a function not only of environmental change but of population growth and unequal social distribution of resources as well (Homer-Dixon *et al.*, 1993). Thus social, economic and environmental issues are very much combined in the current crisis.

Natural resources, both renewable and nonrenewable, are always harvested in the same way—the easiest and cheapest supplies are taken first. The process is called **high-grading** (Coufal *et al.*, 2011). Although few metals are currently facing physical depletion, they are becoming harder to obtain, and the energy, environmental and social cost of acquiring them could constrain future production and usage, while undermining the renewal of so called "renewable resources". The planet is not a bath sponge, which can be wrung out tightly between our fists to extract the last drop of water, and then return to its former absorbent glory. Rather there is a likelihood of increasing damage on ecosystem services as resource quality decreases while quantity demand maintains at current levels (Prior *et al.*, 2012).

2.4 Debate, discussion and further thought

1. Organize a debate taking either a sceptical or positive position on climate destabilization.
2. What are the concerns related to non-linear climate responses? Give examples of potential tipping points.
3. Why is agriculture on of the biggest threats to sustainability? Outline its impacts on climate, habitat and pollution.
4. What challenges do peak minerals pose to industry in the coming century?
5. How are ecosystem services affected by climate destabilization, eutrophication and habitat erosion?
6. Discuss the implications for business practice of the threats confronting our planet.
7. How renewable are renewable resources and what issues does this definition hold for sustainable economics?
8. Prioritize the problems outlined in this chapter and set out a timeline for action.
9. Trace the history, progress and problems of the COP meetings.

References

Adger, W., Kajfe-Bogataj, L., Parry, M., Canziani, O. and Palutikof, J. (2007). *Climate Change 2007: Impacts, Adaptation and Vulnerability.* Cambridge University Press, Cambridge, UK.

Allison, I. and 25 other authors. (2011). The Copenhagen Diagnosis: Updating the world on the latest climate science. The University of New South Wales Climate Change Research Centre (CCRC), Sydney, Australia, 60pp. http://oceanrep.geomar.de/11839/2/Copenhagen_Diagnosis_LOW.pdf

Altizer, S., Ostfeld, R.S., Johnson, P.T., Kutz, S. and Harvell, C.D. (2013). Climate change and infectious diseases: from evidence to a predictive framework. Science 341(6145): 514-19.

Anderegg, W.R., Prall, J.W., Harold, J. and Schneider, S.H. (2010). Expert credibility in climate change. Proceedings of the National Academy of Sciences 107(27): 12107-109.

Archer, D. (2009). *The Long Thaw.* Princeton University Press, Princeton, NJ.

Arrhenius, S. (1908). *Worlds in the Making: the Evolution of the Universe.* Harper, London.

Babbitt, B. (1992). After Rio. world Monitor, June 1992, pp. 28-30.

Bardi, U. (2005). The mineral economy: a model for the shape of oil production curves. Energy Policy 33: 53-61.

Bogaard, A. and 18 other authors. (2013). Crop manuring and intensive land management by Europe's first farmers. Proceedings of the National Academy of Sciences 110(31): 12589-94.

Boulding, K.E. (1945). The concept of economic surplus. The American Economic Review (1945): 851-69.

Boulding, K.E. (1950). Income or welfare? Review of Economic Studies 17: 77-86.

Boulding, K.E. (1966). The economics of the coming spaceship Earth. In: Jarret, H., ed. *Environmental Quality in a Growing Economy.* Johns Hopkins University Press, Baltimore, Maryland, pp. 3-14.

Brandt, A.R. (2007). Testing Hubbert. Energy Policy 35(5): 3074-88.

Breitburg, D.L. and 17 other authors (2009). Nutrient enrichment and fisheries exploitation: interactive effects on estuarine living resources and their management. Hydrobiologia 629(1): 31-47.

Broecker, W.S. (2000). Was a change in thermohaline circulation responsible for the Little Ice Age? Proceedings of the National Academy of Sciences 97(4): 1339-42.

Brown, H. (1954). *The Challenge of Man's Future.* Viking Press: New York, NY.

Brown, L.W. (2011). The new geopolitics of food. Foreign Policy May/June 2011.

Carson, R. (1962). *Silent Spring.* Houghton Mifflin, New York.

Clearfield, M., Pearce, M., Nibbe, Y., Crotty, D. and Wagner, A. (2014). The "new deadly quartet" for cardiovascular disease in the 21st century: obesity, metabolic syndrome, inflammation and climate change: how does statin therapy fit into this equation? Current Atherosclerosis Reports 16(1): 1-11.

Cohen, D. (2007). Earth's natural wealth: an audit. New Scientist 2605: 34-41.

Cordell, D., Drangert, J.O. and White, S. (2009). The story of phosphorus: global food security and food for thought. Global Environmental Change 19(2): 292-305.

Costanza, R., Graumlich, L.J. and Steffen, W.L. (2007). *Sustainability or Collapse? An Integrated History and Future of People on Earth.* MIT Press, Cambridge, MA.

Coufal, J. and other authors. (2011). Consulting Forestry/Certification and Ecosystem Services. Journal of Forestry, 109(8), 530-7.

Cullen, H.M., Hemming, S., Hemming, G., Brown, F.H., Guilderson, T. and Sirocko, F. (2000). Climate change and the collapse of the Akkadian empire: Evidence from the deep sea. Geology 28(4): 379-82.

Deegan, L.A., Johnson, D.S., Warren, R.S., Peterson, B.J., Fleeger, J.W., Fagherazzi, S. and Wollheim, W.M. (2012). Coastal eutrophication as a driver of salt marsh loss. Nature, 490(7420), 388-92.

Diamond, J. (2005). *Collapse: How Societies Choose to Fail or Succeed.* Viking, New York.

Dobson, A., Lodge, D., Alder, J., Cumming, G.S., Keymer, J., McGlade, J., Mooney, H., Rusak, J.A., Sala, O., Wolters, V., Wall, D., Winfree, R. and Xenopoulos, M.A. (2006). Habitat loss, trophic collapse, and the decline of ecosystem services. Ecology 87(8): 1915-24.

Dodds, W.K., Bouska, W.W., Eitzmann, J.L., Pilger, T.J., Pitts, K.L., Riley, A.J., Schloesser, J.T. and Thornbrugh, D.J. (2008). Eutrophication of US freshwaters: analysis of potential economic damages. Environmental Science & Technology 43(1): 12-19.

Drysdale, R., Zanchetta, G., Hellstrom, J., Maas, R., Fallick, A., Pickett, M., Cartwright, I. and Piccini, L. (2006). Late Holocene drought responsible for the collapse of Old World civilizations is recorded in an Italian cave flowstone. Geology 34(2): 101-104.

Duarte, C.M., Conley, D.J., Carstensen, J. and Sánchez-Camacho, M. (2009). Return to Neverland: shifting baselines affect eutrophication restoration targets. Estuaries and Coasts 32(1): 29-36.

Emanuel, K.A. (2013). Downscaling CMIP5 climate models shows increased tropical cyclone activity over the 21st century. Proceedings of the National Academy of Sciences 110(30): 12219-24.

EPA (2011). Electronics waste management in the United States through 2009. US EPA, May 2011, EPA 530-R-11-002.

Ericsson, M. and Söderholm, P. (2010). Mineral Depletion and Peak Production (No. 7). POLINARES working paper.

European Commission (2010). Critical raw materials for the EU, Report of the Ad-hoc Working Group on defining critical raw materials.

FAO (1999). *The State of World Fisheries and Aquaculture 1998.* Food and Agricultural Organization, Rome.

Faure, M., Gupta, J. and Nentjes, A. (2003). Key instrumental and institutional design issues in climate change policy. In: Faure, M., Gupta, J. and Nentjes, A. (eds.), *Climate Change and the Kyoto Protocol: The Role of Institutions and Instruments to Control Global Change.* Edward Elgar Publishing Limited, USA

Flannery, T.F. (1994). *The Future Eaters: An Ecological History of the Australasian Lands and People.* Grove Press, New York.

Fortuna, M.A., Krishna, A. and Bascompte, J. (2013). Habitat loss and the disassembly of mutalistic networks. Oikos 122: 938-42.

Giurco, D., T. Prior, G. Mudd, L. Mason, and J. Behrisch (2010). *Peak Minerals in Australia: A Review of Changing Impacts and Benefits.* Cluster Research Report 1.2, Institute for Sustainable Futures, University of Technology, Sydney.

Hajat, S., Vardoulakis, S., Heaviside, C. and Eggen, B. (2014). Climate change effects on human health: projections of temperature-related mortality for the UK during the 2020s, 2050s and 2080s. Journal of Epidemiology and Community Health 68(7): 641-8.

Hay, M.E. and Rasher, D.B. (2010). Coral reefs in crisis: Reversing the biotic death spiral. F1000 biology reports, 2.

Heck, K.L. and Valentine, J.F. (2007). The primacy of top-down effects in shallow benthic ecosystems. Estuaries and Coasts 30: 371-81.

Heinberg, R. (2007). *Peak Everything; Waking up to the Century of Declines.* New Society Publishers, Canada.

HELCOM (2007). Climate Change in the Baltic Sea Area—HELCOM Thematic Assessment in 2007 Baltic Sea Environmental Proceedings No. 111.

Hodell, D.A., Brenner, M. and Curtis, J.H. (2005). Terminal Classic drought in the northern Maya lowlands inferred from multiple sediment cores in Lake Chichancanab (Mexico). Quaternary Science Reviews 24(12), 1413-27.

Homer-Dixon, T.F., Boutwell, J.H. and Rathjens, G.W. (1993). Environmental change and violent conflict. Scientific American, American Edition 268: 38-45.

Houghton, R.A. (2005). Tropical deforestation as a source of greenhouse gas emissions. In: Moutinho, P. and Schwartzman, S. (eds.), *Tropical Deforestation and Climate Change.* IPAM, Washington DC. pp. 13-22.

Hubbert, M.K. (1956). Nuclear energy and the fossil fuels (Vol. 95). Houston, TX: Shell Development Company, Exploration and Production Research Division.

ILEC/Lake Biwa Research Institute (eds.), *1988–1993 Survey of the State of the World's Lakes.* Volumes I–IV. International Lake Environment Committee, Otsu and United Nations Environment Programme, Nairobi.

IPCC (2007). Summary for policymakers. In: Climate Change 2007: Impacts, Adaptation and Vulnerability. Contribution of Working Group II to the Fourth Assessment Report of the Intergovernmental Panel on Climate Change, pp. 7-22. Cambridge University Press: Cambridge.

IPCC (2014). Climate Change 2014. Synthesis Report. http://www.ipcc.ch/report/ar5/syr/.

Janzen, D.H. (1974) The deflowering of Central America. Natural History 83: 48-53.

Jasinski, S.M. (2006). *Phosphate Rock, Statistics and Information.* US Geological Survey.

Jones, J. and Brett, M.T. (2014). Lake nutrients, eutrophication, and climate change. In: Freedman, B. (ed.), *Global Environmental Change.* Springer, Netherlands. pp. 273-9.

Joralemon, I.B. (1924). Copper and electricity to vanish in twenty years? Engineering and Mining Journal-Press 118(4): 122.

Kellie-Smith, O. and Cox, P.M. (2011). Emergent dynamics of the climate–economy system in the Anthropocene. Philosophical Transactions of the Royal Society A: Mathematical, Physical and Engineering Sciences 369(1938): 868-86.

Kushnir, D. and Sanden, B.A. (2012). The time dimension and lithium resource constraints for electric vehicles. Resources Policy 37(1): 93-103.

Lee, H.F. and Zhang, D.D. (2013). A tale of two population crises in recent Chinese history. Climatic Change 116(2): 285-308.

Lindkvist, M., Gren, M. and Elofsson, K. (2013). A study of climate change and cost effective mitigation of the Baltic Sea eutrophication. In: Singh, B.R. (ed.), *Climate Change—Realities, Impacts over Ice Cap, Sea Level and Risks.* InTech, Croatia. pp. 459-80.

Little, P.E. (1995). Ritual, power and ethnography at the Rio Earth Summit.Critique of Anthropology 15(3): 265-88.

Løvik, J.E. (2009). Operational monitoring of Lake Mjøsa and tributaries (in Norwegian). Annual report for 2008. NIVA report 5758.

Maggio, G. and Cacciola, G. (2012). When will oil, natural gas, and coal peak? Fuel 98: 111-23.

Makarieva, A.M. Gorshkov, V.G. and Li, B.L. (2006). Conservation of water cycle on land via restoration of natural closed-canopy forests: implications for regional landscape planning. Ecological Research 21(6). 897-906.

Marotzke, J. (2000). Abrupt climate change and thermohaline circulation: Mechanisms and predictability. Proceedings of the National Academy of Sciences 97(4): 1347-50.

McGinn, A.P. and Peterson, J.A. (1999). *Safeguarding the Health of Oceans.* Worldwatch Institute.

McGuire, V.L. (2007). Ground Water Depletion in the High Plains Aquifer; Fact Sheet 2007-3029; US Geological Survey: Reston, VA.

McGuire, B. (2010). Climate forcing of geological and geomorphological hazards. Philosophical Transactions of the Royal Society A: Mathematical, Physical and Engineering Sciences 368(1919): 2311-15.

McLeod, E., Chmura, G.L., Bouillon, S., Salm, R., Björk, M., Duarte, C.M., Lovelock, C.E., Schlesinger, W.H. and Silliman, B.R. (2011). A blueprint for blue carbon: toward an improved understanding of the role of vegetated coastal habitats in sequestering CO_2. Frontiers in Ecology and the Environment 9: 552-60.

Meadows, D.H. Club of Rome (1972). *The Limits to Growth; a Report for the Club of Rome's Project on the Predicament of Mankind.* Earth Island, London.

Meadows, D.H., Meadows, D.L. and Randers, J. (1992). *Beyond the Limits.* Chelsea Green Publishing, Post Mills, VT.

Mudd, G.M. (2007). Gold mining in Australia: linking historical trends and environmental and resources sustainability. Environmental Science and Policy 10: 629-44.

Mudd, G.M. (2009). The sustainability of mining in Australia: key production trends and their environmental implications for the future. Research Report No RR5.

Mudd, G.M. (2010). The environmental sustainability of mining in Australia: key mega-trends and looming constraints. Resources Policy 35: 98-115.

Myers, N. (2002). Environmental refugees: a growing phenomenon of the 21st century. Philosophical Transactions of the Royal Society of London. Series B: Biological Sciences 357(1420): 609-13.

Nordhaus W. (2008). *A Question of Balance: Weighing the Options on Global Warming Policies.* Yale University Press, New Haven, CT.

Nordhaus, W.D. and Tobin, J. (1972). Is growth obsolete?. In Economic Research: Retrospect and Prospect Vol 5: Economic Growth (pp. 1-80).

Obama, B. (2009). Remarks by the President on Jobs, Energy Independence, and Climate Change. 26 January 2009. http://www.whitehouse.gov/blog/2009/01 (accessed 2 December 2011).

OECD (2008). Uranium Resources 2003: Resources, Production and Demand. OECD World Nuclear Agency and International Atomic Energy Agency. 2008-03. p. 29.

Paine, R.T., Tegner, M.J. and Johnson, E.A. (1998). Compounded perturbations yield ecological surprises. Ecosystems 1(6): 535-45.

Palmer, G. (1992). Earth Summit: What Went Wrong at Rio. Wash. ULQ, 70, 1005.

Pendleton, L. and 14 other authors (2012). Estimating global "blue carbon" emissions from conversion and degradation of vegetated coastal ecosystems. PLoS ONE, 7(9), e43542.

Percival, V. and Homer-Dixon, T. (1995). *Environmental Scarcity and Violent Conflict: The Case of South Africa.* Population and Sustainable Development Project, American Association for the Advancement of Science & University of Toronto.

Pimentel, D. (2006). Soil erosion: a food and environmental threat. Environment, Development and Sustainability 8: 119-37.

Plato (1961). *The Collected Dialogues of Plato* (Ed. by Hamilton, E. and Cairns, H.). New York: Penguin.

Pretty, J.N., Mason, C.F., Nedwell, D.B., Hine, R.E., Leaf, S. and Dils, R. (2003). Environmental costs of freshwater eutrophication in England and Wales. Environmental Science & Technology 37(2): 201-208.

Prior, T., Giurco, D., Mudd, G., Mason, L. and Behrisch, J. (2012). Resource depletion, peak minerals and the implications for sustainable resource management. Global Environmental Change 22(3): 577-87.

Rabalais, N.N. (2004). Eutrophication. In: Robinson, A.R., McCarthy, J. and Rothschild, B.J. (eds.), Vol. 13 of *The Sea.* Harvard University Press, Cambridge, MA. pp. 819-965.

Ramirez, M. and Butts, K. (2011). Climate Change, Adaptation and Security in Central America and the Caribbean (CSL Issue Paper, Volume 3-11). Army War College Carlisle Barracks PA Center For Strategic Leadership.

Reck, B.K. and Graedel, T.E. (2012). Challenges in metal recycling. Science 337(6095): 690-5.

Reller, A. (2011). Criticality of metal resources for functional materials used in electronics and microelectronics. Physica Status Solidi (RRL)-Rapid Research Letters 5(9): 309-11.

Repetto, R. (2008). The climate crisis and the adaptation myth. Working paper 13.Yale School of Forestry and Environmental Studies, New Haven, Connecticut.

Rosenzweig, C., Elliott, J., Deryng, D., Ruane, A.C., Müller, C., Arneth, A., Boote, K.J., Folberth, C., Glotter, M., Khabarov, N., Neumann, K., Piontek, F., Pugh, T.A.M., Schmid, E., Stehfest, E., Yang, H. and Jones, J.W. (2014). Assessing agricultural risks of climate change in the 21st century in a global gridded crop model intercomparison. Proceedings of the National Academy of Sciences 111(9): 3268-73.

Rosmarin, A. (2004). The Precarious Geopolitics of Phosphorous, Down to Earth: Science and Environment Fortnightly, 2004, pp. 27-31.

Royal Society (2007). Climate change controversies: a simple guide. http://royalsociety.org/policy/publications/2007/climate-change-controversies/

Screen, J.A., Simmonds, I., Deser, C. and Tomas, R. (2013). The atmospheric response to three decades of observed Arctic sea ice loss. Journal of Climate 26(4): 1230-48.

Sepúlveda, A., Schluep, M., Renaud, F.G., Streicher, M., Kuehr, R. Hagelüken, C. and Gerecke, A.C. (2010). A review of the environmental fate and effects of hazardous substances released from electrical and electronic equipment during recycling: Examples from China and India. Environmental Impact Assessment Review 30(1): 28-41.

Shearman, P., Bryan, J. and Laurence, W.F. (2012). Are we approaching "peak timber" in the tropics? Biological Conservation 151: 17-21.

Singh, S.K. (2014). *Viral Infections and Global Change.* Wiley-Blackwell, London.

Smith, J.L. (2012). On the portents of peak oil (and other indicators of resource scarcity). Energy Policy 44: 68-78.

Solarz, A. (2012). *Global Climate and the Security of the European Union.* Army War College Carlisle Barracks, PA. http://www.dtic.mil/cgi-bin/GetTRDoc?AD=ADA561896

Solomon, S., Plattner, G.-K., Knutti, R. and Friedlingstein, P. (2009). Irreversible climate change due to carbon dioxide emissions. Proceedings of the National Academy of Sciences of the United States 106: 1704-709.

Steen, I. (1998). Phosphorus availability in the 21st Century: management of a nonrenewable resource. Phosphorus and Potassium 217: 25-31.

Stern, N. (2006). *Stern Review on the Economics of Climate Change.* Government Economic Service, London.

Stern, N. (2009). *A Blueprint for a Safer Planet: How we can Save the World and Create Prosperity.* The Bodley Head, London.

Stern, N., Peters, S., Bakhshi, V., Bowen, A., Cameron, C., Catovsky, S., Crane, D., Cruickshank, S., Dietz, S., Edmonson, N., Garbett, S-L., Hamid, L., Hoffman, G., Ingram, D., Jones, B., Patmore, N., Radcliffe, H., Sathiyarajah, R., Stock, M., Taylor, C., Vernon, T., Wanjie, H., Zenghelis, D. (2006). *The Economics of Climate Change: the Stern Review.* Cambridge University Press, Cambridge.

Tol, R.S. (2005). The marginal damage costs of carbon dioxide emissions: an assessment of the uncertainties. Energy policy 33(16): 2064-74.

Tol, R.S. (2010). The costs and benefits of EU climate policy for 2020. Copenhagen Consensus Center.

Vereecken, W., Van Heddeghem, W., Colle, D., Pickavet, M. and Demeester, P. (2010). Overall ICT footprint and green communication technologies. In *Communications, Control and Signal Processing* (ISCCSP), 2010 4th International Symposium on (pp. 1-6). IEEE.

WBGU (2007) World in transition: climate change as a security risk. German Advisory Council on Global Change, Earthscan.

Weiss, H. and Bradley, R.S. (2001). What drives societal collapse? Science 291: 609-10.

White, S. and Cordell, D. (2009). Peak phosphorus: the sequel to peak oil. The Global Phosphorus Research Initiative. Online at: http://phosphorusfutures.net

Williamson, H.F. (1945). Natural resources and international policy: prophecies of scarcity or exhaustion of natural resources in the United States. American Economic Review (May, 1945): 97-109.

3
Water, energy and the green paradox

It is an irony that on a planet whose surface area is 73% water, we face a significant threat to water security. Water is essential for all life, and central to many important business sectors including the food and beverage industry, which accounts for over 70% of global water consumption. We examine the significance of water security, both in terms of space and time, exploring the impacts of industrial processes both directly (for example through over-use, pollution or salinization) and indirectly (for example through climate destabilization, deforestation or drainage). The concept of a water footprint is discussed, along with the challenges and opportunities of water import and export. Virtual water flow and trade are explored. Energy is central to all of our activities, in terms of food, power, temperature and pollution. We examine the flow of energy on our planet, before examining the relationship between economic growth and energy. The economics of energy will be analysed with reference to capital market implications, and carbon trading initiatives will be examined to develop an understanding of policy in this area. Finally we discuss issues arising from attempts at legislating for sustainable practice, including the green paradox, carbon leakage, the rebound effect and the porter hypothesis. A bridge case focuses on Caterpillar. The Environmental Kuznets Curve is highlighted in the Discourse section.

Learning aims and objectives

- Define the terms **virtual water**, **water footprint** and **groundwater footprint**
- What do we mean by green, blue and grey water footprints?
- Distinguish between direct and indirect water footprints
- What is meant by hard and soft paths to resource security?
- Define what we mean by **opportunity costs** of a resource?
- Give examples of issues relating to carbon trading
- Define what we mean by an Environmental Kuznets Curve (EKC)

Learning outcomes and experiences

- What are the implications of water insecurity for the planet?
- Discuss the trends, flows and changes in virtual water; comment on the geographical significance and the implications of climate destabilization for virtual water
- Discuss the implications of the water footprint of different energy generating technologies in terms of sustainable energy production within a destabilized atmosphere
- Discuss the positive and negative aspects of personal carbon trading
- Discuss the relationship between energy and economic growth
- Discuss why energy security has become a significant foreign policy driver?
- Discuss the validity of the Environmental Kuznets Curve (EKC)

3.1 Water: the perfect storm

Perhaps no resource integrates the damage on the biosphere like water. Water is the great meeting point of chemistry, where things dissolve and enter food chains. Water therefore conveys the havoc wrecked by our activities on the environment and ourselves. Melted glaciers raise the sea levels, encroaching on the land; carbon dioxide dissolves in water to produce ocean acidification; our fertilizers flow down the streams into the lakes and coastal waters to rob the aquatic life of oxygen; the salt from excessive irrigation poisons the soil; toxic mine tailings enter our rivers; ballast water introduces invasive species from the other side of the planet, decimating local ecosystems; greenhouse gases destabilize the climate, producing the two-edged sword of drought and flood, killing our crops and eroding our soil in turn; dirty water delivers disease to the disaster zones and the refugee camps, where humans are at their lowest ebb anyhow.

Water truly is the conveyor of bad news. It is also essential for our survival. As the universal solvent, it is the solution space for biochemistry. It acts as a temperature regulator, preventing sudden rises in our internal temperatures. It cushions our organs from damage and dilutes our toxic nitrogenous waste as urine. In many organisms it provides the mechanical support as a hydroskeleton. Humans are particularly vulnerable to dehydration, with symptoms becoming apparent when just 2% of our water is lost, with losses above 15% being fatal in most cases.

Water is essential for agriculture. Indeed some of the earliest evidence of farming is represented by the appearance of irrigation ditches in Sumeria and Babylon (Tamburrino, 2010). Today, crop irrigation leads to a build-up of salts, destroying the soil, while drought and flood are equally disastrous.

Deforestation has the potential to greatly disrupt water supply to the plains of Brazil. Water evaporating from tree leaves in the Amazon forest forms the main source of water for rainfall on the Brazil Plains. Removal of the forest means that water is not evaporated, and instead flows out to sea, threatening the Cerrado with extreme drought.

3.1.1 Water security

Civil war, increasing population, deforestation, increasing agricultural pressures and climate destabilization all play a role. In Tanzania the disappearance of the Kilimanjaro glacier will have a significant impact, as will reduced glacial melt for Peru. Many countries will fall below the acceptable minimum levels of water during the next decade. We are draining aquifers of water at a rate higher than their rate of replenishment.

Already, the withdrawal of fresh water in quantities and at rates exceeding natural renewal capacities is documented in many parts of the world including China, India, Mexico, the Middle East, the Mediterranean region, Central Asia, Australia, southern Africa and the USA (UNESCO-WWAP, 2006). The Aral Sea, formerly the fourth largest lake in the world has dried up, due to its feeder rivers being diverted for agriculture (Fig. 3.1). Its disappearance has

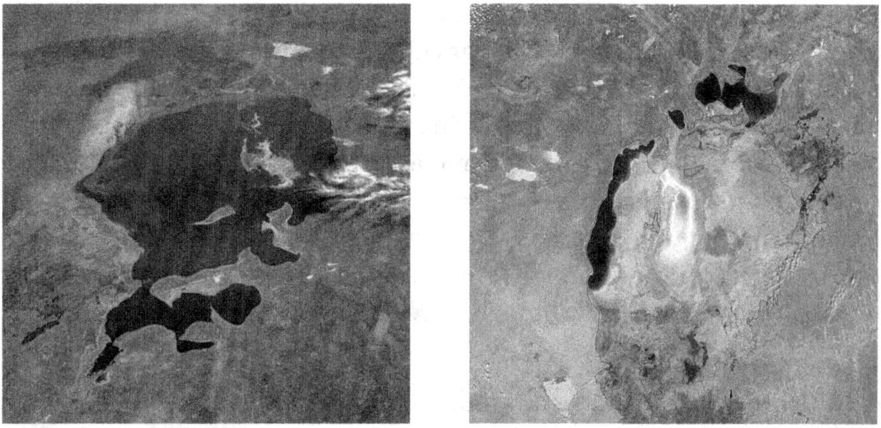

FIGURE 3.1 Differences in the Aral Sea from 1985 to 2009. Due to diversion of water for agriculture, this formerly vast lake has all but disappeared.

Source: NASA Earth Observatory

had wide-ranging impacts, from the collapse of fishing industry to regional climate destabilization.

Meanwhile glacial melt in the Himalayas threatens water flow in the Indus, Ganges, Brahmaputra, Irrawaddy, Mekong, Yangtze, and Yellow rivers, all of which have their sources in the Himalayan range. It is estimated that, by the year 2100, there will be a 30% decline in the Indus, the most important river in Pakistan.

Bogardi *et al.* (2012) observe that our methods of securing human water resources almost always threaten biodiversity, and therefore threaten ecosystem services still further. Indeed we are now in competition for water with nature. Leakage from municipal supply pipes leads to huge loses of drinking water before it even reaches us, akin to the waste of phosphate in agriculture.

Water issues play a central role in any discussion of economic development (UNDP, 2006). The economy is already being impacted by water security issues (including physical scarcity risks, reputational risks and regulatory risks) and a range of recent reports on this issue point to a worsening situation ahead (JPMorgan and Global Equity Research, 2008; Pegram, 2010; SABMiller *et al.*, 2010; WRI, 2011). Gleick and Heberger (2014) trace the history of water conflict over the past 4,500 years.

Vörösmarty *et al.* (2010) found that nearly 80% of the world's population is exposed to high levels of threat to water security. 2.4 billion people (more than the Earth's population in 1940) lack sanitation services equivalent to that experienced in the Roman Empire (Gleick, 2002). Greatest vulnerability comes from areas of high agricultural intensity and dense populations. Expensive investment in water technology enables rich nations to offset water stress without addressing their underlying causes, whereas less wealthy nations remain vulnerable. Habitats associated with 65% of continental discharge are classified as moderately to highly threatened. Drylands become deserts, for example in Argentina, Sahel, Central Asia and the Australian Murray–Darling basin. Elliott *et al.* (2014) estimate a loss of 8–24% in maize, soybean, wheat and rice by 2070 due to irrigation issues.

3.1.2 Virtual water: flow and trade

As a means of measuring the cost of a product in terms of water usage, the concept of virtual water was developed (Allan, 1998). Virtual water is defined as water used in the production of imported goods. The flow of virtual water across the globe began to be mapped, and businesses and nations could be given a water footprint, relating to their water consumption. While some complain that the only water actually traded is the water contained within the product (Iyer, 2012), the point being made here is that water being used in the production of an exported product cannot be used for something else, and therefore should be evaluated as being part of the export cost to a given nation. After all, there would be no apples if there was no irrigation for the tree.

Asia increased its virtual water imports by more than 170%, switching from North America to South America as its main partner, whereas North America oriented to a growing intraregional trade. A dramatic rise in China's virtual water imports is associated with its increased soy imports after a domestic policy shift in 2000. Significantly, this shift has led the global soy market to save water on a global scale, but it also relies on expanding soy production in Brazil, which contributes to deforestation in the Amazon (Dalin *et al.*, 2012). In 2010 Italy had an average net import of 55 km^3 of virtual water (38 km^3 in 1986), a value which places the country among the top net importers in the world. On average each cubic metre of virtual water travels nearly 4,000 km before entering Italy, while export goes to relatively closer countries (average distance: 2,600 km) (Tamea *et al.*, 2012).

Globally, 2,600 km^3 of water are withdrawn each year to irrigate crops, representing over two-thirds of all human withdrawals (FAO, 2004). Strzepek and Boehlert (2010) found that given urban population increase, climate destabilization and economic growth, there will be an 18% reduction in the availability of worldwide water for agriculture by 2050, leading to increasing competition between food supply and other business sectors.

Nations with insufficient water resources to sustain adequate food production are increasingly importing food, leading to virtual water transfer from countries with more water. Thus virtual water allows for an artificially high carrying capacity for human populations in some areas, placing increasing stress on other ecosystem services. The dependence on virtual water trade also leaves countries extremely vulnerable to security issues, relating to politics and war, while undermining their sovereignty and freedom (Suweis *et al.*, 2013; Clark, 2014).

3.1.3 Water footprint (WF)

Following on from the carbon footprint, which became a popular way to envisage the contribution of an individual, business or nation to the greenhouse gas issue, the **water footprint** has become a less populist but increasingly utilized concept, attempting to measure our use and abuse of water. According to Hoekstra *et al.* (2011), the water footprint of a product is an empirical indicator of how much water is consumed, when and where, measured over the whole supply chain of the product. The water footprint of an individual, community or business is defined as the total volume of fresh water that is used to produce the goods and services consumed by the individual or community or produced by the business. For details on how the water footprint is calculated, see the Water Footprint Assessment Manual at www.waterfootprint.org.

Water footprints (WFs) are divided into green WF (rainwater), blue WF (lake, river or ocean water) and grey WF (water used to dilute pollutants). A further division is made between direct (or operational) WF, which is water used by the company itself, and the indirect (or supply chain) WF which is water used by suppliers of that company.

Like all footprints, the water footprint has its weaknesses. Some countries have more renewable water resources than others, and urbanization, recycling and ecological footprints related to products may differ vastly. For example if a country uses more water to produce one apple than another country, but does less damage in other ways, then the overall ecological footprint of that apple may be smaller.

Calculations can also become very cumbersome, and may require a company to share the responsibility of indirect footprints with its suppliers, over whom it has little or no control. However, this internalizing of indirect costs

Product	Quantity	Water footprint (litres per quantity)
Beef	1 kg	15,400 litres per kg
Pork	1 kg	6,000 litres per kg
Apple	1	125 litres per apple
Apple juice	1 litre	1,140 litres water per litre apple juice
Banana	1	160 litres per banana
Orange	1	80 litres per orange
Pizza margherita	1	1,260 litres per pizza
Pasta	1 kg	1,850 litres per kg
Olives	1 kg	3,020 litres per kg
Egg	1	200 litres per egg
Cotton T-shirt	1	2,500 litres per T-shirt
Pair of jeans	1	2,500 litres per pair
Coffee	1 cup	130 litres per cup
Tea	1 cup	30 litres per cup
Chocolate bar	100 g	1,700 litres per 100 g
Cheese	1 kg	5,060 litres per kg
Wine	1 bottle	650 litres per bottle
Beer	0.5 litre	148 litres per 0.5 litre beer

TABLE 3.1 Water footprints of a range of commonly used products

Source: Mekonnen and Hoekstra, 2010; 2011; 2012

sets a useful precedent compared with the usual practice of externalizing responsibility for environmental damage. It also enlightens customers as to the consequences of their economic transactions, and the costs, in natural resources of things they take for granted. Table 3.1 shows the total water footprints of a range of common products. The reaction of many people to this is one of surprise and shock. Most of this water is degraded by the processes used.

Hoekstra and Mekonnen (2012) have calculated that the global annual average WF in the period 1996–2005 was 9,087 Gm^3/y (74% green, 11% blue, 15% grey), of which agricultural production contributes 92%. About one-fifth of the global WF relates to production for export (i.e. virtual water trade). The total volume of international virtual water flows related to trade in agricultural and industrial products combined was 2,320 Gm^3/y (68% green, 13% blue, 19% grey). The WF of the global average consumer was 1,385 m^3/y. The average consumer in the United States has a WF of

Box 3.1

Chapagain and Tickner (2012) suggested four areas of concern relating to WFs:

1. Is it possible to develop robust WF accounting standards?
2. How useful and responsible is it to use results from a WF analysis as a communications tool to facilitate conversations with different audiences about water issues?
3. What are the benefits and dangers of using WF as a business-risk assessment tool?
4. What case is there for shifts in public policy in light of WF analyses?

2,842 m^3/y, whereas the average citizens in China and India have WFs of 1,071 and 1,089 m^3/y, respectively. Consumption of cereal products gives the largest contribution to the WF of the average consumer (27%), followed by meat (22%) and milk products (7%). An example of the use of WF in business is given in the Minicase, below.

3.1.4 Groundwater footprint

While the water footprint gives a volumetric assessment of water use, it does not reflect differences in water availability. For example two countries with equal water footprints may have very different quantities of water available, but the simple figure representing a water footprint gives no indication of this. One way to improve the information value is the **groundwater footprint**. Groundwater is a primary source of drinking water for as many as 2 billion people and it plays a central role in irrigated agriculture and ecosystem health (Gleeson *et al.*, 2012a). The depletion and contamination of groundwater are widespread in both developing and developed nations, creating significant socioeconomic impact (Shah, 2007).

The groundwater footprint (GF) is the land area required to supply sufficient rainwater to underground aquifers in order to replace use of this water, divided by the area of the aquifer. The higher the value, the greater the area needed. Globally, 131 billion km^2 is required to offset groundwater use, which is 3.5 times more area than is available. Thus we are unsustainably using groundwater. This figure rises to >20 for High Plains (USA), north Arabian, Upper Ganges and western Mexican aquifers, indicating that these areas are at high risk of draining aquifers completely, with devastating consequences (Gleeson *et al.*, 2012b). The Ogallala Aquifer (responsible for 30%

Minicase: Use of WF in addressing issues: use of direct versus indirect WF to identify areas of risk to company

The experience of SABMiller with water footprint analyses shows how this approach can greatly assist operational managers within a company to identify the sources of water risks created by the manufacture of a given product. Sometimes a significant proportion of the water risks to the business lie beyond the factory fence. In the case of SAB Ltd. (the company's South African subsidiary) a water footprint analysis of beer production showed that 98.3% of the total water footprint related to crop growth by external suppliers in the Gouritz Water Management Area (SABMiller and WWF, 2009). This new understanding led SAB Ltd. to enter into new stakeholder partnerships aimed at addressing water scarcity issues that threatened to impact on the company's hop supply chain as well as to other water users and to freshwater ecosystems (Chapagain and Tickner, 2012).

of the irrigation water used by the US) is being emptied at record rates, with an average drawdown of 4 m across the eight states it underlies, and water levels have dropped by over 40 m in some areas.

Galli *et al.* (2012) set out the footprint family (ecological, carbon and water) as a means of monitoring the demands we place on the environment at the levels of biosphere, atmosphere and hydrosphere, respectively.

3.1.5 Soft and hard paths

There are two approaches to tackling any resource issue: the soft, demand-oriented path and the hard supply-oriented path. In terms of water, the soft water path aims to reduce use and waste, and decentralizes supply, whereas the hard water path focuses on a centralized approach, building dams and drilling deeper boreholes. Central to either approach is agriculture, which accounts for two thirds of water use. Precision irrigation, soil moisture monitoring and laser levelling of fields have the potential to double productivity per unit of water (Gleick, 2002). Municipal supply leakage is another area of concern, with up to 30% of water entering supply pipelines lost through leaks (Renzetti and Dupont, 2013). The soft water path pursues **backcasting**, asking: "What actions must be taken to achieve a certain groundwater sustainability goal?" Conversely, the hard water path utilizes **forecasting**, predicting the future needs based on current trend analysis. The true value of water may be calculated by using the concept of **opportunity cost**. This evaluates how much value could be derived from water used in one application, if it was instead used in another one. In Australia's Murray Darling Basin, farmers pay US$0.01 per cubic metre of water, while opportunity cost is US$23 (Briscoe, 2009). This would indicate that these farmers are paying far too little for the water.

3.1.6 The water footprint of energy supply

A final sector in which water consumption is often ignored is the energy sector. Focus has been solely on the carbon footprint of energy production, rather than the associated water footprint. In the United States, the Energy Independence and Security Act of 2007 (EISA) ordered the annual production of 56.8 billion L of ethanol from corn by 2015 and an additional 60.6 billion L (16 BGY) of biofuels from cellulosic crops by 2022. This represents 15% of the petroleum used in the USA in 2006 on an energy basis (USDE, 2008). The corn used to supply this quantity is equivalent to 44% of the 2007 US total corn production.

However, more concerning is the vast amount of water needed for this energy production. Table 3.2 shows the water requirements for a range of energy production methods. As can clearly be seen, green fuels such as ethanol use large amounts of water compared with other fuels. Given the already threatened water supplies, this could pose a significant threat to water security and demands re-evaluation in terms of sustainability. Hydraulic power has an additional issue: methane production. When large dams are built the flooded vegetation releases large amounts of methane, a powerful greenhouse gas.

Process	**Litres of water per MWh**
Geothermal	20
Petroleum extraction	40
Oil refining	80–150
Oil shale surface retort	680
Nuclear power plant, closed-loop cooling	950
Nuclear power plant, open-loop cooling	94,600–227,100
Corn ethanol	2,270,000–8,670,000
Soybean biodiesel	13,900,000–27,900,000

TABLE 3.2 Water requirements for energy production by different processes

Source: Dominguez-Faus *et al.*, 2009

3.2 The centrality of energy

3.2.1 The centrality of energy

All life relies on energy for its existence. In fact life is defined as the ability to stay far from thermodynamic equilibrium, which requires the continual through-flow of energy. And for almost all of life (with the exception of hydrothermal vent communities, endoliths and sealed underground lakes), this energy comes from the sun. Light energy is converted into chemical energy (sugar) in plants and algae, which are eaten by herbivores, which in turn are eaten by carnivores. All of these forms of life die, and are eaten by recyclers such as fungi and bacteria. If the light is switched off, as has happened in the past following a comet impact or a huge volcanic eruption, producing dust that envelopes the Earth, blocking the light, then life dies on a massive scale. Just ask the dinosaurs. Energy is also required for warmth. Life dies if it gets too cold. 20,000 years ago, there was nothing living in Scotland, because it was covered in 2 km of ice. Population size is limited by available energy and energy flow lies at the heart of ecosystem function.

The history of humans is tightly linked to the history of our use of energy. Figure 3.2 is a time-line of the sources of energy that we have used through time. We began, like almost all other animals, dependent on solar energy in the form of sugar, and the warmth of the sun. With the discovery of fire, we started burning wood very early in our existence. Around 5000BC, the first sailing boats powered by wind energy emerged, radically transforming transport and fishing. Windmills appeared around AD100. Wind results from heat energy from the sun. By 1000BC, coal was exploited in China, and oil was known to be used as fuel in Ancient Persia around 450BC. Both of these fuels come from plants, built with energy from the sun. In the 1700s, biofuels were discovered, again from plants, and the first engine to run on alcohol was developed in 1826. It was not until 1838 that the first experimental photovoltaic cell was produced. Fully fledged solar panels would not arrive until 1954. These now power many of the satellites so central to the Information Age.

A second strand of energy production appeared in Greece around 300BC, when the waterwheel first appeared. Water has become an important energy source ever since. By 1698, Thomas Savery had developed the first commercial steam engine, combining water and coal to produce a pump. Hydropower turbines were developed in 1848, and in 1878, the first hydroelectric power plant was built. Today, 85% of the electricity needs of Norway, Brazil, Paraguay and the Republic of Congo are met by hydropower.

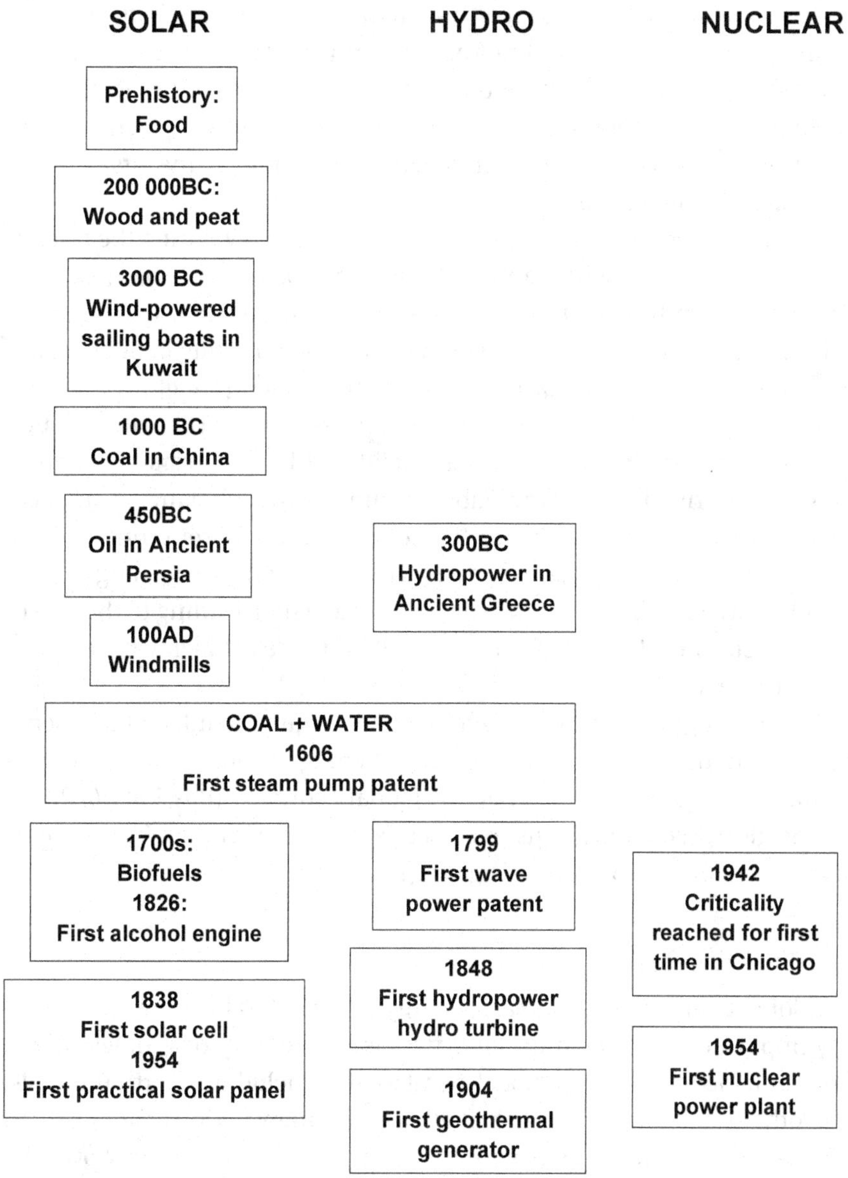

FIGURE 3.2 Energy sources over human history. Humans acquire energy from three sources: the sun, water and nuclear. Key events in energy acquisition through time (not to scale). The sun itself is a giant nuclear fusion reactor.

In 1799, the first patent was taken out on wave power technology, although the first operational units did not appear until 1910. The first geothermal power station opened in 1904. A quarter of the energy needs of Iceland are now met from geothermal power. The most recent form of energy source is nuclear power. Developed from weapons technology, the first nuclear power plant opened in 1954.

The massive increase in energy consumption globally during the last 200 years has led to a huge human population increase. This is because agriculture has been liberated from the constraints of nutrient deficiency by the Haber-Bosch fixation of nitrogen, where huge amounts of energy convert nitrogen gas into fertilizer. Pesticides, herbicides, ploughing and harvesting equipment also require large amounts of energy. The amplification of energy through-flow in our fields, facilitated by fertilizers, has spread beyond our farms into natural habitats, drastically unbalancing the ecosystem energetics, and leading to the collapse of ecosystem function and service. Meanwhile the greenhouse gases released from the burning of fossil fuels play havoc with the energy balance of the planet, leading to the greenhouse effect, where heat is reflected back to Earth, destabilizing the climate, as we have seen earlier.

The other huge change that has happened to humankind, and that separates us from other life forms, is our use of energy in economics. Energy is the foundation of every aspect of our global economy (Bassi *et al.*, 2010). And the global economy consumes vast amounts of energy. Thus energy security is essential for economic growth.

3.2.2 Energy security

As national energy needs increase, energy security has become an increasingly important political and military issue. The lottery of geology, where some countries sit on top of vast mineral wealth, including energy minerals, while others sit on nothing much at all, has led many nations to depend on other nations for their energy supplies. The suppliers have power over the countries that they supply.

Energy security can indeed require military defence, and the opposite is also true. Military superiority requires energy security. The need for secure oil supplies was a motivating factor in Japan's decision to bomb Pearl Harbour and in Germany's decision to invade Russia (Becker, 1981). Germany began the war with an oil production capacity of 9 million barrels per year. By 1943 capacity had been increased to 36 million barrels per year and met the majority of country's demand. However, the facilities proved highly vulnerable to Allied bombing in May 1944, when 90% of the capacity was destroyed. Germany never recovered (Becker, 1981).

When oil shortages led to a tripling of crude oil prices in 1973, most developed countries experienced accelerating inflation, falling economic output and rising unemployment. This led to a new focus on energy security. On 1 January 2006 Russia temporarily cut of the gas supply to Ukraine, and in January 2009, much of western Europe had supplies cut by Russia. This caused considerable unease, and forced countries to once again re-evaluate their energy acquisition security, in an attempt to be less dependent on Russian gas. Other areas of conflict, particularly the Middle East, have impacted on oil supply over many years. The invasion of Kuwait by Iraq sent shock waves across the energy world in August 1990. In this case, one country attempted to take another county's natural resources by military means.

The discovery of significant oil fields in Southern Sudan fuelled the dispute between Animist and Christian rebels in the south and the Muslim government in the north. The oil fields were not only a provocation for the conflict; they ultimately provided the funding for genocide in Darfur (which is also linked to rebel activities following oil discoveries in neighbouring Chad) (Patey, 2010). Indeed, as Simon Dalby observed, the "resource curse" literature "has turned the environmental-scarcity-leading-to-conflict argument on its head suggesting that the connection between resources and violence in the south is a matter of fights over control of resources that are in abundance rather than over ones that are scarce" (Dalby 2002; p. 74).

Policy-makers have tended to equate energy security with energy independence. This can lead to increasing environmental damage, as the pursuit of energy minerals at any cost is justified by the importance of national security. Hydraulic fracturing and the exploitation of oil sands all pose significant concerns, particularly relating to water resources. Other options such as diversifying suppliers and encouraging energy efficiency and substitution are then ignored.

Biofuels and bio-energy pose their own significant problems, in terms of competing with food crops for space, consuming huge amounts of water and costing more energy to produce than they release on combustion. Vast areas of primary rainforest are being removed to make room for the green fuel crops. Furthermore, the plants involved need huge amounts of energy-expensive fertilizers, and are therefore dependent on the energy economy in the first place. Meanwhile palm diesel production is raising emissions by devastating peat forests in Indonesia and Malaysia, along with their animal, plant and human inhabitants (Knudson, 2009). Karp and Richter (2011) suggest that using high input crops as a fuel resource needs to be phased out, instead utilizing crop residues and low input perennial species. The problem with these ideas is that those residues are already often used for other purposes.

The raw fact is that over 80% of the energy used by humans comes from fossil fuels. Oil alone accounts for some 34% of primary energy consumption. Peak oil, as mentioned above, is a characteristic of all oil fields. Peaks have been witnessed in up to 54 of the world's 65 largest oil producing states (Aleklett, 2005). With issues related to all other options, in terms of limited supplies of energy elements needed for things such as batteries and wind turbines, pollution concerns relating to rare earth metals, and huge drawdown of scarce water resources associated with many green fuels, there are serious concerns over energy security.

Furthermore, the threats do not only come from decreasing sources. In fact sinks are posing at least as much concern. As early as 1990, Ronnie Lipschutz and John Holdren wrote:

> It is becoming increasingly likely that the most intractable problems—and the greatest threats to international stability—could come not from the economics or politics of supply but from large-scale environmental and social side effects of energy sources—such as climate change by carbon dioxide from fossil fuels, or the spread of nuclear bomb materials by nuclear energy technology (Lipschutz and Holdren 1990; p. 126).

As with all resource use issues, it is not the increase in population that poses the greatest threat to any concept of a sustainable energetic future. Between 1966 and 2006, the human population has doubled whereas energy consumption has trebled. Much of this energy has not been spent on food, the major contributor to carrying capacity, but on luxury expenditure (i.e. non-essential for our survival). As developing nations expand industrial output, and as standards of living increase, energy use per person in these areas will greatly increase. With 42% of the world's population living in a BRIC state (Brazil, Russia, India and China; World Bank, 2010), if the BRIC countries consumed as much energy as the OECD countries on a per capita basis, holding all else constant, global energy demand would grow by 90%. The latest report from the US Energy Information Administration (EIA, 2010) predicts that between 2010 and 2040, global energy use will increase by 56% (90% in non-OECD countries, 17% in OECD countries).

3.2.3 Energy and economic growth

As energy minerals become less abundant, the efforts to access more difficult sources will increase. This has already been seen in the increase in deep drilling and in hydraulic fracturing. To cover these more expensive, less efficient extraction processes, we create an economic growth paradox: increasing the oil supply to support economic growth will require high oil prices that will undermine that economic growth. Some commentators conclude from this that the economic growth of the past 40 years is unlikely to continue in the long term unless there is some remarkable change in how we manage our economy (e.g. Murphy and Hall, 2011).

All economic processes must require energy and since neither energy nor matter is reproducible they must be captured from the environment with implied environmental disruption. Thus natural capital is degraded. Given that ecosystems work under very carefully balanced energy budgets, energy can be viewed as the most significant pollutant in the world. Excess energy flow has the capacity to destroy ecosystem structure and function in much the same way as insufficient energy flow has been the underlying cause of most of the mass extinctions on our planet to date. Indeed, the current mass extinction of natural capital is unique in the history of our planet, in that it is caused by the insatiable thirst for agricultural and industrial output, fed by excessive energy flow, rather than by insufficient energy flow (Skene, 2011).

In spite of these facts, core mainstream growth models do not include resources or energy (Aghion and Howitt, 2009). Adding nonrenewable natural resources that are essential in production to the basic mainstream growth models brings with it the requirement to substitute lost natural capital with human-made capital. While some argue that technological advance (intelligence capital) could offset natural capital lost, this argument becomes less convincing given that the Information Age has not really delivered any great reduction in environmental damage or in ecosystem service substitution, as we have already noted.

As David Stern and Cutler Cleveland observed:

> The neoclassical production function assumes that an infinite number of efficient techniques coexist at any one point in time. Substitution occurs among these techniques. Changes in technology occur when new more efficient techniques are developed. However, these new techniques really represent the substitution of knowledge for the other factors of production (Stern and Cleveland, 2004).

Indeed, energy is not easily substituted by capital (Wrigley, 1988) and is an essential input in any process within a thermodynamic universe. Energy is important for growth because production is a function of capital, labour, and energy (Stern, 2010). Energy is the bridge between resources and pollution.

Warr and Ayres (2010) found a unidirectional causality runs from energy consumption to GDP, but there was no evidence of causality running from GDP to energy consumption. Thus a reduction of energy consumption, through increased energy efficiency, does not require a reduction (or reversal) in growth. Given energy security concerns and the environmental damage from fossil fuel externalities, reduction in energy use is much more beneficial than driving economic growth by increasing energy through-flow.

In most of western Europe, energy intensity ratios (energy consumption per unit GDP) have decreased significantly between 1990 and 2006. The only countries where this has not been the case are Ireland, Greece and Spain, due mainly to the large growth in transport and construction sectors (Mendiluce *et al.*, 2010). It is interesting to note that these three countries have been most damaged by the global economic recession of 2009.

3.2.4 Carbon trading

As mentioned above, carbon trading emerged from the Kyoto agreement, and has become an extremely contentious and troublesome issue. Yet introducing economics as a tool to solve the economic excesses of the past 200 years, while initially dumbfounding, is clearly the only obvious approach for the business sector to pursue. And so, between 1997 and 2001, the Kyoto Protocol developed into a trading mechanism. As Mike Scott wrote: "What is the best way to tackle climate destabilization? If we have a global carbon price, the market sorts it out" (Scott, 2008). A commodity approach "abstracts from where, how, when and by whom the cuts are made, dis-embedding climate solutions from history and technology and re-embedding them in neoclassical economic theory, trade treaties, property law, risk management and so forth" (Lohmann, 2010).

Environmental taxes certainly facilitate the replacement of natural capital with economic capital, raising money that could be spent on amelioration. However, if the tax is not too punitive, it allows companies to pay their way out of taking any pollution reduction. If taxes are too high, companies may refuse to operate in particular countries, moving to countries with lower environmental taxes.

Direct regulation sets pollution standards, above which some form of punishment is exerted. However, this means that pollution below a particular standard is permitted, and thus licensed as acceptable. Therefore the standard that is set is all-important, and, again, different countries can set different standards, thus forcing governments to raise the allowable levels of pollution or risk losing jobs. Neoliberal governments typically avoid taxes on polluting firms and prefer voluntary agreements. Carbon taxes and direct regulation were, ultimately, viewed as ineffectual, blocked by politics and business. Carbon trading was seen as a better way ahead. Tradable permits offer something of a hybrid between direct regulation and taxation. The concept is to set a standard which is regulated by issuing permissions to pollute. The economic efficiency aspect arises from making the permissions tradable. This pursues the Enlightenment dictum that it is "best to leave it to the invisible hand to work it all out".

The issues with carbon trading are manifold:

1. It assumes that the current economic model is correct, and that applying this model to the problem of greenhouse gas emissions will therefore provide the best solution available.
2. A simple pollution model focusing on a single set of pollutants (greenhouse gases) is likely to increase pollution in other sectors. Here, there is substitution of pollution, rather than substitution of capital.
3. The calculation of the carbon budget is open to manipulation and abuse.
4. Carbon trading does not address social sustainability.
5. There is no agreed approach to substituting the lost natural capital through fiscal means.
6. There is no accounting for heterogeneity in terms of sources of greenhouse gases. For example, comparing the EU with Australia, in the EU (15 member states) sources of GHGs were estimated in 2006 as: 33% energy production, 21% industry, 19% transport, 15% households, 9% agriculture, 3% other (European Commission, 2008; p. 15). In Australia, GHG sources have been estimated as: 50% stationary energy production, 16% agriculture, 14% transport (90% road transport), 7% net land use change (deforestation 11% minus reforestation), 6% oil and gas extraction, 5% industry, 3% other (Australian Government, 2008).

7. Issues relating to the allocation of allowances. Baseline greenhouse gas levels, which are an essential part of the calculations of sink credits and permissions, have been manipulated to favour the submitting nations. Russia and Japan refused to sign the Kyoto protocol in 2001 until they received additional carbon credits for their industrial forests (Lohmann, 2006; p. 53). Famously, under Kyoto, Russia and the Ukraine were awarded excess sink credits because they each used baseline projections calculated for the entire former USSR, arguing that historically this was their right. These permissions became known as "hot air" due to being meaningless in terms of actual carbon.
8. Being able to buy permissions allows the rich to pollute more. It has been compared to indulgences sold by the church, which allowed the rich to be forgiven sins without the need for penance (Spash, 2010).

Lohmann (2006) records that the Czech energy giant CEZ was allocated 30% of the country's carbon allowances. CEZ sold them when their value was high, and bought them back when the price was low. They then used the profit of this trade to expand coal energy production, increasing pollution. From a business point of view, the company cannot be judged badly for doing this. If the rules allow you to behave in a certain way, then the policy-makers are to blame when you do.

Stavins (2004; p. 12) emphasized that a free market approach to environmental destruction could not bring a sustainable outcome:

> If the market is left to itself, too many pollution-generating products get produced. There's too much pollution, and not enough clean air, for example, to provide maximum general welfare. In this case, laissez-faire markets—because of the market failure, the externalities—are not efficient.

Turner (2000; p. 705) similarly concludes that "unfettered markets fail to allocate environmental resources efficiently".

3.2.5 Personal carbon trading (PCT)

Personal carbon trading is an umbrella term covering a range of specific policy proposals which brings the responsibility for energy management down to the individual level. The common features of all PCT schemes are:

- Rights for carbon emissions are allocated to individuals for free.
- Emissions from household energy use and nonbusiness transport are covered (this represents 42% of carbon emissions from energy use in the UK).
- Emissions rights are tradable.
- Emissions allocations should reduce year-on-year in line with a declining national carbon cap (Fawcett, 2010).

Every time a person paid an energy bill, filled up the car with fuel or bought a flight (in the case of PCA), they would have to surrender carbon units from their account, or pay the additional cost of buying carbon units at the market price. By allowing trading, individuals who live low-carbon lives would have a surplus to sell. The scheme has never been implemented because of the difficulties of managing it.

3.2.6 Reducing energy demand

The personal carbon trading scheme is the only one targeting consumers directly. Yet it may offer the most dramatic improvements. Cullen *et al.* (2011) have demonstrated that 73% of global energy use could be saved by applying known engineering best practice to passive systems, transforming useful energy to services. Their assessment of the practical efficiency limits in conversion devices provides an overall global and practical estimate for the reduction potential in demand-side options of 85%.

The Chinese government are world leaders in sustainable economics (see Chapter 6). In their 12th Five-Year Plan, adopted in March 2012, they devoted significant attention to energy issues. Measures included a 16% reduction in energy intensity (following on from a targeted and achieved 20% reduction in the 11th Five-Year Plan), an increase in non-fossil energy to 11.4% of total energy use and a 17% reduction in carbon intensity (carbon emissions per unit of GDP). The 12th Five-Year Plan further targets an increase in the rate of forest coverage by just over 21% and the total forest stock by 12.5 million hectares by 2015. This direct intervention approach while disliked in the West, can be seen as a very effective way of delivering important actions, not only for the benefit of China, but the entire human population on Earth.

3.2.7 The true cost of cheap oil

The collapsing value of a barrel of oil has been the most significant economic event of 2014. From a high of US$112 per barrel in June 2014, Brent Crude oil had fallen to US$47.69 on 20 January 2015. Jonathan Barrett, the CIO of Ayres Alliance Securities, predicts the possibility of a sub-US$40 barrel. Goldman Sachs, Deutsche Bank, ABN AMRO, Intesa Sanpaolo and BNP Paribas have all cut their forecasts, predicting that oil prices will stay at $50 during 2015 and $70 in 2016, according to Thomson Reuters (2015). BP are predicting that prices will remain between $50 and $60 until 2017.

This drop has very significant consequences for the environment. While prices remained high, the non-carbon energy sectors, such as wind, tide and solar, all of which are more expensive to produce at present than oil, could be seen as feasible, in terms of the government subsidies needed to cover costs involved in research and development. However, as the gap increases between oil and non-carbon sources, the increased subsidies need for alternative energy sources to remain even slightly competitive disappears. This current slump delivers a death knell to any chance of a competitive alternative energy supply at a crucial point in the history of renewable energy development.

As the cost of running our cars declines, we may be less likely to cut back on the amount of driving we do. Indeed, cheaper oil will impact on many consumer choices, since the price of oil underpins the price of many highly polluting products. Cost is a powerful controller of consumer decision-making. Increased oil costs means less damage to the environment.

The option of utilizing public transport and rebuilding canals for commercial transport becomes less economically preferable. Meanwhile, the oil industry itself is threatened by low prices since exploration for more complex sources of oil becomes less financially feasible. Emerging markets in commodity-centric countries such as Ecuador, Venezuela (where oil and gas represent some 25% of GDP) and Brazil are particularly vulnerable. Brazil has invested one quarter of a trillion dollars in developing its own oil and gas sector, based on prices at their peak. They now face a financial shortfall at these new low prices. The British economy will suffer as nuclear plants currently being built will be far from cost-effective, and the need to import cheaper gas from overseas may become a necessity. Further development of the North Sea resource will also be challenged.

Cheap oil should benefit heavy carbon-based industries such as manufacturing, but there is little evidence of this occurring. Karl Snyder, Chief Market Strategist with Garden State Securities has observed that: “This is showing you there are greater forces at work. The global economy is really walking a fine line between outright disinflation and deflation".

3.3 The green paradox

Legislation relating to sustainability has been rapidly evolving, and, in many ways, sets the agenda for business response. Indeed environmental legislation will be likely to pose a far greater challenge to business than environmental perturbation in the short to medium term, while also providing the means to ameliorate medium- to long-term environmental destabilization. Here we discuss a number of issues relating to the legislative framework, a topic returned to later in this book.

Pollution legislation began in the 1800s. As Freycinet (1907) documented, manufacturers could be subjected to fines payable to the state as well as damages payable to private entities. This meant that industry had an interest in cleaning up its processes. He wrote (p. 8):

> On the one hand, public authority would be wrong to abandon regulations for fear of harming production ... when these have the goal of stopping serious causes of poor health; on the other hand, manufacturers would be ill-advised to see harmful impediments to their industry in these regulations. They must, on the contrary, tell themselves that the law, while obliging them to improve sanitation, does them a real service most of the time and that for lack of philanthropic considerations, it is in their own interest to respect the security and the well-being of their fellow men.

3.3.1 The green paradox

The green paradox refers to the situation where climate policies and legislation lead to a worsening of environmental damage, rather than an improvement. An example of this is where a given set of restrictive policies are announced to start on a given date in the future, targeting **producers**. These policies may mean that production costs will have to increase because of the demands on manufacturing methods. Industry could well respond by increasing production up until that date in order to maximize the opportunity to use cheaper, but more polluting production methods for as long as they can.

A second facet of the green paradox relates to the situation where legislation targets **consumers**, such as a fuel tax at the pump. Reduced demand leads to reduced fuel prices, thus increasing sales and leading to no change in pollution (Sinn, 2008). However, a decrease in profit to the producer will likely reduce production in this situation, because exploration and exploitation are increasingly expensive under diminishing returns, as we have noted earlier. Thus, prices may not be able to be lowered (Bhattacharyya, 2011). Reduced extraction would then benefit the environment.

A third facet of the green paradox is termed **carbon leakage**. Carbon leakage is where reductions in greenhouse gas production occur in one country, but in another country the pollution levels increase as the first country externalizes its pollution by importing "**dirty goods**" from the second country. Thus the global pollution levels fail to decrease, because while some countries make cuts, others increase production.

A fourth element to the green paradox is called the **rebound effect** (Berkhout *et al.*, 2000). As improved efficiency in the use of energy in manufacturing becomes a reality (i.e. a decline in energy intensity and carbon intensity) costs will decline, given that energy is a key driver of cost. Cheaper production will lead to an increase in consumer spending and an increase in manufacturing, thus leading to a net increase in pollution. If a process becomes twice as efficient as it was in terms of energy efficiency, leading to a significant drop in the consumer cost, then, provided sales increase by more than twice, there will be greater pollution than before.

Greening *et al.* (2000) further defined five different types of rebound effect:

1. The substitution effect: consumers will substitute to achieve the cheapest price for energy.
2. The income effect: dependent on income and financial commitment (e.g. a large mortgage), consumer preferences can vary hugely.
3. Secondary effects (input–output effects, indirect effects). These occur at consumer and producer levels. Consumers, by saving money on fuel, may spend more on other things that consume energy in their production. For industry, the increased demand for nonfuel inputs to their production process may result because of increased demand for output, and production costs of other sectors may be affected by the lower cost of one sector's output. Energy may be substituted for labour or capital inputs, potentially

damaging societal sustainability and impacting on the flow of money (an energy substitute) through the human ecosystem.

4. General equilibrium or economy-wide effects emerge from the technology-induced changes in the effective price per unit of fuel.
5. Transformational effects are large-scale impacts on human behaviour, organization of production and societal changes which may impact on environmental damage in unpredictable ways.

The first two effects can be considered microeconomic and are referred to as direct rebound effects, while the last three effects are macroeconomic.

3.3.2 The Porter Hypothesis

Much controversy surrounds the impact of environmental regulations on the economic performance of firms (Fiorino 2006; Press 2007). Any government needs private and public-sector industry to succeed in order to raise tax revenue, provide employment and strengthen its international trading position. Thus governments struggle to adopt environmental legislation that will both protect natural capital while encouraging economic growth.

The **Porter Hypothesis** was developed by economist Michael Porter (Porter and van der Linde, 1995) and states that properly designed and enforced regulations that actually mitigate environmental harm could trigger innovative responses that would not only fully offset compliance costs, but also result in additional profits, or so-called "win–win" innovations.

The win–win scenario offered by the Porter Hypothesis is the golden egg of environmentally minded governments and environmental movements worldwide. Much effort has been put into trying to convince business that what is good for the environment is good for business, and vice versa. It rests on greater efficiency. Combined with appropriate penalties for non-compliance, thus tilting the playing field sufficiently, a new, leaner, meaner and, most importantly, cleaner industry emerges, with those embracing the new world-view most gaining greatest market share. There is the underlying issue of the **Red Queen** here.

3.3.3 The Red Queen and the Porter Hypothesis

The English author, Reverend Charles Dodgson, better known by his *nom de plume*, Lewis Carroll, described how Alice, his leading character in *Through the Looking Glass*, came upon the Red Queen, a chess piece that became alive. Alice discovered that there was a huge game of chess taking place between a red team and a white team. She asked the Red Queen if she could take part and it was agreed that she could play the role of the white queen's pawn. First, she had to get to the correct square on the giant chess board. The queen and Alice ran as fast as they could, but made no progress. After running and running, all the trees and the bushes were in exactly the same place. The Red Queen explained: "Now, here, you see, it takes all the running you can do to keep in the same place. If you want to get somewhere else, you must run at least twice as fast as that".

Consequently, the advantages offered by the Porter Hypothesis only work if everyone else is standing still. However, if a significant number of your competitors adopt similar environmentally win–win options, then you will be no further on than them, eradicating any advantage. Furthermore, most econometric studies on the topic have yielded inconclusive results on the validity of Porter's idea (Smith and Walsh, 2000; Jaffe *et al.* 2002; Leeuwen and Mohnen, 2013).

Common law principles can be viewed as the optimal approach to controlling environmental harm if only because they will always allow greater freedom and innovation than rigid statutory rules or politically determined punitive measures (Magsig, 2011).

3.4 Bridge case

Since 1973, machinery manufacturer Caterpillar has devoted a whole division of its company to remanufacturing. They remanufacture over 700 products, including those made by competitors. Customers are encouraged to return products through a deposit system. To begin with, Caterpillar sold the remanufactured engines at a large discount. Caterpillar then introduced a scheme where the engines were bought back at a price reflecting their condition and completeness. This led to the quality of the used engines significantly improving. As a result, the remanufactured engines are now sold with the same guarantee and for the same price as new ones (Stahel, 2006).

In 2009, the company took back over 2.1 million end-of-life products and remanufactured over £130 million worth of material. Following disassembly, cleaning and inspection, new engineering updates are then added before full testing and repainting. This can involve laser deposition of material onto worn surfaces and replating (Adler *et al.*, 2007). Remanufactured products such as diesel engines can have 85% lower energy costs and 60% lower material costs than new counterparts. Caterpillar has a 2020 operational goal to eliminate waste by reducing waste generation and re-using and recycling all that remains. It is currently recycling in excess of 80% of its waste and has already achieved zero waste to landfill in two of its UK-based sites. Caterpillar further employs a pricing model which incentivizes customers to return old equipment and get a refurbished replacement at half-price, thus locking in the customer for life (Blus, 2008). Caterpillar annually processes over 2 million used engines and components (Miller, 2004).

3.5 Discourse—the great controversies

3.5.1 The Environmental Kuznets Curve (EKC)

Simon Kuznets was a Belarussian Nobel Prize-winning economist who explored the relationship between inequality and economic growth. In 1955, he set out a theory that with increasing economic growth, inequality first increased to a maximum, but then decreased. This formed an inverted U shape, the **Kuznets Curve** (Fig. 3.3a). Kuznets argued that a nation can grow its way out of inequality. Thus economic growth was seen as being able to deliver social sustainability. This tenet greatly strengthened the position that sustainable development was the best way forward.

In the mid-1990s, several economists (including Shafik and Bandyopadhyay (1992), Panayotou (1993) and Grossman and Krueger (1995)) suggested that the Kuznets Curve could also apply to environmental degradation. They proposed that with economic growth, environmental impact increased up to a point, and then decreased. This inverted U-shaped curve became known as the **Environmental Kuznets Curve** (EKC), with income per capita on the x-axis and the extent of some particular measure of pollution on the y-axis (Fig. 3.3b). The broader field is known as **Ecological Modernization Theory** (EMT) which sets out that modernization, through reason and technology, broadens the rationality of a population which leads to the adoption of a sustainable economy. The drivers are policies invoked by increasingly rational voters (Selden and Song, 1995), structural changes in the economy (Panayotou, 1993) or trade adjustments. This is a very pure Enlightenment dogma. Income then becomes a factor in the production of wellbeing, while also embracing the laissez-faire approach. The markets will sort the environment out, with a little help from society. Torras and Boyce

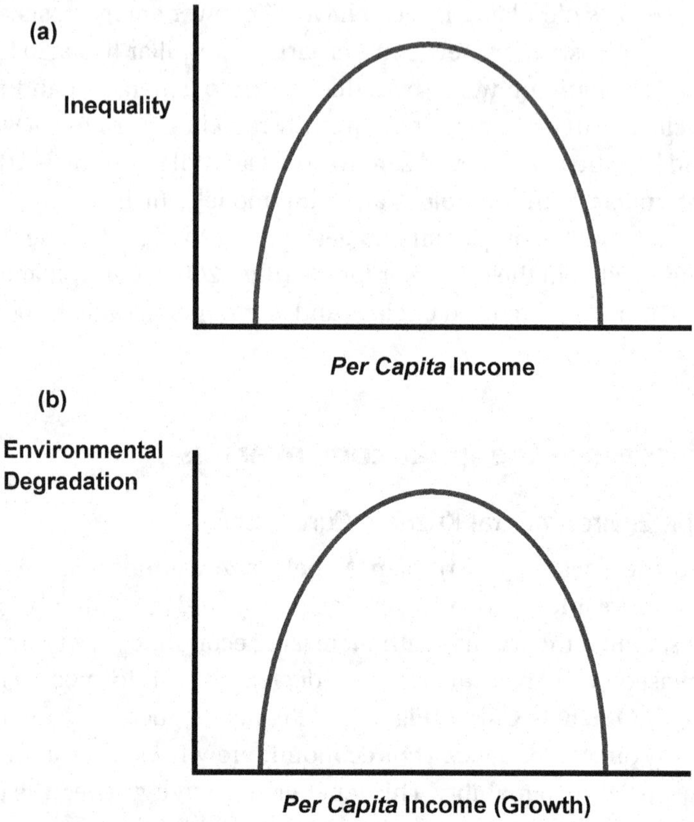

FIGURE 3.3 (a) The Kuznets Curve, which examines the relationship between income per capita and inequality. Inequality initially increases as urbanization increases, then decreases due to the trickle-down effect of wealth diffusing throughout the populace. (b) The Environmental Kuznets Curve (EKC), suggesting that with increasing income, humans spend this money on an increasingly higher energy lifestyle, leading to greater environmental degradation. However, with greater income still, they become aware of this damage and seek to conserve their environment. At even higher incomes, they actively seek to restore the environment. This thinking is strongly aligned with the economic positivism of Adam Smith, but empirical data does not support it (see text for references).

(1998) have argued that education brings a more equitable power distribution, which in turn results in better environmental quality. Thus increased environmental protection will come from increased education, without the need to slow economic growth.

3.5.2 Can economic growth lead to environmental improvements?

The EKC literature seeks to answer the question of whether economic growth will ultimately lead to specific environmental improvements. This is a related but different question to whether environmental constraints in general will limit economic growth.

Increased material wellbeing is the most accepted measure of the human condition, although not agreed by everyone. As GDP rises, spending increases and material wealth increases. Friedman (2005) argues that economic growth provides broader welfare benefits, in that it fosters moral societies, characterized by social and political liberalization. Thus economic growth is argued to bring increases in values (Pezzey, 1992; p. 324). Controversially, according to the EKC, a decrease in growth could well **increase** environmental damage, depending on where on the curve you are. Therefore increased growth is seen as essential to sustainability, less we stall at the damage peak.

Stern (2004) has argued that "developing" countries are not following the same track as "developed" countries, in that they are already taking action to protect the environment. Therefore this will erode any EKC relationship. Caviglia-Harris *et al.* (2009) found no significant EKC relationship between development and growth. Stern (2003; p. 11) also concludes, "The evidence ... shows that the statistical analysis on which the environmental Kuznets curve is based is not robust. There is little evidence for a common inverted U-shaped pathway that countries follow as their income rises." Kuznets' original research was based on only three countries and he freely admitted that his work was "perhaps 5% empirical information and 95% speculation, some of it possibly tainted by wishful thinking" (Kuznets, 1955, p. 26).

He used data from the USA and the UK, as well as from two states within Germany, assuming that rural incomes were lower than industrial incomes, and thus that the transition from the Agrarian to the Industrial Age would bring an increase in incomes and in inequality, between rural and industrial workers. Thus he predicted that the curve would initially go up. Beyond the tipping point, almost everyone will be in industrial sectors, and thus receiving the same, higher wages. This meant that inequality would decrease. And the curve would go downwards. He therefore assumed that inequality was very low in agrarian societies. These assumptions are now questioned, due to evidence emerging from the Roman Empire through to the 1880s, indicating little change in inequality (Milanovic *et al.*, 2007).

Another issue relating to the EKC is that it relies, solely, on economic measures. While industrialization brought greater wealth, the quality of life in cities during the Industrial Revolution was very poor. Cities acted as population sinks, with death rates higher than birth rates, and people drawn in from rural areas maintained urban populations. As early as 1665, some 6,000 people each year moved in to the city of London from surrounding areas (Skene, 2011). Charles Dickens has famously painted a picture of squalor, disease and poverty in urban areas of the 19th century. It is intuitive that workers in a factory in a large city will be less connected to the environment than those working in rural areas and involved in agriculture. Environmental values, thought to be the sole property of increasing GDP per capita, is more likely to emerge from either living within the natural world, or depending on it for your livelihood.

Another issue is that although population growth may be reduced with increasing wealth (although this is a contentious area), the spending power of that population is likely to increase. It is estimated that the global middle class will rise from 1 to 4 billion over the coming 50 years, an so although technology my reduce the pollution per unit manufactured, the huge increase in manufacturing needed to satiate the needs of this huge middle class will mean that absolute levels of pollution may well increase. People's revealed preferences indicate that pollution-intensive material goods are still highly valued (Neumayer, 2002; p. 81).

3.5.3 Humpty Dumpty and the EKC

Environmental perturbation is not necessarily recoverable. On Easter Island, as palm tree forests declined, increases in rat populations led to the tree seeds being eaten. Thus this combination of human and rodent pressure made it impossible for recovery, even if deforestation had halted. This significantly challenges the EKC, which assumes that an easing of pressure on the environment will automatically result in an improvement in environmental health.

Recent research has pointed towards a U-shaped curve, rather than an inverted U (Dietz *et al.*, 2012). In other words increasing economic growth initially leads to a decrease in pollution, but then there is an increase in

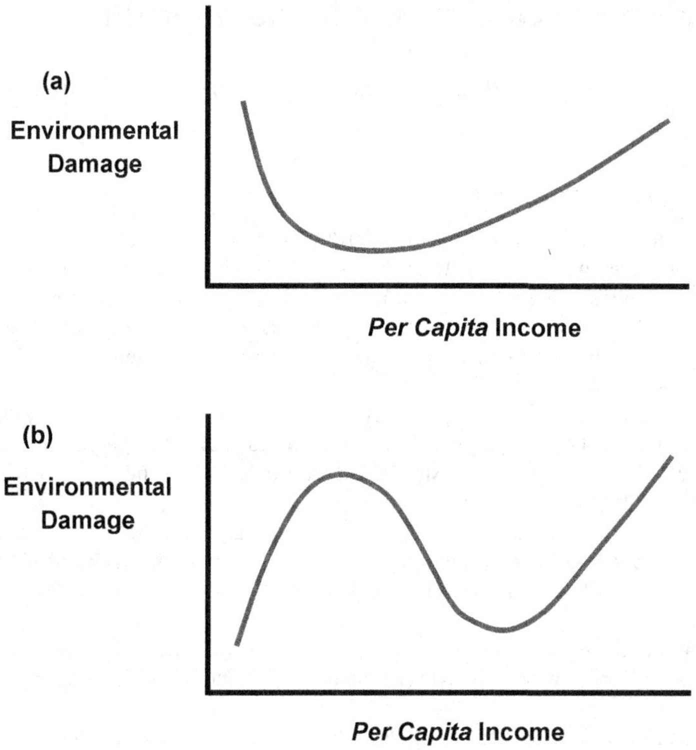

FIGURE 3.4 (a) The "U"-shaped curve, where increasing levels of income lead to improved environmental conditions, but as earnings increase further, damage increases (Dietz *et al.*, 2012). (b) The "N"-shaped curve observed for deforestation (Bhattarai and Hammig, 2001), CO_2 emissions (Fujii and Managi, 2013) and SO_x emissions (Torras and Boyce, 1998), where damage initially increases with initial income improvement, but after a certain level of income, the situation improves, only to worsen again as income reaches higher levels.

pollution at higher levels of growth (Fig. 3.4a). Work by Fujii and Managi (2013) uncovered an N shaped curve for CO_2 emissions from 1970 to 2005 in OECD countries (Fig. 3.4b), while the same pattern was found for deforestation (Bhattarai and Hammig, 2001) and SO_x emissions (Torras and Boyce, 1998).

3.6 Debate, discussion and further thought

Discuss the following, either as debating teams are in small groups:

1. EKC: valid or not?

The following literature may be useful:

Boucekkine, R., Pommeret, A. and Prieur, F. (2013). Technological vs. ecological switch and the environmental Kuznets Curve. American Journal of Agricultural Economics 95(2): 252-60. http://hal.univ-savoie.fr/docs/00/63/30/24/PDF/DTGREQAM2011_41.pdf.

Choumert, J., Combes Motel, P. and Dakpo, H.K. (2013). Is the Environmental Kuznets Curve for deforestation a threatened theory? A meta-analysis of the literature. Ecological Economics 90: 19-28.

Chowdhury, R. and Moran, E.F. (2012). Turning the curve: A critical review of Kuznets approaches. Applied Geography 32(1): 3-11. www.iu.edu/~geog/people/roychowdhury/JournalArticles/RoyChowdhuryMoran2012_Turning%20the%20Curve-A%20critical%20review%20of%20Kuznets%20approaches.pdf.

Dietz, T., Rosa, E.A. and York, R. (2012). Environmentally efficient well-being: Is there a Kuznets curve? Applied Geography 32(1): 21-8. www.sze.hu/fk/kornyezet/Cikkek4/Environmentally-efficient-well-being-Is-there-a-Kuznets-curve_2012_Applied-Geography.pdf.

Eastin, J. and Prakash, A. (2013). Economic development and gender equality: is there a gender Kuznets curve? World Politics 65(1): 156-86. http://faculty.washington.edu/aseem/gkc.pdf.

Esteve, V. and Tamarit, C. (2012). Threshold cointegration and nonlinear adjustment between CO2 and income: The Environmental Kuznets Curve in Spain, 1857–2007. Energy Economics 34(6): 2148-56. ftp://147.156.210.157/RePEc/pdf/eec_1106.pdf.

Fosten, J., Morley, B. and Taylor, T. (2012). Dynamic misspecification in the environmental Kuznets curve: Evidence from CO_2 and SO_2 emissions in the United Kingdom. Ecological Economics 76: 25-33.

Itkonen, J.V. (2012). Problems estimating the carbon Kuznets curve. Energy, 39(1), 274-80.www.isee2012.org/anais/pdf/152.pdf.

Hervieux, M.S. and Darné, O. (2013). Environmental Kuznets Curve and ecological footprint: a time series analysis. http://halshs.archives-ouvertes.fr/docs/00/78/19/58/PDF/LEMNA_WP_201301.pdf.

Thompson, A. (2012). Three essays on the environmental Kuznets curve for water pollution. http://krex.k-state.edu/dspace/bitstream/handle/2097/15073/AlexiThompson2012.pdf?sequence=1.

Other discussion/essay questions

1. Is the water footprint concept fit for purpose? Identify weaknesses and attempt to improve the concept to better respond to criticisms.

2. Footprints are used in many aspects of sustainability. What challenges exist in usefully applying them?

3. Debate whether a soft or hard path is the best approach to delivering resource security. Is there a middle road?
4. How valuable should water be?
5. Summarize the history, implementation and issues related to carbon trading.
6. Could personal carbon trading actually work? Research and write a critique.
7. What is the evidence of a resource curse and what implications does it have?
8. Given the linkage between GDP and energy, how should this be reflected in economic models, considering predicted increasing energy use, especially in BRIC nations, and decreasing energy production.
9. Write a critique of the green paradox. What lessons can be learned by legislators?

References

Adler, D.P., Ludewig, P.A., Kumar, V. and Sutherland, J.W. (2007). Comparing energy and other measures of environmental performance in the original manufacturing and remanufacturing of engine components. In ASME 2007 International Manufacturing Science and Engineering Conference (pp. 851-60). American Society of Mechanical Engineers.

Aghion, P. and Howitt, P. (2009). *The Economics of Growth.* MIT Press. Cambridge, MA.

Aleklett, K. (2005). *The Oil Supply Tsunami Alert.* The Association for the Study of Peak Oil and Gas. Uppsala.

Allan, J.A. (1998). Virtual water: a strategic resource, global solutions to regional deficits. Groundwater 36: 545-6.

Australian Government (2008). *Carbon Reduction Scheme: Australia's Low Pollution Future, Volume 1.* Commonwealth of Australia, Canberra. P. 435.

Bassi, A.M., Powers, R. and Schoenberg, W. (2010). An integrated approach to energy prospects for North America and the rest of the world. Energy Economics 32(1): 30-42.

Becker, P. (1981). The role of synthetic fuel in World War II Germany. Air University Review, July–August 1981.

Berkhout, P.H.G., Muskens, J.C. and Velthuijsen, J.W. (2000). Defining the rebound effect. Energy Policy 28: 425-32.

Bhattacharyya, S.C. (2011). *Energy Economics: Concepts, Issues, Markets and Governance.* Springer, London.

Bhattarai, M. and Hammig, M. (2001). Institutions and the environmental Kuznets curve for deforestation: a cross-country analysis for Latin America, Africa and Asia. World Development 29 (6): 995-1010.

Blus, G. (2008). *Sustainability for Manufacturers: Driving Profitability and Growth.* Autodesk manufacturing white paper.

Bogardi, J.J., Dudgeon, D., Lawford, R., Flinkerbusch, E., Meyn, A., Pahl-Wostl, C., Vielhauer, K. and Vörösmarty, C. (2012). Water security for a planet under pressure: interconnected challenges of a changing world call for sustainable solutions. Current Opinion in Environmental Sustainability 4(1): 35-43.

Briscoe, J. (2009). Water Security: Why it matters and what to do about it. Innovations: Technology, Governance, Globalization 4(3): 3-28.

Caviglia-Harris. J., Chambers, D. and Kahn, J. (2009). Taking the "U" out of Kuznets: A comprehensive analysis of the EKC and environmental limits. Ecological Economics 68(4): 1149-59.

Chapagain, A.K. and Tickner, D. (2012). Water footprint: Help or hindrance? Water Alternatives 5(3): 563-81.

Clark, S., Sarlin, P., Sharma, A. and Sisson, S.A. (2014). Increasing dependence on foreign water resources? An assessment of trends in global virtual water flows using a self-organizing time map. Ecological Informatics. In press.

Cullen, J.M., Allwood, J.M. and Borgstein, E.H. (2011). Reducing energy demand: what are the practical limits? Environmental Science and Technology 45(4): 1711-18.

Dalby, S. (2002). Environmental change and human security. Isuma-Canadian Journal of Policy Research 3 (2): 71-9.

Dalin, C., Konar, M., Hanasaki, N., Rinaldo, A. and Rodriguez-Iturbe, I. (2012). Evolution of the global virtual water trade network. Proceedings of the National Academy of Sciences, USA 109(16): 5989-94.

Dietz, T., Rosa, E.A. and York, R. (2012). Environmentally efficient well-being: Is there a Kuznets curve? Applied Geography 32(1): 21-8.

Dominguez-Faus, R., Powers, S.E., Burken, J.G. and Alvarez, P.J. (2009). The water footprint of biofuels: A drink or drive issue? Environmental Science and Technology 43(9): 3005-10.

EIA (2010). *International Energy Statistics Database.* US Energy Information Agency, Washington, DC.

Elliott, J., Deryng, D., Müller, C., Frieler, K., Konzmann, M., Gerten, D. and 21 other authors (2014). Constraints and potentials of future irrigation water availability on agricultural production under climate change. Proceedings of the National Academy of Sciences, USA 111(9): 3239-44.

European Commission (2008). *EU Action Against Climate Change: EU Emissions Trading.* European Commission.

FAO (2004). *The State of Food Insecurity in the World.* FAO, Rome.

Fawcett, T. (2010). Personal carbon trading: a policy ahead of its time? Energy Policy 38(11): 6868-76.

Fiorino, D.J. (2006). *The New Environmental Regulation.* The MIT Press, Cambridge, MA.

Freycinet, C. de. (1907). *Souvenirs 1848–1878.* Librairie Ch. Delagrave, Paris.

Friedman, B. (2005). *The Moral Consequences of Economic Growth.* Alfred A. Knopf, New York.

Fujii, H. and Managi, S. (2013). Which industry is greener? An empirical study of nine industries in OECD countries. Energy Policy 57: 381-8.

Galli, A., Wiedmann, T., Ercin, E., Knoblauch, D., Ewing, B. and Giljum, S. (2012). Integrating ecological, carbon and water footprint into a "footprint family" of indicators: definition and role in tracking human pressure on the planet. Ecological Indicators 16: 100-12.

Gleeson, T., Alley, W.M., Allen, D.M., Sophocleous, M.A., Zhou, Y., Taniguchi, M. and Vander-Steen, J. (2012a). Towards sustainable groundwater use: setting long-term goals, backcasting, and managing adaptively. Ground Water 50(1): 19-26.

Gleeson, T., Wada, Y., Bierkens, M.F. and van Beek, L.P. (2012b). Water balance of global aquifers revealed by groundwater footprint. Nature 488(7410): 197-200.

Gleick, P.H. (2002). Soft water path. Nature 418: 373.

Gleick, P.H. and Heberger, M. (2014). Water conflict chronology. In *The World's Water, Volume 8*. Island Press/Center for Resource Economics, Washington, DC. pp. 173-219.

Greening, L., Greene, D.L. and Difiglio, C. (2000). Energy efficiency and consumption the rebound effect: a survey. Energy Policy 28: 389-401.

Grossman, G.M. and Krueger, A.B. (1995). Economic growth and the environment. Quarterly Journal of Economics 110: 353-77.

Hoekstra, A.Y. and Mekonnen, M.M. (2012). The water footprint of humanity. Proceedings of the National Academy of Sciences, USA 109(9): 3232-7.

Hoekstra, A.Y., Chapagain, A.K., Aldaya, M.M. and Mekonnen, M.M. (2011). *The Water Footprint Assessment Manual: Setting the Global Standard.* Earthscan, London.

Iyer, R.R. (2012). Virtual water: some reservations. Global Water Forum Discussion Paper 1218, Canberra, Australia.

Jaffe, A.B., Newell, R.G. and Stavins, R.N. (2002). Environmental policy and technological change. Environmental and Resource Economics 22: 41-69.

JPMorgan and Global Equity Research. (2008). Watching water: A guide to evaluating corporate risks in a thirsty world. http://pdf.wri.org/jpmorgan_watching_water.pdf.

Karp, A. and Richter, G.M. (2011). Meeting the challenge of food and energy security. Journal of Experimental Botany 62(10): 3263-71.

Knudson, T. (2009). The cost of the biofuel boom: destroying Indonesia's forests. Yale Environment 360, January 19.

Kuznets, S. (1955). Economic growth and income inequality. American Economic Review 45(1): 1-28.

Leeuwen, G.V. and Mohnen, P. (2013). Revisiting the porter hypothesis: an empirical analysis of green innovation for the Netherlands. CIRANO-Scientific Publications Research Paper (2013s-02).

Lipschutz, R. and Holdren, J.P. (1990). Crossing borders: resource flows, the global environment, and international security. Bulletin of Peace Proposals 21 (2): 121-33.

Lohmann, L. (2006). "Made in the USA": A short history of carbon trading. Development Dialogue 48 (September): 31-70.

Lohmann, L. (2010). Neoliberalism and the calculable world: the rise of carbon trading. In: Birch, K., Mykhnenko, V. and Trebeck, K. (eds.), *The Rise and Fall of neo-liberalism: The Collapse of an Economic Order?* Zed Books, London. pp. 77-93.

Magsig, B.O. (2011). Overcoming state-centrism in water law: regional common concern as the normative foundation of water security. Goettingen Journal of International Law 3: 317.

Mekonnen, M.M. and Hoekstra, A.Y. (2010). The green, blue and grey water footprint of crops and derived crop products. Value of Water Research Report Series No.47, UNESCO-IHE.

Mekonnen, M.M. and Hoekstra, A.Y. (2011). The green, blue and grey water footprint of crops and derived crop products. Hydrology and Earth System Sciences 15(5): 1577-600.

Mekonnen, M.M. and Hoekstra, A.Y. (2012). A global assessment of the water footprint of farm animal products. Ecosystems 15(3): 401-15.

Mendiluce, M., Pérez-Arriaga, I. and Ocaña, C. (2010). Comparison of the evolution of energy intensity in Spain and in the EU15. Why is Spain different? Energy Policy 38(1): 639-45.

Milanovic, B., Lindert, P.H. and Williamson, J.G. (2007). Measuring Ancient Inequality. Munich Personal RePEc Archive, October.

Miller, J. (2004). Old Caterpillars don't die; they come to Corinth, Miss., to be rebuilt. Chicago Tribune, Knight Rider/Tribune Business News, 5 December 2004.

Murphy, D.J. and Hall, C.A.S. (2011). Energy return on investment, peak oil, and the end of economic growth. In: Costanza, R., Limburg, K. and Kubiszewski, I. (eds.), *Ecological Economics Reviews*. Annals of the New York Academy of Sciences 1219: 52-72.

Neumayer, E. (2002). Do democracies exhibit stronger international environmental commitment? A cross-country analysis. Journal of Peace Research 39(2): 139-64.

Panayotou, T. (1993). *Empirical Tests and Policy Analysis of Environmental Degradation at Different Stages of Economic Development.* World Employment Programme Working Paper Number WP238. International Labour Office, Geneva.

Patey, L.A. (2010). Crude days ahead? Oil and the resource curse in Sudan. African Affairs 109(437): 617-36.

Pegram, G. (2010). Shared risk and opportunity in water resources: Seeking a sustainable future for Lake Naivasha. Godalming, UK: WWF and PEGASYS.

Pezzey, J. (1992). Sustainability: an interdisciplinary guide. Environmental Values 1(4): 321-62.

Porter, M.E. and van der Linde, C. (1995). Toward a new conception of the environment-competitiveness relationship. Journal of Economic Perspectives 9(4): 97-118.

Press, D. (2007). Industry, environmental policy, and environmental outcomes. Annual Review of Environment and Resources 32: 317-44.

Renzetti, S. and Dupont, D. (2013). *Buried Treasure: The Economics of Leak Detection and Water Loss Prevention in Ontario.* Environmental Sustainability Research Centre, Brock University. Working Paper ESRC 2013-001.

SABMiller; GIZ (Deutsche Gesellschaft für Internationale Zusammenarbeit) and WWF (2010). *Water Futures: Working Together for a Secure Water Future.* SABMiller, UK.

Scott, M. (2008). Market meltdown? Carbon trading is just warming up. Independent on Sunday Business, 27 July 2008.

Selden, T.M. and Song, D. (1995). Neoclassical growth, the J curve for abatement, and the inverted U curve for pollution. Journal of Environmental Economics and Management 29: 162-8.

Shafik, N. and Bandyopadhyay, S. (1992). Economic growth and environmental quality: time series and cross-country evidence. Background Paper for the World Development Report 1992, World Bank, Washington DC.

Shah, T. (2007). The groundwater economy of South Asia: an assessment of size, significance and socio-ecological impacts. In: Giordano, M. and Villholth, K.G. (eds.), *The Agricultural Groundwater Revolution: Opportunities and Threats to Development.* CABI, Oxford. pp. 7-36.

Sinn, H-W. (2008). Public policies against global warming: a supply side approach. International Tax Public Finance 15: 360-94.

Skene, K.R. (2011). *Escape from Bubbleworld: Seven Curves to Save the Earth.* Ard Macha Press, Angus, UK.

Smith, V.K. and Walsh, R. (2000). Do painless environmental policies exist? Journal of Risk and Uncertainty 21 (1): 73-94.

Spash, C.L. (2010). The brave new world of carbon trading. New Political Economy 15(2): 169-95.

Stahel, W.R. (2006). *The Performance Economy.* Palgrave Macmillan, London.

Stavins, Robert N. (2004). The myth of the universal market. The Environmental Forum 21 (3): 12.

Stern, D.I. (2003). International Society for Ecological Economics Internet Encyclopaedia of Ecological Economics The Environmental Kuznets Curve. Department of Economics, Rensselaer Polytechnic Institute.

Stern, D. (2004). The rise and fall of the Environmental Kuznets Curve. World Development 32(8): 1419-39.

Stern, D.I. (2010). The role of energy in economic growth. CCEP working paper 3.10, Centre for Climate Economics & Policy, Crawford School of Economics and Government, The Australian National University, Canberra.

Stern, D.I. and Cleveland, C.J. (2004). Energy and economic growth. Rensselaer Working Paper in Economics, No. 0410, Rensselaer Polytechnic Institute, Troy, NY.

Strzepek, K. and Boehlert, B. (2010). Competition for water for the food system. Philosophical Transactions of the Royal Society B: Biological Sciences 365(1554): 2927-40.

Suweis, S., Rinaldo, A., Maritan, A. and D'Odorico, P. (2013). Virtual water-controlled demographic growth of nations. Proceedings of the National Academy of Sciences, USA 110: 4230-3.

Tamburrino, A. (2010). Water Technology in Ancient Mesopotamia. In: Mays, L. (ed.), *Ancient Water Technologies.* Springer Netherlands. pp. 29-51.

Tamea, S., Allamano, P., Carr, J.A., Claps, P., Laio, F. and Ridolfi, L. (2012). Local and global perspectives on the virtual water trade. Hydrology and Earth System Sciences 9: 12959-87.

Thomson Reuters (2015). www.cnbc.com/id/102339913#.

Torras, M. and Boyce, J.K. (1998). Income, inequality, and pollution: a reassessment of the environmental Kuznet Curve. Ecological Economics 25: 147-60.

Turner, R.K. (2000). Waste management. In: Folmer, H. and Gabel, H.L. (eds.), *Principles of Environmental and Resource Economics.* Cheltenham (UK): Edward Elgar Publishing Limited, Cheltenham, UK. pp. 700-44.

UNDP (2006). *Beyond Scarcity: Power, Poverty and the Global Water Crisis.* United Nations Development Programme.

UNESCO-WWAP (United Nations Educational Scientific and Cultural Organization: World Water Assessment Programme). (2006). Water: A Shared Responsibility: The United Nations World Water Development Report 2.

USDE (2008). Ethanol Myths and Facts. Department of Energy; Biomass Program; US Department of Energy: Washington, DC. p. 3.

Vörösmarty, C.J., McIntyre, P.B., Gessner, M.O., Dudgeon, D., Prusevich, A., Green, P., Glidden, S., Bunn, S.E., Sullivan, C.A., Reidy Liermann, C. and Davies, P.M. (2010). Global threats to human water security and river biodiversity. Nature 467: 555-61.

Warr, B.S. and Ayres, R.U. (2010). Evidence of causality between the quantity and quality of energy consumption and economic growth. Energy 35(4): 1688-93.

World Bank (2010). The World Bank Data. Indicators. Technical report, The World Bank Group, Washington, D.C.

WRI (World Resources Institute) (2011). *Water Risk Atlas.* Washington, DC: World Resources Institute. http://insights.wri.org/aqueduct/atlas.

Wrigley, E.A. (1988). *Continuity, Chance and Change. The Character of the Industrial Revolution in England.* Cambridge University Press, Cambridge.

4

Business and biology: can we learn from nature?

All models for sustainable business practice have borrowed their inspiration from nature. In this chapter we ask how valid their biological basis is. Many of the models are based on ecological studies from the last century, yet our understanding of ecosystem functioning has altered significantly since then. This chapter will provide students with an understanding of the biological context of sustainable thinking, allowing a critical assessment of the use of biology as an analogy, a model and a blueprint for sustainable economic practice. We demonstrate how our understanding of nature has changed dramatically over the last 40 years, yet this new understanding has not been incorporated into sustainability models. Thus, all current models are based on outdated and incorrect theory. We examine how new theory differs from the old ecology, and what differences this makes to models of sustainable economics.

Learning aims and objectives

- To name and understand the three ages of ecology
- To evaluate the underlying changes which have led to the latest developments in ecology

- To name and to explore the four issues which have defined traditional ecology
- To understand the concept of panarchy and its relevance to succession and sustainability
- To understand the terms inbreeding depression, outbreeding depression and meta-population dynamics
- To understand the different ways of understanding how the biosphere is made and how it functions
- To compare and contrast neo-Darwinism, Gaian theory and thermodynamics in terms of your understanding of how the environment functions and how business operates

Learning outcomes and experiences

- To visualize the changes that have occurred in our understanding of ecological function, and the defining aspects of the three ecological ages
- To understand how the ecological foundations of our economic theories have significant impacts on our approaches to sustainability and business practice
- To appreciate the differences between traditional ecological models, dominated by the four great issues of reductionism, form, balance and circularity, and the non-equilibrium and dynamic equilibrium models of today
- To grasp the repercussions of diversification and insularity on business survival and sustainability
- To understand the differences between neo-Darwinian, Gaian and thermodynamic approaches, both in terms of their underlying philosophies and of the implications for sustainable models of existence

4.1 A brief history of ecology

In the previous chapter, we discussed the changing relationship between humans and the environment. However, the environment has also played another role. It has been used as an **analogy**. The qualitative aspects of the analogy have changed as our understanding of nature has changed. Indeed the journey of our use of nature as a guide is, in many ways, a discourse of the change in that understanding. So how has our perception of nature changed through time, and how has this influenced our use of nature as an analogy, particularly in terms of sustainable economics?

The history of ecological thinking has been marked by four important issues that have provided problems in terms of basing sustainable economic models on ecological theory. While these issues have mostly been resolved in ecology itself, there has been significant inertia in their correction within models of economic sustainability.

4.1.1 Reductionism vs. emergence

While the term ecology (or oecologie) was not used until 1866, the formal study of the interactions of life forms with their biological and physical environment has a long history. Thales is credited as the first naturalist, and the first materialist, who, in the seventh century BC, set out that nature worked without the input of gods or goddesses. Early Greeks endowed the natural world with a rational mind, necessary to explain why it was not a chaotic mess. The Atomists, a later movement led by Democritus, instead asserted no such rational mind, but, rather, aggregations of atoms, where order was a property emergent from inanimate matter itself.

Pythagoras believed that mathematics lay at the heart of nature, and that numerical harmonies represented the order observed. It was Alcmaeon who first applied an ecological theory to a human situation, when he suggested that human health also required a harmonious balance of such opposites as bitter and sweet and hot and cold, and when such balance was destabilized, illness ensued.

Evident here is an emphasis on reductionist thinking, reducing the universe to atoms or humours. However, the ancient Greek approach was one of logic rather than observation. It was Francis Bacon (1561–1626) who challenged this approach. Writing in his *Instauratio Magna Part II: Novum Organum*, published in 1620, he noted that:

> Men have sought to make a world from their own conception and to draw from their own minds all the material which they employed, but if, instead of doing so, they had consulted experience and observation, they would have the facts and not opinions to reason about, and might have ultimately arrived at the knowledge of the laws which govern the material world (Bacon, 2004).

This approach, called **empiricism**, argued that knowledge came from observation. Empiricism became the philosophy of science, represented by the scientific method, where hypotheses were tested through experimentation and observation. In order to do this, experimental systems were designed to compare two almost identical situations, differing in only one way, for example temperature or carbon dioxide levels, in order to determine what impact this one quantity had on the system. In order to achieve this, the experiment would have to be carried out in tightly controlled conditions, something that could not be representative of the real world, with all of its variation.

For example natural soil is so complex that no two teaspoonfuls of material are identical. Thus plants in laboratories are grown in artificial soil or water solutions (hydroponics) to overcome this complexity. However, artificial soil does not represent real soil. Furthermore, over 98% of plants are not plants at all, but a complex organism combining fungi and plants (called a mycorrhiza), and so laboratory experiments using sterile soil or hydroponics without the fungal partner are not reflective of the real world situation.

Most research in microbiology begins with growing the bacteria in nutrient broth, a controllable and repeatable recipe of chemicals. However, in the real world, bacteria mostly grow in biofilms—sheets of living material combining many species of bacteria, algae and fungi. It has been shown that bacteria behave completely differently in these biofilms than in nutrient broth. Thus reductionism may simplify the system, but at the loss of often crucial components, rendering the conclusions irrelevant to the natural world. As Donald Mikulecky observed:

> The nature of the world out there is such that the idea that much is lost by trying to reduce it to parts is paramount. The whole is always more than, and often different from, the sum of its parts (Mikulecky, 2005; p. 98).

Yet this reductionist approach came to pervade most scientific areas, from Newtonian physics to modern evolutionary theory, and from atomic physics to environmental protection. Such dissection allowed for the scientific method to progress. It also allowed laboratory science to advance, legitimizing the use of simplified experiments to replicate natural phenomena. Most modelling is based on similar approaches. Provided you have the basic building blocks, such as genes, species or substrates, you can approach real outcomes.

However, throughout the early history of science, the idea that there was some form of life force pervading matter, and separating living from nonliving was present, a belief called **vitalism**. While almost every religious belief structure recognizes some form of life force, be it *Qi* in Chinese belief to *Ka* in Ancient Egypt, and from *mbec* in the Ghedee energy workers of West Africa to the *Gitche Manitou* of the American Algonchuian people, it was in science that these ideas became most entrenched.

Chemistry was split into organic and inorganic material, the former changing irreversibly when heated, the latter reverting to its original state. Not only did organic matter possess this weightless, invisible substance or **vital force**, but also organic matter could not be made from inorganic matter. It was different and special. Even in the 19th century, important scientists such as Louis Pasteur still believed in Vitalism.

By the 20th century, Vitalism had been discarded. In its place came **emergence**, wherein a level of organization cannot be explained as the sum of its component parts. The term was first coined by the philosopher, George Lewes, in his book *Problems of Life and Mind* (Lewes, 2004). While a steam engine can be seen as an outcome of all the different cogs and bolts, life is an altogether different kettle of fish (as are fish compared with kettles).

Emergent properties are radically new, maintained over a period of time and at a global level, capable of evolution and perception. The greater the number of components, the greater the likelihood of emergent properties arising, although in complex systems, the emergent property may be masked by the vast number of interactions, some of whose outcomes may work against it. One of the most commonly cited examples of emergence is among the social Hymenoptera, such as bees and ants. Individual insects, without direct leadership, work to produce extremely complex outcomes such as the sophisticated termite mounds that even incorporate an air-conditioning system.

Emergence stands in juxtaposition to reductionism, where everything stems from basic components, and thus any process can be reduced to these components. Science generally uses a mechanistic model, wherein all effects have causes. An exception to this is the **New Physics**, where relativity rules the roost and where, as Albert Einstein remarked:

> Even space and time are forms of intuition, which can no more be divorced from consciousness than can our concept of colour or shape or size. Space has no objective reality except as an order or arrangement of objects we perceive in it, and time has no independent existence apart from the order of events by which we measure it (quoted in Barnett, 1949; p. 12).

Emergence allowed a more holistic overview, and, as we will see, became important in more recent ecological models. However, it also meant that laboratory experimentation failed to encompass emergent properties because all components of a natural system cannot be created in a simplified system required for the scientific method to be executed. These missing components mean the laboratory test tube approach cannot produce the emergent properties within a laboratory that occur in the real world, thus potentially undermining the legitimacy of laboratory science in ecological studies.

4.1.2 Form vs. function

Early work used human society as the benchmark, and tended to paint the organization of natural systems in anthropomorphic ways. Terms such as **society** and **community** found their way into early ecological literature and remained there. Form rather than function dominated this early period of biology, with taxonomy playing a leading role, in what we could call the **Age of Descriptive Ecology**. Interestingly, quantitative sociology has been largely dominated by form rather than function too, with emphasis on diversity as a measure of society.

Biological form gained importance when Karl Linnaeus developed the **binomial system of taxonomy**, wherein each type of organism was given a two-part label, the first being the genus, and the second the species. For example, the common poppy was called *Papaver* (genus) *rhoeas* (species). While local names for plants and animals differed from country to country, the Linnaean binomial was a global constant. Thus each life form could be placed in a little taxonomic box and the more forms of life present, the greater the diversity.

Morphological variety (diversity) became the currency of ecosystem health. Decline in diversity was viewed as bad, while increase in diversity was viewed as good. This reductionist approach, viewing ecosystem health as an outcome of the building blocks of taxonomy, made it easy to measure, but would become irrelevant in terms of functional ecology, which requires a more holistic, system approach.

Diversity has become a key aspect of modern ecology, in terms of the measurement of environmental damage and the assessment of the success of our efforts at amelioration. This concept has also found itself applied to society in the form of both sustainable development and post-development. In both frameworks, emphasis on cultural diversity is viewed as a strength.

Box 4.1: Diversity and tribalism: inbreeding, outbreeding and meta-population ecology

In (a), three populations are separated by barriers. This allows them to develop specialization to their own particular environment, but leaves each population at risk of local extinction and inbreeding depression (weakening of individuals due to genetic abnormalities being magnified through breeding with close relatives), since a drop in numbers cannot be recovered from outside the barrier (barriers can be inhospitable habitat, behavioural or areas of increased predation risk due to lack of cover, for example). In (b), the three populations can interact, forming a **meta-population** (a group of interacting populations). This has the advantage of providing greater resilience to extinction and lowering the likelihood of inbreeding depression. However, specialization can be lost, as each population dilutes the others' genetic focus. This is called **outbreeding depression**, and means that no single population within a meta-population is as well-fitted to its environment as it could be. Businesses face similar challenges in terms of whether to share or hide information with competitors, and whether to work with or compete against other companies in attempting to contribute to a sustainable economy, society and environment.

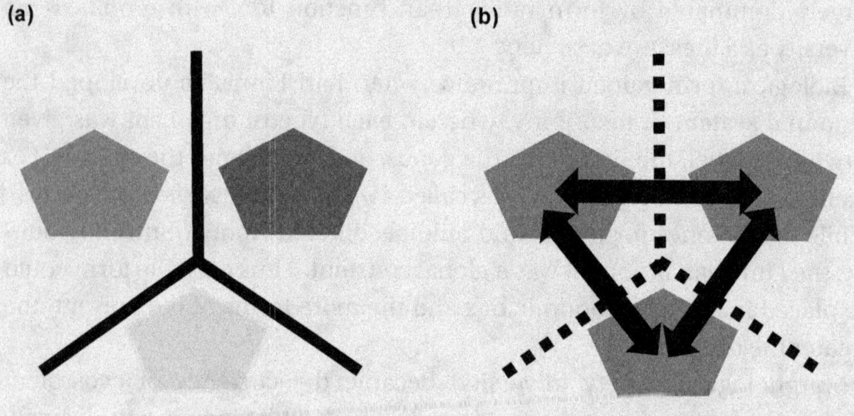

In economics, the need for diversity within financial markets is an alternative to globalization. Localism also promotes diversity. However, as Box 4.1 explores, diversity is a complex and difficult concept to integrate into sustainability.

Jean-Baptiste Lamarck (1744–1829) had set out an evolutionary theory based on function as a driver, wherein the functional need for a giraffe to reach high leaves on a tree drove morphological change. Thus the neck would stretch, and this change would be passed on to the next generation.

Darwinian theory further embraced form over function. Darwin turned Lamarckism on its head, stating that differences in form drove functional exploitation of the environment. It was form, not function that constituted the basis of understanding how diversity emerged. Survival of the fittest forms and the demise of the weakest, through competition, was the basis for natural selection. Darwin further attempted to link together the taxonomic boxes, showing that they represented different branches of a giant tree of diversity, and all were ultimately related to each other, some more closely than others. This relatedness was called **phylogeny**.

Darwinian theory became further reduced to the level of genes, celebrated in the selfish gene hypothesis (most famously propagated by Richard Dawkins). Darwinian theory soon began to be applied to management issues, with forms of management becoming key, rather than function. The idea of competition driving evolution went down well in economic circles also, and many papers have been written using the form-based dogma as a basis and as a defence of globalization and the competitive market. Less positive connotations such as eugenics have also found their roots in Darwinian theory, with Madison Grant, chairman of the Zoological Society of New York, emphasizing that "the laws of nature require the obliteration of the unfit" (Grant, 1916; p. 45). Rudolph Hess claimed that "National Socialism is nothing but applied biology" (Lifton, 1994; p. 129).

Functionalism has been making a comeback of late, both in **post-selectionism** (the theory that natural selection is not the driver of evolution) and in ecology. Conservation has moved from single species protection and diversity conservation to functional ecology, where the emphasis is no longer focused on the forms, but rather on the functionality of an ecosystem. Thus, a more holistic approach has emerged, with monitoring of material flows, outputs and inputs, resilience and recovery all emphasized. The focus is on the physiology of the ecosystem rather than its structure. Little effort has been exerted on applying these ideas to management structure, but undoubtedly this would provide an interesting challenge.

4.1.3 Balance

A third theme that has dominated ecology until the last couple of decades and still prevails within sustainable economics is that of **balance**. The idea that without human interference, nature is in balance and in a state of static equilibrium has a long history. In what has been called the **Ionian enchantment** by E.O Wilson, he refers to it as: "a belief in the unity of the sciences—a conviction, far deeper than a mere working proposition, that the world is orderly and can be explained by a small number of laws" (Wilson, 1999; pp. 4-5).

This concept traces its history back to many religious ideas of a creation that was perfect in its initial state but had somehow been ruined, or unbalanced, by sin. Interestingly, in 1749 Linnaeus published a book called *The Oeconomy of Nature.* In this book, Linnaeus presented his view that nature, while seemingly chaotic and unpredictable, actually existed in a balanced state of order as designed by the creator.

As ecology first began to rise as an academic pursuit at the beginning of the 20th century, ecosystems were seen to go through a number of changes before reaching what was called a **climax community**. The climax community was a destination of sorts. At this stage, nothing would change any further, and the system was viewed as having reached maturity, where it would stay in a balanced, static form unless disturbed. Certainly walking through a mature forest you can easily get the impression that nothing changes from year to year.

As early as 1864, George Perkins Marsh, the American naturalist argued that:

> nature, left undisturbed, so fashions her territory as to give it almost unchanging permanence of form, outline and proportion, except when shattered by geological convulsions; and in these comparatively rare cases of derangement, she sets herself at once to repair the superficial damage, and to restore, as nearly as practicable, the former aspect of her dominion (see Marsh, 1965; p. 12).

This idea was later accredited to Frederic Clements, the American ecologist.

The idea of an unchanging static equilibrium became commonplace among many ecologists. More significantly for this current book, it oozed out into other fields, where applied ecology began to form the basis for a wide number of areas. Closed, regulated, and homeostatic systems formed the basis of population dynamics and carrying capacity with concepts such as maximum sustainable yield and constants in population equations suggesting unchanging aspects. However, things do change, and alter the very constants that these models rely on.

In area versus diversity concepts of island biogeography, the relationship between area and diversity was deemed as a constant, and no other variables were included. This meant that a given area of forest in one location was calculated to be equivalent to a similar area elsewhere, in terms of carbon capture for example. This led to erroneous calculations in the Kyoto

Agreement. Although there may be a given area of forest, much of this may be degraded and thus not functioning well.

4.1.4 Circularity and cycles

The concept of balance is tightly associated with another set of beliefs, that ecosystems are tight, cycling systems, whose efficiency and sustainability can form the basis of economic models. Everything is perfectly recyclable, requiring no additional inputs. People discuss the planet as a "closed system", which couldn't be further from the truth. indeed it is the very open nature of the planetary system which allows life to exist. This huge error may have stemmed from the Spaceship Earth concept of Boulding. The concept of the Earth as a sealed spacecraft was attractive as an analogy. Of course, the first law of thermodynamics does state that energy can neither be created nor destroyed, and the principle of mass conservation states that in a closed system, mass cannot change.

However, the Earth is not a closed system. In fact, only the universe can be considered as a closed system. The sun itself loses mass. When two hydrogen (Deuterium) atoms are joined together to make helium in the sun, a neutron is also produced. However, the mass of the two hydrogen atoms is greater than the helium and neutron. And so mass is lost. The mass is converted to energy ($E=mc^2$). This energy heats the sun and is released from the sun. It is this energy that transforms our planet, where it is converted to sugar.

The bottom line is that nature would not exist as we know it if it wasn't for the continual input of energy. Of course energy cannot be destroyed, but it can be converted into a different form of energy. This form of energy is less useful. Thus life relies on a constant supply of useful energy, and living processes degrade this energy to make things. If the sun's energy is blocked, as has happened in mass extinction events due to it being blocked by dust in the atmosphere, life dies.

So fundamentally, nature is not a closed, tight, circular process, but rather relies on a constant, huge flow of energy and resources through it. This does not represent a closed circular system. The second law of thermodynamics clearly states that any system plus its surroundings tends spontaneously towards increasing disorder. The only way that life can exist is if it takes in enough energy to prevent becoming disordered.

Disorder leads to death. Thus, if you don't eat, you die. Life is like a leaky bucket with a duck floating on it. Energy must continue to flow into the system to allow the duck to stay afloat. Turn the tap off, and the bucket empties. Thus nature needs a continuous input of energy capital in order to stay alive. The second law also means that there can never be such a thing as perpetual motion. Even with continual energy input, chaos continues to enter the system. Thus any concept of lengthening the lifetime of a product, in order to avoid replacing it and thus reducing resource use, will have to be paid for by increased energy input. This challenges any concept of increased life-span of a product as a sustainable outcome.

Decreasing chaos within a product requires increasing the chaos in the product's surroundings. These surroundings are the natural environment. Nature exists in an energetic dynamic equilibrium, but any increase in chaos within the environment leads to disruption and degradation of the system. Thus ecosystems suffer from our attempts to maintain the complex structures that we rely on for our current lifestyles. There is no such thing as a free lunch in thermodynamic terms, and so as we attempt to maintain our highly ordered lifestyles, chaos must be produced out with those lifestyles. It is the environment that ultimately absorbs this chaos, leading to destabilization.

Thus the second law of thermodynamics undermines any suggestion of a circular economy in nature, and refutes the possibility of a circular ecology in economics. Ecosystems do not provide analogies for economics. For in nature there is a huge river of energy flowing through, and this is essential for our survival. It is not some self-sufficient, calm mill pond, but rather a system that is completely dependent on massive external funding, requiring the continuous flow of vast amounts of energy from the sun. Nature relies on hand-outs of cosmic proportions for its survival, hardly a model for economic sustainability.

4.2 The three ages of ecology

The four issues mentioned in the previous section have impacted on ecology in many ways. Their tensions have underpinned the development of the subject. In this section we develop a time-line of changing ecological theory, identifying three ages of ecology and tracing the changes in emphasis through the last 200 years. This is important as it allows us to ultimately understand where the current economic models of sustainability locate their foundations on this time-line.

4.2.1 The Age of Static Equilibrium

As religion, philosophy and science sought an understanding of the natural world, two aspects came to the fore—**ecological succession and stasis**. Succession is the process by which ecosystems develop, from bare soil or rock through a series of different communities of plants, microbes, fungi, algae and animals, to a final, mature phase. It can take hundreds of years to reach this mature stage. At any stage, fire or flood can reset the clock, wiping out the existent ecosystem. The whole process starts again.

Key characteristics of succession include **directionality** (communities change from simple to complex ecosystems), **predictability** (given the location and starting material you can predict roughly what will happen), **replacement** (where a given species thrives for a short time, and then disappears, replaced by a different organism) and **selflessness** (in that no single organism can alter conditions to maintain itself in the succession). The species occurring at the climax stage remain longest, but are not present earlier, and therefore cannot be said to engineer their own longevity. Thus succession lies in opposition to the selfish gene hypothesis of the **modern evolutionary synthesis**, where genes engineer their own survival and fecundity in self-interest. Rather, in succession, the system cannot be reduced to genes, but instead acts in a much more complex way.

The idea that an ecosystem eventually reaches a state which does not change incorporates a number of the issues in ecology mentioned in the previous section. This mature state is characterized as a state of balance. There is no longer a need to change, as perfect order has been established. It is much less chaotic than earlier states. Plants tend to be perennial rather than annual in nature. Diversity is high—the highest of all the stages, with long-living species focused on maintenance and repair, rather than survival and reproduction.

The static equilibrium model also is form-based, in that the changing forms earlier in the succession are replaced by longer living forms, the climax community. While some functional aspects are included, static equilibrium models are mostly based on structure. The mature state is also viewed as being inherently self-contained, a closed set of cycles that are self-maintained and self-regulated. The driver of change in ecological succession is seen as the interaction between organisms and the nonliving environment. On land this is usually soil. Species arrive, altering the soil to such an extent that they no longer can live in it, and are replaced by new species. Eventually a group of species arrives that no longer alters the soil chemistry, and remain there.

Since the 1950s, the static equilibrium model has been applied to **cultural ecology** (Steward 1955), the **ecosystems approach** (Rappaport 1967), and **cultural materialism** (Harris 1979). These theories argue that in the same way that natural environments are homeostatically regulated, so too are societies that rely on nature. Forest and fisheries management became focused on maintaining stock close to but not at static equilibrium, in order to achieve maximum growth, which diminishes at climax. The balance of nature has had a long history within the social sciences, reinforced by functionalist models dependent on stable, equilibrial notions of social order (Scoones, 1999). **Political ecology** was also influenced by the static equilibrium model, expressed as an idea that a balanced, traditional, harmonious system existed in the past and therefore could be re-established.

The "**Golden Age**" conservation movement looks to reintroduce species that were formally in an area and to plant trees in order to re-establish the perfection of nature. The purpose is to return nature to its former glory by putting back in place the original, individual building blocks. This is a form-based approach, and a reductionist concept. Yet planting trees in a field does not make a forest, but rather creates trees in a field. Forests are complex outcomes of succession, and the trees are only a small part of it. Soils must be forest soils, which cannot be made by planting trees in a field. They are created by slow gradual transformation over several hundred years. The forest soil is the outcome of a long succession of different species that grew long before the trees arrived. You cannot fast-track ecological succession. Emergent qualities cannot be constructed.

Environmental economists, ecological economists and institutional economists all reference a static view of the environment and natural resources. Limits to growth and carrying capacity dominate, each reliant on static relationships and constants. Sustainable economics looks to restore the homeostasis to the planet. This restoration generally involves a static philosophy.

4.2.2 The Age of Non-equilibrium

The static equilibrium model has been disputed for over 80 years. In 1930, English ecologist Charles Elton wrote that "the balance of nature does not exist and perhaps never has existed" (Elton 1930; p. 15). This point has been emphasized by many ecologists since. Cronon wrote: "We can no longer assume the existence of a static and benign climax community in nature that contrasts with dynamic, but destructive, human change" (Cronon 1990; pp. 1127-8).

Non-equilibrium ecology stresses that nature is never in a balanced, homeostatic state, because there is always a lag between the ecosystem and its context. Nature, therefore, is continuously catching up (García-Valdés *et al.*, 2013). Large-scale anthropogenic disturbance can also destabilize equilibrium conditions. Depending on conditions during succession, the "**end-point**" may be quite different. It was Henry Gleason who first opposed the static equilibrium approach of his opponent, Frederic Clements, early in the 20th century.

The consequences of this challenge are huge. Gone are the concepts of balance, stasis, homeostasis and order. These principles form the foundation for most of the ecological models used in sustainable economics. Therefore non-equilibrium ecology shakes these foundations to the core, seriously undermining much of the current theoretical basis.

Rather, there is a continual conversation between the components of an ecosystem. One interesting example relates to the **rebound effect** in islands. An island such as Trinidad has only been separated from the continental landmass of South America for around 2,000 years. The impact of this is that the number of species has steadily declined, since the area available has dramatically decreased. However, if this was not taken into account, it could be thought that the decrease in species richness was due to other factors. Instead, it is merely an adjustment to Trinidad having recently (in geological terms) become an island. Thus data on species richness over time must be viewed within a dynamic geological framework.

Variation is viewed as important. For example average rainfall does not indicate the heterogeneity of rainfall events. If two areas have an average annual rainfall of 240 mm precipitation, one location may have 20mm each month, while the other location may have 240mm in one month and no rainfall for the other 11 months. This would have a very different impact on these two areas. Abiotic variation has become important in non-equilibrium ecology. It is estimated that when the coefficient of variation (CV) exceeds 33%, then non-equilibrium dynamics begin to play a significant role in terms rangeland management (Ellis and Smith, 1988).

Social-ecological systems result from a context-driven combination of continuous and discontinuous change, producing non-linear outcomes. Stochasticity plays an important role in non-equilibrium ecology. The change in ecology is reminiscent of the changes in physics at the beginning of the 20th century, leaving behind the reductionist Newtonian approach, and embracing the New Physics, as pioneered by Albert Einstein and Werner Heisenberg. Here, the uncertainty principle led to a breech between observation and the material world. Since observation disturbs the observed, then we cannot be confident that our observations actually reflect reality. Reality itself may be an emergent characteristic.

Non-equilibrium ecology is a holistic science where emergence, variability and uncertainty play significant roles, rather than being viewed as background noise. Central to this is the field of **system biology**, the concept of a community as a superior, emergent hierarchical level of organization.

The impact for other fields that had previously incorporated static equilibrium ecology in their foundations should have been immense. Without a stable, balanced, homeostatic and ordered natural world, standard interventionist approaches in applied management, based on conventional ecological models of cause and effect, became invalid. Furthermore, the debate relating to sustainable development also was challenged.

However, in reality what happened was quite extraordinary. Sustainable economics and management theory decided to ignore the non-equilibrium approach. This was an active process, not some temporary loss of memory, as non-equilibrium theory was written large across the academic sky. Thousands of papers and hundreds of books explore the field, yet in terms of sustainable economics, it was almost as if this body of knowledge was invisible.

Instead concepts such as the closed-loop economy, the circular economy, Cradle to Cradle® and industrial ecology (see Chapter 5 for details on these) all rely on the old school of static equilibrium ecology. It was akin to developing oceanic shipping based on the Earth being flat, or relying on spontaneous generation to procreate.

Of course there have been a few exceptions. Buzz Holling (1978) and Carl Walters (1986) set out **adaptive management** as a non-equilibrium approach, wherein feedback from environmental monitoring allows continuing conversation and response to change. Redclift observed that in terms of sustainable development: "the homeostatic controls that exist within natural communities, and that enable them to achieve succession are only effective if these ecosystems are protected from rapid change" (Redclift, 1987; p. 18).

One of the most challenging outcomes of non-equilibrium ecology is the prediction of tipping points. A tipping point is a threshold of environmental forcing beyond which abrupt and critical changes occur. These changes are often difficult to predict, given the complex nature of any given ecosystem. Examples include the population level of otters in the Pacific Northwest (Dayton, 1985). If the population falls below a critical level, sea urchin populations increase (because predation pressure from otters is no longer strong enough), leading to young kelp plants being over-harvested by the urchins, resulting in the large-scale death of kelp forests. Such changes are often irreversible (Duarte *et al.*, 2012). Tipping points may also lead to species extinctions which are, by their definition, irreversible. These shifts from one ecosystem type to another are explained as alternative equilibria, with the system shifting from one to another (Scheffer *et al.*, 1993).

Interestingly, the origin of the tipping point came not from ecology, but from political science. In 1957, Morton Grodzins identified the percentage of non-white residents living in a previously white neighbourhood that would lead to a phenomenon called "**white flight**", resulting in a switch to a neighbourhood now completely occupied by non-white residents. He referred to this figure as the **tip point** (Grodzins, 1957), a term later changed to **tipping point** (Wolf, 1963). Its application to environmental issues such as climate change has found a place within non-equilibrium ecology, and has become one of its main features.

Given that system theory recognizes the importance of self-organization as the basis of emergence, and that the patterns and processes that result from such organization are central to the identity of the system, then a catastrophic shift in character must reflect a change in self-organization. Dynamic systems theory studies such non-linear behaviour that characterizes tipping points, identifying alternative stable states (Carpenter and Brock, 2006; Mayer, Pawlowski and Cabezas, 2006).

Because the concept of tipping points has emerged from sociopolitical science and from ecology, its application to managerial and economic areas is fairly straightforward. It has been used, for example, to understand why some businesses suddenly collapse, while others remain stable (Gibbs and Deutz, 2005).

It is this very capability of nature to change dramatically and quickly, from one state to another, that delineates non-equilibrium theory from static equilibrium models. The two most concerning issues here relate to the speed at which this can occur and to the irreversibility once changed. Furthermore, it may take very little change to set such events in motion (Lenton *et al.*, 2008), hence the relevance of the term "**tipping point**".

A key theory representing the Age of Non-equilibrium was the concept of **panarchy**, developed by Lance Gunderson and Buzz Holling who defined it "as an antithesis to the word hierarchy (literally, sacred rules). Our view is that panarchy is a framework of nature's rules, hinted at by the name of the Greek god of nature, Pan" (Gunderson and Holling, 2001; p. 21).

While the reference to Pan may have been unfortunate, given the criticism of the use of **Gaia** in the Gaian hypothesis, panarchy really distils the spirit of the Age of Non-equilibrium. Panarchy was much more than an ecological theory. It aimed to explain economic, social and environmental transformation in some form of grand unification. In fact the term had been used several times before Gunderson and Holling's work, in very different contexts.

It was Holling's work on forests that stimulated his thinking. Forests grow, and as they do they become more complex, with increases in the number of species and the connections between these species. Increasing connectedness leads to greater efficiency and greater feedback, in turn increasing stability. As maturity continues, less new species can find roles as most niches are filled. This appears to be drifting towards static equilibrium.

However, this is not how Holling saw the forest progressing. Maturity brings greater vulnerability to outside shock, as increasing complexity requires increasingly narrow variation in conditions. In effect, the old forest becomes brittle and inflexible. The ecosystem becomes less capable of adaptive change, as it is now built up of highly specialist individuals playing a limited role and requiring quite specific conditions in order to play that role. Resilience now decreases. Collapse occurs. However, following collapse, the ecosystem has more freedom. A loss of connectedness allows greater opportunity for exploration of new solution space. This is a period of re-organization, leading to rebirth, whereupon resilience again begins to build.

Thus an adaptive cycle is established: growth (competitive, K phase), collapse (omega phase), re-organization (alpha phase) and rebirth (ruderal, r phase). This allows the ecosystem to be sustainable, evolving in response to changing local and global conditions. The passage through these four stages is represented as a 3D figure of eight (Fig. 4.1).

We start with a basic ecosystem, such as a beach, with some short-lived, rapidly reproducing species. This stage is called a **ruderal or exploitation phase**, represented by "r". It is simple and has high resilience, being able to recover from disruption because of its fast reproductive potential and lack of specialized requirements. Individuals do not live long and so death is not a threat to the overall structure. This is the growth phase, and the ecosystem gradually becomes more complex, gaining connectivity but losing

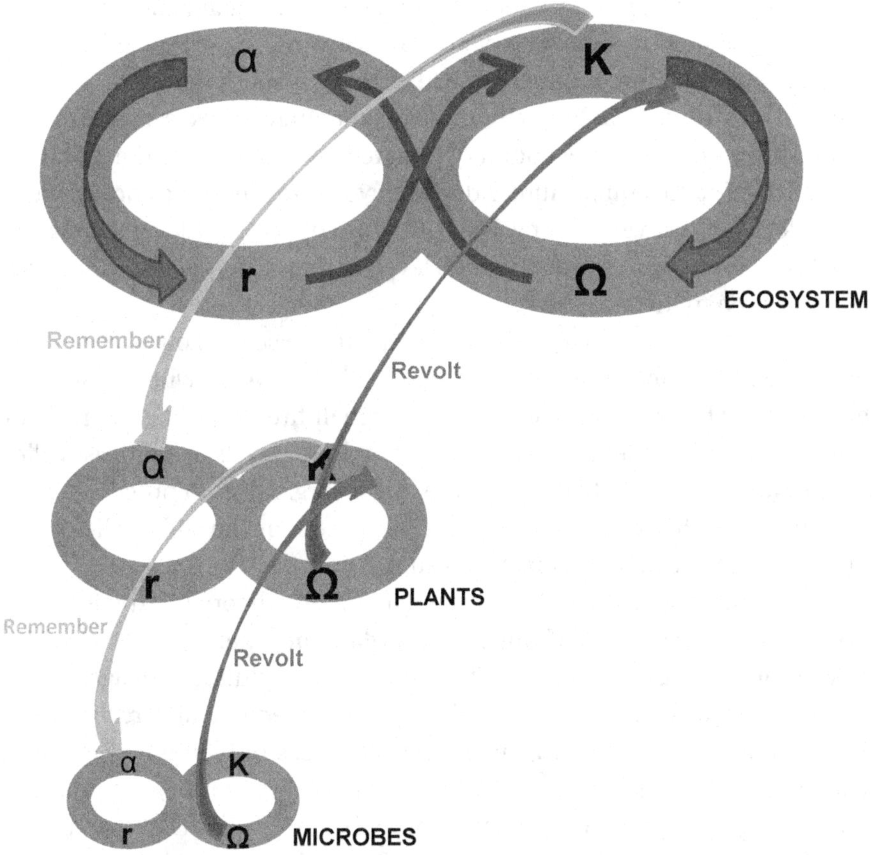

FIGURE 4.1 Panarchy. Each level of organization is seen to cycle through four stages, growth (K), collapse (Ω), re-organization (α) and rebirth (r). Different levels of organization can impact one another through remembering (where previous events such as seed bank build-up impact on re-organization) and revolt (where a collapse event at one level can impact on the stability and growth of another level). Tipping points are extreme revolt cascades.

resilience. Thus the figure swings upwards (increasing complexity) and outwards (loss of resilience).

This transition moves the system from an exploitation phase (r) to a **conservation phase** (K), where all efforts are put into maintaining the status quo. Collapse leads to a reduction in resilience and a decrease in potential, moving to a **release stage** (Ω). From here, the system increases in potential but not resilience, moving to a **re-organization phase**, and then back to an exploitation phase. Generally release and re-organization are rapid, whereas exploitation and conservation are slower.

The second feature of panarchy is that there is more than one adaptive cycle. In fact, somewhat bizarrely, there is a hierarchy of cycles. This is interesting, given that the whole point of panarchy was to replace the hierarchy approach of static equilibrium. Adaptive cycles are viewed as occurring at many levels, from very fast cycles at the microbiological level through to much slower cycles at the continental level. In forest this goes from soil bacteria through to the biosphere.

Each adaptive cycle can interact with other cycles. Lower cycles can impact with higher cycles in a process called "**revolt**", where fast small events overwhelm larger ones (such as a small fire spreading to an entire forest), whereas higher cycles can impact on lower levels in a process called "**remember**" such as when, after a fire, the re-organization process may be influenced by the seed bank still alive in the soil, or the soil quality previously produced by the original forest succession.

While panarchy is meant to represent a unifying theory to explain social, economic and ecosystem change, it is fundamentally an ecological model, relying on analogy to integrate it, rather than any direct linkages. Since adaptive cycles can only be linked through **remember** and **revolt**, there is little way to envisage how three separate stacks of hierarchies of cycles can interact with each other, such as separate ecosystems (e.g. a mountain, river and lake, which are connected through water flow). However, panarchy does at least clearly present the qualities of non-equilibrium ecology. Static ecology only has exploitation and conservation phases, and progress in a straight line from r to K, whereas panarchy represents a cycle. Even so, it relies on the same basic processes as static equilibrium in terms of succession theory, merely adding the impact of disturbance and natural selection in terms of collapse and re-organization respectively. In reality, these ideas have been understood for most of the 20th century, and are not fundamentally new.

Finally, the driver of succession in terms of directionality, is not accounted for. While we can see the stages following on from each other, there is no explanation given for the increasing complexity following rebirth. Why does the system change from r to K? This question, unanswered by the Age of Static Equilibrium, remains unanswered in the Age of Non-equilibrium. The "**why**" question always remains elusive. It would not be until the final age of ecology that we would find answers.

4.2.3 The Age of Ecological Thermodynamics

While non-equilibrium ecology has developed as a significant approach, a third age of ecology has been emerging in recent years, whose seeds trace back to the late 19th century. Focused not on outcomes of destabilization *per se*, this field examines a much more fundamental issue, **entropy**. Entropy is the process of diffusion, leading to a decrease in the ability to do useful work. The second law of thermodynamics states that entropy in the universe must increase.

Thus, over time, the universe becomes more diffuse, expanding and cooling, and this will continue until it reaches a temperature of absolute zero (–460°F or –273° C), at which point it will be completely motionless, with no possibility of further activity (see Appendix for a detailed explanation of thermodynamics). Interestingly, within thermodynamics there exists a very limited but powerful school of economists, which is more than can be said about the previous two ages. However, its application to sustainable economic models remains virtually unexplored.

A shift to an ecophysiological view in ecology, driven by Hutchison and Eugene Odum, took a more functional approach to succession (Drury and Nisbet, 1973), with Noble and Slatyer (1980) attributing **vital attributes** to species, wherein species–environment interactions, rather than the developmental anatomy of the community *per se*, drove community change. From this physiological approach emerged a more fundamental understanding, defined by energy flow, which argued that the ultimate "**strategy**" is to maximize homeostasis against perturbation (Odum, 1969).

Within a universe where entropy is increasing, disorder must increase. The only way to maintain order is if there is a supply of energy available. This energy on Earth comes from the sun, which itself is breaking down. The energy released allows us to do work, and to build things. Of course, work converts useful energy to less useful energy, and contributes to the entropy of our surroundings. In fact the second law of thermodynamics predicts that if an energy source is available, an open system should become more complex, because increasing complexity will produce increasing entropy in its surroundings as a consequence of reducing entropy within itself.

The focus on energy has developed into a fundamental transformation in thinking: that the driver and mechanism of succession lie neither in some fixed association of species, nor in species–environment interactions. Rather, the basis comes from a much more universal set of laws, namely, the laws of thermodynamics (Skene, 2013). Further, there has been a shift within ecological energetics, from a restricted use of the first law (flow and conservation of energy) to the application of the second law (Tiezzi and Pulselli 2008; Nielson 2009).

The significance of thermodynamics in ecology dates back over 100 years, to Ludwig Boltzmann, Sergei Podolinsky and Vladimir Stanchinskii. Alfred Lotka (1922, 1925) and Erwin Schrödinger (1944) developed the concept that evolution was driven by maximization of useful energy flow, and this concept was later to form the basis of much of Howard Odum's work (Odum and Pinkerton, 1955; Margalef, 1963), wherein an ecosystem develops towards maximizing the rate of useful energy transformation (**the maximum power principle**). Not only do ecosystems move to reduce entropy within themselves (hence moving further from energetic equilibrium), but in doing so, they move towards maximizing external entropy increase. Central to this process is the **maximum entropy production principle** (MEPP).

In its modern expression, the MEPP states that "non-equilibrium thermodynamic systems are organized in steady state such that the rate of entropy production is maximized" (Kleidon *et al.*, 2010). The maximum entropy production principle can trace its roots back to 1774, when Pierre-Simon Laplace, in response to Gottfried Leibnitz's **Principle of Sufficient Reason**, developed his **Principle of Insufficient Reason**, originally as part of an elementary mathematics course at a teacher training college. Jaynes (1957) refers to the maximum entropy principle as the translation into mathematics of ancient wisdom.

MEPP has been found to hold for geographic species distributions, trophodynamics, present and past climate, atmospheric circulation, nucleotide sequences, developmental biology, earthquake prediction, linguistics, and macroeconomics (Skene, 2013 and references therein).

Significantly, the MEPP has also been found to hold for the process of ecological succession in Mediterranean lake, marine sediment, and tropical rainforest ecosystems, where entropy production increases during early stages, before reaching a maximum at the climax (Fig. 4.2).

Nicholas Georgescu-Roegen, the Romanian economist, was far ahead of the field when in 1971, he released his book, *The Entropy Law and the Economic Process*. Georgescu-Roegen considered that the neoclassical economic model is based on Newtonian physics, and ignores the principles of energy and matter degradation. He concluded that thermodynamics must be taken into account, emphasizing that the second law of thermodynamics was "the most economical of all natural laws ... in terms of entropy, the cost of any biological or economical venture is always greater than its result. In entropic terms, such activities necessarily translate into some sort of a

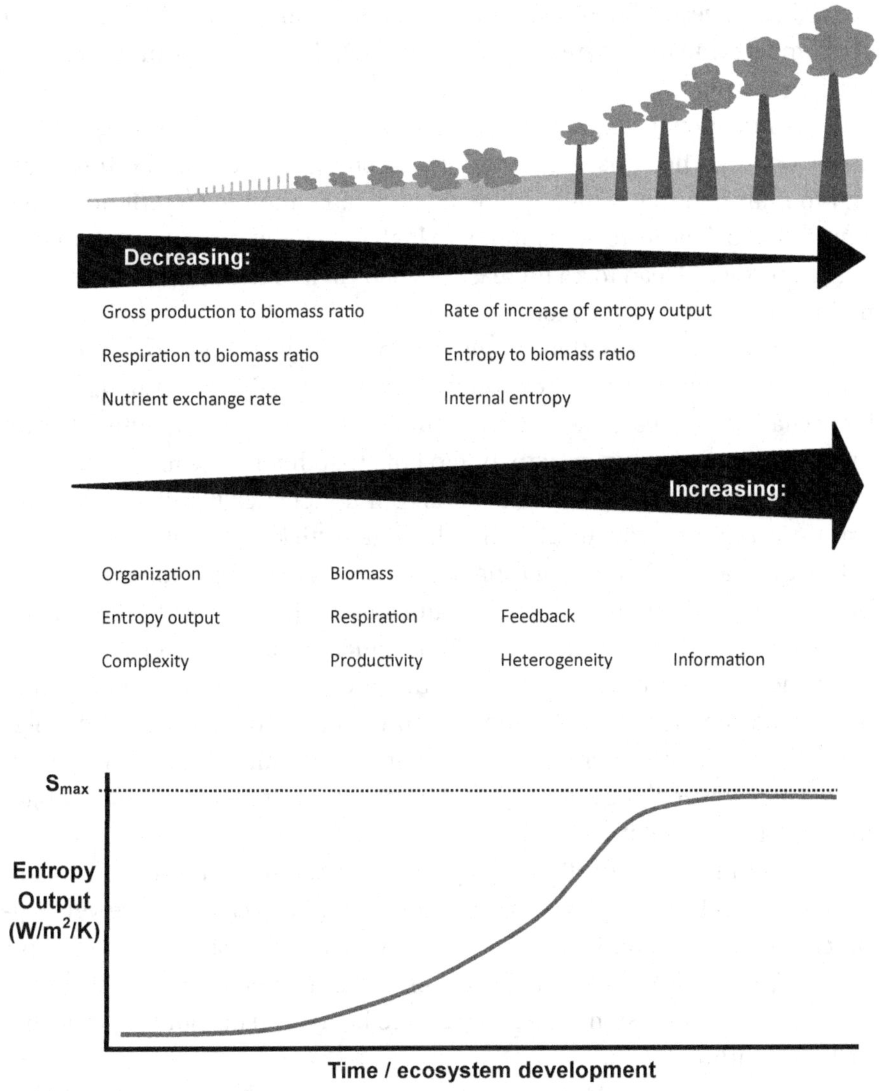

FIGURE 4.2 Succession and thermodynamics. Through time, ecosystems develop and change in nature. Thermodynamically, entropy output increases, approaching a maximum level, S_{max}, as internal entropic levels decrease with increasing complexity and order within the system.

deficit" (Georgescu-Roegen, 1971; p. 85). Other early work on entropy and economics came from Ayres and Kneese (1969), Noll and Trijonis (1971) and Perrings (1986).

Economic growth requires increased conversion of useful energy to less useful energy. The consumption of useful energy is required both to grow and to maintain that which is already grown. Economic growth needs the conversion of low entropy resources to high entropy waste. Thus an expanding economy will lead to an increase in chaos in its surroundings in order to maintain itself far from chaos.

The only problem is that if the flow of energy through our economy should be disrupted, then the economy will begin to die, becoming increasingly chaotic as it loses the energy required to maintain itself. Energy is not just needed to maintain growth, but to hold together that which has already grown. It is the glue that binds together our matchstick world, amid a constant storm. Take away the glue and the match sticks will scatter.

However, a matchstick building, no matter how well glued, can only be built so high. This point is the maximum entropy production of the system. There is an upper ceiling in terms of how much chaos can be created in our surroundings, and in terms of how much order can be maintained within our economic structure. As the environment becomes degraded energetically, it becomes increasingly difficult to maintain the structure of our matchstick tower. For by its very existence, the tower increases the strength of the storm around it.

The natural world itself is dissipative and relies on recycling already. Disturbance of its recycling capacity and its renewal capacity are very significant issues. Not only does the economy fail to recycle, but it interrupts the recycling of nature. Our recycling efforts must not impact on the flow/flux of the natural system. What appears to be neutral output to us may not be to the natural world.

Nordhaus (1992; p. 34) stated that, "as long as the sun shines brightly on our fair planet, the appropriate estimate for the drag from increasing entropy is zero". However, this fails completely to grasp the meaning of entropy output by the economy. Increased dissipation in the natural system cannot be ameliorated by sunlight. For example, when a lake receives nutrients from farmland, the sunlight actually helps create the problem, as the nutrients allow an increase in energy flow which in turn destabilizes the system.

There is no such thing as a free lunch in thermodynamic terms, and entropy output by the economy, required to maintain its very fabric, has devastating effects on the environmental surroundings of the human race, requiring further energy to maintain this fabric and leading to even greater entropy output and environmental degradation. Increasing complexity within the human sphere must lead to increasing chaos within our surroundings.

The Age of Ecological Thermodynamics clearly sets out a new understanding of the cost of our increasing complexity, and challenges any sustainable economic model that is based on circularity, balance and stasis. It also demonstrates unequivocally that economic growth leads to environmental degradation.

It has been argued that consumption of non-material or "intellectual" goods—ideas, art, literature, psychological insight, music—is not bounded by the entropy law in the way that material processes must succumb to the laws of nature. John Stuart Mill asserted that while the material economy would attain a stationary state, our intellectual development could increase indefinitely:

> It is scarcely necessary to remark that a stationary condition of capital and population implies no stationary state of human improvement. There would be as much scope as ever for all kinds of mental culture, and moral and social progress; as much room for improving the Art of Living and much more likelihood of its being improved, when minds cease to be engrossed in the art of getting on (Mill, 1848, p. 129).

As such, it has been suggested that there is no physical limit to the progress of the "intellectual" economy. However, the intellectual economy can only create potential output, and the conversion of these ideas into material output will always produce entropy. The mainstream position has been formulated by Robert Solow, who stated that "Everything is subject to the entropy law, but this is of no immediate practical importance for modelling what is, after all, a brief instant of time in a small corner of the universe" (Solow, 1997, p. 268). Kårberger and Månsson (2001) argue that although the second law may have consequences on a microeconomic scale, it is not relevant on a macroeconomic scale because the Earth is an open system that imports low entropy by solar radiation. Given that global circulation patterns and entire ecosystem development follows the second law, macroeconomics is unlikely to avoid its attention!

Georgescu-Roegen observed that:

> A human being can only avoid the entropic degradation of its own structure. It cannot stop the rise of entropy within the entire system, made up from its very structure and the environment. On the contrary,

> as far as we know today, generally, the entropy of a system rises faster when life exists within it rather than when it is absent (Georgescu-Roegen, 1971; p. 86).

Fundamentally, the second law of thermodynamics means that there can be no such thing as perpetual motion. In other words, energy input will always be required, since dissipation will always occur. The barrel has a hole in it that cannot be plugged. Hence any idea of a truly circular ecology is invalid. The very act of maintaining a system far from equilibrium itself generates greater chaos in the surrounding environment, thus making it increasingly difficult to maintain the order within the system. As heat increases in the surroundings, it becomes more likely that the candle will melt. Eventually the work required to maintain order within an increasingly chaotic universe will be insufficient. The sun will eventually run out of fuel and thus the planet will fall into disorder.

4.3 Biosphere function: how do the pieces fit together?

The central question, in terms of how the biosphere works, relates to how the different levels of organization (namely the genetic material, proteins, cells, organisms, populations, ecosystems and biomes) within the biosphere interact to each other. This is extremely important, as it has major repercussions in terms of referencing the natural world as a model or analogy for sustainable economics and, more importantly, as a reality for our future co-existence. There are three fundamentally different viewpoints here: the **neo-Darwinian approach**, the **Gaian approach** and the **thermodynamic approach**.

4.3.1 Neo-Darwinian theory

The Darwinian theory of evolution suggests that natural selection drives evolution, with the fittest thriving, and the less fit declining. However, Charles Darwin was unable to identify the mechanistic basis by which the fit were differentiated from the less fit. It was Gregor Mendel, the Augustinian monk from Brno, who identified heritable components of individuals, the genes, as being the means by which characteristics were passed from one generation to another. We now know that these genes are pieces of

DNA, and that humans gain just under 50% of their genes from their fathers and just over 50% from their mothers (the difference is because our mitochondrial DNA comes only from our mothers, whereas our nuclear DNA comes from both parents).

Incorporation of the gene into Darwinian theory led to the **modern evolutionary synthesis**, or **neo-Darwinian theory**, wherein the gene was identified as the unit of selection. This is the sacred dogma of neo-Darwinism. It is the gene that ultimately represents the basis of life, and the gene that dictates the success or failure of the organism. This is a purely reductionist approach, wherein everything else in the biosphere stems from the gene. The rest of the biosphere is merely an **extended phenotype** (Dawkins, 1982), the outcome of the selfish gene.

In this view, genes build proteins, individuals, populations and ecosystems. By manipulating the genetic code through genetic engineering or modification, we can construct a better world. Furthermore, since it all stems from the gene, laboratory science can claim to be the best and only way to understand our world. If the biosphere is reductionist, then reductionist science is justified. The building blocks are the genes. They account for the architecture, function and evolution of life. In the life sciences today, departments of molecular biology and genetics dominate university faculties with schools of molecular ecology and conservation genetics representing the conversion of formerly holistic domains into laboratory-based reductionism.

Genes are viewed as resembling self-interested entities, in that their own success in replicating will be reflected in the success of the organism in which they exist. Thus the concept of the "**selfish gene**" has emerged. The selfish gene concept sets out the idea that genes are the primary drivers and beneficiaries of the process of evolution. Their goal is to spread and increase their share of the gene pool. Organisms containing selfish genes will behave in such a way as to support this goal, and everything beyond the gene is merely an extension of this selfish prerogative. Thus you will be more likely to help someone else the more genes you share with them, because you are driven to assist the copies of the genes that you have in common with that person.

This view claims that altruistic behaviour is strongest between organisms that share the closest genetic information, such as next of kin, and that this is because organisms work to protect other organisms with similar genes. The concept is closely married to **inclusive fitness** which represents the global presence of a gene, rather than the presence of related offspring. The gene operates in such a way as to maximize its representation in the global gene pool.

Thus genes selfishly drive their own spread first, by controlling the behaviour of individuals towards closely related family members, even if that leads to the death of the individual in the process of saving another closely related individual with the same gene. Provided more copies of shared genes survive, then the action will be justified and is likely to occur. So if you save your two brothers from drowning, but drown yourself, this is an overall gain in terms of inclusive fitness (or rather a decreased loss). Thus the concept of **kin selection** emerged, wherein kin would be more protected the closer they were related genetically.

The selfish gene allowed the humanizing of the modern evolutionary synthesis, wherein although life was reduced to genes, these genes had, in some way, personalities, and these personalities were complementary to the rawness of the competitive battle that natural selection and the survival of the fittest represented. It also played to the same tune as Adam Smith's observation on economics, where he observed that "It is not from benevolence of the butcher, the brewer or the baker, that we expect our dinner, but from their regard to their own interests" (Smith, 1937; p. 14). In other words these food suppliers are not working for our good, but for their own benefit.

Bernard de Mandeville (1670–1733) had previously written an extremely controversial book, originally called *The Grumbling Hive* (Mandeville, 2007), where he set out that private vice stimulates society, while private virtue ruins it. In other words, there had to be greed in order to drive us on to make money, but that money would then be spent supporting a wide range of workers, providing employment. If this greed didn't exist, Mandeville argued, there would be a sharp decline in the nation's wellbeing. Mandeville went on to argue that society and virtue were merely constructs of a self-centred greed. It was all about selfishness, a theme that neo-Darwinism would adopt, almost four centuries later, in its reductionist explanation for life on Earth.

The neo-Darwinian position posits that the biosphere is made of building blocks, and thus we can build our way to a better future, by replacing ruined building blocks with new ones. Indeed we can develop improved buildings through technology and reason. The reductionist world is a world of the Enlightenment. We can take what nature has done and mimic it, replacing natural capital with human-made capital.

Recent thoughts on climate amelioration have included pouring huge quantities of iron into the oceans to encourage photosynthesis and concomitant absorption of carbon dioxide from the atmosphere into the sediment, or the pumping of sulphur aerosols into the stratosphere to reflect sunlight from the planet surface, thus cooling it. These actions cannot be tested in anything resembling a realistic scenario, and yet have been seriously considered—a worrying proposition given our record of failure in previous cases which have included the use of lead as an antiknock agent, the use of chlorofluorocarbons (CFCs) in aerosols and refrigeration and the release of cane toads in Queensland, Australia. These examples warn that the approach we take to understanding our world can have extremely grave outcomes.

There are no emergent properties in a reductionist universe, and so there should be no surprises, yet there often are. Rather, to the neo-Darwinian school, the biosphere is a predictable outcome of the genetic foundation, an extended phenotype.

Darwinian theory has an elephant in the room, the ecosystem. Incapable of community action, selfish genes must only pursue their own interests of inclusive fitness. However, in ecological succession organisms and genes present at the start of a succession are absent later on, while completely different packages of genes now dominate. Thus the species and the genes are subordinate to the greater picture. This problem resembles the fear of pantheism in the Christian church of medieval times. It recalls an apostasy, one so significant that it resulted in the very concept of a selfish gene in the first place. Vero Wynne-Edwards, a professor in Aberdeen University, had written a book in 1962 entitled *Animal Dispersion in Relation to Social Behaviours* (Wynne-Edwards, 1962), in which he argued that group selection favoured populations that self-regulated themselves in terms of territory and reproduction.

He emphasized the role of group selection over individual selection, opposing the Darwinian view. This led to an almighty backlash from the neo-Darwinians, led by George Williams. In his repost to Wynne-Edwards, entitled *Adaptation and Natural Selection* (Williams, 1966), Williams stressed that selection primarily acts through the individual, and this led to the establishment of the gene as the unit of selection. As a result of the hardening of the gene selection front, any mention of a driver of evolution and ecology beyond the gene is quickly attacked, for fear of the return of group selection to the table.

Adam Smith disagreed with this extreme position. He wrote that virtuous self-interest led to invisible co-operation. There was no need for a human guide. Instead, Smith introduced one of the most interesting and mysterious metaphors in the English literature, the invisible hand. He wrote:

> He intends only his own gain, and he is in this, as in many other cases, led by an invisible hand to promote an end which was no part of his intention. Nor is it always the worse for the society that it was no part of it. By pursuing his own interest he frequently promotes that of the society more effectually than when he really intends to promote it (Smith, 1791; p. 273).

And this invisible hand is explained, in different ways, in the second and third theories of how the biosphere functions.

4.3.2 Gaian theory

James Lovelock worked at NASA in the 1960s, specifically charged with developing a method to ascertain whether there was life on other planets. He began with asking the question: Can the existence of life be recognized from knowledge of the chemical composition of a planet's atmosphere? His approach was to measure the levels of specific gases in the atmosphere of Mars and determine if the gaseous content represented a state of equilibrium, or had the signature of life (chemical disequilibrium), with gases present that are indicative of a living planet.

He developed this idea from the definition of life as one member of the class of phenomena which are open or continuous reaction systems able to decrease their entropy at the expense of substances or energy taken in from the environment and subsequently rejected in a degraded form (Schrodinger, 1944; Bernal, 1951). While organisms were seen as adapting to the environment in which they existed, the environment also was affected by the organisms. Thus there was a feedback process. However, Lovelock went further, suggesting that the planet acted as a superorganism.

This led to the concept that the unit of selection was not the gene but the planet. "The unit of regulation is the Earth system and self-regulation is an emergent property of that system" (Lovelock, 2004; p. 2). By embracing emergence, Lovelock clearly set out his new theory as a holistic approach. This theory was in opposition to neo-Darwinian theory, which denied that organisms could lead to the evolution of planetary self-regulation through natural selection. Indeed Lovelock's theory also crossed the group/gene selection divide, and so was harshly attacked for this reason also. Lovelock called his theory **Gaia** after the primal Greek mother goddess, a suggestion made to him by novelist William Golding. The idea can be traced back to a

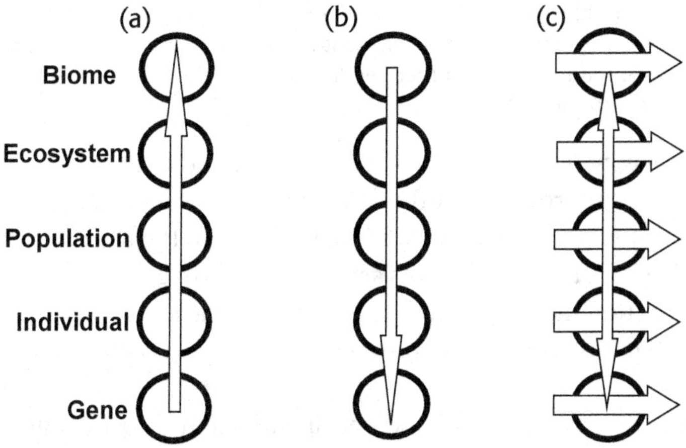

FIGURE 4.3 Scientific theories on how the biosphere evolved and functions. (a) Neo-Darwinism: the biosphere is reduced to selfish genes, the other layers merely representing the extended phenotype; control of the system comes from the gene. (b) Gaian theory: here the planetary superorganism sets the rules, controlling levels below it to maintain homeostasis and advantage to the incumbent regime. (c) Energetic theory: here the laws of thermodynamics speak to each layer of organization individually, while the resultant organizational structures interact with each other to produce the biosphere.

much earlier time, when James Hutton (1726–97) claimed that Earth was a superorganism and that its proper study should be physiology (Hutton, 1788).

Gaia claims to work in the opposite direction of neo-Darwinism, from the top down (Fig. 4.3). The emergence of self-regulation means that the very life processes from which this regulation emerges are controlled by it. Thus Lovelock would see the human race as ultimately being curbed by their destabilizing behaviour, due to environmental regulation. What is interesting about Gaian theory is that it takes a non-equilibrium view of ecology but has a dynamic equilibrium framework. In other words although the planet is maintained far from equilibrium and life is regulated by the environment, with lag acknowledged, there is somehow a stable condition that is maintained over long periods, and restored when necessary.

Lovelock still attempted to maintain some concept of natural selection within Gaia when he wrote:

> Soon after its origin, life was adapting not to the geological world of its birth but to an environment of its own making. There was no purpose in this, but those organisms which made their environment more

> comfortable for life left a better world for their progeny, and those which worsened their environment spoiled the survival chances of theirs. Natural selection then tended to favour the improvers (Lovelock, 2004; pp. 3-4).

This passage indicates that Lovelock favours some form of environmental selection for "**improvers**". Yet this runs into significant problems when we consider the great Oxygen Revolution, whereupon the activities of one set of organisms led to the release of vast amounts of oxygen, wiping out almost completely the anaerobic bacteria. This may have favoured the aerobic bacteria that replaced them, but was devastating for the former dominant regime.

To argue that the advent of oxygen was somehow a positive step forward is a biased concept. Oxygen was a poison for many organisms. It could not be interpreted as an improvement for these organisms, just as humans cannot be seen as an improvement for the many threatened species co-existing with us at present. Yet where was the self-regulation during the oxygen revolution? In whose opinion is improvement assessed?

Gaian theory stresses that the planetary self-regulation maintains the planet in the most favourable state for the life currently on it yet the anaerobes were anything but comfortable with oxygen. What we are left with is a concept of survival of the self-improvers, which differs little from the neo-Darwinian argument that Gaia apparently opposes. Tyrrell (2004; p. 137) has expressed this deep need to align with Darwinian theory when he wrote "A major aim of Gaian research is to explain how large-scale environmental regulation can arise out of principles of natural selection".

4.3.3 Thermodynamic theory

The **thermodynamic theory of biosphere organization** relies neither on biological competition nor chemical comfort, but on a much more basic and fundamental set of laws, the laws of thermodynamics. Based on the concept of diffusion, it does not require itself to fit within Darwinian theory, as there is no unit of selection, neither gene nor planet. Instead, the laws of thermodynamics speak to every level of organization, while complexity is driven by the disorder it must produce. Thermodynamic theory combines the definition of life, above (life as one member of the class of phenomena which are open or continuous reaction systems able to decrease their entropy at the expense of substances or energy taken in from the environment and subsequently rejected in a degraded form), with the **maximum**

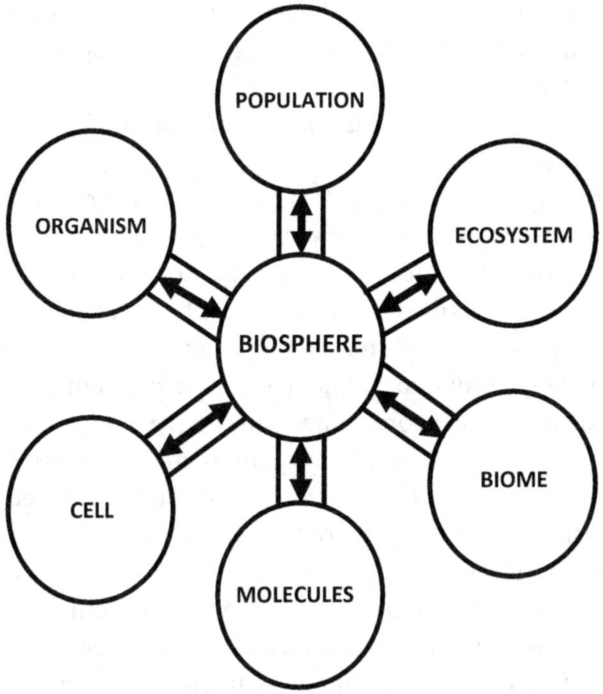

FIGURE 4.4 The see-saw of maximum entropy output, where each level of organization adjusts its output to maintain a dynamic balance within the biosphere, achieved through limited maximum entropy production at each level (Skene, 2011).

entropy production principle (that non-equilibrium thermodynamic systems are organized in steady state such that the rate of entropy production is maximized).

The biosphere is envisaged as being made up of a number of levels of organization, as detailed above, and each of these levels is an open system, with energy flowing through it (Fig. 4.3). Each level self-organizes in such a way as to maximize entropic output, while minimizing internal entropy levels. Because we are dealing with a multilevel system, the biosphere, no single level acts as the unit of organization, but rather a compromise is reached, summed up by the multilevel see-saw analogy of (Fig. 4.4). Here we see that the maximum level of entropy production is defined by the interactions with other levels of organization. For example, populations do not keep growing and growing because they are limited by the energy flow through the system.

Any multilevel system is limited by its environment. It is why food pyramids are pyramids. Energy is lost at each level, meaning that the total biomass that can be supported at the next trophic level is always smaller than the energy flowing into it. There is no such thing as perpetual motion, as we have already observed.

Thus, thermodynamic theory differs greatly from the other theories. Each level is under the control of the laws of thermodynamics, and converses with the levels around it. The environment is also under the laws of entropy. Thus geographic species distributions, food webs, present and past climate, atmospheric circulation and many other complex systems all follow the maximum entropy production principle, as do ecosystems.

A given individual must contribute to the ecosystem energy status at the appropriate place and time, while ecosystems are dependent on the biome location in terms of incoming radiation density and associated rainfall patterns. Organisms contribute to entropic increase in their surroundings, and thus these surroundings are impacted. There is no Gaia or selfish gene, but rather a whole series of interactions between energy and matter, governed by the cosmic laws that dictate architecture and change. This is a complex holistic system, where diffusion rather than selection drives change.

Finally there is no need for a superorganism. Earth, like the rest of the universe, is under a set of laws that determine what can and cannot happen. This applies to the atom and to the biome. Given the nearby star (also under the same laws), we would expect what has happened to happen. And in another galaxy, or elsewhere in our own galaxy, similar events have been, are or will be occurring.

4.4 Implications for economics

4.4.1 Resource/waste issues

Neo-Darwinian theory has no place for concerns relating to sources and sinks. Ultimately, limited resources and harsh conditions merely increase natural selection through increased competition, thus driving evolution forward. Solutions would be found and the fittest would survive. Indeed such crises could be seen as a perfect opportunity to rid the system of imperfect, weak genes, allowing stronger better genes to dominate.

Gaian theory recognizes such perturbations as very significant, not only for the environment but for all of the organisms living within the environment. The importance of self-regulation at the planetary level and of emergent properties places such perturbation at the heart of the issue. Resource flow and waste matter will likely trigger unexpected, complex outcomes. However, waste is seen as a natural glue. As Volk puts it: "The Biosphere is a co-evolved entity consisting of life and what primarily are the by-products of life and the effects of those by-products (such as the waste CO_2 in the soil affecting the weathering rate. It's one big wasteworld" (Volk, 2004; p. 31). Fundamentally, waste is a resource. Or the right kind of waste is a resource.

Additionally, there is an optimal rate of waste production, preferably balancing resource utilization, wherein the entire system can thrive. Significant perturbations are likely to lead to significant repercussions, akin to the Goldilocks story of too little or too much. The intermediate optimum is seen in many spheres, from mutations to disturbance. However, some by-products have more significant impacts than others. Take for example oxygen, carbon dioxide, nitrogen, phosphorus or dimethyl sulphide.

Dimethyl sulphide (DMS) is produced by tiny phytoplankton and is a waste product, produced as a result of its precursor being essential for ion control inside the phytoplankton. It is only released when the phytoplankton are predated on by zooplankton. However, when it reaches the atmosphere, it creates brighter clouds which reflect sunlight away from the planet. In fact DMS is thought to maintain the planet's surface temperature some 5°C lower than would otherwise be the case—a significant amount, given the doomsday scenarios of a 4°C rise in temperature (New *et al.*, 2011). Thus this waste product contributes to the climate of our planet, but was not produced to do so. Gaian theory argues that waste lies at the heart of the biosphere, playing a key role in the conversation between climate and life, though not in a way that can be selected for by selfish genes. The invisible hand lies out with the genetic code.

Thermodynamic theory argues that resource use represents the conversion of low entropy substrates into high entropy waste. Waste in thermodynamic terms represents an increase in chaos. The process leads to the decrease in usefulness of material, generating less energetically utilizable output. This energetic transformation is essential in order to generate the complexity of manufactured goods, whose entropy decreases. Such transformation also requires energy.

Thus waste generation is an outcome of building within an entropic universe. The shift away from thermodynamic equilibrium generates high entropy waste. Ultimately, any form of construction (increase in complexity) must generate waste. While the second law requires an increase in entropy at the level of the universe, energy from the sun allows for complexity to be achieved, provided entropy is released. However, given that the biosphere consists of many levels of organization, there is a maximum entropic production possible (according to the MEPP), and any further increase in entropic production risks destabilizing the biosphere. Thus there is a limit to the amount of waste that can be generated without destabilization.

4.4.2 Micro- and macroeconomics

Darwinian theory is based on reductionist principles (particularly in its current form, neo-Darwinism) and thus espouses that macroeconomics is built from small pieces. Thus microeconomics will ultimately explain macroeconomics. The unit of selection must be at the lowest level of organization, and be governed by competition and differential fitness. Of course inclusive fitness of economic memes will lead to growth in some economic approaches relative to others. However, there is no room for emergent economic characteristics. Due to its reductionist foundations, neo-Darwinism cannot offer any holistic insights into processes beyond the basic building blocks of selfish genes and memes.

Gaian theory espouses the emergence of the invisible hand from within economic activity, meaning that microeconomics will not add up to macroeconomics. Rather, complex interactions will give rise to an apparently different form at different levels of organization. Indeed, Gaian theory would very much align itself with the invisible hand of Adam Smith, wherein virtuous self-interest leads to a benevolent and self-regulating macroeconomic picture, quite distinct from the decision-making at the individual level.

Finally, thermodynamic theory would again recognize significant differences at different levels of economic activity, but not because of some emergent quality. Rather, macroeconomics and microeconomics will respond differently to the laws of thermodynamics, each informed by their contexts and driven by diffusion to a maximum state of complexity (and therefore entropic production), but constrained by all other levels. Aoki (1996) has written on the application of the maximum entropy production principle to macroeconomics.

4.4.3 Economic growth

Darwinian theory views economic growth as an outcome of competition and fitness. Just as successful genes spread, so a successful economy grows.

In this respect, growth is a sign of fitness. Globalization of western economic methods also reflects the inclusive fitness of the dogma underlying this position. Competition drives evolution and therefore the outcome of such competition in terms of market share will reflect fitness. In neo-Darwinian rhetoric, different economic philosophies can be viewed as memes (extra-chromosomal inheritance), and therefore open to natural selection in much the same way as genes.

In Gaian theory, economic growth will be constrained by feedback processes emergent from interactions between economics and all other components of Gaia. However, it would be expected that the economic environment would favour the dominant forms, as predicted by Lovelock. However, ecosystem services are central communication portals for Gaia, and thus if economic growth threatens these channels, then the emergent property of self-regulation could also be threatened. Sir Crispin Tickell has observed: "Markets are marvellous at determining prices but incapable of recognizing costs. Definition of costs requires a Gaian approach to economics and measuring values, and this has to be brought back into pricing" (Tickell, 2004, p. 227).

Thermodynamic theory demonstrates that economic growth increases entropy production, threatening to destabilize the biosphere. While the biosphere has a ceiling, at each level of organization, of maximum entropic production ($\mathbf{S}_{\mathbf{max}}$), sustained economic growth requires continuing increase out with such constraints, driven by greater energy use and waste generation. Thus sustained economic growth cannot deliver sustainability, since sustainability requires a dynamic equilibrium in terms of entropy production. In other words, thermodynamic theory demonstrates that continued economic growth and sustainability are incompatible.

4.4.4 Economic cycles

Darwinian theory again cannot comment on cycles as they represent emergent patterns beyond the consideration of a reductionist theory. Selfish genes nor memes would consider contraction of their fitness. Gaian theory would predict cycling, as feedback and self-regulation within Gaia would operate to produce such cycles. Of course cycles are not replicated, in that the planet is not restored to an identical state at the end of a cycle. Forms are transient, but ecosystem function is long-lasting. Thus after each mass extinction we return to a similar functional planet, though occupied by different forms. The players change, but the play remains the same.

Thus with changing feedback due to a continually changing planet, whose forces emerge from within and out with (both human and cosmic), cycling does not remain cyclical, but more accurately behaves as a spiral. At the most fundamental level, the universe and all that is within it are ageing. The sun has its own cycles in sunspot activity (the 11-year Schwabe cycle and the 80-year Gleissberg cycle), while the distance between the Earth and the sun changes. At the most superficial level, human economic activity has perturbed many of the long established cycles and interrupted many of the self-regulatory pathways of the biosphere. Therefore economic cycles along with natural cycles will become less reliable as Gaia becomes destabilized.

Thermodynamic theory suggests dynamic equilibria exist in all levels of organization in the biosphere, and in other systems too, including economics (Aoki, 1996). Once a stable system emerges, there will be oscillations around a mean value of entropic output. However, if external factors introduce entropy into any particular level of organization, then complexity will also decline, leading to the system having to recover through economic succession, much like an area of land after a forest fire or a volcanic eruption.

Thus economic cycles are of two types: **oscillations** and **crash cycles**. Oscillations occur as part of a dynamic equilibrium, whereas crash cycles result from significant external disturbance. However, human forcing of entropic output (economic growth with costs externalized) is likely to increase the likelihood of violent oscillation and crash economics in the medium to long term, given the increasingly entropy-rich context within which increasing complexity must be maintained. An economic crash cycle has yet to occur in human history and will be part of a greater collapse of all levels of organization, according to thermodynamic theory, as economics is very much a subset of the environmental system. For ultimately, human enterprise is bound by the dimensions of the biosphere (Dilworth, 2010).

4.4.5 Economic succession

The concept of economic succession is an interesting one and merits a small introduction. Neo-Darwinian theory again has no contribution to make to a process such as succession, which operates at a scale mostly beyond the individual. Gaian theory embraces succession as part of the conversation between changing environmental and biotic components, leading to a non-equilibrium state due to lag. The system is always catching up with the environment. Economics, representing an emergent feedback on humans, will change and move towards an increasingly complex state. But constant disturbance will prevent it from stabilizing.

The thermodynamic theory accounts for economic succession in much the same way as ecological succession, with a system moving towards a more complex entity, driven by increasing entropic output. However, economics has the unique character of being driven forward by humans, and thus having the potential to temporarily breech the S_{max} levels that provide stability for the entire biosphere. Thus economic succession, while predictable in terms of function and direction, is unpredictable in terms of form and outcome, given the uncertainties throughout the surroundings, in terms of environmental response to such huge entropic output.

4.4.6 Management

Neo-Darwinian theory clearly states that the fit survive and thrive in a competitive environment. This has had a significant impact on managerial appointments, and pressure is looked on as a refining process. Natural selection, originally stemming from artificial selection and now re-applied to artificial settings such as economics, forms the basis of managerial success and structure.

A Gaian approach to management has not yet been developed, but within this theory, managers should be predominately channels of feedback, facilitating the emergence of characteristics within the company and the greater economy. As transponders and relays, their role is to experience and sense the emergent forces around them.

In the thermodynamic theory, diffusion is the driver of diversity and not competition. Here, management should exist to assist expansion and exploration, and acknowledge succession as a thermodynamic process, where the process is one of dynamic equilibrium. Function, rather than form, is the key to thermodynamic management organization and activity.

4.4.7 Resilience

Resilience represents the ability to bounce back and recover from disturbance. Darwinian theory has no comment on this process as it is a system-level response and begins at low levels of competition (due to simplification during the collapse) which offers little opportunity for selection pressure to operate.

Gaian theory would see resilience as part of the self-regulation and feedback that is central to its thesis. Harding observed that species "are individually vulnerable, but high species diversity ensures that the community as a whole is more likely to persist" (Harding, 2004; p. 265). Of course this depends on the stage of ecological succession that we are examining, but generally more mature phases have higher connectivity. Thus connectivity is central to resilience and resistance in Gaia, as would be expected.

Thermodynamic theory takes a somewhat different view. Resilience is highest in sub-S_{max} environments, because the rate of increase in entropic output is highest at this point. At S_{max}, the system is now in dynamic equilibrium, and the actual rate of increase in entropic output is near zero. Earlier in the succession, there is greater potential for recovery, since the system is operating as a quickly changing unit. Resistance, meanwhile, is likely to be highest at S_{max}.

Any process that reduces the ability of an ecosystem to dissipate entropy will lead to retrogression. The ecosystem will then be shifted to an earlier position on the entropy production curve, and will need to re-organize. Such re-organization may result in further simplification in order to attain a functioning whole. Succession will resume at a point where increasing energetic dissipation can again occur, and this process will continue towards S_{max}. Secondary succession represents an extreme example, where the system may be reset completely. This is equivalent to recovery from an economic crash. Thus retrogression can be understood within an entropic framework. Ecosystems can be considered as possessing thermodynamic self-organizing characteristics that maximize the speed of returning to S_{max} after disturbance versus resistance to being disturbed in the first place.

In terms of Holling's (1986) concept of **creative destruction**, wherein mature ecosystems deconstruct in order to achieve greater complexity, while the ecosystem will reach S_{max}, this is a dynamic equilibrium, and disruption will occur only if entropy *within* the system increases. A rise in internal entropy results in a decrease in complexity, resetting the system to a state further from S_{max}. However, a system can only recover to a *higher* level of complexity than previously (where S_{max} is greater than the original value of S_{max}), as suggested by Holling, if the energetic configuration of the system is altered. Otherwise, S_{max} will remain constant.

Any reversal in ecosystem development can only occur through an increase in entropy *within* the system, thus leading to a decrease in complexity. Thus resistance is viewed as a quality of entropic dissipation. Since ecosystems will naturally move towards a state of S_{max}, then such a change in direction is unlikely to occur without an external agent, disturbance.

Another application using the maximum entropy production principle is to reinvestigate the **intermediate disturbance hypothesis** (Connell

1975; 1978) which suggests that diversity is greatest at some intermediate level of disturbance. How does entropic output and the entropy within systems vary with increasing disturbance? Naveh and Whittaker (1979) and Kratochwil (1999) have suggested that entropic output is at its highest within intermediate disturbance situations. Of course the further above S_{max} an economy grows, the greater the risk of a significant crash, or at least violent oscillation.

4.5 Debate, discussion and further thought

1. "But while they prate of economic laws, men and women are starving. We must lay hold of the fact that economic laws are not made by nature. They are made by human beings" (Roosevelt, 1932). Discuss this statement, developing a defence for or an attack on it.
2. "Economic development is a matter of using the same universal principles that the rest of nature uses. The alternative isn't to develop some other way, some other way doesn't exist" (Jacobs, 2000). Discuss.
3. "The economic system is a subset of the biophysical world" (Gowdy, 1994). Discuss.
4. How relevant is panarchy to business development and its response to sustainability?
5. Are humans separate from or part of nature?
6. How would neo-Darwinism, Gaia and thermodynamic theory each explain the invisible hand of Adam Smith?
7. Are there aspects of nature that act as a super-organism?
8. Is a reductionist or holistic approach more useful and accurate, or do they each give different information?
9. How would sustainability be defined in:
   a. Each of the three ecological ages (static equilibrium, non-equilibrium and dynamic equilibrium)
   b. Each of the three philosophies (neo-Darwinism, Gaia and thermodynamics)?

10. What is the ecological relevance of succession to sustainability and business development and management?

11. Explore Box 4.1. How would your business/work change if it:
    a. Embraced meta-population dynamics to a greater extent?
    b. Embraced isolation to a greater extent?

12. The following set of questions could form the basis of a mini-project or dissertation: explore Box 4.1. Can you identify issues related to inbreeding and outbreeding depression within your management structure and operation? What changes could help this and where should the balance be between open and closed management in your company? How and why might this balance be different in a different type of operation?

13. Explore Figure 4.4. Can you relabel this to incorporate the structure of your company, and identify challenges and solutions to the requirement of suboptimality at each stage in order to achieve a dynamic equilibrium? Contrast this with a static model of management structure, and the difficulties in converting such a structure to a dynamic model.

References

Aoki, M. (1996). *New Approaches to Macroeconomic Modelling: Evolutionary Stochastic Dynamics, Multiple Equilibria and Externalities as Field Effects.* Cambridge University Press, Cambridge, UK.

Ayres, R.U. and Kneese, A.V. (1969). Production, consumption, and externalities. American Economic Review 59: 282-97.

Bacon, F. (2004). *The Instauratio Magna Part II: Novum Organum and Associated Texts.* Rees, G., Wakely, M. (eds.). Oxford University Press, Oxford.

Barnett, L. (1949). *The Universe and Dr Einstein.* The Fanfare Press, London.

Bernal, J.D. (1951). *The Physical Basis of Life.* Routledge and Kegan Paul, London.

Bradley, I. (1999). *Celtic Christianity: Making Myths and Chasing Dreams.* Edinburgh University Press, Edinburgh.

Carpenter, S.R. and Brock, W.A. (2006). Rising variance: a leading indicator of ecological transition. Ecology letters 9(3): 311-18.

Connell, J.H. (1975). Some mechanisms producing structure in natural communities: a model and evidence from field experiments. In: Cody, M.L., Diamond, J. (eds.), *Ecology and Evolution of Communities.* Harvard University Press, Cambridge, Massachusetts. pp. 460-90.

Connell, J.H. (1978). Diversity in tropical rainforests and coral reefs. Science 199: 1302-10.

Cronon, W. (1990). Modes of prophecy and production: placing nature in history. The Journal of American History (1990): 1122-31.

Dawkins, R. (1982). *The Extended Phenotype: the Long Reach of the Gene.* Oxford University Press, Oxford.

Dayton, P.K. (1985). Ecology of kelp communities. Annual Review of Ecology and Systematics 69: 219-50.

Dilworth, C. (2010). *Too Smart for our Own Good: The Ecological Predicament of Pumankind.* Cambridge University Press, Cambridge.

Drury, W.H. and Nisbet, I.C.T. (1973). Succession. Journal of Arnold Arboretum 54: 331-68.

Duarte, C.M., Lenton, T.M., Wadhams, P. and Wassmann, P. (2012). Abrupt climate change in the Arctic. Nature Climate Change 2(2): 60-2.

Ellis, J.E. and Swift, D.M. (1988). Stability of African pastoral ecosystems: alternate paradigms and implications for development. Journal of Rangeland Management 41: 450-9.

Elton, C.S. (1930). *Animal Ecology and Evolution.* Clarendon Press, Oxford.

García-Valdés, R., Zavala, M.A., Araujo, M.B. and Purves, D.W. (2013). Chasing a moving target: projecting climate change-induced shifts in non-equilibrial tree species distributions. Journal of Ecology 101: 441-53.

Georgescu-Roegen, N. (1971). *The Entropy Law and the Economic Process.* Harvard University Press. Cambridge, MA.

Gibbs, D. and Deutz, P. (2005). Implementing industrial ecology? Planning for eco-industrial parks in the USA. Geoforum 36(4): 452-64.

Gowdy, J.M. (1994). *Coevolutionary Economics: the Economy, Society and the Environment.* Kluwer Academic Publishers. Norwell, MA.

Grant, M. (1916). *The Passing of the Great Race or the Racial Basis of European History.* Charles Schribner's Sons, New York.

Grodzins, M. (1957). Metropolitan segregation. Scientific American 197: 33-41.

Gunderson, L. and Holling, C.S. (2001). *Panarchy: Understanding Transformations in Systems of Humans and Nature.* Island Press, Washington DC.

Harding, S.P. (2004). Food web complexity enhances ecological and climatic stability in a Gaian ecosystem model. In: Schneider, S.H., Miller, J.R., Crist, E. and Boston, P.J. (eds.), *Scientists Debate Gaia: the Next Century.* The MIT Press, Cambridge, Massachusetts. pp. 255-66.

Harris, M. (1979). *Cultural Materialism.* New York: Random House.

Holling, C.S. (1978). *Adaptive Environmental Assessment and Management.* John Wiley Chichester, UK.

Holling, C.S. (1986). The resilience of terrestrial ecosystems: local surprise and global change. In: Clark, W.C., Munn, R.E. (eds.), *Sustainable Development of the Biosphere.* Cambridge University Press, Cambridge, UK. pp. 292-317.

Hutton, J. (1788). Theory of the earth. Transactions of the Royal Society of Edinburgh 1(2): 209-304.

Jacobs, J. (2000). *The Nature of Economics.* Random House, New York, NY.

Jaynes, E.T. (1957). Information theory and statistical mechanics. Physical Review 106(4): 620-30.

Jost, L. (2006). Entropy and diversity. Oikos 113: 363-75.

Kårberger, T. and Månsson, B. (2001). Entropy and economic processes—physics perspectives. Ecological Economics 36: 165-79.

Keylock, C.J. (2005). Simpson diversity and the Shannon-Weiner index as special cases of a generalized entropy. Oikos 109: 203-207.

Kleidon, A., Malhi, Y. and Cox, P.M. (2010). Maximum entropy production in environmental and ecological systems. Philosophical Transactions of the Royal Society B 365: 1297-302.

Kratochwil, A. (1999). *Biodiversity in Ecosystems: Principles and Case Studies of Different Complexity Levels.* Kluwer Academic Publishers, Dordrecht, The Netherlands.

Lenton, T., Held, M.H., Kriegler, E., Hall, J.W., Lucht, W., Rahmstorf, S. and Schellnhuber, H.J. (2008). Tipping elements in the earth's climate system.Proceedings of the National Academy of Sciences 105: 1786-93.

Lewes, G.H. (2004). *Problems of Life and Mind.* Kessinger Publishing, Whitefish, MT.

Lifton, R.J. (1988). *Medical Killing and the Psychology of Genocide.* Basic Books, New York.

Lotka, A.J. (1922). Contribution to the energetics of evolution. Proc. Nat. Acad. Sci. USA 8: 147-51.

Lotka, A.J. (1925). *Elements of Physical Biology.* Williams and Wilkins, Baltimore, MD.

Lovelock, J. (2004). Reflections on Gaia. In: Schneider, S.H., Miller, J.R., Crist, E. and Boston, P.J. (eds.), *Scientists Debate Gaia: the Next Century.* The MIT Press, Cambridge, Massachusetts. pp. 1-7.

Mandeville, B. de (2007). *The Fable of the Bees. Or, Private Vices, Publick Benefits.* Penguin Classics, London.

Margalef, R. (1963). On certain unifying principles in ecology. Am. Nat. 97: 357-74.

Marsh, G.P. (1965). *Man and Nature.* Harvard University Press, Cambridge, MA.

Mayer, A.L., Pawlowski, C.W. and Cabezas, H. (2006). Fisher information and dynamic regime changes in ecological systems. Ecological Modelling 195(1): 72-82.

Mikulecky, D.C. (2005). The circle that never ends: can complexity be made simple? In: Bonchev, D.D. and Rouvray, D. (eds.), *Complexity in Chemistry, Biology, and Ecology.* Springer, London. pp. 97-153.

Mill, J.S. (1848). *Principles of Political Economy with Some of Their Applications to Social Philosophy, by John Stuart Mill.* JW Parker, London.

Naveh, Z. and Whittaker, R.H. (1979). Structural and floristic diversity of shrublands and woodlands in Northern Israel and other Mediterranean areas. Vegetatio 441: 171-90.

New, M., Liverman, D., Schroder, H. and Anderson, K. (2011). Four degrees and beyond: the potential for a global temperature increase of four degrees and its implications. Philosophical Transactions of the Royal Society A 369 (1934): 6-19.

Noble, I.R. and Slatyer, R.O. (1980). The use of vital attributes to predict successional changes in plant communities subject to recurrent disturbances. Vegetatio 43: 5-21.

Noll, R. and Trijonis, J. (1971). Mass balance, general equilibrium, and environmental externalities. American Economic Review 61: 730-5.

Nordhaus, W. (1992). Lethal Model 2: The Limits to Growth Revisited. Brookings Papers on Economic Activity 23(2): 1-60.

Odum, E.P. (1969). The strategy of ecosystem development. Science 164: 262-70.

Odum, E.P. (1983). *Basic ecology.* CBS College Publishing, New York, NY, USA.

Odum, H.T. and Pinkerton, R.C. (1955). Time's speed regulator: the optimum efficiency for maximum power output in physical and biological systems. Am. Sci. 43: 331-43.

Perrings, C. (1986). Conservation of mass and instability in a dynamic economy–environment system Journal of Environmental Economics and Management 13: 199-211.

Rappaport, R.A. (1967). *Pigs for the Ancestors: Ritual in the Ecology of a New Guinea People.* Yale University Press, New Haven.

Redclift, M. (1987). *Sustainable Development: Exploring the Contradictions.* Methuen, London.

Rees, W.E. (1999). Consuming the earth: The biophysics of sustainability. Ecological Economics 29: 23-7.

Roosevelt, F.D. (1932). Democratic National Convention Nomination Address, Chicago, Illinois. 2 July 1932. http://newdeal.feri.org/speeches/1932b.htm

Scheffer, M., Hosper, S.H., Meijer, M.-L., Moss, B. and Jeppesen, E. (1993). Alternative equilibria in shallow lakes. Trends in Ecology and Evolution 8: 275-9.

Schrodinger, E. (1944). *What is Life?* Cambridge University Press, Cambridge, UK.

Scoones, I. (1999). New ecology and the social sciences: what prospects for a fruitful engagement? Annual Review of Anthropology 28(1): 479-507.

Shannon, C.E. (1948). A mathematical theory of communication. Bell Syst. Tech. J. 27, 379-423.

Skene, K.R. (2011). *Escape from Bubbleworld: Seven Curves to Save the Earth.* Ard Macha Press, Angus, UK.

Skene, K.R. (2013). The energetics of ecological succession: A logistic model of entropic output. Ecological Modelling 250: 287-93.

Smith, A. (1791). *An Inquiry into the Nature and Causes of the Wealth of Nations, Volume 2.* Tourneisen, Basl.

Smith, A. (1937). *An Inquiry into the Nature and Causes of the Wealth of Nations.* Modern Library, New York.

Solow, R.M. (1997). Georgescu-Roegen versus Solow/Stiglitz. Ecological Economics 22: 267-8.

Steward, J.H. (1955). *Theory of cultural change.* Urbana: University of Illinois.

Tickell, C. (2004). Gaia and the human species. In: Schneider, S.H., Miller, J.R., Crist, E. and Boston, P.J. (eds.), *Scientists Debate Gaia: the Next Century.* The MIT Press, Cambridge, Massachusetts. pp. 223-7.

Tyrrell, T. (2004). Biotic plunder: control of the environment by biological exhaustion of resources. In: Schneider, S.H., Miller, J.R., Crist, E. and Boston, P.J. (eds.), *Scientists Debate Gaia: the Next Century.* The MIT Press, Cambridge, Massachusetts. pp. 137-47.

Volk, T. (2004). Gaia is life in a wasteworld of by-products. In: Schneider, S.H., Miller, J.R., Crist, E. and Boston, P.J. (eds.), *Scientists Debate Gaia: the Next Century.* The MIT Press, Cambridge, Massachusetts. pp. 27-36.

Walters, C. (1986). *Adaptive Management of Renewable Resources.* Macmillan, New York.

White, L. (1967). The historical roots of our ecological crisis. Science 155: 1203-207.

Williams, G.C. (1966). *Adaptation and Natural Selection.* Princeton University, Princeton.

Wilson, E.O. (1999). *Consilience: The Unity of Knowledge.* Alfred A. Knopf, New York.

Wolf, E. (1963). The tipping-point in racially changing neighborhoods. Journal of the American Institute of Planners. 29: 217-22.

Wynne-Edwards, V.C. (1962). *Animal Dispersion in Relation to Social Behaviour.* Oliver and Boyd, Edinburgh.

5

Current schools of sustainable thinking: origins, strengths and weaknesses

At present there are many competing models of sustainability in business, and this chapter introduces the main schools of thought, providing the reader with an understanding of the differences, key principles and strengths and weaknesses. An historical context is first provided, demonstrating how each of these schools of thought emerged and how they are related to each other. The models are then compared to examine their relative emphases on economics, the environment and society, before exploring their historical and political contexts.

Learning aims and objectives

- Become familiar with the major schools of sustainable thinking
- Understand the historical contexts of these schools
- Understand the geopolitical contexts of these schools
- Compare and contrast the strengths and weaknesses of these schools

Learning outcomes and experiences

- Be able to apply the philosophy of any one of these schools of sustainable thinking to your own company or another business
- Reflect on the significance of history and politics on sustainable thinking
- Examine the different emphases of each school and explore the consequences of these differences for any concept of a future built on that particular philosophy
- Develop your own school of sustainable thinking, relating it to a particular historical, geographical and political context

5.1 Introduction

Thoughts relating to finite resources, and the implications of diminishing resources, have been around, most likely, for as long as humans have existed. Ancient writings reflect on the need to set aside some part of the harvest in case of failure in the following season.

Pierre Desrochers (2002a, 2002b, 2008) argues that the principles of sustainability, based on recycling and the efficient use of resources, stem from ancient times—where lack of imported resources meant symbiosis was essential, for example in Asian village life in the middle ages. At these times, globally, there were limited resources, and so people developed tight cycles of material use.

Desrochers demonstrated that closing the loop of resource use and waste was viewed as a good business opportunity in every facet of activity, questioning why such activities have become so "foreign" to modern industry, in which the linear model of raw materials entering at one end of the process and waste materials out at the other end became common practice. He argued that a recycling economy is actually part of our culture, and so it is a matter of reawakening this within society, rather than needing to create a new approach.

Certainly an awareness of the impact of economic activity has been present for several centuries at least. Over this time, various schools of thought have emerged, generally with a set of principles designed to reduce this negative impact. In this chapter we will explore the major ideas currently in circulation, before examining their history and relatedness to each other.

Finally, we will briefly comment on the politics of sustainable economic models.

5.2 Waste is food

Perhaps no concept better demonstrates how apparently recent thinking on sustainable economics has actually been around for a very long time more than **waste is food**. Lying at the heart of industrial ecology, Cradle to Cradle®, the circular economy, closed-loop economy and many of the other major schools of modern thinking, waste is food can be traced back to the beginnings of human civilization. Some of the oldest urban archaeological evidence of resource recovery comes from the late Stone Age city of Çatal Hüyük, in central Turkey. Bones left over from food were used in the manufacture of awls, punches, knives, scrapers, ladles, spoons, bows, scoops, spatulas, bodkins, belt hooks, antler toggles, pins and cosmetic sticks (Mellaart, 1967).

Charles Babbage, the father of programmable computers, wrote in 1835:

> competition between firms spontaneously resulted in a more efficient use of resources, particularly since one of its main results was the care which is taken to prevent the absolute waste of any part of the raw material in order to create as much value as possible out of inputs (Babbage, 1835; p. 217).

Lyon Playfair, chemist and politician, wrote of "methods of utilizing products apparently worthless, or of endowing bodies with properties which render them of increased value to industry" (Playfair, 1852; p. 173), while The Danish writer, Peter Lund Simmonds observed that: "one of the greatest benefits that Science can confer on man is the rendering useful those substances which being the refuse of manufactures are either got rid of at great expense, or when allowed to decompose produce disease and death" (Simmonds, 1862; p. 10). Karl Marx went further, claiming that industrial waste recovery was "the second great branch of economies in the conditions of production", after economies of scale (Marx, 1909; pp. 120-1).

Playfair also pre-empted, by some 150 years, the principles of biomimicry and the circular economy when he wrote that:

> This economy of the chemistry of art is only in imitation of what we observe in the chemistry of nature. Animals live and die; their dead bodies, passing into putridity, escape into the atmosphere, whence

> plants again mould them into forms of organic life; and these plants, actually consisting of a past generation of ancestors, form our present food (Playfair, 1852; pp. 165-6).

Simmonds (1862) discussed the fact that "in every manufacturing process there is more or less waste of the raw material, which it is the province of others following after the original manufacturer to collect and utilize" and he later noted that this practice was widespread throughout Europe and America (Simmonds, 1862; p. 2). Other early references to this can be found in Koller (1918) and Kershaw (1928). It can clearly be seen, then, that the concepts of industrial symbiosis, and eco-industrial parks, have been around for a very long time. As Picasso is famously reported to have said, on viewing the 16,000-year-old cubist cave paintings in Lascaux, France, "We have invented nothing new!" (Rudgley, 1998; p. 182).

Interestingly, concerns about the cost of "**going green**" are also not new. Simmonds, in 1875, wrote "Will it pay, then is, after all, the question usually put when any attempt is made to introduce a new product, or to utilize in an new way any of the residue material used in our popular industries" (Simmonds, 1875; pp. 11-12). In answer to this, the German chemist, Theodor Koller wrote that while some waste products were occasionally "accumulating in such quantity as to injure and retard the continuous progress of a branch of industry," it was also often the case that "the rational treatment and utilization of such waste products either increases very considerably the general profits of an industry or even forms a separate and not inconsiderable source of gain" (Koller, 1918; p. 1).

Other barriers to green manufacturing were also identified early on. The question of industrial architecture was examined, wherein groups of industries are more likely to utilize the **waste is food** approach than a single industry. This pre-empted the concept of industrial symbiosis. Charles Stanton Devas (1901; p. 98) highlighted the role of the "greater growth of subsidiary industries, such namely as supply materials and utilize refuse, to do which for a single factory would not be worthwhile".

The need for a steady supply of waste was also noted. Talbot (1920; p. 303) further pointed out that, in order to be successful, "co-operative and individual methods [of resource recovery] ... can only be conducted upon the requisite scale in the very largest cities where the volume of material to be handled is relatively heavy" because "waste must be forthcoming in a steady stream of uniform volume to justify its exploitation, and the fashioning and maintenance of these streams is the supreme difficulty."

Zimmermann (1933; p. 767) highlighted the role of technological innovation in this respect by pointing out that one of:

> the major functions of modern science [is] to lower the cost of waste elimination; for reduction in such cost may render profitable, and therefore economically justified, practices of waste elimination which otherwise might be technically feasible but unwarranted for economic reasons.

Rudolf Clemen (1935; p. 2) went further, claiming that the **waste is food** approach would provide a competitive edge, again a very modern argument:

> Indeed, the materials from which the by-products in nearly all industries are manufactured today were formerly partially or wholly wasted, and the change to intensive utilization of these materials for by-product manufacture has been brought about by the ever-increasing force of competition in American business, both between individual concerns within a single industry and among different ones.

After pointing out that the "so-called waste plays an important role in almost every industry," Marx argued that rising prices of raw materials were a major impetus behind this process (Marx, 1909).

5.3 Industrial ecology

Perhaps the most significant concept in recent years has been **industrial ecology** (Allenby, 1998). It has been variously described as a process at the level of the regional industrial system and at the societal level where the concept and routines of industrial symbiosis diffuse (Boons *et al.*, 2011), as a collective, multi-industrial approach to improve economic and environmental performance through the use of wastes/by-products as substitutes for raw materials (Costa and Ferrão, 2010) and as an evolving framework for the analysis and design of public policy, corporate strategy, and technological systems and products (Ehrenfeld, 2000).

It has come to incorporate much of the current thinking in sustainable development. It emphasizes flow of materials and energy (White, 1994), and has been described as the network of all industrial processes, much like biological ecology (Frosch, 1992). Indeed, it was Frosch and Gallopoulos (1989; p. 144) who made this comparison clear when they described "**an industrial ecosystem**" as one where "the consumption of energy and materials is optimized and the effluents of one process ... serve as the raw material for another process". In the same year, the eponymous Winter Model laid out 22 clear guidelines for the application of industrial ecology for business management (Winter, 1988). Dijkema and Basson (2009) show the relevance to the three pillars of sustainability, by defining industrial ecology as interacting technical and social networks embedded in the biosphere. As we have seen, all of the foundations were laid 150 years earlier in the **waste is food** concept.

The concept of industrial ecology is normally seen as working on three levels: intra-firm (within a given company), inter-firm (involving a group of companies) and regional.

5.4 Intra-firm industrial ecology

The application of industrial ecology at the individual firm basis incorporates **clean technology**, **cleaner production**, **design for environment** (DfE), **life-cycle assessment** and **green chemistry**.

5.4.1 Clean technology

Clean technology (abbreviated, often, to **Cleantech**) is an economically competitive and productive technology that aims to use less material and/ or energy, to generate less waste and to cause less environmental damage than the alternatives. The term was first used by Keith Raab and Nicholas Parker, founders of the Cleantech Venture Network (now Cleantech Group), and by the journalist, Joel Makower, in 2002, particularly referring to solar, biofuels, fuel cells, water remediation, and renewable power generation (Pernick and Wilder, 2007).

The emphasis went far beyond the environmental or "green" technology of the 1970s, which was consumed with regulations and end-of-pipe issues. Rather, it incorporated new-technology business models, and defined a new investment asset class, making it relevant to business, with market economics at its heart (Bürer and Wüstenhagen, 2009). It includes processes, practices and tools and is seen as a means of uniting grass-roots movements with the business sector (Horwitch and Mulloth, 2010). The term "**greentech**", which is often used interchangeably with "**cleantech**", was popularized by venture capitalists John Denniston and John Doerr from Kleiner Perkins (Rubino, 2009).

Since clean technology involves modification of the processes of production, it has the potential to impact on production efficiency and product performance. However, technology can be developed to produce what Porter and van der Linde (1995) refer to as **innovation offsets**, that is, developments that compensate for additional costs involved in the process.

Oltra and Jean (2005) suggest that there are three strategies that can be taken in practising clean technology. The **productive strategy** focuses on increasing productive efficiency, while maintaining environmental impact at a constant level. Thus you get more product per unit damage, reducing the per product damage. A second approach is the **environmental strategy**. Here, environmental impact is reduced, while productive efficiency remains constant. Again pollution per unit production is reduced. Reduction in waste treatment costs will contribute to innovation offsets. A third approach, entitled the **median strategy**, requires more radical innovations, seeking both a reduction in environmental impact and an increase in productive efficiency.

The Clean Technology Fund (CTF) is administered by the World Bank, and is focused on supporting private-sector action and investment related to mitigating climate destabilization. Nine governments have pledged over US$4.8 billion. The concept emerged from the Gleneagles G8 Summit of 2005, with a stated mission to "help developing countries bridge the gap between dirty and clean technology … and boost the World Bank's ability to help developing countries tackle climate change" (Paulson *et al.*, 2008).

Since its implementation in 2008, progress has been challenging. The programme targeted inputting large amounts of money into a small number of countries in order to maximize the chances of transformation, rather than diluting the impact across many countries. Many countries rejected the involvement of the World Bank in controlling a fund targeting climate change, and also felt that the CTF would prejudice efforts by the United Nations Framework Convention on Climate Change (UNFCCC), becoming yet another western world control (Ballesteros *et al.*, 2010). Another issue involves the fact that much of the CTF funding is from loans, which need to be serviced and which reduce the risks that can be taken in funding creative, innovative projects. Complexities with funding have led to disbursement lagging behind approval, thus jeopardizing the approved projects.

The main drawback of the CTF is its complete and single focus on carbon emissions. By far the largest part of the funding has gone to solar power capture. This ignores completely the majority of the issues facing the planet, and actually contributes to the damage done in other sectors, given the pollution issues associated with much of the green energy production methods that it supports, combined with the resource issues involved.

The CTF addresses energy production, the most political of all aspects of environmental damage and economic concern. For energy underpins everything else, just as in the natural world. Richard Lester calculates that meeting targets for emissions would require an annual expenditure of $250–500 billion, and entail adding roughly 120 gigawatts every year of new low-carbon energy supply. However, the greatest increase in new energy input in the last ten years in the US economy has come not from wind turbines (8.5 gigawatts) nor solar (0.338 gigawatts) but from shale oil and natural gas (67 gigawatts) (Lester, 2009). Hence the current approach is still functioning under an energetic architecture based around the subterranean forest. Even with huge amounts of money being disbursed by the CTF, it is the old technology that holds firm.

Venture capitalists have received huge loans from governments to develop green technology research and innovation (Hargadon and Kenney, 2012). However, these same governments continue to subsidize black energy producers. Furthermore, by giving a small number of venture capital operations vast sums of money, this alters the playing field, meaning smaller innovative companies are unable to compete.

Bréchet and Meunier (2012) argue that global pollution levels are likely to increase with clean companies present because they must operate at higher activity levels, thus creating environmental damage in different ways and of a larger scale than "dirty" companies.

5.4.2 Cleaner production

Cleaner production (CP) was defined by UNEP in 1990 as: "The continuous application of an integrated environmental strategy to processes, products and services to increase efficiency and reduce risks to humans and the environment" (UNEP, 1990). It is also known as **resource-efficient and cleaner production** (RECP), which has three main aims: **production efficiency** (through optimization of productive use of natural resources at all stages of the production cycle), **environmental management** (through minimization of the adverse impacts of industrial production systems on nature and the environment) and **human development** (through minimization of risks to people and communities, and support of their development). As can be seen, it addresses all three pillars of sustainability, the triple bottom line.

Cleaner production practices use highly efficient environmental equipment, and state-of-the-art environmental management measures. CP generally incorporates clean technology. Seven principles define this approach:

1. Good housekeeping
2. Change in raw materials
3. Improved process equipment
4. Technology change
5. On-site recovery/re-use
6. Production of useful by-products
7. Product modification

These principles are summed up by the acronym PPP or **Pollution Prevention Pays**. Although the principles of CP have been in use for over a century, the concept was officially launched as a programme of the United Nations Environmental Programme (UNEP) at the Rio Summit in 1991. While applied to any industrial process, it targeted improvements in industrial production in "developing" nations.

Core characteristics of a given company will determine the most appropriate working methods in order to deliver cleaner production. These are: size, resource intensity and types of process (Van Berkel, 1994). The size of the company is important, as larger companies will be able to dedicate more staff to the task, while small companies may have to have a very different approach.

Companies with high material and energy throughput are likely to have already implemented efficiency measures, as these components will be a large percentage of their total production costs. Thus, to make further savings, a very detailed accounting process would be required. Companies with relatively low material and energy throughput are less likely to have examined strategies of greater efficiency, and in these cases, a more simple assessment process will likely yield cleaner production. Finally, the type of industrial process will affect how easily cleaner production methods can be implemented. Highly specialized companies are less likely to have best practice methods already in use, whereas more generalized companies may well be able to borrow expertise more easily from similar fields.

Numerous problems have faced the implementation of cleaner production globally. A rapidly changing regulatory environment in the "developed" world has obstructed long-term investment into appropriate environmentally friendly actions (Hilson, 2000). This is because money may be spent meeting particular legislative criteria, only for the criteria to be changed, requiring more expenditure with no real gain. In "developing" nations, lack of enforcement of legislation may mean that there is no incentive to adopt cleaner production principles.

Economic support for starter projects may also not be available. Expertise may be lacking or heterogeneously spread across the globe and between sectors, meaning that there is a lack of technical support. Another problem arises from differences in how the business markets operating globally, with large monopolies sometimes limiting market flexibility, while smaller companies have not attained the size to develop certain strategies. Different emphases, for example between self-regulation and central regulation, or laissez-faire and interventionist approaches, also play important roles in impacting on the potential success of cleaner production initiatives.

Another major concern is determining responsibility within a production network. How exhaustive should a cleaner production assessment be, and where are the limits of a company's environmental accountability? While one company's procedures may be clean, are they also responsible for their suppliers, or the suppliers of the suppliers? How practical is it for a computer manufacturer, for example, to validate its supply chain, which may encompass producers of 60 different metals from across the world? Furthermore, "developing" nations often have informal recycling, which is impossible to assess.

There is also the issue of defining what is deemed as "clean". Is it only carbon that is of concern, or do we need to include eutrophication, habitat destruction and diversity? What about social wellbeing? Schaltegger *et al.* (2009) identify three barriers to change:

1. The lack of a one-to-one relationship between organizational change and accounting change
2. The lack of institutional support
3. The belief that cleaner production only applies to manufacturing sectors

5.4.3 Design for environment and ecodesign

Another intra-firm approach is **design for environment** (DfE). Developed as a United States Environmental Protection Agency (USEPA) programme in 1992, though first coined by Branden Allenby (Allenby, 1991), it aims to prevent pollution, and the concomitant risks to humans and the environment, from services, processes and products (Allenby, 1991), from manufacture through to end of life. The environment helps to define the direction of design decisions (van Hemel 1998; Boks, 2000).

The need to design in an ecologically sensitive way had its beginnings in the work of such designers as Victor Papanek and Walter Teague. Central to this approach is to design products and manufacturing processes in such a way as to reduce environmental perturbation, rather than deal with the pollution in an end-of-pipe approach. Production, operation and end-of-life aspects are considered, in an attempt to reduce pollution at every stage of a product's life (Ryan, 1992).

The approach has spawned many subdivisions, such as Design for Supply Chain (Esterman *et al.* 1999), Design for Ownership Quality (Kmenta *et al.* 1999), Design for Assembly (Boothroyd *et al.* 1994, Kmenta 2000), Design for Serviceability (Gershenson *et al.* 1991), Design for Product Retirement (Ishii *et al.* 1994), Design for End-of-Life (Rose *et al.* 2000) Design for Recyclability (Ishii *et al.* 1996) and Design for Product Variety (Martin 2002).

DfE is mirrored in Europe by the concept of **ecodesign** (van Hemel, 1998). Ecodesign in a given type of product can be seen to advance through three stages: **exploration**, **consolidation** and **maturity**. The exploration stage involves diffusion of design at the experimental prototype level. Consolidation involves the emergence of dominant forms from within the mass and maturity involves the diffusion of these forms throughout society (Roy, 1994).

Huge challenges exist in terms of design, both philosophically and practically. Much debate has centred on how much responsibility a designer has, and whether it is the supplier or the demander (the designer or the customer) who is ultimately accountable. Can a person who designed a gun be held responsible for a gun crime? Should Alfred Noble, the person who inspired the Noble prizes and the inventor of dynamite, be held responsible for the deaths of those in explosions caused by dynamite?

A second issue relates to how we view the environment in terms of design demands. For many products, designers face an already large list of design criteria: safety, legality, product life-span, materials, standards, aesthetics, installation, performance, life in service, ergonomics, product cost, quantity, documentation, time-scale, profit, size, shipping, politics, company constraints, manufacturing facility operation, market constraints, competition, maintenance, weight, packing, quality, reliability, shelf-life, storage, patents and disposal to name a few.

Can environmental impact be added as just another criterion, having to be squeezed in with all of the others, or is it a stream that should flow through all of the other criteria? Is it akin to time, which is not a resource, but defines all resources? Certainly all of the criteria above must be fulfilled adequately or the product will likely fail its test in the marketplace. In many ways, environmental issues are the exception, in that ignoring them will be unlikely to impact on the product's success. Indeed, unless the customer demands green production, function and recycling, then should the designer consider these issues at all?

Yet each of the design criteria above must include ecodesign within them. Transport and storage of products should be as environmentally neutral as possible. This means warehouse and distribution methods must be included. Shelf-life should be as long as possible as should life-span, but not so long as to compromise recycling. In fact there will be trade-offs throughout this array of components, and inefficiency at each level will be required to reach an optimal environmental design in its totality. Consequently there is not a single optimal design point to be reached, but rather a surface or subspace in design space, where a range of different solutions can achieve "**adequate design**" (Farnsworth and Niklas, 1995).

Luttropp and Lagerstedt (2006) have identified ten golden rules to help the designer:

1. Do not use toxic substances where possible, and utilize closed loops for necessary but toxic ones
2. Minimize energy and resource consumption in the production and transport phases through improved housekeeping
3. Use structural features and high quality materials to minimize weight in products where possible
4. Minimize energy and resource consumption in the utility phase
5. Promote repair and upgrading, especially for system-dependent products such as cell phones
6. Promote long life, especially for products with significant environmental aspects outside of the utility phase
7. Invest in better materials, surface treatments or structural arrangements to protect products from dirt, corrosion and wear, thereby ensuring reduced maintenance and longer product life

8. Prearrange upgrading, repair and recycling through access ability, labelling, modules, breaking points and manuals
9. Promote upgrading, repair and recycling by using few, simple, recycled, unblended materials and no alloys
10. Use as few joining elements as possible

The European Union has integrated ecodesign into its legislation (Molenbroek *et al.*, 2012). The Ecodesign Directive was originally passed in 2005 (2005/32/EU) and was amended in 2008 (2008/28/EU) and 2009 (2009/125/EU), aiming to reduce the environmental impact of products throughout their entire life-cycle. The Directive applies to companies producing energy-using or energy-related products, with production of over 200,000 units per year.

The directive states that its outcomes should have no (significant) negative impact on (1) functionality, (2) health and safety, (3) affordability and (4) industry's competitiveness, neither should it impose proprietary technology on manufacturers and should not be an excessive administrative burden for manufacturers.

Furthermore, ecodesign parameters should consider all phases of the life-cycle (manufacturing, transport, use, disposal), consider the essential environmental aspects (consumption, material, emission, waste, etc.) for each phase and should determine energy efficiency or energy consumption levels which allow minimum life-cycle cost for end-consumers (Molenbroek *et al.*, 2012).

The biggest problem relating to the Ecodesign Directive is that its success is measured primarily by energy saving. In other words it suffers from **carbon fixation**. This single or dominant goal has the potential to produce damage elsewhere in the biosphere, since it is not a balanced environmental response to all of the threats. If corrosion exists in three links in a chain, then replacing one of those rusty links with a nice shiny new one will not save the chain. Indeed by focusing on only energy savings, we can do more damage, as has been seen with green fuels in Chapter 3. Thus this flaw, placed in the centre of the Directive, will leave ecodesign in a dangerous place, while broadcasting a message of false hope to the consumer.

It has also been argued that ecodesign will provide more jobs. The basis of this is questionable too. In 2011 the ACEEE (American Council for an Energy Efficient Economy) published a study: *Appliance and equipment efficiency standards: a moneymaker and job creator* (Gold *et al.*, 2011). In this report they argue that energy savings achieved through ecodesign will save companies money. These companies will then reduce prices, meaning that consumers save. Consumers then spend this saved money on labour-intensive goods, thus creating more jobs. There are a number of concerns with this line of argument. First, it reiterates the mantra that ecodesign is only about energy saving. Second, it relies on producers reducing prices (i.e. no cartels) and consumers spending their savings on labour-intensive additional products. All of these steps are unproven. Finally there is no guarantee how green these other labour-intensive outputs will be.

Another challenge for ecodesign is the sourcing of components. Highly specialized components may only be available from a single supplier. In this case, it may be impossible to shop around for the greenest equivalent. Furthermore, many components can only be made from damaging materials, such as rare earth metals, and so it becomes very difficult to deliver the product without such costs. Finally, most designs build on a core set of components. To completely redesign these from scratch in order to design the product in a cleaner way would take a huge amount of time and design expertise often unavailable to a given company.

Ecodesign remains focused on form rather than function. Function emerges from many inputs, and requires a holistic approach, much like ecology. Thus **natural design**, a concept developed by Professor Seaton Baxter of Dundee University (Baxter, 2005; Baxter, 2006; Wahl and Baxter, 2008) may be a better way ahead, emphasizing the holistic, functional aspects, rather than the eco-friendly, form-based emphasis of ecodesign. In other words it is not merely about the components or raw materials, but of the impact on ecosystem function, the need for suboptimization, communication and entropic production. However, such an approach needs to be grounded in concrete modern ecological theory.

Function, ultimately, relies on an understanding of thermodynamics, a concept widely misunderstood within many economic models of sustainability, as we have seen in Chapter 4. Walter Teague emphasized this when he wrote:

> The function of a thing is its reason for existence, its justification and its end, by which all its possible variations may be tested and accepted or rejected. It is a sort of life-urge thrusting through a thing and determining its development. It is only by realizing its destiny and revealing that destiny with candor and exactness, that a thing acquires significance and validity of form. This means much more than utility, or even efficiency; it means a kind of perfected order we find in natural organisms, bound together in such rhythms that no part can be changed without wounding the whole (Teague, 1940; p. 32).

5.4.4 Life-cycle assessment

Life-cycle assessment (LCA) is a validation technique, and is a broad methodology for identifying environmental burdens that arise from products from the material suppliers, through manufacture, use and disposal (SETAC 1991, EPA 1993). ISO defines LCA as "a tool to assess the environmental impacts of product systems and services, accounting for the emissions and resource uses during the production, distribution, use, and disposal of a product" (ISO, 1997). LCA has even been promoted by the United Nations General Assembly as the best tool to deliver sustainable consumption and production.

LCA consists of three stages:

1. Determination of the **processes** involved in the production of a given product
2. Determination of the environmental **pressures** emerging from these processes
3. Calculation of **impact indicators**

LCA has been envisaged as a method of informing consumers of the impact of the products they buy, but the information is often overwhelming, given the supply chains associated with any given product. There are three types of LCA:

1. Process LCA
2. Input–output LCA
3. Hybrid LCA

Process LCA is a very detailed inventory approach. Process modelling relies on inventory databases with physical commodity flow units. It uses unit process data and incorporates the complete life-cycle. Its strengths lie in the detail provided, making it the approach of choice for ecological design practitioners.

Input–output LCA (I/O-LCA) lacks process specificity, but has a more complete system boundary understanding (Hall *et al.*, 1992). With I/O-LCA, the product system, which consists of supply chains, is modelled using economic commodity flow databases, accounts and pre-use/consumption life-cycle stages (Joshi, 2000). I/O-LCA works well for big questions addressing the overall impact of a sector, or the introduction of a new technology at a national or regional level. However, it is not very useful in addressing specific, product-related questions.

An LCA based on unit processes is specific and detailed, while generally based on incomplete system boundaries due to the effort for compiling a full data set of the product system. Guinée *et al.* (2002) identify three major system boundaries:

1. Between the technical system and the environment
2. Between significant and insignificant processes
3. Between the technological system under study and other technological systems

On the other hand, I/O-LCAs are more complete in system boundaries but lack process specificity. Attempts to overcome the disadvantages, while combining the advantages of both methods are generally referred to as **hybrid approaches** (Suh and Huppes, 2001).

Hybrid LCA attempts to combine these first two approaches to have both detailed specifics and full system boundary understanding. In principle the approach is straightforward, basically adding far upstream I/O-LCA results to process-LCA results covering near-upstream events (Moriguchi *et al.*, 1993). This approach is termed the **tiered hybrid method**. Another approach is to disaggregate the I/O-LCA data in order to improve resolution. This has been termed the **input–output based hybrid method** (Suh *et al.*, 2004), although it can be thought of as another form of the tiered hybrid method.

All three approaches (Process, I/O and hybrid) are heavily data dependent and issues arise in terms of gaps in the data (e.g. from "**developing**" nations, where informal recycling is commonplace), uncertainties in the data and the validity of the data in the first instance.

LCAs can be used in three different ways. **Attributional LCAs** focus on the environmental burden of a product at a particular point in time. **Consequential LCAs** focus on what difference a change in process would have on future environmental burden (Curran *et al.*, 2005). Consequential LCAs are viewed as being most useful in decision-making situations, allowing comparisons of different strategies. Finally, **social LCAs** focus on the impact of processes and products on society.

A growing consensus is that LCA cannot appropriately separate internal and external issues, which makes the application to industry almost impossible, since cause and effect cannot be separated (Brezet *et al.* 1999; Stevels,

2001). Furthermore, while databases have extensive data on materials and commodities from "**developed**" nations, very little data is available from "**developing**" nations, where much of the industry occurs. Hence the data is biased, and this creates issues with misinforming the consumer (Hertwich 2005).

Björklund (2002) identified 11 potential sources of uncertainty in LCA operation: data inaccuracy, data gaps, unrepresentative data, model uncertainty, uncertainty due to choices, special variability, temporal variability, variability between objects/sources, epistemological uncertainty, human error and estimations of uncertainty.

Perhaps one of the most shocking recent omissions in LCA reporting was the case of life-cycle assessment of wind turbines. In their report, Guezuraga *et al.* (2013) completely omitted rare earth metals, probably the most environmentally damaging of all of the components of a wind turbine. Such an omission will have hugely impacted on the validity of the analysis. Thus LCA must be viewed critically, and not merely accepted for what it is, as there is ample room for error, omission and bias.

5.4.5 Green chemistry

New technology to support firms became important, as predicted by Zimmermann (1933—see section 4.2). In the early 1990s, the United States passed the Pollution Prevention Act of 1990 which established source reduction as the highest priority in solving environmental problems. The US Environmental Protection Agency (Ember, 1991) coined the term **green chemistry**, meaning the promotion of innovative chemical technologies that reduce or eliminate the use or generation of hazardous substances in the design, manufacture and use of chemical products. Later that year, the Office of Pollution Prevention and Toxics in the US Environmental Protection Agency launched the first research initiative of the Green Chemistry Program, the Alternative Synthetic Pathways Program.

By the mid-1990s, there were green chemistry initiatives across Europe, Japan and Australia. Green chemistry is an example of a government-led initiative, later spreading to academia. Soon it was replete with its own Journal, *Green Chemistry*, sponsored by the Royal Society of Chemistry.

Twelve principles of green chemistry have been identified (Anastas and Warner, 1998):

1. Prevention
2. Atom economy

3. Less hazardous synthesis
4. Safer chemicals
5. Safer solvents
6. Energy efficiency in production
7. Renewable raw materials
8. Reduced derivatives
9. Increased catalysis
10. Easier degradation
11. Real-time pollution monitoring
12. Safer production

The recent history of this concept is well discussed in Anastas and Kichhoff (2002). One of the greatest challenges in green chemistry is the use of organic solvents, which are extremely damaging to the environment.

However, while chemistry lies at the foundation of most manufacturing processes, with only physics being more fundamental, green chemistry has faced the usual problem of crossing the barrier between research and industrial practice. Improvements in regulations (particularly relating to hazardous waste), technology transfer, patent longevity and tax incentives are all suggested as important for this barrier to be crossed (Anastas and Kirchhoff, 2002).

Barriers are certainly significant. The share of green chemistry products in industry has been calculated as 1% (Goodman, 2009). Green chemistry products must be both economically and environmentally beneficial for industrial acceptance. Often, the industrial processing plant will need to be overhauled, requiring huge capital expenditure. Margins may not be high enough to allow this. Furthermore, shareholder may not be willing to experience reduced profits in order to complete hardware changes.

Designers are often unaware of advances in green chemistry, and thus do not know of the options available. Regulatory barriers often have an emphasis on reducing exposure to pollutants rather than reducing hazard, thus forcing companies to focus on end-of-pipe solutions, rather than preventative measures. Technological barriers can arise from discoveries being protected for competitive advantage, thus not circulating. Also, organic chemists rarely have any training in chemical engineering, design, ecology or toxicology, due to specialization in school and university courses.

Organizational barriers can result from units within a firm competing with each other, and thus being unwilling to take on additional costs from adopting green chemistry technology. Conflicts of interest can also arise, if a green chemistry product damages sales of another of the company's products.

5.5 Inter-firm industrial ecology

Relationships between firms are viewed as extremely important. In industrial ecology, not only should a single firm take responsibility for environmental impacts of its suppliers and consumers, but also by working in groups, firms can use waste products of other firms, thus reducing resource drain and waste production. This process is called **industrial symbiosis**.

5.5.1 Industrial symbiosis

Industrial symbiosis is defined in the Dictionary of Sociology in 1944 as "a grouping within a community of independent manufacturers, who are able to benefit by using each other's products" (in Fairchild, 1964). The interaction of groups of businesses, connected by waste-substrate linkage, is the domain of industrial symbiosis. Desrochers and Leppälä (2010) refer to some uses of the term from as early as 1930. Industrial symbiosis finds its practical expression in **eco-industrial parks** (EIPs) (Lowe, 1997, Zhu *et al.* 2008). Here, groups of businesses are geographically located in close proximity and share each other's waste materials to use as substrates. The outcomes are:

1. A reduction in the use of virgin materials
2. A reduction in pollution
3. An increased energy efficiency
4. A reduction in the volume of waste products requiring disposal
5. An increase in the amount and types of process output that have market value (Gertler 1995)

Once again there appears to be nothing new under the sun. Evidence from the Roman Empire indicates that businesses located near slaughterhouses turned bones and ivory into items such as pins, tokens, buttons, components of hinges, and wall fittings (Chevalier 1993).

In the 19th century, Charles Babbage wrote that preventing waste in industrial production often caused "the union of two trades in one factory, which otherwise might have been separated" (Babbage, 1835; p. 217). Bernard Ostrolenk also described the conditions for the emergence of EIPS:

> Even the sources of important raw commodities are changing ... The time is not far distant when New York, with its growing production of scrap iron and scrap copper from junked buildings, machinery, automobiles, etc., will be as important a source of raw material for metal industries as is the Mesabi Range or Anaconda (Ostrolenk, 1941; p. 21).

In the first half of the 20th century in the USA, pigs were bred near alcohol distilleries where they were fed on the mash (Bogart 1936; p. 300), while in New York City most of the milk was produced in 260 city stables by cows living on the swill of local distilleries (Miller 1998; p. 78). In Belgium, at the beginning of the early 19th century, most distilleries relocated from the countryside to cities in order to secure markets for their by-products (Dechesne 1945, 51).

Perhaps the most studied example of an EIP is at Kalundborg, in Denmark (Ehrenfeld, 1997; Jacobsen, 2006; Domenech, 2011), which began spontaneously in the early 1960s (Grann, 1997) and combines a coal-fired power plant (Asnæs), a refinery (Statoil), a pharmaceuticals company (Novo Nordisk), a plasterboard manufacturer (Gyproc), as well as the municipal government and a few smaller businesses including a soil remediation company, a sulphuric acid manufacturer, a cement factory and a fish farm.

The power company supplies residual steam to the refinery while the power plant burns the refinery gas to generate electricity and steam. Excess steam is delivered to three sinks: the fish farm, a district heating system and the pharmaceutical plant. Sludge from the pharmaceutical plant and the fish farm is used as fertilizers in local farms. The cement factory receives fly ash from the power plant, while the power plant sends gypsum to the plasterboard manufacturer. The sulphuric acid manufacturer receives sulphur from the oil refinery.

In Kwinana, Australia, an oil refinery, inorganic chemical producer, cement producer, pig iron plant and titanium dioxide producer form part of an EIP with a total of 50 regional synergies. This park also spontaneously developed over time (van Beers *et al.* 2009).

China is now the centre of an industrial revolution embracing sustainability at its heart. Within this context, eco-industrial parks play a significant role in delivering change. These include the Guitang group, which started out some 40 years ago, where a sugar refinery (one of the largest in China), an ethanol producer, a fertilizer plant, a cement works, a pulp mill, a paper plant and a thermoelectricity plant share waste products (Zhu *et al.* 2007). The Pingdingshan Coal Mining Group has coal mining, coal processing, building materials and a chemical plant (Long and Zhang, 2009). The Lubei Chemical Group includes aquaculture, a bromine plant, a salt refinery, a sulphuric acid plant, a cement mill, an ammonium/phosphate plant, and a turbo-generator (Fang *et al.*, 2007). The Suzhou industrial park combines electronics manufacturers and chemical manufacturers (Zhang *et al.*, 2009).

In Ulsan, South Korea, a large eco-park has grown, guided by the Korean National Cleaner Production Center (KNCPC). There are over 70 symbioses, involving collective utility systems, by-product exchanges, shared connections for steam, recycled industrial water, all operating together. Companies include a metals refinery, a paper mill, an oil refinery and a chemical plant (Park *et al.* 2008). In Kawasaki, Japan, a paper mill, a waste-water treatment plant, a steel refinery, a scrap metal plant, and a cement works operate as an EIP (van Berkel *et al.* 2009).

The premise of industrial ecology is that modern industrial economies should mimic the cycling of materials in ecosystems throughout the processes of raw material extraction, manufacturing, product use, and waste disposal. However, Kalundborg is not a self-sustaining island. Rather it relies on exporting some of its by-products as well as its primary products, while still needing to import raw materials, such as gypsum from Germany and Spain.

Some observations have been made on these industrial symbioses. First, they are, generally, not purposefully designed to begin with, but evolve over decades (Mathews and Tan, 2011). One of the great debates concerning EIPs is whether they can be planned. The Kalundborg community and other similar cases developed spontaneously, entirely through market forces. The entire structure emerged from a series of bilateral agreements between pairs of industries, driven by the desire to reduce end-of-pipe costs, converting waste into an exchange currency, while reducing costs related to raw materials. Yet many policy analysts argue that public planners can copy and even improve on Kalundborg. This belief in the superiority of central planning over decentralized decision-making has been called **the pretence of knowledge** by Nobel laureate F.A. Hayek (1980).

China's EIPs are young and will increase in complexity over time. Latecomer status has costs and benefits. State control helps ameliorate fierce competition (Gerschenkron, 1962). Certainly in the United States of America, despite a number of successes, there is a concern that "the vast majority of these projects [were] consigned to the dustbin of history [and] vanished as soon as their funding sources dried up" (Lowitt, 2008; p. 498) and that encouraging existing symbioses has led to "more sustainable industrial development than attempts to design and build eco-industrial parks incorporating physical exchanges" (Chertow, 2007; p. 11).

A shift in emphasis has also been encouraged, moving from a reductionist to a systems-based approach. Gibbs (2008; p. 1140) suggests "cooperation between firms as opposed to focusing on action at the level of the individual firm, seeing firms as nodal points within a networked ecosystem".

5.6 Regional level industrial ecology: industrial metabolism

Finally, at the regional level, comes the field of **industrial metabolism**. Industrial metabolism was most recently introduced by R.U. Ayres in 1989, who compared traditional industry with early life on the planet Earth, where bacteria used the iron and sulphur from hydrothermal vents to power their metabolisms (Ayres, 1989). Instead, Ayres suggested that industry needed to mimic more advanced life, where nutrients were cycled through the biosphere, powered by the Sun. Thus the global economy should run like the modern biosphere, interconnected and recycling material throughout the entire system.

This concept actually goes back more than 150 years and developed from an understanding of material and energy exchange (the 19th century meaning of biological metabolism) rather than the functional substrate-product cycle of modern biochemistry (Fischer-Kowalski, 2003). Karl Marx first made use of the concept of metabolism with regards to socioeconomics. He emphasized that our subsistence must come through an exchange with nature, which demands social organization and labour. This concept was extended to societal production methods and consumption, which further define the relationship.

Recent work highlights the importance of regional aspects of industrial ecology (Matsunaga, 2000; Liu *et al.*, 2012). A number of regional studies have been recorded in the literature, such as Dalian (Geng *et al.*, 2009) and Liaoning (Xu *et al.*, 2008).

Some confusion in the literature exists as to whether industrial metabolism is a subset of industrial ecology, or the other way around: Korhonen (2003; p. 301) wrote "The method is applied to common industrial metabolism tools of ecological footprints (EF), environmental life cycle assessment (LCA) and industrial ecology (IE)", whereas Tang *et al.* (2011; p. 380) state that "Three methods analogous to nature systems are used to conduct research on industrial ecology: industrial metabolism, life cycle management and industrial symbiosis".

In addition to industrial ecology two other major fields exist in sustainable development: **environmental economics** and its younger sibling, **ecological economics**. Before examining these schools, we must first have an understanding of two different forms of sustainability, weak and strong.

5.7 Weak and strong sustainability

Sustainable development is defined as development that meets the needs of the present without compromising the ability of future generations to meet their own needs (Brundtland, 1987). Sustainable development has been variously conceived in terms of vision expression (Lee, 1993), value change (Clark, 1989), moral development (Rolston, 1994), social re-organization (Gore, 1992) or transformational processing (Viederman, 1994) towards a desired future or better world. Mason (2011) defined sustainability as intra- and intergenerational justice, with the prevention of social and ecological harm.

Two different operational concepts have developed: **economic sustainability** (the continuance of economic growth and capital maintenance, both produced and natural) and **ecological sustainability** (reduction in source and sink impacts on the environment by dematerializing the economy) (Bartelmus, 2001).

Weak sustainability seeks to maintain levels of total capital from generation to generation, through substitution. Thus if natural capital declines, provided that man-made capital increases by the same amount, then total capital will be maintained.

Neoclassical economists view sustainability as a problem of controlling the national portfolio of capital to maintain it at a constant level. It allows for virtually unlimited substitution between man-made and natural capital (see Pearce *et al.*, 1990). The initial problem was sketched out by Salow

(1974), who demonstrated that if a nonrenewable resource was a factor of production, consumption falls to zero eventually, as the resource runs out. Hartwick (1977) resolved this issue by suggesting that earnings derived from nonrenewable resource depletion should be reinvested in produced capital. The Hartwick-Solow models therefore required either abundant nonrenewable resources or reversible substitution between natural and human-made capital stocks

Weak sustainability finds its roots in **new welfare economics** (NWE) and the **Pareto efficiency**. Pareto efficiency is achieved when resources are shared in such a way that no individual can improve their share of resources without impacting negatively on another individual. Generally this occurs when resource availability is maximized, meaning that there is a drive to exploit resources in order for each individual to have an equally large share of the greatest whole. NWE sought to maximize individual wellbeing by optimizing economic input and output. An immediate problem arises here: the measurement and comparison of wellbeing. How can we compare wellbeing between individuals at one time, and how can we compare wellbeing of individuals from different generations (Suzumura, 1999)? Can wellbeing really be reduced to economic utility, or do we need to include such ambiguous issues as happiness and contentment?

Weak sustainability can equate to intergenerational equity if we accept that gross economic output and gross consumption equate to welfare (Ayres *et al.*, 1998). Another point is that trade can mask decline in natural capital provided it maintains economic output. Trade can be seen to decouple national natural capital from man-made capital, by supplementing local natural resource supply with imported natural resources. Provided economic activity is maintained, then the whole can be labelled as sustainable.

A further criticism is that the transformation of natural capital into man-made capital is likely to be a one-way process, in that nature cannot be bought back. Once a habitat is polluted by mine waste, a wetland drained or a rainforest removed, it can be many hundreds of years before the ecosystem can be restored. Basic life-support systems are likely to be impossible to substitute (Barbier *et al.*, 1994). Ott (2003; p. 63) states that "Natural capital is characterized by internal and dynamic complexity. Its components form a network of relationships. In principle, they are mutually non-substitutable". Thus once an ancient forest has gone, it has gone for good. No matter how much man-made capital is accrued from its destruction, there will be no possibility of bringing the ancient forest back.

Krysiak (2006) demonstrates that the second law of thermodynamics casts doubt over the feasibility of weak sustainability. "Weak sustainability relies on an infinite elasticity of substitution between the different stocks, that is, it is always possible to exchange resource stock for capital stock" (Krysiak, 2006; p. 189).

Strong sustainability requires the maintenance, or sustaining, of each pool of capital (human, man-made, economic and natural) with no substitution between pools. It is often misrepresented as only applying to natural capital, but this is not its meaning. For opportunity to continue for all, each pool of capital should be maintained (Daly and Cobb, 1989; p. 72; Brekke, 1997; p. 91).

Strong sustainability theorists argue that substitution between different forms of capital is limited by complementarity (i.e. the fishing boat is no use without the fish, nor the sawmill without the forest), irreversibility (once gone, it is difficult to restore natural capital), uncertainty (as to the needs of future generations that need to be sustained) and discontinuous change (such as climate destabilization and resource availability) (Ng and Wills, 2002; Gowdy, 2004).

To counteract these issues, the concept of **consilience** was developed by the biologist E.O. Wilson. He defines consilience as "the linking of facts and fact-based theories across disciplines to create a common groundwork for explanation" (Wilson, 1998; p. 8). Consilience demands that the most superior theory will work across the most subject areas, making sense in all of these different contexts. Thus a truly sustainable economy must operate within social and environmental contexts, not merely economic contexts. Many new models of economic sustainability are now using consilience as a test (Ayres *et al.*, 2001; Glimcher and Rustichini, 2004; Tietenberg, 2011).

Both weak and strong sustainability have been criticized on common grounds (Douai, 2009). First, they both discuss the environment in terms of natural capital, thus putting a financial value on nature, and suggesting nature is a tradable commodity. Many argue that this is wrong, given the complexity of the natural world. In other words, if an ecosystem cannot be bought or mimicked by human-made capital, then it cannot have a value. Furthermore, ecosystems emerge from an energetic context and contribute to the overall structure of biomes and the biosphere, as well as forming crucial definitional space for populations and individuals. Ecosystems become priceless.

Raudsepp-Hearne *et al.* (2010) reported that although ecosystem services have been degraded, human wellbeing has increased. They termed this effect the **environmental paradox**. This paper was viewed as supporting weak sustainability over strong sustainability. However, this conclusion hinges on the definition of human wellbeing (see above). This work has been critiqued by Ang and van Passel (2012) who point out that it relies on a stock-flow framework that is fundamentally unsuitable for understanding the environment/wellbeing relationship. Furthermore Raudsepp-Hearne *et al.* (2010) also contradict weak sustainability theory by demonstrating that declining natural capital, without substitution, still improves human wellbeing. Thus their work undermines both weak and strong sustainability.

A second paradox, the **paradox of plenty** (also called the **natural resource curse**), creates significant issues for weak sustainability (Autyraudsepp, 1993). The resources of the world are not homogeneously spread throughout the planet. Some countries have much greater wealth than others. Yet as Frankel (2012) points out, countries with oil, mineral or other natural resource wealth, on average, have failed to show better economic performance than those without. This anomaly is known as the paradox of plenty. It stands as an important challenge to the concept of weak sustainability, wherein greater resource exploitation generates greater capital which can then be used to replace natural capital, thus saving the planet. Because greater use of natural resources does not guarantee an increase in available capital to replace lost natural capital, then this casts doubt over a fundamental argument of weak sustainability.

5.8 Environmental economics

Environmental economics attracts economists, and stresses weak sustainability, looking at economic growth as essential, while facilitating environmental considerations through technology. It is set within the neoclassical school of economics. Whereas the classical school, represented by Adam Smith and Robert Malthus, emphasized population levels as the significant threat, the neoclassical school pointed towards nonrenewable resources (Jevons, 1865), damaged ecosystems and economic growth (Mill, 1857) as of prime concern.

The school of environmental economics really took shape following the oil crisis of the early 1970s (Seneca and Taussig, 1974; Nijkamp, 1977), although the core values had been in place long before (see Cropper and Oates, 1992). The foundations of environmental economics were laid in the

1950s by the work of Siegfried von Ciriacy-Wantrup, who introduced the concept of uncertainty and the safe minimal standard (e.g. Ciriacy-Wantrup and Schultz, 1957).

Largely based on the theory of market failure, the field of environmental economics focuses on how various types of market failure create environmental damage (Cropper and Oates, 1992; Dorfman, 1993). Environmental economics approaches pollution primarily as an economic problem. Environmental economists are fundamentally concerned with the means of eradicating market failure because they believe that this will reduce environmental degradation and enhance economic and ecological sustainability.

The founding of the Association of Environmental and Resource Economists in 1974 established two subdisciplines. Resource economists dealt with resource depletion (source issues), while environmental economists dealt with pollution (sink issues). Environmental economics approaches pollution primarily as an economic problem. Environmental economists are fundamentally concerned with the means of eradicating market failure because they believe that this will reduce environmental degradation and enhance economic and ecological sustainability. Government intervention into price structure has historically been associated with this approach, setting it in contradiction with institutional ecological economics and free market environmentalism (see below).

A perceived lack of input from social sciences has recently been attacked (Folmer and Johansson-Stenman, 2011). Another criticism of environmental economics is its fundamental reliance on cost–benefit analysis, wherein environmental damage can be given a value, allowing its integration into a weak sustainability position. As early as 1970, Karl Kapp, one of the founders of ecological economics, warned against the valuation of environmental damage and improvement, insisting that the consequences of each is highly heterogeneous and cannot be compared with the other nor with control costs (Kapp, 1970). He emphasized that it is wrong to replace natural capital with human-made capital, nor human capital with human-made capital. His work represented some of the earliest economic arguments for strong sustainability against weak sustainability. It can be argued that it is impossible to value diversification potential in nature, that is, the inherent ability for nature to restore diversity in the face of significant extinction, because any measure of diversity is form-based and thus fails to adequately account for function (Skene, 2011a).

5.9 Ecological economics

By the 1980s, frustration with progress in environmental economics led to a second school of thought, **ecological economics**, separating itself and developing a more ecologically centred approach (Daly and Farley, 2004). From this group emerged a third school, who felt that the social aspects of sustainability were not sufficiently recognized. This was called **socio-ecological economics** (Jacobs, 1996; Cameron, 1997).

Ecological economics places its emphasis on ecology, and its proponents are mostly ecologists. Its seat of power rests in the University of Maryland's Institute of Ecological Economics, although with chapters spread throughout the world. It emerged as a response to a perceived failure of environmental economics to penetrate mainstream economic thinking into the 1980s. In Europe, the emphasis is somewhat different, and includes social considerations, whereas the American school is fundamentally science-based (Spash, 2009).

The history of ecological economics, and the infighting that accompanied it, has been recorded by Røpke (2004; 2005). Its emphasis is on strong sustainability economics, wherein ecosystem services should be prioritized, rather than technological mimicry (Daly and Farley, 2004). Economies are recognized as open subsystems within a closed biosphere system (Victor, 2010). Fundamentally, ecological economics views GDP as an inappropriate measure of wellbeing (van den Bergh, 2009). Ecological economics is more interdisciplinary than environmental economics, and both fields have a distinct group of authors and journals (Ma and Stern, 2006).

A second school within ecological economics is called **institutional ecological economics** (Young, 2002; Gowdy and Erickson, 2005; Paavola and Adger, 2005). This school emphasizes the role of institutions as important determinants of values and preferences in human behaviour. Institutions are also seen as helping to deliver property and management regimes that provide incentives for environmental protection. Institutional ecological economics advocates a middle ground between decentralized and centralized government, with numerous decision-making centres (**poly centres**) acting independently (Ostrom, 1999). In this respect, this school shares a philosophy with **localism** and **territoriality** (see below).

Gerber *et al.* (2009) and Hardy and Patterson (2012) raise concerns that while ecological economics covers two of the three pillars of sustainability (namely, the environment and the economy), there is, again, insufficient attention paid to the social implications. Indeed, a new field, called

socio-ecological economics (Jacobs, 1996; Cameron, 1997), or **social ecological economics** (Spash, 2009), has developed to counter this. As socioeconomists began to take interest in ecological economics, they demanded an increased emphasis on society. A workshop was organized at the Wuppertal Institute in 1995, resulting in a call for socio-ecological economics. Socio-ecological economics has emerged as a new movement within ecological economics that overtly takes account of the sociological and political bases of economic activity as well as the biophysical base (Cameron, 1997).

5.10 Free market environmentalism

Free market environmentalism holds closely to Adam Smith's concept of laissez-faire economics, and emphasizes the need for individual property rights for environmental resources. It fundamentally believes that the mechanism of supply–demand–marketplace will ensure environmental protection (Anderson and Leal, 2001; Block, 1990). This relies on individuals in the marketplace demanding improved environmental conditions. A central belief is that the only reason markets fail is because of state intervention, and that state intervention also lies at the heart of environmental damage, not the free market economy (Raeder, 1998).

Governments can externalize losses in natural capital as often the true costs are not apparent until long after that particular government is gone. The 4/5-year political cycle allows governments to act in such a way as to be unaccountable in anything but the immediate future (Huffman, 1994). However, free market environmentalism would not adhere to smaller government localism, unlike institutional ecological economics, but rather would lean towards globalization and sustainable development. Only with homogeneity can the free market run perfectly.

5.11 Closed-loop economy and Cradle to Cradle®

The concept of **Cradle to Cradle®** has been disputed in terms of its origins. McDonough and Braungart say, in their book *Cradle to Cradle: Remaking the Way We Make Things* (McDonough and Braungart, 2002: p. 104), "Products can either be composed of materials that biodegrade and become food for biological cycles, or of technical (sometimes toxic) materials that stay in closed-loop technical cycles, where they continually circulate as valuable nutrients for industry." The term "C2C Certification" is now a protected term of the McDonough Braungart Design Chemistry (MBDC) consultancy. However, supporters of Walter Stahel claim that he coined the term in the 1970s (Product-Life, 2008). There is no doubt in the literature that Stahel first used the term "economy in loops" (Stahel, 1976).

Stahel founded the Product Life Institute in Geneva whose main goals were product-life extension, long-life goods, reconditioning activities and waste prevention. Kodak, DuPont, the BBC and Bosch are among its clients. The concept of delaying death of products by investing in longevity and service was very much an idea of Stahel, who said that an improved service industry could balance a loss in manufacturing, thus allowing this approach to be a financial success (Stahel, 2003). He also introduced the concept of a performance economy which he defined as economic actors achieving sustainable profits in the long-term without an externalization of the costs of risk and of waste (Stahel, 2006).

The idea that we can design much longer-lasting products appears useful, but design may be compromised and, in nature, appropriate flow is important. In order to continue to defy the second law of thermodynamics, by not breaking down, products must consume more useful energy, and release more entropy than otherwise would be the case. It could be energetically less disruptive to design towards a more natural outcome, likely with shorter life. In nature, turnover rather than stasis is the rule.

For example a bamboo chopstick would be better than a highly synthesized plastic fork, as it could easily be recycled and would only briefly be removed from the biosphere. Furthermore, the bamboo chopstick uses only natural nutrients, not technical nutrients, and therefore is more easily reassimilated back into the environment. By building long-lasting materials, we will be likely to use more technical nutrients than natural nutrients, which is likely to make their ultimate breakdown more difficult and energetically expensive. This is because long-lasting products are actually moving further away from a natural economy, not towards one. The issue of flux should be central to all of this, and delaying the cycle through exotic chemistry or prolonged servicing may well not be an appropriate strategy.

Braungart and McDonough went further, stressing that the long-life approach merely delayed the inevitable reintroduction of toxins back into the environment. Instead they proposed a redesign of the industrial processes altogether. This became known as the **waste equals food** approach, where "one organism's waste is food for another, and nutrients and energy flow perpetually in closed-loop cycles of growth, decay and rebirth (McDonough and Braungart, 2003). Waste includes energy, water, material and information. However, as we have already noted, this concept has been around for at least 150 years.

McDonough and Braungart point out that the total biomass of ants on Earth is greater than the total biomass of humans, yet no "pollution" or ecological degradation results from their activities (McDonough and Braungart, 2002). However, this viewpoint fails to realize that humans are warm-blooded, large mammals that require much greater energy flow-through to maintain themselves far from equilibrium than ants do. Second, we are much more vulnerable and require a much narrower range of conditions to remain alive than ants do, meaning that to sustain the current population, we need to spend huge energy to maintain favourable conditions (in terms of food, shelter, water, heating, cooling, medical aid and transport). Our population would crash if we attempted to reduce energy expenditure to antlike levels.

5.12 Biomimicry and natural capitalism

Biomimicry is a concept that has recently gained much ground in sustainability thinking. Janine Benyus, a scientist and author of *Biomimicry: Innovation Inspired by Nature,* defines biomimicry as "a new discipline that studies nature's best ideas and then imitates these designs and processes to solve human problems" (Benyus, 1998). She thinks of it as "innovation inspired by nature". Biomimicry relies on three key principles:

1. Nature as model: study and emulate natural forms, processes, systems and strategies to solve human problems
2. Nature as measure: using environmental monitoring to judge the sustainability of our innovations
3. Nature as mentor: using nature as a source of information, not of material

Benyus suggests that nature is designed around nine specific principles: (i) runs on sunlight (ii) uses only the energy it needs (iii) fits form to function (iv) recycles everything (v) rewards co-operation (vi) banks on diversity (vii) demands local expertise (viii) curbs excesses from within (ix) taps the power of limits (Benyus, 2002, p. 7).

Several of these assumptions are problematic. First, nature does not use only the energy it needs. Supplying more energy to an ecosystem may well destroy it, but the destruction comes because it cannot constrain its use of energy. This is why eutrophication has such disastrous effects on ecosystem function. The excess nutrients release parts of the ecosystem, which then generates too much chaos within the surroundings, thus destabilizing the entire system.

Nature responds to the conditions available, but there is no Gaian self-control apparent in a eutrophied lake with its dead fish and poisoned water. Thus nature is also unable to curb excesses from within under such conditions. It is not merely in response to human pollution that we see such loss of control. During the Great Oxygen Event of 2 billion years ago, huge levels of extinction occurred within the anaerobic bacteria. As can be seen, the same issues arise here as we found with the Gaian hypothesis (Chapter 4), and this points to the fact that biomimicry references Gaia. It also references the static equilibrium model of ecology, where restoration of nature's balance will restore the biosphere to a healthy place.

Applications span a mesmerizing range of subjects, from using beehive structure to inform capsule hotel design in Tokyo (Fragkou and Stevenson, 2012) to water skaters being mimicked to design cocktails (Burton *et al.*, 2013). Lovins (2008; p. 11) reports that:

> Now, a Canadian biotechnology company and the United States Army research centre have spliced spider genes into cells from cows and hamsters and induced the cells to churn out silk. The silk, grown in tissue cultures, has been spun into threads that are comparable to those produced by spiders.

Most papers on biomimicry focus on one or two design aspects in nature that can be incorporated into human life, improving our quality of life while not impacting strongly on the environment. Although nature does indeed give us innovative solutions to problems that we face, such as Velcro and photosynthetic cells, we cannot rebuild the biosphere through lots of little mimics. Biomimicry is fundamentally a reductionist approach, but since all natural processes emerge due to holistic interactions, then mimicking nature in isolation is unlikely to achieve sustainability. Surely sustainability should include nature as part of the tripartite bottom line, rather than replacing it with nature-inspired technology?

In a similar way that neo-Darwinian theory cannot contribute to an understanding of the holistic entity that is the biosphere, neither in terms of its function nor sustainability, so biomimicry is unable to address these issues as it is a reductionist collection of bite-sized solutions. Also akin to neo-Darwinism, these bite-sized pieces leave no room for ethics. Although the spider and hamster cells can be used to make weblike material, should we be making it? Are cocktails based on biomimicry of water skaters really necessary?

Biomimicry claims that it will introduce a second industrial revolution, wherein industrial production will regenerate nature (Mathews, 2011; p. 372), a fundamentally weak sustainability notion. This is an extraordinary claim, and it is based on the concept that human consumption is not the problem and so reducing economic growth is not necessary. It sits uncomfortably with the stated aim of acting within nature. True ecology does not work in this way, and indeed, in ecology, the bite-sized pieces are merely outcomes of much deeper principles.

Finally, Janine Benyus observes that nature doesn't make waste (Benyus, 1997). This could not be further from the truth. Nature produces entropy (i.e. energy waste) very effectively. Energy requires constant replenishment because waste production is so extreme. Life, in many ways, is a **waste generator**. This is why, during the last mass extinction, when the energy source was cut off, the entire biosphere collapsed. If nature made no waste, it could have kept going without any additional input. And the energy is needed because nature produces high entropy material waste as well (such as carbon dioxide), which must be re-energized to be useful. Without energy, the CO_2 would not be able to be converted back into sugar. According to the second law of thermodynamics, in order to create complexity and stay far from thermodynamic equilibrium, waste must be produced. So Benyus is wrong. Nature is very wasteful.

Amory and Hunter Lovins have endeavoured to incorporate the ideas of biomimicry into economics, in a school of thought called **natural capitalism**. Indeed, its authors have defined it as the second great intellectual shift in the last 40 years, the other being the fall of communism (Lovins and Lovins, 2000)! Natural capitalism is based on three principles:

1. By using resources more productively (eco-efficiency), we buy time to address the issues of the future. The target is a fourfold increase in efficiency (Von Weizsäcker *et al.*, 1998).

2. Redesign how to make products and provide services using biomimicry and Cradle to Cradle®.

3. Manage all institutions to be restorative of human and natural capital (Lovins, 2008).

Eco-efficiency is defined as:

- A reduction in material intensity
- A reduction in energy intensity
- Reduced dispersion of toxins
- Improved recyclability
- Maximum use of renewable resources
- Greater durability
- Increased service intensity (Schmidheiny, 1992)

Amory Lovins sums up natural capitalism as follows:

> If capitalism is a productive use of and reinvestment in capital, we can't deal only with financial and physical capital—money and goods. We also need to productively use and reinvest in two more valuable kinds of capital—people and nature. If you play with a full deck, using all four kinds of capital, then you make more money, do more good, and have more fun (Lovins in Hopkins, 2009; p. 36).

Problems arise with this approach. Nature is extremely wasteful, converting low entropy resources into high entropy waste, which requires huge energy to recycle. It produces vast amounts of toxins, such as oxygen. It has high energy intensity and it doesn't generally work towards greater durability, but rather fast recycling.

Another issue is that eco-efficiency is limited by the chemical properties of the periodic table. For example, lithium and graphite are currently irreplaceable in the batteries that power electric cars. Rare earth metals, central to wind power, require complex and toxic processes to release and concentrate them from their source materials. Their chemistry again makes them irreplaceable in terms of alternatives. Thus they are not replaceable by renewable resources. The concept of renewable resources is questionable anyway (see Chapter 2).

And this returns us to a core issue with the biomimicry approach—the centrality of the concept of maintaining both profit and comfort. Unless we are willing to completely revisit how we live, the concept of eco-efficiency will be constrained by the chemistry that underpins most of our modern technology such as mobile phones, flat-screen monitors and wind turbines. Energy will always be needed in manufacturing, as complexity demands the externalization of waste. With increasing energy use in BRIC countries, any cutbacks in the West will be a drop in the ocean.

A significant issue is that natural capitalism is very much targeted at the Western world, whereas most people on the planet live relatively eco-efficient lives at present, with small carbon footprints per capita. The future is highly uncertain in that even if the majority of the population globally take on a western eco-efficiency, this would represent a huge **increase** in consumption compared with the current situation.

Biomimicry and natural capitalism have lots of examples of good practice, but they fail to explain how we can continue to feed the world without the Haber-Bosch process, how we truly power the economy with green energy (without destroying the rainforests, mining rare earth metals or polluting the planet with photovoltaic technology), and how this school approaches the subject of ethics, in terms of such areas as genetic engineering, human community sovereignty or ecosystem function.

Finally there is huge redundancy and suboptimality in nature, which is an essential aspect of it (Skene, 2011b). Nature is, by its nature, inefficient. Suboptimality is a characteristic of multilevel systems, wherein the solutions at one level are compromised by the solutions at another. If a squirrel remembered where it had buried all of its nuts, then the forest would not renew, and there would be no more nuts, nor squirrels. If DNA repaired itself perfectly, there would be no mutations and no genetic variation and evolution.

This creates issues in terms of any concept of eco-efficiency, as at the ecosystem level, excess redundant diversity can provide protection against disturbance (Alison, 2004; Jones *et al.*, 2004; Virah-Sawmy *et al.*, 2009; Schindler *et al.*, 2010). Natural capitalism is an evolution of traditional economics, in that it relies on the same industrial overarching logic (Sánchez, 2013).

Biomimicry implies that we need to pretend to be biological, rather than actually *being* biological. It is very much a weak sustainability argument, where technology can replace what nature has lost. Indeed, in many ways it is merely a restatement of weak sustainability. A different approach would be **bioparticipation**, where we learn to play our role within the existent biosphere, rather than mimic aspects of that biosphere, while still existing in technological exclusion (Skene, 2011b). Bioparticipation, also called **biosynergy**, would allow nature to design our desires and lifestyles, whereas biomimicry currently advocates using natural design to provide new ways of maintaining our current lifestyles (Mathews, 2011).

5.13 The blue economy

A green economy was defined, at Rio +20, as an economy that "should contribute to eradicating poverty, as well as sustained economic growth, enhancing social inclusion, improving human welfare and creating new opportunities for employment and decent work for all, while maintaining the healthy functioning of the earth's ecosystems" (UNOSD, 2012). The Small Island Developing Nations (SIDS) renamed this economy as the blue economy, emphasizing the importance of the oceans to their existence.

Gunter Pauli, the Belgian entrepreneur and author of *The Blue Economy: 100 Innovations—Ten Years—100 Million Jobs* (Pauli, 2009), adopted the term blue economy in a different way. He challenged the concept of a green economy, claiming that a green economy is perceived as requiring investment by industry and delivering extra cost to consumers, a combination particularly unpalatable during economic downturn.

Pauli claims that the green economy relies on externalizing environmental costs, citing the increased consumption of shiitake mushrooms in the western world as driving oak forest destruction in China, and palm oil consumption in the West as leading to the decimation of rainforest in Borneo. Instead he suggests that three core ecosystem characteristics can help us transform our approaches, leading to a sustainable future that costs neither industry nor the consumer:

1. Energy and matter cascades
2. Physics-based thinking
3. Waste as a food

He further points out that a green economy requires continual subsidies, which he views as economically unsustainable. He views the green economy as substituting one resource with a different one (e.g. palm oil for petroleum) and instead argues for substituting something with nothing, reducing our burden on the planet. **The p2p Foundation** claims that the blue economy creatively works with what is available and aims at catalysing a shift from scarcity to abundance (http://p2pfoundation.net/).

As we have seen in section 5.2, the concept of waste as food is not new. The use of physics in economics has been around for at least 40 years, dating back to the work of Nicholas Georgescu-Roegen (see Chapter 4). The concept of energy and matter cascades is intriguing but occurs in other schools of sustainable thinking. In its use in the blue economy, as a foundation for greatly reducing costs yet saving the planet and thus being attractive to business and consumer alike, it runs into two significant obstacles: the first and second laws of thermodynamics. Unfortunately, the physics used in the blue economy is wrong.

Pauli's idea that there is no such thing as waste in nature is contradicted by physics which clearly demonstrates that life is a dissipative process by its very nature, in that it exists by converting useful energy to less useful energy, creating entropy. For example he claims that a cascade is like a waterfall, requiring no power to generate, since it flows because of gravity. However, this is fundamentally flawed. Newton's apple did indeed fall, but the tree used huge resources not only to form the apple but to grow tall enough so that the apple was above the ground.

Within an entropic universe (see Appendix), order must be paid for, and entropy must be generated. As the first law says, there is no such thing as a free lunch. Water in the river above a waterfall got there from the processes of evaporation and precipitation. This required energy. The waterfall is ultimately powered by the sun. Often in gardens an artificial fountain is built, powered by an electric pump. Switch off the electricity and the fountain will stop. Yet in spite of this very simple fact, *The Blue Economy* claims "Nature uses physics and biochemistry to build harmoniously functioning whole systems, cascading abundantly, transforming effortlessly, and cycling efficiently without waste or energy loss" (Pauli, 2009; p. 11). This forms the basis for his conclusion that the blue economy will be cheap, because it uses so little energy. This is fundamentally flawed.

5.14 Post-development

The concept of development and its more recent offspring, sustainable development, are viewed by many as being northern hemisphere-based, top-down, controlling and politically motivated, used to deliver globalization and the Western philosophy of the Enlightenment rather than improving living standards (Rahnema and Bawtree, 1997; Hart, 2001, Matthews, 2004). Sachs refers to development as "a ruin in the intellectual landscape" (Sachs, 1991; p. 1).

Development as an economic and political school, emerged from the Age of Modernity, whose own foundations lie in the Enlightenment. As such, development is viewed by some as representing an extension of Western colonialism, much like orientalism. Arturo Escobar suggests that "development can be described as an apparatus (dispositif) that links forms of knowledge about the Third World with the deployment of forms of power and intervention, resulting in the mapping and production of Third World societies" (Escobar 1992b; p. 23).

It is argued that development has led to worsening societal and environmental conditions, with increased gaps between rich and poor, continued child exploitation, significant people-trafficking and increases in extremist politics. The GDP of sub-Saharan Africa between 1975 and 1999 shrank by 1%—i.e. Africa actually became economically weaker in spite of countless development projects launched from the West (UNDP 2001; p. 10). It is further argued that sustainable development merely camouflages the underlying values of development, while relying on a growth-based global economy that can only damage the environment further, allowing greater externalization of natural capital losses. It has also been suggested that cultural differences mean that several of the assumptions forming the foundation of post-World War II development theory are not universally accepted, and as a result efforts to implement Western development fails to work in many locations (N'Dione *et al.*, 1997).

These criticisms are bound together in a movement that has been labelled as **post-development**. However, to understand what post-development means, we must first determine what we mean by development. The **Western model**, developed after World War II, as the victorious western allies took on the responsibility to "enlighten" the rest of the world to their philosophy of progress, is the target of post-developmental theorists. The Cameroonian sociologist, Jean-Marc Ela puts it this way, when explaining why Western development projects often fail in Africa:

> Africa is not against development. It dreams of other things than the expansion of a culture of death or an alienating modernity that destroys the fundamental values so dear to Africans ... Africa sees further than an all-embracing world of material things and the dictatorship of the here and now, that insists on trying to persuade us that the only valid motto is "I sell, therefore I am". In a world often devoid of meaning, Africa is a reminder that there are other ways of being (Ela, 1998; p. 3).

"**Developing**" nations are seen as being forced to adopt "**developed**" approaches, without any input whatsoever. Schumacher (1973), in his controversial book *Small is Beautiful,* clearly highlighted this issue. The impression that development is not merely a set of policies that have failed to work by accident, but is a deliberate political tool, has led to the subject of post-development taking on a radical political identity itself, akin to some form of Marxism in the 19th century. Development is viewed as an imposition from an elite minority on a majority whose voice is deemed too outdated to contribute anything of value. Arturo Escobar has written: "The question in this [sustainable development] discourse is what new manipulations can we invent to make the most out of nature and 'resources'? But who is this 'we' who knows what is best for the world as a whole?" (Escobar, 1996; p. 329).

Post-development does not call for an alternative form of development, but rather an eradication of any attempt to train the "**developing**" world, arguing that indigenous people are likely to have better solutions within the context of their natural and cultural landscape for the problems facing them than will Western thinkers. This concept aligns post-development with neo-romanticism, postmodernism and post-structuralism in their broadest expressions.

The post-development practitioner would point to the empires of the West as being at the base of most of the problems now experienced in the so-called "**third world**". Furthermore, the Western world can be seen to have been responsible for most of the destruction of the environment and society, and thus is no model for sustainability.

Since post-development began as a school of protest, it is a diverse church. Finding a single concrete definition of its vision for the future is difficult if not impossible (although it should be mentioned that there are also many different schools within the broad church of development, including capitalist development, Marxist development, state-led development and market-led development (Matthews, 2004)).

Indeed many adherents claim that the purpose of post-development is to oppose development, not to come up with an alternative (Nustad, 2001). However, among the more constructive practitioners, terms such as **radical democracy** (Ziai, 2004) and **endogenous discourse** (Escobar, 1992a) are used to set out a society where diversity and sovereignty belong to the communities and where identity is landscape-oriented. Such movements as **buen vivir**, **localism** and **communalism** (see below) all share ground with post-development theory.

As discussed in Chapter 3, the Environmental Kuznets Curve, which would have environmental damage decreasing with increasing prosperity, is not supported, and thus post-development theorists argue that one of the core foundation stones of development, namely prosperity (tied to economic growth), cannot deliver a sustainable future (Rupasingha *et al.*, 2004; Bousquet and Favard, 2005).

Post-development is largely (though not exclusively) focused on society and culture, rather than the environment or economics, and so it lacks the breadth to offer a truly global resolution of the economics–society–environment challenge. However, its value lies mostly in its critique of current practice.

5.15 Communalism

Edward Goldsmith, philosopher, environmentalist, founder of the Green Party in the UK and former editor of *The Ecologist* magazine, claimed that:

> the problems facing the world today can only be solved by restoring the functioning of those natural systems which once satisfied our needs, i.e. by fully exploiting those incomparable resources which are individual people, families, communities and ecosystems, which together make up the biosphere or real world (Goldsmith, 1988; p. 189).

E.F. Schumacher emphasized that sustainability would not work under neoliberal, socialist nor liberal approaches, but rather required a new economy, stressing appropriate technology, ownership and national self-sufficiency (Schumacher, 1973). Hopkins (2008) and Estill (2008) go further, saying that small is not only possible, but inevitable.

The **decentralized communalist approach** emphasizes local, communal organization using sustainable technologies and local sharing of wealth. It is fundamentally a form of anarchism. Here, a national government is unnecessary and unwanted. Instead, local communities work together to produce that which the communities themselves require (Gallopin, 2001; Meadowcroft, 2001; Raskin, 2008; Foster, 2009).

Communalism represents the extreme collective on the individual–collective axis, and as such, defies neo-Darwinism in rejecting selfish needs for the greater good, while embracing group selection of Wynne-Edwards. This is a holistic social structure, decrying self-interest, personal achievement, self-reliance and individual rights, while embracing community welfare, solidarity, ascription and co-ordination (Gudykunst and Ting-Toomey, 1988).

Community characteristics are seen to emerge over time, and thus cannot be created artificially. This makes it very difficult to apply communalism to a modern planet where many such communities have been lost. Indeed this need for time and heritage means that to many, communalism can only be conserved, not introduced. Given this, it is not surprising that communalism is the cultural foundation of nations with preserved heritages, such as Canadian Indians, Caribbean island nations, Arctic Indians, much of continental Africa, South-East Asians, American Indians and Australian Aborigines, where the guiding dictum is "I am because we are" (Mbiti, 1969; p. 108).

However, a broader approach may posit the notion that in all of us lie the ungerminated seeds of communalism, preserved from when all of us were part of a truly communalist heritage. This heritage may not be lost but dormant, and so communalism may be able to be reawakened rather than created. It may also be that our attraction to collectives, even though they may be not exactly liberating, such as tribal identities or religious cults, may stem from this deep desire to be part of a community of sorts.

Communalism has been most fiercely attacked by Hardin (1968) in his analogy of the **tragedy of the commons**, where unregulated communities are viewed as irresponsible and unable to stop themselves from overexploitation. However, advocates would argue that the central tenet of communalism is the health of the community, and thus Hardin's model only applies to societies in which there is a communal vacuum, where individualism dominates.

Individual needs are met within the context of the community, rather than being the dominant force, as theorized and practised during the period of Reaganomics and Thatcherism. However, the system is anarchic, in that it is the community and not some higher order of organization of centralized government that is the decision-making unit. This does not mean, however, that communalism is not truly holistic, as the community-environment relationship places the individuals and communities within much greater levels of organization than government, namely the ecosystem, biome and biosphere.

Thus globalization is represented by the natural planetary context, rather than the philosophy of development. This sets communalism apart from **collectivism**. Collectivism is an artificial, designed structure adopted by societies, usually with some form of government. Even within individualistic cultures such as the Western world, collectives are formed rarely with any awareness of the value of environment (which often is transcribed through culture). However, communalism is a completely different approach, with culture playing a very significant role, and thus community actions are enriched by environmental awareness.

Kim (1994) has observed that family communalism has transferred into corporate communalism in South Korean economics. The application of communalism to economics has not really been examined, and could offer some interesting insights. One exception to this is the concept of pluralism (see below).

A final point of interest relates to the impact of the Information Age on communalism (Kalathil, 2002). While initially seeming to dilute communalism by globalizing culture and diluting community identity, there are clear examples where national diaspora are brought together through the Internet. These include the exiled Burmese nationals, who used the Internet to organize and put pressure on the military leadership of Burma, contributing to the re-establishment of democracy within the country and the possibility of return of much of the diaspora.

5.16 Localism

Localism is also an anarchic movement, but separates itself from the decentralized communalist approach, stressing community and sustainability over appropriate technology, and targeting the middle class rather than working class. It incorporates some neoliberal values of the market (albeit locally applied), and of decentralized government. It can be seen as liberal in that it calls for government support.

Local ownership is socialist and local food networks are communalist but, importantly, it is built from grass roots, hence diversity plays a key role. It targets the large corporation-society interaction. Its focus is on restoring community-based sovereignty in order to find social justice and equality, empowering individuals and communities. Localism also allows escape from the global economy and its drivers (McIntyre and Rondeau, 2011).

The history of humankind has been a history oscillating between localism and centralization (Fig. 5.1). Hunter-gatherers are thought to have lived in an equitable society, but with the onset of agriculture and economics, inequality and power entered into the system.

Aristotle recognized the importance of intermediary groups as essential components in societal structure to oppose tyranny. This he referred to as the *Koinonia politike*. Ancient Greece itself had numerous city-states,

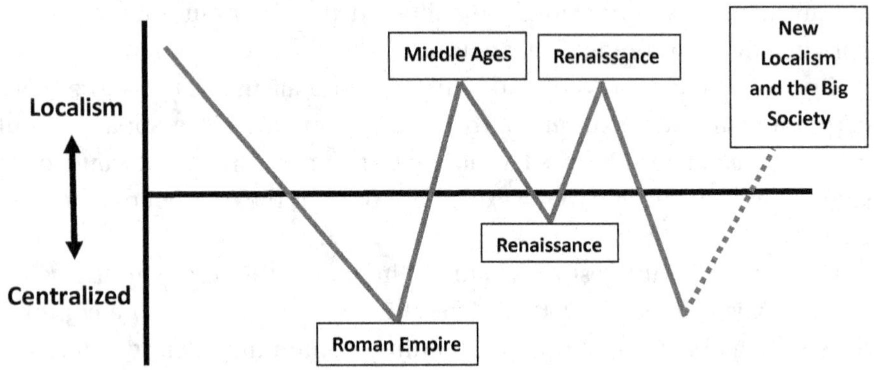

FIGURE 5.1 Swings between localism and centralized control over history.

reflecting localized power. The Roman Empire transitioned from a city-state to a centralized empire. However, by the end of the Roman Empire, land was being divided up and auctioned to private citizens, on leasehold, called *latifundia* (large farms forming part of the *agri publici*), many becoming self-sufficient coloniae, similar to the haciendas of South America.

This evolved into the manorial system of the Middle Ages. Italian city-states developed. However, with the onset of the Renaissance, centralization returned to Europe. During these centuries, the Roman Catholic Church acted as an alternative Roman Empire, with centralizing power reaching over western Europe. Hobbes wrote "If man consider the original of this great ecclesiastical dominion, he will easily perceive that the Papacy is no other than the ghost of the deceased Roman Empire, sitting crowned upon the grave thereof" (Coulton, 1942: p. 23). However, the structure of the church also encouraged a form of localism, with the local priest presiding over most activities in a particular activity.

In Britain, kings and queens generally ruled in a centralized fashion until the onset of parliament. At this point, a tension was introduced between the Royal family and the Houses of Parliament, with the church playing a lessening role over time. As revolution spread through mainland Europe and America, the remaining royal households struggled to maintain centralized control of their nations. However, even in countries such as France and the USA, centralized royal control was replaced with centralized government control.

The 19th century saw some revival of localism. Alexis de Tocqueville (1805–59) became an advocate for the presence of intermediate groups such as municipal institutions. Edmond Burke (1729–97) developed the concept of "small platoons as the pillars of the state". However, following World War II, centralization returned to Britain, first in the form of the welfare state, and then in the form of privatization by Thatcherism.

Leopold Kohr, the economist and political scientist, observed:

> There seems to be only one cause behind all forms of social misery: bigness. Oversimplified as this may seem, we shall find the idea more easily acceptable if we consider that bigness, or oversize, is really much more than just a social problem. It appears to be the one and only problem permeating all creation. Whenever something is wrong, something is too big (Kohr, 1978; p. xviii).

He was joined by Ernst Shumacher, Chief Economic Adviser to the Coal Board in the UK, who wrote his book, *Small is Beautiful*, following a trip to Burma, where he developed an interest in Buddhist economics (Schumacher, 1973).

At the beginning of the 21st century, British politics again embraced localism, which was seen as a vehicle to combat civic disengagement, meet individual and community needs more precisely, deliver more and better for less and encourage community cohesion. Born out of local communities feeling the brunt of globalization and privatization, where communities were forced to compete against each other for private capital, the Labour Party embarked on a series of white papers to set out some localist ideals. This was initially termed **new localism**, with the term "**Double devolution**" replacing it in 2006. This term, developed by the Young Foundation, described how governance would change from central to local, and then from local to very local, moving from Whitehall to councils to neighbourhoods.

The 2007 Lyons Inquiry led to the concept of **place-shaping**, defined as the creative use of powers and influence to promote the general well-being of a community and its citizens. The first white paper, released in 2008 (*Communities in Control*), was designed to increase citizen influence and participation in local affairs. It placed a duty to involve people on local councils. Local partnerships were sought to expand consultations with citizens. It also provided funding for community groups and proposed measures to require councils to consider citizen petitions.

A second paper, *Total Place*, was released in 2009 and examined how public services and agencies in the locality can pool strategic effort and budgets. With a change of government in 2010, from Labour to a Conservative–Social Democrat coalition, the drive towards localism was maintained, despite the very different political philosophies of the parties involved. The new coalition promised a fundamental shift of power from Westminster to the people and in December 2010, the government introduced the Decentralization and Localism Bill as a key component of the government's flagship "**Big Society**" policy. This has been mirrored in the states by the Tea Party, which is pushing for decreased central government control. The ethos was localism, decentralization was the mechanism and Big Society was the outcome. The Localism Act (2011) followed, emphasizing the community right to challenge, and the community right to bid, with proposals for local referendums and the right to veto excessive council tax rises.

What is interesting about localism from a political point of view is that so many different political ideologies are drawn towards it, from revisionist neoliberalism to post-Marxism. Post-Marxism emphasizes conscientious and collective identity formation around common experience, with collective action and bottom-up change, driven by inequality, whereas revisionist neoliberalism sees institutional involvement (top down) helping to drive reduced dependence on the state, thus reducing government expenditure. A leading critic, David Walker (Walker, 2002; p. 6), has gloomily stated that "We are all localists now".

Localism has many schools, including agrarianism, eco-feminism, bioregionalism, grass-roots democracy, cellular democracy, subsidiarity and urban secession. In Europe, two different approaches have emerged:

1. Legal localism where increased powers are given to local authorities. This tends to be most common in Northern Europe.
2. Political localism where increased representation of individuals at the national level is emphasized. This tends to be most common in Southern Europe.

Interestingly, localism is written into the Lisbon Treaty of the EU, which states that "The Treaty creates a basis for a more decentralized and transparent approach to implementing EU policies to help ensure that decisions are taken as close as possible to the citizen" (http://europa.eu/lisbon_treaty/faq/).

While the discussion up to now has focused on political localism, there is a parallel development of economic localism. This takes the form of local currencies. Advocates argue that local currencies tend to circulate more quickly than national currencies, thus increasing economic activity. If set with a small negative interest rate, spending is encouraged. Improved economic activity improves employment and encourages local trade, delivering community empowerment. The Information Age also is beginning to play a role, with the potential of global communities to develop their own currencies through the Internet, e.g. QQ coins in China. Critics of economic localism claim there is an increased potential for tax evasion, a prevention of economy of scale and difficulties with import–export issues.

None of the rhetoric emerging from the Big Society and the Tea Part references the environment. However, there has been much separate discussion on environmental localism. The most significant worker in this area has been Patrick Geddes (1854–1932) who discussed this under the theme of "Think Global, Act Local". He wrote that "Environment and organism, place and people, are inseparable" and set out the concept of sympathy, synthesis and synergy:

- **Sympathy** for the people and environment affected by any social remedy
- **Synthesis** of all the factors relevant to the case
- **Synergy**: the combined co-operative action of everyone involved (Berger, 1987; MacDonald, 1994)

Geddes was an ecologist, a town planner and a sociologist and brought thinking from each of these fields together in his work.

A more recent school of thought, heavily influenced by Geddes, and developed by Alberto Magnaghi (b.1941), is the **Territorialist** school. This urban and regional planning approach is based on the balance between self-reliance, enhanced environmental quality and self-government by local society, emphasizing **place consciousness** (Magnaghi, 2005).

Localism, if merely about local governance, is incapable of producing a sustainable future, nor the restoration of individual sovereignty. Big fish in small ponds are as problematic as very big fish in very big ponds. While removing the economy of scale with its consequent intensive destruction of nature, it fails to re-establish a relationship within the biosphere. A fully functioning version of localism has the advantage of not externalizing ecological damage, and thus communities would be under greater pressure to develop truly sustainable approaches. Until political localism references environmental localism, then a sustainable economic localism cannot emerge.

5.17 Pluralism

Pluralism can be defined as some degree of acceptance of two or more mutually inconsistent theoretical frameworks which pertain to the same or overlapping domains of reality. In this sense it is not a theory *per se*, but a method.

Pluralism has arisen in response to a perceived drive towards monism over the last 60 years. Its most recent development can trace its roots back to an advertisement which appeared in the American Economic Review (vol. 82(2); p. xxv) in 1992, signed by 44 leading economists of the time, which called for "a new spirit of pluralism in economics, involving critical conversation and tolerant communication between different approaches between the disciplines."

The following year the International Confederation of Associations for Reform in Economics (ICARE) was founded with a stated aim of promoting "a new spirit of pluralism in economics, involving critical conversation and tolerant communication among different approaches, within and across the barriers". By 2000, this organization had changed its name to Confederation of Associations for Pluralism in Economics (ICAPE). A Journal emerged, called the Post-autistic Economic Review, representing the post-autistic economics movement, whose stated aim is: "about reopening economics for free scientific inquiry, making it a pursuit where empiricism outranks a priorism and where critical thinking rules instead of ideology" (www.paecon.net/HistoryPAE.htm).

Thus, modern economic pluralism, born out of academia, immediately took on a political face, setting itself up as an institution to take on a more orthodox opponent, Neoclassicism. What sets it apart from other schools is that in its most recent form, it has been largely driven by students, rather than academics. The Paris group (June 2000), The Cambridge 27 (June 2001), the 17 nation group (August 2001, in Kansas), and a group of students from Harvard (March 2003), all wrote open letters demanding adoption of economic pluralism in the teaching they received. This represented an unprecedented attempt to revolutionize teaching of an academic subject from within the student body.

However, economic pluralism can trace its history to a much earlier time. Prior to World War I, The Social Gospel movement supported both neoclassical and institutionalist economics, provided both led to social reform (Bateman, 1998). The Great Depression, quickly followed by World War II, provided the perfect launch pad for Neoclassicism to take centre stage, setting itself out as the only "-ism" on the table. The new global community, whose birth was celebrated by the launch of such global institutions as the World Bank and the United Nations, also embraced a new global economy, and institutionalism was seen as not fit for purpose.

Monism in economics was further strengthened by the marriage between Darwinian evolution, empiricism and economic thinking, where competition drove out "weaker" theories, leading to a single model, as befitting a reductionist landscape (ignoring the fact that there are probably as many as 30 million different species on the planet). As the scientific method became dominant in economic theory, the individual became the building block, with microeconomics dominating. This move towards microeconomics was reflected in biology, where neo-Darwinism focused on the selfish gene as its unit of selection.

Yet as Bob Coats observed: "the process of internationalization has by no means obliterated national differences" (Coats 1996; p. 4). Furthermore, a microeconomic approach struggled to explain many macroeconomic phenomena. This came to a head in the 1960s in what became known as the Cambridge controversies in the theory of capital (identifying the two protagonists, economists from Cambridge University in the UK arguing against the individual as the unit of construction, with Cambridge Massachusetts economists arguing for the microeconomic foundation (Harcourt, 1969). This was reminiscent of the group selection versus gene selection debate occurring simultaneously in evolutionary biology. Further research (e.g. Sonnenschein 1972; Mantel 1976; Rizvi 1994) led Wade Hands to conclude "the standard micro model has almost no implications for macrobehavior" (Hands, 1995; p. 617). From all of this, it became apparent that there was a necessity to re-examine neoclassical economics, and to be more open to other explanations. Pluralism then, had a focus, and has become established as an important methodology.

5.18 Buen vivir

Buen vivir (Spanish for "good life") or *vivir bien* means living as part of the natural world, both embracing indigenous knowledge and criticizing western developmental philosophy. The rights of nature point towards a biocentric rather than an anthropocentric framework. *Buen vivir* has been defined as the "organized, sustainable, and dynamic ensemble of economic, political, socio-cultural, and environmental systems" (Walsh, 2010; p. 15) in such a way as to maintain human living within the biosphere.

Buen vivir is currently a government-driven school of environmental economics, although it represents a grand unifying theory, enveloping social environmental and economic issues. Prevalent in the South American Andes region, the movement is typified in the new constitutions of Ecuador and Bolivia, introduced in 2008 and 2009 respectively, which emphasize the rights of nature and the subordination of economic objectives to ecological criteria, human dignity and social justice (Escobar, 2012).

Buen vivir can be viewed as more of an umbrella term than a fixed set of beliefs, given the diversity of thoughts within its family of philosophies. One objective is to replace western development theory with a completely different approach. Value-based ethical perspectives dominate, where value can be denoted in a number of currencies, including spiritual, historical, environmental, cultural and aesthetic. Nature becomes a subject rather than an object, and has its own set of values, as opposed to being valued as natural capital. Citizenship includes actors other than humans. Generally, *buen vivir* thinking moves towards decolonization, making it relevant to much of the "**developing**" world, which was subject to colonization by the "**developed**" world for centuries. Another trait is a move away from instrumental and manipulative rationality and linear unidirectional history.

The *buen vivir* movement arose from a socialist, humanist emphasis, where human quality of life was seen not as a product of capitalism, but rather as an outcome of a balanced equation, marrying our own happiness with that of the environment. Undoubtedly framed to offer an alternative to Western colonialist materialism, *buen vivir* also drew on indigenous knowledge, setting out a post-development approach to economics. In Ecuador, the movement uses the indigenous *kichwa* words, *sumak kawsay*, while in Bolivia the *aymara* term *suma qamaña* is used. Other indigenous peoples have had the principles of *buen vivir* enshrined within their beliefs for centuries, including *shiir waras* of the Shuar people of Ecuador, and the idea of harmonious living, *küome mongen*, of the Mapuches of Chile (Gudynas, 2011).

Buen vivir views our relationship with our natural environment as key, where social change can only occur when our relationship with our environmental context is correct, reflecting elements of communalism. The Ecuadorian Constitution emphasizes this biocentric view, highlighting the rights of nature, both in terms of its existence, maintenance, regeneration, reparation and restoration.

However, a significant difference with communalism exists. *Buen vivir* places the emphasis for change on the individual, whose responsibility it is to life positively. Four key criteria underpin the ability of the individual to realize his personal development: liberty, autonomy, co-existence, and social inclusion. These four criteria represent the importance of individual sovereignty (liberty and autonomy) combined with the need for social integration (co-existence and social inclusion). This latter effect has been termed **functional interculturality** (Walsh, 2010). Development itself is redefined as achieving *buen vivir*. The movement is fundamentally pluralist, setting out a **pluriverse**, wherein different ecological contexts will demand different societal function.

5.19 Comparative economics

Comparative economics in its original form refers to the comparison between socialist and capitalist economic systems. With the fall of the Berlin Wall, socialist economics was placed in the grave (although still thriving in China), and comparative economics fizzled out. However, a new form has risen from the ground, and in its present state involves the comparison of different capitalist models (a form of economic pluralism).

Particular axes of comparison focus on property rights, a central pillar of capitalism, and these axes are degrees of **disorder** (risk of losing property to another person) and degrees of **dictatorship** (risk of losing property to the state) (Djankov *et al.*, 2003). The belief is that neither extreme disorder nor extreme dictatorship is healthy for a capitalist economy, and some intermediate point will deliver the best economic returns. However, this approach runs into problems in terms of China, with its strong state control but extremely successful economy.

Confusingly, another version of comparative economics also exists, combining the description and underlying explanation of human and nonhuman variations with that of the relationship between life and its living and nonliving environment (Vermeij, 2009). This form of comparative economics sets out to explore similarities and differences between human economics and the economics present in nature. This is viewed as important in order to understand how much of natural science is applicable to economics.

While some take the view that each organism represents a unique narrative that cannot be compared to other narratives (e.g. Popper, 1964; Monod, 1971; Gould, 2002), this viewpoint is very much based on form, rather than function. Functionally, the biosphere is united thermodynamically, and thus shares identical boundaries and drivers. Thus functionally there is a unity that pervades all life forms. Hence, it very much depends what view of economics you take, a structural or a functional one. Since natural economies relate to the transformation of matter and energy, then we are dealing primarily with a functional situation.

One problem with this version of comparative economics arises from the fact that humans have a natural economy, in terms of their own biological metabolism. Thus the economy involving capital is a second human economy, and operates at a population level. The energetic economy operates at an individual level, and partly overlaps with the capital economy, because work entails biological energy use at the individual level. Thus the capital economy is dependent on the human individual economy in terms of human labour. Obviously some sectors, such as construction, require more human labour (in terms of biological energy) than other sectors, such as information technology.

Thus we run into a problem in terms of trying to compare economies that are actually inextricably linked. Furthermore, the true accounting of the capital economy involves somehow incorporating natural capital, further complicating things. If we view the capital economy as a behavioural subset of the human experience, which itself is grounded in the physiological economy of nature, then we cannot really compare the capital economy to this physiological economy, since the latter economy is bounded, through the laws of thermodynamics, to all other natural economies, while the capital economy is bounded, through human labour, to those same natural economies.

5.20 Emphases of different schools

Figure 5.2 places the major schools of sustainability within a triangle whose apices represent economics, society and the environment. A point on any one of the three edges represents a school that is focused on the two apexes at either end of that edge, whereas a point within the body of the triangle has some emphasis on all three topics. The closer a point lies to a particular apex, the more dominant is that apex in that particular school.

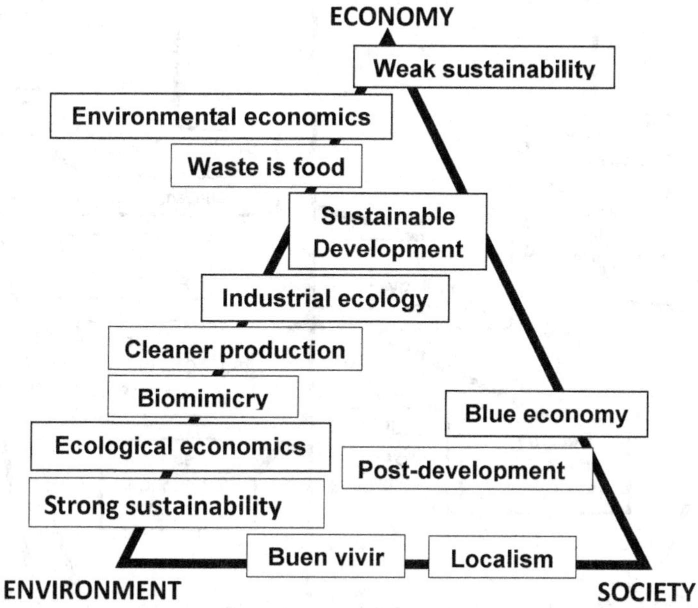

FIGURE 5.2 The triangle of sustainability. The emphasis of major schools of sustainability with each of the three pillars of sustainability.

Ecological economics is more environment-weighted, unsurprisingly, as its advocates have often come from mainly biology backgrounds, whereas **environmental economics**, which draws mainly from economists, is placed further towards the economy locus. **Weak sustainability**, with its emphasis on technology replacing ecosystem services, is dominated by economics, whereas **strong sustainability** states that ecosystem services must be protected at all costs, and is nearest the environment locus.

A group of schools align along the economics–environment axis, including industrial ecology, biomimicry, cleaner production and waste is food.

Along the society–environment axis lie *buen vivir* and localism, representing truly biocentric approaches, with localism lying nearest the Society locus. Post-development lies much closer to the environment–society axis than does sustainable development. Finally the blue economy is much further towards the economy–society axis, given its greater emphasis on human needs. Free market environmentalism lies near the economics apex, with socio-ecological economics positioned at the centre of the triangle.

The triangle demonstrates the range of different drives across the major schools of sustainability. What is interesting is that most of the schools are

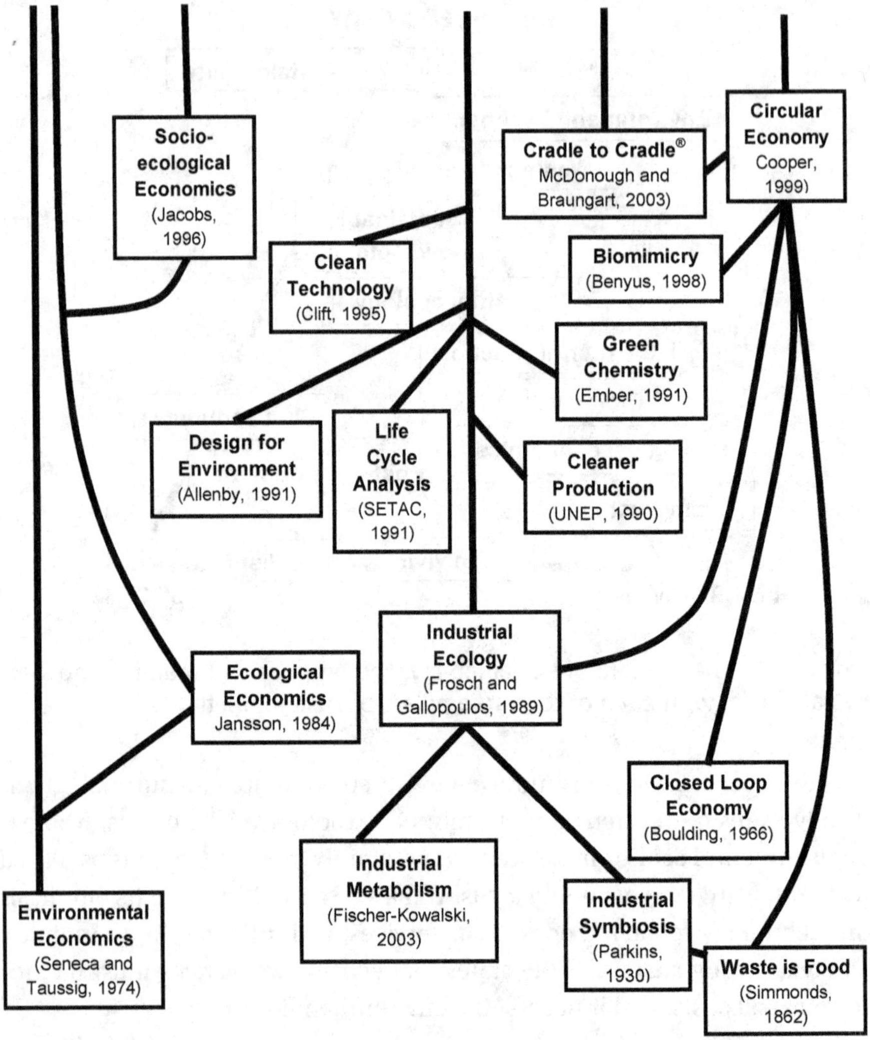

FIGURE 5.3 The shrubbery of sustainable thinking: a chronological map of the interrelatedness of sustainability concepts, tracing the emergence of current models. References denote early records of each concept.

associated with edges, rather than occupying central positions at the centre of the triangle. In other words, most schools ignore at least one of the three major aspects of sustainability. This can be understood when we consider that these three areas (economics, ecology and social sciences) represent very different academic subjects, usually in different faculties within a university.

New schools tend to emerge in two ways, either as children of previous fields or as divorces. The former pattern generally results in clusters of similar sets of ideals, whereas the latter will result in distinctively different ideals. Furthermore, as in many academic disciplines, new schools of thought tend to separate themselves from existent views, both on academic grounds and because of the need to stake out new territories for funding. Figure 5.3 explores the relatedness of the schools of sustainability described in this chapter, providing a phylogeny and a temporal context of their development.

5.21 Political emphases

Given that there are a great range of government styles and political movements currently on our planet, the type of political philosophy underpinning any given government will have huge implications into how sustainable economics can be implemented. Government support for a given school of sustainability will only occur if that school shares some common ground with the political philosophy of the particular political party in office. Figure 5.4 examines the relationship between some of the major political philosophies and two particular aspects: the importance of globalization and the importance of government intervention.

Strong centralized government control, such as state-centred socialism, allows for powerful, enforceable legislation, producing high levels of uptake. This has many benefits in terms of implementing centrally decided policy, and enabling change across the many departments of government. China represents this approach, and is certainly the most active and significant player in development of sustainable policy. It's most significant challenge lies in remaining globally competitive.

A milder form of centralization, which includes some state-controlled input, but also responds to the global markets, is a common model, allowing the invisible hand to operate, with help. The extent of the help depends on the form of political philosophy adopted. Social democracy (welfare state liberalism) has greater emphasis on government control, whereas neoliberalism will have a greater emphasis on globalization, with much less government intervention (Hawken *et al.*, 1999). Post-neoliberalism signals a return to closer government control. This model has dominated the Western world for much of the last century.

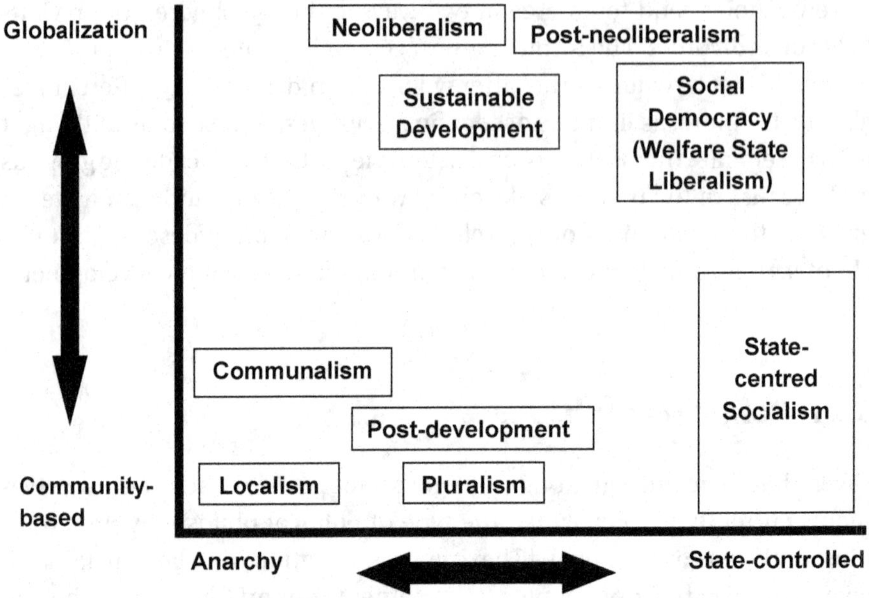

FIGURE 5.4. The relationship between globalization, state control, political philosophy and sustainability approach.

On the opposite end of the scale lies complete decentralization. This expresses itself as an anarchic, community-based approach, relying on the local community to take responsibility for its own interactions with the environment and to build its own economy. Movements such as localism, communalism, post-development and the *buen vivir* approach of Ecuador and Bolivia represent this much more socio-environmental approach (Escobar, 2012). Interestingly, the release from centralized government also appeals to neoliberalism, as can be seen in the Big Society and Tea Party movements of Britain and the USA respectively. Here, the drive is the sovereignty of the individual, the power of community and the relevance of local policies to local conditions.

Finally, an extreme version of laissez-faire exists, where market forces drive everything and where globalization is the major objective. Guided by the invisible hand, with no government intervention at all, this model relies on conversation between the three pillars of sustainability, responding appropriately. It requires non-intervention. Extreme forms of neoliberalism, represented by **free market environmentalism**, are examples of this. Many political groups with global leanings, such as the **Globalist Social Democracy** (Martell, 2007) would embrace this approach. Sustainable development, in its purest form, also aligns with the globalist approach of this school, although it would emphasize a global governance to steer "**under-developed**" nations towards the set of ideals. Post-development moves away from this position, seeking the restoration of individual sovereignty and the recognition of diversity (Escobar, 2000).

5.22 Journals

Many of these schools of sustainable economics have their own journals, such as the *Journal of Industrial Ecology, Progress in Industrial Ecology, Journal of Environmental Economics, The Journal of Environmental Economics and Management, Review of Environmental Economics and Policy, Ecological Economics, The International Journal of Ecological Economics and Statistics, Journal of Cleaner Production, The International Journal of Life Cycle Analysis, Clean Technologies and Environmental Policies, Green Chemistry, Journal of Sustainable Development, Journal of the Society for International Development, Journal of Economics and Sustainable Development, Journal of Development Studies, Journal of Comparative Economics, Journal of Pluralism and Economics Education, Journal of Post-autistic Economics* and *Bioinspiration & Biomimetics.*

A number of these schools have also formed their own societies including The International Society for Industrial Ecology and the International Society for Ecological Economics, the Association of Environmental and Resource Economics and the Green Economics Institute for Green Economics (representing Ecological Economics). It will doubtless not be long until we see a dedicated journal and institute for the most recent school, discussed in the next chapter, circular economics (CE).

5.23 Debate discussion and further thought

1. "Technology exists now to produce in virtually inexhaustible quantities just about all the products made by nature ... We have in our hands now ... the technology to feed, clothe, and supply energy to an ever-growing population for the next seven billion years" (Simon, 1995; p. 5). Discuss.

2. "For all its apparent mathematical sophistication, the core model of theoretical economics, that of competitive general equilibrium, is premised on an entirely faulty view of the modern world" (Paul Ormerod, 1994). Discuss.

3. Compare and contrast how your company would operate using any two of the schools of sustainability discussed in this section. What would be the main challenges and how could these be resolved in each case?

4. Some researchers believe that the human race were originally skilled in sustainable living. Examine this idea, and comment on the challenges of applying those basic principles to our current time.

5. You are a member of the management team of a business. The team consists of three people. One believes in weak sustainability, while the other is a strong sustainability advocate. Design a presentation to deliver to these members that attempts to bring them together in a strategy for sustainable business practice.

6. Explore the impact of politics on sustainable economic strategy. What are the strengths and weaknesses of different political philosophies in terms of delivering sustainability across the three sectors (economics, society and environment).

7. Identify the main stakeholders of each school of sustainability (students, business, government, academia, etc.) and explore how these different stakeholders impact on how the school functions.

8. Possible mini-project. Can you identify which school of sustainability would most resemble your own company, or a company of your choice? Now undertake a planning policy to transition your company to a different school of sustainability of your choice. Assess all of the changes needed across the entire structure.

9. "We have in our discipline been led up the wrong path by the invisible hand of the demon, and because it takes both time and money to make an engine, we are producing on a large scale—aeroplanes which have no engine" (Morishima 1984; p. 51). Discuss.

References

Alison, G. (2004). The influence of species diversity and stress intensity on community resistance and resilience. Ecological Monographs 74: 117-34.

Allenby, B.R. (1998). *Industrial Ecology: Policy Framework and Implementation.* Prentice Hall, Upper Saddle River, NJ.

Allenby, B.R. (1991). Design for Environment: a tool whose time has come. SSA Journal, September 1991. pp. 5-10.

Anastas, P.T. and Kirchhoff, M.M. (2002). Origins, current status, and future challenges of green chemistry. Accounts of Chemical Research 35(9): 686-94.

Anderson, T.L. and Leal, D.R. (2001). *Free Market Environmentalism* (revisited edition). Palgrave, New York.

Ang, F. and Passel, S.V. (2012). Beyond the environmentalist's paradox and the debate on weak versus strong sustainability. BioScience 62(3): 251-9.

Auty, R.M. (1993). *Sustaining Development in Mineral Economies: The Resource Curse Thesis.* London: Routledge.

Ayres R.U. (1989). Industrial metabolism. In: Ausubel, J. and Sladovich, H.E. (eds.), *Technology and the Environment.* The National Academies Press, Washington DC, pp. 23-49.

Ayres, R.U., van den Bergh, J.C. and Gowdy, J.M. (1998). Viewpoint: weak versus strong sustainability (No. 98-103/3). Tinbergen Institute.

Ayres, R.U., van den Berrgh, J.C. and Gowdy, J.M. (2001). Strong versus weak sustainability: economics, natural sciences, and consilience. Environmental Ethics 23 (2): 155-68.

Babbage, B. (1835). *On the Economy of Machinery and Manufactures.* Charles Knight, London.

Ballesteros, A., Nakhooda, S., Werksman, J. and Hurlburt, K. (2010). Power, responsibility, and accountability: rethinking the legitimacy of institutions for climate finance. Climate Law 1(2): 261-312.

Barbier, E.B., Burgess, J.C. and Folke, C. (1994). *Paradise Lost? The Ecological Economics of Biodiversity.* Earthscan, London.

Bartelmus, P. (2001). Accounting for sustainability: greening the national accounts. In: Tolba, M.K. (ed.), *Our Fragile World, Forerunner to the Encyclopaedia of Life Support System.* Vol. II. Kluwer Academic Publishers, Dordrecht, Netherlands. pp. 1721-35.

Bateman, B.W. (1998). Clearing the Ground: The Demise of the Social Gospel Movement and the Rise of Neoclassicism in American Economics. In: Morgan, M.S. and Rutherford, M. (eds.), *From Interwar Pluralism to Postwar Neoclassicism.* Annual Supplement to Volume 30, History of Political Economy. Duke University Press, Durham. pp. 29-52.

Baxter, S. (2005). Deep Design and the Engineers Conscience: A Global Primer for Design Education. In: Rodgers, P., Brodhurst, L. and Hepburn, D. (eds.), *Crossing Design Boundaries: Proceedings of the 3rd Engineering and Product Design Education International Conference, 15–16 September 2005, Edinburgh, UK.* Taylor & Francis, London. pp. 283-7.

Baxter, S. (2006). The way to natural design: learning to see and confront the bigger design questions. In: *Enhancing Curricula.* The 3rd International CLTAD Conference, Lisbon, Portugal. pp. 405-15.

Benyus, J.M. (1997). *Biomimicry: Innovations Inspired by Nature.* William Morrow, New York.

Benyus, J.M. (2002). *Biomimicry: Innovation Inspired by Nature.* Harper Collins Publishers Inc., New York.

Berger, J. (1987). Guidelines for landscape synthesis: some directions—old and new. Landscape and Urban Planning 14: 295-311.

Björklund, A.E. (2002). Survey of approaches to improve reliability in LCA. The International Journal of Life Cycle Assessment 7(2): 64-72.

Block, W.E. (1990). Environmental problems, private property rights solutions. In: Block, W.E. (ed.): *Economics and the Environment: A Reconciliation.* The Fraser Institute, Vancouver, B.C. pp. 281-318.

Bogart, E.L. (1936). *Economic History of the American People* (2nd ed.). Longmans, Green and Co., New York.

Boks, C. (2000). Assessment of future end-of-life scenarios for consumer electronic products. Design for sustainability. Delft University of Technology, Delft, NL.

Boons, F., Spekkirk, W. and Mouzakitis, Y. (2011). The dynamics of industrial symbiosis: a proposal for a conceptual framework based upon a comprehensive literature review. Journal of Cleaner Production 19: 9-10.

Boothroyd, G., Dewhurst, P. and Knight, W. (1994). *Product Design for Manufacture and Assembly.* M. Dekker, New York.

Bousquet, A. and Favard, P. (2005). Does S. Kuznets's belief question the Environmental Kuznets Curves? Canadian Journal of Economics 38(2): 604-14.

Bréchet, T. and Meunier, G. (2012). *Are clean technology and environmental quality conflicting policy goals?* (No. Ec-01/12). European University at St Petersburg, Department of Economics.

Brekke, K.A. (1997). *Economic Growth and the Environment: On the Measurement of Income and Welfare.* Edward Elgar, Cheltenham.

Brezet, H., Stevels, A.L.N. and Rombouts, J. (1999). LCA for Ecodesign: the Dutch experience. Ecodesign '99: First International Symposium on Environmentally Conscious Design and Inverse Manufacturing, Published by IEEE Computer Society Piscataway NJ USA, Tokyo, Japan, pp. 36-40.

Brundtland (1987). *Our Common Future.* Oxford University Press, Oxford.

Burton, L.J., Cheng, N., Vega, C., Andrés, J. and Bush, J.W. (2013). Biomimicry and the culinary arts. Bioinspiration and Biomimetics 8(4): 1-6.

Bürer, M.J. and Wüstenhagen, R. (2009). Which renewable energy policy is a venture capitalist's best friend? Empirical evidence from a survey of international cleantech investors. Energy Policy 37: 4997-5006.

Cameron, J.I. (1997). Applying socio-ecological economics: a case study of contingent valuation and integrated catchment management. Ecological Economics 23(2): 155-65.

Chertow, M.R. (2007). "Uncovering" industrial symbiosis. Journal of Industrial Ecology 11: 11-30.

Chevalier, R. (1993). *Science and Technology in Rome.* Presses Universitaires de France, Paris.

Ciriacy-Wantrup, S.V. and Schultz, A.M. (1957). Problems involving conservation in range economics research. Journal of Range Management 10(1): 12-16.

Clark, W.C. (1989). Managing planet Earth. Scientific American 261: 47-54.

Clemen, R.A. (1927). *By-Products in the Packing Industry.* University of Chicago Press, Chicago.

Coats, A.W. (1996). *The Post-1945 Internationalization of Economics, Annual Supplement to Volume 28, History of Political Economy.* Durham: Duke University Press.

Costa, I. and Ferrão, P. (2010). A case study of industrial symbiosis development using a middle-out approach. Journal of Cleaner Production 18: 984-92.

Coulton, G.G. (1942). *Studies in Medieval Thought. Discussion Books No. 65.* Thomas Nelson and Sons Ltd., London.

Cropper, M.L. and Oates, W.E. (1992). Environmental economics: a survey. Journal of Economic Literature 30: 675-740.

Curran, M.A., Mann, M. and Norris, G. (2005). The international workshop on electricity data for life cycle inventories. Journal of Cleaner Production 13 (8): 853-62.

Daly, H.E. and Cobb Jr., J.B. (1989). *For the Common Good: Redirecting the Economy Toward Community—the Environment and a sustainable Future.* Boston, MA., Beacon Press.

Daly, H.E. and Farley, J. (2004). *Ecological Economics: Principles and Applications.* Island Press, Washington DC.

Dechesne, L. (1945). *The Location of Various Manufacturing Activities.* Les Éditions Comptables, Commerciales et Financières, Brussels.

Desrochers, P. (2002a). Cities and industrial symbiosis: Some historical perspectives and policy implications. Journal of Industrial Ecology 5: 29-44.

Desrochers, P. (2002b). Industrial ecology and the rediscovery of inter-firm recycling linkages: Historical evidence and policy implications. Industrial and Corporate Change 11: 1031-57.

Desrochers, P. (2008). Did the invisible hand need a regulatory glove to develop a green thumb? Some historical perspective on market incentives, win–win innovations and the Porter Hypothesis. Environmental Resource Economics 41: 519-39.

Desrochers, P. and Leppälä, S. (2010). Industrial symbiosis: old wine in recycled bottles? Some perspective from the history of economic and geographical thought. International Regional Science Review 33: 338-61.

Dijkema, G.P.J. and Basson, L. (2009). Complexity and industrial ecology: Foundations for a transformation from analysis to action. Journal of Industrial Ecology 13: 157-64.

Djankov, S., Glaeser, E., La Porta, R., Lopez-de-Silanes, F. and Shleifer, A. (2003). The new comparative economics. Journal of Comparative Economics 31(4): 595-619.

Domenech, T. and Davies, M. (2011). Structure and morphology of industrial symbiosis networks: The case of Kalundborg. Procedia, Social and Behavioral Sciences 10: 79-89.

Dorfman, R. (1993). Some concepts from welfare economics. In: Dorfman, R., Dorfman, N.S. (eds.), *Economics of the Environment: Selected Readings.* W.W. Norton, New York. pp. 79-96.

Douai, A. (2009). Value theory in ecological economics: The contribution of a political economy of wealth. Environmental Values 18: 257-84.

Ehrenfeld, J.R. (2000). Industrial ecology: paradigm shift or normal science. American Behavioral Scientist 44: 229-44.

Ehrenfeld, J.R. and Gertler, N. (1997). Industrial ecology in practice: the evolution of interdependence at Kalundborg. Journal of Industrial Ecology 1: 67-79.

Ela, J. (1998). Western development has failed: looking to a new Africa. Le Monde Diplomatique, October.

Ember, L. (1991). Chemical Engineering News 1991, 8 July, pp. 7-16.

EPA (1993). *Life-Cycle Assessment: Inventory Guidelines and Principles.* US Environmental Protection Agency, Office of Research and Development, Washington, DC.

Escobar, A. (1992a). Reflections on "development": grassroots approaches and alternative politics in the Third World. Futures 24: 411-36.

Escobar, A. (1992b). *Imagining a Post-Development Era? Critical Thought, Development and Social Movements.* Social Text, No. 31/32, Third World and Post-Colonial Issues (1992), pp. 20-56 Published by: Duke University Press Stable URL: http://www.jstor.org/stable/466217

Escobar A. (1996). Construction nature. Elements for a post-structuralist political ecology. Futures 28(4): 325-43.

Escobar, A. (2012). *Encountering Development: the Making and Unmaking of the Third World.* Princeton University Press, Princeton.

Esterman, M. and Ishii, K. (1999). Challenges in robust concurrent product development across the supply chain. ASME Design for Manufacture, Las Vegas, NV. pp. 1-10.

Estill, L. (2008). *Small is Possible: Life in a Local Economy.* New Society Publishers, Gabriola Island, BC, Canada.

Fang, Y., Cote, R.P. and Qin, R. (2007). Industrial sustainability in China: practice and prospects for eco-industrial development. Journal of Environment Management 83: 315-28.

Farnsworth, K.D. and Niklas, K.J. (1995). Theories of optimization, form and function in branching architecture in plants. Functional Ecology 9: 355-63.

Fischer-Kowalski, M. (2003). On the history of industrial metabolism. In: Bourg, D. and Erkman, S. (eds.), *Perspectives on Industrial Ecology.* Greenleaf Publishing, Sheffield, pp. 35-45.

Folmer, H. and Johansson-Stenman, O. (2011). Does environmental economics produce aeroplanes without engines? On the need for an environmental social science. Environmental and Resource Economics 48: 337-61.

Foster, J.B. (2009). *The Ecological Revolution: Making Peace with the Planet.* Monthly Review Press, New York, NY.

Fragkou, D. and Stevenson, E.V. (2012). Study of Beehive and its potential" biomimicry" application on Capsule hotels in Tokyo, Japan. http://orca.cf.ac.uk/37671/1/MC12-32_Fragkou.pdf.

Frankel, J.A. (2012). The Natural Resource Curse: A Survey of Diagnoses and Some Prescriptions. HKS Faculty Research Working Paper Series RWP12-014, John F. Kennedy School of Government, Harvard University.

Frosch, R.A. (1992). Industrial ecology: a philosophical introduction. Proceedings of the National Academy of Sciences, USA 89: 800-803.

Frosch, R.A. and Gallopoulos, N.E. (1989). Strategies for manufacturing. Scientific American 266: 144-52.

Gallopin, G.C. (2001). The Latin American world model (a.k.a. the Bariloche model): three decades ago. Futures 33: 77-89.

Geng, Y., Zhu, Q., Doberstein, B. and Fujita, T. (2009). Implementing China's circular economy concept at the regional level: A review of progress in Dalian, China. Waste Management 29: 996-1002.

Gerber, J.-F., Veuthey, S. and Martínez-Alier, J. (2009). Linking political ecology with ecological economics in tree plantation conflicts in Cameroon and Ecuador. Ecological Economics 68: 2885-9.

Gerschenkron, A. (1962). *Economic Backwardness in Historical Perspective, a Book of Essays.* Harvard University Press, Cambridge, Mass.

Gershenson, J. and Ishii, K. (1991). Life-cycle serviceability design. ASME Design Theory and Methodology Conference, Miami, FL. pp. 127-34.

Gertler, N. (1995). *Industrial Ecosystems: Developing Sustainable Industrial Structures.* M.S. Thesis (Technology and Policy), Massachusetts Institute of Technology.

Gibbs, D.C. (2008). Industrial symbiosis and eco-industrial development: an introduction. Geography Compass 2: 1138-54.

Glimcher, P.W. and Rustichini, A. (2004). Neuroeconomics: the consilience of brain and decision. Science 306 (5695): 447-52.

Gold, R., Nadel, S., Laitner, J.A. and de Laski, A. (2011). Appliance and equipment efficiency standards: a moneymaker and job creator. American Council for an Energy-Efficient Economy.

Goldsmith, E. (1988). *The Great U-Turn: De-Industrializing Society.* Green Books, London.

Goodman, S. (2009). "Green chemistry" movement sprouts in colleges, companies. The New York Times, 25 March 2009.

Gore, A. (1992). *Earth in Balance: Ecology and the Human Spirit.* Houghton Mifflin, New York.

Gould, S.J. (2002). *The Structure of Evolutionary Theory.* Belknap Press of Harvard University, Cambridge, MA.

Gowdy, J. (2004). The revolution in welfare economics and its implications for environmental valuation and policy. Land Econonomics 80: 239-57.

Gowdy, J. and Erickson, J. (2005). Ecological economics at a crossroads. Ecological Economics 53(2): 17-20.

Gudykunst, W.B. and Ting-Toomey, S. (1988). *Culture and interpersonal communication.* Sage, Beverly Hills, CA.

Gudynas, E. (2011). Buen vivir: today's tomorrow. Development 54(4): 441-7.

Guezuraga, B., Zauner, R. and Pölz, W. (2012). Life cycle assessment of two different 2 MW class wind turbines. Renewable Energy 37(1): 37-44.

Guinée, J.B., Gorrée, M., Heijungs, R., Huppes, G., Kleijn, R., de Koning, A., van Oers, L., Wegener Sleeswijk, A., Suh, S., Udo de Haes, H.A., de Bruijn, J.A., van Duin, R., Huijbregts, M.A.J. (2002). *Handbook on Life Cycle Assessment: Operational Guide to the ISO Standards. Series: Eco-efficiency in Industry and Science.* Kluwer Academic Publishers, Dordrecht.

Hall, C., Cutler, C. and Kaufmann, R. (1992). *Energy and Resource Quality.* University Press of Colorado; Boulder, CO, USA.

Hands, D.W. (1995). Social epistemology meets the invisible hand: Kitcher on the advancement of science. Dialogue 34: 605-21.

Harcourt, G.C. (1969). Some Cambridge controversies in the theory of capital. Journal of Economic Literature 7(2): 369-405.

Hardin, G. (1968). The tragedy of the Commons. Science 162: 1243-8.

Hardy, D.J. and Patterson, M.G. (2012). Cross-cultural environmental research in New Zealand: Insights for ecological economics research practice. Ecological Economics 73: 75-85.

Hargadon, A.B. and Kenney, M. (2012). Misguided policy? Following venture capital into clean technology. California Management Review 54(2): 118-39.

Hart, G. (2001). Development critiques in the 1990s: Culs de sac and promising paths. Progress in Human Geography 25(4): 649-58.

Hartwick, J.M. (1977). Intergenerational equity and the investing of rents of exhaustible resources. American Economic Review 67(5): 972-4.

Hawken, P., Lovins, A. and Lovins, H. (1999). *Natural Capitalism: Creating the Next Industrial Revolution.* Rocky Mountain Institute, Snowmass, Colorado.

Hayek, F.A. (1980 [1948]). *Individualism and Economic Order.* Chicago: University of Chicago Press, Chicago.

Hertwich, E.G. (2005). Life cycle approaches to sustainable consumption: a critical review. Environmental Science and Technology 39(13): 4673-84.

Hilson, G. (2000). Barriers to implementing cleaner technologies and cleaner production (CP) practices in the mining industry: a case study of the Americas. Minerals Engineering 13(7): 699-717.

Hopkins, M.S. (2009). What executives don't get about sustainability (and further notes on the profit motive). MIT Sloan Management Review 51(1): 34-40.

Horwitch, M. and Mulloth, B. (2010). The interlinking of entrepreneurs, grassroots movements, public policy and hubs of innovation: the rise of Cleantech in New York City. The Journal of High Technology Management Research 21: 23-30.

Huffman, J.L. (1994). The inevitability of private rights in public lands. University of Colorado Law Review 65: 241-77.

Ishii, K. and Lee, B. (1996). Reverse fishbone diagram: a tool in aid of design for product retirement. ASME Design Technical Conference, Aug., 1996, Irvine, CA. ASME Paper 96-DETC/DFM-1272.

Ishii, K., Eubanks, C.F. and Di Marco, P. (1994). Design for product retirement and material lifecycle. Materials and Design 15: 225-33.

ISO (1997). *ISO 14040: Environmental Management—Life Cycle Assessment—Principles and Framework.* International Organization for Standardization: Geneva, 1997.

Jacobs, M. (1996). What is Socio-Ecological Economics? Ecological Economics Bulletin 1: 14-16.

Jacobsen, N.B. (2006). Industrial symbiosis in Kalundborg, Denmark. Journal of Industrial Ecology 10: 239-55.

Jevons, W.S. (1865). *The Coal Question: An Inquiry Concerning the Progress of the Nation and the Probable Exhaustion of our Coal Mines.* Macmillan, London.

Jones, J.C., Myerscough, M.R., Graham, S. and Oldroyd, B.P. (2004). Honey bee nest thermoregulation: diversity promotes stability. Science 305: 402-404.

Joshi, S. (2000). Product environmental life-cycle assessment using input–output techniques. J Ind Ecol 3: 95-120.

Kalathil, S. (2002). Community and communalism in the information age. Brown J. World Aff. 9: 347-53.

Kapp, K.W. (1970). Environmental disruptions and social costs: A challenge to economists. Kyklos 23: 833-47.

Kershaw, J.B.C. (1928). *The Recovery and Use of Industrial and Other Waste.* Ernest Benn Limited, London.

Kmenta, S., Fitch, P. and K. Ishii (1999). Advanced failure modes and effects analysis of complex processes. ASME Design for Manufacture, Las Vegas, NV.

Kohr, L. (1978). *The Breakdown of Nations.* Dutton, New York.

Kim, U.M. (1994). Significance of paternalism and communalism in the occupational welfare system of Korean firms: A national survey. Cross Cultural Research and Methodology Series-Sage 18: 251-66.

Koller, T. (1918) [1902]. *The Utilization of Waste Products: A Treatise on the Rational Utilization, Recovery, and Treatment of Waste Products of all Kinds* (3rd revised edition, translated from the 2nd revised German edition). D. Van Nostrand Company, New York.

Korhonen, J. (2003). On the ethics of corporate social responsibility—considering the paradigm of industrial metabolism. Journal of Business Ethics 48: 301-15.

Krysiak, F.C. (2006). Entropy, limits to growth, and the prospects for weak sustainability. Ecological Economics 58(1): 182-91.

Langdon, W., Renner, C. and Renner, G.T. (1936). *Geography: an Introduction to Human Ecology.* Appleton-Century Company, New York.

Lee, K.N. (1993). Greed, scale mismatch and learning. Ecological Applications 3: 560-4

Lester, R.K. (2009). America's Energy Innovation Problem. MIT-IPC-Energy Innovation Working Paper 09-007.

Liu, C., Ma, C., Zhang, K. (2012). Going beyond the sectoral boundary: a key stage in the development of a regional industrial ecosystem. Journal of Cleaner Production 22: 42-9.

Lovins, L.H. (2008). Rethinking production. *State of the World: Innovations for a sustainable economy,* 34-44. The Worldwatch Institute. W.W. Norton and Company, London.

Lovins, L.H. and Lovins, A.B. (2000). Harnessing Corporate Power to Heal the Planet. World and I 15(4): 152-61.

Lowe, E.A., Moran, S.R. and Holmes, D.B. (1996). *Fieldbook for the Development of Eco-Industrial Parks: Final Report.* Research Triangle Institute, Research Triangle Park, New York.

Lowitt, P. (2008). Devens redevelopment: the emergence of a successful eco-industrial park in the United States. Journal of Industrial Ecology 12: 497-500

Luttropp, C. and Lagerstedt, J. (2006). Ecodesign and The Ten Golden Rules: generic advice for merging environmental aspects into product development. Journal of Cleaner Production 14(15): 1396-408.

Ma, C. and Stern, D.I. (2006). Environmental and ecological economics: a citation analysis. Ecological Economics 58: 491-506.

MacDonald, M. (1994). The Outlook Tower: Patrick Geddes in context: glossing Lewis Mumford in the light of John Hewitt. The Irish Review (1986-) (16): 53-73.

Magnaghi, A. (2005). *The Urban Village: A Charter for Democracy and Sustainable Development in the City.* Zed Books, London.

Mantel, R.R. (1976). Homothetic preferences and community excess demand functions. Journal of Economic Theory 12 (2): 197-201.

Martell, L. (2007). The third wave in globalization theory. International Studies Review 9(2): 173-96.

Martin, M.V. (2002). Design for variety: developing standardized and modularized product platform architectures. Research into Engineering Design 13: 213-35.

Marx, K. (1909). *Capital: A Critique of Political Economy. Volume III: The Process of Capitalist Production as a Whole.* Ed. Federick Engels. Trans. from the 1st German edition by Ernest Untermann. Charles H. Kerr and Company Cooperative, Chicago.

Mason, M. (2011). The sustainability challenge. In: Brady, J., Ebbage, A. and Lunn, R. (eds.), *Environmental Management in Organizations.* Earthscan, London, UK. pp. 525-32.

Mathews, J.A. and Tan, H. (2011). Progress towards a circular economy in China: the drivers (and inhibitors) of eco-industrial initiative. Journal of Industrial Ecology 15: 435-57.

Mathews, F. (2011). Towards a deeper philosophy of biomimicry. Organization and Environment 24(4): 364-87.

Matthews, S. (2004). Post-development theory and the question of alternatives: a view from Africa. Third World Quarterly 25(2): 373-84.

Matsunaga, H. (2000). Regional characteristics and challenges of the eco-town projects. Kanmon Regional Studies 9: 1-13.

Mbiti, J.S. (1969). *African Religions and Philosophy.* Heineman, London.

McDonough, W. and Braungart, M. (2002). Design for the triple top line: new tools for sustainable commerce. Corporate Environmental Strategy 9(3): 251-8.

McDonough, W. and Braungart, M. (2003). Towards a sustaining architecture for the 21st century: the promise of cradle-to-cradle design. UNEP Industry and Environment April–September 2003. pp. 13-16.

McIntyre, L. and Rondeau, K. (2011). Individual consumer food localism: A review anchored in Canadian farmwomen's reflections. Journal of Rural Studies 27: 116-24.

Meadowcroft, J. (2001). Green political perspectives at the dawn of the twenty-first century. In: Freeden, M. (ed.), *Re-assessing political ideologies: the Durability of Dissent.* Routledge, London. pp. 175-92.

Mellaart, J. (1967). *Çatal Hüyük. A Neolithic Town in Anatolia.* McGraw-Hill Book Company, New York.

Mill, J.S. (1857). *Principles of Political Economy.* Parker, London.

Miller, B. (1998). Fat of the land: New York's waste. Social Research 65(1): 75-100.

Molenbroek, E., Cuijpers, M and Blok, K. (2012). Economic benefits of the EU Ecodesign Directive: Improving European Economies: 1-24.

Monod., J. (1971). *Chance and Necessity. An Essay on the Natural Philosophy of Modern Biology.* Knopf, New York.

Moriguchi, Y., Kondo, Y. and Shimizu, H. (1993). Analyzing the life cycle impact of cars: the case of CO_2. Industry and Environment 16: 42-5.

Morishima, M. (1984). The good and bad uses of mathematics. In: Wiles, P.J.D. and Routh, G. (eds.), *Economics in Disarray.* Basil Blackwell, Oxford. pp. 51-73.

Ng, Y.K. and Wills, I. (2002). *Welfare economics and sustainable development. Knowledge of Sustainable Development: an Insight into the Encyclopedia of Life Support Systems.* UNESCO Publishing, Paris.

Nijkamp, P. (1977). *Theory and Application of Environmental Economics. Studies in Regional Science and Urban Economics Volume 1.* Andersson, A. and Isard, W. (eds.). North-Holland Publishing Company, Elsevier North-Holland, Inc., New York, N.Y.

Nustad, K.G. (2001). Development: the devil we know? Third World Quarterly 22(4): 479-89.

N'Dione, E.S., De Leener, P., Perier, J., Ndiaye, M. and Jacolin, P. (1997). Reinventing the present: the Chodak experience in Senegal. In: Rahnema, M. and Bawtree, V. (eds.), *The Post-Development Reader.* David Philip, Cape Town. pp. 364-76.

Oltra, V. and Jean, M.S. (2005). The dynamics of environmental innovations: three stylised trajectories of clean technology. Economics of Innovation and New Technology 14(3): 189-212.

Ormerod, P. (1994). *The Death of Economics*. Faber and Faber, London.

Ostrolenk, B. (1941). *Economic Geography*. Richard D. Irwin, Inc., Chicago.

Ostrom, E. (1999). Revisiting the Commons. Local lessons, global challenges. Science 284: 278-82.

Ott, K. (2003). The case for strong sustainability. In: Ott, K. and Thapa, P.P. (eds.), *Greifswald's Environmental Ethics: from the Work of the Michael Otto Professorship at Ernst Moritz Arndt University 1997–2002.* Steinbecker Verlag Ulrich Rose, Greifswald. pp. 59-64.

Paavola, J. and Adger, N.W. (2005). Institutional ecological economics. Ecological Economics 53: 353-68.

Park, H.-S., Rene, E.R., Choi, S.M. and Chiu, A.S.F. (2008). Strategies for sustainable development of industrial park in Ulsan, South Korea: from spontaneous evolution to systematic expansion of industrial symbiosis. Journal of Environmental Management 87: 1-13.

Pauli, G. (2009). *The Blue Economy: 10 Years, 100 Innovations. 100 Million Jobs.* Paradigm Publications, New Mexico, USA.

Paulson, H, Darling A. and Nukaga, F. (2008). Financial bridge from dirty to clean. Financial Times. 7 Feb. 2008.

Pearce, D.W. and Turner, R.K. (1990). *Economics of Natural Resources and the Environment.* Harvester Wheatsheaf, Hemel Hempstead

Pernick, R. and Wilder, C. (1997). *The Clean Tech Revolution: The Next Big Growth and Investment Opportunity.* Collins, London.

Playfair, L. (1852). On the chemical principles involved in the manufactures of the Exhibition as indicating the necessity of industrial instruction. In: *Lectures on the Results of the Great Exhibition of 1851.* Royal Society of Arts Great Britain, London. pp. 147-208.

Popper, K.R. (1964). *The Poverty of Historicism.* Harper and Row, New York, NY.

Porter M. and Van Der Linde C. (1995). Toward a new conception of the environment-competitiveness relationship. Journal of Economic Perspectives 9(4): 97-118.

Product-Life (2008). http://product-life.org/en/cradle-to-cradle. Last accessed 28/02/12

Raeder, L.C. (1998). Liberalism and the common good—a Hayekian perspective on Communitarianism. The Independent Review, II(4): 519-35.

Rahnema, M. and Bawtree, V. (1997). *The Post-development Reader.* Zed Books, London.

Raskin, P.D. (2008). World lines: A framework for exploring global pathways, Ecological Economics 65: 461-70.

Raudsepp-Hearne, C., Peterson, G.D., Tengö, M., Bennett, E.M., Holland, T., Benessaiah, K., Macdonald, G.K. and Pfeifer, L. (2010). Untangling the environmentalist's paradox: why is human well-being increasing as ecosystem services degrade? BioScience 60: 576-89.

Rizvi, S.A.T. (1994). *The Microfoundations Project in General Equilibrium Theory.* Cambridge Journal of Economics 18 (4): 357-77.

Rolston, H. (1994). *Conserving Natural Value.* Columbia University Press, New York.

Røpke, I. (2004). The early history of modern ecological economics. Ecological Economics 50: 293-314.

Røpke, I. (2005). Trends in the development of ecological economics from the late 1980s to the early 2000s. Ecological Economics 55: 262-90.

Rose, C.M., Stevels, A.L.N. and Ishii, K. (2000). A new approach to end-of-life design advisor (ELDA). 2000 IEEE International Symposium on Electronics and the Environment, IEEE Piscataway NJ USA, San Francisco, CA, USA. pp. 99-104.

Roy, R. (1994). The evolution of ecodesign. Technovation 14(6): 363-80.

Rubino, J.A. (2009). *Clean Money: Picking Winners in the Greentech Boom.* Wiley and Sons, Hoboken, NJ.

Rudgley, R. (1998). *Lost Civilizations of the Stone Age.* Century, London.

Rupasingha, A., Goetz, S.J., Debertin, D.L. and Pagoulatos, A. (2004). The environmental Kuznets curve for US counties: A spatial econometric analysis with extensions. Papers in Regional Science 83(2): 407-24.

Ryan, C. (1992). (Re)designing cleaner products: factors affecting the ecodesign of manufactured products and some implications for the UNEP cleaner production program, *Mimeo.* Centre for Design at RMIT, Royal Melbourne Institute of Technology, Melbourne, Australia (October 1992).

Sachs, W. (1992). *The Development Dictionary: A Guide to Knowledge as Power.* Zed Books, London.

Sánchez, R.R. (2013). The complex political economy of natural capitalism: the case of whole foods, Stonyfield Farms and Walmart. Online Journal of Communication and Media Technologies 3 (3), July 2013.

Schaltegger, S., Bennett, M., Burritt, R.L. and Jasch, C. (2009). *Environmental management accounting (EMA) as a support for cleaner production.* Springer Netherlands. (pp. 3-26).

Schindler, D.E., Hilborn, R., Chasco, B., Boatright, C.P., Quinn, T.P., Rogers, L.A. and Webster, M.S. (2010). Population diversity and the portfolio effect in an exploited species. Nature 465: 609-12.

Schmidheiny, S. (1992). *Changing Course.* The MIT Press, Cambridge, MA.

Schumacher, E.F (1973). *Small is Beautiful: a Study of Economics as if People Mattered.* Harper and Row, New York.

Seneca, J.J. and Taussig, M.K. (1974). *Environmental Economics.* Prentice and Hall Inc. Englewood Cliffs, NJ.

SETAC (1991). *A Technical Framework for Life-Cycle Assessments.* Society of Environmental Toxicology and Chemistry, Washington D.C.

Simmonds, P.L. (1862). *Waste Products and Undeveloped Substances.* R. Hardwicke, London.

Simmonds, P.L. (1875). *Waste Products and Undeveloped Substances: A Synopsis of Progress Made in their Economic Utilisation During the Last Quarter of a Century at Home and Abroad.* Hardwicke and Bogues, London.

Simon, J. (1995). The state of humanity: steadily improving. *Cato Policy Report,* Vol. 17: 5. Cato Institute, Washington, DC.

Skene, K.R. (2011a). Form, function and forests: sustainability revisited. Contemporary Review 293: 462-72.

Skene, K.R. (2011b). *Escape from Bubbleworld: Seven Curves to Save the Earth.* Ard Macha Press, Angus, UK.

Spash, C.L. (2009). *Social Ecological Economics.* CSIRO Working Paper Series, June 2009. CSIRO Sustainable Ecosystems, Canberra.

Stahel, W.R. and Reday-Mulvey, G. (1976). Jobs for Tomorrow: The Potential for Substituting Manpower for Energy; study no. 76/13, for DG Manpower, European Commission, Brussels.

Stahel, W.R. (2003). The functional society: the service economy. In: Bourg, D. and Erkman, S. (eds.), *Perspectives on Industrial Ecology.* Greenleaf Publishing, Sheffield. pp. 264-82

Stahel, W.R. (2006). *The Performance Economy.* Palgrave McMillan, London.

Suh, S., Lenzen, M., Treloar, G.J., Hondo, H., Horvath, A., Huppes, G., Jolliet, O., Klann, U., Krewitt, W., Moriguchi, Y., Munksgaard, J. and Norris, G. (2004). System boundary selection in life-cycle inventories using hybrid approaches. Environmental Science & Technology 38(3): 657-64.

Solow, R.M. (1974). Intergenerational equity and exhaustible resources. Review of Economic Studies Symposium: 29-46.

Sonnenschein, H. (1972). Market excess demand functions. Econometrica 40 (3): 549-63.

Stevels, A.L.N. (2001). Integration of ecodesign into business. In: Hundal, M.S. (ed.), *Mechanical Life Cycle Handbook: Good Environmental Design and Manufacturing.* CRC Press, Boca Raton, Florida. pp. 509-27.

Suzumura, K. (1999). Paretian welfare judgements and Bergsonian social choice. Economics Journal 109: 204-21.

Talbot, F.A. (1920). *Millions from Waste.* J.B. Lippincott Company, Philadelphia.

Tang, Y.Q. and Tang, Z.B. (2011). Exploration of industrial ecology growth base on Po Yang Lake ecological economic zone. Key Engineering Materials 458: 380-5.

Teague, W.D. (1940). *Design This Day: The Technique of Order in the Machine Age.* Harcourt, Brace & Co., New York.

Tietenberg, T. (2011). Reflections—in praise of consilience. Review of Environmental Economics and Policy 5(2): 314-29.

United Nations Development Programme (UNDP) (2001). *Human Development Report 2001.* Oxford University Press, Oxford.

UNOSD (2012). Future We Want: outcome document of United Nations Conference on Sustainable Development, Rio+20. www.unosd.org/index.php?menu=242.

van Beers, D., Bossilkov, A. and Lund, C. (2009). Development of large-scale reuses of inorganic byproducts in Australia: The case study of Kwinana, Western Australia. Conservation and Recycling 53: 365-78.

Van Berkel, C.W.M. (1994). Comparative evaluation of cleaner production working methods. Journal of Cleaner Production 2(3): 139-52.

van den Bergh, J.C.J.M. (2009). The GDP paradox. Journal of Economic Psychology 30: 117-35.

van Hemel, C. (1998). *Ecodesign Empirically Explored: Design for Environment in Dutch Small and Medium Sized Enterprises.* Technische Universiteit Delft, Delft, NL.

Vermeij, G.J. (2009). Comparative economics: evolution and the modern economy. Journal of Bioeconomics 11: 105-34.

Viederman, S. (1994). The economics of sustainability: challenges. Paper presented at the workshop: The Economics of Sustainability. Fundacao Joaquim Nabuco, Recife, Brazil.

Victor, P.A. (2010). Ecological economics and economic growth. Annals of the New York Academy of Sciences 1185: 237-45.

Virah-Sawmy, M., Gillson, G. and Willis, K.J. (2009). How does spatial heterogeneity influence resilience to climatic changes? Ecological dynamics in southeast Madagascar. Ecological Monographs 79: 557-74.

Von Weizsäcker, E., Lovins, A.B. and Lovins, L.H. (1998). *Factor Four: Doubling Wealth, Halving Resource Use.* Earthscan, London.

Wahl, D.C. and Baxter, S. (2008). The designer's role in facilitating sustainable solutions. Design Issues 24(2): 72-83.

Walker, D. (2007). *Real Localism.* The Smith Institute, London.

Walsh, C. (2010). Development as Buen Vivir: Institutional arrangements and (de) colonial entanglements. Development 53(1): 15-21.

White, R.M. (1994). Preface. In: Allenby, B.R. and Richards, D.J. (eds.), *The Greening of Industrial Ecosystems.* National Academy Press, Washington, DC. pp. v-vi.

Winter, G. (1988). *Business and the Environment; A Handbook of Industrial Ecology with 22 Checklists for Practical Use and a Concrete Example of the Integrated System of Environmentalist Business Management (the Winter Model).* McGraw-Hill, London.

Wilson, E.O. (1998). *Consilience.* Alfred Knopf, New York.

Xu, M., Jia, X.-P., Shi, L. and Zhang, T.-Z. (2008). Societal metabolism in Northeast China: case study of Liaoning Province. Resources, Conservation and Recycling 52: 1082-6.

Young, O.R. (2002). *The Institutional Dimensions of Environmental Change—Fit, Interplay and Scale.* The MIT Press, Cambridge, MA.

Zhang, H., Hara, K., Yabar, H., Yamaguchi, Y., Uwasu, M. and Morioka, T. (2009). Comparative analysis of socio-economic and environmental performances for Chinese EIPs: Case studies in Baotou, Suzhou, and Shanghai. Sustainability Science 4: 263-79.

Zhu, Q., Lowe, E.A., Wei, Y.-A. and Barnes, D. (2007). Industrial symbiosis in China: a case study of the Guitang Group. Journal of Industrial Ecology 11: 31-42.

Zhu, Q., Sarkis, J., Cordeiro, J.J. and Lai, K.-H. (2008). Firm-level correlates of emergent green supply chain management practices in the Chinese context. Omega 36: 577-91.

Ziai, A. (2004). The ambivalence of post-development: between reactionary populism and radical democracy. Third World Quarterly 25(6): 1045-60.

Zimmermann, E. (1933). *World Resources and Industries: A Functional Appraisal of the Availability of Agricultural and Industrial Resources*. Harper & Brothers, New York.

6
The circular economy

This chapter is dedicated to the most recent school of economic sustainability, the circular economy, and explores how this concept emerged and became the model of choice for the Chinese government and the EU. Tracing its origin from Germany and Japan, we examine how this rapidly growing school of thought applies to modern business, and the implications of its application, in terms of business strategy, finance and operations. We explore the differences between the Eastern model and the more embryonic Western model. Significant issues with the underlying biological foundations are also examined.

Learning aims and objectives

- To define the circular economy and compare it with a linear economy
- To understand the issues related to this definition
- To understand the historical development of the circular economy in China and South Korea
- To catalogue the legislation supporting the circular economy in Japan, China and Europe

Learning outcomes and experiences

- Having considered the issues related to its definition, attempt to develop an improved definition of the circular economy
- Compare and contrast the eastern and western approaches to this school of sustainability
- Discuss the main issues relating to delivering a sustainable future utilizing the circular economy
- Identify the strengths and weaknesses of the circular economy relative to other schools of sustainability
- Determine what novelty the circular economy represents relative to industrial ecology

6.1 Semantics and substance

The term **circular economy** has both a linguistic and a descriptive meaning. Linguistically it is an antonym of a **linear economy**. A linear economy is one defined as converting natural resources into waste, via production. Such production of waste leads to the deterioration of the environment in two ways: by the removal of natural capital from the environment (through mining/unsustainable harvesting) and by the reduction of the value of natural capital by pollution from waste. Pollution can also occur at the resource acquisition stage. This is a one-way system and an economy based on such a system was referred to as a **cowboy economy** by Boulding (1966).

The term **linear economy** was brought into popular use by those writing on the circular economy and related concepts. Thus, in many ways, the origin has been deliberately set, in framing the antonym to promote the term **circular economy**. By circular, an economy is envisaged as having no net effect on the environment, but, rather, restoring any damage done in resource acquisition, while ensuring little waste is generated throughout the production process, nor in the life history of the product.

The word **circular** has a second, inferred, meaning, which relates to the concept of the cycle. There are two cycles of particular importance here:

1. The biogeochemical cycles
2. The recycling of products

6.1.1 Biogeochemical cycles and product recycling

Many basic molecules and atoms pass through cycles on the planet. Water evaporates from the oceans, forms rain clouds, falls on land as rain, runs into rivers and flows back to the ocean. Carbon dioxide dissolves in rainwater, forming a slightly acidic solution which weathers landmasses, releasing material that flows in the rivers to the sea, forming sediment on the ocean floor. From here it may form sedimentary rock which is later uplifted into the air, or be subducted, later re-emerging through volcanic activity. Indeed the hydrological cycle is the great transport system on our planet.

Phosphorus is weathered by water from rocks into soil, taken up by plants, eaten by animals, released by decomposition, returned to the soil and back into plants. It may also flow from the land into the ocean as part of the hydrological cycle, fall to the ocean floor, eventually become rock, be subducted into the deeper crust and mantle, and then be released by volcanic activity to form surface rock, where it is weathered to form soil. In fact the planet has many such cycles.

The length of time that it takes to complete a lap of the cycle varies. For example, it takes nine days for all of the atmospheric water to cycle through the atmosphere, while it takes 37,000 years for the oceans to complete a cycle (Murray, 1992). Phosphorus takes 2,000 years to cycle through the soil (Jahnke, 1992), as does nitrogen (Jaffe, 1992). Carbon dioxide takes four years to cycle through the atmosphere (Siegenthaler and Sarmiento, 1993) while atmospheric oxygen takes 3.7 million years (Keeling *et al.*, 1993). Faster turnover times mean greater susceptibility to change, and so atmospheric carbon dioxide is much more sensitive than atmospheric oxygen, partly due to the size of the pool. Thus, flux is a very important issue in biogeochemical cycles (Schlesinger, 1993).

Almost every biogeochemical cycle has been altered by human activity, be it carbon dioxide, phosphorus, nitrogen, water, sulphur or uranium. The circular economy seeks to restore fluxes to their natural levels, reducing the excessive removal of material from a cycle, and the excessive release of materials into a cycle. Cycles can cope with change, but it is the rate of change that is the important issue. Thus CE is centrally concerned with flux.

The concept of **recycling** has been a significant part of sustainable practice for centuries, and it is fundamental to the circular economy. Indeed, the Chinese transformation was significantly informed by several recycling laws in Japan (The Basic Law for Establishing a Sound Material-cycle Society, 2002) and Germany (The Waste Avoidance and Management Act, 2002). CE is ultimately linked to resource cycling. These ideas are further developed in industrial symbiosis (where firms use each other's waste as resources) and in the service economy, where work is done to slow down cycles of use, in order to delay resource input and waste output. By increasing longevity of products through better manufacturing and maintenance, then the rate of replacement decreases, and so resource use is reduced. Thus the waste-is-food concept and the three Rs of reduce, re-use, recycle have become central to the circular economy. In the UK, the Biffaward programme, which ran between 1999 and 2008, focused on material flow accounting of business sectors in the United Kingdom (Hill, 2015), providing focus on industry-specific issues relating to material cycling within the economy. The Waste and Resource Action Programme (WRAP) continues to spotlight material flows as important in any audit of sustainable economics (WRAP, 2014).

The recently arranged marriages between biology and economics that form the parents of the circular economy, namely environmental economics, ecological economics and industrial ecology (all developed in the latter half of the 20th century) find earlier precedents in industrial symbiosis and industrial metabolism, which arose in the mid-19th century and early 20th century (Parkins, 1930; Fischer-Kowalski, 2003).

However, comparisons between economics and biology go much further back. The **physiocrats** (meaning literally "government of nature") held that agriculture was the source of all wealth, and François Quesnay first set out the concept of a **circular flow of income**, in his book, *Tableau Économique*, in 1758 (Quesnay, 1972). This circular flow was inspired by the work of William Harvey (in 1628) and Marcello Malpighi (in 1661) on blood circulation. The circular flow of blood around the body was viewed as a useful metaphor for the flow of money through an economy.

Of course, in terms of etymology, the word "economy" (*οἰκονομία*, "household management"), comes from the same ancient Greek origin as "ecology" (*οἶκος*, "house"; *-λογία*, "study of") meaning study of the household. This makes it all the more fitting that these concepts should come together. Indeed, the circular economy has as its main concern the management of the economy in such a way as to leave the house undamaged.

6.2 A range of definitions

Tim Cooper, one of the earliest protagonists of the circular economy in the United Kingdom, comments that:

> The model of a linear economy, in which it is assumed that there is an unlimited supply of natural resources and that the environment has an unlimited capacity to absorb waste and pollution, is dismissed. Instead, a circular economy is proposed, in which the throughput of energy and raw materials is reduced (Cooper, 1999; p. 10).

In its most basic form, a circular economy can be loosely defined as one which balances economic development with environmental and resources protection (UNEP, 2006) and in this form, it appears to be inseparable from industrial ecology, or, indeed, sustainable development. Its uniqueness comes from two interconnected ideas, the closed-loop economy and Cradle to Cradle® thinking.

UNEP developed its definition of the circular economy as featuring low consumption of energy, low emission of pollutants and high efficiency, using it as a generic term for an industrial economy which is, by design or intention, restorative and in which material flows are of two types—those which are biological nutrients, designed to re-enter the biosphere safely, and technical nutrients, which are designed to circulate at high quality without entering the biosphere. The aims are to "design out" waste, to return nutrients and to recycle durables, using renewable energy to power the economy (UNEP, 2006).

The Ellen MacArthur Foundation also defines the circular economy as an industrial system that is restorative or regenerative by intention and design. It replaces the "end-of-life" concept with restoration, shifts towards the use of renewable energy, eliminates the use of toxic chemicals which impair reuse, and aims for the elimination of waste through the superior design of materials, products, systems and, within this, business models (EMF, 2012).

The use of the word "**restorative**" is important, as the circular economy is not merely a preventative approach, reducing pollution, but also aims to repair previous damage (Cooper, 1997; Nakajima, 2000; Pitt, 2011). Drawing on concepts such as Cradle to Cradle®, biomimicry and industrial ecology, the circular economy focuses on optimizing systems rather than components. This is reflected in a change from **eco-efficiency** (minimization of material use within a linear economy) to **eco-effectiveness** (cyclic Cradle to Cradle® metabolisms with synergistic relationships between ecological and economic systems), representing positive recoupling. The circular economy is viewed as a grand harmonization between industrialization and its natural limits (Moriguchi, 2007).

The circular economy demonstrates new concepts of system, economy, value, production and consumption (Wu, 2005), leading to sustainable development of the economy, environment and society (Wu, 2005). The ultimate objective of the CE approach is to achieve the decoupling of economic growth from natural resource depletion and environmental degradation. In many ways, the circular economy is a general term covering all activities that reduce, re-use, and recycle (3R) materials in production, distribution, and, consumption processes (Cooper, 1999). According to the definition in the Law to Promote Circular Economy in the People's Republic of China, the circular economy is the integration of activities of reduction, re-use and recycling during production, exchange and consumption (Shen and Qi, 2012). Liu (2012) sums up the core characteristics of a circular economy under the following headings:

- The principle of three Rs
  - **Reduce** means an efficient method should be implemented such that at a given level of output, input can be reduced so that efficiency could be increased
  - **Recycle** means an efficient method should be implemented such that waste together with normal output can be collected and transformed for further use
  - **Re-use** means an integrated system should be implemented such that recycled material (or recaptured energy) can be utilized in the input stage, allowing a reduction in dependence on virgin raw materials
- The principle of balanced and sustainable growth

In Germany and Japan the interpretation of CE is based on the management of waste through 3R. The underlying vision is that the present linear flow of materials (resource–product–waste) needs to be transformed into a circular flow (resource–product–recycled resource). Hu *et al.* (2011) stress the focus of the circular economy is on resource productivity and eco-efficiency improvement, and uses the "4R" approach: **reduce**, **re-use**, **recycle** and **recover**.

Felix Preston, writing for Chatham House, summarized the circular economy as resting on five columns:

1. Closed-loop thinking
2. Maintenance of distinct technical and biological material cycles
3. Extended manufacturing cycle

4. Zero waste
5. Renewable energy as basis (Preston, 2012)

Feng and Yan (2007) describe CE as a mode of economic development based on ecological circulation of natural materials, requiring compliance with ecological laws and sound utilization of natural resources to achieve economic development. Feng (2004) explains that there is a feedback process of resource–product–renewed resource, and that the ultimate objectives of optimum production, optimized consumption and minimum waste can be achieved in production. The role of the CE has been identified as a means of decoupling economic growth from environmental degradation (Liu *et al.*, 2009; Xue *et al.*, 2010).

Baily *et al.* (2013) clearly distinguish the circular economy from the "**take–make–dispose**" business model for use of materials in manufacturing. The circular economy maximizes the productivity of materials and energy and minimizes the impact of their extraction and processing. According to Baily *et al.*, the circular economy is built on four principles:

1. **Designing** products with their entire life-cycles in mind
2. **Maximizing** product life-cycles
3. **Recycling** materials from end-of-life products
4. **Re-using** materials across diverse industries and value chains (Bailey *et al.*, 2013)

As described by Jones *et al.* (2011), in a circular economy material loops need to be closed by direct recycling of pre-consumer manufacturing scrap/residues (e.g. steel slags), urban mining of post-consumer end-of-life products (e.g. recovery rare earth metals from electronic waste), and landfill mining of historic (and future) urban waste-streams.

Reverse logistics is the process of moving goods from their typical final destination for the purpose of capturing value, or proper disposal. There are eight types of recovery/disposal option: direct re-use/resale, repair, refurbishing, remanufacturing, cannibalization, recycling, incineration, and landfilling (Graczyk *et al.*, 2013). Reverse logistics is playing a significant role in circular economy implementation, particularly in terms of end-of-life options.

Li and Su (2012) summarize the circular economy as having four distinctive features:

1. Minimum investment

2. Minimum effluents
3. Maximum exploiting of resources
4. As little influence on environment as possible

The Ellen Macarthur Foundation (EMF, 2012) emphasize four central themes:

1. "Designing out" waste
2. Returning nutrients and recycle durables
3. Using renewable energy to power economy
4. Replacing consumer with user

These in turn provide four sources of value creation:

1. **Power of the inner circle**: less cost in production
2. **Power of circling longer**: less goes longer
3. **Power of cascading use**: waste is food
4. **Power of pure circles**: uncontaminated material streams reduce costs

Indeed value creation has become a very important element of western circular economy models, seen as key to winning over private-sector involvement. The EMF in particular emphasizes this, as evidenced by their 2012 paper, which was researched and written neither by economists nor scientists but by a global management consulting firm, McKinsey and Company. CE claims to create more value from resources, support companies in meeting changing market requirements, lower environmental costs, increase consumer convenience and secure supplies (Preston, 2012).

An almost unique emphasis on society appears in EMF (2013) which states: "CE aims for a redesign of linear processes and flows of "materials, energy, labour and information" to more circular ones, thereby rebuilding natural and social capital" (EMF 2013, p. 26). However, there is no integration of social sustainability in the vast majority of definitions, models nor legislation pertaining to the circular economy (Murray *et al.*, 2015).

Niederberger *et al.* (2013) have compared the circular economy approach (CEA) to the carbon trading approach (CTA), as exemplified by the Kyoto agreement. They examined this under seven headings, and summarized their results as follows:

1. Paradigm
   - CEA: from **waste management** to **resource management**, leading to most productive use of resources.
   - CTA: flexibility in fulfilling GHG mitigation obligations. Market forces identify least cost mitigation actions, leading to reduced cost of climate protection.
2. Ultimate objective
   - CEA: overall long-term sustainability.
   - CTA: avoid dangerous anthropogenic interference with climate system.
3. Targeted outcomes
   - CEA: less material inputs; reduced toxicity; recover more.
   - CTA: absolute emissions reductions or sink enhancement.
4. Environmental impacts considered
   - CEA: inputs and outputs from/to the environment (incl. use of materials, energy and water), plus multiple environmental impacts.
   - CTA: (selected) greenhouse gas emissions and their global warming potential.
5. Currency
   - CEA: relative impact rankings, aggregated across multiple impact criteria (environmental impacts; material, energy and water use; material waste) and for different supply chain perspectives.
   - CTA: 1 tonne CO_2e.
6. Boundary considerations
   - CEA: not geographically constrained; considers all life-cycle stages of a material or product.
   - CTA: defined by territory (geographic), facility (ownership/management control) or project scope.
7. Responsibility:
   - CEA: all parties involved globally in the life-cycle of a material or product, including consumers and manufacturers.
   - CMA: nations (for territorial emissions); capped entities (for their Scope 1 and 2 emissions), typically large energy users.

This analysis is interesting, since most other sustainable economics models focus on carbon, whereas the circular economy puts much more weight on resource flux and industrial function. As can be seen, there are significant differences between a carbon-fixated approach and a broader resource flux approach. Mathews (2012) argues that the circular economy, as practised in South Korea and China, is much more likely to deliver carbon emission reduction than is the Kyoto agreement, which although running for over 16 years, has actually led to an increase in carbon emissions.

Recent literature has provided analysis of the application of circular economy thinking to agriculture (Song *et al.*, 2014), design (Bakker *et al.*, 2014), recycling (Prendeville *et al.*, 2014; Sevigné-Itoiz *et al.*, 2014) and product-service systems (Tukker, 2013). For a recent, detailed review of the development of the concept of the circular economy, Hill (2015) and Murray *et al.* (2015) should be referenced.

6.2.1 Emphases within the three pillars

Figure 6.1 places the circular economy within the triangle of emphasis, as presented in Chapter 5. As before, the major schools of sustainability are placed within a triangle, representing the emphasis of each school, in terms of economy, environment and society. We see that CE emerges as closest to the environment–economy axis, about halfway along, but appears to show less relevance to society. This is understandable, as it is based on an analogy with ecology, and, in particular, involves biogeochemical cycling at its heart. There is still a need to develop a social angle, but this may prove difficult, given the emphasis on biogeochemistry. And so we are faced with a significant problem. None of the schools of sustainable thinking provide a balanced approach to sustainability (with the exception of socio-ecological economics, whose name suggests everything, but has virtually no content to examine it by). Yet each field defies any form of combination with another field. And so we are left with highly specialized, polarized approaches, each failing to provide the necessary integration within society, economics and environment.

One interesting difference between CE and most of the other schools of sustainable thought is that it has largely emerged from legislation, rather than from a group of academics, who have split from one field and have started a new one (for example, the tortuous birth of ecological economics from environmental economics, as described by Røpke, 2004; 2005). This may explain why CE has not yet had a journal, editorial board and a group

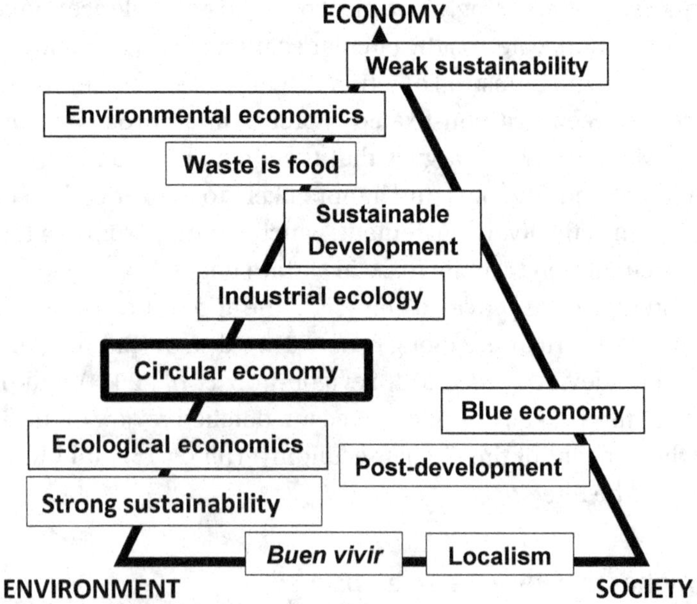

FIGURE 6.1 The circular economy within the triangle of sustainability, in comparison with other schools of sustainable thinking. Note the lack of social sustainability, like many of the schools.

of faculties of its own, as these are the normal territorial markings of a group of academics. Having said this, EMF is setting its stall out to represent western circular economics, while a number of academic faculties specializing in the subject have emerged in China, including the Circular Economy and Industrial Ecology Research Group in the Institute of Applied Ecology at the Chinese Academy of Science.

6.3 Origins and meaning

6.3.1 The origin of the circular economy

The origin of the term CE itself is debated. Certainly, the idea behind a circular economy has existed for a long time. As early as 1848, R.W. Hofmann, the first President of the Royal Society of Chemistry, stated "In an ideal chemical factory there is, strictly speaking, no waste but only products. The better a real factory makes use of its waste, the closer it gets to its ideal, the bigger is the profit" (Lancaster, 2002; p. 10).

Greyson (2007) claims that Kenneth Boulding was the originator. Boulding (1966; pp. 7-8) wrote: "Man must find his place in a cyclical ecological system which is capable of continuous reproduction of material form even though it cannot escape having inputs of energy". The term circular economy was first used in the Western literature in 1980s (Pearce and Turner, 1990) to describe a closed system of economy–environment interactions. David Pearce, known in the field of environmental economics, has also been credited with coining the term circular economy (Andersen, 2007). Concepts such as Cradle to Cradle® and biomimicry, which were inspired by nature as well, also had an influence on the development of the circular economy concept (Sherwin, 2013).

Park *et al.* (2010) claim that the CE concept originated from eco-industrial development (EID) theory and thought, based on a win–win philosophy of economic and environmental health.

It was Walter Stahel in 1976 who authored jointly a research report to the European Commission, *The Potential for Substituting Manpower for Energy* (co-authored with Genevieve Reday), presenting their vision of an economy in loops (or circular economy) and its impact on job creation, economic competitiveness, resource savings, and waste prevention. Stahel's idea of improved durability actually was drawn directly from Boulding (1966; p. 12) who wrote: "I suspect that we have underestimated, even in our spendthrift society, the gains of increased durability". In the late 1980s, Walter Stahel as well as Michael Braungart and William McDonough revived the idea of an economy functioning in loops and discussed its impact on economic competitiveness, resource savings, job creation and waste prevention. German chemist Michael Braungart went on to develop (together with American architect Bill McDonough) the Cradle to Cradle® concept and certification process.

All three claim that in an ideal closed-loop system, waste would not exist as it would be feedstock for other processes (Stahel and Reday-Mulvey 1981; McDonough and Braungart 2002). Mathews and Tan (2011; p. 436) stated that "the goal of the ecoinitiatives is to eventually establish a so-called circular economy, or what is otherwise known as a 'closed-loop' economy", while Yang and Feng (2008) called CE an abbreviation of Closed Materials Cycle Economy or Resources Circulated Economy. Certainly the CE concept can be seen to have emerged from established sustainable economics thinking, including such schools of thought as performance economics, industrial ecology, biomimicry, Cradle to Cradle®, eco-efficiency and waste is food (Andersen, 2007; EMF, 2013).

Liu *et al.* (2009) claim it was originally a Chinese concept. Yuan *et al.* (2006) also claim first use of a circular economy concept was in China and occurred in a paper by Zhu (1998), inspired by German and Swedish loop-closing, and arising from the industrial ecology paradigm. The inclusion of Sweden is interesting here, as most literature attributes the inspirations as stemming from Germany and Japan. More bizarrely, in a brazenly revisionist swoop, Baily *et al.* (2013: p. 10) accredit the McKinsey Global Institute for coining the term, stating "circular economy is another term coined by the McKinsey Global Institute". There is no evidence of this elsewhere in the literature.

Another more reasonable claim for early use is by Robèrt (1991; p. 3) who wrote: "Most environmental problems are based on the same systemic error, linear processing of material. Until resources are processed in cycles either by society or by biogeochemical processes, the global economy and public health will continue to deteriorate".

6.4 The circular economy in China

China is the world leader in sustainability economics, having developed and executed an ambitious programme of measures, using the circular economy as a model (Zhou *et al.*, 2014). In this section we will examine the history of the circular economy in China, and the way in which this most populous nation on Earth has implemented the most advanced programme of environmental economic measures in the history of our planet. Given its population of 1.35 billion people as of 2011, around 19% of the global population (UN, 2011), the economic practices of China are of vital interest for the rest of the globe. First, a few words on the industrial activity of China.

Chinese chemical industries are severely challenged by resource shortages and environment problems. Although China is rich in resources and energy, the per capita amount is no more than half the average of the entire world (Tan, 2008); 40% of petrol and more than 70% of natural rubber are imported, and the main chemical minerals are in short supply, especially calcium, phosphorus, sulphur, and boron. China's GDP has grown in 30 years from \$106 billion to \$2.4 trillion, making it the fourth largest economy in the world. Over the last 25 years, China has experienced an average annual economic growth rate of 8.7% (Tan, 2008).

The history of the adaptation of the circular economy as a central theme in sustainable economics in China can be traced back to 1973, when the first National Environmental Protection Conference formulated environmental protection policies and guidelines. 1979 saw the enactment of the Environmental Protection Law of the People's Republic of China (for Trial Implementation). In 1983, the second National Environmental Protection Conference was held, making environmental protection a core national policy. In 1989, the Environmental Protection Law of the People's Republic of China was enacted.

In 2002 the 16th National Congress of the Communist Party of China set out an ambitious development plan: quadrupling of GDP, social equality, and the recovery and protection of environmental integrity. This was to be called a **circular economy**. In China, the CE is defined in legislation as a generic term for reducing, re-using and recycling activities conducted in the process of production, circulation and consumption.

What is interesting about these three goals is that the Chinese model formally attempted to address all three pillars of sustainability, unlike most of the other schools (though the reality has been, so far, disappointing in terms of social inclusion).

This *bauplan* for China's development targeted the realization of an overall *shao kong* ("comfortable" or, literally, "less empty") society by the year 2020. It was to Germany and Japan that Chinese leaders looked for inspiration (Triebswetter and Hitchens, 2005; Moriguchi, 2007). At the request of the National Development and Reform Commission (NDRC), a Japanese document, the Recycling-Based Society Law, was translated into Chinese as one of a number of models for the formulation of this development plan. The document had more than 100,000 words, and took six months to translate.

The Japanese Recycling-Based Society Law incorporated a number of different laws which were formulated and passed during the period 1990 to 2002. These included:

- On the resources and reutilization of end-of-life automobiles (2002)
- Waste collection, transportation and re-use of home appliances (2001)
- The law for promotion of efficient utilization of resources (formulated from July 1999 to April 2001)

- The basic direction for reutilization and recycling of foodstuffs (2001)
- The law for the promotion of national procurement of environmentally friendly products (2001)
- The basic law for establishing a sound material-cycle society (2000)
- The major contents on the mechanism for green procurement (2000)
- Legislation on the reutilization of construction materials (2000)
- The basic guidelines for promoting waste classification of specific construction materials including concrete, wood and other recoverable materials (2000)
- The law for the promotion of the recycling of foodstuffs (2000)
- The fundamental directions for the promotion law: objectives for waste minimization, production, consumers and society (2000)
- The recycling of packaging materials, e.g. PET bottles, paper products (2000)
- The law on classification of packaging materials and re-use for commercial products (1999)
- The recycling of home appliances (1998)

The reconciliation of these three policy goals (GDP, society and environment) would be achieved through the establishment of a circular economy, underpinned by a cleaner production strategy. Three new laws were introduced to move the agenda forward:

- Cleaner Production Promotion Law (passed on 29 June 2002 and put into effect on 1 January 2003)
- The Law of the People's Republic of China on Appraising Environmental Impacts (passed on 28 October 2002 and put into effect on 1 September 2003)
- The Law on Pollution Prevention and Control of Solid Waste (April 2005)

These laws appear to be the first in the world to make the circular economy a national strategy of economic and social development. The Ministry of

Environmental Protection initiated eco-industrial parks (EIPs) as early as 2002, releasing an EIP standard. Currently, 50 such parks exist.

Guiyang was chosen as the pilot city for implementing a circular economy. First led by the local Mayor of Guiyang (capital city of south-west China's Guizhou Province) in 2002, the first definition of a circular economy with legal bearings was offered by a decree issued by Guiyang and promulgated by the local people's congress on 25 September 2004. The Guiyang Circular Economy Development Plan focused on six sectors: coal, phosphorus, aluminium, herbal medicine, tourism and organic agriculture. Guiyang government also worked with Prodev, a project co-ordinated by UNEP and funded by the EU, involving the Wuppertal Institute Collaborating Centre on Sustainable Consumption and Production, whose stated objective is "to improve the policy framework and promote a more integrated decision-making process in the local government to support sustainable development and Circular Economy" (www.scp-centre.org/projects/basic-projects-data/29-prodev.html).

Ma Kai, head of the National Development and Reform Commission and, currently, a vice-premier of China, stated, at a national conference on the circular economy in 2004, that the circular economy had a highly efficient use of resources and recycling as the core:

> [The] reduction, re-use, resource principle would lead to low consumption, low emission, high-efficiency features, in line with the concept of sustainable development. The circular economy was to be a closed feedback process of resource–product–renewable resource, and finally achieve optimal production, optimal consumption, minimum waste (Zhao *et al.*, 2012; p. 438).

The law of the People's Republic of China on Renewable Energy was passed on 28 February 2005 (enacted on 1 January 2006), marking an important step in terms of **conversion** of energy. The Energy Conservation Law of the People's Republic of China revised on 28 October 2007 and put into effect on 1 January 2008, marked the second stage, impacting on energy **consumption**.

The incorporation of a circular economy into the Outline of the 11th Five-Year Plan for National Economic and Social Development was an important step, allowing much greater support and focus on sustainability (Wu *et al.*, 2014). The importance of the five-year plan cannot be overemphasized here, as it forms the medium term focus for government policy in China. China is governed using five-year plans, focusing on social and economic development. The first of these began in 1953, under Mao Zedong, inspired by the soviet model of economic and industrial development. Currently, the 12th Five-Year Plan is being implemented, running from 2011 to 2015.

The Law for the Promotion of the Circular Economy, which was issued on 29 August 2008 and came into effect on 1 January 2009, promotes resource utilization efficiency, natural environment protection and sustainable development.

It operates at three levels:

1. Individual firms: ecodesign and cleaner production. Results of environmental performance must be publicly released.
2. Eco-industrial parks: waste is food concept.
3. Eco-city and eco-province level: creation of recycling society.

Key objectives were:

- The government to closely monitor energy consumption and pollution emissions in heavy industries.
- Government departments to promote recycling and improve energy-saving and waste-reutilization standards and develop policies to divert capital into environment friendly industries.
- Industrial enterprises to introduce water-saving technologies, strengthen management, and install water-saving equipment in new buildings and projects.
- Crude oil refining, power generation, steel and iron production plants to stop using oil-fired fuel generators and boilers, in favour of clean energy, such as natural gas and alternative fuels.
- Enterprises and government departments to adopt renewable products in new buildings, such as solar and geothermal energies.
- Recycling and use of coal mine waste, coal ash, and other waste materials.
- Agricultural sector to recycle straw, livestock waste, and farming by-products to produce methane.

China has also needed to resort to financial incentives in order to encourage businesses to partake in the circular economy. As of 2011, tax incentives have been further expanded, including variable rates of VAT on specific products. For example construction sand and cement made from construction waste is VAT-exempt, recycled graphite earns a 50% VAT refund and, more bizarrely, wigs made from human hair earn an 80% VAT refund.

The main responsibility for CE implementation in China now rests with the National Development and Reform Commission, who released the first CE indicators in 2007 (see below), the first in the world. While the National Development and Reform Commission is leading the circular economy strategy at the national level, implementation on the ground is the responsibility of local authorities. Under the NDRC's guidance, a circular economy is promoted through a score of legislative, political, technical and financial measures. The overall responsibility for environmental policy now rests with the vice president of China (the first ranked vice-premier), indicating the importance placed on this area. Academic institutions have also been formed to provide support, including the Circular Economy and Industrial Ecology Research Group in the Institute of Applied Ecology at the Chinese Academy of Science.

Tan (2008) explains that the current Chinese model is based on the 3–2–1 model which refers to:

- Three industrial systems (the eco-industrial system, the eco-agricultural system and the eco-service system important in that the middle stage refers to agriculture, an area rarely addressed in sustainable economic models, but one of significant importance).
- Two domains (production and consumption).
- One industrial chain of renewable resources (referred to as the **venous industry** in Japan).

6.4.1 12th Five-Year Plan

In the 12th Five-Year Plan (2011–15), the priority is a shift from the resource efficiency of heavy industries to recycling of metals and minerals and remanufacturing of products, especially the exchange of materials between companies (Preston, 2012). China's 12th Five-Year Plan has dedicated huge resources towards the implementation of a circular economy.

Key outcomes include:

- Increased domestic consumption, relaxing growth targets to 7%
- Resource efficiency and recirculation
- Seven new industries for strategic promotion

- Investment of US$468 billion
- Internalization of sustainability goals
- New growth pattern based on lower resource intensity, renewable energy
- Pricing of inputs to reflect ecological value
- Focus on green cities and green buildings
- Development of "**Internet of Things**" containing resource history of products; GG (Green Growth) strategy

6.4.2 Indicators

China has developed a system of indicators to provide feedback on progress in the circular economy (Geng *et al.*, 2012). These operate at two levels. At the macro-level and the meso-level. Macro-level indicators allow evaluation of regional and national progress, providing guidance in terms of development and planning. Meso-level indicators operate at the eco-industrial park level. In both cases, there are four categories: resource output, resource consumption, integrated resource utilization and waste disposal/pollution emission.

A third set of indicators, eco-city indicators, consist of 28 different categories, including such subjects as local ecosystem value, land greening rate and biodiversity. Finally a group of CO_2 indicators provides feedback on climate mitigation policies. Usefully, CO_2 indicators are disaggregated, allowing proper focus on different aspects of the bigger problem, rather than the carbon fixation so prevalent in most western models of sustainability. Of note is the fact that there are no social sustainability indicators in the Chinese national standards, nor any industrial/urban symbiosis indicators relating to scavenger and decomposer activities (Geng *et al.*, 2012).

6.4.3 South Korean programme

China is not the only eastern nation adopting a circular economy style. South Korea has recently launched its own ambitious programme of change. In 2008, the 60th Anniversary of South Korea, President Lee Myung-bak reflected on 60 years of growth and committed his government to 60 years of greenhouse gas reduction. This was framed as a five-year plan (2009–13). Targets included becoming the seventh-greenest economy by 2020 and the fifth greenest by 2050. The programme encompassed the following goals:

- Public investment in infrastructure
- Mandatory guidelines for procurement
- Public research and development in low-carbon technology
- Regulations/incentives
- Market correction measures
- Supported with US$20 billion from private businesses
- GG (Green Growth) (Kim, 2009)

Several indicators, such as energy and material efficiency indicators, have been set up for the first five-year plan (2009–13) of the Republic of Korea, with the application of input/output tables for calculating the expected economic and environmental gains (UNEP 2010). For a review of the progress of the circular economy in Asia, reference Murray *et al.* (2015).

6.5 Western approaches

While China has led the way in terms of adopting a circular economy, Europe, which originally had been world leaders with eco-industrial parks such as Kalundborg in Denmark established in the early 1970s and Germany's recycling laws providing important inspiration in China, has fallen behind in terms of national policy. However, the Chinese experience has reawakened interest, and this has been most clearly demonstrated in recent EU developments.

The European Commission is an important driver for new policies regarding resource usage: the concept of a circular economy is an essential component of the resource efficiency initiative of the EU2020 strategy (The Parliament, 2012). In 2008 for instance, the European Commission presented the **Sustainable Consumption and Production and Sustainable Industrial Policy (SCP/SIP) Action Plan** which is supposed to lead to an improved environmental performance of products and increase the demand for more sustainable production technologies (EC, 2012). Furthermore, a "Cradle to Cradle® network" has been established in 2010, providing a platform for cooperation of EU regions for sharing their knowledge and experiences "in the areas of innovation, the knowledge economy, the environment and risk prevention" (C2C Network, 2010). Hill (2015) provides an excellent review of the emergence of circular economic concepts within the European Union.

The EU has agreed a strategy for a resource-efficient Europe under its **Europe 2020 Strategy** and introduced an initiative to address raw materials security (European Commission, 2011). Relevant national strategies include the National Resource Efficiency Programme in Germany (BMU, 2011) and the proposed "materials roundabout"—a hub for the high grade recycling of materials and products—in the Netherlands (Van de Wiel, 2011).

Joke Schauvliege (president of EU Environment Council 2010) stated: "We must deal with our materials, and with our energy, more efficiently. At the end of their life we must be able to reuse materials as new raw materials. This is called completing the cycle." (EMF, 2012).

The EU, initially in collaboration with the USA, but later unilaterally, recognized the importance of being able to audit the costs of pollution, a key externality related to market failure, as identified early in the 20th century by Pigou (1920). To do this they set up **ExternE**, which focuses mainly on damage from energy and transport sectors on the environment in terms of sink issues. This type of audit is seen as essential if a circular economy is to be assessed and implemented in Europe (Andersen, 2007). This developed into what became known as **material flow accounting** (MFA) (Bringezu, 2001). Important institutes involved with MFA in Europe currently include the Wuppertal Institute in Germany and RIVM in the Netherlands. MFAs are now regularly calculated. Detailed national calculations have been available for several years for countries such as the UK, Germany, Denmark, Austria, and Finland. Germany additionally publishes annual input/output tables.

Eurostat, the EU's statistical organization published both a detailed methodological guide on MFA and a retrospective analysis of key material use indicators (Eurostat 2001; Bringezu, 2001). The European Environment Agency's reports include assessments of policy progress and an analysis of key material flow trends. The importance of MFA was examined in a report commissioned under the EU's 6th Environmental Action Programme (EAP), which aimed to review resource use patterns across the EU 25 and to provide information that could be used in setting targets (Moll, Bringezu and Schütz, 2005).

The ELV (end-of-life vehicle) EU directive was passed in 2000, and would inform Chinese policy (Chen and Zhang, 2009). The WEEE (waste electrical and electronic equipment) EU directive was enforced in 2003. This has been updated ever since.

Finally on 17 December 2012, the EU released the following statement: "In a world with growing pressures on resources and the environment, the

EU has no choice but to go for the transition to a resource-efficient and ultimately regenerative circular economy" (EU, 2012).

They identified six action points (EU, 2012):

1. Encouraging innovation and accelerating public and private investment in resource-efficient technologies, systems and skills, also in SMEs, through a dynamic and predictable political, economic and regulatory framework, a supportive financial system and sustainable growth enhancing resource-efficient priorities in public expenditure and procurement.

2. Implementing, using and adopting smart regulation, standards and codes of conduct that a) create a level playing field, b) reward front-runners and c) accelerate the transition, and d) take into account the social and international implications of our actions.

3. Abolishing environmentally harmful subsidies and tax-breaks that waste public money on obsolete practices, taking care to address affordability for people whose incomes are hardest-pressed. Shifting the tax burden away from jobs to encourage resource efficiency, and using taxes and charges to stimulate innovation and development of a job-rich, socially cohesive, resource-efficient and climate-resilient economy.

4. Creating better market conditions for products and services that have lower impacts across their life-cycles, and that are durable, repairable and recyclable, progressively taking the worst performing products off the market; inspiring sustainable lifestyles by informing and incentivizing consumers, using the latest insights into behavioural economics and information technology, and encouraging sustainable sourcing, new business models and the use of waste as raw materials.

5. Integrating current and future resource scarcities and vulnerabilities more coherently into wider policy areas, at national, European and global level, such as in the fields of transport, food, water and construction.

6. Providing clear signals to all economic actors by adopting policy goals to achieve a resource-efficient economy and society by 2020, setting targets that give a clear direction and indicators to measure progress relating to the use of land, material, water and

greenhouse gas emissions, as well as biodiversity. Such indicators must go beyond conventional measures of economic activity, help guide the decisions of all actors, and assist public authorities in timely action. All organizations above a meaningful size and impact must be held accountable to measure and report key non-financial progress indicators on a comparable basis.

In 2013, European Union (EU) environment commissioner Janez Potocnik set out a parallel path with China, undoubtedly with the hope of encouraging trading relations with China through a shared sustainability approach: "When I look to China's 12th five-year plan and compare it with the EU's political documents, I see a lot of similarities ... It is a really good basis for cooperation" (Potocnik, 2013).

The British-based Waste and Resources Action Programme (WRAP, 2014), in its annual conference in 2013, focused on the circular economy, as evident in their EU2020 vision. It highlighted:

- Business competitive improvements of £330 billion
- Improved trade balance of £90 billion
- Extra 160,000 jobs in recycling
- 500 million tonnes CO_2 saved
- 190 million tonnes reduction in extracted materials
- 220 million tonnes less waste produced
- 350 milion tonnes more recycled material

WRAP further predict that a circular economy could halve domestic waste by 2025 (WRAP, 2014).

The Ellen MacArthur Foundation (EMF), set up by the round-the-world yachtswoman in 2010 and funded in the first place by the companies who had sponsored her sailing career, including Renault, Cisco, BT, National Grid and B&Q, also identified financial benefits as being central to any meaningful circular economic framework. Economic, company and consumer benefits have been emphasized by the EMF. Europe, along with nations around the world, has agreed the Ten Year Framework of Programmes on Sustainable Consumption and Production (10YFP) at the Rio+20 conference, which emphasizes circular economy-like principles.

This approach taken by the EU, Rio+20 and EMF clearly highlights some key differences between China and western Europe. While China set out their principles to guide government and in order to communicate the rationale and implementation of their programme to its citizens as *ipsum factum*, setting up new EIP projects continuously and funding from central funds, the capitalist West relies much more on the private sector (as evidenced, for example by the funding of the EMF by a group of companies), who they must convince of the merit of such a thing (Murray *et al.*, 2015).

The private sector is predominately profit-driven. Hence the emphasis on the financial benefits of the circular economy lies at the heart of these approaches. Western governments are also elected, and so attractive political references relating to jobs, standard of living and the environment play well on national and European stages. Europe also faces the difficulty of significant differences between its member states, partly geopolitical, and partly historical. This makes progress extremely difficult at an EU level. However, many countries are pursuing their own approaches.

Progress has also been threatened by the recent severe recession that particularly impacted on Europe, with several states facing bankruptcy. Europe also has less space and resources available for development. One common facet between Europe and China is the dependence on external sources for much of their material and energy needs.

There is a huge variation between individual nations within the EU both in terms of pollution output and industrial profile. Many nations are mostly agrarian, others industrial, while others are firmly in the Information Age. Earnings vary radically, while poverty levels also vary widely. All of this heterogeneity provides a massive challenge for the EU, reliant as it is on a capitalist approach to governance and economics, whereas in China, things are more easily organized within its socialist economics approach. However, the circular economy has some more fundamental issues facing it in terms of its potential as the state-of-the-art economic model for sustainability. The next section examines some of these issues.

6.6 Issues with the circular economy

6.6.1 Confusion with semantics

Felix Preston observes that currently, "the term 'Circular Economy' is inconsistently used by governments and companies—and awareness of the concept is relatively low" (Preston 2012: p. 3). The use of the word "circular", and, indeed, "linear", in association with the word "economy" is potentially confusing as both have been used in completely different contexts.

The **linear stages of growth model** is set out by Rostow (1960) in his book *A Non-Communist Manifesto*, wherein he describes five successional seres that developing nations all pass through: the traditional society, the preconditions for take-off, the take-off, the drive to maturity and the age of high mass-consumption. Other examples include **linear economic models**, which are mathematical tools used to analyse economic behaviour, be it in closed or open systems (Gale, 1989).

Furthermore there is the concept of **circular flow of income**, dating back to 1758 (Quesnay, 1972). Here, income, production and expenditure cycle through consumers and producers. Thus the term circular economy has significant baggage.

6.6.2 Thermodynamics

The circular economy builds on a thermodynamic foundation which is completely fictional (Rammelt and Crisp, 2014). A circular economy is not actually possible at all, neither in nature nor in human trade. Systems deteriorate with time, and require constant energetic flow to maintain themselves. Complexity exists only if waste is generated. Indeed, the second law demands that waste must increase. The longer something exists, the more energy is required to allow this. Since energy flow through our biosphere is one of the greatest problems (for example in eutrophication), then any strategy that demands increased energy flow is not environmentally friendly. This brings to mind the perpetual motion machines of the 19th century. They couldn't actually exist.

Furthermore, the idea of circular economics has its origins in the *Spaceship Earth* of Boulding (1966), where it is suggested that we live in a closed system, at least in terms of mass. This idea has been repeated ad nauseam in much of the environmental literature. It is not true. Earth is an open subsystem, part of a greater closed system called the universe. Earth relies on a huge river of energy flowing through it, as shown by the consequences of closing off that flow during mass extinctions (when the Earth is closest to a closed system, and fails to function properly).

Mass also can leave the planet, or be added to it. The fact that our entire industrial revolution relied on metals that were available within the crust of the planet is wholly dependent on external sources. A planet such as Earth would be expected to have much lower levels of metals such as gold and silver at its surface than is the case, as these metals would be attracted to the iron in the core. However, meteorites bombarding the surface at the time when the crust neared formation led to incorporation of much higher levels of metals (Willbold *et al.*, 2011).

Furthermore, some of the water on the planet is thought to have come from comets or chondrites colliding with the Earth (Robert, 2001). Matter is also lost from Earth. For example, helium is continuously lost (Hunten, 1973). So our planet is certainly not a **closed system**. If it were, we would have less water and few available metals!

Of even greater significance is the fact that energy is continuously lost from the planet in the form of heat, and that energy is continuously arriving on the planet, in the form of solar radiation (Daly, 1985). Indeed, the biosphere plays the role of absorbing this energy, and re-releasing it in a less useful form (waste), as entropy. The first law of thermodynamics says energy can neither be created nor destroyed (basically, you can only break even) while the second law says that energy is continuously converted to a less useful form (basically, you can't even break even). This means that nothing lasts forever. Indeed, many things last a lot less time than that. This has repercussions for the service industry and long-life ideas that are often suggested as part of a circular economy, as we shall see later.

Not only does the circular economy rely on a complete breach of the laws of thermodynamics, but it also references a static equilibrium model (see Chapter 4), reliant on some state of perfection, attainable by reducing waste to zero. This emphasis on the eradication of waste creates a significant clash with the parallel concept of waste as food. For the waste-is-food principle to work, a reliable, continuous, homogeneous supply of waste is essential. Otherwise, the waste-dependent economy will literally starve to death.

Thus by decreasing waste production, with increasing resources trapped in long-life products, and more efficient production methods leading to a decline in waste, EIPs that are reliant on this waste will begin to fall apart at the seams. This can be seen in Figure 6.2. You can't eradicate the cake *and* eat it! Another point is that a circular economy cannot promote recycling in perpetuity (Andersen, 2007). No recycling process can be 100% efficient. In reality the figure is much less than this. Furthermore the energetic costs of recycling are significant, partly because of the need to restore functionality to degraded materials. The production of this energy will in itself produce waste. There is no such thing as perpetual motion, nor a free lunch.

This problem of reliable waste provision for secondary industry was first identified as early as 1920, by Talbot (1920; p. 303), who pointed out that, in order to be successful, industrial symbiosis relied on the foundation that "waste must be forthcoming in a steady stream of uniform volume to justify

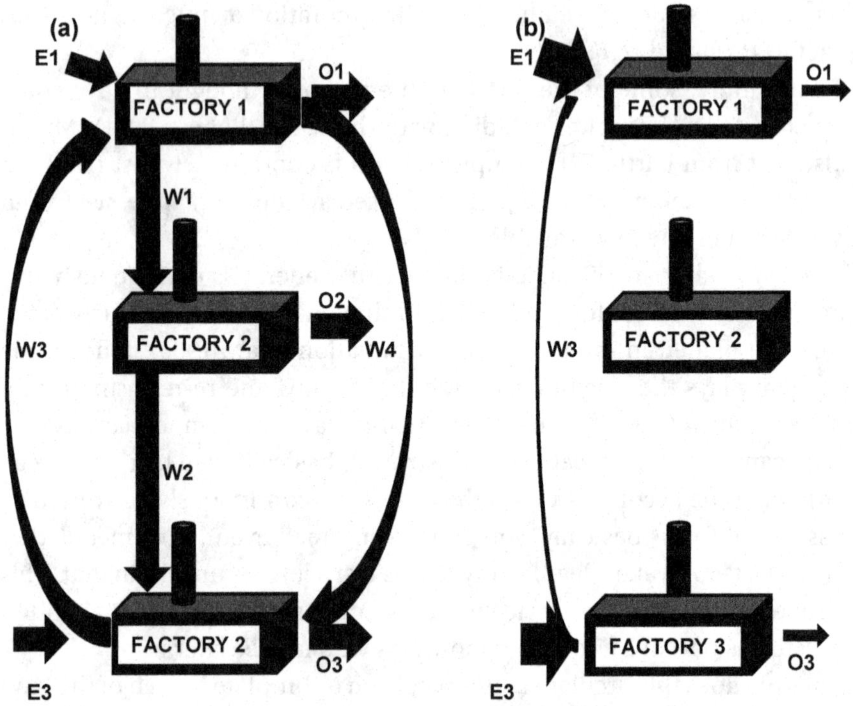

FIGURE 6.2 Waste is food versus zero waste: the impact on an eco-industrial park. In (a), three factories co-exist, utilizing waste from each other. Factory 1 has inputs from external sources (E1) and internal sources (Factory 3). Factory 2 is dependent on waste from Factory 1. Factory 3 is dependent on waste from factories 1 and 2 as well as external materials (E3). In (b) new laws are issued that force Factory 1 to change its operations and reduce waste dramatically. This has a disastrous impact on all three factories, with waste supply routes W1 and W4 reduced to zero, leading to waste supply route W2 and W3 also collapsing, impacting on all three factory outputs O1, O2 and O3. Factory 2 closes and factories 1 and 3 must greatly increase external supplies, significantly impacting on profits and on pollution in source countries. Jobs are lost throughout the park.

its exploitation, and the fashioning and maintenance of these streams is the supreme difficulty".

Not only must the market and production methods for the product concerned remain constant, but the market and production methods of all the other products, whose associated waste creates the substrate for the original product, must also remain constant. Finally, as in Kalundborg, no EIP can be circular (as neither can any economy be circular) and thus externalities will always exist, unless there is a dramatic shift in the manufacturing of all the products. However, such a change will likely alter the quantitative and qualitative aspects of waste, meaning that unless product development is completely unified within an EIP, it will be impossible to avoid externalities.

Externalities are a significant issue for industrial symbiosis, since they usually involve significant resource use and waste generation out with the symbiosis. Ecologists find similar problems trying to audit ecosystem externalities that include flow of such things as migrating species, nutrients, water and heat. Furthermore a forest fire upstream of a feeder stream can have significant impact on the balance of a lake far removed from such a forest.

Advocates of a circular economy would appear to view the energetics of an ecosystem as a cube, where what goes in comes out, and the whole system is a robust, leak-free passage of energy from level to level. However, food chains do not work like this. They form food pyramids, not food cubes (Fig. 6.3), where energy and material are increasingly lost as we move through the food chain. Externalities have a significant role here, particularly relating to weathering and respiration, releasing heat, CO_2 and nutrients to external markets. Industries work in similar ways. Externalities not only impact on raw materials. Britain exports 60% of its recycled metals overseas, meaning that any direct benefit from recycling leaks away.

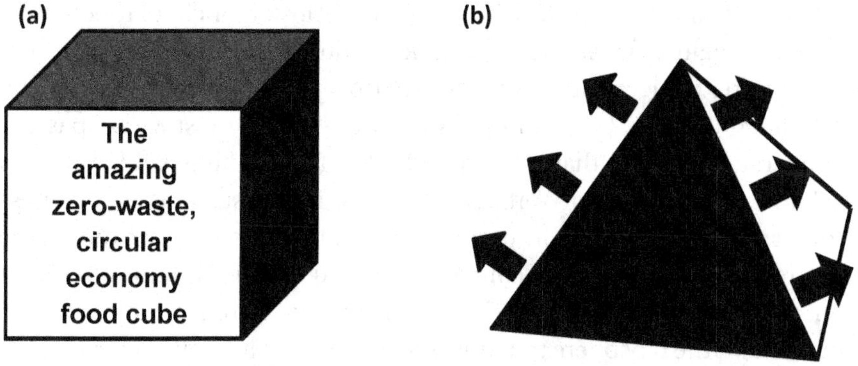

FIGURE 6.3 The circular economy and ecological reality. (a) The circular economy, like many other schools of sustainability, strives for zero waste. In this rationale, a food chain would be a cube, with no waste. (b) a real ecosystem has a food chain that is a pyramid, with 90% loss of biomass at each stage, supporting fewer and fewer organisms. The peak predators will be few in number. Waste of biomass and energy is de rigueur in the real natural world.

The goals of a circular economy must be achieved within the unyielding constraints of resource availability, dynamic environmental carrying capacity and the limits of eco-efficiency. Many nonrenewable natural resources have limited reserves regionally, nationally, and globally. The capacity for renewable resources to regenerate is compromised by pollution and overuse, as with ocean fisheries. There are natural limits to eco-efficiency in human systems, including the energy demand of resource recovery, the number of cycles through which materials can be recycled and maintain value, and dissipative uses of materials where they become unrecoverable by the nature of their use (e.g. particles from the surface of tires dissipate along roadways).

6.6.3 Ecological succession

Missing from much of the ecological content of economics is the subject of ecological succession. The most dominant form of succession moves from a simple system, through an increasingly complex system with increasing growth, to a dynamic state of balance, where net growth is greatly reduced.

This latter state is a resilient system, with equilibrium conditions applying. However, it involves a significant reduction in growth, a point often not understood by ecological economists. This is because the system reaches what is known as maximum entropy production (Chapter 2), and it is limited from further growth by its context: a functioning biosphere (Skene, 2013). This climax community is probably as close to a circular economy as can be imagined, given the importance of flux and dynamic equilibrium, but it requires a huge reduction in growth (to a point where net growth = 0).

Ehrenfeld (2005; p. 23) defines sustainability in the most encompassing way as “the possibility that human and other forms of life will flourish on the Earth forever”. Adam Werbach (2009) defines a sustainable business as one capable of thriving in perpetuity, an idea very much at the centre of a circular economy. These concepts demand a static equilibrium rather than a dynamic equilibrium. This has no place within a natural order. Functionally, the biosphere remains unchanged, but in terms of form, there is regular change. Many more species have come and gone over the history of the planet than exist on it today.

A failure to grasp the true meaning of succession is no more evident than in Donella Meadows’ hugely influential book, *Beyond the Limits*. Meadows quotes from a World Bank Environment Working Paper which clearly recognizes the problems with treating economic growth as part of, or analogous to, development. It states that "Our planet develops over time without growing. Our economy, a subsystem of the finite and non-growing earth, must eventually adapt to a similar pattern of development" (Meadows *et al.*, 1992; p. xix). This is entirely wrong and references some imaginary alternative universe where thermodynamics does not occur. Succession involves increasing complexity and increasing entropic output (i.e. growth) up to a point, thereafter net growth approaches zero, but gross growth will continue in dynamic equilibrium with gross collapse. In other words, this is not a static system, and natural disturbance will provide opportunities for growth continuously. Once again the static model of Chapter 4 lies at the heart of these misconceptions, based on old ecological, flat-Earth thinking.

6.6.4 Is longevity good?

The concept of longer-lasting products with greater emphasis on maintenance has been mooted as an important element of the circular economy by such advocates as EMF, Stahel and Cooper (e.g. Cooper, 2010, EMF, 2012; Stahel, 2012). It has been suggested that the benefits include removing technical nutrients from the environment for longer, reducing the flow of material through the industrial cycle and replacing manufacturing jobs with service sector jobs.

There are a number of significant issues that arise from such an approach. First, longer-lasting products will, by definition, be more difficult to break down. Second, longer-lasting products will, by definition, slow the flow of all associated materials through the overall cycle. Third, the environmental footprint associated with the service sector is not insignificant, in terms of transport, repair and inventory needed to support it. Fourthly, the energy required to produce longer-lasting products will inevitably be much greater than for short-lived products and most likely involve materials further removed from the natural cycle.

It would surely be energetically less disruptive to design towards a more natural outcome, likely with *shorter* life. For example a bamboo chopstick would be better than a highly specialized plastic fork, as it could easily be recycled and would only briefly be removed from the biosphere. Furthermore, the bamboo chopstick uses only natural nutrients, not technical nutrients, and therefore is more easily reassimilated back into the environment. The plastic fork may last for a long time (if carefully handled) but has birth and death consequences. In fact, its very durability causes issues in terms of its difficulty in recycling.

The more natural the product, the faster it's breakdown, and the more complete its reintegration within the environment. Thus durability is not a profit-only approach, and the costs are likely to move us further away from an improved integration within the environment (i.e. sustainability), rather than closer towards it. By building long-lasting materials, we will be likely to make their ultimate breakdown more difficult and energetically expensive. The issue of flux should be central to all of this, and delaying the cycle through exotic chemistry or prolonged servicing may well not be an appropriate strategy.

There is no such thing as a free lunch. Servicing engineers require transport, replacement parts, long-lasting materials, service centres and a large support network, all of which goes against the natural way of quick turnaround. Turnover is king in the natural world. If you pursue a strategy that dismisses turnover in nature, you end up with a bog instead of forest.

It is why rainforest soils are so fragile. Rainforest soils are brief repositories of the rainforest's true riches. Most of it is stored in the trees themselves, and cycling happens very quickly. Take away the trees and the remaining soil in no way reflects the biodiverse treasure that once stood upon it. In bogs, material is locked away in acidic, wet soil, where bacteria are unable to break it down. Little grows on a slow-cycling bog, but lots of things thrive in a fast cycling rainforest.

Human societies can be seen as "**flow structures**" (Prigogine, 1980), meaning that their existence depends on flows of matter, energy and information. However, all levels of biosphere organization, from single cells to biomes, are also flow structures. Thus the alteration of flow at any one point is likely to significantly impact on all other levels, whether it be matter, energy or information. Thus flow is central to sustainability, and any alteration of flow must be carefully examined in terms of its consequence on the environment, which surely feeds back to us.

Leeuw claims that the flows of matter, energy and information do not follow the same pattern. Matter and energy are subject to the laws of conservation, and cannot be shared. They could therefore never have created durable human social institutions, let alone societies. Information, on the other hand, can be shared (Leeuw, 2011). However, the impact of altering the flow of energy and material through human industry *does* impact all else, and fundamentally informs society.

Concern exists that an obsession with technology, incorporating rare and limited metals, is overshadowing simpler supply and demand issues. Reducing consumption is a better way, more natural, not less natural, bioparticipation not biomimicry. A circular economy focuses on a status quo, maintaining levels by recirculation, and on perfect efficiency. It defies dynamic equilibrium and the laws of thermodynamics in its present form, and misses almost entirely the third pillar, that of society. Hislop and Hill observe that "a large part of the shift to a more circular economy may need to come from our values and behaviour, which might be independent from or else reinforced by an economic motive" (Hislop and Hill, 2007; p. 1).

In a market economy, prices of natural resources will be lower than they should be if they reflected depletion and environmental damage. Andersen (2007) argues that this means that only a limited range of circular economy options will make sense. Indeed, most industry will already recycle up to a point that makes economic sense, meaning that many of the calculations of win–win models are overenthusiastic. Only with truly environmentally relative pricing can a capitalist economy consider embracing more rigorous recycling.

6.6.5 Green energy

Within the circular economy, emphasis has been placed, by both western and eastern models, on using green fuels. However, this is problematic, as no fuel is truly green in terms of its ecological footprint. The green fuel drive has led to large areas in Borneo being cleared of forest in order to plant oil palm. This has led to devastation of crucial habitat for clouded leopards and orang-utans, among many other species (Fitzherbert *et al.*, 2008). Another issue is the reliance of much green technology on rare earth metals, such as neodymium, which is mined at considerable environmental cost (Zhang, 2000).

Ethanol production requires more fossil fuel than it produces ethanol, while biofuels use the equivalent of ten acres for every car per year (Pimentel, 1998). Moreover, demand for biofuel has contributed directly to the loss of millions of acres of tropical forest that are replaced by soy fields, for biofuel production (Farigone *et al.*, 2008). Even without forest destruction, essential farmland is being displaced for green energy production, putting huge pressure on food production and water resources in poor countries (Gardner, 1997).

Beyond revealing the significant and often hidden cost of biofuels, this discussion is of critical importance because the global availability of grain producing land is only about three-tenths of an acre per person and appears to be shrinking under the pressure of biofuel demand (Gardner, 1997).

A circular economy should seek to correct a problem with carbon markets, where impacts up and downstream of a regulated entity are generally excluded from consideration. However, there has been little integration between circular economy thinking and climate mitigation policy. Indeed, interestingly, Geng *et al.* (2012) report that carbon reduction indicators are not included in China's Circular Economy Evaluation Indicator System (see also Niederberger *et al.*, 2013).

The circular economy in western Europe, particularly that set out by EMF (2012), paints a "win–win" solution: to corporate actors, more efficient resource and energy use; to employees and communities, less pollution; and to governments, investment patterns in line with ambitious productivity and regulatory targets. However, these deliverables fall short of the economic dematerialization and decarbonization gains necessary for delivering environmental sustainability (Mason, 2011).

In China, the economic requirements of implementing a circular economy have caused concerns. This is interesting and reveals how different the approaches in the West and East are. While western approaches focus on the profitability of a circular economy as a win–win situation (essential rhetoric to attract the private sector and voters, as indicated by EMF's choice of partner in their 2012 report, namely McKinsey and Company), Chinese government will bear the brunt of financial management of the transition. Thus while parallels can be drawn between these two versions of the circular economy, and while both versions meet, both in terms of a globalized market and in terms of mutual externalities (i.e. trade between Europe and China), there are many significant differences both in terms of implementation and finance.

6.7 Debate, discussion and further thought

1. How can circular economics embrace social sustainability?
2. Given the issues raised in section 6.6, what are the challenges facing the circular economy in terms of ecological realism and public reaction?
3. Compare and contrast the application, geopolitical context and governance of eastern and western CE programmes. What does the future hold for these two approaches?

4. Is the circular economy any different from the other schools of sustainable economics, and is the eastern version so different that it should be treated differently?

5. The circular economy would appear to be unique in that it has been adopted by two completely different political systems. What barriers and strengths do each system represent in terms of a fully implemented sustainable future across environment, economics and society?

6. Compare and contrast strengths and weaknesses of the circular economy with that of the other schools encountered in Chapter 5.

7. Design an appropriate set of indicators to monitor progress of a circular economy programme in a particular country of your choice. Discuss the principles that you have employed to develop this set of indicators.

8. Write a defence or an attack on the circular economy in China.

9. Examine the following paper:

   Chen, T., Lin, R. and Lin, W. (2011) The construction of a new rice industrial chain: a case study from the view of circular economy. Journal of Resources and Ecology 2: 51-5. www.jorae.cn/fileup/PDF/20110108.pdf.

   What are the challenges of implementing a circular economy in the agriculture sector in China and in Europe?

References

Andersen, M.S. (2007). An introductory note on the environmental economics of the circular economy. Sustainability Science 2(1): 133-40.

Baily, M.N., Manyika, J.M. and Gupta, S. (2013). US productivity growth: an optimistic perspective. International Productivity Monitor, Spring 2013. pp. 3-12.

Bakker, C., Wang, F., Huismann, J. and den Hollander, M. (2014). Products that go round: exploring product life extension through design. Journal of Cleaner Production 69: 10-16.

Boulding, K.E. (1966). The economics of coming spaceship Earth. In: H. Jarret (ed.), *Environmental quality in a growing economy*. Johns Hopkins University Press, Baltimore, Maryland. pp. 3-14.

Bringezu, S. (2001). Material flow analysis—unveiling the physical basis of economies. In: Bartelmus, P. (ed.), *Unveiling Wealth*. Kluwer, Dordrecht. pp. 109-34.

BMU (2011). Röttgen: Germany aims to become world champion in resource efficiency. 12 October 2011, www.bmu.de/english/current_press_releases/pm/47870.php.

C2C Network. (2010). The Project. www.c2cn.eu/content/project (last accessed: 15 November 2014).

Chen, M. and Zhang, F. (2009). End-of-life vehicle recovery in China: consideration and innovation following the EU ELV directive. JOM 61(3): 45-52.

Cooper, T. (1997). Creating an economic infrastructure for sustainable product design. In: *Towards Sustainable Product Design, 2nd International Conference, London, July 1997.*

Cooper, T. (1999). Creating an economic infrastructure for sustainable product design. Journal of Sustainable Design 8: 7-17.

Cooper, T. (2010). Longer lasting products: alternatives to the throwaway society. Gower, Farnham, Surrey.

Daly, H.E. (1985). The circular flow of exchange value and the linear throughput of matter-energy: a case of misplaced concreteness. Review of Social Economy 43(3): 279-97.

EC (2011). Non-energy Raw Materials. http://ec.europa.eu/enterprise/policies/raw-materials/.

EC (2012). Sustainable Development: European Sustainable Consumption and Production Policies. http://ec.europa.eu/environment/eussd/escp_en.htm (last accessed: 15 November 2014)

EMF (2012). *Towards the circular economy. Executive Summary.* Ellen MacArthur Foundation, Isle of Wight.

EMF (2013). Towards the Circular Economy Vol. 2: Opportunities for the Consumer Goods Sector. www.ellenmacarthurfoundation.org/business/reports/ce2013 (last accessed: 15 November 2014).

Ehrenfeld, J.R. (2005). The roots of sustainability. MIT Sloan Management Review 46: 23-5.

EU (2012). Manifesto for a Resource-efficient Europe. http://europa.eu/rapid/press-release_MEMO-12-989_en.htm (last accessed: 15 November 2014).

Eurostat (2001). *Economy-wide Material Flow Accounts and Derived Indicators. A Methodological Guide.* Statistical Office of the European Union, Luxembourg.

Farigone, J., Hill, J., Tilman, D., Polasky, S.and Hawthorne, P. (2008). Land clearing and the biofuel carbon debt. Science 319: 1235-8.

Feng, Z. (2004). *An Introduction to the Circular Economy.* People's Press, Beijing.

Feng, Z.J. and Yan, N.L. (2007). Putting a circular economy into practice in China. Sustainability Science 2(1): 95-101.

Fischer-Kowalski, M. (2003). On the history of industrial metabolism. In: Bourg, D. and Erkman, S. (eds.), *Perspectives on Industrial Ecology.* Greenleaf Publishing, Sheffield. pp. 35-45.

Fitzherbert, E.B., Struebig, M.J., Morel, A., Danielsen, F., Brűhl, C.A., Donald, P.F. and Phalan, B. (2008). How will oil palm expansion affect biodiversity? Trends in Ecology and Evolution 23: 538-45.

Gale, D. (1989). *The Theory of Linear Economic Models.* University of Chicago Press, Chicago, IL.

Gardner, G. (2007). *Shrinking Fields, Cropland Loss in a World of Eight Billion.* Worldwatch Institute: Washington, DC.

Geng, Y., Fu, J., Sarkis, J. and Xue, B. (2012). Towards a national circular economy indicator system in China: an evaluation and critical analysis. Journal of Cleaner Production 23(1): 216-24.

Graczyk, M., Burchart-Korol, D. and Witkowski, K. (2013). Reverse logistics processes in steel supply chains. 21st International Conference on Metallurgy and Materials (METAL).

Greyson, J. (2007). An economic instrument for zero waste, economic growth and sustainability. Journal of Cleaner Production 15: 1382-90.

Gunderson, L. and Holling, C.S. (2002). *Panarchy: Understanding transformations in Human and Natural Systems.* Island Press, Washington DC.

Hill, J.E. (2015). The circular economy: from waste to resource stewardship, part I. Waste and Resource Management 168 (1): 4-14.

Hislop, H. and Hill, J. (2011). *Reinventing the Wheel: A Circular Economy for Resource Security.* Green Alliance, www.green-alliance.org.uk/grea_p.aspx?id=6044.

Hu, J., Xiao, Z., Zhou, R., Deng, W., Wang, M. and Ma, S. (2011). Ecological utilization of leather tannery waste with circular economy model. Journal of Cleaner Production 19: 221-8.

Hunten, D.M. (1973). The escape of light gases from planetary atmospheres. Journal of Atmospheric Sciences 30: 1481-94.

Jaffe, D A. (1992). The nitrogen cycle. In: Butcher, S.S., Charlson, R.J., Orians, R.J. and Wolfe, G.V. (eds.), *Global Biogeochemical Cycles.* Academic Press, San Diego, CA. pp. 263-84.

Jahnke, R A. (1992). The phosphorus cycle. In: Butcher, S.S., Charlson, R.J., Orians, R.J. and Wolfe, G.V. (eds.), *Global Biogeochemical Cycles.* Academic Press, San Diego, CA. pp. 301-15.

Jones, P.T., Van Gerven, T., Van Acker, K., Geysen, D., Binnemans, K., Fransaer, J., Blanpain, B., Mishra, B. and Apelian, D. (2011). CR3: cornerstone to the sustainable inorganic materials management (SIM2) research program at K.U. Leuven. Journal of Metals 63 (12): 14-15.

Keeling, R.F., Najjar, R.P., Bender, M.L. and Tans, P.P. (1993). What atmospheric oxygen measurements can tell us about the global carbon cycle. Global Biogeochemical Cycles 7: 37-67.

Kim, S-J. (2009). *Korean Strategy for Green Growth and IT.* Information Technology and Innovation Foundation, Washington, DC.

Lancaster, M. (2002). Principles of sustainable and Green Chemistry. In: Clark, J. and Macquarrie, D. (eds.), *Handbook of Green Chemistry and Technology.* Blackwell Science, Oxford. pp. 10-27.

Leeuw, S.E. van der. (2011). VI. Long-term study of complex society–environmental interactions. In: An Emerging Research Program for Global Systems Science: Assessing the state of the Art. At: http://gsdp.eu/fileadmin/images/about/GSDP_1st-year-deliverables.pdf#page=56 (last accessed: 15 November 2014).

Li, R.H. and Su, C.H. (2012). Evaluation of the circular economy development level of Chinese chemical enterprises. Procedia Environmental Sciences 13: 1595-601.

Liu, Q., Li, H.M., Zuo, X.L., Zhang, F.F. and Wang, L. (2009). A survey and analysis on public awareness and performance for promoting circular economy in China: A case study from Tianjin. Journal of Cleaner Production 17(2): 265-70.

Liu, J.Y.S. (2012). Circular economy and environmental efficiency: the case of traditional Hakka living system. Procedia-Social and Behavioral Sciences 57: 255-60.

Luhmann, N. (1992). *Ecological Communication.* Polity Press, London.

Mason, M. (2011). The sustainability challenge. In: Brady, J., Ebbage, A. and Lunn, R. (eds.), *Environmental Management in Organizations,* 2nd edition. Earthscan, London. pp. 525-32.

Mathews, J.A. (2012). Green growth strategies: Korean and Chinese initiatives. Carbon Management 3(4): 353-6.

Mathews, J.A. and Tan, H. (2011). Progress towards a circular economy in China: the drivers (and inhibitors) of eco-industrial initiative. Journal of Industrial Ecology 15: 435-57.

McDonough, W. and Braungart, M. (2002). Design for the triple top line: new tools for sustainable commerce. Corporate Environmental Strategy 9(3): 251-8.

Meadows, D. and Randers, J. (1992). *Beyond the Limits: Confronting Global Collapse, Envisioning a Sustainable Future.* Chelsea Green Publishing Company: Boulder, CO, USA.

Moll, S., Bringezu, S. and Schütz, H. (2005). *Resource use in European countries: an estimate of materials and waste streams in the community, including imports and exports using the instrument of material flow analysis* (No. 1). Wuppertal Report, Wuppertal Institut für Klima, Umwelt, Energie.

Moriguchi, Y. (2007). Material flow indicators to measure progress toward a sound material-cycle society. Journal of Material Cycles and Waste Management 9(2): 112-20.

Murray, A., Skene, K.R. and Haynes, K. (2015). The circular economy: an interdisciplinary exploration of the concept and its application in a global context. Journal of Business Ethics *In Press.*

Murray, J.W. (1992). The oceans. In: Butcher, S.S., Charlson, R.J., Orians, R.J. and Wolfe, G.V. (eds.), *Global Biogeochemical Cycles*. Academic Press, San Diego, CA. pp. 176-211.

Nakajima, N. (2000). A vision of industrial ecology: state-of-the-art practices for a circular and service-based economy. Bulletin of Science Technology Society 20: 154-69.

Niederberger, A.A., Shiroff, S. and Raahauge, L. (2013). Implications of carbon markets for implementing circular economy models. European Journal of Business and Management 5(3): 187-99.

Park, J., Sarkis, J., Wu, Z.H. (2010). Creating integrated business and environmental value within the context of China's circular economy and ecological modernization. Journal of Cleaner Production 18: 1494-501.

Parkins, E. (1930). The geography of American geographers. The Journal of Geography 33: 229.

Pearce, D.W. and Turner, R.K. (1990). *Economics of Natural Resources and the Environment.* Harvester Wheatsheaf, Hemel Hempstead.

Pigou, A.C. (1920). *The Economics of Welfare*. Macmillan, New York.

Pimentel, D. (1998). Energy and dollar costs of ethanol production with corn. Hubbert Center Newsletter #98-2; M. King Hubbert Center for Petroleum Supply Studies: Golden, CO. pp. 1-7.

Pitt, J. (2011). Beyond Sustainability? Designing for a circular economy. 10th Hatter Technology Seminar Teaching Design through Technology: www.ort.org/uploads/media/10th_Hatter_booklet.pdf (last accessed: 15 November 2014).

Potocnik, J. (2013). Interview: EU eyes circular economy, global partnership. http://news.xinhuanet.com/english/indepth/2013-10/25/c_132828284.htm (last accessed: 15 November 2014).

Prendeville, S., Sanders, C., Sherry, J. and Costa, F. (2014). Circular Economy: is it enough? Ecodesign Centre, CMU, Cardiff.

Preston, F. (2012). *A Global Redesign? Shaping the Circular Economy. Energy, Environment and Resource Governance.* Chatham House, London.

Prigogine, I. (1980). *From Being to Becoming*. Freeman, San Francisco.

Quesnay, F. (1972). *Tableau Économique, 1758–59 Editions*. MacMillan, London

Rammelt, C.F. and Crisp, P. (2014). A systems and thermodynamics perspective on technology in the circular economy. Real-world Economics Review 68: 25-40.

Robert, F. (2001). The origin of water on Earth. Science 293 (5532): 1056-8.

Robèrt, K.-H. (1991). The physician and the environment. Reviews in Oncology: European Organisation for Research and Treatment of Cancer 4 (2): 1-3.

Røpke, I. (2004). The early history of modern ecological economics. Ecological Economics 50: 293-314.

Røpke, I. (2005). Trends in the development of ecological economics from the late 1980s to the early 2000s. Ecological Economics 55: 262-90.

Rostow, W.W. (1960). *The Stages of Growth: a Non-Communist Manifesto.* Cambridge University Press, Cambridge.

Schlesinger, W.H. (1993). *Biogeochemistry: an Analysis of Global Change.* Academic Press, San Diego, CA.

Sevigné-Itoiz, E., Gasol, C.M., Rieradevall, J. and Gabarrell, X. (2014). Environmental consequences of recycling aluminium old scrap in a global market. Resource, Conservation and Recycling 89: 94-103.

Shen, X. and Qi, C. (2012). Countermeasures towards circular economy development in west regions. Energy Procedia 16: 927-32.

Sherwin, C. (2013). Sustainable design 2.0: new models and methods. www.guardian.co.uk/sustainable-business/blog/sustainable-design-modelsmethods-biomimicry-cradle (last accessed: 15 November 2014).

Siegenthaler, U. and Sarmiento, J.L. (1993). Atmospheric carbon dioxide and the ocean. Nature 365: 119-25.
Skene, K.R. (2013). The energetics of ecological succession: A logistic model of entropic output. Ecological Modelling 250: 287-93.
Song, Z., Zhang, C., Yang, G., Feng, Y., Ren, G. and Han, X. (2014). Comparison of biogas development from households and medium and large-scale biogas plants in rural China. Sustainable Energy Reviews 33: 204-13.
Stahel, W.R. and Reday-Mulvey, G. (1981). *Jobs for Tomorrow, the potential for substituting manpower for energy.* Vantage Press, New York.
Stahel, W.R. (2012). *The business angel of a circular economy: higher competitiveness, higher resource security and material efficiency.* 15 May 2012. Geneva: The Product-Life Institute.
Talbot, F.A. (1920). *Millions from Waste.* J.B. Lippincott Company, Philadelphia.
Tan, Z. (2008). Circular economy and renewable resource industry in China. CESC Contribution for the 4th EU–China Round Table on Recycling Industries.
The Parliament (2012). Europe must operate a "circular economy" to improve resource efficiency. www.theparliament.com/policyfocus/energy/energy-article/newsarticle/europe-must-operate-a-circular-economy-toimprove-resource-efficiency/#.UPqJ3fKa-4Z (last accessed: 15 November 2014)
Triebswetter, U. and Hitchens, D. (2005). The impact of environmental regulation on competitiveness in the German manufacturing industry: A comparison with other countries of the European Union. Journal of Cleaner Production 13(7): 733-45.
Tukker A. (2013). Product services for a resource-efficient and circular economy—a review. Journal of Cleaner Production 30: 1-16.
UN (2011). UN Data Country Profile: China. http://data.un.org/CountryProfile.aspx?crName=CHINA (last accessed: 15 November 2014).
UNEP (2006). *Circular Economy: an Alternative for Economic Development.* UNEP, DTIE.
UNEP (2010). Overview of the Republic of Korea's National Strategy for Green Growth. UNEP DTIE Economics and Trade Branch, Geneva, Switzerland.
Van de Wiel, H. (2011). The Netherlands as materials roundabout. Waste Forum special edition, January 2011. www.wastematters.eu/uploads/media/The_Netherlands_as_materials_roundabout.pdf (last accessed: 15 November 2014).
Werbach, A. (2009). *Strategy for sustainability: A business manifesto.* Harvard Business Press, Boston, MA.
Willbold, M., Elliott, T. and Moorbath, S. (2011). The tungsten isotopic composition of the Earth's mantle before the terminal bombardment. Nature 477: 195-8.
WRAP (2014). WRAP's vision for the UK circular Economy to 2020. www.wrap.org.uk/content/wraps-vision-uk-circular-economy-2020 (last accessed: 15 November 2014).
Wu, J.S. (2005). *New Circular Economy.* Beijing: Tsinghua University Press, Beijing.
Wu, H.Q., Shi, Y., Xia, Q. and Zhu, W.D. (2014). Effectiveness of the policy of circular economy in China: A DEA-based analysis for the period of 11th five-year-plan. Resources, Conservation and Recycling 83: 163-75.
Xue, B., Chen, X.P., Geng, Y., Guo, X.J., Lu, C.P., Zhang, Z.L. and Lu, C.Y. (2010). Survey of officials' awareness on circular economy development in China: based on municipal and county level. Resources, Conservation and Recycling 54(12): 1296-302.
Yang. S. and Feng, N. (2008). A case study of industrial symbiosis: Nanning Sugar Co., Ltd. in China. Resources, Conservation and Recycling 52(5): 813-20.
Yuan, Z., Bi, J. and Moriguichi, Y. (2006). The circular economy: A new development strategy in China. Journal of Industrial Ecology 10: 4-8.

Zhang, H., Feng, J., Zhu, W., Liu, C., Xu, S., Shao, P., Wu, D., Yang, W. and Gu, J. (2000). Chronic toxicity of rare-earth elements on human beings. Biological Trace Element Research 73(1): 1-17.

Zhao, Y., Zang, L., Li, Z. and Qin, J. (2012). Discussion on the model of mining circular economy. Energy Procedia 16: 438-43.

Zhou, K., Bonet Fernandez, D., Wan, C., Denis, A. and Juillard, G.M. (2014). *A Study on Circular Economy Implementation in China.* Working papers 2014-312, Department of Research, Ipag Business School, Nice, France

Zhu, D. (1998). Sustainable development appeals for cycle economy. Science and Technology Review 9: 39-43.

7
Design to redesign

The relationship between product design and sustainability lies at the foundation of the circular economy, as it does for most schools of sustainability. Workplace design and organizational design also play important, though less vaunted roles in any sustainable approach, and we explore the latest thinking in these areas. However, design has been included in what are called wicked problems, i.e. difficult to solve due to inadequate information and complex interdependences. In this chapter we trace the history of this relationship and explore what the future hold for design towards sustainability.

Learning aims and objectives

- Summarize the history of design, highlighting the key stages and the degree of interaction with the environment at each stage
- List the seven levels of design
- Define conceptual, cognitive and detailed design
- List some difficulties of sustainable design

Learning outcomes and experiences

- Discuss the key events in sustainable design since 1960
- Discuss the challenges posed at each of the seven levels of design

- Discuss the interactions between the seven levels of design
- What are the challenges of sustainable design?

7.1 Introduction

From our earliest times, humans have solved problems, as many other organisms do. However, the manipulation of our environment has increased rapidly over our history, and central to this has been the process of **design**. Papenek (1985; p. 4) defined design as "the conscious and intuitive effort to impose meaningful order". Steffen (2006; p. 86) states that "Design is also about the way things are used; how they are committed to the world, and the way they are produced".

While design has delivered solutions to humans, the implications of design products on the rest of the planet have often been problematic:

> Everything was fine in the ancient past. Nature produced no embarrassing shapes and colours, humans were busy struggling for survival and had no time to decorate their first wedges with scrolls. Everything was fine, because in the ancient past there were no designers (Schmidt and Donnert, 2009 as translated in Spangenberg *et al.*, 2010; p. 1485).

Papanek has observed that (1985; p. ix) "There are professions more harmful than industrial design, but only a very few of them ... Today, industrial design has put mass murder on a mass production basis". Julie Hill (2011), in her challenging and stimulating book, *The Secret Life of Stuff*, points to the failure to design, manufacture and utilize products within the planetary boundaries as being underpinned by a lack of knowledge relating to how such products are created in the first place.Whiteley (1993) argues that designers have a moral and ethical obligation to be responsible for their designs, and the social and environmental impacts of their work.

Datschefski (2001; p. 17) reports that:

> most environmental problems are caused by unintentional side effects of the manufacture, use, and disposal of products. For example, according to one source, over 30 tonnes of waste are produced for every one tonne of product that reaches the consumer and then 98 percent of those products are thrown away within 6 months.

Yet the story of design is the story of our relationship with the environment in many ways. In the next section we trace the relationship between design and sustainability across the short history of the human race.

7.2 A brief history of design and sustainability

No clearer example of changes in design can be found than on the now deserted St Kilda archipelago, far off the north-west shores of Scotland. This World Heritage Site (unusually listed under both natural and cultural criteria) is the remnant of an extinct volcano, rising, some 60 million years old, from the surrounding 3 billion years old Lewisian gneiss.

Home to the largest northern gannet population in the world, 300,000 puffins, 90% of Europe's Leach's petrels, 40,000 guillemot, 10,000 kittiwake and one of the largest populations of the northern fulmar, it is truly an ornithologist's paradise. The Soay sheep point to a more relevant life form: humans. Soay sheep represent the last link to the original Neolithic sheep, and some of the earliest experiments in animal breeding by humans. The Soay sheep are thought to have been on the islands for some 4,000 years. These sheep moult rather than needing shearing, and wool is gathered by plucking.

Since the sheep didn't swim to St Kilda, humans must have occupied these islands for at least 4,000 years. The men were notably different from mainland men in one interesting way. St Kilda men did not have facial hair growth until the age of 30 years. This all changed in 1726, when a male St Kildan died of smallpox on the isle of Harris. His clothes were of good quality and were returned to his family. The result was a smallpox epidemic that killed almost all of the ancient people. The island was repopulated from the mainland with "bearded" males.

It was to be another mainland import that would serve as a lesson in the history of design. Prior to the 1860s, St Kilda existed in glorious solitude. In 1838 Lachlan MacLean wrote "Where is the land which has neither arms, money, care, physic, politics, nor taxes? That land is St Kilda" (MacLean, 1838, p. 1). The people survived on birds and their eggs and plumage, sheep and fish. They paid their rent, under a feudal communalism system, to the Macleods of Skye, in wool, feathers and fish. The local parliament consisted of all of the males on the island and met every morning.

Their houses, blackhouses or *taigh-geal*, were double-walled dry-stone structures with the cavity packed with earth, with turf roofs covered in cereal straw. These structures were well insulated against the atrocious winter weather, and heated by turf fires. The St Kildans were self-sufficient. As early as 1698, Martin observed: "The inhabitants of St Kilda are much happier than the generality of mankind, being almost the only people in the world who feel the sweetness of true liberty" (Martin, 1698).

In the 1860s all of this would change. Corrugated iron was introduced onto the island as a new roofing material. Much lighter and easier to assemble, the material became very popular. The only problem was that it meant less insulation. Soon coal had to be imported in order to heat the new house designs sufficiently, as peat didn't release sufficient heat. Coal imports required money, and so capitalism finally reached this outlier of the British Isles, requiring an intensification of exploitation, and the spiral of increasing imports.

Thus a change in design led to a radical transformation of life on St Kilda. This is a lesson on several levels. First, early humans designed within their environmental context, and lived sustainably as a result. Although the Earth was relatively underpopulated and full of resources, man's ability to exploit these resources was limited and nature constrained our activities and design approach. As humans overcame the barriers imposed by nature, their design activities were freed to create an easier life (for surely, laziness is the mother of invention today, not necessity?), while exhausting natural capital and spiralling ever more quickly towards ecological crisis.

Mass production of designs soon was needed to satiate consumer demand with production lines developing. The Ford Motor Company was one of the earlier leaders in this scale transformation. The market was huge, and resources were increasingly liberated from nature's grasp thanks to a great increase in energy availability from the subterranean forests. Energy was needed to realize the designs, as complexity requires energy flux, and the generation of waste. Thus waste production increased dramatically, not just in terms of production waste and end-of-use waste, but also energy waste from energy sources (sulphur, carbon dioxide, mercury and nitrogen oxides, in addition to particulate pollution).

By the 1960s, a more sinister design approach had emerged as consumer markets became saturated, entitled **designed to fail** or **planned obsolescence**. The mantra was all about the need to replace outdated objects with new, improved versions. Designers played a central role in this process. This approach greatly increased end-of-use waste, while maintaining production and energy waste. Interestingly, this trend led to a response from several schools of sustainability, which today advocate increasing the life-span of products. As many reactionary concepts prove to be, this approach could well prove to be erroneous, as we have seen in Chapter 6. Longevity certainly has no basis in natural ecosystem function, where fast turnover is key.

Another sinister design approach is lock-in design where consumers are deliberately forced to buy further hardware, software and service products from the manufacturer. Many computer firms follow this practice. Agricultural companies producing herbicide-resistant genetically engineered crops design them so that you must also buy the herbicide from them. Such locking-in means that the consumer loses much freedom of choice.

Thus if a company makes a product that is environmentally friendly, the consumer may then be forced to buy further products associated with the original purchase that are not necessarily as sustainable as competing models, but with no choice now available, the consumer cannot select. Of course, lock-ins also greatly inhibit new less damaging companies from entering the market, unless they can provide the entire package of associated equipment, an unlikely scenario for a new small enterprise. As ratio of labour costs to material costs increased, it also became less attractive to repair products.

Another change that emerged in the 20th century is that designers began to focus on luxury detail rather than basic function in the mass consumer market. Mainwaring (2001) suggests that more positional goods will have a greater negative impact on the environmental than less positional goods, as status is most frequently demonstrated by exhibiting material goods. While ownership has always signified wealth, as reflected in the extraordinary archaeological record of human artefacts, style and detail has become the norm for everyone. Whiteley (1993; p. 18) cites designer Terence Conran: "There was a strange moment around the mid-1960s when people stopped needing and need changed to want. Designers became more important in producing 'want' products rather than 'need' products, because you have to create desire".

Cooper (1999) points to the 1980s as an age of conspicuous consumption, where status was celebrated by wealth. He observed that designers became sucked into materialism. This materialism can be traced back to the onset of the Agrarian Age, with many artefacts not at all related to function, but rather communicators of power. However, until recently, this was the arena of the powerful.

While Whiteley described the 1980s as holding to a view of design as "the yuppy fun of a moneyed minority" (Whiteley, 1993, p. 1), the reality was that a mass produced image of these designs began to pour into the high streets, with huge environmental damage following in its wake. Design had previously brought exclusivity, but now brought the semblance of exclusivity by association.

While sustainability began to impact on economics, design was slow to respond. There have been numerous phases in environmental design. **Green design** emerged in the 1970s, focused on what materials were used in the production of products. The first Green Consumer Guide was published in 1988, revealing the real costs of a range of products. Green consumerism still represented a form of materialism, and allowed companies to "play green" with marketing tricks giving cursory recognition of a green market rather than incorporating an environmentally friendly practice.

Ecodesign emerged around this time, where the focus was on the entire product life-cycle, not just manufacturing. Ecodesign is an approach dealing mainly with environmental and economic effects (and thus with eco-efficiency), based on a life-cycle analysis (LCA) and life-cycle costing (Romli *et al.*, 2014). Criticisms of ecodesign include:

- Underlying production systems are inherently unsustainable, thereby any changes to the design of products will have minimal effect, or in some cases negative consequences.
- Product usage and user behaviour may have significantly negative side- or so-called "rebound" effects (be they social or environmental) outside the product's manufacture, direct use and disposal.
- Ecodesign does not question whether or not a product makes a meaningful and responsible contribution to the system as a whole, resulting in products that may be produced using "eco-friendly" attributes (such as materials, etc.), but ultimately provide limited societal and environmental benefit.

Design for environment (DfE) aims to achieve the human satisfaction the consumption process is motivated by while minimizing the negative and maximizing the positive impacts on nature, humans and society. A major challenge for DfE is to design low-impact positional goods, i.e. to make consumption efficiency a positional value. In both green and ecodesign, solutions tended to focus on eco- and techno-centric approaches, missing out on socio-centric approaches (Humphries-Smith, 2010). Of the three Rs, emphasis also tended to focus on recycling, rather than reduction and re-use.

Design for sustainability (D4S) differs from ecodesign in that it has evolved to include both the social and economic elements of production, embracing how to meet consumer needs in a more holistic, sustainable way (Crul and Diehl, 2006). However, it still focuses on the product, rather than incorporating a system approach needed for real impact on social and environmental sustainability. The key D4S approaches are: redesign, benchmarking (incremental design), new product design and radical design.

The goal of D4S **redesign** is to sustainably redesign an existing product for which the specific market and manufacturing conditions are already known. This may involve adapting a product for a different cultural or technological context. Thus redesign is important in "developing" nations. **Benchmarking** compares similar products, taking the best sustainable elements of each and recombining these strongest elements to improve any single product. Because the initial products are similar, incorporating new elements into any one of them will likely be relatively easy, not requiring complete redesign. Thus benchmarking differs from D4S redesign in that it starts with existing products in the market before moving into the design phase. **Radical design** requires a clean sheet, beginning with conceptual design and a freedom not necessarily available to all designers (Clark *et al.*, 2009).

Deep redesign is concerned with finding creative and sustainable ways to integrate nature's wisdom into the design and management of all industrial operations (Hill, 2005), but this position could be argued in the opposite direction (i.e integrating technology into a natural context), which would be more properly related to deep ecology (i.e. **bioparticipation** rather than biomimicry).

Deep redesign initiatives aim to use ecological insights to create self-maintaining and self-regulating optimally productive healthy systems. Fourteen significant differences in how humans behave compared to ecosystems can be identified:

1. Humans wait for crises while ecosystems are responsive to early indicators
2. Humans use linear material flows while ecosystems utilize cyclical, regenerative relationships
3. Humans see lengthened product life-cycles as sustainable, whereas ecosystem utilize fast cycling
4. Humans have limited financial capital while ecosystems have huge energetic capital
5. Humans operate in a closed energy system while ecosystems operate in an open, cosmic energetic system
6. Humans pursue reduced internal entropy as a driver while ecosystems have increased external entropy as a driver

7. Humans pursue unlimited growth (unsustainable) while ecosystem growth is subject to limiting factors (S_{max}—see Chapter 4)
8. Production is overemphasized in human economics while most resources are used for maintenance in mature ecosystems
9. Humans are reliant on fossil fuels and nuclear power, while ecosystems are based on solar and renewable energy
10. Competition is emphasized in human systems while mutualism and interconnectivity is favoured in ecosystems
11. Humans operate within simplified, highly controlled systems (dependent and unstable) while ecosystems have functional diversity and complexity, which confer stability
12. Humans tend to have few specialists and roles whereas in ecosystems, a rich diversity of specialists, generalists, roles and niches are found
13. Humans universalize structures and processes (everything the same, everywhere, all the time) whereas with ecosystems, there is a uniqueness of time and place (reflected in all structures and processes)
14. For humans, we encounter rapid, forced change with few beneficiaries and many "casualties" while for ecosystem gradual co-evolutionary structural change is the norm, with occasional bursts of creativity

Sustainable product design (SPD) became an important approach in the 1990s. This is the process which creates product designs that are sustainable in terms of the environment and resource use while considering the need for the product. SPD embraces:

- Resource use efficiency
- Product quality
- Production organization and efficiency
- Local culture and capacity
- Market
- End of life

This represented a shift beyond design for environment or ecodesign, where the focus is on product attributes, to SPD, which requires a broader approach. In SPD the relationship between the product, suppliers, stakeholders, and external economic and social factors are taken into account, enabling more radical option to be considered (Cooper, 1999).

Sustainable design emerged next, embracing ethical and societal issues and working at the system level, rather than with individual products. Here, local and global impacts on both society and the environment were important. Madge (1997; p. 52) claims that sustainable design is "a broader, long-term vision of eco-design". Diegel *et al.* (2010; p. 68) define sustainable design as:

> design which aims to achieve triple-bottom line ideals by striving to produce products that minimize their detriment to the environment while, at the same time, achieving acceptable economic benefits to the company and, wherever possible, having a positive impact on society.

Dewberry and Goggin (1994; p. 49), discussing the transition from ecodesign to sustainable design, observed: "The concept of sustainable design, however, is much more complex [than ecodesign] and moves the interface of design outwards toward societal conditions, development and ethics ... and involves a general shift from physiological to psychological needs".

This shift towards psychology led to the development of a number of new approaches. **Emotionally durable design** focused on reduction of resource via increasing consumer–product bonds, leading to longer ownership (Chapman, 2005). **Persuasive technology** again targets motivation of consumer through design (Lockton *et al.*, 2008) while **slow consumption**, like emotionally durable design, aims to build linkages between product and consumer, again contributing to longevity (Cooper, 2005). **Design for behaviour** considers how user behaviour can be influenced through product and service features designed to curb unsustainable practices (Campbell, 2009).

In reviewing literature relating to behaviour change through design, Lilley, Lofthouse and Bhamra (2005, p. 7) identify three primary methodologies:

1. **Scripts and behaviour steering**: products or systems that contain "scripts" or prescriptions for use to encode the designer's use intention

2. **Eco-feedback**: feedback that informs users of their impact in an attempt to persuade them to modify their behaviour

3. **"Intelligent" products and systems**: those that circumvent rebound effects by ceding decision-making to an "intelligent" product which mitigates controls or blocks inappropriate user behaviour

In late 1991, The **Design Principles of Environmental Stewardship** were generated through the efforts of several member organizations of the American Design Council, a coalition of 12 major US design organizations (including the Design Management Institute), based on the CERES Principles from 1989, created by the Coalition of Environmentally Responsible Economies (www.ceres.org):

- The protection of the biosphere
- Sustainable use of natural resources
- Reduction and disposal of wastes
- Energy conservation
- Risk reduction
- Safe products and services
- Environmental restoration
- Informing the public
- Management commitment
- Audits and reports

There was a growing movement to transform the throwaway economy to a service economy, and design had a significant seat at the table.

A more recent design school is that of **co-design** or **co-creation** (Faud-Luke, 2007). Sanders and Simons (2009, p. 1) define these concepts;

> co-creation as any act of collective creativity that is experienced jointly by two or more people. How is co-creation different from collaboration? It is a special case of collaboration where the intent is to create something that is not known in advance. The concept of co-design is directly related to co-creation. By co-design we refer to collective creativity as it is applied across the whole span of a design process.

By involving consumers in the design phase, this is likely to tie them in emotionally, mentally and physically to the product, creating a sense of ownership of the design. This in turn is likely to encourage the adoption and advocacy of the design outcome within the end-user group.

Design is now viewed as a key aspect of business success, not merely a servant. This broadened conception of design is referred to using a variety of labels including **design thinking**, **service design**, **experience design**, **user- or human-centred design**, **integrative thinking**, **transformative design** and **social innovation**.

Young (2010) defines design thinking as possessing the following characteristics:

- **Human-centred**: places people at the centre of the design process, rather than tackling design challenges from internal/organizational or technical frames
- **Research-based**: qualitative, ethnographic and observational research techniques applied in the aid of responding to design challenges
- **Broader contextual view**: expanding the design "question" to a wider frame of reference, to examine the system and context in which design challenges exist
- **Collaborative and multidisciplinary**: exploratory, and at times playful, approaches to problem-solving, including co-design methods specifically designed to encourage participation from a broad array of stakeholders and multidisciplinary design teams
- Iterative delivery and prototyping: use of iterative project management approaches and prototyping, incorporating rapid feedback loops from end-users, to evaluate and evolve ideas and prospective designs

The *Design with Intent Toolkit* (Lockton, 2010) identifies seven lenses that design can incorporate:

1. **Architectural lens**: use of environmental design to steer behaviour in transport, urban planning and crime prevention
2. **Error-proofing lens**: treats deviations as errors, which are either discouraged or prevented by design
3. **Interaction lens**: users interactions with product impact on behaviour
4. **Ludic lens**: uses common game elements such as collections, cores and levels to encourage suitable behaviour

5. **Cognitive lens**: use of cognitive psychology and behavioural economics to understand decision-making

6. **Machiavellian lens**: end justifies the means approach, with planned obsolescence, pricing, etc.

7. **Security lens**: countermeasures to protect environment at product/system/environment level

Certainly significant environmental policies such as the Kyoto agreement now incorporate design as a significant player. The Kyoto report highlights six themes seen as problem areas suitable for design activity: quality of life, efficient use of natural resources, protecting the global commons, managing human settlements, the use of chemicals and the management of human and industrial waste, and fostering sustainable economic growth on a global scale (Margolin, 1998).

In concluding this section, we have observed that the history of design and sustainability is one of a relationship formerly close, and then lost, but finally being rediscovered, albeit in a very different context, where economic growth is still the dominant ethos, a century after it was a resource-relevant approach. The Earth is now full of people and resources are scarce. Yet this resembles early times, when although there were few humans, their ability to access resources was also very limited. Design has moved through three stages:

1. **Form-based** (aesthetic): colour, shape, texture, smell, etc. This phase was consumed with want rather than need, and with desire rather than purpose. Natural forms are mimicked, as in biomimicry.

2. **Function-based**: biochemistry, levers, physiology, etc. This phase has moved away from form as the dominant area, embracing function at both the unit and system level. Ecosystem function is now recognized, with products designed to limit their life-cycle impact on the functioning of the biosphere. Natural function is explored.

3. **Fusion-based**: here, designs that fit into nature, in terms of temporal and spatial context are emphasized, leaving reduced ecological footprints, and energizing environmental progression appropriately. Design occurs within the context of nature, rather than inspired by it. This is a phase of bioparticipation rather than biomimicry. Fusion design should not only function within

acceptable environmental boundaries, but also draw society towards integration with the environment.

7.3 Design as a driver of economic growth

While we have focused on the impact of design on the environment and society, it is worth briefly highlighting some thinking related to the putative impact of design on economics. Austrian economist Joseph Schumpeter claimed that economic growth is not merely accompanied by new technology and the expansion of such innovation, but it primarily depends on technological innovation (Schumpter, 1939). More recent work has been undertaken by Freeman and others at the University of Sussex, exploring the relationship between technological innovation and cyclical trends in the economy known as "long waves" (Freeman, 1984, 1992). The impact of a new sustainable design phase has the capacity to herald economic growth in line with historical trends.

7.4 Designing what? The seven levels of design

Design has traditionally been associated with specific products and early environmental design approaches were focused on the manufacture (green design) and end of life (ecodesign). Yet as Figure 7.1 indicates, design impacts on many different processes related to the product. This section explores the design challenges and opportunities in each of these areas.

7.4.1 Product design

What is a sustainable product? What parameters do we use to measure this? Can sustainable products deliver a sustainable future? What of the context of these products, both spatially and temporally? Is the product form-based, function-based or fusion based? These and many other questions face the designer of a particular object.

Product architecture has a profound impact on the entire product lifecycle (Fixson, 2005). Product architecture has been identified as the crucial factor that links product design and supply chain activities for environmental decision-making (Kwak *et al.*, 2009; Chu *et al.*, 2009). Product design

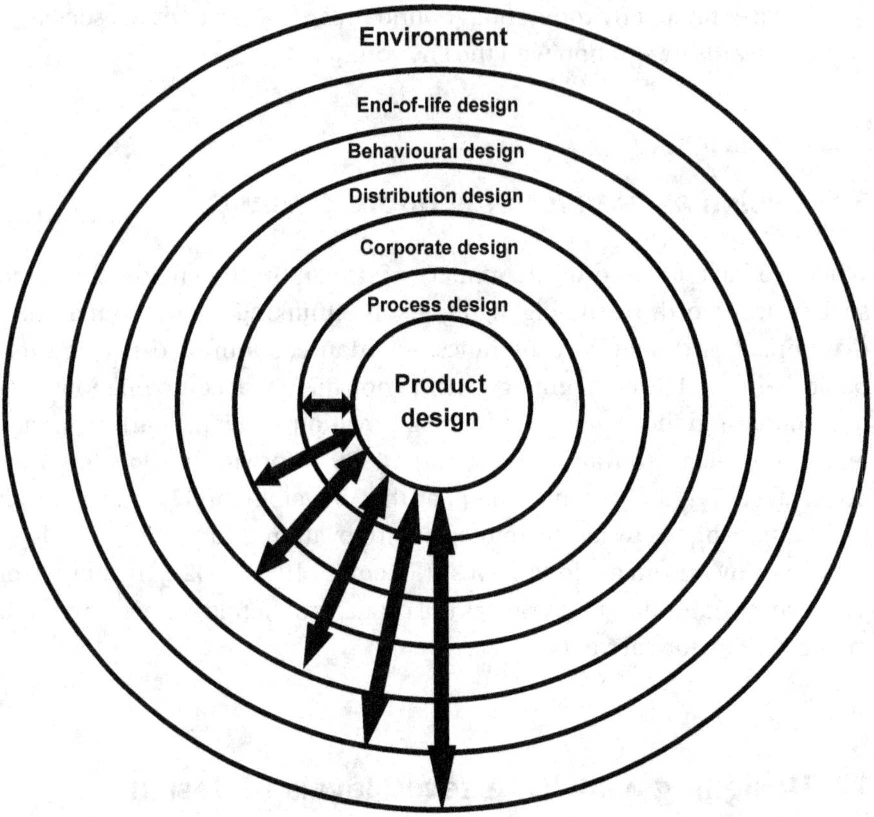

FIGURE 7.1 The inner circle of product design. Designers face huge challenges meeting sustainability targets at each level of design, all of which impact on the environment. The product is only a part of the overall design challenge. Each level has repercussions on all of the other levels.

also is the focus of most legislation, both in terms of manufacturing and recycling. Thus there are considerable constraints. Meanwhile, companies rely on product design for market share and profitability. It is the sale of the product and the cost of production that ultimately determine the success of the particular business enterprise. Thus while design has significant implications for all of the processes detailed in this section, pressure from industry is focused on product design.

7.4.2 Process design

Almost all products consumed by people are outputs of the product development process. Production system design is hugely important as it is not just what you do, but the way that you do it. The machinery used in product manufacture, from mining raw resources, preparing these resources for manufacturing, product assembly, product distribution and sales and product recycling all require specific design, with environmental consequences. While product design dictates much of this cost, there are usually different ways of approaching the same manufacturing task, some with less environmental impact than others.

The 6R approach (i.e. the traditional reduction, re-use, and recycling, along with the modern recovery, redesign, and remanufacture) attempts to signpost areas for attention within the production system (Yan and Feng, 2014).

- **Reduce** refers to activities required to simplify the current design of the product in order enable post-use capabilities. This will incorporate modular assembly, universal fitting and add-on facilities.
- **Re-use** incurs the least environmental burden and economic costs of all end-of-life activities, meaning that there is little human labour expenditure.
- **Recycling** refers to reintroducing used materials or modules into the manufacturing stage through a range of methods (i.e. smelting, shredding, separating, etc.). Three core characteristics must be considered relating to service modularity in order to realize its full benefits: (1) maintaining independence between components in different modules, (2) encouraging similarity in all components in modules, and (3) maintaining interchangeability between modules. Recycling thus reduces mining of limited resources.
- **Recovery** can be facilitated by initial design, reducing the cost of the cycling of products at the end of their lives (includes transportation, disassembly and dismantling costs).
- **Redesign** involves altering the product in order to simplify future post-use processes.
- **Remanufacture** involves the subsequent manufacturing steps required to implement redesign (Jaafar *et al.*, 2007). It has been reported that the automotive industry could save an annual energy equivalent of five nuclear power plants by adopting remanufacturing pathways (Steinhilper, 1998).

Decisions during the conceptual design phase account for nearly 70% of the entire cost of a product's development, it can be inferred that the ecological footprint is significantly fixed based on these decisions. Thus the repercussions of decisions made at this stage must be adequately assessed, in order to understand the implications. Central to this are an understanding of the processes needed to deliver a particular design and the freedom available to reduce environmental impact throughout the life-cycle of the product (Gmelin and Seuring, 2014). The designer is like an Egyptian pharaoh, who should spend most of his life designing and planning for the afterlife. By the time a design is in place, the process design is hugely constrained, as are the end-of-life options. Thus process design diversification must pre-empt product design, delivering tools for the designer to use in order to shape the product in an environmentally sensitive way.

By the detailed design phase, i.e. when dimensions, tolerances, and geometrical features of a product/process are known, few options remain in terms of minimizing the environmental impact (e.g. dematerialization, production optimization, efficient transport routes, etc.). For example, a highly modular design will bias the chosen end-of-life strategy towards modular recycling (Ramanujan *et al.*, 2011).

Problems arise when we examine the design tools focused on conceptual compared to detailed design. There are over 30 ecodesign tools available to designers (Masui *et al.*, 2003) which fall into three broad categories:

1. LCA based tools. While life-cycle assessment is quantitative, it is hugely affected by uncertainties associated with conceptual design, including fundamental characteristics such as shape and component interaction (Ramani *et al.*, 2010). LCA is not really optimized towards the design process but rather, product evaluation, particularly in terms of functional and fusion design, and has little capacity to embrace social issues.

2. Checklist-based tools. By far the most user-friendly approach, utilized commonly among small companies, these tools generally consist of a number of simple questions such as "will this design be more easily broken down than a current product?" Checklists are more likely to be subjective, and struggle with trade-offs and system suboptimality issues (i.e. a design may be less good at certain things, but overall better for the environment).

3. Quality function deployment (QFD)-based tools. These generally operate as follows: customer and environmental needs are

assessed, and then these are correlated with product quality characteristics. Finally a functional analysis is carried out whereby quality and engineering characteristics are correlated. The focus is on product specification development, but issues arise relating to the reliance on the designer to carry out such correlations and analysis, without consideration for life cycle qualities (Bouchereau and Rowlands, 2000).

There is a lack of quantitative content during conceptual design, where it would be most useful.

Product design features, such as material properties, product architecture, functional performance and reliability, greatly affect what types of used product can be collected, what options there are for re-use, what recovery operations are needed to produce them, and how profitable the recovered units can be.

A significant area of research has been the development of design metrics for assessing the remanufacturing potential of product designs. In order for profitable re-use and remanufacturing, a product design should incorporate efficiency in assembly, testing, repair, cleaning, inspection, refurbishing, disassembly and replacement (Bras and Hammond, 1996).

Reducing material diversity in a product, using less toxic materials and employing biodegradable material are well-known design guidelines applicable in the design stage to help with recycling.

Clockspeed (i.e. the speed of change within an industry that influences a company's new product development activities as well as the existing product's life-cycle length) is now recognized as an important issue. Four problems emerge:

1. A short clockspeed and a product with limited modular architecture alone or in combination complicate reverse logistics. Varying clockspeeds in individual modules also increases the relative difficulty in the organization of subsequent recovery, repair, and re-use functions.

2. The higher the degree of modularity, the more opportunity there is to recover parts of the product economically, although under a certain level there does not seem to be a viable recovery alternative. In other words, as first hypothesized, modularity directly relates to the recoverability of a product.

3. For every organization, there is a company-specific optimal clockspeed at which a reverse logistics framework would operate seamlessly.
4. Clockspeed of supply chain also comes into effect—fundamental concerns relating to consistent supply.

Similar to **computer-aided design** (CAD), **computer-aided process planning** (CAPP) when combined with **computer-aided manufacturing** (CAM) is effective in optimizing processes in terms of their temporal and spatial arrangements. However, it usually offers limited help at the early stages of process planning. The availability of a range of processes may be compromised by limited equipment availability, meaning that it would be prohibitively expensive to alter the processes themselves. However, process redesign may be possible. Furthermore if processes are designed in a modular way universally, it may be possible to build greater flexibility into production methods. Rather than product focus, factory or network focus may provide a very different approach, where system-based environmental performance lies at its core. Here product and factory life-cycles can be harmonized.

Life-cycle management (LCM) considers the product life-cycle as a whole and optimizes the interaction of product design, manufacturing and life-cycle activities (Westkämper *et al.*, 2000). Supply chain management is not just the property of the buyer. It works both ways. Companies may refuse to buy from unsustainable suppliers, but suppliers can also refuse to supply unsustainable producers.

Performing a **5S evaluation** of sorting, setting, shining, standardizing, and sustaining will help to create new benchmarks for improved processes (Dulhai, 2008):

- **Sorting** means distinguishing between the necessary and the unnecessary, eliminating the unnecessary as required
- **Setting** involves the establishment of an efficient factory layout optimized in spatial and temporal terms
- **Shining** involves maintaining a clean workplace
- **Standardizing** refers to clear, constant systems of management
- **Sustaining** involves deploying sustainability criteria throughout the entire workforce

An example of sustainable process design comes from the advent of **additive manufacturing**. Additive manufacturing is the process of manufacturing a physical object through the layer-by-layer selective fusion, sintering or polymerization of a material (Diegel *et al.*, 2010). Subtractive manufacturing involves the removal of material to produce forms and generates more waste. Less waste means less cost (Wohlers, 2009). Additive manufacturing also allows mass customization, while also having the potential to increase freedom of design.

However, additive manufacturing has a number of limitations. Powder can be left inside enclosed voids, surface finish can be stepped due to layers (particularly obvious in low gradient slopes) strength and flexibility may be compromised and material and machine costs can be prohibitive. While additive manufacturing may produce freedom of design, there has been no assessment of recycling potential. Given the fusion of small amounts of different materials, it is unlikely that these products will be easily recycled.

7.4.3 Supply chains

Operations management is now central to sustainability (Kleindorfer *et al.*, 2005). About 1% of all material that originates at the top of the supply chain serving the United States remains in use six months after the sale of the products containing it (Hawken *et al.*, 1999). Thus there is huge potential for value creation relating to the supply chain. Interest in sustainable supply chains has been growing for over a decade and the topic is becoming a significant area of research and practice (see Corbett and Kleindorfer 2003; Corbett and Klassen 2006; Kannegiesser and Günther, 2014).

Kleindorfer *et al.* (2005, p. 484) report:

> The US faces a tidal wave of e-waste. Some three-quarters of all the computers, televisions, and PDAs ever sold in the US are no longer in use and await disposal. These devises all contain substantial amounts of toxic materials and are thus prohibited from most landfills. Disposal cost estimates already stand at $50 billion with no clear solution on how these costs will be covered.

Increasing concern over waste has led to the concept of **closed-loop supply chains** (CLSCs).

To design profitable CLSCs, the underlying accounting issues must be understood (for example, valuing recovered products or components) and the related marketing issues must be grasped (for example, how remanufactured products affect primary markets for those products and how to price them). One significant issue is **loop leakage**. For example in the United Kingdom, much of the recycled material is exported.

Supply chains generally cover a large geographical area and as transport costs increase due to oil prices, this becomes an environmental issue. Furthermore, since the supply chain has roots in many different countries, social issues can play a significant role, with problems relating to gender discrimination, child exploitation and low wages all coming into play. Clockspeed may also be variable and dynamic over time. Life-cycle analysis data is only available for a small number of western nations, and so the globalized resource market leads to significant blind spots in LCA. Variability in environmental legislation across regions can also be problematic. From purchasing decisions to reverse logistics, the whole supply chain will be reshaped by changes and differences in these environmental regulations (Björklund, 2012).

Network design decisions are central to supply chain sustainability. This complex area operates in a constantly changing playing field with constantly changing rules. Supply chains not only require collaboration with different companies. Each company may well be in a different country with a very different business culture. It is this heterogeneity that poses the greatest challenge to network designers.

The reconfiguration of the supply network needs to take into account the trends to globalization with lengthening pipelines and local differences in customer requirements. There is a need to balance economic advantage with local market requirements. Companies have to combine local responsiveness, global efficiency and a capability to develop and share knowledge management. Sustainability is becoming a key priority in supply chain operation and design (Chopra and Meindl, 2009).

No company is an island, and changes in a supplier's working practice and national regulations can have significant implications for the entire supply chain. Supply chain capabilities are a significant determinant of competitiveness and Christopher (2005) has argued that competition is at the level of the supply chains, not the individual companies. Supply chain network design decisions determine the physical configuration of the supply chain, including transportation-related facilities, storage, location of manufacturing and the allocation of capacity and markets to each facility (Ravet, 2012; 2013).

Lee (2010) has identified three elements that are important in a sustainable network:

1. The **inbound supply chain** relates to the raw materials or substrates that are essential for the manufacturing process, both quantitatively and qualitatively. This can have great complexity, due to the number of different interest groups involved, including consolidators, traders, commission agents, wholesalers and retailers. With greater accountability and transparency, the consumer will have access to data relating to this area. Thus the inbound supply chain impacts on company reputation and sales. Other environmental issues arise from social issues related to employees of the suppliers. Of course product design will have huge implications for the inbound supply chain. Recycling, modularity and reuse can all impact on the inbound supply chain.
2. **The manufacturing supply chain or internal supply chain** involves factory design and the 5S approach, wherein production methods and the production process are optimized to reduce environmental damage. Areas such as additive manufacturing, as opposed to subtractive manufacturing, can play a significant role here and the internal supply chain is open to technological improvement. Again, product and process design such as modularity and remanufacturing can play a significant role here.
3. Finally, the **outbound supply chain** is important, particularly with regards to product distribution, storage and sales. Achieving more sustainable production must include these post-production aspects, as environmental damage in this phase is still associated with the product and the producer. Large supercooled warehouses are extremely environmentally damaging. Huge shops demanding customers to drive long distances are also damaging, but so are courier delivery services.

Bernon (2009) stresses that firms should measure and report on four manufacturing outcomes:

1. Energy consumption
2. Water consumption
3. Greenhouse gas emissions
4. Waste generation

Opportunities for improving supply chain sustainability come by matching these categories with the supply chain driver such as transportation or facilities (Bernon, 2009).

Simchi-Levi and Fine (2010) have identified six trends that have impacted on supply chain design: globalization, increase in logistics costs, increase in risk, increase in labour cost in developing countries, increase in the volatility of commodities, and an increasing focus on sustainability. Companies throughout the supply chain, not just at the end, should take a holistic approach to sustainability and pursue broader structural changes than they typically do (Lee, 2010). It is only with shared responsibility that a truly sustainable and successful supply chain can be put in place. One certainty is that the greatest threat to supply chain function is environmental perturbation.

7.4.4 Systems design

System thinking addresses the condition, not just the symptoms. Eco-design at the product level only addresses the symptoms. Products do not exist in isolation. While their design and manufacture may be optimized, it is the consequences of these products on society and the environment as a whole that systems design is concerned with. Furthermore, a single product may be part of a number of different systems, hence complicating the design challenge at both levels. The need for sustainable systems has long been recognized. Just as an ecosystem is not merely the sum of the species present, so a sustainable system cannot be built from individual products. System design incorporates behavioural design as an important element. In contrast to "**disabling solutions**" Manzini (2006, p. 4) refers to designs that support such behavioural change at a systems level as "**enabling solutions**".

Vezzoli and Manzini (2008) describe four different **levels of intervention** with increasing potential to achieve system sustainability and to transform society and economics.

- Level 1: environmental redesign of existing products—incremental innovation
- Level 2: designing new products and services—radical innovation
- Level 3: designing new production-consumption systems—behavioural innovation
- Level 4: creating new scenarios for sustainable lifestyles—system innovation

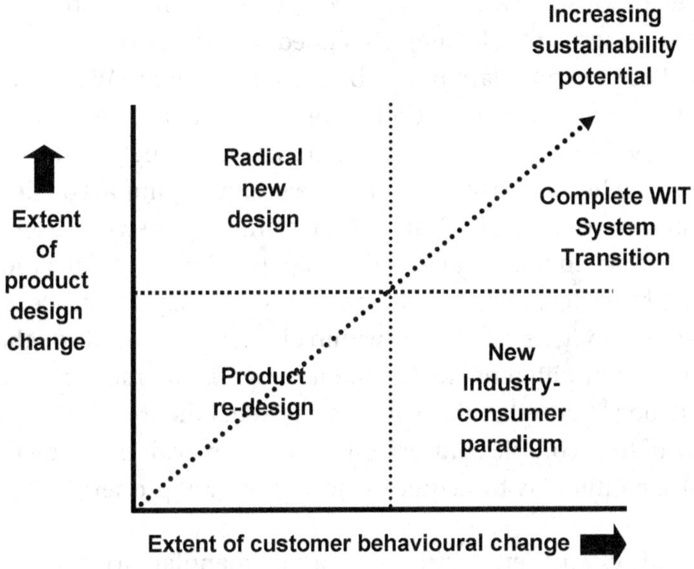

FIGURE 7.2 The relationship between sustainability potential, change in design and change in customer behaviour. Only with a radical transition involving world-view, institutions and technologies (WIT) can maximum sustainable potential be reached (based on Dusch *et al.*, 2010).

In this context, the term **system innovation** was coined, meaning "far-reaching changes in technology [which may influence] several branches of the economy [or even] give rise to entire new sectors" (Freeman and Perez, 1988) (see Fig. 7.2).

Instead of focusing purely on the function and form of a product or service, design teams today must consider a broad range of system-level issues (Anastas and Zimmerman, 2003).

Inventing a hydrogen-powered car will be of no use unless hydrogen supply and production is also in place, and that these processes are sustainable in themselves.

A system can be defined as a unit of functional value. While reductionist thinkers would not recognize system design as relevant, ecologists recognize life as being composed of a series of levels of organization, each interacting and modulating the other levels. Goals may be quite different at each level, and so tensions must be resolved. This points towards suboptimality at each level, since no one level can be optimal, given the differences in goals of each level.

Another problem relates to how we can establish realistic boundaries for system design. This challenge is shared by ecologists, when they try to delineate between populations and between ecosystems. Where does a lake ecosystem stop? Do we include all of the feeder streams even though they begin in very different montane ecosystems? Do we include the estuary or coastal areas where deposits from the lake eventually impact on deposition, current and nutrient levels? What of the salmon that swims from the sea, through the lake to the stream, or the migratory bird that visits the lake for a few months each year before moving to a completely different ecosystem?

With some products interacting within different systems throughout their life-cycle, and in different ways, system design is the most complex of all design schools. Central to this subject is **systems theory**. Systems theory is the study of how complex entities interact openly with their environments and evolve continually by acquiring new, **emergent** properties (Heylighen, 2003).

Industrial systems (energy, transportation, manufacturing, food production), societal systems (urbanization, mobility, communication) and natural systems (soil, atmospheric, aquatic, biotic) are linked by information flow, labour, wealth, materials, energy, and waste. Such interactions produce complex dynamics and the non-linear nature of these interdependent systems imply that the notion of sustainability as a steady-state equilibrium is not realistic (Fiksel, 2006).

Modelling and decision-making frameworks must embrace dynamic rather than static function, examining how such systems can remain resilient yet responsive.

7.4.5 Architecture and construction

Sustainable architecture has been present for a long time and only lost in recent times, as the example of the blackhouses on St Kilda has illustrated. It was the advent of plentiful energy and resource sources that freed architecture from its previously constrained state and thus its environmentally harmonious origins. It was the liberation from these constraints that led to unsustainable approaches. Construction is America's largest manufacturing activity, using 60% of the nonfood, nonfuel raw materials consumed each year (US Geological Survey, 1998). Architecture is the underlying design school responsible for this.

Once built, a structure has significant impact on the environment, in terms of consumption of energy and water as well as sink-related issues of waste and habitat fragmentation. Buildings generate 35–40% of the nation's carbon dioxide emissions (greenhouse gases), along with 49% of sulphur dioxide emissions, 25% of nitrous oxide emissions, and 10% of particulate emissions.

Landscape architecture contributes to the problems. Most gardens, for example, are packed with exotic species which are often useless as a wildlife resource, while indigenous species (often called weeds) are constantly removed. These exotic species can escape the boundaries of these gardens, becoming significant threats to native species. In terms of urban design (next section), architecture lies at the heart of this area. Architecture has a huge impact on system-level sustainability, having the potential to transform human attitudes and actions. It forms the grid within which we live our lives and maps the landscape in which many of us spend most of our lives. Architecture thus straddles many of the key issues facing us in terms of sustainability.

The definition of a green building can be found in the Leadership in Energy and Environmental Design (LEED) programme developed by the nonprofit, non-governmental US Green Building Council. The LEED programme evaluates the sustainable features of new construction by awarding points in six areas:

1. Location and siting
2. Water efficiency
3. Energy and atmosphere
4. Materials and resources
5. Indoor environmental quality
6. Innovation and design (US Green Building Council, 2003)

Land use regulation tends to be at the local level. With 75% of housing needing replaced in the US in the next 20 years (Bureau of National Affairs, 2007), the need to introduce green housing (structurally and functionally) is essential, given the environmental impact that building design creates, Bronin (2008) asks how useful is local control in terms of delivering this challenge?

Local control rests on two arguments: the historical argument and the autonomy argument. While state laws enforce zoning and design controls, these are the responsibility of local government. The autonomy argument is based on the observation that locals understand local landscapes best.

These two positions vie for power, creating a vacuum within which sustainability becomes lost. Local building design controls often make it difficult to install solar panels, energy-efficient windows and landscaping (traditional lawns use huge amounts of water), while federal level legislation may prove too blunt to apply across such a diversity of landscapes and communities. Combined state and federal input to local building control may be necessary to establish even progress across the country. There is also the risk of politicizing the issue, with localism and centralist interest groups using it to pursue their agendas.

Margaret Jane Radin (1982; p. 957) links property ownership and the associated rights with "**personhood**". She argues that "to achieve proper self-development—to be a person—an individual needs some control over resources in the external environment" Local governance is viewed as allowing greater individual representation.

Architecture has followed the pattern of general design relating to sustainability. To begin with, it was form-oriented, increasingly using renewable building materials and reducing environmentally damaging materials. This was followed by a function-oriented approach, reducing energy and material flux while providing important feedback systems. What is yet to fully emerge is a fusion-oriented approach, where designs of nature and humans merge. A recent movement called **bioarchitecture** has developed whose central thesis is that all life responds well to design that is energetically harmonious with nature (Gunning, 2012).

7.4.6 Urban design

In many ways, **urban design** represents a system approach to architecture. **Sustainable urbanism**, reduced to its most basic principles, is walkable and transit-served urbanism integrated with high-performance buildings and high-performance infrastructure. Key areas of focus include compactness, walkable streets and networks, open space, storm-water systems, integration of transportation, land use and energy, impact of planning on building energy usage and large district energy systems (Farr, 2012).

Optimal sustainable urban development is not possible at densities below seven or eight dwelling units per acre. To free inhabitants from reliance on cars, a density of 15 dwelling units per acre makes a trolley service worthwhile, while a compactness of 20 units per hectare makes a light railway feasible. Sustainable corridors require a 1:1 ratio of housing to employment (Farr, 2012).

Design plays a very important role in sustainable urbanism acting as a basis for socially sustainable settlements. Sustainable urbanism approaches tend to fall into two categories: behavioural approaches (e.g. biophilia) and structural approaches (design). Supply chains to and from cities are important in terms of sustainability, due to the huge sinks and sources that urban hot spots represent for manufactured goods. Cities also form significant sources of waste.

Alusi *et al.* (2011) note that urbanization is one of the most pressing and complex challenges of the 21st century. Cities are supplied by a complex array of supply chains servicing an immense spectrum of economic activities from food stores and restaurants, office supplies and high-tech equipment, clothing, construction materials, as well as raw materials. The sustainability of supply chains is, therefore, a precursor to the sustainability of our cities.

The need for new theories of flows and networks for cities exists. Geroliminis and Daganzo (2005) emphasize that the environmental impacts of logistical activities are most severe where population densities are highest, that is, in cities. Poor environmental performance at any link of the supply chain network can have significant implications on the urban market (a powerful, if under-used, lobby group) and may damage what is considered a firm's premier asset—its reputation (Nagurney, 2006).

7.4.7 Corporate design

Corporate design relates to the purpose of the firm. Modern firms can be considered as the most powerful social institutions of our time. Economics has engulfed society and undermined environment. The central question is: "**What are companies for?**" The context of any business is the corporate environment within which it trades. Within a given company, particularly the larger operations, corporate culture is extremely important. Certain elements are common to all cultures, but in other cases, culture can play an important role is determining the form of corporate design in practice. The corporate design impacts on every aspect of the business, and acts as a constraint or thermostat. The very process of problem-solving design will be shaped fundamentally by corporate structure.

A regime shift in corporate culture cannot occur without changing worldviews, institutions, and technologies (WIT) together, as an integrated system. Current corporate culture evolved during the **empty world** period of the 19th century, when resources were plentiful and population low. Market institutions are geared towards economic growth and provide only private goods at the expense of public goods (Beddoe *et al.*, 2009).

There would appear to be two routes to regime change—collapse or evolution. If we continue to flaunt the warning signs, the environment will eventually force the issue. However, we have the option of a controlled descent and landing. Examples of the evolutionary approach include:

- Tikopia Islanders have developed and maintained a sustainable food supply while maintaining their population at a stable, non-increasing level. They have a bottom-up social structure (Diamond, 2005).
- New Guinea features a silviculture system dating back some 7,000 years. The islanders have developed an extremely democratic, bottom-up, decision-making structure (Diamond, 2005).
- Japan's top-down forest policies in the Tokugawa-era arose as a response to an environmental and population crisis, bringing peace and prosperity (Diamond, 2005).
- The Moche civilization in northern Peru suffered severe drought in the 6th century AD followed by flooding. This led to the decimation of their capital city, fields, and irrigation system with disastrous consequences. In response, the Moche moved their capital city and developed new, adaptive agricultural and architectural approaches (Weiss and Bradley, 2001).

A change to the corporate structure and associated institutional values will require integrated, system-level redesign of our entire socio-ecological regime, with the goal of sustainable quality of life rather than the obsession with unlimited economic growth. This will, obviously not be straightforward. We will address this in greater detail in Chapter 9.

As we have mentioned, corporate design stems from "**empty world**" times of plenty. Being dominated by the return of profit to owners, however increasingly dispersed such owners are, leaves little room for environmental concerns. Short termism, both in business, academia and politics, prevents long-term strategies necessary for environmental improvement. Corporate redesign requires both external and internal transformation, involving changes to the law, charter, governance, internal incentives and interactions with capital markets.

Corporate design lacks the structures of political design, or constitutions, which have two key guiding lights: sets of shared principles and an array of operating elements. Corporations have transcended governments and politics, often controlling them, yet they lack these guiding lights. An absence of accountability operates throughout, externalizing responsibility up and down the supply chain. Actions have addressed the symptoms not the causes. Core corporate values have remained unchanged. They create wealth disparity and devastate communities through acquisition and mergers.

Self-regulation through feedback has been lost, akin to a runaway train. While the rights of corporations have increased over the last 200 years, the obligations on them have decreased. Free trade is encouraged but the invisible hand has been paralysed. The iron triangle of short term pressure comes from stock analysts, hedge funds and stock options, according to Citigroup CEO John Reed (in Kelly and White, 2007; p. 768).

Kelly and White (2007) have identified six foundations for corporate redesign:

1. **Purpose**: the purpose of the corporation is to harness private interests to serve the public interest
2. **Capital**: corporations shall accrue fair returns for shareholders, but not at the expense of the legitimate interests of other stakeholders
3. **Sustainability**: corporations shall operate sustainably, meeting the needs of the present generation without compromising the ability of future generations to meet their needs
4. **Wealth**: corporations shall distribute their wealth equitably among those who contribute to wealth creation
5. **Governance**: corporations shall be governed in a manner that is participatory, transparent, ethical and accountable
6. **Policy**: corporations shall not infringe on the right of natural persons to govern themselves, nor infringe on their universal human rights

In addition to business, government and nonprofit sectors, a fourth sector, where social and financial gains are equal, is emerging. Examples include:

- New York Times Company: publicly owned but family-controlled via dual shares
- John Lewis Partnership: 100% employee-owned; employee-partners' happiness is focus

- Organic Valley: owned by farmer families; co-operative
- Grupo Nueva: public and private ownership; profits targeted at South American sustainability; targets 10% of profit from socially inclusive businesses

These alternative models are growing in number, challenging the traditional corporate design structure.

7.5 The process of design: conceptual, cognitive and detailed design

Seven cognitive steps to broach the attitude-behaviour gulf in pro-environmental behaviour have been developed by MacDonald and She (2012):

1. **Responsibility**: designing products that have interactive curtailing features, e.g. more perforations in rolls of paper towels to allow choice of smaller or larger sheets depending on need.
2. **Complex decision-making skills**: designs that encourage decision-making through pricing incentives and feedback, communicating environmental interaction in a comprehensible fashion, e.g. Toyota Prius incentivizes improved fuel efficiency by encouraging the driver to beat previous efficiency.
3. **Decision heuristics**: short cuts to optimize and simplify decision-making—often hardwired through evolution—impacted by urban myths, e.g. the idea that bottled water is better for you than tap water ignores plastics pollution. Designers should co-ordinate complex trade-offs by design, rather than rely on customer education, e.g. carbon fluorescent light bulbs contain mercury which is released on breaking. Mercury should be excluded or contained rather than relying on attempts to educate the public of the tiny risks posed compared with carbon released from burning coal. The concepts of **crux** and **sentinel design attributes** is important here. Crux attributes represent important but difficult to assess qualities, while sentinel attributes are related to crux, but are more easily grasped.

4. **Altruism-sacrifice link**: products need to meet self-interested and altruistic positions. Sustainability tends to be painted as sacrifice. Designs should not portray substandard inferiority, but should really be better products.

5. **Trust**: is the product really green or merely greenwashing? Designs should include semantics and heuristics that communicate trust.

6. **Cognitive dissonance and guilt**: a gap can open between beliefs and actions, called cognitive dissonance. If a person experiences guilt on realizing his behaviour is not adequately helping the environment, he may change his behaviour to match his cognition (improving his impact) *or* change his cognition to match his behaviour (move from an environmentally concerned position). Thus guilt can be resolved in either way and so it can be a game of Russian roulette. Thus designers should avoid the guilt-trip message. "Use predominately positive, rather than negative reinforcements" when trying to change user behaviour (Lilley, 2009).

7. **Motivation**: sustainable product purchase decisions are best motivated with incentives that are short-term, repetitive, and small in size: "reward schedules that are just sufficient to initiate behavior change are more likely to produce longer-term behavior change than more powerful rewards" (Geller *et al.*, 2002). This promotes a change from extrinsic to intrinsic motivation, which becomes self-sustainable.

Creativity is generally accepted in cognitive psychology as the capacity to perform mental work which leads to an outcome both novel and applicable. **Creative thinking** produces a useful outcome while **original thinking** produces a novel outcome. Designers are faced with wicked problems (Rittel and Webber, 1973) and operate in constrained reality. We can never say that function follows form since it is the inner built experience of use that remains central in the design process. Function is much more difficult to conceive than form.

Encouragement of divergence and discouragement of inhibition has been the dogma of creative thinkers such as Osborn (1953), Gordon (1961) and de Bono (1992). Issues relating to these approaches involve the problem that creative design cannot merely deliver a concept, but must produce a tangible outcome. Furthermore, limits within an individual mind cannot all be overcome, in that we are shaped by the limited number of experiences we encounter which themselves act as constraints. Lateral thinking is unlikely to allow adventure beyond certain perimeter fences imposed by genetics and experience/trauma/attachment.

It is now well accepted that representations follow a path of progressive elaboration through the design process. A **perceptual sphere** offers a greater likelihood of tangible outcome than does a **conceptual sphere**, since perceptual meaning is a direct reproduction of the experience in the mind while conceptual meaning is a metaphorical construction based on experience. With the first we can deduct, generalize and build coded knowledge, with the second we can directly feel if something works or not (Lakoff and Johnson 1999). The search for conceptual meaning is not connected to solution finding but to problem finding and, by being so, the originality may reside in the way we locate problems and not in the way we generate solutions.

Bernstein *et al.* (2010) highlight conceptual design as the most important stage in the design process. The foundations are laid, and cannot be undone during detailed design. Life-cycle assessment is not useful during conceptual design, as the details required are not yet in place. LCA is unable to support a holistic approach to ecologically sound idea generation (Kobayashi, 2005). Available methods to help inform conceptual design include quality function deployment (QFD), functional component analysis, and the Pugh chart (Matzler and Hinterhuber, 1998).

The **function–impact matrix** is another useful tool (Bernstein *et al.*, 2010). The function–impact matrix allocates the life-cycle environmental impacts to the functions performed by the product. A main role of the function–impact matrix is to identify which product functions are important from an environmental perspective, and which functions need to be re-examined to achieve a better ecodesign. It focuses on function rather than form. By benchmarking a range of competitors, the lowest functional impacts can be drawn from the range of approaches and combined to give a new, low-impact fusion.

Psychological and artificial intelligence research suggests that the cognitive mechanisms that support conceptualization are imagination and associations (Madanshetty, 1995). Function is more difficult to conceptualize than form, creating difficulties for sustainable conceptualization. The process of conceptual design produces the input for the other design activities, such as embodiment, detailing and documentation.

Though in principle the complete product conceptualization process could be covered with the available specific techniques, the difference in the supporting theories and representations practically prevents it. It is obvious that all pieces of knowledge needed for conceptual design cannot be included in any single model at the same level of abstraction. That is the reason why the issue of meta-models has come into the working life of many researchers. However, as opposed to the market of computer-aided design systems, the market of the computer-aided conceptual design (CACD) tools is dormant. The conceptual design techniques available are generally sophisticated, but synthetic solutions are not in harmony with the natural thinking and working of the designers in the course of conceptualization.

7.6 Difficulties in sustainable design

There are a number of significant issues facing designers working to contribute towards a sustainable outcome. First, there is the problem of **emphasis**, both at stakeholder and at content levels. The designer does not work in isolation. He who pays the piper calls the tune, and so the designers will find themselves compromised by the various stakeholders, either directly (the manufacturer, machinery, logistics, financial/time budget, the designer's own knowledge and training) or indirectly (consumers, legislation, shareholders, suppliers, etc.).

This creates a problem in terms of identifying how to incentivize sustainable design. Putting pressure on any one member of this consortium will be a strategy of doubtful value. Thus one of the biggest barriers to change is the multifaceted structure of the stakeholder context. A designer may be trained and educated enough to produce sustainable designs, but the company he is hired by may not support this work. Thus we have a wicked problem, reliant on knowledge transfer and world-view/institutional/technological transformation.

Another problem arises from the fixation of humans with carbon dioxide (Skene, 2010). Currently, most models are focused on greenhouse gas output, and a successful sustainable product is one that emits the lowest levels of these gases (e.g. Chu *et al.*, 2011). Unfortunately, there is more damage done than merely greenhouse gas emissions. As we noted in Chapter 3, much "green" technology actually has devastating impacts on the environment, be it the destruction of rainforest for growth of oil palm or the use of rare earth metals in wind-generated power. Another area that passes under the radar is agriculture, possibly the most destructive of all of our activities, with habitat destruction, salinization, soil erosion and nutrient pollution.

Thus models used in design must incorporate all aspects of ecological change and not just those associated with climate change. This is partly the problem of the science communities and large organizations such as the United Nations, where more effort is put into climate change than all of the other serious threats put together. Yet habitat destruction, nutrient pollution and water shortage will be as likely to damage human prospects as will climate change.

Designers are targeting longevity of product life-cycle as equalling sustainability, leading to reduced material flow. However, ecology would disagree. Material flow is central to nature. Nature has many examples of planned obsolescence such as generation times, fire-promoting strategies of eucalypts (where highly flammable bark of these trees gradually peels off over years, building up a highly flammable layer on the forest floor awaiting ignition), smoke responsive seeds and turnover rates. While ecosystems such as woodland and coral reefs may look unchanging, in reality there is a dynamic, fast cycling system, a bit like the legs of a duck, paddling madly beneath the flowing water to maintain the duck in its position.

This is the reality of nature—huge waste production (as the recipient of entropy ejected from life forms in order to maintain their order) and the conversion of that waste, utilizing mostly solar energy, into useful material. Switch off the light (as in many of the mass extinction events) and you will achieve a low rate of waste production, but only because everything is dead.

This also applies to a raised mire. These areas slowly rise as waste material is added over thousands of years, and is not broken down. This is because the mire is highly acidic and waterlogged, and therefore none of the organisms charged with recycling waste materials can survive. Yes, the life-cycle is slow, but only because of the abiotic conditions and low productivity.

In nature there is constant waste, entropic release and breakdown. Indeed complexity (such as life) can only exist if entropy increases within its surroundings. As we have seen, only thanks to energetic flux does this waste become reinvigorated. It is akin to jumping off a diving board. In order to experience the pleasure of free-falling again, you have to release energy by climbing back up the ladder. Life is, ultimately, a waste producer. It has to be in order to maintain order within a living organism. Thus design should not be obsessed with reducing waste, but by the nature of that waste and its potential for recycling. Many recent schools of sustainability, such as Cradle to Cradle®, biomimicry, biomimetics, bionics and the transition initiative movement are obsessed with reducing waste (bionics means "the use of biological prototypes for the design of man-made synthetic systems" (Papanek, 1971; p. 185)).

The extended life-cycle argument relies on the growth of the service sector, but this is problematic due to free trade combined with wage disparities. Many of the major industrial producer countries have very low wages, exporting their products to countries with very high wages. Thus production is cheap in the country of origin, but service engineers, living in more affluent countries, must be paid a high wage. Hence it is financially much easier to replace a product with a new one than to pay for the servicing of an ageing product, no matter how well designed that product is in terms of service potential. But, in the industrialized world, high labour costs encourage labour efficiency rather than resource efficiency.

This is a serious problem, and will only be corrected if the product owner could carry out the maintenance. However, this would then lead to the collapse of the service industry, which is a central pillar of the sustainability argument in terms of replacing manufacturing jobs. Finally, the loss of manufacturing jobs will not be in the same countries as the increase in service sector jobs anyway, and so this system of extended life-cycle would punish many of the poorer countries while enriching many of the already rich countries wherein the servicing takes place. Thus socially, economically and environmentally, extended life-cycle is problematic.

7.7 Bridge case

Sustainable product development (SPD) in furniture manufacture, rural Mexico. Research reference: Masera, D. (2001) Sustainable product development: a strategy for developing countries. In. Charter, M. and Tischner, U. (eds.), *Sustainable Solutions: Developing Products and Services for the Future.* Greenleaf Publishing, Sheffield. pp. 203-19.

Sustainable product development (SPD) is the process which creates product designs that are sustainable in terms of the environment and resource use while considering the need for the product. Sustainable product development in small enterprises offers unique challenges, given the lack of specialized staff and training. SPD considers the intensity and optimization of resource use for product design, while involving local culture and tastes, and the overall production efficiency, with the aim of improving the product's quality to increase market opportunities.

Design schools tend to produce courses targeted at employment within large industries which have the luxury of design departments specializing in design resolution. There are a limited number of designers working with small enterprises in "developing" countries. Small enterprises in "developing" nations tend to copy other products, often exploiting the luxury goods mimic market.

The Purépecha, the largest indigenous group of people in the Michoacán state in south-western Mexico, specialize in the production of wooden handicrafts which employs about 150,000 people. Local forests are highly diverse, with more than ten species of *Pinus* (pines) and 12 species of *Quercus* (oaks), among many other tree species. Currently, however, a rapid deforestation process, reaching close to 2% per year (1,880 ha per year), and a degradation of a large fraction of the remaining forested area is taking place.

Problems stem from the high density of wood workshops, low product quality and diversity, inefficiencies in the manufacturing processes, a lack of technical training, a lack of support from official institutions, a lack of organization and training opportunities and a lack of financial resources. The search for cheaper prices for raw materials has favoured the use of illegally harvested timber because of its lower price.

Forest eco-production has been introduced, aimed at sustaining supply of quality timber while increasing value to producers, ranging from forest management through to marketing. This involves quantitative measurement of production costs, both in economic and environmental terms. Product designs can be compared based on a series of ad hoc indicators, including material intensity, profit margins and cost per unit length of timber used.

As a result a new chair design, the Casas Blancas model (called after the community in which it was developed), was introduced. The new chair consumes four times less timber than the common Opopeo model (again named after the community where it was built). In terms of pesos by board foot used, the returned value per unit of timber used was four times higher than other models. Finally, the profit margins achieved with the Casas Blancas chair were 65% compared with an average of 40% for other models.

SPD training is essential in the reduction of the environmental impact of small enterprises in "developing" countries. Artisans require training to be able to improve their current situation and designers should become more actively involved in SPD training for small enterprises in "developing" countries.

7.8 Debate, discussion and further thought

1. Debate the following topics (or write a balanced account of the arguments in each case):
   - Extended life-cycle vs. shortened life-cycle.
   - Incentivizing sustainable design—who gets the carrot and who gets the stick?
2. Compare and contrast the constraints on conceptual and detailed design. How does this inform the larger sustainability argument in terms of developing meaningful design practice?
3. How can a local firm have any control on an international supply chain?
4. Can a service sector replace manufacturing?
5. According to a 2007 study, American consumers use their mobile phones on average for only 17.5 months [J.D. Power and Associates, 2007). Central to improving sustainable cell phones, human–computer interactions (HCI) will be essential. While refurbishing and resale of donated phones can extend their life-spans and additionally fund charities, the phones are often sent to areas such as Latin America for resale, where they may eventually be thrown in the trash, thus shifting the location of the waste problem (Most, 2003). Participatory design with phone owners may yield further ideas about to make better use of old phones. Extend functionality instead of replacing it, facilitated by modular functionality. Contract renewal could encourage keeping the old phone rather than replacing it (Huang and Truong, 2008). What opportunities exist for applying design as a way to close the gap between the functional lifetime and the perceived lifetime of mobile phones? How would you approach the challenges that mobile phone technology poses for the environment in terms of systems design?
6. How important is design if we are to achieve a sustainable world?
7. Compare and contrast the challenges of environment, economics and society for sustainable design practitioners.
8. What are the most important elements of sustainable design?

9. What are the challenges of WIT (world-views, institutions and technologies) transformation in terms of design?

10. Design a sustainable design course for an Art College. What other subject areas would you want to involve?

11. What can we learn from St Kilda?

References

Alusi, A., Eccles, R.G., Edmondson A.C. and Zuzul T. (2011). Sustainable cities: Oxymoron or the shape of the future? Harvard Business School, working paper, 11-062, Cambridge, MA.

Anastas, P. and Zimmerman, J.P. (2003). Design through the 12 principles of green engineering. *Environmental Science and Technology* 37: 94A-101A.

Beddoe, R., Costanza, R., Farley, J., Garza, E., Kent, J., Kubiszewski, I., Martineza, L., McCowen, T., Murphy, K., Myerse, N., Ogden, Z., Stapleton, K. and Woodward, J. (2009). Overcoming systemic roadblocks to sustainability: The evolutionary redesign of worldviews, institutions, and technologies. *Proceedings of the National Academy of Sciences,* USA 106(8): 2483-9.

Bernon, M. (2009). Building sustainable supply chains for the future. In: Gattorna, J. (ed.), *Dynamic Supply Chain Alignment.* Gower, London. pp. 299-310.

Bernstein, W., Ramanujan, D., Devnathan, S., Zhao, F., Ramani, K. and Sutherland, J. (2010). Development of a framework for sustainable conceptual design. In: CIRP (ed.), *17th CIRP International Conference on Life Cycle Engineering.* CIRP, Hefei, China.

Björklund, M., Martinsen, U. and Abrahamsson, M. (2012). Performance measurements in the greening of supply chains. Supply Chain Management: An International Journal 17(1): 29-39.

Bouchereau, V. and Rowlands, H. (2000). Methods and techniques to help quality function deployment (QFD). Benchmarking: An International Journal 7(1): 8-20.

Bras, B. and Hammond, R. (1996). Towards design for remanufacturing: metrics for assessing remanufacturability. In: Flapper, S.D. and de Ron, A.J. (eds.), *Proceedings of the 1st International Workshop on Reuse.* Eindhoven, The Netherlands. pp. 11-13.

Bronin, S. (2008). The quiet revolution revived: sustainable design, land use regulation, and the states. Minnesota Law Review 93: 231.

Bureau of National Affairs (2007). Green buildings helping the environment, the bottom line. Environmental Compliance Bulletin, 18 June 2007, p. 208.

Campbell, E. (2009). You know more than you think you do: Design as resourcefulness and self-reliance. www.thersa.org/__data/assets/pdf_file/0006/215457/RSA_designandsociety_pamphlet.pdf Last accessed: 15 November 2014.

Chapman, J. (2005). *Emotionally Durable Design—Objects, Experience and Empathy.* Earthscan, London.

Chopra, S. and Meindl P. (2009). *Supply Chain Management.* 4th edition. Pearson Educational, London.

Christopher, M. (2005). *Logistics and Supply Chain Management: Creating Value-adding Networks.* Third edition. Financial Times, New York.

Chu, C.H., Luh, Y.P., Li, T.C. and Chen, H. (2009). Economical green product design based on computer-aided product structure variation. Computers in Industry 60(7): 485-500.

Clark, G., Kosoris, J., Hong, L.N. and Crul, M. (2009). Design for sustainability: current trends in sustainable product design and development. Sustainability 1(3): 409-24.

Cooper, T. (1999). Creating an economic infrastructure for sustainable product design. Journal of Sustainable Design 8: 7-17.

Cooper, T. (2005). Slower consumption reflections on product life spans and the "throwaway society". Journal of Industrial Ecology 9(1-2): 51-67.

Corbett, C.J. and Kleindorfer, P.R. (2003). Environmental management and operations management: introduction to the third special issue. Production and Operations Management 12(3): 287-9.

Corbett, C.J. and Klassen, R.D. (2006). Extending the horizons: environmental excellence as key to improving operations. Manufacturing and Service Operations Management 8(1): 5-22.

Crul, M. and Diehl, J. (2006). *Design for Sustainability: A Practical Approach for Developing Economies.* UNEP&TU Delft: Paris, France.

Datschefski, E. (2001). The Total Beauty of Sustainable Products. RotoVision, Crans-Pres-Celigny, Switzerland. P. 17.

De Bono, E. (1992). *Serious Creativity: Using the Power of Lateral Thinking to Create New Ideas.* HarperCollins, New York.

Dewberry, E. and Goggin, P. (1994). *Ecodesign and Beyond: Steps Towards Sustainability.* Open University and Nottingham Trent University.

Diamond, J. (2005). *Collapse: How Societies Choose to Fail or Succeed.* Viking, New York.

Diegel, O., Singamneni, S., Reay, S. and Withell, A. (2010). Tools for sustainable product design: additive manufacturing. Journal of Sustainable Development 3(3): 68.

Dulhai, G. (2008). The 5S strategy for continuous improvement of the manufacturing processes in autocar exhaust. Management and Marketing 3(4): 115-20.

Dusch, B., Crilly, N. and Moultrie, J. (2010). Developing a framework for mapping sustainable design activities. Paper presented at Design and Complexity, Montreal. www.drs2010.umontreal.ca/data/PDF/033.pdf Last accessed 15 November 2014.

Farr, D. (2012). *Sustainable Urbanism: Urban Design with Nature.* Wiley, London.

Faud-Luke, A. (2007). Redefining the purpose of (sustainable) design: enter the design enablers, catalysts in co-design. In: Chapman, J. and Gant, N. (eds.), *Designers, Visionaries and Other Stories.* Earthscan, London.

Fiksel, J. (2006). Sustainability and resilience: toward a systems approach. Sustainability: Science Practice and Policy 2(2): 14-21.

Fixson, S. (2005). Product architecture assessment: a tool to link product, process and supply chain decisions. Journal of Operations Management 23 (3-4): 345-69.

Freeman, C. (1984). *Design Innovation and Long Cycles in Economic Development.* Royal College of Art, London.

Freeman, C. and Perez, C. (1988). Structural crises of adjustment, business cycles and investment behaviour. In: Dosi, G., Freeman, C., Nelson, R., Silverberg, G. and Soete, L. (eds.), *Technical Change and Economic Theory.* Pinter, London. pp. 38-66.

Freeman, C. (1992). *The Economics of Hope.* Pinter, London.

Geller, E.S., Bechtel, R.B. and Churchman, A. (2002). *The Challenge of Increasing Proenvironmental Behavior. Handbook of environmental psychology.* J.Wiley, New York. pp. 525-40.

Geroliminis, N. and Daganzo, C.F. (2005). *A Review of Green Logistics Schemes Used Around the World.* U.C. Berkeley Centre for Future Urban Transport.

Gmelin, H. and Seuring, S. (2014). Determinants of a sustainable new product development. Journal of Cleaner Production 69: 1-9.

Gordon, W.J.J. (1961). *Synectics: the Development of Creative Capacity.* Harper & Row, New York.

Gunning, P. (2012). Bioarchitecture: the organization and regulation of biological space. Bioarchitecture 2(6): 200-203.

Hawken, P., Lovins, A.H. and L.H. Lovins, L.H. (1999). *Natural Capitalism*. Little, Brown and Company, Boston, MA.

Heylighen, F. (2003). The science of self-organization and adaptivity. In: Kiel, L.D. (ed.), *The Encyclopedia of Life Support Systems*, EOLSS Publishers, Oxford. http://pcp.vub.ac.be/Papers/EOLSS-Self-Organiz.pdf Last accessed 15 November 2014.

Hill, S.B. (2005). Redesign as deep industrial ecology: lessons from ecological agriculture and social ecology, in: Cote, R., Tansey, J. and Dale, A. (eds.), *Industrial Ecology: A Question of Design?* University of British Columbia, Vancouver, BC. pp. 29-49.

Hill, J.E. (2011). *The Secret Life of Stuff: a Manual for a New Material World*. Vintage, London.

Huang, E.M. and Truong, K.N. (2008). Breaking the disposable technology paradigm: opportunities for sustainable interaction design for mobile phones. In: Czerwinski, M. and Lund, A. (eds.), Proceedings of the SIGCHI Conference on Human Factors in Computing Systems. ACM. pp. 323-32.

Humphries-Smith, T. (2010). Several Shades of Green: do you do eco-design or sustainable design or neither. Engineering Designer (2010): 10-12.

Jaafar, I.H., Venkatachalam, A., Joshi, K., Ungureanu, A.C., de Silva, N., Dillon Jr., O.W., Rouch, K.E. and Jawahir, I.S. (2007). Product design for sustainability: a new assessment methodology and case studies. In Kutz, M. (Ed.), *Handbook of Environmentally Conscious Mechanical Design*. John Wiley & Sons, London. pp. 25-65.

Kannegiesser, M. and Günther, H.O. (2014). Sustainable development of global supply chains—part 1: sustainability optimization framework. Flexible Services and Manufacturing Journal 26(1-2): 24-47.

Kelly, M. and White, A. (2007). Corporate design: the missing organizational and public policy issue of our time. New England Law Review 42: 761-86.

Kleindorfer, P.R., Singhal, K. and Wassenhove, L.N. (2005). Sustainable operations management. Production and Operations Management 14(4): 482-92.

Kobayashi, H. (2005). Strategic evolution of eco-products: a product life cycle planning methodology. Research in Engineering Design 16: 1-16.

Kwak, M.J., Hong, Y.S. and Cho, N.W. (2009). Ecoarchitecture analysis for end-of-life decision making. International Journal of Production Research 47(22): 6233-59.

Lakoff, G. and Johnson, M. (1999). *Philosophy in the Flesh*. Basic Books, New York.

Lee, H.L. (2010). Don't tweak your supply chain—rethink it end to end. Harvard Business Review, October 2010: 64-9.

Lilley, D. (2009). Design for sustainable behaviour: strategies and perceptions. Design Studies 30(6): 704-20.

Lilley, D., Lofthouse, V. and Bhamra, T. (2005). Towards instinctive sustainable product use. Paper presented to 2nd International Conference: Sustainability Creating the Culture, Aberdeen, 2–4 November 2005.

Lockton, D. (2010). *Design With Intent Toolkit*. www.danlockton.com Last accessed 15 November 2014.

Lockton, D., Harrison, D. and Stanton, N. (2008). Design with intent: Persuasive technology in a wider context. In: Oinas-Kukkonen, H., Hasle, P., Harjumaa, M., Segerståhl, K. and Øhrstrøm, P. (eds.), *Persuasive Technology*. Springer, Berlin Heidelberg. pp. 274-8.

MacDonald, E. and She, J. (2012). Seven cognitive concepts for successful sustainable design. International Design Engineering Technical Conferences and Computers and Information in Engineering Conference, Chicago, IL, Aug. 12–15.

MacLean, L. (1838). *Sketches on the Island of St Kilda*. McPhun, Glasgow.

Madanshetty, S.I. (1995). Cognitive basis of conceptual design. Research in Engineering Design 7 (4): 232-40.

Madge, P. (1997). Ecological design: a new critique. Design Issues 13 (2): 52.

Mainwaring, L. (2001). Environmental values and the frame of reference. Ecological Economics 38 (3): 391-401.

Manzini, E. (2006). *Design, Ethics and Sustainability: Guidelines for a Transition Phase.* DIS-Indaco, Politecnico di Milano.

Margolin, V. (1998). Design for a sustainable world. Design Issues 14 (2): 83-92.

Martin, M. (1698). *A Late Voyage to St Kilda.* Gent, London www.undiscoveredscotland.co.uk/usebooks/martin-stkilda/chapter01.html Last accessed: 15 November 2014.

Masui, K., Sakao, T., Kobayashi, M. and Inaba, A. (2003). Applying Quality Function Deployment to Environmentally Conscious Design. International Journal of Quality Reliability Management 20: 90-106.

Matzler, K. and Hinterhuber, H.H. (1998). How to make product development projects more successful by integrating Kano's model of customer satisfaction into quality function deployment. Technovation 18(1): 25-38.

Most, E (2003). Calling all Cell Phones: Collection, Reuse, and Recycling Programs in the US. www.informinc.org. Last accessed: 15 November 2014.

Nagurney, A. (2006). *Supply Chain Network Economics: Dynamics of Prices, Flows and Profits.* Edward Elgar Publishing, Cheltenham, England.

Nagurney, A. (2012). Design of sustainable supply chains for sustainable cities. Isenberg School of Management, University of Massachusetts, Amherst, MA.

Osborn, A.F. (1953). *Applied Imagination* (Revised Edition). Scribner's, New York.

Papanek, V. (1971). *Design for the Real World: Human Ecology and Social Change.* Thames and Hudson, London.

Papanek, V. (1985). *Design for the Real World: Human Ecology and Social Change.* 2nd edition. Academy Chicago, Chicago, Ill.

Power, J.D. and Associates (2007). *Wireless Customers Are Keeping Their Mobile Phones Longer as Term Contracts Impact the Replacement Cycle.* US Wireless Mobile Phone Evaluation Study. http://businesscenter.jdpower.com/news/pressrelease.aspx?ID=2007079 Last Accessed: 15 November 2014.

Radin, M.J. (1982). Property and personhood. Stanford Law Review 34(3): 957-1015.

Ramani, K., Ramanujan, D., Bernstein, W Z., Zhao, F., Sutherland, J., Handwerker, C., Choi, J.K., Kim, H. and Thurston, D. (2010). Integrated Sustainable Life Cycle Design: A Review. Journal of Mechanical Design 132: 1-15.

Ramanujan, D., Bernstein, W.Z., Zhao, F. and Ramani, K. (2011). Addressing Uncertainties Within Product Redesign for Sustainability: A Function Based Framework. Proceedings of ASME Design Engineering Technical Conference Vol. 9: 1057-64.

Ravet, D. (2012). An exploration of facility location metrics in international supply chain. In: Němečková, I. (ed.), Proceedings of 3rd International Joint Conference on Business Strategies on Global Markets Trends in International Business 2012. p. 19.

Ravet, D. (2013). Delivering sustainability through supply chain distribution network redesign. Central European Business Review 3: 22-9.

Rittel, H.W. and Webber, M.M. (1973). Dilemmas in a general theory of planning. Policy Sciences 4(2): 155-69.

Romli, A., Prickett, P., Setchi, R. and Soe, S. (2014). Integrated eco-design decision-making for sustainable product development. International Journal of Production Research (2014): 1.

Sanders, L. and Simons, G. (2009). A social vision for value co-creation in design. Open Source Business Resource (December 2009).

Schmidt, P. and Drommert, J. (2009). Klein design. LH Exclusive 12: 38-46.

Schumpter, J.A. (1939). *Business Cycles: a Theoretical, Historical and Statistical Analysis of the Capitalist Process* (2 vols.). McGraw Hill, New York.

Simchi-Levi D. and Fine C.H. (2010). Your next supply chain. MIT Sloan Management Review Winter 2010: 17-21.

Skene, K.R. (2010). After Copenhagen: carbon is not the planet's greatest threat. Contemporary Review 292: 15-22.

Steinhilper R (1998). *Remanufacturing: The Ultimate Form of Recycling.* Fraunhofer IRB Verlag, Stuttgart.

Spangenberg, J.H., Faud-Luke, A. and Blincoe, K. (2010). Design for Sustainability (DfS): the interface of sustainable production and consumption. Journal of Cleaner Production 18(15): 1485-93.

Steffen, A. (2006). *Worldchanging: a User's Guide for the 21st Century.* Abrams, New York

US Geological Survey (1998). *Materials Flow and Sustainability.* Fact sheet, US Geological Survey.

US Green Building Council (2003). Green building rating system for new construction and major renovations (leed-nc) version 2.1 v–vi (2002, rev. 2003), available at www.usgbc.org/Docs/LEEDdocs/LEED_RS_v2-1.pdf Last accessed 15 November 2014.

Vezzoli, C. and Manzini, E. (2008). *Design for Environmental Sustainability.* Springer, London.

Weiss H. and Bradley, R.S. (2001). What drives societal collapse? Science 291: 609-10.

Westkämper, E., Alting, L. and Arndt, G. (2001). Life cycle management and assessment: approaches and visions towards sustainable manufacturing. Proceedings of the Institution of Mechanical Engineers Part B: Journal of Engineering Manufacture 215(5): 599-626.

Whiteley, N. (1993). *Design for Society.* Reaktion Books, London.

Wohlers, T. (2009). Worldwide progress report on the rapid prototyping, tooling and manufacturing state of the industry. Wohlers Report 2009, Wohlers Associates, USA.

Yan, J. and Feng, C. (2014). Sustainable design-oriented product modularity combined with 6R concept: a case study of rotor laboratory bench. Clean Technologies and Environmental Policy 16(1). 95-109.

Young, G. (2010). Design thinking and sustainability. http://zum.io/wp Last accessed 15 November 2014.

8
Generic barriers to change

Change is difficult in any setting. This chapter examines the structure and psychology of resistance to change, identifying key elements that represent this resistance. We explore generic aspects of change at different levels of business organization. All managers face the challenge of delivering change, and this is particularly complex in the area of sustainability, where legislation places demands on working practice at every level, but where knowledge relating to the causes and consequences of environmental change are often poorly understood.

Learning aims and objectives

- Name and define the major barriers to sustainability
- Distinguish barriers from limitations
- Discuss the reasons for and doorways through each type of barrier
- Understand the importance of psychology in creating and overcoming barriers

Learning outcomes and experiences

- What characteristics of sustainability are particularly prone to barriers?
- Discuss why change is difficult for humans

- Discuss the centrality of psychology in each of the types of barrier
- Give examples of barriers created by some schools of sustainability themselves
- Discuss the significance of industry–consumer interactions in overcoming barriers to sustainability

8.1 The challenge of change

> At every level the greatest obstacle to transforming the world is that we lack the clarity and imagination to conceive that it could be different.
>
> Roberto Unger, Brazilian Philosopher

A rich literature reflects on the barriers to implementing a sustainable business model. These barriers divide into two types: generic barriers, that apply to all or most situations, and specific barriers, that apply to particular sectors of the economy. In this chapter we will examine generic barriers.

What is a barrier? Moser and Ekstrom (2010; p. 22028) differentiate between limits and barriers as follows:

> [limits are] obstacles that tend to be absolute in a real sense: they constitute thresholds beyond which existing activities, land uses, ecosystems, species, sustenance, or system states cannot be maintained, not even in a modified fashion. Barriers are ... obstacles that can be overcome with concerted effort, creative management, change of thinking, prioritization, and related shifts in resources, land uses, institutions.

However, some barriers at a given level of organization may be required to set limits that ensure the survival of another level of organization. For example, if a fox caught all the rabbits available, there would be no more rabbits, and ultimately no more foxes. If we were able to catch all the fish due to improved technology, we would soon be fishless. Thus barriers to hunting efficiency may actually limit the possibility of mutual extinction of fox *and* rabbit, or fish *and* piscivore. Therefore overcoming all barriers does not guarantee a successful conclusion. Unfortunately, focus solely on improved technology can bring down the very barriers that ensure our futures.

D'Este *et al.* (2012) further divide barriers into **revealed** and **deterring** barriers. Revealed barriers are those of which the firm is aware and believes that innovative solution space exists, whereas deterring barriers are viewed by the firm as limits which cannot be solved, even though they are solvable.

Thus these barriers are all about perception. Research has shown that more innovative firms are more likely to encounter revealed barriers, whereas firms that do not innovate encounter deterring barriers (Iammarino *et al.*, 2009; D'Este *et al.*, 2012). Larger, established firms experience barriers to innovation from lock-ins and organizational inertia (Ferriani *et al.*, 2008). Small, new firms face problems from a lack of finance, specialization and market structure (Katila and Shane, 2005).

8.2 The psychology of change

Ultimately, individual change begins in the mind. Stimulus from our surroundings impact on this process, and thus the realm of psychology is central in our understanding of some of the most significant barriers to change. Gifford (2011) has identified seven psychological barriers or "**dragons**" opposing a transition to sustainability.

8.2.1 Limited cognition

The first dragon is **limited cognition**. Gifford believes that human thinking can act as a barrier to sustainability. Our ancestors were mainly concerned with their immediate group, immediate dangers and exploitable resources. This poses difficulties in responding to invisible future threats. The feedback loop is long and apparently infinite. However, we can challenge Gifford here. Faith-based religions abound (and have done so for thousands of years) across our planet, inspiring much of the architecture and art throughout the ages, and so we do have the capacity to respond to the invisible and imagined. Since much of the evidence is highly scientific, many people do not have a foundation on which to lay the bricks of evidence, due to ignorance. Science does not help here, often, given the reductionist, empirical principles on which it is based. Indeed the very rational thought process that allows us to comprehend the invisible is often rejected by science (Skene, 2009).

Complacency and environmental numbness can play a role, as the "Matilda cries wolf" syndrome sets in. Climatic heterogeneity can throw a cold winter or a cold summer at us, and the cries of "where's your climate change now?" begin to resound around staff rooms and kitchen tables. Our brains are wired in such a way as to prioritize dangers, and so invisible concepts such as climate may be pushed back down the list in terms of requiring urgent action, while food, health, education, facilitating technology, transport and leisure activities all rise to the top. This is called **judgemental discounting** and is re-enforced if the threat is externalized geographically. The disappearance of the Maldives is not an imminent threat to someone living in the steppes of Russia.

Uncertainty creates a significant barrier as we are fed different messages, many built on outdated ecological models, or unrealistic assumptions (such as zero waste, closed loops and the circular economy). Scientists oversimplify the real world, either as a consequence of the empirical philosophy they follow, or the need to deliver hard hitting bullet points in order to prise funding from government and the private sector. Businesses may utilize green wrapping that may be ultimately exposed as false, while other companies will downplay the impact of climate destabilization and lobby government to ease restrictive legislation, particularly if their products contribute to the problem. This all confuses the population at large.

Optimism bias is another innate characteristic, where we assume things won't be as bad for us as for others. Research indicates that while we do expect environmental conditions to worsen over the next 25 years, we assume that it will be worse elsewhere than where we live (Gifford *et al.*, 2009).

Perceived behavioural control refers to the confidence a person has that their behaviour will affect a particular outcome. Low perceived behavioural control will lead to a person feeling that it is not worthwhile wasting energy on a cause that they are unlikely to be able to change. This can be particularly relevant to consumers, faced by multinational co-operatives within a globalized economic system. Switching a light off isn't going to help at all. **Fatalism** reinforces this barrier to action. Extremely negative sustainability predictions can strengthen fatalism. **Threat messaging** (change or we are doomed) is much less likely to work than **challenge messaging** (we have a problem, but we can solve it) (O'Neill and Nicholson-Cole, 2009).

8.2.2 Ideology

The second great dragon, **ideology**, is most commonly represented by the philosophical world-view held, be it scientific, religious, humanist or political philosophy. Free market capitalism is a particularly destructive philosophy that is global in its distribution, resulting in the tragedy of the commons. Others turn to **techno-salvation**, an Enlightenment-based idea, where education and technology can overcome all limits imposed by nature. Indeed the Enlightenment as a philosophy, and its bedfellow, humanism, have spawned a set of principles that form the greatest barrier to sustainability, the belief that humans, freed from nature, can progress through technology and reasoning, to a utopia (Skene, 2011). This is the signature of modern civilization and the cornerstone of almost all political philosophy today. If nature begins to "misbehave" we will control it. Indeed, we now believe that we can improve nature, through genetic engineering, geo-engineering and river engineering.

Another ideological barrier is that of **system justification**. System justification theory combines three needs that humans experience: the need to be part of a group, the need to maintain the status quo within that group and the need for security and stability. These three needs lead to behaviour that rejects an alternative challenging view, and system justification theory is thought to be a significant contributor to climate destabilization denial. Some 39% of Americans reject the claim that our actions are detrimentally impacting on our climate, including some 59% of republican voters (Dunlap, 2008).

The activities that damage our planet are often tied into core beliefs, including economic growth, freedom to trade, equality, globalization, comfort and improvement. The very concept of development is closely tied to economic growth. Thus the status quo for many of us is unsustainable. This creates a need to justify it.

Feygina *et al.* (2010) demonstrated that if people perceive sustainability activity as part of their system, they are much more likely to adopt it. This explains the Ellen MacArthur Foundation's emphasis on the profitability of the circular economy, demonstrating that it is a truly capitalist pursuit (EMF, 2012).

8.2.3 Comparisons with other people

In the third psychological dragon, people derive their social norms from sampling their immediate circle of friends and neighbours. "Keeping up with the Jones" is a common reference to this, but psychologists refer to it as **planned behaviour** or the **value-belief-norm model**. There is also the issue of perceived inequity, where sacrifice on one person's behalf is not matched by similar sacrifice from another actor. This is further exacerbated by concerns over the cheater or free-rider, who may benefit from our sacrifice but not contribute.

8.2.4 Sunk costs

In this dragon, if a consumer has invested heavily in, say, a car, he/she will be reticent to reduce their use of it and switch to public transport. **Cognitive dissonance** can act to turn the actor away from environmentally friendly actions if sunk costs create too big a barrier for the consumer to deal with. This can then spin into other areas of activity, creating a more polluting individual (Skinner, 1987; p. 5). **Behavioural momentum** or habit is also a significant barrier. It acts as a resistance to change that is considered to be one of the major barriers to change, particularly in terms of climate change (Carrus *et al.*, 2008). **Incompatible goals** also create issues. We deal with incompatibilities and inconsistencies in all aspects of our lives, and sustainability is merely added to this mix. It will not be judged on its own merit, but rather will contribute to the suboptimal solution base available when multiple challenges are offered. Each new challenge added leads to an increasing number of decreasingly optimal solutions.

8.2.5 Discredence

Discredence is the fifth dragon. Mistrust or distrust of an organization greatly effects how well we respond to that organization. In sustainability, this can come from embarrassing behaviour, such as the email leakage from The University of East Anglia's climate research group. This has not only questioned the integrity of the group involved, but hugely undermined the public trust in climate science.

Cognitive dissonance can be important here, with denial becoming increasingly common as the debate polarizes and mud is thrown from each side. Fundamentally, there is an inherent mistrust of science and government. Scientists have been regularly portrayed in the media as boffins or, worse, as Dr Frankenstein-like characters. Opposition parties work to undermine government, with selective media outlets supporting and mediating this view to the public. In many ways, disagreement is the foundation of modern politics and science, contributing to a sense of discredence within the public. Finally, powerful lobbies, such as the fossil fuel industry, have significant impact on government, and will seek to undermine the message of science.

An important element here is the process of justice. As more decisions are taken to the courts, in terms of whether a wind farm or a fracking site can open in a local community, and as government policy on sustainability is challenged, it is important for people to feel empowered and have a sense that the system is fair. Three kinds of justice have been identified by Fischer *et al.* (2012):

1. **Distributive justice**: has there been a requirement, equity and equality in the outcome?
2. **Procedural justice**: is the process fair, inclusive and effective?
3. **Interactional justice**: how are people treated during the process?

Fischer *et al.* (2012) stress the importance of ensuring that the process of justice meets these requirements, otherwise the justice system itself will become a significant barrier.

8.2.6 Perceived risk

This is the sixth psychological dragon. What could the cost of sustainability actually be? These risks include concerns over time (would public transport take me longer?), society (what will others think?), psychology (will my self-esteem be damaged by driving a smaller car?), functionality (will it really work as well as my more polluting model?) and finance (will the cost be more?).

8.2.7 Rebound effect

The final psychological dragon is called the **rebound effect**. Here, having made savings, we then relax and go back to our damaging lifestyles. We may have a greener car, but now we do many more miles in it. The rebound effect is also termed the Jevons paradox (Jevons, 1866) and the Khazzoom–Brookes postulate (Khazzoom, 1980; Brookes, 1990).

Shove (2010) argues that by portraying the issue of climate destabilization as a psychological one based on attitude, behaviour and choice (the ABC approach), we risk marginalizing the debate, excluding social theories such as transition and practice. While Paul Stern suggests that "behavior (B) is an interactive product of personal-sphere attitudinal variables (A) and contextual factors (C)" (Stern, 2000; p. 415), Shove argues that the ABC approach suits government as it places responsibility back onto the consumer, a form of Big Society that avoids government responsibility. The powerful psychological lobby can produce context-free models, wherein habit drives behaviour, even though habit is itself a behavioural property. Shove (2010; p. 1277) concludes: "In effect, the idea that desires and attitudes drive behaviour produces a blind spot at a particularly crucial point, making it impossible to see how the contours and environmental costs of daily life evolve".

8.3 Fundamental issues I: knowledge barriers

Knowledge and information are viewed as essential if consumers are to move towards sustainable consumption (Valor, 2008; Hill, 2011). A significant generic barrier relates to a lack of information and a lack of clarity relating to sustainability. Lorenzoni *et al.* (2007) identify a number of difficulties relating to information, including:

- A lack of knowledge about where to find information
- A lack of desire to seek information
- A perception of information overload
- A confusion revolving around conflicting information or partial evidence
- A perceived lack of locally relevant information
- Information that is not accessible to nonexperts
- A perceived lack in credibility relating to the source of information
- Confusion relating to links between environmental issues and their respective solutions
- Information that is in conflict with values or experience

At the most basic level, there is confusion over what sustainability itself means. Given the multitude of schools of thought pertaining to sustainable development, each emphasizing a different set of criteria for progress, this is not surprising. As we have seen in earlier chapters, these schools range from technocratic or weak positions through to ecocentric or strong positions, and evolutionary through to revolutionary ideas. **Discursive confusion** is seen as a significant issue in the knowledge–action gap that is apparent (Markkula and Moisander, 2012).

Further confusion comes from inherent contradictions between different schools of thought. For example some advocate zero waste, while at the same time advocating a waste-is-food approach. There are contradictions between ecological knowledge and applied ecology within business models. For example the concept of renewable natural capital focuses on reducing use of the given resource, but pays no attention to the functions that underpin renewal (Fig. 8.1). Environmental degradation impacts on the capacity to renew the resource. So even if you reduce usage, damage such as salinity (on agriculture), soil erosion (on forests), ocean acidification (on shellfish)

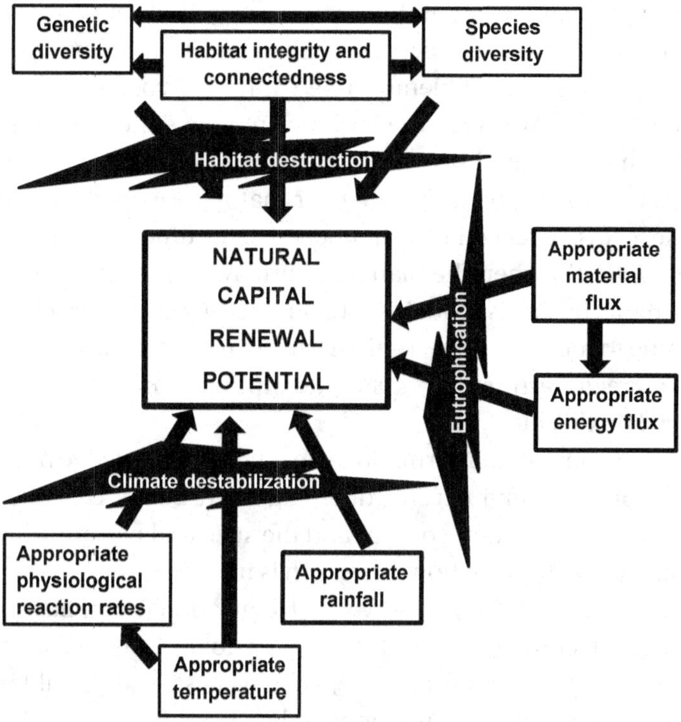

FIGURE 8.1 Recovery potential of renewable natural resources. Even if we stopped all of our negative activities today, the damage already done means that renewable natural capital is less likely to be renewed. Eutrophication, habitat destruction and degradation and climate destabilization have already damaged the key contributors to renewal and many of these contributors will take centuries to restore. The concept of renewable natural capital is questionable therefore, as we have damaged the very process of renewal as well as consuming the capital itself.

and eutrophication (on coral and fish) may well destroy the capacity for resource renewal.

Another point of confusion related to this is the idea that if we reduce carbon dioxide emissions, we will solve the crisis (Skene, 2010). Almost all the models and plans related to environmental destruction measure only carbon as their parameter. The carbon footprint dominates discussion. Yet it is the much larger and more complex ecological footprint that really matters. There is no point in having reduced carbon emissions if energy flux, nutrient pollution, toxic run-off and habitat destruction carry on as before. Making one metal link in a chain really strong and shiny will not prevent the chain snapping if one or more of the other links are still corroded.

The erroneous concept that the Earth is a closed system has also created much confusion, making it feel that we can resolve problems because the answers as well as the problems all lie within the cosy space we call our planet. But as we have seen, the Earth is an open system, within a closed universe, where material has and continues to come and go, and where energy flows through the leaky colander that represents the planet. If you don't believe this, reflect on what happened to the dinosaurs (and some 65% of all life on Earth) when the planet did briefly, approach a closed system. Yet sustainable business models such as closed-loop and circular economics continue to repeat the Spaceship Earth error of Earth as a closed system, leading to greater errors in terms of attempting to frame economic solutions based on this idea.

Studies often find that information can increase knowledge but has minimal effects on behaviour (e.g. Gardner and Stern, 2002). This reiterates the importance of information content and the style and pattern with which it is communicated. Information on its own is not enough.

Frisk and Larson (2011) observe that educational emphasis needs to change from technological and ecological to a more balanced knowledge content, embracing procedure, effectiveness, and social knowledge. Information-based educational approaches have failed to deliver transformative behavioural change (Finger, 2010). Some of the key barriers to sustainable education lie, according to Frisk and Larson (2011), in:

- Assembly line fragmentation of subjects, oversimplifying issues to a multiple choice true-or-false level, rather than embracing interconnectedness and system-based thinking
- One-size-fits-all, instant solutions which prevent understanding of long-term foresighted thinking
- Evaluation of students based on individual activities and outcomes, rather than group collaboration and stakeholder engagement
- Informational learning based solely on declarative knowledge rather than action-orientation and change-agent skills

Short class periods that prevent community-based projects along with restrictive and quarantined curricula also contribute to difficulties with exploring sustainability. However, the problem is not isolated to this subject. This is positive news, as many other disciplines would benefit from addressing the barriers mentioned above.

While values, ethics and norms have been viewed as areas to be avoided in modern curricula, these practices must be reintegrated if we are to fully explore sustainability in the curriculum (Sipos *et al.*, 2008). This nervousness around ethics and beliefs, while central to behavioural sociology, may have been closed out from sustainability theory because the reductionist model lies at the "heart" of science and engineering.

Frisk and Larson (2012) recommend a combination of knowledge approaches to deliver sustainability and other system-based areas of the curriculum:

- **Declarative knowledge**: to study social-ecological system dynamics, interactions and impacts
- **Procedural knowledge**: to study local action strategies and processes of change
- **Effectiveness knowledge**: to study personal efficacy and consequences of actions
- **Social knowledge**: to study cultural/moral norms and perceptions

Gaps are particularly apparent in forecasting, observing, confining and managing environmental perturbation. Hasnain and Jasimuddin (2012) divide knowledge into two forms, tacit and explicit. **Tacit knowledge** (that which is difficult to write down) has a number of barriers not found in **explicit knowledge**, including perception, language, time, value and distance.

While risk managers tend to solve problems holistically, climate science relies on reductionist methods, resulting in a disconnection between science and end-users. This is because the information from science lacks relevance within a holistic solution space occupied by end-users (Kiem and Austin, 2013).

Davenport and Prusak (2000) identify a number of **cultural factors** as impacting on knowledge transfer, including lack of trust, different cultures, vocabulary, frames of reference, giving status and rewards to the knowledge owners, treating knowledge as a prerogative of particular groups, and lack of time and meeting places. These issues are often magnified within a globalized economy.

Knowledge transfer from academia to stakeholders can be restricted by the vast array of terminology and unclear taxonomy (Axelsson, 2009). Hammer and Söderqvist (2001) comment that universities have failed to meet the societal need for integrated education. The reductionist emphasis that has dominated academia for the last century is a powerful barrier preventing the training and hiring of trans-disciplinary scientists needed to deliver and communicate system-based knowledge. Bringing together specialists in small areas of knowledge has failed to address the requirements of the knowledge transfer challenges facing us (Axelsson, 2010).

Government assessments of universities, which are central to their funding and reputations, have also failed to reward trans-disciplinary studies, focusing instead on specialist research. Indeed many faculties are likely to steer away from collaborations out with their areas of specialism for fear of being downgraded in research assessment exercises. Blue sky research and innovation are similarly punished as grants awarded and papers published are the main criteria for success in such assessment exercises, leaving no room for speculative work with a risk of failure (Garfield, 2005; von Bothmer *et al.*, 2009). High ranking academic journals tend to be highly specialized, preventing high impact collaboration across disciplines from being awarded equally or higher than specialist collaborations.

8.4 Fundamental issues II: co-ordination barriers

Boons and Baas (1997) identify a lack of co-ordination within companies as creating a significant hurdle. Political divisions, segmented responsibility and protective departmental interests can shield organizations from identifying the potential economic benefits of sustainability initiatives. These are termed organizational silos and form significant barriers to transition in companies (Lovins and Lovins, 1997; Whiteman *et al.*, 2011).

Moon *et al.* (2011) identify the following barriers to strategic integration of more financially orientated management control systems (MCSs) with sustainability control systems (SCSs):

- Organizational barriers:
  - Lack of co-ordination across multiple internal businesses, functions and management levels
  - Lack of leadership commitment
  - Latent silo effects
  - Underinvestment in sustainability data collection and development
  - Insufficient systems and structures enabling staff collaboration

- Cognitive barriers:
  - Uncertainty surrounding costs and risks related to sustainability
  - Uncertainties surrounding the relationship between sustainability and mainstream business performance
  - Incompatibilities between the design logics of MCSs and SCSs
  - Lack of understanding of their respective objectives and operations
  - Insufficiently developed commitments to and understandings of sustainability
- Technical barriers
  - Challenges in development of integrative and comparable key performance indicators (KPIs) and other metrics
  - Difficulties in measuring and accounting for the various impacts caused by company activities as well as the value created through sustainability measures
  - Unavailability of appropriate IT, particularly to integrate sustainability and financial data

8.5 Fundamental issues III: financial barriers

Capital budgets can prevent plant managers from making wise long-term decisions, related to total life-span costing of plant equipment. Capital planning is often designed around economic metrics that encourage actions which damage the environment or ignore social consequences (Hoffman and Bazerman, 2007).

Bai *et al.* (2010) report that financial barriers have significant impacts on urban sustainability development projects. Feasibility studies can first come upon economic and financial barriers. Funding from the World Bank and other international funders can bring with it requirements that a country may not be able or willing to meet, and a lack of trust can also impact on securing funding from outwith the country concerned (Nguyen, 2006). Failure to secure ongoing funding, risking financial sustainability, can also be problematic, given the unreliability of world markets (Mabbitt, 2006).

8.6 Fundamental issues IV: policy framework barriers

A lack of a cohesive policy framework at a government level can be problematic. For example, in their recent report, *Seizing the Sustainability Advantage,* Consult Australia state that leading Australian firms in the built and natural environment sectors raised concerns about national and state policies inhibiting transition to a sustainable economy (Consult Australia 2011). Policy strategies have also been implicated in slowing eco-innovation (del Rio *et al.*, 2010). Business tends to be reactive rather than proactive towards sustainable development, particularly if it is enforced by policy (Chatterton and Style, 2001). The lack of involvement of the consumer in any analysis has also been identified as problematic (Hertwich, 2005). Often, pro-environmental attitudes already exist within business, but converting this into operational changes has been identified as a key obstacle (Revell and Blackburn 2007).

The obstacles to sustainability become increasingly important when companies, operating globally, have to deal with the added factors of international legalities and the need to cater to different cultures, because these can require a different suite of corporate responsibility activities (Vidal and Kozak, 2008).

Local planning has long been recognized as being constrained by limited information (Mukheibir and Ziervogel, 2007), institutional context (wherein municipal authorities have no constitutional standing) and resource limitations (Pini *et al.*, 2007). However, Measham *et al.* (2011) point to deeper issues within the structure and function of municipal policy decision-making. Local authorities have a tendency to place climate destabilization response within environment departments, whereas a cross-sectoral approach is actually required for proper response. **Institutional silos** make for tidy administration, but not for system-level action.

Land use planning often works within a framework of a stable climate, preventing adaptation towards future variation. Resource limits also impact in terms of competition. Roads, schools and childcare facilities may well be viewed as more urgent priorities than climate destabilization adaptation. The political platform on which the leaders of local authorities stand will also impact on decisions taken. The fact that so few politicians represent the Green Party and similar environmental political groupings indicates the priorities of the voters globally, and thus the difficulty in gaining support for local environmental policies and plans.

In terms of implementing sustainable urban development projects, Bai *et al.* (2010) report that political barriers were most significant during project formulation, relating to fund allocation and rent agreements. Resentment from local government towards national government can also play a significant role (Mathur, 2006), particularly where party politics differ between the two levels of administration. Institutional barriers were most pronounced during project implementation. Bai *et al.* (2010) highlighted lack of competence, workplace culture, and resistance to change as particularly problematic.

Negro *et al.* (2010) focus on six barriers facing the introduction and spread of sustainable practice:

1. **The valley of death barrier**: many innovations become trapped in the so called "valley of death" at a point on their development path just prior to large-scale market introduction. Risks and doubts come to the fore just as final commitment is called for, both financially and institutionally. Surprisingly, policy instruments are generally not available to assist in tackling this barrier.

2. **Attention shift**: Johnson and Jacobsson (2000) demonstrated that development and diffusion of new innovations takes a long time; 25 years for the formative phase and another 25 years for diffusion. During this time, policy objectives can shift, meaning that by the time the new concept is ready to roll out to the market, there is no longer the policy framework to support it. For example changes in financial markets and oil prices alter the policy context over time, and can alter the support for particular technologies (e.g. Sandén and Jonasson, 2005).

3. **Unstable policy instruments**: policy-makers expect technological investment and research and development to quickly produce market-ready solutions. When this does not happen, the flavour of the month can shift, leading to instability in policy direction. A classic example of this was the abolition of the Fossil Energy Tax in Holland in 2001, and the subsequent, sudden collapse of two replacement subsidies, the MEP (*Milieukwaliteit Elektriciteitsproductie subsidie*) and the SDE (*Stimuleringsregeling duurzame energieproductie*), greatly damaging the renewable energy market (Suurs and Hekkert, 2009).

4. **Delegitimization**: powerful incumbent companies may see new sustainable innovations as a threat and can seek to delegitimize them at three levels:
   - Undermining the performance of each unit (e.g. in terms of environmental impact).
   - Undermining the potential (physically, technically or economically).
   - Undermining the functionality (in terms of technology and cost).
5. **Lack of knowledge in policy-makers**: universities generally have weak relationships with policy-makers, particularly in terms of sustainability issues, reducing knowledge diffusion. This can lead to wrong technology choices and a lack of appropriate market instruments.
6. **Size matters**: policy-makers tend to compare large-scale incumbent technologies to new innovative technologies. This is unfair, as new technologies cannot possible produce an equivalent impact until scaled up, and so their potential contribution is ignored based on their current output.

International bodies often attempt to roll out western policies in "developing" nations, where they are not relevant. The inability to implement appropriate technologies and to understand historical, cultural and geographical differences means that the globalization of sustainable development, with a one-size-fits-all approach, is likely to create significant barriers (Sarkar and Singh, 2010).

Bauer *et al.* (2012) highlight four significant barriers facing government policy-makers.

1. Climate destabilization poses challenges that cut horizontally across policy sectors. Policy fields that are particularly affected include water and coastal management, housing, spatial planning, public health, tourism, public infrastructure, agriculture and forestry. There is a lack of policy integration, underpinned by political incoherence.
2. Challenges also cut vertically across different jurisdictional levels of government. Adger *et al.* (2005: p. 80) note that "the dynamic nature of linkages between levels of governance is not

well-understood, and the politics of the construction of scale are often ignored".

3. Huge uncertainty surrounds the field of climate destabilization, both in terms of the science and its transformation into policy.
4. Issues involve a large number of non-state actors with limited capacities to respond. Governments are keen to pursue informative participation, but are less keen to take part in neither consultative participation nor decisional participation.

8.7 Fundamental issues V: technological barriers

Another generic problem, in terms of it affecting all sectors of business, is the use of inappropriate technology in particular cultural contexts. Examples include large-scale hydro-electric projects, that displace thousands of people and change landscapes and ecosystems, or the introduction of mechanized straight line harvesting in areas where agriculture is small scale, community-owned and engaged in polyculture (Black, 2007).

Ryan and Vivekananda (1993) discuss a number of smaller scale inappropriate approaches including the introduction of grinders powered by bicycles into villages where, normally, women grind flour, but only men use bicycles. They also cite the promotion of smokeless cooking stoves into areas where smoke from fires plays a major role as a deterrent to malaria-carrying mosquitoes, and building solar-powered stoves in locations where, traditionally, cooking takes place after sunset. Yet the use of appropriate technology is often perceived as a "**poor person's**" technology and too difficult for a multinational company to accommodate (Zelenika and Pearce, 2011).

8.8 Fundamental issues VI: organizational barriers

Habitual routines, fear of the unknown, resource limitations and threats to established power bases all form resistance to transition (Hoffman and Bazerman, 2007). Indeed the corporate sector has been identified as a significant barrier, due to its emphasis on economic growth. Directors are politically powerful, while growth and cost cutting lead to profits (McGregor, 2006). Financial markets can also present significant barriers to change.

Doppelt (2003) emphasized a patriarchal approach from senior management, preventing new thinking, as the most serious intra-firm barrier to transition. In addition, confusion over cause and effect (i.e. treating the symptoms rather than the underlying causes) and a failure to institutionalize sustainability, create impediments to change (Doppelt, 2003). An assumption referred to as the **mythical fixed pie of negotiation** (the belief that negotiators are fighting over a finite pool of resources and that there can only be a win–lose outcome) is often accompanied by the belief that environmental change will always be bad for the company (Pruitt and Rubin, 1986). Lorenzoni *et al.* (2007) highlight denial, lack of faith in alternatives, faith in technology to solve problems and being too busy to change as sticking points.

In Europe, small and medium enterprises (SMEs) account for 64% of environmental damage (Calogirou *et al.*, 2010). In the UK alone, 45% of total UK business energy use is by SMEs, broadly in proportion to their share of the economy (Vickers *et al.* 2009). SMEs are responsible for some 43% of the serious industrial pollution incidents and generate 60% of the commercial waste in England and Wales (Blundel *et al.*, 2011).

Important differences in scale emerge, and small and medium enterprises (SMEs) can have very different obstacles compared with large businesses (Burch *et al.*, 2011). In surveys, most SMEs recognized the importance of environmental issues, but few could envisage remaining as competitive (Taylor *et al.*, 2003). Unless there were regulatory and political checks, market-led actors are under pressure to externalize social and environmental costs (Stern, 2009). Also environmental legislation was not clear to many SMEs (Vickers *et al.*, 2009).

Working as part of a network greatly improves the success of SMEs in terms of meeting sustainability targets, while isolated SMEs are unlikely to be able to implement sustainable practice. Thus isolation can be a significant organizational barrier. Cost is a considerable issue, due to effect of scale of being a small company. Time is also a barrier, as there may be less or no staff with dedicated job descriptions related to sustainability implementations. Again a network could provide a dedicated person, shared between a group of SMEs, thus reducing the cost for each business.

The organization for Economic Co-operation and Development (OECD) highlights the importance of clustering, stating that: "Knowledge-based strategies stand out as a key element of new regional policy ... National and regional governments are reorienting their policies to emphasize the role and interaction among economic actors" (OECD, 2005, p. 9). The concept of business clusters has a long history, going back almost a century (for example the industrial districts of Marshall (1920)), and received recent interest in the form of eco-industrial parks, but competitiveness and data protection have deterred it, fundamentally based on the application of Darwinian competition and selection, rather than the system-based ecological approach of synergy and interaction more commonly seen in nature.

Barriers to cluster formation (Potter and Miranda, 2009) include:

- Weak entrepreneurial cultures
- Weak involvement of small firms in cluster projects
- Lack of seed capital
- Problems of congestion and social divisions
- Shortages of qualified labour
- Poor co-ordination of policies

Willard (2005) identified the three most significant barriers for SMEs, when undergoing transition towards greater sustainability, as perceived/actual costs, lack of awareness of business benefits and resources (time, money and knowledge). Barriers such as cost implications, management time, and other priorities have been listed as significant obstacles to sustainability in a survey of 800 small businesses in New Zealand (Lawrence *et al.*, 2006). SMEs are often in leased buildings, and thus do not have complete control over infrastructure. Concerns relating to growing the business also forced prioritization of focus, due to small size, which means that small businesses would be less willing to put time into sustainable practice as opposed to investing in customer recruitment and expansion (Herren, 2010).

Kotter (1995) identified eight barriers to successful corporate transformation:

1. **A lack of urgency**: in order to begin a process of transformation, there needs to be aggressive co-operation between many individuals, with high motivation. A sense of urgency can only be distilled if there is a hard case to be made, and woolly thinking of much of the sustainability literature, along with the invisibility of the threat, make this difficult to achieve. However, urgency doesn't

mean rushing headlong into change. Urgency is a driver, not an accelerator, and each step must be carefully managed.

2. **A lack of a powerful coalition**: deconstructing the present system is not enough. A new system must be presented alongside the negative message relating to the old system, otherwise a vacuum, often quickly filled with paralysis, results. A new system requires leadership, and so transformation is hindered by a management structure inhabited by weak leaders. It is essential to have a consensus for change.

3. **A lack of clear vision**: a myriad of plans and programmes often accompany attempts at transformation, but unless there is a clear, comprehensible, easily communicated vision that can be pictured and understood, failure will follow. It is essential that the wording of this vision is carefully developed and tested before launch.

4. **A lack of communication**: a single company-wide meeting is insufficient. Indeed, Kotter (1995) suggests that the average effort to communicate the vision is tenfold too small. Improved communication may be strengthened by changes in existing communication channels—e.g. redesigned newsletters, improved feedback channels to increase ownership, new structures to team meetings, etc.

5. **Failure to remove obstacles to the new vision**: these obstacles may be within the minds of individuals, in management structure or in job descriptions.

6. **Lack of short-term wins**: momentum is crucial in achieving transformation, but if a workforce does not sense progress, then perceived cost and risk may overpower perceived gain, undermining the entire process. These clear and communicable successes should be carefully planned for, and not just stumbled upon.

7. **Declaring victory too soon**: again, a loss of momentum, even after a few years, can be catastrophic. Failed transformation also plants seeds of doubt for future efforts.

8. **Failure to anchor changes within the corporate structure**: this can arise from a failure to communicate how the new thinking at every level has achieved the positive change, and the failure to appoint new managers who embrace the vision.

An unclear business model is also a significant barrier. According to Chesbrough and Rosenbloom (2002; pp. 533-4), a business model should:

- Articulate the value proposition (i.e., the value created for users)
- Identify a market segment and specify the revenue generation mechanism (i.e., users to whom technology is useful and for what purpose)
- Define the structure of the value chain required to create and distribute the concept and complementary assets needed to support position in the chain
- Detail the revenue mechanism(s) by which the firm will be paid
- Estimate the cost structure and profit potential (given value proposition and value chain structure)
- Describe the position of the firm within the value network linking suppliers and customers (incl. identifying potential complementers and competitors)
- Formulate the competitive strategy by which the innovating firm will gain and hold advantage over rivals

Barriers to introducing a new business model include conflicts with the prevailing business model and conflicts with the assets dedicated to the previous model.

Chowdhury *et al.* (2012) highlight a number of organizational barriers facing implementation of sustainable practice. Internal social barriers within a company included lack of awareness between employees and employers, absence of sustainability content within strategic and policy thinking, inadequate governance within the supply chain members, lack of written policies and reporting practices, absence of social and environmental reporting and lack of a regulatory framework and compliance with the law. External issues include dependence on material imported from uncertified sources, fluctuations of raw material and currency and lack of choice of supplier.

The **competing vales framework** (CVF) provides an interesting insight into business organization (see Fig. 8.2) (Linnenluecke and Griffiths, 2010).

An **internal process culture** will focus on growth, long-term productivity and economic performance. A **human relations culture** might experience a tension between creating a business venture and pursuing a social purpose. A **rational goal culture** focuses on how to organize systems rationally while facing varying environmental demands and emphasizing the efficient use

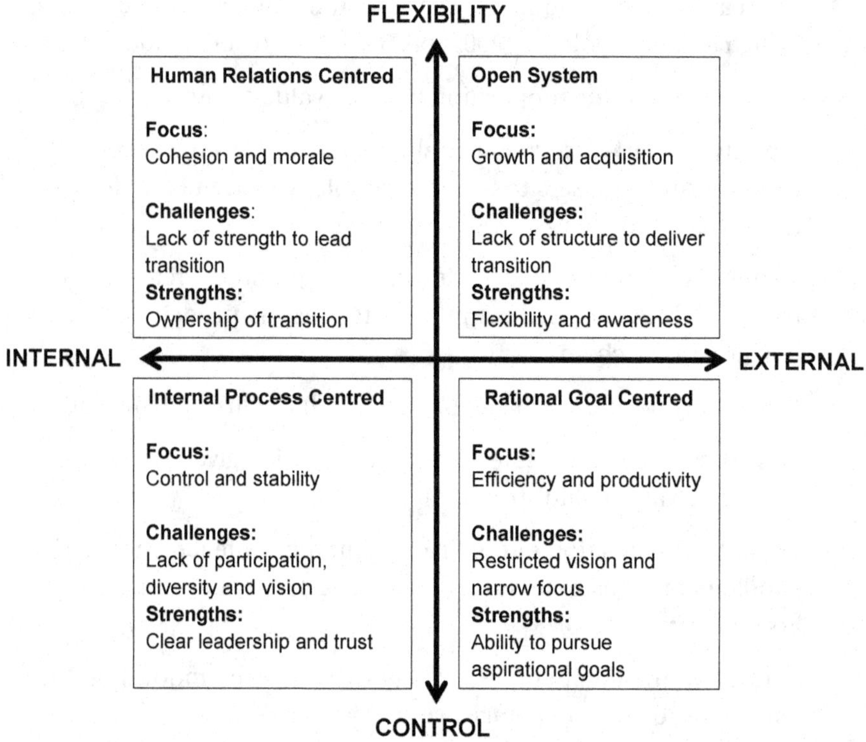

FIGURE 8.2 Consequences of the competing vales framework (CVF), based on Linnenluecke and Griffiths (2010), for transition to sustainable practice. Businesses that have strong top-down control have the ability to embed management decisions related to sustainability and to implement policies. More flexible management approaches provide greater willingness to change and the staff are more likely to adapt to change. Flexibility brings issues related to a lack of strong rudder control, while control prevents visionary participation and exploration of the full diversity of the workforce. Companies who focus on their staff and business structure and function will likely have greater trust from their employees and will be in closer contact with staff, whereas companies with an external focus will be more able to adjust to market demands and to plan in a broader context.

of resources, planning and goal setting and the adequacy of organizational structures in light of the environment. An **open systems culture** will place greater emphasis on innovation for achieving ecological and social sustainability in their pursuit of corporate sustainability.

8.9 Fundamental issues VII: consumer barriers

Consumers participate in two forms of damaging consumption: conspicuous and inconspicuous consumption. Each has very different motivations. **Conspicuous consumption** (the possession of noticeable, environmentally damaging possessions) relates to status, a sense of self-importance and, at a higher level, affirmation of the particular world-view adopted by the consumer. It also can involve peer-pressure. Inconspicuous behaviour relates to everyday activities, such as heating, air conditioning, washing machines, cookers and fridges. **Inconspicuous consumption** is interpreted as "**need**", and therefore is a much more sensitive issue to address in terms of change.

In Sweden, social issues, habits, price, lack of information and low self-efficacy were deemed as the most significant barriers by consumers (Isenhour, 2010). Paetz *et al.* (2012) point to confirmed habits, high expenses, doubts on ecological sense, data privacy protection and technical complexity as the main barriers to people adopting smart technology in homes to monitor sustainable living.

While consumers are the source of a number of barriers to sustainability, they also encounter barriers. These include:

- A lack of suitable transport options.
- A lack of suitable employment options, forcing long working hours on consumers and a spiral of earn and spend. Holland has introduced the Hours Adjustment Act 2000, which allows workers to decide how many hours they work, leading to one third of the Dutch working part time (de Graaf, 2009 p. 274). The New Economic Forum (2010) suggests a 21-hour working week.
- Insufficient product information, preventing conscientious consumption.
- Excessive exposure to consumer temptations can destroy the neoclassical reliance on an invisible hand acting to control economics. Customers are not allowed to make private preferences, but can

be controlled by advertising (Brulle and Young, 2007). Consumers can encounter 3,000 advertisements everyday (de Graaf *et al.*, 2005: p. 165).

- A lack of sustainable yet affordable housing is a significant barrier. Cost, proximity to work and schools, proximity to environmentally friendly retail outlets and leisure options are all sustainable qualities, but this would require a complete alteration of city plans and property rights. Yet if everyone had property large enough to grow their own vegetables, the urban sprawl would increase, destroying nature. Expensive houses require more work to pay for them. Housing is looked on as the most difficult consumer area to change as a result of these problems (Alexander, 2012).

Young *et al.* (2010) interviewed consumers as to the barriers preventing them from basing their consumer decisions on the sustainability of the company and product. The following hurdles were prominent:

- Insufficient time for research, decision-making and purchase.
- Extra cost of sustainable products.
- Lack of information on, for example, supply chain. Focus of available information is on running cost, not manufacture and recycling potential.
- Sustainability must compete with nongreen criteria, such as specification, recognized brand, size, price, information source reliability, model, appearance, availability, design, colour, age, mileage, sales technique and service history.

Critics have highlighted the injustice of expecting consumers to lead the fight for greater sustainability in a global market. Halkier (2001; p. 205) noted: "it has become increasingly common to call upon so-called ordinary consumers to solve a range of societal and political problems. Environmental policies and food policies are no exception to this pattern".

8.10 Fundamental issues VIII: legislative barriers

Dernbach and Mintz (2011) highlight the fact that:

> in many cases, the legal rules for a particular sustainability objective at a higher level of government are completely separate from the relevant legal rules at a lower level of government. As a result, the lower level of government can make decisions that frustrate or impede sustainability goals.

Thus the use of law to require integrated decision-making is emphasized, given the need not only to focus on carbon-based issues, but on broader environmental, social and economic considerations. While the need for new laws and modifications to current laws are required, existent laws can also have significant roles to play in delivering sustainability (Craig and Ruhl, 2010; Medina and Tarlock, 2010). **Comparative law** (employing laws from other jurisdictions) can also be used to pursue sustainable outcomes (Abbott and Marchant, 2010; Ross, 2010).

Adler (2010) expects that as drought and flood issues increase due to climate destabilization, national governments will move to displace local authorities from controlling water laws and other legislation pertinent to adaptation and resilience. Thus subnational governments, the sources of many barriers to change, may find their positions weakened legally. The need for law to protect ecological integrity directly is also an area of concern. While laws pertaining to our activities are important, the primacy of functional ecology cannot be overlooked.

Compliance time-frames are often too short to accommodate green infrastructure. For example mature trees can absorb the first 13mm of rainfall, but take time to grow. Grey infrastructure takes a known short time to construct. A barrier arises because of the uncertainty related to the outcomes of green infrastructure, and thus proponents of these approaches must develop methods of demonstrating compliance with regulatory standards by quantifying their costs and measuring the various benefits yielded by green infrastructure (Dunn, 2010).

8.11 Other barriers

8.11.1 Carbon lock-ins

Countries with large supplies of fossil fuels and other important resources (often referred to as mineral-energy complexes), such as South Africa, have low coal prices, and so it is more difficult for alternative technologies to compete economically. The low energy price means there is little incentive to develop alternative energy sources or energy efficiency (Fine and Rustomjee, 1996; Winkler and Marquand, 2009).

8.11.2 Barriers to investing in natural capital

Wackernagel and Rees (1997) identify 14 barriers to investing in natural capital:

1. Slow but steady decline in environmental health are imperceptible to humans
2. The business-as-usual model is supported by casual observations that the birds are still singing (i.e. spring is not silent)
3. The exploitative relationship between man and nature is normalized by tolerance to exploitation in cultural, spiritual and gender relations (e.g. turning a blind eye to child labour participation in supply chains and other externalized miseries)
4. The belief that maximizing utility is good
5. Conservation biology portrays humans as capable of saving nature
6. Industrialization and growth will deliver development
7. Body–mind and people–nature splits represent denial of cause and consequence; mimicry rather than participation prevents recognition of our place within nature
8. Money represents wealth, while nature and money are interchangeable (weak sustainability)
9. Resource price is perceived as equating to resource scarcity. Thus if water is cheap, then it can't be scarce
10. Marginal value (not total value) determines market price

11. There is an increasing gap between what we need to know and what we know
12. Enlightenment philosophy re-enforces technology as saviour and solution to all problems, while paving the way to a human-made utopia (nature holds no limits)
13. Main resource conservation tool is efficiency, even though increased efficiency at an individual level increases resource throughput at a societal level
14. Trade is assumed to be mutually beneficial, bringing wealth to all, but in reality it increases the risk to all of environmental collapse

8.11.3 Barriers to recycling

The Engineering Employers' Federation (EEF) has written a report on issues relating to recycling in industry in the UK (EEF, 2011), which concludes that businesses find the regulatory framework confusing. It is unclear if environmental permits are required, for example, when repairing, re-using and recycling waste, such as wooden pallets. The regulatory framework could impede manufacturers recovering their own or their customers' waste by actual or perceived regulatory barriers because of the uncertainty of compliance.

Manufacturers of all sizes are struggling to recycle low volumes of segregated wastes. Solutions are required to enable economies of scale to be achieved cost-effectively in order to unlock these resources. Resources required to segregate some waste-streams are labour intensive and uneconomic.

The EEF recommends that governments should reflect this in how they measure the success of the Waste Framework Directive waste hierarchy and its range of waste policies. Finding markets for materials remains an issue. Furthermore, much of the recycled material is exported, limiting the value to the internal market.

Finally, access to commercial capacity is still limited. The number of facilities may be on the increase for domestic waste, but that does not address shortfall in capacity for commercial and industrial wastes. Waste recovery facilities need to be convenient, cost-effective and reflect the costs to businesses of segregating materials. Clustering of firms could help here.

8.11.4 Barriers to green procurement of services

Procurement of services by governments represents a huge global market and one where sustainability has the potential of having a huge impact (Taylor, 2006; Sustainable Procurement Task Force, 2006). Spending is now at historically high levels of 40% of gross domestic product (GDP) in OECD countries (Hall 2010), 49.1% of GDP in 27 European countries (Eurostat 2012) and rising in "developing" countries (Islam and Siwar, 2013).

However, a number of barriers exist. Economies of scale put pressure on procurement in terms of buying in bulk, rather than in small parcels, the latter considered to be more expensive. This forms both a barrier and a lock-in, preventing sustainable development (Morgan, 2008). EU procurement rules mean it is illegal to specify "local" food in public catering contracts (Morgan, 2008). Through creative procurement policies, public bodies in Italy and France are able to purchase local food without specifying it as such (Morgan and Morley, 2002; Morgan and Sonnino, 2007).

There is a supply and demand problem, where small organic producers are unable to meet large contracts, or to expand quickly enough, such as with organic produce. Other barriers to localism include EU hygiene regulations which have made small local abattoirs uneconomic (Morgan, 2008), preventing localism from developing. The National Audit Office (2005) considers cost, knowledge, awareness, risk, legal issues, regulatory ambiguity, and leadership inertia to be key obstacles in the implementation of sustainable procurement. In one of the most comprehensive studies of sustainable procurement in the UK, the Sustainable Procurement Task Force (2006) added two further barriers: a lack of whole life costing and a lack of sustainable procurement skills. They further identify the following barriers:

- Higher upfront, capital costs of sustainable products
- Higher costs of a more specialized labour force for installing and maintaining sustainable technologies
- Long payback periods
- Lack of financial incentives, including tax relief and grant funding
- Lack of financial benefits for developers and contractors (benefits tend to accrue for the end-user)
- Lack of economies of scale for sustainable products
- Cost savings of innovative products are difficult to prove

In China, Qiao and Wang (2011) identified the following barriers to the implementation of green public procurement:

- **Unfavourable marketing, legal and production contexts**: the most recent Government Procurement Method regulations state that government should give priority to high-tech products and eco-friendly products, but there is no definition of what is meant by an eco-friendly product. There are not many choices in the market in terms of green alternatives or any subsidies available to neither producers nor procurers. Furthermore producers of sustainable products must go through a long process before they are allowed to sell products. While this protects against greenwashing, it also works as a barrier to green production.
- **Issues with the management of programmes**: China lacks a single agency with responsibility for green procurement. This produces policy overlaps, management duplication and competition between the agencies involved.
- **Lack of uniformity** in green production definition and evaluation criteria.
- **Insufficient resources**: given the difficulty in gaining legal rights to produce green products, the outcome is that these products are very expensive initially, and unless a company can somehow survive and grow, there is a real danger of not being able to compete with regards to pricing.

8.11.5 The business case for sustainability

Sazmann *et al.* (2005) sum up the challenges facing anyone attempting to construct a business case for sustainability (BCS):

- **Complexity**: the nature of the BCS is extremely complex because of its reliance on a number of very different parameters (e.g. technology, regime and visibility) that vary hugely between firms, sectors, nations and development phases.
- **Materiality**: the BCS may exist but may often be marginal in practice and/or difficult to detect. Such approaches are extremely limited, focusing on eco-efficiency and on reducing downside operational risk.

8.12 Debate, discussion and further thought

1. Why are psychological barriers so important in preventing change? What particular aspects of sustainability make it particularly susceptible to such barriers?
2. Evaluate which barriers most impede change in your own or another company.
3. How could you suggest tackling information barriers?
4. Why are organizational barriers so difficult to overcome?
5. What are the barriers associated with WIT (world-view, institution and technology).
6. In what ways has the Enlightenment contributed to the barriers to sustainability?
7. What barriers exist in politics?
8. Examine Figure 8.2. Identify your company or a company of your choice with one of the four systems, and examine what challenges come from the management style employed, in terms of sustainability.
9. Compare and contrast the relevance of different barriers to social, environmental and economic sustainability.
10. What are the limits to sustainability?

References

Abbott, K.W. and Marchant, G.E. (2010). Institutionalizing sustainability across the federal government. Sustainability 2: 1924-42.

Adger, N.W., Arnell, N.W. and Tompkins, E.L. (2005). Successful adaptation to climate change across scales. Global Environmental Change Part A 15: 77-86.

Adler, R.W. (2010). Drought, sustainability, and the law. Sustainability 2: 2176-96.

Alexander, S. (2012). Degrowth implies voluntary simplicity: overcoming barriers to sustainable consumption. Simplicity Institute Report.

Axelsson, R. (2009). Landscape approach for sustainable development. Doctoral dissertation, School for Forest Management, SLU. Acta Universitatis agriculturae Sueciae Vol. 2009: 94.

Axelsson, R. (2010). Integrative research and trans-disciplinary knowledge production: A review of barriers and bridges. Journal of Landscape Ecology 4 (2): 14-40.

Bai, X., Roberts, B. and Chen, J. (2010). Urban sustainability experiments in Asia: patterns and pathways. Environmental Science and Policy 13(4): 312-25.

Bauer, A., Feichtinger, J. and Steurer, R. (2012). The Governance of Climate Change Adaptation in 10 OECD Countries: Challenges and Approaches. Journal of Environmental Policy and Planning 14(3): 279-304.

Black, M. (2007). *The No-Nonsense Guide to International Development.* New Internationalist, London.

Boons, F.A. and Baas, L.J. (1997). Types of industrial ecology: the problem of coordination. Journal of Cleaner Production 5(1-2): 79-80.

Blundel, R.K., Spence, L.J. and Zerbinati, S. (2011). Entrepreneurial social responsibility: scoping the territory. In: Spence, L.J. and Painter-Morland, M. (eds.), *Ethics in Small and Medium Sized Enterprises: a Global Commentary.* Springer Netherlands. pp. 123-45.

Burch, C., Shaw, A., Zerriffi, H. and Meyer, R. (2011). Harnessing the entrepreneurial power of small business: New strategies for reducing greenhouse gas emissions (briefing note 2011-28). University of Victoria: Pacific Institute for Climate Solutions.

Brulle, R. and Young, L. (2007). Advertising, consumption levels, and the natural environment. Sociological Inquiry 77: 522.

Brookes, L. (1990). The greenhouse effect: The fallacies in the energy efficiency solution. Energy Policy 18: 199-201.

Calogirou, C., Sorensen, S.Y., Larsen, P.J. and Alexopolou, S. (2010). *SMEs and the Environment in the European Union.* Main report, PLANET & Teknologisk Institute.

Carrus, G., Passafaro, P. and Bonnes, M. (2008). Emotions, habits and rational choices in ecological behaviours: The case of recycling and use of public transportation. Journal of Environmental Psychology 28: 51-62.

Chatterton, P. and Style, S. (2001). Putting sustainable development into practice? The role of local policy partnership networks. Local Environment 6(4): 439-52.

Chesbrough, H. and Rosenbloom, R.S. (2002). The role of the business model in capturing value from innovation: evidence from Xerox Corporation's technology spin-off companies. Industrial and Corporate Change 11(3): 529-55.

Chowdhury, M., Dewan, M.N.A., Hossain, M.M. and Quaddus, M.A. (2012). An AHP-QFD integrated approach for mitigating barriers of corporate sustainability. In: Pillai, R., Ozbilgin, M., Harley, B. and Hartel, C. (eds.), *Managing for Volatility and Stability.* The 26th Australian and New Zealand Academy of Management Conference (ANZAM), 5–7 Dec. 2012. ANZAM, Perth, Australia.

Consult Australia (2011). *Seizing the Sustainability Advantage.* Consult Australia, Sydney.

Craig, R.K. and Ruhl, J.B. (2010). Governing for sustainable coasts: complexity, climate change, and coastal ecosystem protection. Sustainability 2(5): 1361-88.

Davenport, T.H. and Prusak, L. (2000). *Working Knowledge: How Organizations Manage What They Know.* Harvard Business School Press, MA.

De Graaf, J. (2009). Political prescriptions. In: Alexander, S. (ed.), *Voluntary Simplicity: The Poetic Alternative to Consumer Culture.* Stead and Daughters Ltd., New Zealand. P. 274.

De Graaf, J., Wann, D. and Naylor, T. (2005). *Affluenza: the All-Consuming Epidemic.* Berret-Koehler, San Fransisco. 2nd Edition.

Del Río, P., Carrillo-Hermosilla, J. and Könnölä, T. (2010). Policy strategies to promote eco-innovation. Journal of Industrial Ecology 14(4): 541-57.

Dernbach, J.C. and Mintz, J.A. (2011). Environmental laws and sustainability: an introduction. Sustainability 3(3): 531-40.

D'Este, P., Iammarino, S., Savona, M. and von Tunzelmann, N. (2012). What hampers innovation? Revealed barriers versus deterring barriers. Research Policy 41(2): 482-8.

Doppelt, Y. (2003). Implementation and assessment of project-based learning in a flexible environment. International Journal of Technology and Design Education 13(3): 255-72.

Dunlap, R. (2008). Partisan gap on global warming grows. Gallup Poll. Retrieved 8 February 2014, from www.gallup.com/poll/107593/Partisan-Gap-Global-Warming-Grows.aspx. Last accessed: 15 November 2014.

Dunn, A.D. (2010). Siting green infrastructure: legal and policy solutions to alleviate urban poverty and promote healthy communities. Boston College Environmental Affairs Law Review 37: 41-66.

EEF (2011). *Ascending the Waste Hierarchy*. EEF, London.

EMF (2012). *Towards the Circular Economy: Economic and Business Rationale for an Accelerated Transition*. Ellen MacArthur Foundation, Isle of Wight.

Eurostat (2012). General Government Expenditure Statistics. reviewed 20 July 2012.

Ferriani, S., Garnsey, E. and Probert, D. (2008). Sustaining breakthrough innovation in large established firms: learning traps and counteracting strategies. In: Bessant, J., Venables, T. (eds.), *Creating Wealth from Knowledge: Meeting the Innovation Challenge*. Edward Elgar, UK. pp. 177-202

Feygina, I., Jost, J.T. and Goldsmith, R.E. (2010). System justification, the denial of global warming, and the possibility of "system-sanctioned change." Personality and Social Psychology Bulletin 36: 326-38.

Fine, B. and Rustomjee, Z. (1996). *The Political Economy of South Africa: From Minerals-Energy Complex to Industrialisation*. Westview Press, Boulder, CO.

Finger, M. (2010). From knowledge to action? Exploring the relationships between environmental experiences, learning, and behavior. Journal of Social Issues 50(3): 141-60.

Fischer, J., Dyball, R., Fazey, I., Gross, C., Dovers, S., Ehrlich, P.R., Brulle, R.J., Christensen, C. and Borden, R.J. (2012). Human behavior and sustainability. Frontiers in Ecology and the Environment 10(3): 153-60.

Frisk, E. and Larson, K.L. (2011). Educating for sustainability: Competencies and practices for transformative action. Journal of Sustainability Education, 2. http://journalofsustainabilityeducation.org/. Last accessed: 15 November 2014.

Gardner, G.T. and Stern, P.C. (2002). *Environmental Problems and Human Behavior* (2nd ed.). Pearson Custom, Boston, MA.

Garfield, E. (2005). The agony and the ecstasy: the history and meaning of the journal impact factor. Paper presented at the international congress on peer review and biomedical publication. Chicago, 16 September 2005.

Gifford, R. (2011). The dragons of inaction: psychological barriers that limit climate change mitigation and adaptation. American Psychologist 66(4): 290-302.

Gifford, R., Scannell, L., Kormos, C., Smolova, L., Biel, A., Boncu, S., Corral, V., Hanyu, K., Hine, D., Kaiser, F.G., Korpela, K., Mertig, A.G., Mira, R.G., Moser, G., Passafaro, P., Pedrosa, L., Pinheiro, J.Q., Saina, S., Sako, T., Sautkina, E., Savina, Y., Schmuck, P., Schultz, W., Sobeck, K., Sundblad, E.-L. and Uzzell, D. (2009). Temporal pessimism and spatial optimism in environmental assessments: An 18-nation study. Journal of Environmental Psychology 29: 1-12.

Halkier, B. (2001). Consuming ambivalences: consumer handling of environmentally related risks in food. Journal of Consumer Culture 1(2): 205-24.

Hall, D. (2010). Why we need public spending? PSIRU, October 2010, viewed 20 July 2012. www.psiru.org/reports/2010-10-QPS-pubspend.pdf.

Hammer, M. and Söderqvist T. (2001). Enhancing trans-disciplinary dialogue in curricula development. Ecological Economics 38: 1-5.

Hasnain, S.S. and Jasimuddin, S.M. (2012). Barriers to Knowledge Transfer: Empirical Evidence from the NGO (Non-Governmental Organizations)-Sector in Bangladesh. World Journal of Social Sciences 2(2): 135-50.

Herren, A. (2010). Barriers to environmental sustainability facing small businesses in Durham, NC (Doctoral dissertation, Duke University).

Hertwich, E.G. (2005). Consumption and the rebound effect: an industrial ecology perspective. Journal of Industrial Ecology 9(1-2): 85-98.

Hill, J.E. (2011). *The Secret Life of Stuff: a Manual for a New Material World.* Vintage, London.

Hoffman, A.J. and Bazerman, M.H. (2007). Changing practice on sustainability: Understanding and overcoming the organizational and psychological barriers to action. Organizations and the Sustainability Mosaic. Crafting Long-Term Ecological and Societal Solutions: 84-105.

Iammarino, S., Sanna-Randaccio, F. and Savona, M. (2009). The perception of obstacles to innovation foreign multinationals and domestic firms in Italy. Revue d'Economie Industrielle 125: 75-104.

Isenhour, C. (2010). On conflicted Swedish consumers, the effort to stop shopping and neoliberal environmental governance. Journal of Consumer Behaviour 9(6): 454-69.

Islam, M.M. and Siwar, C. (2013). A comparative study of public sector sustainable procurement practices, opportunities and barriers. International Review of Business Research Papers 9(3): 62-84.

Jevons, W.S. (1866). *The Coal Question: an Inquiry Concerning the Progress of the Nation, and the Probable Exhaustion of Our Coal Mines.* Macmillan and Company, London. Second Edition.

Johnson, A. and Jacobsson, S. (2000). Inducement and blocking mechanisms in the development of a new industry: the case of renewable energy technology in Sweden. In: R. Coombs, R., Green, K., Richards, A. and Walsh, V. (eds.), *Technology and the Market: Demand, Users and Innovation.* Edward Elgar Publishing Ltd, Cheltenham. pp. 89-111.

Katila, R. and Shane, S. (2005). When does lack of resources make new firms innovative? Academy of Management Journal 48 (5): 814-29.

Khazzoom, D.J. (1980). Economic implications of mandated efficiency standards for household appliances. The Energy Journal 1: 21-40.

Kiem, A.S. and Austin, E.K. (2013). Disconnect between science and end-users as a barrier to climate change adaptation. Climate Research 58: 29-41.

Kotter, J.P. (1995). Leading change: Why transformation efforts fail. Harvard Business Review 73(2): 59-67.

Lawrence, S.R., Collins, E., Pavlovich, K. and Arunachalam, M. (2006). Sustainability practices of SMEs: the case of NZ. Business Strategy and the Environment 15: 242-57

Linnenluecke, M.K. and Griffiths, A. (2010). Corporate sustainability and organizational culture. Journal of World Business 45(4): 357-66.

Lorenzoni, I., Nicholson-Cole, S. and Whitmarsh, L. (2007). Barriers perceived to engaging with climate change among the UK public and their policy implications. Global Environmental Change 17(3): 445-59.

Lovins, A. and Lovins, H. (1997). *Climate: Making Sense and Making Money.* Rocky Mountain Institute, Snowmass, CO.

Mabbitt, R. (2006). Urbanization and sustainability in Lao PDR. In: Roberts, B.H., Kanaley, T.K. (eds.), *Urbanization and Sustainability in Asia: Case Studies of Good Practice.* Asian Development Bank and Cities Alliance (World Bank), Manila, Philippines.

Markkula, A. and Moisander, J. (2012). Discursive confusion over sustainable consumption: a discursive perspective on the perplexity of marketplace knowledge. Journal of Consumer Policy 35(1): 105-25.

Marshall, A. (1920). *Principles of Economics.* Macmillan, London.

Mathur, O.P. (2006). Urbanization and sustainability in India. In: Roberts, B.H. and Kanaley, T.K. (eds.), *Urbanization and Sustainability in Asia: Case Studies of Good Practice*. Asian Development Bank and Cities Alliance (World Bank), Manila, Philippines. pp. 135-54.

McGregor, I.M. (2006). Corporate capitalism: A major barrier to ecologically and socially sustainable development alternatives. PORTAL Journal of Multidisciplinary International Studies 3(1).

Measham, T.G., Preston, B.L., Smith, T.F., Brooke, C., Gorddard, R., Withycombe, G. and Morrison, C. (2011). Adapting to climate change through local municipal planning: barriers and challenges. Mitigation and Adaptation Strategies for Global Change 16(8): 889-909.

Medina, R. and Tarlock, A.D. (2010) Addressing climate change at the state and local level: using land use controls to reduce automobile emissions. Sustainability 2: 1742-64.

Moon, J., Grubnic, S., Herzig, C. and Gond, J.P. (2011). Management control for sustainability strategy. CIMA Research Executive Summary Series 7(12): 1-20.

Morgan, K. (2008). Greening the realm: sustainable food chains and the public plate. Regional Studies 42(9): 1237-50

Morgan, K. and Morley, A. (2002). *Relocalising the Food Chain, the role of Creative Public Procurement*. Regeneration Institute, Cardiff.

Morgan, K. and Sonnino, R. (2007). Empowering consumers: the creative procurement of school meals in Italy and the UK. International Journal of Consumer Studies 31(1): 19-25.

Moser, S.C. and Ekstrom, J.A. (2010). A framework to diagnose barriers to climate change adaptation. Proceedings of the National Academy of Sciences, USA 107(51): 22026-31.

Mukheibir, P. and Ziervogel, G. (2007). Developing a Municipal Adaptation Plan (MAP) for climate change: the city of Cape Town. Environment and Urbanization 19(1): 143-58.

National Audit Office (2005). *Sustainable Procurement in Central Government*. National Audit Office, London.

Negro, S., Hekkert, M. and Alkemade, F. (2010). Seven typical system failures that hamper the diffusion of sustainable energy technologies. In Summer Conference: Opening Up Innovation: Strategy, Organization and Technology. Imperial College London Business School, June 16–18, 2010 (pp. 16-18).

Neto, P. and Serrano, M.M. (2011). Clusters, governance and sustainability. Journal of Modern Accounting and Auditing 7(5): 509-23.

New Economics Foundation (NEF) (2010). 21 hours: why a 21-hour work week can help us all flourish in the 21st century. Available at www.neweconomics.org last accessed on 15 November 2014.

Nguyen, T.L. (2006). Urbanization and sustainability in Vietnam. In: Roberts, B.H. and Kanaley, T.K. (eds.), *Urbanization and Sustainability in Asia: Case Studies of Good Practice*. Asian Development Bank and Cities Alliance (World Bank), Manila, Philippines. pp. 369-401.

OECD (2005). *Building Competitive Regions: Strategies and Governance*. OECD Publishing, Paris.

O'Neill, S. and Nicholson-Cole, S. (2009). "Fear won't do it": promoting positive engagement with climate change through visual and iconic representations. Science Communication 30: 355-79.

Paetz, A.G., Dütschke, E. and Fichtner, W. (2012). Smart homes as a means to sustainable energy consumption: A study of consumer perceptions. Journal of Consumer Policy 35(1): 23-41.

Pini, B., Wild River, S., McKenzie, F.M.H. (2007). Factors inhibiting local government engagement in environmental sustainability: case studies from rural Australia. Australian Geographic 38(2): 161-75.

Potter, J. and Miranda, G. (eds.) (2009). *Clusters, Innovation and Entrepreneurship*. OECD Publications, Paris.

Pruitt, D.G. and Rubin, J.Z. (1986). *Social Conflict: Escalation, Stalemate, Settlement.* Random House, New York.

Qiao, Y. and Wang, C. (2011). Issues and Challenges in Implementing China's Green Public Procurement Program. Journal of Environmental Protection 2(8): 1034-45.

Revell, A. and Blackburn, R. (2007). The business case for sustainability? An examination of small firms in the UK's construction and restaurant sectors. Business Strategy and the Environment 16(6): 404-20.

Ross, A. (2010). It's time to get serious—why legislation is needed to make sustainable development a reality in the UK. Sustainability 2: 1101-27.

Ryan, F.A. and Vivekananda, F. (1993). *Finding new routes in old paths: Linking cultural needs to technical knowledge. Appropriate technology inspires developing societies: concept, controversy, and clarification.* Bethany Books, Stockholm, Sweden.

Salzmann, O., Ionescu-Somers, A. and Steger, U. (2005). The business case for corporate sustainability: literature review and research options. European Management Journal 23(1): 27-36.

Sandén, B. and Jonasson, K. (2005). Variety creation and co-evolution of contenders: The case of alternative transport fuels in Sweden 1974–2004. Environmental Systems, Analysis Department of Energy and Environment, Chalmers University of Technology, Göteborg, Sweden.

Sarkar, A. and Singh, J. (2010). Financing energy efficiency in developing countries—lessons learned and remaining challenges. Energy Policy 38(10): 5560-71.

Shove, E. (2010). Beyond the ABC: climate change policy and theories of social change. Environment and planning A 42(6): 1273-85.

Sipos, Y., Battisti, B. and Grimm, K. (2007). Achieving transformative sustainability learning: Engaging head, hands, and heart. International Journal of Sustainability in Higher Education 9(1): 68-86.

Skene, K.R. (2009). *Shadows on the Cave Wall: a New Theory of Evolution.* Ard Macha Press, Angus, UK.

Skene, K.R. (2010). After Copenhagen: carbon is not the planet's greatest threat. Contemporary Review 292: 15-22.

Skene, K.R. (2011). *Escape from Bubbleworld: Seven Curves to Save the Earth.* Ard Macha Press, Angus.

Skinner, B.F. (1987). *Upon Further Reflection.* Prentice Hall. Englewood Cliffs, NJ.

Stern, P. (2000). Toward a coherent theory of environmentally significant behavior. Journal of Social Issues 56: 407-24.

Stern, S. (2009). How to build trust when it is in short supply. Financial Times, 16 June, p. 14.

Sustainable Procurement Task Force (2006). *Procuring the Future: Sustainable Procurement National Action Plan: Recommendations from the Sustainable Procurement Task Force,* June 2006.

Suurs, R.A.A. and Hekkert, M.P. (2009). Cumulative causation in the formation of a technological innovation system: The case of biofuels in the Netherlands. Technological Forecasting and Social Change 76(8): 1003-20.

Swim, J.K., Stern, P.C., Doherty, T.J., Clayton, S., Reser, J.P., Weber, E.U., Gifford, R. and Howard, G.S. (2011). Psychology's contributions to understanding and addressing global climate change. American Psychologist 66(4): 241-50.

Taylor, I. (2006). *A Modern Integrated and Collaborative Supply Chain for the Supply of Fresh Local Food to Education: Why Not?* DfES, London.

Taylor, N., Barker, K. and Simpson, M. (2003). Achieving "sustainable business": a study of perceptions of environmental best practice by SMEs in South Yorkshire. Environment and Planning C: Government and Policy 21 (1): 89-105

Valor, C. (2008). Can consumers buy responsibly? Analysis and solutions for market failures. Journal of Consumer Policy 31: 315-26.

Vickers, I., Vaze, P., Corr, L., Kasperova, E. and Fergus, L. (2009). SMEs in a low carbon economy. Centre for Enterprise and Economic Development Research, London.

Vidal, N.G. and Kozak, R.A. (2008). Corporate responsibility practices in the forestry sector. Journal of Corporate Citizenship 31: 59-75.

von Bothmer, R., Schnürer, J., *Åström*, B., Vrede, K. and Andersson P. (2009). Evaluation of quality and impact at SLU (KoN 09). SLU, Uppsala.

Wackernagel, M. and Rees, W.E. (1997). Perceptual and structural barriers to investing in natural capital: Economics from an ecological footprint perspective. Ecological Economics 20(1): 3-24.

Whiteman, G., de Vos, D.R., Chapin, F.S., Yli-Pelkonen, V., Niemelä, J. and Forbes, B.C. (2011). Business strategies and the transition to low-carbon cities. Business Strategy and the Environment 20: 251-65.

Willard, B. (2005). *The Next Sustainability Wave: Building Boardroom Buy-in.* New Society Publishers, Gabriola Island, BC, Canada.

Winkler, H. and Marquand, A. (2009). Changing development paths: from an energy-intensive to low-carbon economy in South Africa. Climate and Development 1: 47-65.

Young, W., Hwang, K., McDonald, S. and Oates, C.J. (2010). Sustainable consumption: green consumer behaviour when purchasing products. Sustainable Development 18(1): 20-31.

Zelenika, I. and Pearce, J.M. (2011). Barriers to appropriate technology growth in sustainable development. Journal of Sustainable Development 4(6): 12-22.

9
Transition to a sustainable economy

There is a growing literature on transition, and this addresses a most important issue: how best should the transition to a sustainable economy be implemented, given the barriers that exist. Based on the findings of a World Bank-supported study, four areas were viewed as being crucial to transition: a balanced mix of policy instruments, the appropriate participation of the government (politics) and the participation by both industry and the public in the CE approach. There is a significant literature on policy, politics and participation. We examine previous transitions, exploring what these transitions tell us. Can such transitions be managed or are they emergent events? Does economic change act as a driver or is it an outcome of transition?

Learning aims and objectives

- Define the concept of transition
- List the goals of sustainable transition across environment, society and economics
- List the differences between weak and strong sustainability concepts of transition
- Characterize the Dutch and Viennese schools of transition
- Define the role of protective spaces
- Understand the role and challenges relating to the concept of transition management

Learning outcomes and experiences

- Explain what makes a sustainable transition different from other transitions
- Why is technology such a contentious issue relating to a sustainable transition?
- What are the strengths and weaknesses of socio-metabolism when applied to transition?
- Explain why the geography of transition is important

9.1 Introduction

Given the unprecedented expansion of the human impact on our planet in terms of habitat, meteorology and nutrient pollution, and the increasing pressure on ecosystem services (as outlined in Chapter 1), there is clear evidence that our current trajectory must be changed if we are not to face serious repercussions for our economy, our society and our environment. As early as 1954, Harrison Brown, Professor of geochemistry, wrote presciently that:

> A substantial fraction of humanity today is behaving as if it ... were engaged in a contest to test nature's willingness to support humanity and if it had its way it would not rest content until the earth were covered completely and to a considerable depth with a writhing mass of human beings much as a dead cow is covered with a pulsating mass of maggots (Brown, 1954, p. 16).

Of course the problem is not really population growth *per se*, but rather the rapid increase in resource use and waste production that the average human uses. The vast majority of people on Earth live a financially much poorer existence than do western nations, but are rapidly improving their standard of living, particularly in BRIC nations. This will lead to a huge increase in source and sink issues within the next 50 years, even without population increase. Increases in meat consumption mean increases in land required for grazing. WWF suggests that lifestyles in the developed world at present require the resources of around two planets to sustain them and if emerging economies follow the same trajectory this will rise to 2.5 by 2050 (WWF 2010).

Energy consumption is set to soar. Water supplies are increasingly under stress. Waste fertilizers herbicides and pesticides threaten the fundamental functioning of whole ecosystems. Fisheries and forests are being increasingly decimated. As supply diminishes, demand increases. It was Ehrlich and Holdren (1971) who developed an equation to express the impact, I, of the human population on the planet:

$$I = PAT$$

where P represents **population**, A represents **affluence** as defined by GDP, and T represents eco-efficiency from improved **technology** (i.e. the resources consumed per unit GDP). With a 30% population growth and 300% growth of average per capita income predicted by the midst of the century (OECD, 2012), only improved technological eco-efficiency can stabilize or reduce human impact. Professor Tim Jackson, University of Surrey, has calculated that if the global economy grows at an average of 2% per year (as a comparison, the average annual GDP growth from 1990 to 2006 was 3.3%) and population reaches 9 million by 2050 as expected, there would need to be a 130-fold improvement of efficiency by 2050 (Jackson, 2009).

This level of improvement is beyond possibility. Any hope of technological intervention is further undermined by what Westley *et al.* (2011) refer to as the **ingenuity gap**, where our interventions in the broader life-supporting environment are based on a limited knowledge of that environment, and our impact on that environment has many dimensions that are unknown to us. IPAT points to a difficult conclusion, that technology will not pave the road of progress through this particularly deep valley of our own making. Indeed, our interventions have been responsible for some of the mess we find ourselves in.

Given this challenge to the Enlightenment thinking that has guided our economic progress for two centuries or more, there is a realization that incremental change, bolted on to the existing modus operandi will not suffice. What is needed is a transition.

9.2 What is transition?

A **transition** is a transformation process "in which existing structures, institutions, culture and practices are broken down and new ones are established" (Loorbach, 2007; p. 17). Temporally, transitions do not occur quickly.

De Haan (2007) observed that "A transition is defined as a long term process—it may take one or more generations—of non-linear social change leading to new constellations of actors, structures and practices, which determine the functioning of the system".

Eckel *et al.* (1998) provide the following definition of transformative change:

- Alters the culture of the institution by changing underlying assumptions and overt institutional behaviours, processes and structures
- Is deep and pervasive, affecting the whole institution
- Is intentional
- Occurs over time

A **sustainability transition** is a "radical transformation towards a sustainable society as a response to a number of persistent problems confronting contemporary modern societies" (Grin *et al.*, 2010; p. 1). This definition points to the society as the home of the transition. Geels (2011) points out that sustainability transitions differ from other transitions in that:

- First, sustainability transitions are goal-oriented or "purposive".
- It is therefore unlikely that environmental innovations will be able to replace existing systems without changes in economic frame conditions.
- The major areas where change is needed such as energy, food and car manufacturing are occupied by large incumbent firms with strong positions *vis-à-vis* pioneers that often first develop environmental innovations.

Institutional commitments, shared beliefs and discourses, power relations, and political lobbying by incumbents stabilize existing systems (Unruh, 2000).

The Nobel Laureate in physics, Murray Gell-Mann, has proposed seven kinds of interdependent transition "to a more sustainable world"; the demographic transition, the technological transition, the economic transition, the social transition, the institutional transition, the ideological transition and finally, the information transition (Gell-Mann 1994; pp. 345-66).

As humans embrace the new Sustainable Age, the impact will resonate in the economic and environmental arenas. Torjman summed up the difficulties facing us, commenting that: "From a social perspective in particular, human wellbeing cannot be sustained without a healthy environment and is equally unlikely in the absence of a vibrant economy" (Torjman, 2000; p. 2).

Given the unrealistic expectations placed on technology in terms of counter-balancing the impact of population and affluence, the transition required is unlikely to bear significant resemblance to other transitions often cited as examples for study. This is because these other examples had technology at their heart, be it farming methodology underlying the green revolution, steam engines underpinning the industrial revolution or liquid petroleum underpinning the automobile revolution.

In other words, it is not all about science. Societal transformations not only involve new technological artefacts, but also require new regulations, infrastructures, markets, cultural meanings and user practices (Elzen *et al.*, 2004; p. 1). Seidl *et al.* (2013; p. 5) observe that:

> Interdisciplinary scientific knowledge is necessary but not sufficient when it comes to addressing sustainable transformations, as science increasingly has to deal with normative and value-related issues. A systems perspective on coupled human–environmental systems (HES) helps to address the inherent complexities. Additionally, a thorough interaction between science and society (i.e., transdisciplinarity) is necessary.

The economic arena is also likely to require a transition, as we will discuss later in this chapter. Given that it is a human creation, this should not be surprising. The human transition covers both economics and society. However, the environment may not transition, since the major objective of a sustainable transition is to ease pressure on the environment, thus allowing it to carry on as "normal".

Major structural transitions in the natural world tend to happen after mass extinctions, where the life forms can be replaced by very different life forms. However, interestingly, function is little changed. Although the flying reptiles and dinosaurs were removed 60 million years ago, the functional world, before and after the mass extinction, was little changed, with primary producers, primary consumers, omnivores, carnivores and detritivores all still there, but in different clothing. The players changed, but the functional play remained the same. Ultimately, this should not be surprising, as the functional environment is merely an extension of the laws of thermodynamics that envelop the entire Universe, applied locally.

Thus the outcomes of transition on the environment are much more predictable than the outcomes on society and economics, since the environment is answerable to the laws of physics, and not to human bidding. In the cold light of physics, we do not damage the environment, but rather we facilitate the expression of these laws of physics, akin to opening the window of a car that is submersed in a river. Physics always delivers the outcomes that we should expect. If we drop a Ming Dynasty vase onto a rock, it will break. Interestingly, Rotmans (1994; p. 1) emphasized the structural aspect of human transitions when he defined transition as "a gradual, continuous process of societal change, changing the character of society (or a complex part) structurally".

The idea of sustainability transitions not only includes the challenge of orchestrating a change of systems (transportation, agriculture, energy) but also a change in criteria that we use to assess the appropriateness of products, services and systems. Kemp and van Lente (2011) argue that transitions that do not fundamentally change criteria by which decisions are made are unlikely to lead to sustainability. Compared with the transitions of hygiene and waste, the transition to sustainable mobility and sustainable energy can be expected to be much more difficult because the systems of transport and fossil fuel-based energy are deeply embedded. Furthermore, they are almost trivial tips of the much greater iceberg underpinning them, whose fundamental scale includes the dominant philosophies of much of the population: humanism and the Enlightenment.

Some confusion emerges from the literature relating to the use of the terms **incremental change**, **transition** and **transformation**. Roggema *et al.* (2012) refer to incremental change as a slow process, which modifies the landscape only slightly. Transition is seen as a fluent change towards a new future, which is an improved version of the existing system. Transformation is seen as a change towards a future that is fundamentally different from the existing system. Walker *et al.* (2004; p. 3) describe a transformation as "the capacity to transform the stability landscape itself in order to become a different kind of system, to create a fundamentally new system when ecological, economic, or social structures make the existing system untenable".

However, given the complexity of existence and actor-network interactions, there has been a different interpretation, highlighting the difficulties of prediction and management in any attempted planned transition. **Complex systems theory**, emerging out of the Santa Fé Institute in New Mexico, contends that systemic thinking is required in order to understand any given element within an interactive whole. These elements co-evolve through their interaction with each other and with the outcome of the system as a whole, leading to the emergence of new structures and new configurations.

Central to complex systems theory is the concept that societal structures remain stable and optimized for long periods, followed by relatively shorter periods of structural transition. Here, a transition is defined as "a shift or 'system innovation' between distinctive socio-technical configurations encompassing not only new technologies but also corresponding changes in markets, user practices, policy and cultural discourses and governing institutions" (Geels *et al.*, 2008; p. 521).

A more extreme version of this approach is found in **Markov chains**, defined as a series of transitions between different states, such that the probabilities associated with each transition depend only on the immediately preceding state, and not on how the process arrived at that state. These are stochastic processes, where the future state is unaffected by the history of the chain. Thus a Markov chain wanders about in space unaffected by its journey.

Patterns can emerge, giving the appearance of order, but are really outcomes of stochastic drift. Markov processes have been used to understand noisy transitions in ecology, ranging from bottle nose dolphin behaviour (Lusseau, 2003) to rural sustainability (Kamusoko *et al.*, 2009) and sustainability forecasting (Xiaojian and Rong, 2010). However, they pose significant challenges to any understanding of human transitions, as they posit a situation where stochastic processes lie at the heart of a transition in a truly anarchic situation, making it impossible to manage.

Thus, depending on how we view transitions, they can either be managed or merely observed. This fundamental disparity of views means that there are very different opinions within transition theory. However, the problems relating to transition run even deeper when we consider what we are transitioning from and what we consider the destination of our journey to be.

9.3 What kind of a transition: a sustainable future?

In attempting to envisage what kind of a transition is needed, we must first identify what the goals of such a transition are. Rockström *et al.* (2009) point to three transgressions of the "**planetary borders**": biodiversity destruction, nitrogen and phosphorus flooding of ecosystems, and greenhouse gas emissions causing climate destabilization. This list is probably slightly ill-conceived. Habitat destruction should replace biodiversity collapse, because biodiversity collapse is an outcome of the three other transgressions (habitat destruction, eutrophication and climate destabilization), and ultimately impacts on ecosystem function in collaboration with chemico-physical imbalances such as heat and nutrient concentration. Humans are generally not seeking to actively destroy biodiversity and so this is an indirect effect of the other three activities. This collapse in species numbers then acts as a vector, passing on the damage to ecosystem function.

Given the source and sink issues detailed in Chapter 1 and the five security issues in Figure 1.4 (food, water, energy, resource and national security), it is clear that environmental, social and economic instability results from the breakdown of ecosystem services. These services themselves emerge from a functioning suit of ecosystems, whose outputs emerge from complex interactions within the ecosystem and with its environmental and energetic context. As human activity alters this context, ecosystem function changes.

Thus from an environmental perspective, the transition must deliver an environmental and energetic context that allows ecosystems to function in such a way as to not threaten our own existence. Of course, ecosystems are not museum pieces that can be preserved. Indeed dramatic changes in ecosystem structures permitted primate evolution in the first place, with the demise of the dinosaurs. Thus the dynamic ever-changing aspect of the biosphere must be recognized.

Even the trilobites eventually went extinct, after 270 million years of swimming in the oceans. In other words, the biosphere is not designed to maintain and conserve particular species. Thus any attempt to transition to a sustainable planet defined as supporting our own existence in perpetuity will not equate to a natural biological state. A planet designed to promote a single species' survival is not the same as a planet with a healthy functioning environment. Indeed a planet that sustains humans will require a transformation of the environment to a state never before realized, one whose sole aim is the support of human life. We have no evidence that this is even possible. Early attempts, such as Biosphere I, led to the exclusion of the human representatives. Given the dynamic nature of the biosphere over its 2 billion years or more of existence, there has never been a single species that has sustained. It just doesn't work like that.

Van Vuuren *et al.* (2012) suggest the following targets for a sustainable transition:

- Universal access to electricity and clean cooking by 2030
- Energy for development by 2050
- Reducing air pollution in compliance with the WHO air quality guidelines
- Limiting global average temperature change to 2°C above pre-industrial levels
- Energy security

Raskin *et al.* (2010) set out the following deliverables and outcomes of a successful transition:

- People living in hunger: by 2100, 6% of today's levels
- People living with water stress: <2 billion people by 2100 (currently 1.73 billion)
- Atmospheric CO_2 concentration: 350 ppm (currently 391 ppm)
- Percentage of land under cultivation: 15% (currently 12%)
- Extinctions per million species per year: 10 (currently 100–1,000 extinctions per million species per year)

The EC have set a 20–20–20 target, representing a 20% reduction of greenhouse gases emissions, a 20% share of renewable energy resources and a 20% rise in energy efficiency, with all three to be delivered by 2020 (EC, 2007).

The very concept of sustainable development is highly questionable on several fronts. First, what equates to human sustainability does not represent environmental sustainability. Second, the idea of what the end-point of "development" actually represents is ill-defined. Does it mean that impoverished, unsuccessful, backward, uneducated nations should be converted to western lifestyles, values and practices? If that is the case, how sustainable would such a development actually be? Third, how realistic is it to assume that this journey of development can be delivered through the same technological pathway, economic model and philosophical framework which have delivered the current crisis in the first place? Finally, how big a transition are we actually prepared to acknowledge?

The responses to these questions sublimate into two visions of transformation, **weak and strong sustainability** (as encountered in Chapters 1 and 5). Transition based around weak sustainability (WS) is hardly any sort of transition at all. WS represents the dominant social paradigm, operating within the Enlightenment philosophy of technology, reasoning and human-led recovery. The answers lie within us. Capitalist materialism, supported by economic growth will fund the sustainable development of the planet towards a globalized unity, founded on Western philosophy. The environment can be managed and, where this is difficult, should be replaced with technology mimicking and improving on the natural world.

Core values of competition, convergent thinking, free market economics and self-enhancement lie at the core of WS, with emphasis on progress and improvement. The focus is on what businesses should do in order to deliver sustainable production, and sustainable production must be profitable, in order that growth can continue. This has led to the concept of green growth, an idea strongly supported by the Stern Report and the Ellen Macarthur Foundation. WS also focuses on carbon as the single issue, reducing all of our problems to this one element.

Almost every strategy and approach is focused on carbon reduction, and success is measured by the decline in emissions. There is a belief, deeply ingrained in organizations such as the United Nations, that if we reduce carbon emissions to a reasonable level, then all of our problems will be solved. Economic growth is not a problem provided it does not contribute to carbon emissions. Indeed, climate destabilization is the only issue on the table and green energy is the key focus. No matter that a 20% reduction in meat consumption would have the same impact on emissions as would the purchase of a hybrid car. Agriculture is generally ignored in terms of problem and solution space. Such Iceberg thinking avoids the problems of habitat destruction and eutrophication, yet even if we cleaned up our energy production, these issues still threaten our sustainability. Weak sustainability relies on a technological solution, a reductionist rationale and a humanist foundation.

Strong sustainability (SS) challenges the current capitalist paradigm, placing the environment at the top of the agenda, and pressing for economic de-growth and abandonment of our reliance on human ingenuity. It stresses ecological and social sovereignty and accountability and the view that economics should serve nature, rather than the other way around. These statements are easily read and scanned over, but their import is revolutionary and, to many, extremely unpalatable. SS points towards a complete transition of human behaviour, requiring a break from traditional, core values. It threatens central institutions of business, government and wealth, undermining accepted values of progress such as GDP and westernization. Few if any of the main schools of economic sustainability would adhere to strong sustainability, with its avowed opposition to economic growth, development and globalization.

However, as research on sustainable transitions gathers momentum, and government funding begins to follow this new field, there is an increasing realization that old school weak sustainability is unlikely to deliver enough of a change to reduce carbon emissions, let alone address any of the other major challenges. Let's revisit the debate on economic growth.

9.3.1 Economic growth vs. de-growth

Probably the most significant and hotly debated difference between WS and SS is situated around whether a decrease in economic output, as measured by GDP, is necessary to realize a sustainable transition, or whether green growth is possible. Alber (2002) points out that there is no correlation between economic growth and poverty reduction, yet there is a strong correlation between the existence of a welfare state and a reduction in poverty. The current economic paradigm is competition-based, and thus there are losers as well as winners. It is argued that these losers are represented in society by poverty, and thus any theory of sustainability for a society must clearly act towards greater equity, which is unlikely to result from a competition-based free market economy.

Indeed SS advocates would argue that the poverty of the "**developing**" world permits the "**developed**" world to reduce its manufacturing burden and thus its pollution, while switching to a more service-based economy. Highly toxic mine pollution in China, associated with rare earth metal production, causes significant harm, while the rare earth metals produced are used by western governments in the production of large offshore wind turbines. Here, the green economy is powered by very polluting extraction processes. The decimated rainforests of Borneo are another hidden externalized cost behind green fuels from palm oil plantations.

However, the green energy from these technologies is then used as an example of how the West has reduced its pollution, and thus developed a superior economy, setting itself up as the ideal which sustainable development aims to deliver to the entire planet. This argument fails to recognize that the western economy has externalized the highly polluting practices underpinning its green economy to "developing" nations. If these nations become "developed" where will all the dirt be externalized to then?

So while sustainable development holds the redistribution of wealth, health, environment and income as an important and central target, such considerations play no part in the OECD green growth concept which is essentially built around a resource economics concept, and merely represents the fundamentals of neoclassical economics while acknowledging that nature is an important capital stock and should be accounted for as part of the national wealth. This is a dangerous concept, as it allows economic value to be placed on nature, which reduces it to a tradable commodity with no inherent value beyond that which the markets place on it. Nature as a tradable structure rather than as an irreplaceable function is a much more easily managed but abused concept.

Weak sustainability also faces a significant problem related to potential competition between social and environmental sustainability in "**developing**" countries. Since competition is a central ethos, and sustainability within a green economic approach has a currency of money, then the financial demands of environmental and social improvement will compete for funding. If money is scarce, then social rather than environmental sustainability is the more likely winner. The very fact that environmental sustainability is viewed as buyable in the first place reiterates the tenet of WS: that technology can replace the environment and that nature is a commodity.

However, we have seen that a sustainable transition does not actually involve the environment in terms of actively managing environmental sustainability, but rather applies to the human arenas of society and economics. Nature is best left to recover itself, following the removal of pressure from the human sector. WS fails to recognize this point, and asserts its claim that humans can engineer the required transition through interventionist policies and technologies, biomimicry as opposed to bioparticipation, as advocated by SS. Within a strong sustainability perspective, society and the environment are not seen as competitors for economic salvation. Rather, society and economics must work together to reintegrate their activities *within* an environmental context.

From the Stern Report (Stern, 2006) to the EMF report (EMF, 2012), there has been a strong emphasis on green growth. This is understandable, as businesses cite financial concerns as significant barriers to embracing sustainability (see Chapter 8). Lebel and Lorek (2008) identify 11 ways in which the sustainable production-consumption system can be encouraged: produce with less, validate green supply chains, co-design, produce responsibly, service rather than sell, certify and label products honestly, trade fairly, advertise ethically, buy responsibly, use less and increase wisely.

Economic growth is seen as essential if we are to finance the changes needed to deliver a sustainable transition, as WS advocates believe that recovery can be bought through investment in technology rather than through the recuperation of the environment functionally. Furthermore society defines itself in terms of earnings. The Human Development Index has GDP at its core. Consumption is no longer a means of fulfilling material needs but a method to create a personal identity. The emphasis of many WS advocates is on maintaining the output of products, but in greener ways, rather than asking if we need these products and if we require so much water, meat and energy.

Emphasis has been placed on decoupling economic growth from environmental damage. Suggestions have included:

- Eco-intelligent production systems
- Resource-light infrastructures
- Appropriate technologies

However, under conditions of permanent economic growth (defined in the traditional sense of GDP growth), the gains from eco-efficiency will be eroded by growth in volume.

To avoid this problem the following steps are suggested by Banuri *et al.* (2005):

- Lower performance expectations
- Regional rather than global markets and sources
- Community resource rights
- Intensify product use, not resource use

Banuri *et al.* (2005) see a sustainable society as flowing from two decoupling processes: **decoupling growth from resource flows**, and **decoupling well-being from production.**

A key stumbling block for any consideration of economic de-growth resides in the institution of property, and the growth in property, which overrides any factor that limits the exploitation of humans and natural resources. Property, as a guarantee for credit, is dependent on economic growth. Credit accumulates interest, and thus property must also accumulate value to match this. A mortgage only works if the lender makes some profit. However, if property devalues, then it can become worth less than the credit awarded, leading to negative equity. The collapse of property markets was central to the economic recession of 2009. Property sets a pattern of growth for growth's sake (or rather for repaying credit), that is not easy to resolve within any discussion of economic de-growth or steady-state economics (van Griethuysen, 2010).

In order to raise consumption in the developing world to western levels and to eradicate poverty, taking into account population growth, the Brundtland report argues for a five- to tenfold increase in manufacturing output (Brundtland, 1987; p. 15). Development is equated here with economic growth, because growth provides resources to pay for environmental measures and technologies, and can help solve poverty problems. The main driver is business and the main instruments are markets and technology. Eco-efficiency through technology is the key strategy.

The emphasis on economic growth as essential for any meaningful sustainable transition is disparaged by SS advocates. Sustainable de-growth will involve a decrease in GDP as currently measured, because of a reduction in the large-scale, resource-intensive productive and consumptive activities that constitute a big portion of GDP. However, the "**Easterlin paradox**" states that GDP per capita does not correlate with happiness above certain levels of satisfaction of basic needs (Easterlin, 1974).

If we calculate the **environmentally sustainable national income**, eSNI (defined as the maximum attainable production level which allows vital environmental functions to remain available for future generations), rough estimates of eSNI show that world eSNI is at 50% of the world national income, meaning that production must be halved in order to reach a sustainable level (Hueting, 2010). So there is a call for economic de-growth. Economic de-growth may be defined as "an equitable downscaling of production and consumption that increases human wellbeing and enhances ecological conditions at the local and global level, in the short and long term" (Schneider *et al.*, 2011; p. 512). Victor (2010) calls for de-growth by design, not by disaster, warning that ecosystem failure and resource decline will ultimately cause economic collapse anyway, and so the options are a controlled landing or a crash landing. Instead, consumers are asked to reduce the demand on the natural world. Less demand will drive less supply.

Many of the sustainability schools currently appear to protect the core trajectories rather than challenge them—e.g. increased efficiency to make product A and increased recycling of product B, rather than challenging the need for A and B. Greening of energy supply rather than decrease in energy supply and profitable green growth rather than decreased growth all steer away from a meaningful transition. Sustainable development is taken as a dogma rather than challenging the development criteria. Hamilton points out that one-fifth of the population of the UK and Australia, a class he calls "**downshifters**", have voluntarily reduced their income and consumption to spend more time with family and friends (Hamilton, 2010). Thus the entirety of the human race is not addicted to economic growth.

The recent economic downturn of 2009 can be used as a model of de-growth. While hardship has indeed spread across wealthy nations (though still in a state of incomparable affluence in comparison with 75% of the world's population), this period of de-growth has had significant impacts on the environment. Because of the economic crisis, and despite continued economic growth in India, China and Indonesia during the recession, the 3% annual global increase in carbon dioxide emissions was reversed, with a 3% observed decrease (IEA, 2009). This is too little compared with the IPCC recommended reduction of over 60% but it shows that economic de-growth achieved what the Kyoto agreement failed to do. In the first four months of 2009, cement demand dropped by about 45% in Spain. Similarly, because of the decrease in external demand for exports, the decline in the Amazon rainforest slowed significantly (Schneider *et al.*, 2010). Economic de-growth allowed us to reach goals that 20 years of intercontinental panels and meetings failed to do.

Concerns have been voiced relating to the prospects of employment in a sustainable age. The number of jobs can only increase if the economy grows faster or de-grows slower than per capita productivity and resource consumption can only decrease if the economy grows slower or de-grows faster than resource productivity. Spangenberg (2010) explores two options for escaping from this catch-22 situation. The first one involves capping resource throughput, and the second involves capping wealth creation. The latter is capable of meeting environmental objectives, but would lead to significant social tensions and hardships. The political appetite for such unpalatable policy may not be adequate. Reductions in the length of the working week would help, but Spangenberg (2010) warns that this would involve significant financial investment in the social security system and redistributive taxation as costs shift from labour to capital.

9.3.2 The place of technology

Perhaps nothing divides weak from strong sustainability more than the place of technology. Technology is sacred to weak sustainability advocates. Technology is the sword of human intellect that transfers our ideas into the physical world, builds the bulwarks of knowledge and constructs the cathedrals of reasoning. Technology not only creates reality from dreams, but it inspires all around to reach for the skies. Technology will deliver us from any challenge that nature can throw at us.

Indeed, technology can replace nature. We can use nature as a starting point and, through biomimicry, take the best bits and make them even better: genetic engineering, cloud seeding, iron-enrichment of the oceans. For over 50 years we have dreamt of **terraforming** (literally, Earth-making) an inhospitable planet, creating habitats for humans. Now we may have to terraform our own planet, as it becomes inhospitable for us. However, the technocrats believe that we can do this. Pour enough money and resources at anything and the science will clear the way through.

Indeed the very concept of "transition" is not really recognized by weak sustainability advocates. The Enlightenment philosophy of reasoning and technology remains central to progress, and so there is no requirement to change the system. Continuing with the same approach as the last 300 years will service the human race adequately. This view is summed up in the transition concept of **technological innovation systems** (TIS). TIS represents a significant field in weak sustainability transition, and is principally concerned with emerging new technologies and their potential contribution to future sustainability. Sustainability transitions are therefore characterized by substantially enhanced ecological efficiency within new socio-technological configurations. From such a perspective, new technologies and products crowd out established technologies, delivering the necessary changes to ensure sustainability (Coenen *et al.*, 2012).

While sociological solutions such as localism, communalism and sustainable behaviour patterns must be developed gradually and against the incumbent economic and sociological model, advanced engineering solutions can be rolled out at any scale because they are a continuation of mass-production technology, whether in biotechnology (to produce high-yielding crops to feed 9 billion people) or geo-engineering and low-carbon energy technologies (to mitigate climate destabilization). Sustainable development approaches embrace these large-scale solutions, as they can be shown to make a difference without any sacrifice on behalf of the human race.

However, there is a recognized need to communicate the processes of science and technology to people in order to win the hearts and minds of those unsure. Philosophers and sociologists of technology emphasize that an improvement in the relationship between society and technology "is the key to building a better world" (Johnson and Wetmore 2009, p. 441). The socio-technical transitions literature provides insights as to how technology can deliver the transition towards more sustainable systems and societies.

Instrumentalist technology ascribes to the viewpoint that technology is neutral, and can be transferred from industrialized to "developing" worlds without any difficulty. This neutrality hypothesis emphasizes increased efficiency as the universal panacea, allowing already neutral technology to deliver better, cheaper and more sustainable products. Eco-efficiency is not a challenging concept to companies, as most would view efficiency as a common sense business model anyhow.

Instrumental technologists hold that a combination of solar energy, genetic engineering and the Internet will solve poverty in the world; the only problem is to make them cheap and universally available. "The development and diffusion of new technologies is perhaps the most robust and effective way to reduce GHG emissions", state Banuri *et al.* (2005, p. 83); "any response to climate change will depend critically on the cost, performance, and availability of technologies that can lower emissions in the future" (Halnaes *et al.* 2007, p. 147).

Colonization refers to society's deliberate interventions into natural systems in order to create and maintain a state of the natural system that renders it more useful socially. The classic reading of Marx leads to a discussion of changing modes of appropriation of nature through the development of new means of production, i.e., technology. Godelier (1986) stresses the fact that human appropriation of nature modifies nature and this modified nature in turn stimulates social change.

Substantivist technology advocates that technological development exists within its own bubble, one invention building on the other, without anyone or any institution being able to stop, slow or redirect it. From this perspective, technology is not neutral. Technology changes our culture and shapes the whole of social life, introducing new values. Some analysts argue that we are currently locked into a carbon-based technological system, as our economies strongly rely on the use of exhaustible fossil fuels. We are also addicted to an abundant energy lifestyle as a result, making it almost impossible to conceive of life at a much lower energy flux. The average internal temperatures in UK homes has risen from 13.8°C in 1970 to 18.2°C in 2004, while the average number of electric appliances owned has increased from 17 to 47 over the same time-period (Healy, 2008; Martiskaïnen, 2008).

To many, modern technology is visualized as part of "the central myth of European modernity" (Ulrich, 1992, p. 278), along with the dominant economic model and other global institutions. Geographical issues mean that technology cannot be rolled out across the planet, without changing forever the very landscape that contributes to the diversity of our environments.

Thus technology is seen as a globalizing tool, designed to eradicate differing opinions, cultures and landscapes. To post-development advocates and strong sustainability practitioners, technology is seen as a means to further exploiting natural resources and generating cultural imperialism. Clean technologies are viewed similarly, because they also "force their laws upon society in such a way that cultural self-definition and autonomy cannot be maintained for long" (Ulrich, 1992, p. 284). The problem facing the substantitive technology theory arises from its claim that technology is self-driven and uncontrollable. If this is the case, how can the behemoth be stopped? Surely it is impossible? The only conceivable way would be to alter the entire system. Thus, strong sustainability advocates would pursue a complete transformation, of philosophy and practice.

9.3.3 Globalization vs. pluriverse

The Brundtland Report stressed the importance of the common future of our planet, requiring us to all pull in the same direction. Sachs uses the term "**astronaut's perspective**" (Sachs, 1999; p. 83) to refer to this global approach for sustainability. From a transformation viewpoint, the socio-ecological problem is rooted in the economic and power structures of our society and in the way humans interrelate with nature.

Important incentives for strong sustainable consumption are quite likely to come from social innovation. A countless number of initiatives are on the way including food co-operatives, public gardening, the provision of services with explicit sustainable character, neighbourhood centres, barter trading platforms and local currencies (Seyfang and Smith, 2007; Seyfang, 2009). It is argued by these authors that calls to scale up such approaches miss the whole point, as they work best as small scale approaches. This resembles Sachs's "**home perspective**" where the stress is on developing sustainable local livelihoods and radically restructuring the development patterns of the North (Sachs, 1999, p. 88).

This localist approach is interesting. In Chapter 5 we saw that localism has repeatedly come and gone through history, and has alternated with strong centralization. At present there is a rise in localism, and so it is not surprising that strong sustainability embraces this concept. This is an interesting example of an historical cycle resonating with a period of change, impacting on the solution space. This current upwelling of localist thinking also coincides with the apogee of economic globalization, a credos of opposite values. Indeed, the entire concept of sustainable development follows a globalist approach.

Post-development has attacked the value of globalization as being ill-equipped to deliver the changes needed for any transition. Recent movements such as the **buen vivir** approach in South America offer alternative paths towards sustainability. Escobar (2011) discusses the emergence of **transition discourses** (TDs) in recent years. A hallmark of contemporary TDs is the fact that they posit radical cultural and institutional transformations, often involving a transition to an altogether different world. Such terms as a "paradigm shift", a "change of civilizational model", or even the coming of an entirely new era beyond the modern dualist, reductionist, and economic age are frequently encountered. One example is Thomas Berry's notion of *The Great Work*, a transition which he called the **Ecozoic**, "from the period when humans were a disruptive force on the planet Earth to the period when humans become present on the planet in a manner that is mutually enhancing" (Berry, 1999: 11). Vandana Shiva (2008) refers to the key to the transition as being from oil to soil, increasingly emphasizing localism. These writers all call for a diverse economy that has a strong base on communities (Gibson-Graham, 2006).

In emphasizing the profound interconnectedness of life, landscape, society and activity, as in complex systems theory, and in demonstrating that no single approach can be applied across the globe in the face of the great cultural, geographic and climatic ranges, these newer tendencies point towards an ontology for which the world is always multiple, a pluriverse. The pluriverse can be described as "a world where many worlds fit". Escobar suggests that "To accomplish this goal, we need to start thinking about human practice in terms of ontological design, or the design of other worlds and knowledges" (Escobar, 2011; p. 140).

Thus the WS advocates would see globalization economically and socially as the best way ahead, whereas the SS advocates would see localism as a fundamentally better option. This presents a problem, as both approaches are exclusive, and offer little in the way of a middle road.

9.3.4 Our carbon fixation

Countless papers refer to the reduction of carbon footprints as the main issue facing us, and transitions are often judged in terms of how this can be achieved. Only true system-based models recognize that there are two other very significant issues facing us, habitat degradation and nutrient pollution. Neither of these will be prevented by reducing greenhouse gas emissions. They need completely different approaches.

Yet a succession of summits has ignored these equally threatening issues, and we remain focused on carbon. "**Green**" equates to low carbon emissions. Unless we dramatically shift our focus and begin work on addressing these other issues, it will not matter how low carbon dioxide atmospheric levels reach. Ecosystem function along with its life-preserving services will cease to provide the little bear's porridge that Goldilocks requires in order to survive. This fixation with carbon is perhaps the greatest threat to the realization of a sustainable transition. You can have all the green fuel you want, but if it continues to be used to make nitrogen fertilizers which are poured on the damaged soils of our planet, dispersing into our ecosystem, then it matters not.

Atmospheric gas perturbation is only one third of the problem. We are ignoring two rather large, increasingly angry elephants in the room. Why is this the case? It suits the reductionist science and the reductionist political process. Focusing on one single threat, with one single letter, C for carbon, means politicians can easily sell their policies to the electorate, and deliver nice clean messages, while being seen to be making nice clean progress. It's a bit like the crew of a ship all gathered around a hole in the bow of the ship, repairing the damage and bailing out the water, while two equally large holes go unattended in the stern.

The problems facing any transition planner are multiple, and the solution space is a difficult and hazardous terrain, with gullies and crevasses all around. By simplifying things, scientists and politicians do the human race a great disservice. Unless we recognize the issues at hand as legion, intertwined and complex, we will have no possibility of putting in place a meaningful response. Indeed such ignorance could well make matters worse. For example many green energy alternatives create huge problems in terms of habitat destruction and pollution.

9.4 The mechanics of transition—transitional models

What are the mechanics of transition, and how can we plan the process? It really depends on two things. Is it a random, ahistorical event or is there a predictable, determinate and applicable formula that can be seen through history? What drives transition to its conclusion? How much flexibility is there and is it a selective or diffusional process? Can we base the design of a sustainable transition on previous transitions? This latter question is extremely important. If we do model it on previous examples, then how relevant are those other examples for this current transition?

Unsurprisingly, there are many different viewpoints. In this section we will examine some of the key models.

9.4.1 The Dutch model

The Dutch Scientific Network on Transitions (KSI) focuses on driving system innovation forward by achieving sociocultural, institutional, economic, and technological changes. The status quo is visualized as a dynamic rather than a static equilibrium, which is then disturbed. In this respect, transition resembles secondary succession, wherein external disturbance leads to renewal and development of the ecosystem through a series of steps. These steps combine to give a **multiphase transition**. This multiphase transition describes the dynamics of transitions in terms of four different stages: predevelopment, take-off, acceleration and stabilization (Rotmans *et al.*, 2001, Rotmans, 2005):

1. The **predevelopment phase** arises from a dynamic state of equilibrium in which continuous perturbation is occurring, but within an envelope of overall stability and these perturbations are not visible
2. The **take-off phase** represents the actual point of ignition after which the process of structural change gathers pace
3. The **acceleration phase** in which structural changes become obvious
4. The **stabilization phase** where a new dynamic state of equilibrium is achieved (Rotmans *et al.* 2001)

If we consider the present era, we would identify it as nearing the end of the acceleration phase, with technology, production and population all expanding rapidly. And so we are yet to emerge into a new equilibrium. However, the industrial and technological advances are coming into collision with ever-increasing natural threats (ecosystem service collapse and resource exhaustion) which threaten to alter this cycle. Thus the Dutch model may not be relevant as there has never been such unprecedented consequences of human behaviour in the past, placing us in a new situation.

The Dutch approach holds that transitions cannot be steered or controlled due to their complexity. However, there is a belief that the speed and direction of change can be guided. There is also no possibility of conceiving of it as subsystem of an ecosystem, in contrast to more natural science-based sustainability research (e.g., Berkes and Folke 1998), because the human race is viewed as a self-referencing closed system, or Bubbleworld (Skene, 2011). Transitions can be classified into eight types based on three axes:

1. Teleological vs. emergent
2. Degree of co-ordination (from high to low)
3. Level of aggregation (high vs. low)

For example, the Internet is viewed as an emergent, hardly co-ordinated, and highly aggregated transition, while the transition from coal to gas is classed as a teleological, highly co-ordinated, and slightly aggregated transition. Transitions are not thought of as emerging from a single point, and diffusing outwards, but rather they occur in different locations, akin to Young's moduli in wave mechanics, and modulate into a significant change. These ideas are difficult in terms of differences in starting points, cultures and geopolitical heterogeneity across the planet. Indeed, currently, all four ages (hunter-gatherer, agrarian, industrial and information) exist on our planet. Thus to envisage a series of waves, coming together to deliver a global transition is not particularly straightforward.

The Dutch approach envisages a dominant existing state as being overthrown in three ways:

1. A bottom-up change, where niches emerge at the micro level, cluster and attack the existent dominant state, leading to transformation
2. A squeezed path change, where contrasting approaches eventually influence each other, leading to gradual incorporation and slow transition to a new state
3. A top-down change, where a dramatic change alters the landscape completely

This approach is called the **multilevel concept**. The multilevel concept describes the dynamics of a transition as the interactions between three different scale levels: a microlevel of niches, innovations and alternatives to the existent regime, a meso-level, where a regime of dominant structures, culture and practices operates and a macro-level of societal trends and developments. MLP has been used to examine transitions from the shift from open to closed sewage systems in Netherlands (Geels, 2006) to the shift from crooners to rock 'n' roll (Geels, 2007)!

A final approach is the **multi-pattern concept**, which aims to describe the way in which systems transform (Rotmans, 2005). It focuses on how a certain transformative change progresses, for instance through a bottom-up dynamic or a top-down dynamic. An underlying assumption is that a transition can be explained by only a limited set of patterns of transformative change.

Two types of pattern have been identified. Geels and Schot (2007) suggest a group of four paths:

1. **Reconfiguration path**: niches are adapted, giving rise to further niches; this represents a process of gradual change
2. **Transformation path**: a lack of niches means actors must respond individually
3. **Dealignment/realignment path**: following disillusionment, actors discover a new approach
4. **Technological substitution path**: new niche replaces incumbent regime

De Hahn (2007) sets out three possibilities:

1. **Re-constellation**: where a large-scale alternative is forced on an incumbent regime
2. **Empowerment**: where a small niche grows and eventually replaces the incumbent
3. **Adaptation**: where an incumbent regime responds to new niches

The Dutch approach utilizes an array of tools, including complex systems theory, adaptive governance, and socio-technical studies. Complex adaptive systems have unique features such as: co-evolution, emergence, and self-organization. The principle of "**radical change in incremental steps**" is a paradox that is derived from complexity theory. Immediate radical change, however, would lead to maximal resistance from the deep structure (Grin *et al.*, 2010; p. 145).

9.4.2 The Viennese school

The **Viennese School** of sustainable transition analyses contemporary and historical phenomena of radical change in societies linked to change in their relations to the environment. Sociology and history are core tools of this approach, and are used to calculate **socio-metabolic profiles** (that is, social structures and their use of resources). Krausmann *et al.* (2009) sum up this approach as follows: "In world history certain modes of human production/subsistence can be broadly distinguished that share, at whatever point in time and irrespective of bio-geographical conditions, certain fundamental systemic characteristics derived from the way they utilize and thereby modify nature". For the Viennese social-ecology approach, socio-metabolic regimes in world history correspond to human modes of subsistence (Boyden, 1992).

According to the Viennese approach, the key to a transition is a society's energy system, and the impact of changes in this energy system is different across scale levels. At the foundation of their approach lies the reconstruction of metabolic profiles of social systems through time. It was noted that major changes in socio-metabolic profiles were characterized by substantial increases in metabolic rates (in terms of joules and tonnes of socioeconomic input per capita population).

What is clearly observed from Table 9.1 is that there has been a huge increase in population, energy consumption and material use over the last two millennia, with a transition from an active solar-powered society to a fossil fuel-powered society (Sieferle, 2003). Socio-metabolic regimes represent dynamic equilibria of society–nature interactions and are characterized by typical patterns of material and energy flows (metabolic profiles).

However, what is also clear is that today on our planet there exist nations that have metabolisms similar to the Agrarian Age and intermediate between the Agrarian and Industrial ages. What this means is that the previous transition is still very much ongoing, and has not reached its own equilibrium as yet. And so we find ourselves striving to create the next transition before the last one has reached maturity. This fact has not been fully appreciated by many. How this observation will interfere with any plans for a new transition is an important though as yet unexplored issue.

The next transition cannot continue along this path of increase of the last 10,000 years, not only because it would further destabilize a creaking planet, but because we do not have the fossil fuels left to power such an increase. The most recent socio-metabolic phase has only lasted 300 years, compared with the 9,000-year reign of the Agrarian Age and the >300,000-year innings of the Hunter-Gatherer Age. The Stockholm-centred resilience movement (e.g. Gunderson and Holling 2002), would say that the potential to maintain a certain socio-metabolism is key to the resilience of a particular

	Agrarian regime	Industrial regime	LD[1]	DC[2]	EU[3]
Population density (per capita per km^2)	30–40	100–300	40	76	116
Energy use per capita (GJ per capita per year)	50–70	150–400	33	64	205
Energy/area (GJ per ha per year)	20–30	200–600	13	49	216
Fossil fuels (%)	0–5	60–80	8	50	77
Material use per capita (t per capita per year)	2–5	15–25	4.2	6.8	16
Material use/area (t per ha per year)	1–2	20–50	1.3	4.8	18

TABLE 9.1 Metabolic profiles of the agrarian and industrial socio-ecological regimes (based on data from Fischer-Kowalski *et al.*, 2007; p. 231)

[1] LD = least-developed countries
[2] DC = developing countries (according to UN definitions)
[3] EU = 15 member countries of the European Union

social-ecological system. Since our energy source is diminishing, the social-ecological system that it maintains will also decline.

The concept that the ages of humankind are some sort of universal history from which we can learn to transition again is questionable for a number of reasons:

- The narrative flowing through the first three ages is merely an account of gradual development, with the Industrial Age being an extension of the Agrarian, and the Information Age further extending the drives and aspirations of the early agrarian settlers. Only the Hunter-Gatherer to Agrarian transition is noteworthy, where a complete change in system occurred.
- None of them were planned.
- None of them were universal—we have all four ages present today.
- None of them were transformative—we have all four ages here today.
- None of them form a model for salvation.
- None of them utilized extrapolated data.
- There were three very different horses of the apocalypse (famine, war and disease).

Various mechanisms behind the directionality of time may be distinguished. Akin to successional theory, it can either imply consecutive stages of a "developmental" type (akin to Herbert Spencer's (1876) notion of evolution or Marxist historical materialism (Marx 1976)), or it may follow a Darwinian or Gouldian type of evolutionary theory by assuming the future to be contingent on the past but principally unpredictable. As we have seen in Chapter 4, more recent approaches, including thermodynamic post-selection, also exist, with predictable physiology, and a diffusion of form, encompassing the maximum entropy production principle (MEPP). This latter theory would consider transition as an outcome of disturbance, wherein functional integrity is restored following an increase in entropy *within* the structure.

In the case of the sustainability transition, this would involve economic breakdown, driven by excessive entropy within the surroundings, preventing continued maintenance of order through available energy flux. However, a thermodynamic transition is a destructive outcome, and although the "**crash landing**" scenario is inevitable if a "**planned landing**" transition is not put in place, will be an extremely unpleasant experience.

Darwinian theory has difficulty coping with transition. Gradual incremental changes based on genetic mutation and competition are very much the grounds for business as usual. Competition will deliver the best of all possible worlds, as nature selects the best outcomes. However, the reductionist approach of the selfish gene leaves no room for transition in all of its complexity. Indeed it is the application of this thinking that has underpinned the disastrous journey of recent centuries. A system change requires the ousting of the incumbent philosophy, and thus it is unlikely that Darwinian architecture can help support the significant transition required in order to avoid the **thermodynamic transition** ahead. The Gaian hypothesis also struggles for a meaningful comment on transition as it holds to an "equilibrium at all costs" phenomenon at the planetary level.

Mauser *et al.* (2013) outline three important stages in transition all of which acknowledge the importance of stakeholder involvement:

1. **Co-design** of the research agenda through integration between stakeholders and decision-makers from the relevant societal sectors and science to develop a viable research strategy for the broader scientific community.

2. **Co-production**: during this phase, integrated research is conducted as a continuous exchange among the participating scientists and with the stakeholders.

3. **Co-dissemination**: the last step consists of the dissemination of the findings among the different societal groups for review, feeding back into the next cycle of co-design.

These steps target the importance of inclusion and involvement of everyone, preventing ivory towers of academia and business from seclusion, and increasing the opportunity for cross-fertilization and feedback. This approach exemplifies the broader church of **co-evolutionary transition**, wherein the firm has a symbiotic, co-evolving relationship with society and ecosystems (Korhonen and Seager, 2008), avoiding the dangers of supporting the incumbent regime as is feared will be the result from eco-efficiency strategies (Korhonen and Seager, 2008) and incremental change (Könnölä and Unruh, 2008) leading to suboptimal innovation trajectories.

Marechal and Lazaric (2010) emphasize the following concepts as being important for delivering a transition:

- The maintenance of solution diversity is important for allowing climate-friendly technologies to emerge
- Motivate consumers with other measures than the usual incentives to shift from the existing carbon-, nitrogen- and phosphorus-based socio-technological system
- Target "lead users" (those with a habit of looking for novelty) and pave the way for a transition towards a sustainable future

9.4.3 Transition by evolution

As early as 1898, Thorstein Veblen was already wondering why economics is not an evolutionary science (Veblen, 1898). Of course it all depends what we mean by evolution. A number of evolutionary models exist: neo-Darwinian thinking, focused on the gene, Gouldian evolution, focused on contingency and punctuated equilibrium, Ganong's concept of evolution down the path of least resistance and post-selection. Certainly the modern evolutionary **synthesis**, with its reliance on a reductionist single unit of selection and its emphasis on the extended phenotype (i.e. everything is built from the gene and behaves selfishly) has little to contribute to a complex transition system. The opposite approach, exploring thermodynamics as a cosmic force acting as an agent of organization, as envisioned by Georgescu-Roegen, offers a more interesting option, where systems theory contributes to understanding change. However, such an approach has never been applied to transition theory.

Within a sustainable transition, the philosophy of business must change, according to Nelson and Winter (1982). A company is no longer seen as being driven only by the primary goal of profit maximization but also by its survival, given the environment in which it operates. Here, innovation still plays an important role for growth and development, but "satisfying" (i.e. not necessarily optimizing) strategies such as organizational routines also play a significant role (Becker *et al.*, 2005). It becomes survival of the fitting, not of the fittest. Suboptimality becomes important in system-based thinking, because each level of organization is part of another level, and so solution space will be compromised, leading to reduced optimality for any given level, but overall optimality at the system level.

Another concept plucked from evolutionary theory is the idea of hopeful monstrosities or hopeful monsters (Gould, 1977) where niches may offer protective space for new innovations that otherwise would be out-competed by incumbents. The difficulty is that it is unlikely that the luxury of protective space exists. One way to help potentially brilliant ideas to survive the competitive business world of today is to engineer protective space. These spaces would provide protection against particular selective characteristics of the incumbent regime (Smith and Raven, 2012):

- The cultural significance attached to a specific regime forms a selection environment
- Public policies and political power
- Markets and infrastructures
- Established industry structures
- Dominant user practices
- Guiding principles and socio-cognitive processes in the established knowledge base
- Dominant technologies

Smith and Raven (2012) further identify two types of protective space:

1. **Passive protective spaces**: generic spaces that pre-exist deliberate mobilization by advocates of specific innovations, but who exploit the shielding opportunities they provide
2. **Active protective spaces**: those spaces that are the result of deliberate and strategic creation by advocates of specific path-breaking innovations

One concern relating to protective spaces is that it they could become forms of protectionism, protecting one type of hopeful monster but killing off others. This also brings with it the possibility of corrupt practice and an even more uneven playing field. Another issue is that of the captive breeding analogy, wherein animals captive bred in a zoo rarely survive reintroduction in the wild.

Modern business organizations face numerous demands out with the sustainability issues relating to the transition. They are tuned to these challenges, both structurally and in terms of strategic management. However, traditional models of organization design are ill-equipped to cope with the challenges of a sustainable transition. Businesses need to be strategically agile. They need to be designed to react and adjust rapidly. This is summed up in the built to change (B2C) approach. The ability to change drives performance because no single advantage lasts long enough to warrant the investment.

Worley and Lawler (2006) identified some basic features of the B2C model: strategizing, organizing, and creating value. In fast-changing environments such as transitions, an overzealous pursuit of efficiency slows change and threatens long-term effectiveness (Van Alstyne, 1997). Efficiency and predictability do not share common ground with diversity, which is essential for adaptation and innovation. Organizations with efficiency (even eco-efficiency) at their hearts will often sacrifice deep sustainability for current performance.

The innovation challenge essentially relates to processes of search (for innovation trigger signals), selection (resource allocation) and implementation. "Core competences" may become "core rigidities", limiting the organization's ability to deal with changing conditions (Leonard-Barton, 1995; p. 335). A key point is that the search and selection space is not one-dimensional. As Henderson and Clark (1990) point out, it is not just a question of searching near or far from core knowledge concepts but also across configurations—the component/architecture challenge.

Leach *et al.* (2012) emphasize three key attributes of any mechanism of transition:

1. **Determination of the specific direction of change**: this means being clear on the particular goals and principles driving policy and innovation.
2. **The importance of diversity** is also crucial. Protective space without protectionism is essential if the breadth of thinking is to be

explored. For truly diffusive thinking, selection cannot be present. Under post-selectionist thinking, selection is an outcome of dynamic equilibrium but has no role in an evolving transition. "Evolution occurs not in the crowded back-alleys but in the empty market places" (Skene, 2009; p. 224). Brusatte *et al.* (2008; p. 1485) observe that "historical contingency rather than prolonged competition or general 'superiority' was the primary factor in the rise of dinosaurs". Professor Sam Alizon and colleagues note that under resource competition, there is an exponential slowdown of the apparent rate of evolution (Alizon *et al.*, 2008). And so it is with innovation. Nurturing more diverse approaches and forms of innovation (social as well as technological) allows us to respond to uncertainty and surprise. Competition and selection crush such opportunity.

3. **Distribution**: this means taking seriously how the safe operating space is shared between different people, and asking about who gains and who loses from particular policies and innovations aiming to navigate within it. There are often trade-offs at stake, between contrasting environmental and poverty reduction goals, for instance, or national and local interests.

Finally, it is important to recognize that transition mechanisms cannot just be rolled out across the world, oblivious to geography. The geography of transition is important because:

- There is a territorial sensitivity towards transitions
- Significant differences may require a pluriverse approach with multiple transition pathways

One of the strengths of transition analysis lies in its capacity to deal with structure–agency duality. However, it can be argued that what is gained in a historical treatment has come at the expense of a neglect of geographical factors (Coenen and Truffer, 2012). Geographical networks define and create spaces with their own institutional arrangements, power relations, governance institutions and dynamics, which offer "proximity" between actors (Boschma, 2005). Coenen *et al.* (2012) have observed that "Transition analyses, whether through the lens of technological innovation systems or the multilevel perspective, should start to explore, and partly revisit, the meaning played by particular places in the evolution of transitions".

9.5 Transition management

If transition can be managed (and this will be the first transition to be carried out with the support of a large academic community dedicated to transition management), then some management strategies will be needed. Unlike most business management, the goals are not increased economic growth, competitive edge and profit for investors. However, some attributes are shared: importance of teamwork, good communication, good staff training, appeal to the consumer, legislative support and goal-oriented focus.

We have seen that there is much uncertainty about the "market". How will voters respond to the required legislation? Will politicians be brave enough to pass said legislation? How will the natural environment respond to our actions? However, the central issue is the generation of innovative solutions in order to solve the wicked problem that we face. Therefore in order to have a transition to manage at all, we must manage the innovative process itself.

Loorbach *et al.* (2007) suggest the following transition management cycle:

- Problem structuring, establishment of a transition arena, and envisioning
- Developing coalitions, transition agendas, transition images, and related transition paths
- Establishing and carrying out transition experiments and mobilizing transition networks
- Monitoring, evaluating, and learning lessons from the experiments and, based on these, adjust vision, agenda and coalitions

Avelino (2007) has identified six important principles of transition management. The first principle is that of **creating space for niches** in so-called **transition arenas** or **protective spaces**, an idea we have already discussed. The second transition management principle involves **focus on the front-runners**. In complex system terms, front-runners are agents with the capacity to generate dissipative structures and operate within these deviant structures. This can only be achieved if these front-runners are not dependent on the structure, culture and practices of the incumbent regime. Thus managing opportunity and supporting outliers is important.

A third principle of transition management is **guided variation and selection**. A continuously selective, competitive environment will not work, but some selection may be necessary at times. Thus there needs to be a flexible approach. A fourth principle is that of **radical change in incremental**

steps. Too much change too quickly will lead to an immune response from the incumbent regime. Fifth, the importance of **empowering niches** is an important principle of transition management. Hopeful monsters need resources such as knowledge, finances, abilities, lobby mechanisms, exemption from rules and laws, and space for experimenting. What was started within a transition arena must now be able to germinate and grow beyond that arena. Finally, **anticipation and adaptation** are required. Being receptive to feedback and review, in co-operation with all stakeholders, and being diversified enough to be adaptable to unknown futures are key aspects of good transition management, embracing collective intelligence (Bonabeau, 2009).

Jantsch (1972) put forward the idea that knowledge creation should be organized and co-ordinated in hierarchical systems at four levels: purposive (meaning values), normative (social systems design), pragmatic (physical technology, natural ecology, social ecology) and empirical (physical inanimate world, physical animate world).

The key steering philosophy underlying transition management is that of "anticipation and adaptation, starting from a macro-vision on sustainability, building upon (micro) initiatives, meanwhile influencing the meso-regime" (Loorbach *et al.*, 2007; p. 82). This reflects Patrick Geddes's concept of **think global act local**. Reinforcement is, therefore, an important management exercise. In order to express this philosophy, a more local emphasis has begun to develop in sustainable transition management.

Non-governmental organizations (NGOs) may have an important role to play in local transition management, especially those involved in environmental, development and consumer issues. Their ace card is that they generally have much greater trust within society compared with business or political parties. Most NGOs, in their consumption-related work, are focusing on carbon, without exploring the embeddedness of energy use within larger sociocultural and institutional structures. Furthermore, few if any are targeting habitat destruction and eutrophication. In times of political green growth promotion, campaigns for reduced, sustainable consumption will struggle to find donors, and those that do, will likely have to follow the new incumbent green movement: carbon fixation. There is a need to manage a move away from carbon.

An even more local level of management, ignored in transition management literature is the civil society. Civil society is an arena that encompasses the collective activities by which associations of people develop and assert shared values, identities and interests, without direct recourse to market transactions or the authority of the state in the first place (Hargreaves *et al.*, 2011; p. 4).

Civil society acts to intervene in the dynamics of practice, rather than challenging regimes or developing new niches. It brings into tight focus the issue of who should manage transition. Is it the state and the modern church that is neoclassical economics, driven by popularity and growth, or should this revolution be led by the people?

Obviously the answer to this will depend on who you ask. Certainly localism movements have been growing rapidly across the political spectrum. From the Big Society of David Cameron, the Tea Party of Republican America to communalism and slow food, the trend of returning sovereignty to communities and relinquishing control, has demonstrated itself in legislation and in action. However, when such movements begin to threaten the institutions, such as when local currencies begin to appear, then localism can appear to be less welcomed (Aldridge and Patterson, 2002).

A key movement in delivering local transition, particularly in urban areas, is the **transition culture** (TC), which emphasizes the reduction in the economic dependence of towns and cities on distant communities (Malpass *et al.*, 2007). However, TC also includes a moral care-of-vulnerable-proximate-others within its codes of practice. The movement works towards developing communities that are more locally resilient by reducing the reliance on global oil production, while locally responding to environmental issues. Transition culture is more focused on strong sustainability responses rather than centralized weak sustainability approaches (Bernstein 2000). Self-mobilizing elements of civil society are cast as the key agents of metropolitan and global change.

Transition culture bears many similarities with **international municipalism**. Pierre-Yves Saunier (2002) sets out four postulates that underpin international municipalism:

1. The future is an urban one
2. The municipality is the basic cell of any political structure in any human culture or civilization
3. Local government is seen as essentially technical, a pursuit of the common good with no allegiance other than to the "Municipal Party"
4. They belong to a shared universe of rules and values in which they can compare themselves to, or rival others

Transition culture seeks to rescale urban space into networked communities of low-energy living of approximately 15,000 people. In this, it appears to be more a form of international localism or territorialism than international municipalism. However, one of the greatest challenges within TC is the struggle with whether or not to network with other urban units for the transfer of skills, ideas, resources and currency. There is a fear within transition culture that networking can lead to a situation where the State is, in a sense, replaced by a similar beast: networked municipalities.

Libertarian municipality, as outlined in *Remaking Society* by Murray Bookchin (1989), is built around the concept of the *polis* as "large enough so that its citizens could meet most of their material needs, yet not so large that they were unable to gain a familiarity with each other and make policy decisions in open, face-to-face discourse" (Bookchin 1989:180). To this extent, libertarian municipalism is a manifestation of social anarchism.

All of these movements are political and revolutionary. Their potential to deliver a transition relies on some form of conversation, and some interaction with academic, government and business actors, but their separatism precludes this. Furthermore rural aspects appear not to feature, and so it is difficult to see how issues relating to habitat destruction and agricultural pollution can be addressed, in addition to climate destabilization.

Given that 40% of the world's population live in large cities and that all the food and water is sourced from out with these cities, a more integrated approach may be necessary than is offered by transition culture and its bedfellows. Think global, act local. There are two parts to this very significant statement.

Finally, the psychology of transition should be mentioned. Gifford *et al.* (2011) highlight the importance of behaviour in transitions. **Curtailment behaviour** consists of repetitive actions that reduce consumption (e.g., turning off a light switch), whereas **efficiency behaviours** are one-time actions involving the adoption of an efficient technology (e.g., purchasing energy-efficient light bulbs). The former are over-represented among reported intervention studies, yet the latter have greater energy-saving potential although more likely to be subject to the rebound effect. An advantage of efficiency behaviours is that they do not require behavioural maintenance.

Two broad types of behavioural intervention strategy may be distinguished: **antecedent strategies** and **consequence strategies** (Schultz, 1999). Antecedent strategies (e.g., increasing knowledge or problem awareness) are assumed to influence the determinants of behaviour prior to its performance. In contrast, consequence strategies (e.g., feedback, rewards, and punishment) are thought to have their influence on the determinants of a target behaviour after reflection, in the hope of changing that behaviour. In contrast, **structural strategies** aim to alter the circumstances under which the behaviourally relevant decision is made (Messick and Brewer, 2005).

9.6 Debate, discussion and further thought

1. "From a social perspective in particular, human wellbeing cannot be sustained without a healthy environment and is equally unlikely in the absence of a vibrant economy" (Torjman, 2000; p. 2). Discuss.
2. Can a sustainable transition be controlled or merely encouraged?
3. Compare and contrast transitional space within weak and strong sustainability.
4. "There has only been, so far, a single transition in the human race, from hunter-gatherer to agrarian." Discuss.
5. Compare the strengths and weaknesses of localism versus centralization in the delivery of a sustainable transition.
6. Transition: evolution or revolution?
7. Write a critique on Leach *et al.* (2012)'s three key attributes of transition.
8. When is a transition not a transition?
9. What are the challenges of transition management?
10. Why is the geography of transition so important, and what implications does it have on transition planning?
11. Mini-project: research and outline a blueprint for transition, clearly defining the underlying philosophical framework utilized and the challenges to be addressed. Include a time-line.

References

Alber, M. (2002). *Poverty Eradication and Sustainable Development.* HSRC Publication, Pretoria.

Aldridge, T.J. and Patterson, A. (2002). LETS get real: constraints on the development of Local Exchange Trading Schemes. Area 34(4): 370-81.

Alizon, S., Kucera, M. and Jansen, V.A.A. (2008). Competition between cryptic species explains variations in rates of lineage evolution. Proceedings of the National Academy of Sciences, USA 105: 12382-6.

Avelino, F. (2011). *Power in Transition: Empowering Discourses on Sustainability Transitions.* Doctoral dissertation, Erasmus University Rotterdam.

Banuri, T., Weyant, J., Akuma, G., Najam, A., Pinguelli R.L., Rayner, S., Sachs, W., Sharma, R. and Yohe, G. (2001). Setting the Stage: Climate Change and Sustainable Development. In Metz, B., Davidson, O., Swart, R. and Pan, J. (eds.), *Climate Change 2001: Mitigation, Contribution of Working Group III to the Third Assessment Report of the Intergovernmental Panel on Climate Change.* Cambridge University Press, Cambridge.

Becker, M.C., Lazaric, N., Nelson, R.R. and Winter, S.G. (2005). Applying organizational routines in understanding organizational change. Industrial and Corporate Change 14(5): 775-91.

Berkes, F., Kislalioglu, M., Folke, C. and Gadgil, M. (1998). Exploring the basic ecological unit: ecosystem-like concepts in traditional societies. Ecosystems 1: 409-15.

Bernstein S (2000). Ideas, social structure and the compromise of liberal environmentalism. *European Journal of International Relations* 6: 464-512

Berry, T. (1999). *The Great Work: Our way into the Future.* Bell Tower, New York.

Bookchin, M. (1989). *Remaking Society.* Black Rose Books, New York.

Bonabeau, E. (2009). Decisions 2.0: the power of collective intelligence. MIT Sloan Management Review 50 (2): 45-52.

Boyden, S. (1992). *Biohistory: the Interplay Between Human Society and the Biosphere, Past and Present.* UNESCO.

Boschma, R.A. (2005). Proximity and innovation. A critical assessment. Regional Studies 39(1): 61-74.

Brown, H. (1954). The challenge of man's future. Engineering and Science 17(5): 16-36.

Brundtland, G.H. (1987). *Brundtland Report. Our Common Future.* Comissão Mundial.

Brusatte, S.L., Benton, M.J., Ruta, M. and Lloyd, G.T. (2008). Superiority, competition and opportunism in the evolutionary radiation of dinosaurs. Science 321: 1485-8.

Coenen, L., Benneworth, P. and Truffer, B. (2012). Toward a spatial perspective on sustainability transitions. Research Policy 41(6): 968-79.

Coenen, L. and Truffer, B. (2012). Places and spaces of sustainability transitions: Geographical contributions to an emerging research and policy field. European Planning Studies 20(3): 367-74.

de Haan, J. (2007). *Pillars of Change: A Theoretical Framework for Transition Models.* The ESEE 2007 Conference: Integrating Natural and Social Sciences for Sustainability. Leipzig, Germany.

Easterlin, R.A. (1974). Does economic growth improve the human lot? In: David, P.A. and Reder, M.W. (eds.), *Nations and Households in Economic Growth: Essays in Honor of Moses Abramovitz.* Academic Press, New York.

EC, 2007. Presidency Conclusions of the Brussels European Council. 8/9 March 2007, (7224/1/07) REV 1, CON 1.

Eckel, P., Hill, B. and Green, M. (1998). On change: en route to transformation. Occasional Paper Series of the ACE Project on Leadership and Institutional Transformation. American Council on Education, Washington DC.

Ehrlich, P. and Holdren, J. (1971). Impact of population growth. Science 171: 1212-17.

Elzen. B., Geels, F.W. and Green, K. (2004). System Innovation and the Transition to Sustainability: Theory, Evidence and Policy. Edward Elgar, Cheltenham, Glos.

Escobar, A. (2011). Sustainability: Design for the pluriverse. Development 54(2): 137-40.

EMF (2012). *Towards the Circular Economy: Economic and Business Rationale for an Accelerated Transition.* Ellen MacArthur Foundation, Cowes, Isle of Wight.

Geels, F.W. (2006). The hygienic transition from cesspools to sewer systems (1840–1930): The dynamics of regime transformation. Research Policy 35(7): 1069-82.

Geels, F.W. (2007). Analysing the breakthrough of rock 'n' roll (1930–1970): multi-regime interaction and reconfiguration in the multi-level perspective. Technological Forecasting and Social Change 74: 1411-31.

Geels, F.W. (2011). The multi-level perspective on sustainability transitions: Responses to seven criticisms. Environmental Innovation and Societal Transitions 1(1): 24-40.

Geels, F.W. and Schot, J. (2007). Typology of sociotechnical transition pathways. Research Policy 36(3): 399-417.

Geels, F., Hekkert, M. and Jacobsson, S. (2008). The dynamics of sustainable innovation journeys. Technology Analysis and Strategic Management 20(5): 521-36

Gell-Mann M. (1994). *The Quark and the Jaguar.* WH Freeman, New York.

Gibson-Graham, J.K. (2006). *"The" End of Capitalism (as We Knew It): A Feminist Critique of Political Economy; with a New Introduction.* University of Minnesota Press, Minneapolis, MN.

Gifford, R., Kormos, C. and McIntyre, A. (2011). Behavioral dimensions of climate change: drivers, responses, barriers, and interventions. Climate Change 2(6): 801-27.

Godelier, M. (1986). *The Mental and the Material: Thought Economy and Society.* Blackwell Verso, London.

Gould, S.J. (1977). The return of hopeful monsters. Natural History 86(6): 22-30.

Grin, J., Rotmans, J. and Schot, J. (2010). *Transitions to sustainable development: New directions in the study of long term transformative change.* Routledge, New York.

Gunderson, L. and Holling, C.S. (2002). *Panarchy: Understanding transformations in Human and Natural Systems.* Island Press, Washington DC.

Hamilton, C. (2010). Consumerism, self-creation and prospects for a new ecological consciousness. Journal of Cleaner Production 18(6): 571-5.

Hargreaves, T., Haxeltine, A., Longhurst, N. and Seyfang, G. (2011). Sustainability transitions from the bottom-up: Civil society, the multi-level perspective and practice theory (No. 2011-01). CSERGE working paper EDM.

Healy, S. (2008). Air-conditioning and the "homogenization" of people and built environments. Building Research and Information 36(4): 312-22.

Henderson, R. and Clark, K. (1990). Architectural innovation: The reconfiguration of existing product technologies and the failure of established firms. Administrative Science Quarterly 35: 9-30.

Hueting, R. (2010). Why environmental sustainability can most probably not be attained with growing production. Journal of Cleaner Production 18(6): 525-30.

IEA (2009). Fatih Birol, chief economist. Press conference, 6 October 2009.

Jackson, T. (2009). *Prosperity Without Growth.* Earthscan, London.

Johnson, D.G. and Wetmore, J.M. (2009). *Technology and Society: Building our Sociotechnical Future.* The MIT Press, Boston, MA.

Jantsch, E. (1972). Towards interdisciplinarity and transdisciplinarity in education and innovation. *Interdisciplinarity. Problems of Teaching and Research in Universities.* OECD, Paris. pp. 97-121.

Kamusoko, C., Aniya, M., Adi, B. and Manjoro, M. (2009). Rural sustainability under threat in Zimbabwe—Simulation of future land use/cover changes in the Bindura district based on the Markov-cellular automata model. Applied Geography 29 (3): 435-47.

Kemp, R. and van Lente, H. (2011). The dual challenge of sustainability transitions. Environmental Innovation and Societal Transitions 1(1): 121-4.

Könnölä, T. and Unruh, G.C. (2007). Really changing the course: the limitations of environmental management systems for innovation. The Journal of Business Strategy and the Environment 16 (8): 525-37.

Korhonen, J. and Seager, T. (2008). Beyond eco-efficiency: a resilience perspective. Business Strategy and the Environment 17: 411-19.

Krausmann, F., Fischer-Kowalski, M., Schandl, H. and Eisenmenger, N. (2009). The global socio-metabolic transition: past and present metabolic profiles and their future trajectories. Journal of Industrial Ecology 12(5-6): 637-56.

Leach, M., Rockström, J., Raskin, P., Scoones, I., Stirling, A.C., Smith, A., Thompson, J., Millstone, E., Ely, A., Around, E., Folke, C. and Olsson, P. (2012). Transforming Innovation for Sustainability. Ecology and Society 17(2): 11.

Lebel, L. and Lorek, S. (2008). Enabling sustainable production-consumption systems. Annual Review of Environmental Research 33: 241-75.

Leonard-Barton, D. (1995). *Wellsprings of Knowledge: Building and Sustaining the Sources of Innovation.* Harvard Business School Press, Boston, MA.

Loorbach, D. van Bakel, J.C., Loorbach, D.A., Whiteman, G.M. and Rotmans, J. (2007). *Business Strategies for Transitions towards Sustainable Systems* (No. ERS-2007-094-ORG). Erasmus Research Institute of Management (ERIM).

Loorbach, D., Frantzeskaki, N. and Thissen, W. (2011). A transition research perspective on governance for sustainability. In: *European Research on Sustainable Development.* Springer, Heidelberg. pp. 73-89.

Lusseau, D. (2003). Effects of tour boats on the behavior of bottlenose dolphins: using Markov chains to model anthropogenic impacts. Conservation Biology 17(6): 1785-93.

Malpass, A., Cloke, P., Barnett, C. and Clarke, N. (2007). Fairtrade cities. International Journal of Urban and Regional Research 31: 633-45.

Marechal, K. and Lazaric, N. (2010). Overcoming inertia: insights from evolutionary economics into improved energy and climate policies. Climate Policy 10(1): 103-19.

Martiskaïnen, M. (2008). Household energy consumption and behavioural change: the UK perspective. In: Ken, T.G., Tukker, A., Vezzoli, C. and Ceschin, F. (eds.), *Proceedings of the SCORE Conference Sustainable Consumption and Production: Framework for Action.* 10–11 March, Brussels. pp. 73-90.

Marx, K. (1976). *Capital. Volume 1* (Originally published 1867).Vintage, New York.

Mason, K. and Whitehead, M. (2012). Transition urbanism and the contested politics of ethical place making. Antipode 44(2): 493-516.

Mauser, W., Klepper, G., Rice, M., Schmalzbauer, B.S., Hackmann, H., Leemans, R. and Moore, H. (2013). Transdisciplinary global change research: the co-creation of knowledge for sustainability. Current Opinion in Environmental Sustainability 5(3): 420-31.

Messick, D.M. and Brewer, M.B. (2005). Solving social dilemmas: a review. In: Bazerman, M.H. (ed.), *Negotiation, Decision Making and Conflict Management.* Vol. 1–3. Edward Elgar Publishing; Northampton, MA. pp. 98-131.

Nelson, R.R. and Winter, S.G. (1982). *An Evolutionary Theory of Economic Change.* Harvard University Press, Cambridge, MA.

OECD (2012). *OECD Environmental Outlook to 2050. The Consequences of Inaction.* OECD, Paris.

Raskin, P.D., Electris, C. and Rosen, R.A. (2010). The century ahead: searching for sustainability. Sustainability 2: 2626-51.

Rockström, J., Steffen, W., Noone, K., Persson, Å., Chapin, F.S., Lambin, E.F., Lenton, T.M., Scheffer, M., Folke, C., Schellnhuber, H.J., Nykvist, B., de Wit, C.A., Hughes, T., van der Leeuw, S., Rohde, H., Sörlin, S., Snuder, P.K., Costanza, R., Svedin, U., Falkenmark, M., Karlberg, L., Corell, R.W., Fabry, V.J., Hansen, J., Walker, B., Liverman, D., Richardson, K., Crutzen, P. and Foley, V. (2009). A safe operating space for humanity. Nature 461: 472-5.

Roggema, R., Vermeend, T. and Dobbelsteen, A.V.D. (2012). Incremental change, transition or transformation? Optimising change pathways for climate adaptation in spatial planning. Sustainability 4(10): 2525-49.

Rotmans, J. (1994). *Transitions on the Move. Global Dynamics and Sustainable Development.* Dutch National Institute of Public Health and the Environment (RIVM), Bilthoven, The Netherlands.

Rotmans, J. (2005). Societal innovation: Between dream and reality lies complexity. Inaugural speech, Erasmus University Rotterdam.

Rotmans, J., Kemp, R. and Van Asselt, M.B.A. (2001). More evolution than revolution. Transition management in public policy. Foresight 3(1): 15-31.

Sachs, W. (1999). *Planet Dialectics. Explorations in Environment and Development.* Zed Books, London.

Saunier, P.-Y. (2002). Taking up the bet on connections. Contemporary European History 2: 507-27.

Schneider, F., Kallis, G. and Martinez-Alier, J. (2010). Crisis or opportunity? Economic degrowth for social equity and ecological sustainability. Introduction to this special issue. Journal of Cleaner Production 18(6): 511-18.

Schultz, P.W. (1999). Changing behavior with normative feedback interventions: a field experiment on curbside recycling. Basic Applied Social Psychology 21: 25-36.

Seidl, R., Brand, F.S., Stauffacher, M., Krütli, P., Quang Bao Le, Q.B., Spörri, A., Grégoire Meylan, G., Moser, C., González, M.B. and Scholz, R.W. (2013). Science with society in the Anthropocene. Ambio 42: 5-12.

Seyfang, G. (2009). *The New Economics of Sustainable Consumption.* Palgrave Macmillan, New York.

Seyfang, G. and Smith, A. (2007). Grassroots innovations for sustainable development: towards a new research and policy agenda. Environmental Pollution 16 (4): 584-603.

Shiva, V. (2008). *Soil Not Oil: Environmental Justice in an Age of Climate Crisis.* South End Press, New York.

Sieferle, R.P. (2003). Sustainability in a world history perspective. In: Benzing, B. (ed.), *Exploitation and Over-exploitation in Societies Past and Present.* LIT Publishing House, Münster, Germany. pp. 123-42.

Skene, K.R. (2009). *Shadows on the Cave Wall: a New Theory of Evolution.* Ard Macha Press, Angus, UK.

Skene, K.R. (2011). *Escape from Bubbleworld: Seven Curves to Save the Earth.* Ard Macha Press, Angus, UK.

Smith, A. and Raven, R. (2012). What is protective space? Reconsidering niches in transitions to sustainability. Research Policy 41(6): 1025-36.

Spangenberg, J.H. (2010). The growth discourse, growth policy and sustainable development: two thought experiments. Journal of Cleaner Production 18(6): 561-6.

Spencer H. (1976). *The First Principles of Sociology.* Appleton, New York

Stern, N. (2006). *Stern Review on ehe Economics of Climate Change.* Executive Summary. HM Treasury, London.

Torjman, S. (2000). The social dimension of sustainable development. Caledon Institute of Social Policy.

Ulrich, O. (1992). Technology. In: Sachs, W. (ed.), *The Development Dictionary. A Guide to Knowledge as Power*. Zed Books, London. pp. 275-87.

Unruh, G.C. (2000). Understanding carbon lock-in. Energy Policy 28: 817-30.

Van Alstyne, M. (1997). The state of network organizations: A survey in three frameworks. Journal of Organizational Computing and Electronic Commerce 7: 83-151.

van Griethuysen, P. (2010). Why are we growth-addicted? The hard way towards degrowth in the involutionary western development path. Journal of Cleaner Production 18(6): 590-5.

Van Vuuren, D.P., Nakicenovic, N., Riahi, K., Brew-Hammond, A., Kammen, D., Modi, V., Nilsson, M. and Smith, K.R. (2012). An energy vision: the transformation towards sustainability—interconnected challenges and solutions. Current Opinion in Environmental Sustainability 4(1): 18-34.

Veblen, T. (1898). Why is economics not an evolutionary science? Quarterly Journal of Economics 12(4): 373-97.

Victor, P. (2010). Questioning economic growth. Nature 468: 370-1.

Walker, B., Holling, C.S., Carpenter, S.R. and Kinzig, A. (2004). Resilience, adaptability and transformability in social-ecological systems. Ecology and Society 9(2): 1-9.

Westley, F., Olsson, P., Folke, C., Homer-Dixon, T., Vredenburg, H., Loorbach, D., Thompson, J., Nilsson, M., Lambin, E, Sendzimir, J., Banerjee, B., Galaz, V. and van der Leeuw, S. (2011). Tipping toward sustainability: emerging pathways of transformation. Ambio 40(7): 762-80.

Worley, C.G. and Lawler, E.E. (2010). Built to change organizations and responsible progress: Twin pillars of sustainable success. Research in Organizational Change and Development 18: 1-49.

WWF (2010). *Living Planet Report 2010. Biodiversity, Biocapacity and Development*. Gland, Switzerland: WWF International.

Xiaojian, G. and Rong, L. (2010). Green house demand forecasting model based on markov chains. In Intelligent Computation Technology and Automation (ICICTA), 2010 International Conference Vol. 2, IEEE. pp. 407-409.

10
Appropriate indicators of a sustainability transition

In this chapter, we address the issue of how to measure the progress of our efforts towards a sustainable future. We examine what makes an appropriate indicator, what we should measure in order to assess progress (or lack of it), and the particular challenges of measuring a sustainable transition. With environmental, economic and social aspects to be evaluated, is there really any objective approach? We then examine whether a single indicator is realistic, and if not, what combination of indicators should be used.

Learning aims and objectives

- What are the two categories of indicator, and what are the three dimensions within which they exist?
- What are the objectives of a good indicator?
- Differentiate between an index and an indicator
- Give some examples of commonly used sustainability indicators, providing a description of how they are calculated, what they are used for and what issues relate to them
- Explain the difference between absolute and relative decoupling

Learning outcomes and experiences

- Why are sustainability indicators difficult to develop and what issues particularly arise in terms of transition indicators?
- Explain why geography is a challenge for national indicators
- Discuss the challenges posed in terms of designing indicators of social, economic and environmental sustainability

10.1 What is an indicator?

Indicators are measurable characteristics of a given entity or system. They are particularly useful in monitoring change and impact. Indicators both inform and communicate. They inform policy-makers, planners, scientists and engineers, allowing them to benchmark a particular approach with another, provide early warning, and help anticipate and extrapolate historic patterns. In terms of communication, indicators form important bridges between experts and nonexperts, having the potential to simplify complex concepts into more easily digested figures. Indicators are also important in research planning, programme evaluation and public reporting. José Barroso, president of the European Community, recently stated:

> The appropriate choice of indicators is key to boost our understanding of the complexity of our diverse societies within the European Union, to better communicate on it, and to better respond to new policy needs as for example with the "GDP and beyond" initiative to include measurement of wellbeing (Barroso, 2011).

Indicators fall into two categories:

1. **Common scale indicators**: usually involving scientific measurements and reported as common units of measurements
2. **Composite indices**: using subjective measurements with no associated units

Common scale (or objective) indicators primarily measure quantity while composite indices primarily measure quality.

Indicators can be thought of as having three dimensions, more or less of which may be occupied depending on the nature of the given indicator:

1. The **normative dimension** includes cultural aspects which should be understood before applying conclusions to other contexts
2. **The systemic dimension** includes relationships between the measured characteristic(s) and the overall system within which the characteristics(s) abide, including social, economic and environmental contexts
3. **The procedural dimension** involves structural elements and their interactions

Care must be taken in any attempt to aggregate a number of indicators into an index, as key structural information can be lost (Binder *et al.*, 2010).

Environmental indicators are environmental measures that provide information about potential or realized effects of human activities on environmental phenomena of concern (Heink and Kowarik, 2010). **Sustainability indicators** can be defined as measurable aspects of environmental, economic, or social systems that are useful for monitoring changes in system characteristics relevant to the continuation of human and environmental wellbeing. McCool and Stankey (2004, p. 298) write of the need to link "**specific measurable variables**" to sustainability goals. Dennis Meadows has commented that "an environmental indicator becomes a sustainability indicator with the addition of time, limit or target" (Meadows, 1998).

The need for appropriate indicators was identified early in the short history of sustainable development. The Rio agreement in 1992 called on governmental and non-governmental organizations to develop indicators that could provide a solid basis for decision-making at all levels and for the harmonization of efforts to develop such indicators, in Article 21 (UNCED, 1992). The Commission on Sustainable Development (CSD) approved its Work Programme on Indicators of Sustainable Development in 1995 (UN, 1996).

Hay *et al.* (2014) set out the following four categories of sustainability indicators:

1. **Accounting indices** (AIs), which focus mainly on the resource use, yield production, waste production, and social impacts of **economic activities** in the Earth system
2. **Energetic and physical flow indicators** (EPFIs), which focus mainly on the resource use and yield production behaviour of **production activities** in the Earth system

3. **Sustainable development indicators** (SDIs), focusing primarily on the resource use, yield production, waste production, and social impacts of **development activities** in the Earth system
4. **Ecological indicators** (EIs), which are holistic measures focusing on the resource use and yield production behaviour of **whole systems**

These indicators can be used in four ways:

1. **Description/explanation** of the state of spatial systems and its deviation from some reference state
2. **Impact assessment/evaluation** of the effect of particular actions on the state of spatial systems and its deviation from some reference state
3. **Prediction** of future conditions of spatial systems under various scenarios of socioeconomic and environmental change
4. **Monitoring** to keep track of changes in the state of spatial systems and to support appropriate corrective actions (Briassoulis, 2001)

The European Environmental Agency (EEA, 1999) classified its sustainable development indicators into four groups which address the following questions:

1. What is happening to the environment and to humans?
2. Does it matter?
3. Are we improving?
4. Are we on the whole better off?

Sustainable transition indicators measure progress in a major system-wide change that envelops technical, economic and social subsystems. Challenges here are huge, as we shall see in the next section.

10.2 Challenges of indicating sustainable transition

"More and more often, availability of data, i.e. obtaining the value of sustainability indicators, is not a problem. The main difficulties relate to selection, interpretation and the use of indicators" (Moldan *et al.*, 2012; p. 7).

This is particularly relevant to sustainability transition indicators. Given all that was discussed in Chapter 9, it is clear that the concept of sustainable development is not globally accepted and that we have not yet agreed on what exactly a sustainable transition should consists of, how far it should go, how quickly it should happen, how it should operate and how it can be managed. Thus, developing a set of indicators to help deliver and communicate this transition is even more intangible.

Sustainable development is quite different from a sustainable transition. Sustainable development is a steady, directional, progressive journey towards some global point in the future where society achieves equity in a way that ceases to harm the environment, supported by economic growth. A sustainable transition is a much more fundamental shift, where philosophy, practice, ethics and behaviour are transitioned into a new state, reaching through every level of society. The transformation is not restricted to some global identikit, but rather reserves the option of a pluriverse with geographical and cultural diversity. The economic model is not a given either. Indeed the only pillar of sustainability that is not envisaged as transforming is the very pillar that has driven the transition movement, the environment. Indeed, many experts predict that if society and economics do not transform, then the environment will transition to a new people-free state.

It is also ironic that by far the majority of indicators currently available are focused on the environment, the arena where no change is a sign of moderate success. Yet a transition requires indicators of social and economic change, which can operate out with current models of society and economics, since these very models are likely to be replaced. This is a significant challenge in that since we cannot predict what the final state of a transition will be accurately, we find it difficult to develop indicators that demonstrate the proximity to that destination. While quantitative indicators are relatively straightforward, at least within a reductionist approach, qualitative, system-based, context-specific indicators are rare, and yet are central to crucial aspects of transition such as changes in values, beliefs and norms, and their time duration. Further difficulties arise in terms of embodying a scientific approach that is more relativistic (akin to the New Physics) and capable of dealing with highly complex, holistic areas such as ecology and sociology. Social sciences and natural science may share a common word in their titles, but there is very little if any meaningful interaction between them at an academic level.

The Board on Sustainable Development summed up the present predicament, finding that:

> there is no consensus on the appropriateness of the current set of indicators or the scientific basis for choosing them. Their effectiveness is limited by the lack of agreement on what to develop, what to sustain, and for how long (National Research Council, 1999; p. 9).

The reliance on economic growth to deliver sustainable development may be the greatest barrier to sustainable transition. However, new indicators and indices are emerging. Brundtland *et al.* (2012) have observed that:

> More than three dozen new, multidimensional indexes and indicators have been proposed in the last decades (e.g., the Human Development Index, Happy Planet Index, Global Innovation Index, and the Genuine Progress Indicator). These indexes are more salient, credible, and legitimate than GDP because they relate to the social and environmental pillars of sustainable development.

The call for more inclusive wealth indicators, including built, financial, social, human and natural capital, is gaining momentum. One such example is the Declaration of the Planet under Pressure Conference (Planet Under Pressure, 2012).

10.3 A single indicator of transition?

As is becoming clear, transition is an extremely complex topic, requiring both quantitative and qualitative indicators. Even by 2001, Briassoulis (2001) assessed that the hope of developing ideal indicators has faded and that there was an increasing move towards micro-indicators. Yet in 2003, the impact assessment (IA) system was introduced by the European Commission (EC), replacing and integrating all sectoral assessments of direct and indirect effects of proposed measures into one global, integrated instrument (De Smedt, 2010).

While an integrated indicator or index is convenient for purposes of communication and tracking, it reduces transparency by collapsing a variety of substantive information into a single index. But given that there are hundreds of indicators available, how do you decide which ones should be integrated into a given index? Furthermore since system theory predicts that emergent properties can arise unexpectedly from the complex interactions of different levels and elements within the system, and since the objective of a transition is to change completely, it may be difficult to know what can be justified as a valid measurement.

Finally, there is the risk of changing what we measure by the very process of measuring (the observer effect). Whether it is a questionnaire or an invasive experiment, we can effect what we are trying to measure. Furthermore, the reductionist approach of science, where we can only vary a very few parameters, does not in any way replicate the real world, where many different variables are present, including a large proportion that we do not even know about. For example only 5% of bacterial and fungal species have been classified and named, yet they play central roles in ecosystem functioning.

When we examine the indicators and indices, there are certain ones that dominate, particularly in economics. GDP, as we have seen, holds a sacred spot. Another set of important economic indicators is the group of financial indices such as the FTSE, the Dow Jones Average, the CAC and the DAX, which chart the share prices of a range of companies. Carbon footprint in terms of anthropogenic pollution also springs to mind readily. Species diversity is another measure that many people will be familiar with. What we want to know is whether things are getting better or worse.

A significant problem exists: what is good for one sector can be bad for another, or even for the same sector. A higher economic growth rate may mean lower species diversity in the forest that has been cut down and sold. An increase in green fuel supply (good environmentally) may have led to the local extinction of orang-utans in Borneo, whose habitat has been converted to palm oil plantations (bad environmentally). The closure of a huge iron mine (bad economically and socially, good environmentally) may lead to the formation of a set of localist communities built on a nearby meadow area (good socially, bad environmentally, neutral economically). No one index could sum these impacts up in a meaningful way. However, it is easier to communicate a single number than a whole list of them, and so indices have become popular.

10.3.1 Some current indices

There follows a list (intentionally not exhaustive) of some of the key indicators currently used, with an early reference and a more recent one in each case.

- **The Environmental Sustainability Index** incorporates 21 elements of environmental sustainability covering natural resource endowments, past and present pollution levels, environmental management efforts, contributions to protection of the global commons, and a society's capacity to improve its environmental performance over time (Sands *et al.*, 2000; Esty *et al.*, 2005).

- **The Environmental Performance Index** ranks countries on performance indicators tracked across policy categories that cover environmental, public health and ecosystem vitality (Färe *et al.*, 2004; Hsu *et al.*, 2013).
- **The Environmental Vulnerability Index** (EVI) was developed by UNEP and SOPAC (South Pacific Applied Geoscience Commission) The EVI uses 50 biophysical or natural environment indicators grouped into three subindices (hazards; resistance; damage) and then applies these to the following issues or threats: climate change, biodiversity, water, agriculture and fisheries, human health, desertification, and exposure to natural disasters (Kaly *et al.*, 1999; Barnett *et al.*, 2008).
- **The Human Development Index** was developed by the United Nations Development Programme, starting in 1990, in an effort to go beyond income as a measure of wellbeing. It combines measures of health, education and income in a single index (Trabold-Nübler, 1991; Palazzi and Lauri, 2013).
- **The Human Wellbeing Index** also includes measures of community (political rights, crime, Internet users, and peace and order), and social equity (gender and income) (Prescott-Allen 2001; Yang *et al.*, 2013).
- **The Genuine Progress Indicator** (GPI) takes everything the GDP uses into account, but also adds other figures that represent the cost of the negative effects related to economic activity (such as the cost of crime, cost of ozone depletion and cost of resource depletion, among others) (Hamilton, 1999; Kubiszewski *et al.*, 2013).
- **Adjusted Net Saving** was developed by the World Bank in the late 1990s, and measures the true rate of savings in an economy after taking into account investments in human capital, depletion of natural resources and damage caused by pollution (Gnègnè, 2009).
- **The Prevalent Vulnerability Index** (PVI) is a social vulnerability index that concentrates on social, economic, institutional, and infrastructural capacity to recover from natural hazards, focusing on socioeconomic fragility and social resilience. It was developed by the Inter-American Development Bank (Cardona 2005; Ciurean *et al.*, 2013).

- **The Energy Performance Index** (EPI) indicates the specific energy usage of a building. It is basically the ratio of total energy used to the total built-up area. This total energy used includes both purchased electricity as well as that generated on-site, but excludes renewable sources such as solar photovoltaic, etc. The total built-up area excludes basement and parking areas (Boussauw and Witlox, 2009; Zhang *et al.*, 2013).

One attempt at bringing together all three pillars of sustainability in one analysis has been the **Life Cycle Sustainability Assessment** (LCSA) framework, established by the UNEP/SETAC Life Cycle Initiative (Valdivia *et al.*, 2011). An LCSA is defined as the summed outputs from life-cycle analysis of economics, society and the environment: the environmental Life Cycle Assessment (LCA), the life-cycle costing (LCC), and the social LCA (S-LCA). It is noteworthy, if for nothing else, in its effort to cover all aspects, although there have been significant criticisms of each and every aspect (e.g. Hertwich, 2005; Reap *et al.*, 2008).

10.4 Major issues

As we have already mentioned, there are some significant issues in terms of developing indices of sustainable transition. Before looking at a few specific examples in the next section, we will first examine some of the central issues here.

10.4.1 Time-lag

The current state of a system does not necessarily reflect the impact of the current conditions. Due to the complexity of systems, it can take a while before changes in the environment are seen in a given measurable variable. In populations, for example, depending on the reproductive cycle, it can be over a year before changes in prey numbers are seen in predator numbers. But changes can be much more delayed than this. Take, for example, an island, such as Trinidad, which has been separated from mainland South America for 2,500 years or so. Before separation it had a much higher species diversity, as species richness is proportional to area, and, as part of South America, its area was huge.

Since separation, it has a relatively tiny area compared with previously, and so the species diversity is still adjusting to this change, thousands of years later. If you measured the species richness 100 years ago and again today, it would be less. Some of this decline may, of course, be due to human impact, but some of it is due to the geographical isolation of the island. Now if we used a species richness index here, we would see a decline in species. But even if we had no human impact, there would still be a decline. In another 500 years, the rebound effect may have stopped and species decline will be reduced, not because of any improvement in our sustainable actions, but because the island's biodiversity had come into equilibrium with the greatly reduced area.

A forest may have been burned away 200 years ago, but today it may look no different from a neighbouring forest that was planted anew 200 years ago. However, the very different histories will mean that these two forests, although apparently the same age, size, area and tree density, are actually quite different in terms of soils and water relations. As we have seen in Chapter 4, there are huge differences between habitats at different points in a succession in terms of many parameters. If we do not know at what point a given ecosystem is at in its succession, then if we measure it over time, we will not know how much of the change in indicator values is due to natural change associated with ecological succession and how much is due to environmental policy that we have implemented.

So an indicator or index will be highly unlikely to include such important biogeographical elements within its calculations. However, given the significance of history in terms of diversity, this means that these indices cannot be used to give us a meaningful measure of the impact of human behaviour on biodiversity. Moreover, short-term changes in certain indicators are not necessarily evidence of the longer-term changes required for transitions to different modes of socioeconomic functioning (Briassoulis, 2001). Given that nature reports on the past because of such time-lags, our current concerns relating to the environment are most likely underestimates.

Ultimately, there is no such thing as a control in nature, as every particle of soil is unique at any given moment in time. It is estimated that each gram of soil contains 1 billion bacteria, and so the likelihood is that each gram of soil is a unique biological community. This is another significant issue. Given how we measure the parameters needed to generate our data, much of this management is questionable when related to real world, complex, emergent functioning as is common in the fields, lakes and forests, but non-existent in the labs and greenhouses of the scientific community.

10.4.2 Decoupling

Decoupling occurs when the growth rate of an environmental pressure is less than that of its economic driving force (e.g. GDP) over a given period, and is viewed as an important means of maintaining economic growth and achieving sustainability, according to weak sustainability advocates. Decoupling indicators are of two types:

1. **Absolute decoupling** occurs when the environmentally relevant variable is stable or decreasing while the economic driving force is growing
2. **Relative decoupling** occurs when the growth rate of the environmentally relevant variable is positive but less than the growth rate of the economic variable (OECD, 2006)

However, a significant issue arises here. Unless a threshold or limit is established for a particular indicator relating to sustainable use, then it is impossible to demonstrate that either relative or absolute decoupling represent more sustainable practice (Moldan *et al.*, 2012). Establishing such a threshold is problematic, given what we have discussed above. At what point in history should we refer to in terms of providing an environmentally acceptable level of economic growth. Furthermore, measures of economic growth are extremely problematic, since many economies have unreported economic activity that may significantly damage the environment and society, but fails to register in any economic analysis (often to avoid taxes). For example plastic is burned from old computers in order to free up the metals within, leading to release of dioxins (significant carcinogens).

The use of national indicators creates a number of problems, including:

- Most spatial systems are more open than nations
- Governance structures differ between spatial levels
- Conceptual definitions of indicators may differ between spatial levels
- Nations are not always appropriate units for studying sustainable development
- Data availability and quality problems are encountered at other than the national levels, especially in countries with incomplete information systems and thriving informal economies (Briassoulis, 2001)

Here, geography, anthropology and politics come into play. Another irritation with national indicators is their use in tables of fame and shame. Who ranks highest and who ranks lowest? These indicators rarely if ever provide any information on variation within countries, underlying issues nor historical, cultural or geographical context. The "developed" world tends to occupy the top of the league while members of the "developing" world vie for the wooden spoon. Yet indices such as the Human Development Index are measured in terms of northern, western strengths, with little or no credence given to eastern, southern hemisphere strengths. The social, institutional, cultural and political values are the less represented dimensions of sustainable development.

Most indicators tend to be uni-dimensional, focusing either on economics, environment or social parameters, or on a single business sector, or a single aspect of the environment (species richness, air quality, etc.). Such indicators are also aggregate, not distinguishing between social or economic status, sex, or variation within any given data set. Little reference is made to the environmental damage caused, historically, to achieve such high GNP, nor of the slavery, persecution, externalized damage and environmental degradation in other countries underpinning the current high status.

Furthermore, there is a scarcity of indicators in key areas such as social demand on economics and the environment and no integration of society–environment–economics. This void is disturbing, as if a transition is to occur, it will operate across the entire planet, not in isolated "sectors". Ultimately there is no point in excelling in one aspect while having no idea what repercussions this achievement has on the other areas of importance.

Dennis Meadows comments that "Indicators arise from values (we measure what we care about), and they create values (we care about what we measure)" (Meadows, 1998; p. viii). This circularity is dangerous, as a value-based process is unavoidable yet undesirable, given the likelihood of a range of value systems within a given set of people. Thus indicators are greatly weakened in terms of subjectivity, particularly if they are viewed as objective. You can always find what you are looking for, and as the saying goes, there are lies, damn lies and statistics. In an attempt to be objective, there is a concern that science has become ultra-reductionist, failing to be able to cope with the holistic, multi-dimensional challenge such as sustainable transition. Many of the indices and indicators are built around values that represent the incumbent system. For example GDP lies at the heart of the calculations of such indicators as the Human Development Index of the United Nations. As we shall see in the next section, there are significant concerns over this indicator, particularly in terms of the importance given to it by sustainable development organizations such as the UN.

Another significant concern rests with the fact that some very damaging aspects of our economy do not get covered at all by indicators of sustainable transition. **Nanomaterials** are being used increasingly in various products such as electronics, clothing, or personal care products; yet, the resulting releases of nanoparticles and the associated impacts on environment are still not covered in life-cycle inventories and LCA methods, while the relevance of such inclusions has been explicitly proved. Copper oxide nanoparticles have been found to be particularly harmful (Bulcke *et al.*, 2014). Another issue relates to the chemicals released from new products in terms of impacting the health of a consumer. For example the interior of a new car is particularly toxic (Faber *et al.*, 2014). Yet assessments of interior pollutants are still not operational in current LCA practice.

10.5 Examples of indicator failures

As we have already mentioned, **gross domestic product** (GDP) does not take into account nonmarket, community economies, where no registered financial activity takes place, thus undervaluing activity in many countries. GDP favours industrialized countries and systematically highlights the poverty of regions whose economies included a large component of non-recorded activities (Borowy, 2013). Voluntary work is also not registered by GDP. GDP treats the depletion of natural capital (i.e. environmental damage) as income. GDP increases during the clean-up of pollution disasters, due to the costs involved. Natural disasters also register as positive due to rebuilding expenditure. GDP takes no account of income distribution, therefore hiding wealth inequality. Strong sustainability advocates would strongly disagree with the incorporation of GDP into any indicator of sustainability, arguing that it is this measure more than any other that has supported and empowered the current economic model.

One such example is the **economic energy intensity** (EEI). The EEI of a nation, defined as the ratio between the energy consumed and the GDP of that country, is receiving wide interest (El Anshasy and Katsaiti, 2014; Voigt *et al.*, 2014). However, an indicator such as EEI, based on a ratio, should be considered a **white noise indicator** rather than a measure of economic efficiency. EEI represents the amount of primary energy needed to generate one unit of GDP in a given country and year. The indicator is used to demonstrate increases in energy efficiency. The consumption of energy for producing and consuming goods and services does not translate into the generation of a relative amount of GDP since a large fraction of these goods and services are not market-traded. For this reason, the EEI of some of these countries tend to be much higher than the rest (Fiorito, 2013). Given the flaws already associated with GDP, as mentioned above, the EEI is further flawed.

The **carbon footprint** is one of the most well-known indicators of environmental impact, having entered popular culture. However, when the details of this particular indicator are examined, it, and the closely associated **ecological footprint** (below), can be seen to be highly questionable. The carbon footprint is the amount of carbon dioxide released into the atmosphere in a given amount of time per person, family, school, city or other group of individuals. As assessed by the Global Footprint Network (2011), the carbon footprint is the additional area of forest (expressed in gha) needed to sequester all net anthropogenic emissions of carbon dioxide after subtracting the fraction of CO_2 estimated to be absorbed by oceans (currently 28%). A large footprint means that you generate a lot of CO_2, while a small footprint means you do not generate much CO_2. Carbon footprints have also been applied to nations. The ecological footprint is a measure that combines all environmental costs to indicate the cost of externals (Rees, 1992; Wackernagel and Rees, 1997; van den Berg and Verbruggen, 1999).

So what is the issue with the carbon footprint? First, it focuses all attention on carbon, meaning that other highly significant problems, such as habitat destruction and agricultural run-off are ignored. Thus it is a reductionist approach and contributes negatively to any hope of a system transition so necessary if we are to discover a means to achieving a sustainable future.

Second, it is largely based on energy sources, wherein a country with geothermal energy, such as Iceland, will have a much lower footprint than a coal-dependent country. This may sound good, but it is what the energy is used for, for example aluminium smelting, rather than merely the energy production method itself that can have huge impacts on the health of the planet.

Third, much of a country's carbon costs are often externalized to nations through imports. For example, Australia moves its aluminium ore to Iceland in boats for smelting to take advantage of cheaper energy costs. Nations reliant on nuclear power, such as France, have a much lower carbon footprint than others reliant on coal, but run the risks of significant environmental damage due to a meltdown. Another issue is that a resident in a particular country may not have a choice as to how the energy they use is manufactured. Thus their personal footprint may be affected by this. Furthermore, urbanization, mobile phone use, limited public transport and hospital use may all adversely impact on a carbon footprint.

Products or systems fulfilling similar functions in a society's activities may show similar carbon footprints but differ by orders of magnitude with respect to other equally relevant environmental impacts. In a decision-making context, this indicates a real risk of selecting the least environmentally friendly solution, i.e. the one having the largest environmental impact, if the decision is based on the CFP alone.

Another great problem with the carbon footprint is the popular concept of planting forest to offset the damage. This offset is calculated on an average forest. However, such a forest rarely exists. What type of forest should we plant? Tropical rainforest consumes 7 tonnes of carbon per hectare per year while boreal forest consumes only 0.2 tonnes of carbon per hectare per year. Thus the further from the equator that you live, the more forest you need to plant. The forest planting approach uses a value based on a weighted average of the annual increment of merchantable timber per hectare in a sample of existing forest biomes, calculated at 0.97 tonnes of carbon per hectare per year. This uncertainty relating to forest location on the planet is increasingly exacerbated by the effects of climate change, nitrogen deposition, and other forms of global change (Schaphoff *et al.*, 2006). If the world's forests were to become a net *source* of carbon later in this century—as some scenarios suggest (Schaphoff *et al.*, 2006)—then the universe could not contain the trees needed to offset carbon footprints.

The age of the forest also matters. If the offset mechanism of choice were old growth forests (an important target of conservation efforts and ecologically most diverse, but for which respiration rates often equal sequestration), the net balance of carbon sequestration from such forests is zero or close to it. Another universe full of trees would be needed (Gibson *et al.*, 2011). New growth forests on the other hand are just about ecologically useless, but do absorb lots of carbon. Old trees contain lots of carbon but grow very slowly and so do not consume much "new" carbon. The carbon they do consume is re-released when they burn sugar to keep their big old bodies alive. So gross photosynthetic rate approaches respiration rate, hence no growth and no net carbon absorption. However, the problem is that new growth forests become old growth forests, and so you would need to continually keep planting trees to replace the ageing forest before even beginning to offset your footprint.

A genuine correlation between carbon footprint and all the other environmental impact indicators can be observed if and only if all impacts from the product life-cycle predominantly stem from one or few key processes that co-vary. Carbon footprint has particularly weak correlations with toxicity to ecosystems and humans, depletion of resources, and land use.

The **ecological footprint** (EF) represents the amount of biologically productive land and sea area necessary to supply the resources a human population consumes, and to assimilate associated waste (Laurent *et al.*, 2012).

The EF has influenced the policies and communications of many governmental and non-governmental organizations. EF is calculated as net **biocapacity**, involving the net productivity minus harvest of five categories (cropland, grazing land, forest, fishing, and built-up land) plus the carbon footprint. The productivity minus harvest tends to approach zero, showing no net footprint, in all of these five categories, leaving only the carbon footprint. Thus there is little difference between the EF and the carbon footprint. This means that criticisms of the carbon footprint are equally targeted at the ecological footprint. This is very disappointing, as a true ecological footprint would be extremely useful. Instead, we are back to carbon. The carbon fixation dominating most sustainability discussions continues apace.

Forest productivity is limited to merchantable forests. This means that issues such as soil fertility and erosion, water scarcity and groundwater lowering are not included. The EF attempts to provide a single index by measuring a subset of net primary productivity, regardless of its source, quality, or ecological relevance. EF fails to indicate whether forest area is increasing or decreasing, whether biodiversity is being lost or gained, and whether ecosystem services are improved or damaged.

10.6 What makes a good indicator of transition?

Having examined the challenges to and failures of sustainability indicators, we now examine what makes a good suite of indicators and indices. First, it must be stressed that there is no golden arrow here, piercing the heart of the issue. The best that can be hoped for is **transparency**. All designs are ultimately subjective, and so we should have health warnings attached to any indicator, highlighting shortcomings, motives, what they do and do not say and their ability to interlock with other measures in order to arrive at a fuller picture of where we are.

The importance of involving **multiple stakeholders** in discussions on sustainability indicators cannot be overstressed. This will help in balancing subjective choices and will bring fresh and different heads to the table (Celino and Concilio, 2010).

The **geography of sustainability** must be reflected in the use of indicators. Human, physical and historical geography all must play an important role. Indicators should reflect huge differences across the globe, and seek to incorporate the various drivers and drags that vary from region to region. Understanding units of regionalization is also important here (Parris and Kates, 2003). A country may be made up of several quite different regions, or may be a part of a larger region. National league tables are not helpful here. These tables only re-enforce concerns of colonialism targeted by post-development advocates and strengthen racial discrimination, while providing little useful information for policy-makers.

Moldan *et al.* (2012) identify four key areas of importance in designing and using indicators: the choice of baseline level, the choice of target, the integration of a measure of variation and the integration of some temporal level. Dale and Beyeler (2001) emphasize the following criteria:

- Easy to measure
- Sensitive to stresses on system
- Responsive to stress in a predictable manner
- Anticipatory: signify an impending change in the environmental system
- Integrative: the full suite of indicators provides a measure of coverage of the key gradients across the environmental systems (e.g., soils, vegetation types, and temperature)
- Possess a known response to natural disturbances, anthropogenic stresses and changes over time
- Have known variability/spread in response to given environmental changes

The importance of **systems theory** must be high on the agenda of indicator design and implementation. It is crucially important that social, economic and environmental input and output are balanced and integrated, and this may well mean starting anew. Plugging in **old favourites** just because they worked in the past is insufficient justification for their inclusion. Each indicative element must justify its place within the context of the whole.

Binder *et al.* (2010) have stressed that to obtain adequate system representation, three issues should be considered when selecting the indicators to be used in the assessment:

1. Parsimony: as much simplicity as possible
2. Sufficiency: as much complexity as necessary
3. Indicator interaction

Fiksel *et al.* (2012) emphasize the following system-based foci:

- **Adverse Outcome Indicator** (AOI): indicates destruction of value due to impacts on individuals, communities, business enterprises, or the natural environment
- **Resource Flow Indicator** (RFI): indicates pressures associated with the rate of consumption of resources, including materials, energy, water, land and biota
- **System Condition Indicator** (SCI): indicates state of the systems in question, i.e., individuals, communities, business enterprises and the natural environment
- **Value Creation Indicator** (VCI): indicates creation of value (both economic and wellbeing) through enrichment of individuals, communities, business enterprises, or the natural environment

Given that many hundreds of sustainability indicators exist, what criteria should we base our selection on, in order to choose a suite of sustainability performance indicators? Fiksel (2009) has suggested the following criteria:

- Relevant to the interests of the intended audiences, reflecting important opportunities for enhancement of social and environmental conditions as well as economic prosperity
- Meaningful to the intended audiences in terms of clarity, comprehensibility and transparency
- Objective in terms of measurement techniques and verifiability, while allowing for regional, cultural and socioeconomic differences
- Effective for supporting benchmarking and monitoring over time, as well as decision-making about how to improve performance
- Comprehensive in providing an overall evaluation of progress with respect to sustainability goals

- Consistent across different sites or communities, using appropriate normalization and other methods to account for their inherent diversity
- Practical in allowing cost-effective, non-burdensome implementation and building on existing data collection where possible

The Green Book (NRC, 2011) states that indicators should have the following attributes:

- **Actionable**, so that practical steps can be taken to address contributing factors
- **Transferable and scalable**, so that they are adaptable at regional, state, or local levels
- **Intergenerational**, reflecting fair distribution of costs and benefits among different generations
- Durable, so that they have long-term relevance

Finally, Blomqvist *et al.* (2013) highlight the following principles for improved indicators:

- Indicators should illuminate pathways towards attaining sustainability goals that make both ecological and common sense
- Indicators of the sustainability of natural capital consumption should be able to record depletion or surpluses
- A set of indicators, each pertaining to an identifiable and quantifiable form of natural capital or ecosystem service, is likely to be more comprehensible and useful than a single aggregate index
- Indicators must take into account the geographical scale of the phenomena they are measuring
- Ecological indicators should, where possible, include estimates of uncertainty

However we choose to identify, communicate and measure change in our world, we face three issues relating to our perception of the world around us. First, **the veracity of the observer** must be considered. Our journey is a human one, with all of the limits, illusions and conditioning that this entails. Our swollen cerebral cortex provides much room for subjectivity. Our attempts at imbuing our observed world with meaning will always be influenced by the experiences that we have participated in prior to the point in time at which the interpretation takes place, both in our own lives, and within the context of accumulated knowledge through our species' existence. Thus the veracity or purity of the interpretation will be a product of these experiences, which in turn define the observer.

Almost all of life's activities are arranged around resources. As humans we may be seen to have separated ourselves from the madding crowd, that is the rest of life, yet this denial does not alter the fact that we are, essentially, resourcers akin to everything else. We must therefore recognize that our thinking will also reflect these drives. By understanding our universe, we can attempt to understand our place within it. Yet our attempts to understand this universe are coloured by human nature, by drives that are much older than we are and by motives that may distort the initial observation.

The **validity of our observations** questions what is reality anyway? What is it we are attempting to measure and to transition? All statements about reality rely on a huge step of faith—that what we sense is actually there. This theme has been explored many times throughout the history of philosophy. Scientific thinking relies on our perception of reality being taken as a fundamental truth: that what our minds interpret from the multitude of identical nerve impulses corresponds to the outside world. This is called **mechanistic materialism**. Without this premise, the scientific method is meaningless.

Finally the **vicissitude of the observed** focuses on what we want to measure. The world as we observe it is a snapshot of a journey, a brief moment in time. One of the challenges in studying anything is that time is as important as space. Time can impact on our interpretation in a number of ways. First, the observer is part of a culture or society, and, since no man is an island, the surrounding culture will impact on the observer, depending on the moment in time within which they exist. The contexts of their upbringing, education and belief structure may well impact on how they interpret what they observe. Second, things change over time, as we have noted in terms of diversity on an island such as Trinidad. Tectonic plates move, with the current city of London having been at a similar latitude to present day Ghana some 50 million years ago, as evidenced by fossil palm trees in the London Clay beneath the river Thames. A third important aspect of the temporal context of the observer is that the system which is being observed will be within an evolutionary setting and its historical context will be at least as important as its present context in terms of what is happening.

Thus the very act of observing, which is pivotal to indication, is filled with its own minefield of issues that should at least be acknowledged.

10.7 Debate, discussion and further thought

1. "More and more often, availability of data, i.e. obtaining the value of sustainability indicators, is not a problem. The main difficulties relate to selection, interpretation and the use of indicators" (Moldan *et al.*, 2012; p. 7). Discuss.
2. Dennis Meadows comments that "Indicators arise from values (we measure what we care about), and they create values (we care about what we measure)" (Meadows, 1998; p. viii). Discuss.
3. What are the strengths and weaknesses of each of the following indicators? (i) Carbon footprint; (ii) ecological footprint; (iii) GDP; (iv) economic energy intensity.
4. In what ways does geography impact on indicator design?
5. What are the difficulties in an indicator attempting to inform both policy and the general public? How can these issues be resolved?
6. Index or indicator? Which is best?
7. Discuss the different challenges presented in terms of designing indicators for social, environmental and economic sustainability.
8. Mini-project: design a suite of indicators to monitor progress in a sustainability transition, highlighting the issues addressed.

References

Barnett, J., Lambert, S. and Fry, I. (2008). The hazards of indicators: insights from the environmental vulnerability index. Annals of the Association of American Geographers 98: 102-19.

Barroso, J. (2011). President of the European Commission, in his opening speech at the Eurostat Conference *Statistics for Policy Making: Europe 2020* on 10 March 2011 in Brussels.

Binder, C.R., Feola, G. and Steinberger, J.K. (2010). Considering the normative, systemic and procedural dimensions in indicator-based sustainability assessments in agriculture. Environmental Impact Assessment Review 30(2): 71-81.

Blomqvist, L., Brook, B.W., Ellis, E.C., Kareiva, P.M., Nordhaus, T. and Shellenberger, M. (2013). Does the Shoe Fit? Real versus Imagined Ecological Footprints. PLoS Biology 11(11) electronic journal: www.plosbiology.org/article/info%3Adoi%2F10.1371%2Fjournal.pbio.1001700 Last accessed: 15 November 2014.

Borowy, I. (2013). Global health and development: conceptualizing health between economic growth and environmental sustainability. Journal of the History of Medicine and Allied Sciences 68(3): 451-85.

Boussauw, K. and Witlox, F. (2009). Introducing a commute-energy performance index for Flanders. Transportation Research Part A: Policy and Practice 43: 580-91.

Briassoulis, H. (2001). Sustainable development and its indicators: through a (planner's) glass darkly. Journal of Environmental Planning and Management 44(3): 409-27.

Brundtland, G.H. and 15 other authors (2012). Environment and development challenges: the imperative to act. Blue Planet Synthesis paper for UNEP. London.

Bulcke, F., Thiel, K. and Dringen, R. (2014). Uptake and toxicity of copper oxide nanoparticles in cultured primary brain astrocytes. Nanotoxicology 8(7): 775-85.

Cardona, O.D. (2005). *Indicators of Disaster Risk and Risk Management: Summary Report.* Inter-American Development Bank, Washington, D.C.

Celino, A. and Concilio, G. (2010). Explorative nature of negotiation in participatory decision making for sustainability. Group Decision and Negotiation 20: 255-70.

Ciurean, R.L., Schröter, D. and Glade, T. (2013). Conceptual Frameworks of Vulnerability Assessments for Natural Disasters Reduction. In: Tiefenbacher, J. (ed.), *Approaches to Disaster Management: Examining the Implications of Hazards, Emergencies and Disasters.* InTech, Rijeka, Croatia. pp. 3-32.

Dale, V.H. and Beyeler, S.C. (2001). Challenges in the development and use of ecological indicators. Ecological Indicators 1: 3-10.

Demou, E., Hellweg, S., Wilson, M.P., Hammond, S.K. and McKone, T.E. (2009). Evaluating indoor exposure modeling alternatives for LCA: A case study in the vehicle repair industry. Environmental Science and Technology 43: 5804–5810.

De Smedt, P. (2010). The use of impact assessment tools to support sustainable policy objectives in Europe. Ecology and Society 15(4): 30-8.

EEA (1999). *Environmental Indicators: Typology and Overview. Technical report No 25.* European Environmental Agency, Copenhagen.

El Anshasy, A.A. and Katsaiti, M.S. (2014). Energy intensity and the energy mix: what works for the environment? Journal of Environmental Management 136: 85-93.

Esty, D.C., Levy, M., Srebotnjak, T. and A. de Sherbinin (2005). *Environmental Sustainability Index: Benchmarking National Environmental Stewardship.* Yale Center for Environmental Law & Policy, New Haven, CT.

Faber, J., Brodzik, K., Gołda-Kopek, A. and Łomankiewicz, D. (2013). Air pollution in new vehicles as a result of VOC emissions from interior iaterials. Polish Journal of Environmental Studies 22(6): 1701-709.

Färe, R., Grosskopf, S. and Hernandez-Sancho, F. (2004). Environmental performance: an index number approach. Resource and Energy Economics 26: 343-52.

Fiksel, J. (2009). *Design for the Environment. A Guide to Sustainable Product Development.* Second edition. McGraw-Hill., New York, NY, USA.

Fiksel, J., Eason, T. and Frederickson, H. (2012). A Framework for Sustainability Indicators at EPA. National Risk Management Research Laboratory Office of Research and Development US Environmental Protection Agency.

Fiorito, G. (2013). Can we use the energy intensity indicator to study "decoupling" in modern economies? Journal of Cleaner Production 47: 465-73.

Gibson, L., Lee, T.M., Koh, L.P., Brook, B.W., Gardner, T.A., Barlow, J., Peres, C.A., Bradshaw, C.J.A., Laurance, W.F., Lovejoy, T.E. and Sodhi, N.S. (2011). Primary forests are irreplaceable for sustaining tropical biodiversity. Nature 478: 378-81.

Global Footprint Network (2011). *National Footprint Accounts.* 2011 Edition. Oakland, CA: Global Footprint Network.

Gnègnè, Y. (2009). Adjusted net saving and welfare change. Ecological Economics 68: 1127-39.

Hamilton, C. (1999). The genuine progress indicator methodological developments and results from Australia. Ecological Economics 30: 13-28.

Hay, L., Duffy, A. and Whitfield, R.I. (2014). The sustainability cycle and loop: models for a more unified understanding of sustainability. Journal of Environmental Management 133: 232-57.

Heink, U. and Kowarik, I. (2010). What are indicators? On the definition of indicators in ecology and environmental planning. Ecological Indicators 10(3): 584-93.

Hertwich, E.G. (2005). Life cycle approaches to sustainable consumption: a critical review. Environmental Science and Technology 39(13): 4673-84.

Hsu, A., Lloyd, A. and Emerson, J.W. (2013). What progress have we made since Rio? Results from the 2012 Environmental Performance Index (EPI) and Pilot Trend EPI. Environmental Science and Policy 33: 171-85.

Iribarren, D., Hospido, A., Moreira, M.T. and Feijoo, G. (2011). Benchmarking environmental and operational parameters through eco-efficiency criteria for dairy farms. Science of the Total Environment 409(10): 1786-98.

Kaly, U., Briguglio, L., McLeod, H., Schmall, S., Pratt, C. and Pal, R. (1999). Environmental vulnerability index (EVI) to summarise national environmental vulnerability profiles. SOPAC Tech. Rep. 275. South Pacific Applied Geoscience Commission, Suva, Fiji.

Kubiszewski, I., Costanza, R., Franco, C., Lawn, P., Talberth, J., Jackson, T. and Aylmer, C. (2013). Beyond GDP: Measuring and achieving global genuine progress. Ecological Economics 93: 57-68.

Laurent, A., Olsen, S.I. and Hauschild, M.Z. (2012). Limitations of carbon footprint as indicator of environmental sustainability. Environmental Science and Technology 46(7): 4100-108.

McCool, S.F. and Stankey, G.H. (2004). Indicators of sustainability: challenges and opportunities at the interface of science and policy. Environmental Management 33: 294-305.

Meadows, D. 1998. *Indicators and Information Systems for Sustainable Development.* The Sustainability Institute, Hartland VT, USA.

Moldan, B., Janoušková, S. and Hák, T. (2012). How to understand and measure environmental sustainability: Indicators and targets. Ecological Indicators 17: 4-13.

National Research Council (1999). *Our Common Journey.* National Academies Press, Washington DC.

NRC (2011). *Sustainability and the US EPA.* The National Academies Press, Washington DC.

OECD (2006). Decoupling Indicators. In: *Decoupling the Environmental Impacts of Transport from Economic Growth.* OECD Publishing.

Palazzi, P. and Lauri, A. (2013). The human development index: Suggested corrections. Banca Nazionale del Lavoro Quarterly Review 51(205): 193-221

Parris, T.M. and Kates, R.W. (2003). Characterizing a sustainability transition: goals, targets, trends and driving forces. Proceedings of the National Academy of Sciences, USA 100(14): 8068-73.

Planet under Pressure (2012). State of the Planet Declaration. Planet under pressure: new knowledge towards solutions. (29 March 2012) Available: www.planetunderpressure2012.net/pdf/state_of_planet_declaration.pdf. Last accessed: 15 November 2014.

Prescott-Allen, R. (2001). *The Wellbeing of Nations.* Island Press, Washington D.C.

Reap, J., Roman, F., Duncan, S. and Bras, B. (2008). A survey of unresolved problems in life cycle assessment. The International Journal of Life Cycle Assessment 13(5): 374-88.

Sands, G.R. and Podmore, T.H. (2000). A generalized environmental sustainability index for agricultural systems. Agriculture, Ecosystems and Environment 79: 29-41.

Schaphoff, S., Lucht, W., Gerten, D., Sitch, S., Cramer, W. and Prentice, I.C. (2006). Terrestrial biosphere carbon storage under alternative climate projections. Climate Change 74: 97-122.

Trabold-Nübler, H. (1991). The human development index—a new development indicator? Intereconomics 26: 236-43.

UNCED (1992). Agenda 21, Programme of Action for Sustainable Development, adopted at the United Nations Conference on Environment and Development, Rio de Janeiro, Brazil, 1992.

UN (1996). *Indicators of Sustainable Development Framework and Methodologies.* United Nations Sales Publication No. E.96.II.A.16 (New York, August 1996).

Wackernagel, M. and Rees, W.E. (1996). *Our Ecological Footprint: Reducing Human Impact on the Earth.* New Society Publishers, Gabriola Island, B.C. Canada.

Valdivia, S., Ugaya, C.M.L., Sonnemann, G. and Hildenbrand, J. (2011). *Towards a Life Cycle Sustainability Assessment: Making Informed Choices on Products.* UNEP/SETAC Life Cycle Initiative, Paris.

Voigt, S., De Cian, E., Schymura, M. and Verdolini, E. (2014). Energy intensity developments in 40 major economies: Structural change or technology improvement? Energy Economics 41: 47-62.

Yang, W., Dietz, T., Kramer, D.B., Chen, X. and Liu, J. (2013). going beyond the millennium ecosystem assessment: an index system of human well-being. PLoS ONE, 8(5). At: http://www.plosone.org/article/info%3Adoi%2F10.1371%2Fjournal.pone.0064582. Last accessed 15 November 2014.

Zhang, N., Zhou, P. and Choi, Y. (2013). Energy efficiency, CO_2 emission performance and technology gaps in fossil fuel electricity generation in Korea: a meta-frontier non-radial directional distance function analysis. Energy Policy 56: 653-62.

Appendix: a brief guide to thermodynamics

The basics

Thermodynamics (*therme*, "heat"; *dynamis*, "power") describes and relates the physical properties of energy and matter. As such it is the fundamental science of everything. It is not so much to do with the form of the universe. Rather, it explains how the universe functions. In doing this, it answers the otherwise elusive "**why**" questions.

Thermodynamics revolves around two major laws.

The First Law

The First Law of Thermodynamics states that energy can neither be created nor destroyed. This is a fundamental rule. You can't get something from nothing. Of course, energy can change from one type to another. Energy can be converted from light energy to chemical energy. Plants do this, making sugar from sunlight. Energy can also be transferred from one object to another. For example a cup of coffee cools down (loses energy) but this warms up the atmosphere (a relatively tiny amount!). In a more complex example, imagine you find yourself in a completely flat airfield of tarmac. You are on a bicycle and start pedalling. The bicycle speeds up.

Energy transfers from you to the bicycle. You then stop peddling. You have lost energy through the work you have done in pedalling. The bike slows down and eventually stops. The bicycle has lost energy to the airfield through friction and heat. You eat a chocolate bar containing sugar to restore your energy balance. The sugar was made by a plant that converted sunlight into glucose. The sunlight came from the sun, which is constantly losing energy to its surroundings and will eventually collapse. In this situation the total energy in the universe has not changed, but the sun loses energy to the plant which loses energy to the human. The human loses energy to the bicycle, and then the bicycle loses energy to the surroundings which in turn loses energy to the universe. Overall energy has flowed from the sun, through a plant, a human, a bicycle the surrounding airfield to the universe.

The universe is viewed as a **closed system**. The first law ultimately applies to the universe. The total universal energy doesn't change. In this respect the universé represents a circular economy. Energy flows through various parts of the universe (such as ourselves and our bicycles). The Earth is an **open system**. Energy flows into it from the sun, and also flows to the surface of the planet from the core of the Earth (which is the same temperature as the surface of the sun), through volcanoes, earthquakes, hot springs and mudpots. Energy leaves the Earth as heat.

The planet's energy balance is a very tight budget. Even slight increases in the distance between the Earth and the sun lead to ice ages. Our seasons can lead to a 60° difference between summer and winter temperatures at high latitude, caused merely by the tilt of the Earth's axis.

Following the impact of a large asteroid or comet onto the Earth, clouds of dust can fill the atmosphere for years, blocking the sun's energy and leading to what is termed an impact winter. Not only does the temperature drop, but energy no longer flows into the biosphere, and many species starve to death. Thus the first law has a very dark side. Insufficient energy from the sun, but continued heat loss from the planet leads to an imbalance: less energy in than out. Because the Earth is an open system, it continuously loses energy as heat, just as your cup of coffee loses heat. And so if energy input from the sun decreases, there is just not enough energy to go around. Dinosaurs went extinct because of the first law, and because the Earth is an open system (Fig. A.3).

Many papers on economics claim that the Earth is a closed system. This is a fundamental error.

The Second Law

The Second Law of Thermodynamics states that the universe will continue to expand until energy and matter are spread evenly throughout it. It is best observed in a glass of water where you add a drop of ink or concentrated colour. Over the next few minutes, the drop will spread until the solution is evenly coloured, reaching a state called equilibrium. Now each molecule of dye is equally separated from each other molecule (Fig. A.1). There is a driver, a law that directs things in this direction: ashes to ashes, dust to dust. The second law is that signpost. Things head to equilibrium (even distribution). Things become increasingly chaotic as the universe heads to absolute equilibrium. The average temperature of the universe also cools down, eventually reaching absolute zero.

Because the Earth is an open system, the second law pervades all that happens on our planet. Examples include the deterioration of manufactured goods, the increasing untidiness of a child's bedroom, and many more things. The direction is towards increasing chaos. Tightly linked to the second law is the concept of entropy. Entropy is a measure of the amount

(a)

(b)

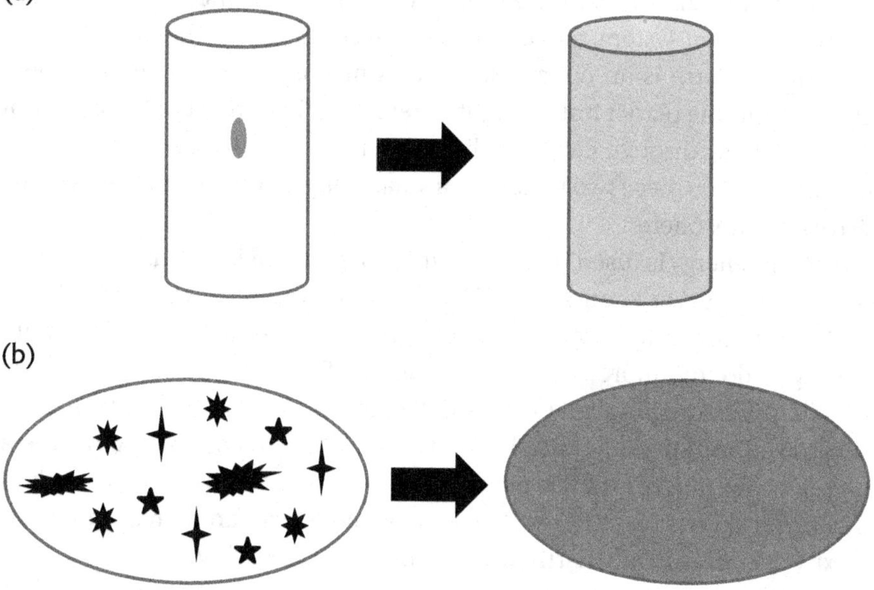

FIGURE A.1 The Second Law of Thermodynamics drives any system towards equilibrium, be it (a) a drop of orange in a glass of water or (b) the entire universe. Entropy increases as the system loses order and moves towards a state of equilibrium, by the process of diffusion.

of disorder in a system. In other words it tells us how close a system is to absolute equilibrium. The release of heat from a steam engine or of perfume from a bottle is viewed as being irreversible (because you could never put all the escaped heat back into the engine, nor every perfume molecule back into the bottle), and in these cases there is an **irreversible increase in entropy**. So the Second Law can also be stated as: **the entropy in the universe increases up to the point of equilibrium**. And here on planet Earth, we experience it. Energy is leaking away into the universe as a whole. The planet, the sun and the whole show is heading steadily towards absolute chaos.

Building things in an entropic universe

So if the universe is heading towards absolute chaos, how do we explain the complexity of human civilization on our planet? Surely this defies the second law? Also, why has life gradually become *more* complex on the planet, starting with bacteria and evolving into dinosaurs, whales and humans? To understand this apparent anomaly we must remember two things: the Earth is an open system, and complexity takes energy to build it.

First, the Earth is an open system. This means that not only does heat escape from the planet but sunlight enters it. In fact there is a huge river of energy flowing through Earth: sunlight flooding in and heat energy flooding out. In-between these two fluxes lies a small eddy on this river where energy drives the biosphere.

And this energy is "used" to make things. Of course it is not "used" in terms of being used up, as energy can neither be created nor destroyed (First Law). Rather it is converted, from useful energy to less useful energy. The more work you do, the more energy is converted. The secret to understanding what happens on our planet lies here. The second law demands that energy should diffuse, spreading until it is evenly distributed across the universe (Fig. A.1). Events that diffuse more energy will be more likely to occur than those that diffuse less energy. Thus we would expect an increase in complexity over time in any Earth process, and that is exactly what we see.

So the law that requires increasing chaos (called entropy) in the universe also leads to increasing complexity, provided free energy is available. The more energy that passes through a system, the more entropy is produced. Of course, the total entropy contributed by the Earth is infinitesimal relative

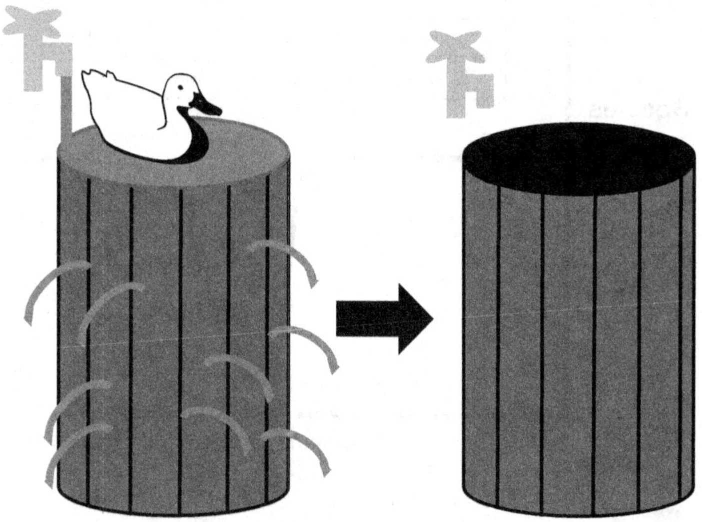

FIGURE A.2 Turning the tap off. In (a), the Earth receives sunlight which balances the loss of energy to the universe. In (b), the tap is turned off and the energy, along with the duck, is lost. The Earth is an open system, like a leaky barrel, and a circular economy is not possible, neither in nature nor in economics.

to the universe as a whole, but this isn't the point. The laws of thermodynamics reach down to the minutia of our planet. Of course not only is entropy released during the building of a complex structure, but also in the maintenance of that structure. Thus long-lasting products will need energy input to maintain them.

I often think that a duck in a leaking barrel is a nice analogy here. The second law demands leakage, and so water must be continually added to keep the duck afloat (Fig. A.2). As economic growth continues, the laws of physics still apply, and more and more structure requires more and more energy flux.

In terms of evolution, if we look at the number of species over time (Fig. A.3), we find that when incoming energy levels drop, species diversity drops too. These energy drops are called mass extinctions. When the lights come back on, life diversifies again, diffusing into the empty niches and species numbers increase. Thus the planet does fall apart unless the sunlight keeps flowing. The sunlight itself represents the gradual death of our star, as it uses up its fuel and heads towards its own fuel crisis, eventually expanding to consume the Earth, in about 5 billion years in the future. Entropy

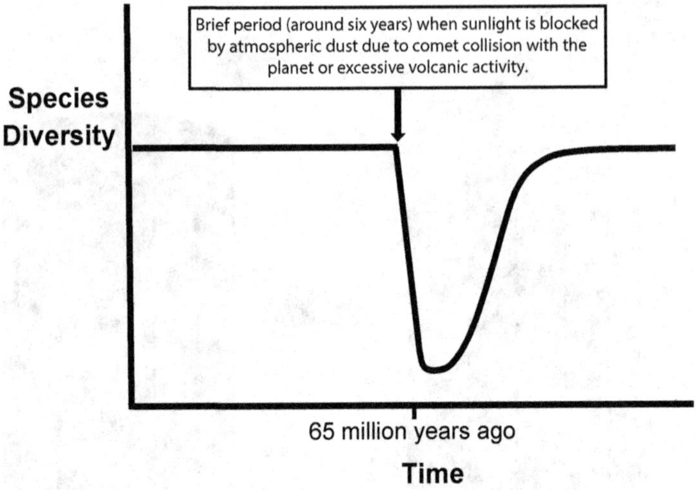

FIGURE A.3 The fact that the Earth is clearly an open system is demonstrated by the collapse of the biosphere 65 million years ago when incoming energy flux from the sun was blocked by clouds of dust thrown into the atmosphere by either an extraterrestrial object colliding with the earth or excessive volcanic activity. This wiped out 60% of nonbacterial life on Earth. The planet continued to lose energy (contributing to the entropy of the universe), but the energy balance was destabilized due to the lack of energy entering the system. The leaky barrel went dry.

is increasing within the star, and the dying star will one day consume the Earth, as the whole show heads towards equilibrium.

A final point to make relates to internal and external entropy. In living organisms, chaos is reduced internally and order is increased internally. In this way we can say that life is a process of maintaining a given organism in **a state far from equilibrium**. This means being far from the point where the whole universe is heading. To do this requires a deal with the energetic devil called the Second Law. Only by converting useful energy to less useful energy, by doing work, can we maintain order within ourselves, creating disorder out with ourselves. When we die, disorder creeps into our ordered internal structure, reducing it to dust.

Systems and thermodynamics

If the sun keeps shining and the Second Law continues to hold, then surely there is no ceiling to the complexity possible, as more and more complexity increases the entropy of the universe. We can keep growing economically, and run along progress world to our enlightened utopia that lies just up ahead. We can also facilitate the development of the "developing" world along this merry path. More is good. This, however, is not the case. Jack's beanstalk won't keep growing and skyscrapers are a long way from reaching outer space. There are limits to reproduction and growth in nature and economics.

Measurement of the release of entropy from complex open systems shows that initially, entropy output increases rapidly, as complexity increases, but the slows and levels off at a particular level. This is referred to as the maximum entropy production principle, and as we saw in Chapter 4, applies to an amazing array of different systems, from linguistics to macroeconomics, and from weather circulatory systems to ecosystem development. Open systems increase in complexity, and internal order up to a point, then level off, oscillating around some dynamic equilibrium called S_{max}, or the state of maximum entropy production for that system. Thus entropy production follows a **logistic curve** (Skene, 2013). Why does this happen?

Open systems are usually made up of several interacting levels of organization. Each level will move towards maximizing its entropic output, as decreed by the second law, and its internal order and complexity as a consequence. However, each level is dependent on other levels, and, like a group of people on a multi-armed see-saw, will need to make some compensation if the whole system is to achieve dynamic balance. Why does it have to achieve dynamic balance? This is because the whole system will increase the entropy of the universe by more than would be possible with no system. And so it is in better agreement with the second law that the system as a whole exists than that it doesn't. Of course, events happen that release huge amounts of entropy, such as a forest fire. But the continued cycling of nature over hundreds of years will produce more entropy than the burning of all the assets at any one point, as cycles go further the more the wheels go around. When a fire or a mass extinction does occur, the system builds up again to the maximum entropy production state.

Thus the second law of thermodynamics is a driver of ecosystem function and development, forming the crucial arrow that points sand dunes in the general direction towards the forest. You can chop the forest down, but if you leave it alone it will regrow. Nature has a direction, which is energetic and functional. A mass extinction will be followed by a rebuilding that re-establishes the functioning planet of before.

So what lessons do we learn for economics and sustainability? First, the Earth is an open system, plain and simple. Second, if we disturb the planet's function sufficiently, it will collapse and rebuild without us. Third, we are challenging the laws of the cosmos when we try to redirect things for our own survival. Fourthly, continued economic growth will require more and more energy flux to maintain order within the system. Fifthly, there is a maximum level beyond which we cannot maintain complexity. Sixthly, a circular economy is not possible, according to the laws of thermodynamics. Finally, a sustainable future will only be possible if we find a sustainable entropic production level, S_{max}, for the human race, and live within its dynamic equilibrium.

References

Skene, K.R. (2013). The energetics of ecological succession: a logistic model of entropic output. Ecological Modelling 250: 287-93.

Glossary

Absolute decoupling: an economy where global resource use declines in absolute terms, no matter whether there is economic decline or otherwise. See *Relative decoupling*.

Adaptive management: highly structured and feedback-dependent management approach, particularly suited to rapidly changing environments that present novel challenges. Relies on using experience to learn from, resulting in changes in structure and function. Pioneered by Frederick Taylor at the beginning of the 20th century.

Additive manufacturing: industrial process wherein material is added, often in powder form and then fused in place, to build complex forms, rather than beginning with a block of material and removing some of it (subtractive manufacturing) e.g by lathing. Additive manufacturing therefore greatly reduces waste.

Agrarian Age: period during which a group of people practises agriculture, utilizing solar energy to power society. Different parts of the world have entered and left an agrarian phase at different times. Currently, there are many people who still live in an agrarian age. Agrarianism is preceded by a Hunter-Gatherer Age, and followed by an Industrial Age. The onset of agrarianism is viewed by many as the onset of modernism in terms of culture and economics.

Agroforestry: the practice of combining silviculture (tree farming) and agriculture (animal and crop farming), with the aims of reducing environmental degradation, external inputs and loss of nutrients. Trees can help release nutrients from the soil, fix nitrogen, reduce soil erosion and reduce water-logging.

Anthropocene: a suggested new geological epoch, representing the time during which humans have impacted the planet in such a way as to leave a geological record, in terms of changes to weathering, sedimentation and deposition of radioactive elements. The concept has been around in different forms for 200 years, but has recently been popularized by Paul Crutzen and Eugene Stoermer.

Astronaut's perspective: term developed by Wolfgang Sachs, referring to a global approach to sustainability. Since many of the impacts of environmental damage act at a global level (such as sea level rise, atmospheric perturbation, climate destabilization and economic growth), there is a need for a global adjustment in order to respond to environmental and justice crises. See also *Home perspective*.

Benchmarking: using best practice as a cannon against which to measure a company's processes and products. Issues arise relating to a definition of "best".

Bioarchitecture: the merger of science and art in creating a built environment which harnesses and replicates the principles found in nature and in so doing, enhances the life experience and living systems.

Bio-energy: energy derived from biological sources that are renewable. Issues relating to what "renewable" actually means exist. For example trees may take 200 years to regrow, by which time the community of species living in the original trees will have disappeared, while ecosystem function may also be lost.

Biofuel: a fuel that is produced from recently fixed carbon, particularly relating to transportation. Ethanol is an example.

Biogeochemical cycle: the movement of elements or molecules associated with life through the hydrosphere, atmosphere, biosphere and geosphere. Turnover time is important, as are sink sizes and flux. Disturbance of such cycles, in terms of temporal aspects, can greatly impact on the life-support system of the planet. Examples include the carbon cycle and the water cycle.

Biome: the sum of all ecosystems of a particular type on the planet. For example, the tropical rainforest biome includes all tropical rainforest ecosystems on Earth. The sum of all the biomes is called the biosphere.

Biomimicry: a school of sustainability developed by Janine Benyus, which advocates the application of natural processes and designs to human production, aspiring to bring human activity into greater synchrony with the natural world.

Bioparticipation: rather than borrowing processes and designs for human use (see *Biomimicry*), bioparticipation advocates the reintegration of humans within the biosphere, where participation rather than knowledge transfer ensures a deeper symbiosis.

Biosphere: the sum of all life on the planet.

Blue carbon: carbon contained in coastal ecosystems such as lagoons, estuaries and mangrove swamps, sea-grass beds and marshes, which can be released into the atmosphere if these ecosystems are disturbed.

Blue economy: initially referring to marine-based human civilizations (in particular small island populations), the term has recently been used as the name of a school of sustainability developed by Gunter Pauli, set up to replace the concept of a "green economy", which he sees as merely externalizing damage. Instead he emphasizes physics as the central element of his thinking.

BRIC nations: a term referring to the nations of Brazil, Russia, India and China, representing the largest national populations on the planet and also the most rapidly expanding economies, with the potential to create a significant acceleration in environmental damage.

Buen vivir: a school of sustainability predominately in the Andes region of South America (particularly Ecuador and Bolivia), emphasizing the importance of local geography, ecology and culture in terms of economic functioning.

Built to change (B2C): designed for change, rather than stability, this ethos emphasizes change capability within management, with strong feedback loops in place, emphasizing open, adaptive processes over hierarchical, historic structures.

Capital

- **Human**: the human workforce in terms of numbers, skills, health and functionality.
- **Social**: the intensity, resilience, outputs and patterns of networks among people.
- **Human-made**: the material output of human activities.
- **Natural**: the resources available in the environment.

Carbon footprint: variously defined as the sum of all carbon dioxide or carbon—based greenhouse gases released by an individual, organization, event or nation. Attempts to associate a measurable area, reflecting a footprint, with this metric involve the area of a forest needed to absorb the said amount of carbon, but this doesn't work well for other greenhouse gases, and runs into complications in terms of what age the trees are, as this greatly effects net carbon absorption.

Carbon leakage: the externalization of carbon emissions, wherein a country may reduce its own carbon footprint by importing carbon emission-rich products from another country, whose own footprint then increases.

Carbon trading (see also *Personal carbon trading*): the concept of trade of carbon emissions rights within the setting of limits on the quantity of carbon emissions allowed by a given country, person or other grouping. If your emissions are below the limited quantity, you can sell the unused quantity to someone who has reached their limit. However, the potential to reduce emissions globally is questionable, as it encourages carbon leakage, in terms of finance facilitating excess pollution.

CFCs: chlorofluorocarbons are gases that lead to the destruction of ozone in the atmosphere, resulting in increased UV radiation reaching the planet's surface. While emissions have greatly reduced, CFCs can function for 100 years.

Circular economy: a school of sustainability unique in terms of its incorporation into central policy by the governments of China and South Korea, with emphasis on recycling, resource use efficiency and longer life product functionality, in order to reduce the use of natural capital.

Clean technology: school of sustainability that emphasizes reduction in resource use and waste production, utilizing technology to improve efficiency and profitability at the same time. It emphasizes its difference from green technology.

Cleaner production: school of sustainability adopted by the United Nations and emphasizing the continuous application of an integrated environmental strategy to processes, products and services to increase efficiency and reduce risks to humans and the environment.

Climax community: a concept from static equilibrium ecology, wherein an ecosystem stops developing at a point called the climax, which represents the end-point, beyond which no change is observed. Concept has since been discredited by dynamic and non-equilibrium models, but still persists in sustainable economics.

Clockspeed: the time needed for an industry to adapt to new circumstances or alter a product to respond to changes in the market.

Closed system: a thermodynamic term, referring to a system that is self-contained with no transfer of mass nor energy into or out of it. The Universe represents a closed system, while Earth is an open system, with both mass and energy transferring across its boundaries. Many schools of sustainability incorrectly look on Earth as a closed system.

Co-design: design school that incorporates end-users in the design process, usually beyond mere feedback, and builds a synergy between designer, producer, product and customer. Emphasis is placed on the design process, rather than the designer *per se*.

Co-evolutionary transition: the process of transition where different sub-systems are shaping but not determining each other, each evolving within the context of the other.

Common property resource model: large-scale resources, such as fisheries, which are subtractable and accessible by many individuals (common property), are likely to be used at a greater rate than they are replaced, leading, ultimately, to the disappearance of the resource.

Common scale indicators: a measurable quantity, such as number, density or rate, using common units, applicable to a single property of a system, that allows a comparison between two situations at a simple mathematical level.

Communalism: a school of philosophy emphasizing the importance of the social community in delivering a sustainable future. Can have a strong reference to historical culture, wherein a line of common descent plays an important role in defining the commune, since community properties are seen to emerge over time-scales beyond a single generation.

Comparative economics: refers to two different schools. The first rests on a comparison between socialist and capitalist systems, while the second compares human economics with economies in non-human natural settings.

Composite indices: single numbers representing the combination of a number of indicators, to provide a combined reference value for a complex system, as opposed to a common scale indicator, which references a single property of that system.

Complex systems theory: examines how the interactions of subsystems give rise to system-level properties.

Conceptual design: the initial stage of design, where hypothetical function, aesthetics and initial manufacturing concepts are defined.

Conspicuous consumption: the purchase of luxury, non-essential goods, designed to advertise wealth and power.

Corporate design: the management structure and operation of a company, which greatly impacts on such issues as adaptability, resilience and transition.

Cradle to Cradle®: protected term of the McDonough Braungart Design Chemistry (MBDC) consultancy, referencing a school of sustainability built around recycling and material flow patterns, centred around an economy of loops, or closed-loop economics, wherein leakage of waste is reduced at every level of production, product life and death.

Creaming curve: plots the number of successful resource discoveries (Y axis) against the number of attempts at finding that resource (x-axis). As the number of attempts at finding the resource increases, successful discoveries initially remain constant but then begin to decline, as the resource runs out.

Creative intelligence: the design discipline of creating through understanding the creative process. Championed by Bruce Nussbaum, but heavily referencing Edward de Bono in terms of learned creativity.

Dead man walking ecosystem: refers to an ecosystem that has been degraded to such an extent that it has ceased to function as an ecosystem, although from a distance it may still look like one. This is often a consequence of a decline in diversity, at the population and species level, due to pollution, over-harvesting or environmental perturbation.

Deep ecology: radical approach to conservation, developed by Arne Naess, which stresses the sovereignty of all living things and the restructuring of human practice and thinking to reflect this truth.

Design for behaviour: a design school that targets the consumer, in terms of attenuating their behaviour through the design of the product.

Design for sustainability (D4S): product-based school of design, incorporating social, environmental and economic contexts.

Design for environment (DfE): design school targeting consumer satiation but with low-impact products.

Design thinking: a discipline that uses the designer's sensibility and methods to match people's needs with what is technologically feasible and what a viable business strategy can convert into customer value and market opportunity. More recently applied to sustainable design issues. Now being replaced by *Creative intelligence*.

Deterring barriers: barriers that are viewed as unsolvable.

Development: as applied to economics, the deliberate, funded and directed transformation of agrarian or early industrial nations into the Information Age, with emphasis on globalization and western values. Nations not yet transformed are often referred to as "developing" while those that belong to the transformed set are referred to as "developed" nations. See Post-development.

Dynamic equilibrium: a school of thought that recognizes that no subsystem can reach a climax or static state, given the continued change of the overall system (the universe) and the ongoing interactions with other subsystems. Change is constant and results from feedback. An equilibrium represents a hypothetical state around which real subsystems oscillate.

Ecodesign: a European version of the American *Design for environment*, based around exploration, consolidation and maturity.

Eco-effectiveness: cyclic synergistic relationship between ecology and economics.

Eco-efficiency: reduction in end-of-pipe pollution by improved manufacturing process.

Eco-industrial park (EIP): spatial grouping of companies that can use each other's waste-streams as substrates for their production streams, reducing the consumption of resources and the production of waste.

Ecological economics: school of economic sustainability with greater emphasis on ecology, emerging from discontent with *Environmental economics*.

Ecological footprint: represents the amount of biologically productive land and sea area necessary to supply the resources a human population consumes, and to assimilate associated waste. Issues relate to what is considered as a reference habitat, as land and sea vary greatly in their ability to absorb waste depending on many factors.

Ecological intelligence: the ability to understand the Earth system and our place within it. This set of skills is thought to have weakened as we have become more distanced from the natural environment through technology.

Ecological thermodynamics: the application of thermodynamics to ecology, with particular emphasis on the process of ecological succession and the driver of complexity, resilience and change.

Ecology: the study of the Earth system in terms of the interactions between material flows, energetics and the biosphere. Subdisciplines include population ecology, molecular ecology, community ecology, physiological ecology and human ecology.

Economic energy intensity (EEI): the ratio between the energy consumed and the GDP of a country.

Economics: the study of the production, consumption and transfer of wealth.

Ecosystem: the abiotic and biotic environment of an organism, consisting of all of the interactions and representing a self-organizing unit, formed from populations of organisms and being part of a biome.

Ecosystem services: key functional outcomes of an ecosystem that are of importance to the survival and aesthetics of organisms, including humans, within that ecosystem and in the larger biosphere.

Emergence: outcomes which are different from the sum of the parts of a subsystem or system, such as imagination, life and ecological succession.

Emotionally durable design: a term coined by Jonathan Chapman, referencing product designs that engender emotional attachment within the consumer, meaning that they are less likely to throw it away. The concept assumes that lengthening lifetime of products is a positive outcome for the environment.

Empiricism: a school of philosophy that asserts that knowledge is derived mostly from sensual experience rather than reasoning (rationalism). Empiricism forms the basis of the scientific method and of reductionism (that higher levels of organization are merely products of lower levels).

Empty world: the representation of a world relatively empty of people, where resource supply far exceeded demand, as represented by the time before the 20th century.

Endarkenment: a word coined to reflect the position that the Enlightenment actually set the human race on a road to environmental destruction, leading to the current crisis, by advocating our superiority over nature and our use of its resources to pave the way to a human utopia.

Energy intensity: energy used per unit GDP

Enlightenment: the philosophical revolution of the 18th century that set out a road of progress based on reason and technology, whose destination would be a utopian human society. Embracing social sciences, economics, education and science, it generally celebrated the individual and decried that which would restrain individual progress, including religion and state intervention. Nature was also viewed as an unnecessary hindrance to this progress. The Enlightenment shaped the modern world as we know it. See also *Endarkenment*.

Entropy: the unavailability of a system's thermal energy for conversion into mechanical work, also defined as diffusion or, more loosely, disorder. The second law of thermodynamics states that the entropy within a closed system (the universe) will increase until equilibrium is achieved.

Environmental economics: a school of sustainability, mostly populated by economists, stresses weak sustainability, emphasizing that economic growth is essential.

Environmental paradox: the observation that although ecosystem services have been degraded, human wellbeing has increased.

Environmentally sustainable national income (eSNI): the maximal attainable production level by which vital environmental functions remain available for ever, based on the technology available at the time.

Eutrophication: enrichment of a water body with nutrients to such a level as to destabilize ecosystem function.

Existential risk: a threat so great as to have the potential of delivering the extinction of the human race.

Experience design: design school targeted at enhancing the user experience, often aimed at enforcing a bridge between the individual customer and a particular brand through emotional resonance. In terms of sustainability, the experience may be related to environmental awareness and synergy.

Flow structures: structures such as living organisms that can exist thermodynamically only because energy is continuously flowing through them.

Also referred to as dissipating structures, because the energy is converted to a less useful form by passing through these structures. Concept developed by Ilya Prigogine.

Forecasting: predicting the future needs based on current trend analysis.

Free market environmentalism: school of sustainability which believes that if markets are allowed to operate freely, they will ultimately act to preserve the environment. For example, as resources become less available, price increases will lead to reduced consumption.

Function–impact matrix: a design tool which allocates the life-cycle environmental impacts to the functions performed by the product. A main role of the function–impact matrix is to identify which product functions are important from an environmental perspective, and which functions need to be re-examined to achieve a better ecodesign.

Fusion-based design: designs that fit into nature, in terms of temporal and spatial context, are emphasized, leaving reduced ecological footprints and energizing environmental progression appropriately.

Gaian hypothesis: the idea that the Earth is a self-organizing superorganism, with feedback favouring the status quo. A top-down control of life processes, achieving homeostasis, sets this theory apart from reductionist theories. Named after the Greek goddess, Gaia. Developed by James Lovelock and Lynn Margulis.

Globalization (economic): the ultimate free market economy, where all nations freely trade with each other using the same economic model, under the auspices of the invisible hand, for maximum benefit. Globalization can also extend to cultural, legal and educational fields. Globalization is strongly opposed by many, who argue that diversity is essential for resilience, and that the model being used is a western colonial one.

Green accounting: an economic index that includes environmental damage.

Green chemistry: the promotion of innovative chemical technologies that reduce or eliminate the use or generation of hazardous substances in the design, manufacture and use of chemical products.

Green design: design school focused on environmentally sustainable manufacturing processes.

Green fuel: fuel produced from renewable biological resources. Issues come from a definition of renewable, and the observation that fields used to produce the fuel plants displace agriculture and natural habitats, such as in Borneo.

Green IS: the use of information systems to enhance sustainability across the economy.

Green IT: the study and practice of designing, manufacturing, using and disposing of computers, servers and associated subsystems, efficiently and effectively with minimal or no impact on the environment.

Green paradox: refers to the situation where climate policies and legislation lead to a worsening of environmental damage, rather than an improvement.

Greenhouse gases: any gas that contributes to the greenhouse effect, wherein heat escaping from the planet is absorbed by greenhouse gas molecules and re-radiated back to Earth, contributing to the warming of the planet.

Gross domestic product (GDP): the monetary value of all the finished goods and services produced within a country's borders in a specific time-period.

Groundwater footprint: the land area required to supply sufficient rainwater to underground aquifers in order to replace use of this water, divided by the area of the aquifer.

Growth (economic): a long-term expansion of a country's productive potential.

Haber-Bosch process: the industrial production of nitrogen fertilizers from dinitrogen gas. Requires large amounts of energy to generate 200 atmospheres of pressure and the 300°C needed. Nitrogen fertilizer is a significant contributor both to greenhouse gas emission during its production, and eutrophication during its use.

Habitat erosion: the gradual degradation of habitat, through local species extinctions, leading to a loss in ecosystem function and the services supplied.

Hartwick-Solow sustainability: states that the total sum of all changes in capital stocks must be zero.

High-grading: natural resources, both renewable and nonrenewable, are always harvested in such a way so that the easiest and cheapest supplies are taken first.

Home perspective: concept developed by Wolfgang Sachs, wherein a local driver of sustainability is seen as the best response to a heterogeneous landscape, allowing local context to provide inspiration for adaptive response. See also *Astronaut's perspective.*

Hopeful monsters: originally an evolutionary theory set out by Stephen Jay Gould, where unusual mutants may survive if conditions change in such a way that their competitors are no longer able to survive.

Hubbert Curve: the curve of production of any finite resource over time (years) will fundamentally be described by the Gaussian Error Curve which starts at zero, rises to a maximum and then returns to zero. The area under the curve from zero to infinity represents the total available mass of that resource measured in tonnes.

Human Development Index (HDI): an index that combines measurement of education, earnings (measured by gross national income per capita) and health.

Hunter-Gatherer Age: period of time that a given group of individuals spend foraging and hunting, often in a nomadic existence, with neither settlements, economics nor agriculture. Strong feedback between the environment and human population exists, given that no food is stored. The natural state of most animals on Earth. Humans have spent at least 97% of their existence in this state, and there are still small numbers of humans who live in this Age.

Inbreeding depression: genetic abnormalities produced by sexual reproduction between close relatives, leading to phenotypic abnormalities that often prevent reproduction, such as egg casings in birds which are so thin, the egg cannot survive.

Inclusive fitness: theory in evolutionary biology in which an organism's genetic success is believed to be derived from co-operation and altruistic behaviour.

Inconspicuous consumption: relates to everyday consumption, such as heating, air conditioning, washing machines, cookers and fridges. Inconspicuous consumption is interpreted as essential rather than luxury consumption.

Industrial Age: the period of time a human population spends wherein mechanized production is central to the survival and expansion of the population, and where fossil fuels drive the machinery. Pre-dates the Information Age and follows on from the Agrarian Age.

Industrial ecology: an interdisciplinary framework for designing and operating industrial systems as living systems interdependent with natural systems. The concept of industrial ecology is normally seen as working on three levels: intra-firm (within a given company), inter-firm (involving a group of companies) and regional.

Industrial metabolism: managing the total use of materials and energy throughout an entire industrial process, in such a way as to reduce waste and raw materials.

Industrial symbiosis: a grouping within a community of independent manufacturers, who are able to benefit by using each other's waste products.

Information Age: the period of time a human population spends wherein computer technology controls the economic, manufacturing, food production and societal aspects of a culture's existence.

Ingenuity gap: situation where our interventions in the broader life-supporting environment are based on a limited knowledge of that environment, and our impact on that environment has many dimensions that are unknown to us.

Institutional silo: an attitude where several departments or groups do not want to share information or knowledge with other individuals in the same company leading to reduced efficiency and acting as a contributory factor to a failing corporate culture.

Instrumentalist technology: the viewpoint that technology is neutral, and can be transferred from industrialized to "developing" worlds without any difficulty.

Integrated economic and environmental satellite accounts (IEESA): an attempt at green accounting in the USA, wherein environmental damage was included as a loss. Ceased to be used in 2005.

Invisible hand: much debated concept, developed by Adam Smith, wherein free market economies would be controlled by an invisible hand, which is thought to reference moral sentiments within individuals, the subject of an earlier book by Smith.

Ionian enchantment: the conviction that the world has a unified order and can be explained by natural laws. The term was suggested by E.O. Wilson.

Jet stream: ribbons of very strong winds, travelling at 9–16 km above the surface of the planet, at 200 mph, which move weather systems around the globe.

Judgemental discounting: process whereby invisible concepts such as climate may be pushed back down the list in terms of requiring urgent action, while food, health, education, facilitating technology, transport and leisure activities all rise to the top.

Kin selection: refers to apparent strategies in evolution that favour the reproductive success of an organism's relatives, even at a cost to their own survival and/or reproduction.

Kuznets Curve: with increasing economic growth, inequality first increases to a maximum, but then decreases. This forms an inverted U shape.

Laissez-faire economics: as set out by Adam Smith, a globalized economy should be allowed to operate without interference (*laissez-faire* is a French term meaning to leave alone).

Life-cycle analysis (or assessment) (LCA): compilation and evaluation of the inputs, outputs and the potential environmental impacts of a product system throughout its life-cycle.

Life-cycle management (LCM): monitoring and reduction of environmental impact at each stage of a product's life-cycle.

Linear economy: the make–take–dispose mantra of consumerism, wherein no thought is given to resource use or waste disposal. Products travel along a linear path from production to destruction.

Localism: a school of sustainability that places community and sustainability over appropriate technology. An anarchic movement, opposing centralization, it has flourished in many different forms throughout human history.

Malthusian: named after the writing of Thomas Malthus, it refers to the idea that the human population will one day become so large that it will outgrow the available resources, leading to the collapse of the human race.

Mass extinction: the extinction of a large number of species within a relatively short period of geological time, thought to be due to factors such as a catastrophic global event or widespread environmental change that occurs too rapidly for most species to adapt. There have been five such events in the history of life on Earth, and some suggest that we are in the midst of a sixth event, caused by humans.

Material flow accounting (MFA): an estimation of all the physical inputs entering the economy and the outputs of products, waste and emissions resulting from the production and consumption activities of the economy.

Maximum entropy production principle (MEPP): non-equilibrium thermodynamic systems are organized in steady state such that the rate of entropy production is maximized.

Meta-population: a group of populations connected reproductively.

Modern evolutionary synthesis: linking Darwinism to genetics, the synthesis sets out the gene as the unit of selection, and the phenotype as the outcome of the genes. Increasing frequencies of genes in populations represents genetic fitness.

Multilevel transition: describes the dynamics of a transition as the interactions between three different scale levels: a microlevel of niches, innovations and alternatives to the existent regime, a meso-level, where a regime of dominant structures, culture and practices operates and a macro-level of societal trends and developments.

Multi-pattern transition: aims to describe the way in which systems transform. It focuses on how a certain transformative change progresses, for instance through a bottom-up dynamic or a top-down dynamic. An underlying assumption is that a transition can be explained by only a limited set of patterns of transformative change.

Multiphase transition: describes the dynamics of transitions in terms of four different stages: predevelopment, take-off, acceleration and stabilization.

Multi-stakeholder sustainability alliances (MSSAs): a long-term partnership involving multiple participants from two or more categories of stakeholders (government, business, societal organizations, and knowledge institutions) with the objective of jointly defining and reaching sustainability objectives.

Natural capitalism: a school of sustainability which extols the recognition of natural capital and human capital, in contrast to traditional industrial capitalism, which primarily recognizes the value of money and goods as capital.

Natural design: a design concept developed by Seaton Baxter, emphasizing the holistic, functional aspects, rather than the eco-friendly, form-based emphasis of *Ecodesign*.

Natural resource curse: countries with oil, mineral or other natural resource wealth, on average, have failed to show better economic performance than those without such resources. Also known as the *Paradox of plenty*.

Neo-Darwinism: Darwinian evolution embracing the *Modern evolutionary synthesis* and focused on the gene as the unit of selection and selfish.

Niche construction theory: describes how organisms alter the environmental conditions of their surroundings (their niche) to their own benefit. This behaviour has been considered as a key contributor to ecological complexity.

Non-equilibrium ecology: stresses that nature is never in a balanced, homeostatic state, because there is always a lag between the ecosystem and its context.

Non-linear climate response: due to positive feedback, climate may change more rapidly than expected. For example as the climate warms, permafrost regions melt, releasing large amounts of methane previously trapped in the frozen soil, which leads to accelerated warming.

Noosphere: Teilhard de Chardin saw increasingly complex social networks, currently facilitated by the Internet, as contributing to the noosphere, leading eventually to the Omega point, which he felt was the goal of history, akin to the destination of the path of progress of the Enlightenment. The noosphere is represented by integration and unification.

Opportunity cost: evaluation of how much value could be derived from a resource such as water, used in one application, if it was instead used in another one.

Optimism bias: assumption that things won't be as bad for us as for others.

Outbreeding depression: situation where genes from another population dilute specialized genes in a given population, so that this population is no longer specialized in coping with its local environmental conditions.

Palaeolithic: stretching from 3.4 million years ago up until 10,000 years ago, the Palaeolithic coincided with the hunter-gatherer period in Europe, a period where humans based most of their technology on stone tool-making.

Panarchy: an ecological theory initially, it went on to attempt to explain economic, social and environmental transformation in some form of grand unification, incorporating ecological succession with resilience theory. Advocates include Buzz Holling.

Paradox of plenty: see *Natural resource curse.*

Pareto efficiency: is achieved when resources are shared in such a way that no individual can improve their share of resources without impacting negatively on another individual. Generally this occurs when resource availability is maximized, meaning that there is a drive to exploit resources in order for each individual to have an equally large share of the greater whole.

Peak resources: the concept that a point is reached in nonrenewable resource extraction, beyond which harvesting becomes increasingly inefficient and supply declines.

Perceived behavioural control: refers to the confidence a person has that their behaviour will affect a particular outcome. Low perceived behavioural control will lead to a person feeling that it is not worthwhile wasting energy on a cause that they are unlikely to be able to change.

Personal carbon trading (PCT): a concept that involves individuals being give a certain quantity of carbon pollution that they are allowed to produce, and if they do not use all of this, they can trade the spare capacity.

Persuasive technology: targets motivation of the consumer through design.

Phylogeny: the grouping of species together based on shared characteristics in such a way as to map relatedness.

Planned obsolescence: products designed to fail, requiring replacement.

Pluralism: defined as some degree of acceptance of two or more mutually inconsistent theoretical frameworks which pertain to the same or overlapping domains of reality.

Pluriverse: the concept that different ecological contexts will demand different societal function and economic models. Contrasts with *Globalization*.

Porter Hypothesis: properly designed and enforced regulations that actually mitigate environmental harm could trigger innovative responses that would not only fully offset compliance costs, but also result in additional profits, or so-called "win–win" innovations.

Positive feedback: where the consequences of an action lead to an intensification of that action.

Post-development: a school of sustainability that does not call for an alternative form of development, but rather an eradication of any attempt to train the "developing" world, arguing that indigenous people are likely to have better solutions within the context of their natural and cultural landscape for the problems facing them than will western thinkers.

Post-selectionism: a set of evolutionary theories that do not hold that natural selection is a useful way of understanding evolution. The gene is not viewed as the unit of selection, and evolution is not understood within a reductionist framework, but a holistic one. Alternative models include thermodynamic diffusion.

Progress: the Enlightenment mantra that humans continue to improve and that there is nothing to be learned from our imperfect past. Rather, reasoning and technology will continue to deliver an ever-improving context for human existence.

Protective space: a concept in transition management, where protection is provided for new innovations that otherwise would be out-competed by incumbents before realizing a critical mass. Hugely controversial topic in terms of what should be protected and how such innovations will eventually survive in the big wide world.

Radical design: requires a clean sheet, beginning with conceptual design and a freedom not necessarily available to all designers

Rebound effect (ecology): changes in population sizes due to an island separating from a larger landmass or joining one. Based on area-species richness theory of island biogeography, where larger areas have larger numbers of species and smaller areas have less species. A new island may take thousands of years before species numbers adjust to the greatly diminished land area.

Rebound effect (resources): as improved efficiency in the use of energy in manufacturing becomes a reality (i.e. a decline in energy intensity and carbon intensity), costs will decline, given that energy is a key driver of cost. Cheaper production will lead to an increase in consumer spending and an increase in manufacturing, thus leading to a net increase in pollution.

Reductionism: the philosophy that more complex levels are merely outcomes of the building blocks at the most basic level. Thus we can understand more complex levels by studying greatly simplified levels.

Relative decoupling: an economy where resource use per unit growth declines. If economic growth increases sufficiently rapidly, absolute resource use may still increase, unless resource use efficiency increases enough.

Resilience: the ability to bounce back and recover from disturbance.

Revealed barriers: barriers of which the firm is aware and believes that innovative solution space exists. See also *Deterring barriers*.

Reverse logistics: the process of moving goods from their typical final destination for the purpose of capturing value, or proper disposal.

Right-skewed: a binomial curve with an extended tail on the right side, meaning that as value x increases, value y ceases to behave as would be expected in a normal distribution, and instead has increased values.

Servitization: the innovation of an organization's capabilities and processes to better create mutual value through a shift from selling product to selling product-service systems.

Sink issues: environmental concerns relating to end-of-life product management and waste production throughout product life-cycle.

Slow consumption: design approach which aims to build linkages between product and consumer, contributing to longevity.

Socio-metabolic profile: social structures and their use of resources (material and energy).

Source issues: issues related to resource use, particularly in terms of habitat destruction, diminishing nonrenewable resources and pollution associated with mining/harvesting.

Spaceship Earth: the idea that Earth is a closed system (incorrect) and that we must recycle resources to survive.

Static equilibrium: the idea that change in ecosystem development eventually stops, when the ecosystem reaches a climax. Since rejected by ecology, but still integrated into most sustainable economics models.

Strong sustainability: a school of sustainability that states that natural capital must be protected at all costs and cannot be replaced with human-made capital. It sees little role for technology in any sustainability discourse.

Suboptimality: each level of organization is part of another level, and so solution space will be compromised, leading to reduced optimality for any given level, but overall optimality at the system level.

Substantivist technology: advocates that technological development exists within its own bubble, one invention building on the other, without anyone or any institution being able to stop, slow or redirect it. From this perspective, technology is not neutral.

Subterranean forest: a reference to fossil fuels, reflecting a shift from using wood to using coal and oil as the main fuel.

Succession: the process of ecosystem development, from bare soil or sand to forest in the example of lowland succession.

Surplus theory of social stratification: surplus of food supply allows populations to increase while allowing greater leisure time, particularly for those no longer involved directly in food production. This surplus can support a new urban population of specialized craftsmen, merchants, priests, officials, and clerks.

Sustainability: the maintenance of capital. Social sustainability maintains human capital, economic stability maintains human-made capital and environmental stability maintains natural capital. Two more general forms exist: *Strong sustainability* and *Weak sustainability*.

Sustainable development (SD): development that meets the needs of the present without compromising the ability of future generations to meet their own needs.

Sustainable product design (SPD): the process which creates product designs that are sustainable in terms of the environment and resource use while considering the need for the product. SPD embraces resource use efficiency, product quality, production organization and efficiency, local culture and capacity, market and end of life. This represented a shift beyond *Design for environment* or *Ecodesign*, where the focus is on product attributes, to SPD, which requires a broader approach. In SPD the relationship between the product, suppliers, stakeholders, and external economic and social factors are taken into account, enabling more radical options to be considered.

Sustainable urbanism: walkable and transit-served urbanism integrated with high-performance buildings and high-performance infrastructure. Key areas of focus include compactness, walkable streets and networks, open space, storm-water systems, integration of transportation, land use and energy, impact of planning on building energy usage and large district energy systems.

System biology: the study of biology as a system with subsystems which interact, producing emergent properties.

System justification theory: combines three needs that humans experience: the need to be part of a group, the need to maintain the status quo within that group and the need for security and stability. These three needs lead to behaviour that rejects an alternative challenging view, and system justification theory is thought to be a significant contributor to climate destabilization denial.

Technological innovation systems (TIS): principally concerned with emerging new technologies and their potential contribution to future sustainability.

Thermodynamic equilibrium: the point where atomic motion ceases, at absolute zero, and no free energy remains.

Thermohaline circulation: involves the gradual evaporation of surface water, increasing the salt concentration, until the more salty water becomes so dense that it sinks down. A loop forms, driven by the sinking, a bit like a fan belt that is turned by the rotation of a wheel. A second wheel involves the temperature. As the water moves into cooler areas, it cools and becomes denser.

Threat multiplier: that which exacerbates threats caused by persistent poverty, weak institutions for resource management and conflict resolution, fault lines and a history of mistrust between communities and nations, and inadequate access to information or resources.

Tipping point: a threshold of environmental forcing beyond which abrupt and critical changes occur.

Tragedy of the commons: the observation that if a resource of limited quantity is accessed by a population, then there is likelihood that the resource will be over-exploited, to the detriment of the population, because individuals will continue to use the resource with no concern for the greater population.

Transition: a transformation process in which existing structures, institutions, culture and practices are broken down and new ones are established.

Transition culture (TC): emphasizes the reduction in the economic dependence of towns and cities on distant communities.

Virtual water: virtual water is defined as water used in the production of imported goods. The flow of virtual water across the globe began to be mapped, and businesses and nations could be given a water footprint, relating to their water consumption.

Waste hierarchy: the waste hierarchy emphasizes the preferred ways to deal with waste. While modern theory emphasizes reduce, re-use and recycle, resisting the acquisition of the product in the first place is the preferred option.

Waste is food: the idea that waste can be fed into the manufacturing process as raw material for another industry.

Water footprint: an empirical indicator of how much water is consumed, when and where, measured over the whole supply chain of the product. The water footprint of an individual, community or business is defined as the total volume of fresh water that is used to produce the goods and services consumed by the individual or community or produced by the business.

Weak sustainability: a school of sustainability that seeks to maintain levels of total capital from generation to generation, through substitution. Thus if natural capital declines, provided that man-made capital increases by the same amount, then total capital will be maintained.

About the authors

Keith Skene was born in Northern Ireland in 1965, in the beautiful city of Armagh. Keith was educated at the Royal School, Armagh, before gaining a First Class Honours degree in Botany at the University of Dundee. He completed his PhD in 1997, specializing in evolutionary ecology and developmental biology. He has carried out fieldwork in the Americas, Asia, Africa, Europe and Australia. Keith taught for 13 years at the prestigious College of Life Sciences in Dundee. During this time, he carried out field research across the planet, from Kenya to the Carpathian Mountains, from the Scottish highlands to southwest Australia and from Vietnam to Trinidad. He was appointed as Convenor of the Board of Environmental and Applied Biology in 2008.

In 2010, Keith established the Biosphere Research Institute (www.biosri.org), becoming its first director. The Biosphere Research Institute works with businesses, educators and communities in areas of economic and ecological function, and focuses on a fundamental dialogue on our place in the earth system. He is the author of four books and over thirty peer-reviewed journal articles, and his work has been translated into four languages. Writing on ecosystem structure and function, thermodynamics, evolutionary biology, sustainability, design and economics, he believes that human dignity can only be found within our ecology. He works with a number of business schools, including visiting fellowships at the University of Leeds Business School and Winchester Business School. He teaches at a number of universities across Europe, including MENDELU in Brno, and collaborates with numerous academics on research. Keith lives in Angus with his wife, young son and foster children.

Before entering academic life, Professor **Alan Murray** gained wide managerial and business experience through careers in both the public and private sectors. Having undertaken an undergraduate degree in his forties, he then embarked on a PhD study focusing on the role of social information in capital markets. He founded the British Academy of Management Special Interest Group on CSR in 2007, and went on to organize a number of conferences to support the growing number of researchers and teachers in the CSR and sustainability field. In 2008, he co-authored, with Michael Blowfield, *Corporate Responsibility: A Critical Introduction*, which quickly established itself as a leading textbook in the area. A second edition was published in 2011, and was awarded the Chartered Management Institute's "Management Book of the Year 2011–12" in the Leadership and Management Textbook category.

In 2006 Professor Murray was part of the United Nations Taskforce that developed the Principles of Responsible Management Education (http://unprme.org), and was elected Chair of the PRME Regional Chapter for the UK and Ireland in May 2013. He is also active within the UN Global Compact UK Network. In April 2013 he was invited to join a research consortium based at Kedge Business School, in Marseilles, France, examining concepts of the "Circular Economy" and its application in French industry and commerce. He is on the organizing committee of the Third International Symposium of Corporate Responsibility and Sustainable Development and is Track Chair of the Sustainable and Responsible Business Track at British Academy of Management in September 2015.

Index

Printed in the United States
by Baker & Taylor Publisher Services